HOW TO USE THE NEW EDITION 1998/99

The 25th edition contains a number of additions and enhancements to make this an even more useful reference source.

NEW INFORMATION AND NEW SECTIONS

'SELLING' ESTABLISHMENTS. Where this information has been supplied, establishments have been marked 'C' for a purely commercial enterprise, 'P' for a public gallery or museum, and 'PS' for a public gallery or museum holding selling shows.

PRICE RANGE. Again where this has been supplied, in addition to showing the media stocked and sold by each establishment, entries now also show the price range of the work.

VIRTUAL GALLERIES. This section lists galleries which may be accessed purely by the Internet and a complete listing of all Internet sites listed in the directory.

ART UNDER £1,000. Establishments where work priced at under £1,000 may be purchased.

ART EDUCATION. Details on where to study 23 different visual arts based courses. Full address and contact details, awards and course types.

REGIONAL GALLERIES. The English regional galleries section is now organised by REGION, making it even easier to plan your visits.

ARTISTS INDEX. Fully revised and expanded. Now lists more than double the number of previous entries. Over 3,700 individual artists - where to buy their work.

HIGHGATE
Fine Art

26 Highgate Street, London N6 5JG
Telephone / Facsimile 0181 340 7564

"Dance Music" by **Richard Robbins** Oil on canvas 48x48ins

1998 EXHIBITION SCHEDULE

Rosemary Lowndes MA FSCD	**Mar 26** - **Apr 9**		**Anthony Atkinson** ARCA	**Apr 16** - **May 2**
Julian Jaen, E. Cascajosa				
and Doug Patterson	**May 7** - **May 23**		**Claude Harrison** ARCA	**May 28** - **Jun 13**
Ishbel McWhirter	**Jun 18** - **Jul 4**		**Summer Show Part I**	**Jul 9** - **Aug 1**
Summer Show Part II	**Aug 6** - **Sep 5**		**Arthur Easton** ROI	**Sep 10** - **Sep 26**
Bruno Guaitamacchi	**Oct 1** - **Oct 17**		**Richard Robbins**	**Oct 22** - **Nov 7**
Andrew Flint-Shipman	**Nov 12** - **Nov 28**		**Mixed Christmas Show**	**Dec 3** - **Jan '99**

Tues - Sat 10am - 6pm Tube: Archway Buses: 143, 210, 271

CONTENTS

Art consultants, art management, digital graphics, electronic services, information services, marketing services & PR, public art agencies

THE ART WORLD
DIRECTORY
1998/99 25TH EDITION

LAMONT GALLERY

Dear Reader,

It is with great pleasure I introduce the 25th edition of this book. Like its sister title, Art Review magazine, The Art World Directory has undergone significant changes in the last few years and we trust that you will find the silver anniversary edition an even more useful and user friendly publication.

We have added a number of new sections and enhanced others (the artists' index now contains some 3,700 individual names) and have reorganised many of the elements to make it easier and faster to find the gallery, medium or artist of your choice.

We are indebted to our many readers and advertisers for their advice and encouragement in preparing this new edition and to Nautilus Fine Art Foundry for their kind support.

Now, please go and buy something!

David Fox Publisher

Elisabeth Frink
Walking Man

The Nautilus foundry prides itself on making a casting so perfect that art and craft are invisible

Contemporary sculpture exists in an ever increasing range of materials. It can be carved out of alabaster or cast in zinc; it can be formed in fibre optics or fluorescent tubes. For anyone wishing to commission a piece as a private individual, a collector, a company or a public sector patron the choice is bewildering. However, most sculpture demands detail, colour and durability, and this is best expressed in bronze.

Casting is a kind of rebirth. The sculptor's initial vision (be it in clay , plaster or some other material) must be reborn, recreated, reconstructed - in whatever material the sculptor has chosen. Exactly and precisely, in every minute detail - to make a perfect match with the sculptor's concept.

This is the essence of fine art casting, and a major moment of truth for the sculptor. Because the whole intricate, complex process is now in the hands of others.

A fine art foundry must be a centre of excellence, where diverse craft skills of the highest order can combine to produce a perfect cast.

But superb skills are not enough. At every stage, these craftsmen must also be able to communicate; to generate trust, must respect and certainly that they share the sculptor's vision.

Such men are rare. It is rarer still, to find them in a fine art foundry Rarest of all, is to find a foundry which is linked to such an established and successful business that is also a closely related commercial enterprise.

Finch Seaman made an inspired decision to acquire Nautilus because they recognised the potential of complementing the advanced foundry techniques an the facilities they could offer with established traditional skills.

Nautilus manager Paul Joyce sums it up, "It's like two cultures coming together, giving us the best of both worlds".

When Finch Seaman re-located Nautilus from south-east London to their industrial foundry in Braintree, they designed and built a facility of some 3,500 sq ft which matched exactly the particular needs of then team. the light and spacious Fine art foundry, is equipped with an overhead crane, furnaces which can fire up to a ton at a time, 1,000 sq ft of storage space, and studio facilities both here and in London.

Sculptures as large as 20 feet high and 25 feet long can be assembled here, and transporters can back right in to the foundry itself. The whole facility has direct access to the adjacent Finch Seaman industrial foundry. that means not only instant access to the induction furnace technology and sand casting expertise, but also the bulk raw material purchasing power, financial resources, commercial acumen and business skills of an established company.

Why not give Paul Joyce a ring for more information on 01 376 343 222

ALBEMARLE GALLERY

Elena & Michel Gran   *Chapeau de Cartes*

After a successful opening in November 1996, the Albemarle Gallery is now thriving, with new and varied exhibitions every three to four weeks. 1998 sees a number of exciting exhibitions by artists exclusive to the gallery. Figurative paintings by the American artist Malcolm Liepke are on show in March, which is followed by an exhibition of 'Trompe-l'Oeil' by Elena and Michel Gran in April. In May, the outstanding Bosnian artist Mersad Berber will have his first London exhibition. Then we see the return of the Spanish artist Fabio Hurtado on May 28.

The Summer months pass by with two marvellous mixed exhibitions; the first, The Scottish Show, will be an opportunity to see four of Scotland's fine figurative artists, from 25 June. The second, The Still Life Show, (16 July to 1 August), will be a group exhibition of international artists. From September onwards the gallery will mount a number of solo shows, by artists including Robert Saunders, Csaba Markus, Jincheng Liu, Jeremy Barlow and Goyo Dominguez.

The Albemarle Gallery draws its inventory of artists from a broad international spectrum, representing artists from America, China, France, Italy, Holland, Croatia, and in particular an outstanding group from Spain.

For further information please contact Tony Pontone or Kate Daniel on 0171 499 1616.

49 Albemarle Street London W1X 3FE

Tel 0171 499 1616 Fax 0171 499 1717 Opening Hours: Mon – Fri 9.30 – 5.30 Sat 10 – 4

CALENDAR OF EXHIBITIONS

There's a Whole New World In UV Picture Framing Glass.

Introducing *New* Museum Image Perfect® Single-Strength Anti-Reflective Glass
The Highest UV blockage-*99%*-over the full UV light spectrum

In case you haven't heard, we've introduced Museum Image Perfect, arguably the finest framing glass available in the world. Why is it so? Just take a look at a mere sampling of its attributes:

- 99% UV blockage over the **entire** UV light spectrum compares with less than 93% blockage of other UV glass products (entire UV spectrum is 300–400 nanometers).
- Single-strength, 2.5 mm glass.

LIGHT BLOCKAGE COMPARISON

| MUSEUM IMAGE PERFECT® UV ANTI-REFLECTIVE GLASS *99% UV BLOCKAGE UP TO 400NM* | |
| OTHER UV GLASS | HARMFUL UV LIGHT NOT BLOCKED BY OTHER UV GLASS |

300   380   400
UV WAVELENGTH IN NANOMETERS

Image Perfect is, to our knowledge, the only framing glass that has passed The Image Permanence Institute (Rochester NY) Photographic Activity Test for image preservation.

- The ultimate in conservation protection; effectively delays fading and deterioration of artwork.
- Literally invisible to the eye, it eliminates the mirror effect of plain glass and the dull, hazy look of no-glare glass.
- The only non-coated anti-reflective glass at a lower price.

Too good to be true? We can prove it isn't. Call or fax us today. You can have the world of picture framing glass in

This is a selection of exhibitions, both selling and non-selling, due to take place over the coming year at public and commercial galleries. Exhibitions are listed under the month in which they start, so if you want to know what's on in a particular month, don't forget also to check previous months for continuing exhibitions. It is advisable to contact the venue before visiting in order to ensure that details have not changed since publication.

CONTINUING FROM EARLIER MONTHS ...

Paintings & Drawings from the First World War
Imperial War Museum, London SE1
0171-416 5000
ongoing.

Unofficial Flowers: Art of the Second World War
Imperial War Museum, London SE1
0171-416 5000
ongoing.

Inventing America: A Year of American Culture
Barbican Art Gallery, London EC2
0171-638 8891
throughout 1998 (see later months for individual exhibitions).

Carving Mountains: Modern Stone Sculpture in Britain 1910-1937
Kettle's Yard, Cambridge
01223 352124
to 26 April.

Roger Hilton (1911-75): sketchbooks & related paintings
Tate Gallery, St. Ives.
01736 796543
to 26 April.

Shaker: The Art of Craftsmanship
Barbican Art Gallery, London EC2
0171-638 8891
to 26 April.

The Art of the Harley: Harley Davidsons 1945-1998
Barbican Art Gallery, London EC2
0171-638 8891
to 26 April.

Talking Heads: Old Master Drawings and Prints
Christ Church Picture Gallery, Oxford
01865 276172
to 29 April.

Scottish 19th & early 20th C paintings & watercolours
Calton Gallery, Edinburgh
0131-556 1010
to 30 April.

Chocolate in contemporary art
Collins Gallery, Glasgow
0141-548 2558
to 2 May.

Angels and Urchins: The Fancy Picture in 18th C British Art
Djanogly Art Gallery, Nottingham
0115-951 3189
to 3 May.

Let's All Sing Together: photographs of football supporters
Herbert Art Gallery, Coventry
01203-832410
to 3 May.

Paolozzi – Life in Art: Art in Life
Crawford Arts Centre, St. Andrews
01334 474610
to 3 May.

Caro: Sculpture from Painting
National Gallery, London WC2
0171-747 2885
to 4 May.

Christopher Le Brun
Marlborough Fine Art & Graphics, London W1
0171-629 5161
to 8 May.

3rd International Miniature Print Exhibition
Gracefield Arts Centre, Dumfries
01387 262084
to 9 May.

John Bellany: a Scottish Odyssey
Beaux Arts, London W1
0171-437 5799
to 9 May.

A Great Teacher: Valette & Lowry
Manchester City Art Galleries
0161-236 5244
to 10 May.

Weaving Pictures: Masterpieces of 20th-Century Tapestry
Sainsbury Centre for Visual Arts, Norwich
01603 456161
to 10 May.

William MacTaggart (1903-1981)
Scottish National Gallery of Modern Art, Edinburgh
0131-556 8921
to 10 May.

Richard Newton: satirical prints from the 1790s
Whitworth Art Gallery, Manchester
0161-275 7450
to 17 May.

Future Systems: futuristic architecture and design group
Institute of Contemporary Arts, London
0171-930 3647
to 24 May.

Italy in the Age of Turner
Dulwich Picture Gallery, London SE21
0181-693 5254
to 24 May.

Pre-Raphaelite Women Artists
Birmingham Museum and Art Gallery
0121-303 2834
to 24 May.

Turner Watercolours
Whitworth Art Gallery, Manchester
0161-275 7450
to 24 May.

Bird Swallowing a Fish by Gaudier-Brzeska, at Kettle's Yard, Cambridge, to 26 April.

FAIRFAX GALLERY
TUNBRIDGE WELLS

British Contemporary art by established and emerging artists

Theo Matoff "Devon Wedding" Acrylic on paper

The Fairfax Gallery provides a striking juxtaposition of contemporary art with its setting in the heart of the historic Pantiles.

FAIRFAX GALLERY
23 The Pantiles
Tunbridge Wells
Kent TN2 5TD
Tel/Fax
01892 525 525

Gallery opening hours:
Tuesday – Saturday
10am – 6pm
Sunday 11am – 4pm

Arts of Nepal
British Museum, London WC1
0171-636 1555, 0171-323 8599/8299
to 31 May.

Birmingham Arts Lab: 1970s youth culture
Birmingham Museum and Art Gallery
0121-303 2834
to 31 May.

Brigitte Kraemer: photographs
Wakefield Art Gallery
01924 305796
to 31 May.

Bruce Weber: Branded Youth and Other Stories – photographs
Walker Art Gallery, Liverpool
0151-207 0001
to 31 May.

Design for Living: Art and Industry in the 1930s
Manchester City Art Galleries
0161-236 5244
to 31 May.

The Science of the Face
Scottish National Portrait Gallery, Edinburgh
0131-556 8921
to 31 May.

The Whitechapel Open & Open Studios
Whitechapel Art Gallery, London E1
0171-522 7878/7888
to 31 May.

Art Textiles
Leighton House, London W14
0171-602 3316
to 2 June.

Henri Cartier-Bresson – Portraits: Tête-à-Tête
National Portrait Gallery, London WC2
0171-306 0055
to 7 June.

The Art of Holy Russia: Icons from Moscow 1400-1660
Royal Academy of Arts, London W1
0171-300 8000
to 14 June.

Black Power: photographs by Donald A. MacLellan
National Portrait Gallery, London WC2
0171-306 0055
to 14 June.

High Society: Edwardian Life in Photographs
National Portrait Gallery, London WC2
0171-306 0055
to 21 June.

Homes of Football
Dick Institute, Kilmarnock
01563 526401
to 11 July.

John Singer Sargent: Gassed 1918
Imperial War Museum, London SE1
0171-416 5000
to end August.

Fortuny Fabrics
Whitworth Art Gallery, Manchester
0161-275 7450
to September.

Survival Patterns: wallpapers from 1793 onwards
Whitworth Art Gallery, Manchester
0161-275 7450
to November.

APRIL 1998

Metropolitan: paintings by Richard Walker
New Academy Gallery, London W1
0171-323 4700
2 April to 1 May.

The Power of the Poster
Victoria & Albert Museum, London SW7
0171-938 8349/8441
2 April to 26 July.

Mittel Europa by Richard Walker, at the New Academy Gallery, London, 2 April to 1 May

Flights of Fancy: contemporary children's book illustrations
Cambridge Contemporary Art
01223 324222
3 April to 18 April.

Leon Morrocco: recent paintings
Roger Billcliffe Fine Art, Glasgow
0141-332 4027
3 April to 28 April.

Artists for Mencap: work by accomplished contemporary artists
Cromwell Hospital, London SW7.
Details: 0181-964 5444 (Wendy De Souza, Kensington & Chelsea Mencap)
3 April to 1 May.

David Williams: Findings ... Bitter/Sweet – photo-animation
Scottish National Portrait Gallery, Edinburgh
0131-556 8921
3 April to 3 May.

Vong Phaophanit: new commission
Royal Festival Hall, London SE1
0171-921 0600
3 April to 17 May.

Henry Moore and the National Gallery
Room 1, National Gallery, London WC2
0171-747 2885
3 April to 31 May.

Avril Paton: paintings
The People's Palace, Glasgow
0141-550 0892
3 April to 18 October.

Walls & Windows: colour photographs by Dorothy Bohm 1994-8
Octagon Galleries, Royal Photographic Society, Bath
01225 462841
4 April to 17 May.

Going Modern and Being British: Art, Architecture and Design in Devon c1910-1960
Royal Albert Memorial Museum, Exeter
01392 265858
4 April to 30 May.

Invention, Imagination, Interpretation: the Prague Surrealists 1970-1997
Glynn Vivian Art Gallery, Swansea
01792 655006
4 April to 31 May.

art ^{with} *attitude*

Twentieth century British painting at the Imperial War Museum

Edward Burra *Skull in Landscape, c.1946*

Imperial War Museum
Lambeth Road
London SE1 6HZ

Department of Art
Research and Archives
10.00 – 17.00
Monday to Friday

Museum open
seven days a week
10.00 – 18.00
admission £4.70
free after 16.30

For further information
telephone 0171 416 5211
fax 0171 416 5215

Shoji Hamada (1894-1978): Master Potter
Ditchling Museum, Ditchling
01273 844744
4 April to 7 June.

Darkness into Light: Craig McPherson and the Art of Mezzotint
Hunterian Art Gallery, Glasgow
0141-330 5431
4 April to 20 June.

Carroll Through the Viewfinder: photographs by Lewis Carroll
National Museum & Gallery of Wales, Cardiff
01222 397951
4 April to 21 June.

Barbara Rae: new paintings; Lucy Casson: tin sculpture;
The Scottish Gallery, Edinburgh
0131-558 1200
6 April to 29 May.

Touching Dust: works in pigment on paper by Siân Bowen
Cafe Gallery, London SE16
0171-237 1230
8 April to 26 April.

Handmade in India: contemporary crafts from India
Crafts Council, London N1
0171-278 7700
8 April to 28 June.

A Million Brushstrokes 1998: miniature oils, watercolours & pastels by over 150 artists
Llewellyn Alexander, London SE1
0171-620 1322
9 April to 9 May.

Dawoud Bey portraits 1975-1995
Barbican Concourse Gallery, London
0171-638 8891
9 April to 31 May.

John Kobal Photographic Portrait Award
Scottish National Portrait Gallery, Edinburgh
0131-556 8921
9 April to 31 May.

Ferdinand Porsche: Design Dynasty – the history of the Porsche
Design Museum, London SE1
0171-403 6935
9 April to 31 August.

Silver from the Gilbert Collection
The Burrell Collection, Glasgow
0141-469 7151
10 April to 31 May.

Jan Wightman & Liz McCarthy: recent paintings
Frames Contemporary Gallery, Perth
01738 631085
11 April to 2 May.

Drawing show; Paintings by James McDonald
Glasgow Print Studio
0141-552 0704
11 April to 9 May.

The Edge: art from the northernmost area of Europe
City Art Centre, Edinburgh.
0131-529 3993
11 April to 23 May.

Vital Patterns: new paintings & sculptures by Margaret Hunter
Art First, London W1
0171-734 0386
15 April to 14 May.

Elizabeth Zollinger
An Lanntair, Stornoway
01851 703307
18 April to 16 May.

Henry Moore in Perspective
Yorkshire Sculpture Park, Wakefield
01924 830302
(National Touring Exhibition: call 0171-921 0837 for details of further venues)
18 April to 31 May.

Paula Rego
Midlands Arts Centre, Birmingham
0121-446 4372
18 April to 31 May.

Dal-Dale: photographic installation by Tone Myskja
City Art Gallery, Leeds
0113-247 8248
18 April to 30 June.

Illustrators of the 1860s: The Forrest Reid Collection
Ashmolean Museum, Oxford
01865 278000
21 April to 21 June.

Ariel Luke: recent landscapes
Lumley Cazalet, London W1
0171-491 4767
22 April to 22 May.

Georgia and Trina by Dawoud Bey, at the Barbican Concourse Gallery, 9 April to 31 May.

David Sinclair: new oil paintings
Ewan Mundy Fine Art, Glasgow
0141-248 9755
23 April to 14 May.

Leonard Marchant RE: paintings & prints
Bankside Gallery, London SE1
0171-928 7521
24 April to 2 May.

Forts and Palaces: paintings by Jenny Robinson
The Ice House, Holland Park, London
0171-603 1123
25 April to 10 May.

Willie Rodger; Carola Gordon
Open Eye Gallery, Edinburgh
0131-557 1020
25 April to 14 May.

Artists' Books from Scotland
art.tm, Inverness
01463 712240
25 April to 30 May.

Sacred & Profane: constructed photography by Calum Colvin
Scottish National Gallery of Modern Art, Edinburgh
0131-556 8921
25 April to 28 June.

A Surreal Life: Edward James (1907-1984)
Brighton Museum & Art Gallery.
01273-603005
25 April to 26 July.

Bosch in Britain: 100 Years of German Design
Design Museum, London SE1
0171-403 6935
25 April to 16 August.

The Grizedale Society
Britain's Premier Sculpture Trail
Prudential Award Winners 1990

"Taking a Wall for a Walk" Andy Goldsworthy

In the heart of Lakeland's Grizedale Forest, are over 80 site-specific sculptures. Artists, responding to this special environment, use indigenous materials to make works, some permanent, some ephemeral.

Guidemaps, updated annually, enable visitors to find sculptures along more than 9 miles of the Silurian Way.

The Grizedale Society arranges residencies for sculptors, painters, and craft workers whose work is reflected in an exhibition gallery (10 - 4 daily, admission free). The society also runs the celebrated Theatre in the Forest.

"1250 Willows..."
Kristaps Gulbis

"Picea"
Charles Poulsen

"One of 'Em"
Steven Siegal

**The Grizedale Society, Theatre in the Forest, Grizedale, Hawkshead, Cumbria, LA22 0QJ.
Tel 01229 860291 • FAX 01229 860050 • Registered Charity 500253**

Paul Huxley
Jason & Rhodes, London W1
0171-434 1768
29 April to 30 May.

Goddesses: Earthy Women – new ceramics by Melanie Keevil
The Orangery, Holland Park, London W8
0171-603 1123
30 April to 13 May.

Anish Kapoor
Hayward Gallery, London SE1
0171-921 0600
30 April to 14 June.

MAY 1998

Heretical Diagrams: prints by Ian Howard
Compass Gallery, Glasgow
0141-221 6730
during May.

Lesley Banks & Frances MacDonald: recent paintings
Cyril Gerber Fine Art, Glasgow
0141-221 3095
during May.

Relative Values: contemporary portraiture
Harris Museum & Art Gallery, Preston
01772 258248
May to July.

Spring Exhibition: recent work by 12 Scottish artists
Logie Steading Art Gallery, Forres
01309 611378
1 May to 17 May.

Mary Armour, Christine McArthur, Rupert Spira
Roger Billcliffe Fine Art, Glasgow
0141-332 4027
1 May to 28 May.

Colours of the Indus: Costumes and Textiles of Pakistan
Royal Museum of Scotland, Edinburgh
0131-225 7534
1 May to 28 June.

Philip Jackson: Sculpture
Parkview Fine Paintings, Bristol
0117-970 6265
1 May to 31 May.

Scrolls from the Dead Sea
Kelvingrove Art Gallery and Museum, Glasgow
0141-287 2699
1 May to 30 August.

Susan Betty: paintings
Aberdeen Arts Centre Gallery
01224 635208
2 May to 3 June.

In the Mind's Eye: Surrealist works on paper
Hove Museum & Art Gallery
01273 779410
2 May to 5 July.

John Wells (b.1907): The Fragile Cell – paintings
Tate Gallery St. Ives
01736 796543
2 May to 1 November.

172nd Annual Exhibition
Royal Scottish Academy, Edinburgh
0131-225 6671
3 May to 5 July.

Medina Hammad
Usher Gallery, Lincoln
01522 527980
3 May to 5 July.

Royal Society of Portrait Painters
Mall Galleries, London SW1
0171-930 6844
7 May to 25 May.

Edward Piper: Circles of Stones – black and white photographs, 1978
Scottish National Portrait Gallery, Edinburgh
0131-556 8921
7 May to 5 July.

Masters of Light: Dutch Painting from Utrecht in the Golden Age
National Gallery Sainsbury Wing, London WC2
0171-747 2885
7 May to 2 August.

The Print in Stuart Britain
British Museum, London WC1
0171-636 1555, 0171-323 8599/8299
8 May to 20 September.

Dilwyn Smith: paintings
Djanogly Art Gallery, Nottingham
0115-951 3189
9 May to 14 June.

Layers of Meaning: the rag rug – a contemporary approach
Collins Gallery, Glasgow
0141-548 2558
9 May to 20 June.

Colin Fraser: new work – egg tempera
Gatehouse Gallery, Glasgow
0141-620 0235
10 May to 4 June.

Garden Party: paintings of gardens & flowers
Portal Gallery, London W1
0171-493 0706
11 May to 30 May.

Critical Interventions: Evil
John Hansard Gallery, University of Southampton
01703 592158
12 May to 27 June.

Quantum Contemporary Art Spring Show: affordable paintings by contemporary fine artists
Atrium Gallery, Whiteley's, London
Details: 0171-834 7767 (Orange Square)
13 May to 17 May.

Rimpa Art from the Idemitsu Collection, Tokyo
British Museum, London WC1
0171-636 1555, 0171-323 8599/8299
13 May to 26 July.

Crucifixion with the Virgin and Saint John by Hendrick ter Brugghen, at the National Gallery, 7 May to 2 August.

POINT OF SALE
RETAIL DISPLAYS
INTERIOR DECOR
SIGNAGE

LIVING BRIDGES EXHIBITION
ROYAL ACADEMY OF ARTS
BRANSON COATES ARCHITECTURE

GRAPHIC DISPLAYS
EXHIBITIONS
TV & FILM STUDIO SETS
THEATRICAL SCENERY
PROMOTIONAL BANNERS
CONFERENCE STAGE SETS
MUSEUMS DISPLAYS
OUTDOOR EVENTS
FASHION DESIGN
COSTUMES
FLAGS

HORNIMAN MUSEUM & GARDENS
CARTER WONG & PARTNERS

Giant **Images**

THE ENDURING IMAGE

NATIONAL MUSEUM, NEW DELHI, INDIA · TIM HARVEY

REPLICA PAINTING, TORBAY BOROUGH COUNCIL

01799 531049

The Power of Print: work by Royal Society of Painter-Printmakers
Bankside Gallery, London SE1
0171-928 7521
14 May to 7 June.

The Collector's Eye: From Romney to Renoir: a private collection revealed
Holburne Museum, Bath
01225 466669
15 May to 5 July.

The Quest for Albion: Monarchy and the Patronage of British Painting – from the collection of HM Queen Elizabeth II
The Queen's Gallery, Buckingham Palace, London SW1
0171-839 1377
15 May to 11 October.

John Renton
The Edinburgh Gallery
0131-557 5227
16 May to 9 June.

The Rock Drill and Beyond: Epstein's *Rock Drill* (1913) and contemporary responses to it
Inverness Museum and Art Gallery
01463 237114
16 May to 13 June.

Sally Carson: portraits
Balbardie Gallery, Bathgate
01505 777585
16 May to 23 June.

Patterns of Africa
Elgin Museum, Elgin
01343 543675
16 May to 12 July.

Lari Pittman: large decorative canvases
Cornerhouse, Manchester
0161-228 7621
17 May to 5 July.

Ian McKeever: woodcut monotypes
Alan Cristea Gallery, London W1
0171-439 1866
20 May to 20 June.

Hitchin Sink: humorous paintings by Michael Paramore
The Orangery, Holland Park, London W8
0171-603 1123
21 May to 3 June.

Photography: An Independent Art – exhibition marking the opening of the new Canon Photography Gallery
Victoria & Albert Museum, London SW7
0171-938 8349/8441
21 May to November.

Scottish Artists & Artist Craftsmen
Perth Art Gallery and Museum
01738 443505
22 May to 20 June.

Syzygy: paintings by Philip Mead & Alan Rodgers
Newport Museum & Art Gallery
01633 840064
23 May to 4 July.

Image & Icon: New Greek Photography
Octagon Galleries, Royal Photographic Society, Bath
01225 462841
23 May to 19 July.

John Newling: site-specific project for Art Transpennine
Cornerhouse, Manchester
0161-228 7621
23 May to 6 August.

Art Transpennine '98
Commissions for public locations from Liverpool to Hull
Call the Tate Gallery, Liverpool (0151-709 3223) for details
23 May to 16 August.

Cubism: exhibition marking the reopening of the Tate Liverpool
Tate Gallery, Liverpool
0151-709 3223
23 May '98 to April '99.

James McDonald & Angus McEwan
The Leith Gallery, Edinburgh
0131-553 5255
26 May to 6 June.

The Warhol Look, 1940s-1980s
Barbican Art Gallery, London EC2
0171-638 8891
28 May to 16 August.

William Littlejohn, Emilio Coia, Anne Wegmuller, Simon Manby,
Kingfisher Gallery, Edinburgh
0131-557 5454
29 May to 26 June.

Angela de la Cruz: new commission
Royal Festival Hall, London SE1
0171-921 0600
29 May to 5 July.

Robert Capa: photographs
Scottish National Gallery of Modern Art, Edinburgh
0131-556 8921
30 May to 12 July.

First Swansea Annual Open Exhibition
Glynn Vivian Art Gallery, Swansea
01792 655006
30 May to 26 July.

JUNE 1998

Degree Shows
Most art colleges: check with individual colleges for specific dates
during June.

Matisse: drawings & paintings
Lumley Cazalet, London W1
0171-491 4767
June to July.

Lowry Drawings
Whitworth Art Gallery, Manchester
0161-275 7450
early June to end August.

John Greenwood
Jason & Rhodes, London W1
0171-434 1768
1 June to 4 July.

230th Summer Exhibition
Royal Academy of Arts, London W1
0171-300 8000
2 June to 16 August.

Ethel Walker
Gatehouse Gallery, Glasgow
0141-620 0235
7 June to 3 July.

Not the Royal Academy 1998: a Salon des Refusés (a percentage of proceeds goes to the British Heart Foundation)
Llewellyn Alexander, London SE1
0171-620 1322
8 June to 5 September.

David Eyre: new work
The Cree Gallery, Castle Douglas
01557 814458
10 June to 28 June.

GALLERY DUNCAN TERRACE

24 DUNCAN TERRACE LONDON N1 8BS
TEL 0171 837 5856   FAX 0171 278 2140

TOM ESPLEY "AMANDA ON RED" OIL ON CANVAS 41" X 66"

HEPHZIBAH RENDLE-SHORT "LIVE AND LET LIVE" OIL ON CANVAS 20" X 24"

DIDO CROSBY "STEEL ANTELOPE" 55" X 39"

ARTISTS INCLUDE:

BRIAN NICOL

VICKI OLVERSON

TOM ESPLEY

JOHN O'DONNELL

PETER CLOSSICK

DIDO CROSBY

JO VOLLEY

ANYA KING

DOM THEOBALD

ANDREW CARNEGIE

JOHN HOLDEN

GEOFFREY OLSEN

COLIN McCALLUM

JIM JACK

ARTHUR NEAL

LUCY SPANYOL

HEPHZIBAH RENDLE-SHORT

PETER CLOSSICK "HILLA"
OIL ON CANVAS 40" X 45"

Jack Vettriano: Between Darkness and Dawn
Portland Gallery, London SW1
0171-321 0422
10 June to 10 July.

Hughie O'Donoghue: prints & works on paper
Purdy Hicks Gallery, London SE1
0171-401 9229
12 June to 11 July.

Aubrey Williams: paintings
Whitechapel Art Gallery, London E1
0171-522 7878/7888
12 June to 16 August.

Peter Doig: new figurative paintings
Whitechapel Art Gallery, London E1
0171-522 7878/7888
12 June to 16 August.

Light Sensitive: silver gelatin works by contemporary artists
York City Art Gallery
01904 551861
13 June to 20 July.

Jim Malone: Artist Potter
Birmingham Museum and Art Gallery
0121-303 2834
13 June to 30 August.

David McNae Boyne: paintings, prints & ceramic slipware
Tolbooth Art Centre, Kirkcudbright
01557 331643
16 June to 28 June.

Lee Jones
Hanover Galleries, Liverpool
0151-709 3073
17 June to 27 June.

Invited Members of the Royal Institute of Painters in Watercolours
Linda Blackstone Gallery, Middlesex
0181-868 5765
17 June to 4 July.

Paula Rego: recent paintings
Dulwich Picture Gallery, London SE21
0181-693 5254
17 June to 19 July.

Royal Scottish Watercolour Society
Bankside Gallery, London SE1
0171-928 7521
18 June to 12 July.

University of Nottingham Summer Exhibition
Djanogly Art Gallery, University of Nottingham
0115-951 3189
20 June to 12 July.

Matisse: Jazz;
Adrian Wiszniewski
Glasgow Print Studio
0141-552 0704
20 June to 25 July.

Scottish Landscapes
The Original Print Shop, Glasgow
0141-552 1394
20 June to 25 July.

William Blake and His Circle
Birmingham Museum and Art Gallery, Birmingham
0121-303 2834
22 June to 6 September.

Henri Matisse: original prints
Alan Cristea Gallery, London W1
0171-439 1866
24 June to 1 August.

Carlos David: paintings
Morley Gallery, London SE1
0171-450 9226
25 June to 17 July.

Artists of Today and Tomorrow, Part 1: 30th Anniversary Show
New Grafton Gallery, London SW13
0171-748 9818
25 June to 18 July.

Effigies and Ecstasies: Roman Baroque Sculpture and Design in the Age of Bernini
Scottish National Gallery, Edinburgh
0131-556 8921
25 June to 20 September.

A Celebration of Glass
Contemporary Applied Arts, London W1
0171-436 2344
26 June to 1 August.

Drawings from the Weld-Blundell Collection (16th to 18th C)
Walker Art Gallery, Liverpool
0151-207 0001
26 June to 20 September.

BP Portrait Award 1998 & BP Travel Award 1997
National Portrait Gallery, London WC2
0171-306 0055
26 June to 27 September.

A Bridge Between East and West: paintings by Isao Miura
The Ice House, Holland Park, London W8
0171-603 1123
27 June to 12 July.

Maori
British Museum, London WC1
0171-636 1555, 0171-323 8599/8299
27 June to 1 November.

Claude Lorrain (1604-82): drawings
Ashmolean Museum, Oxford
01865 278000
30 June to 19 September.

The Circle of the Lustful by William Blake, at Birmingham Museum & Art Gallery, 22 June to 6 September

Marj Bond *Crusader* Oil on canvas 24 × 24 ins

Julian Trevelyan *Low Tide* 1974 Etching 35 × 47.9 cm

23 March – 21 April
25th Anniversary Exhibition Part II
Artists include Maggi Hambling, John Hoyland, Jack Knox, Neil MacPherson, Robert Maclaurin, Simon Palmer, June Redfern

27 April – 26 May
Marj Bond
New Paintings

1 June – 25 July
John Piper
Watercolours

19 October – 10 November
Julian Trevelyan 1910-1988
A Retrospective Exhibition of Etchings
To coincide with the publication of a Catalogue Raisonné of the Prints of Julian Trevelyan co-published by Scolar Press and Bohun Gallery

16 November – 8 December
John Houston
New Paintings

Bohun Gallery
15 Reading Road Henley-on-Thames
Oxfordshire RG9 1AB
Telephone/fax 01491 576228
Closed Sunday and Wednesday

JULY 1998

Lari Pittman: paintings
Institute of Contemporary Arts, London
0171-930 3647
July and August.

**New Generation: this year's
graduates from Scottish art colleges**
Compass Gallery, Glasgow
0141-221 6730
July and August.

Lux: Work in Light
Harris Museum & Art Gallery, Preston
01772 258248
July to September.

**Home Sweet Home: depictions of
houses and castles;
What's Happening Here Then? –
figurative and narrative painting**
Perth Art Gallery and Museum
01738 443505
July to October.

**Little Sparta: photographs by Robin
Gillanders**
Scottish National Portrait Gallery,
Edinburgh
0131-556 8921
July to October.

The Reformation in Europe
The Burrell Collection, Glasgow
0141-469 7151
July to October.

Printmaking in Paris
Hunterian Art Gallery, Glasgow
0141-330 5431
(National Touring Exhibition: call 0171-921 0837 for details of further venues)
during July.

Chagall: Love and the Stage
Royal Academy of Arts, London W1
0171-300 8000
2 July to 4 October.

**Francis Boag, James Spence,
Sarah Beeny, Paul Spence**
Kingfisher Gallery, Edinburgh
0131-557 5454
3 July to 24 July.

**Elemental! – artists respond to the
four elements**
Towner Art Gallery, Eastbourne
01323 417961/725112
4 July to 2 August.

Maria Braggins: paintings
Aberdeen Arts Centre Gallery,
Aberdeen
01224 635208
4 July to 5 August.

Annual Marine Exhibition
The Leith Gallery, Edinburgh
0131-553 5255
7 July to 1 August.

Pop Art in Spain
Sainsbury Centre, Norwich
01603 456161
7 July to 30 August.

Rose Warnock
Jason & Rhodes, London W1
0171-434 1768
8 July to 14 August.

Summer Festival: new British crafts
Crafts Council, London N1
0171-278 7700
8 July to 31 August.

Lewis Carroll
National Portrait Gallery,
London WC2
0171-306 0055
10 July to 11 October.

William Brown: paintings & prints
Newport Museum & Art Gallery
01633 840064
11 July to 15 August.

Robert Faulkner: watercolours
Tolbooth Art Centre, Kirkcudbright
01557 331643
14 July to 26 July.

Venice Through Canaletto's Eyes
National Gallery, London WC2
0171-747 2885
15 July to 11 October.

Scottish Marine & Coastal Paintings 1800-1950
Calton Gallery, Edinburgh
0131-556 1010
16 July to 5 September.

Bruce Nauman
Hayward Gallery, London SE1
0171-921 0600
16 July to 6 September.

Mary Newcombe
Djanogly Art Gallery, Nottingham
0115-951 3189
18 July to 23 August.

View from the Window in the Country,
Zaolshye by Chagall, at the Royal
Academy of Arts, 2 July to 4 October.

**High Summer: paintings, ceramics
& sculpture by established artists &
graduates**
Mainhill Gallery, Ancrum, Jedburgh
01835 830518
19 July to 2 August.

**An Indian Summer: watercolours
by Charlotte Viscountess Canning
in India, 1856-61**
Holburne Museum & Crafts Study Centre, Bath
01225 466669
21 July to 13 September.

**Out from Under: Land, Myth &
Power in Australian Art**
Cecil Higgins Art Gallery, Bedford
01234 211222
21 July to 11 October.

Society of Wildlife Artists
Mall Galleries, London SW1
0171-930 6844
23 July to 7 August.

**Artists of Today and Tomorrow,
Part 2**
New Grafton Gallery, London SW13
0171-748 9818
23 July to 5 September.

S. J. Peploe (1871-1935)
Kirkcaldy Museum & Art Gallery
01592 412860
25 July to 11 October.

COMPUTER CONSULTANCY

"Progress Through Perception...."

• ART GALLERIES • COLLECTORS • MUSEUMS •
• ARTISTS • ART DEALERS • FRAMERS •
• RESTORERS • ART SUPPLIERS •
• ART STORAGE FACILITIES •

For the last fifteen years we have specialised in all the above from Single Users PC's to Multi-User Networks for our Clients in the UK and around the world.

We design and setup Stock Databases, comprehensive Client Files, Accounts Systems, Invoicing Systems, Word Processing, Desk Top Publishing, eMail and Laptop/Pc Communications Packages along with the complete training program in a range of today's most popular software.

So please telephone or fax us for more information. Wherever you are, whatever the problem... we can help.

Tel: 0181 - 462 7740
Fax: 0181 - 462 7739

LMR... *The Computer Name In Art*

JOHN BLOXHAM FINE ART

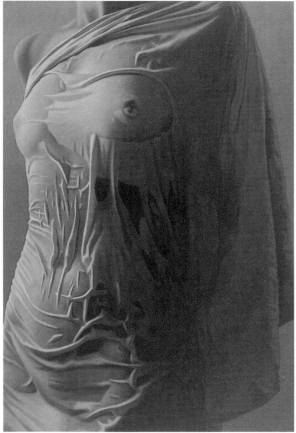

Torso III, oil on board, 100cm x 65cm, £5500.00

WILLI KISSMER
PAINTINGS & ETCHINGS
FROM £175.00 TO £8000.00

Other artists include: Liu Haiming, Nigel Cladingböel, Geraldine Hayward,
Piao Chun Zi, Martin Gowar, Linda Sutton, Russell Gilder

117 ST JOHN'S HILL, LONDON SW11 1SZ
TEL 0171 924 7500 FAX 0171 585 3901
WEB SITE www.art-com/john_bloxham

OPEN 10AM - 6PM MON TO SAT OR BY APPOINTMENT

Graham Clarke

Etching and the Prints of Whales

Produced entirely by hand in a worldwide edition of 300 copies plus 30 artist's proofs. Image size 248mm x 212mm.

Contact: Wendy Clarke or Dawn Masters, Graham Clarke (Prints) Ltd, Boughton Monchelsea, Maidstone, Kent ME17 4LF

Phone: 01622 743938 Fax: 01622 747229
E-mail: info@grahamclarke.co.uk Website: www.grahamclarke.co.uk

Druie Bowett

Accent Perimeter, 179cm x 183cm, Oil on Canvas, £5000   Pachalafaka Art Agency & Virtual Gallery

BLOND FINE ART

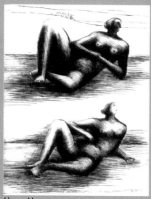

Henry Moore
Two Reclining Figures 1977

John Hoyland
Composition 1983

British original prints 1920 – 80, including:

Bawden, Buckland Wright, Burra, Caufield, Clough, Davie, Denny, Fedden, Frink, Gibbings, Gill, Gross, Hayter, Hepworth, Hermes, Heron, Hodgkin, Hockney, Hoyland, Hughes-Stanton, Allen Jones, David Jones, Kitaj, Anita Klein, Claire Leighton, Mackley, Moore, Nash, Paolozzi, Pasmore, Piper, Raverat, Ceri Richards, Rothenstein, Scott, Smith, Sutherland, Tilson, Trevelyan, Turnbull.

By appointment.
Barnat Works, 1a Upper Redlands Road
Reading RG1 5JJ Tel 0118-926-0880

Halo: interactive video projection
by Simon Biggs
Terrace Gallery, Harewood House, Leeds
0113-288 6331
25 July to 1 November.

AUGUST 1998

Robert Kelsey; sculpture by
Christopher Bailey; Moray Miller
Kingfisher Gallery, Edinburgh
0131-557 5454
August (Festival Exhibition)

Richard Wright & Dave Allen:
site-specific project
Centre for Contemporary Arts, Glasgow
0141-332 7521
August to September.

Sketches by Joseph Crawhall
Bourne Fine Art, Edinburgh
0131-557 4050
August to September

The Society of Eight: PW Adam,
FCB Cadell, David Alison, James
Paterson, Henry Lintott, John Dun-
can, William Gillies
Bourne Fine Art, Edinburgh
0131-557 4050
August to September

The Basketmaker's Art: exhibition
to opening the new Craft Gallery
Royal Museum of Scotland, Edinburgh
0131-225 7534
August '98 to January '99.

Jewellery Moves: contemporary
sculptural jewellery
Royal Museum of Scotland, Edinburgh
0131-225 7534
August '98 to January '99.

Highland Open Exhibition
art.tm, Inverness
01463 712240
1 August to 29 August.

Brian Craig
Glasgow Vennel Art Gallery, Irvine
01294 275059
1 August to 4 September.

Interactive sculpture by Jan Niedo-
jadlo (aimed at children)
York City Art Gallery
01904 551861
1 August to 13 September.

The Scottish Colourists in France,
1890s to 1960s
City Art Centre, Edinburgh
0131-529 3993
1 August to 3 October.

William Gillies: A Centenary Celebration
Royal Scottish Academy, Edinburgh
0131-225 6671
1 August to 11 October.

Mona Hatoum: installations,
sculptures, photographs and videos,
1983 to the present
Scottish National Gallery of Modern
Art, Edinburgh
0131-556 8921
1 August to 25 October.

Summer Exhibition: fine Scottish
18th-20th C and contemporary
wildlife
McEwan Gallery, Ballater
01339 755429
3 August to 31 October.

A Scottish Panorama: 19th- &
20th-century oils & watercolours
Malcolm Innes Gallery, Edinburgh
0131-558 9544/5
5 August to 29 August.

Masterpieces of Modern Printmaking
Alan Cristea Gallery, London W1
0171-439 1866
5 August to 12 September.

Northern Graduates: work selected
from the 15 Northern universities
New Academy Gallery and Curwen
Gallery, London W1
0171-323 4700
6 August to 29 August.

Elizabeth Blackadder: new paintings; Gordon Baldwin: ceramics
The Scottish Gallery, Edinburgh
0131-558 1200
7 August to 2 September.

British Figurative Art: Sculpture
Flowers East, London E8
0181-985 3333
7 August to 20 September.

Josephine Graham
The Edinburgh Gallery
0131-557 5227
8 August to 22 August.

Fiona Hudson: recent work
Aberdeen Arts Centre Gallery
01224 635208
8 August to 2 September.

John Brown RSW;
Contemporary Scottish Masters
Open Eye Gallery, Edinburgh
0131-557 1020
*8 August to 3 September
(Festival Exhibition).*

Jock McFadyan: paintings
Talbot Rice Gallery, Edinburgh
0131-650 2211
mid-August to mid-September.

Buddhist Arts of Japan
British Museum, London WC1
0171-636 1555, 0171-323 8599/8299
mid-August to mid-November.

Frank Watkins & Tony Alcock:
paintings & assemblages
Newport Museum & Art Gallery
01633 840064
22 August to 3 October.

Emergence: ceramic sculptures by
Catrine Ballie
The Ice House, Holland Park, London
W8
0171-603 1123
29 August to 13 September.

Paintings by Pan Tianshou (1897-
1971)
Ashmolean Museum, Oxford
01865 278000
29 August to 25 September.

Lee Grandjean & Jeremy Hooker
Djanogly Art Gallery, Nottingham
0115-951 3189
29 August to 27 September.

Willie Doherty: photographic and
video work
Tate Gallery, Liverpool
0151-709 3223
29 August to 4 October.

SEPTEMBER 1998

Jack Knox: Retrospective;
Margaret Morris (1891-1980):
designs & drawings
Cyril Gerber Fine Art, Glasgow
0141-221 3095
during September.

Maggie Beveridge, John Lowrie
Gallery Heinzel, Aberdeen
01224 625629
during September.

Secret Victorians
The Minories, Colchester
01206-577067
(National Touring Exhibition from the
Hayward Gallery: call 0171-921 0837
for details of further venues)
during September.

The Real David Mellor
Design Museum, London SE1
0171-403 6935
September to November.

Contemporary American Basketry
Barbican Art Gallery, London EC2
0171-638 8891
1 September to 11 October.

Vessels: paintings by Robin Richmond
Curwen Gallery, London W1
0171-323 4700
2 September to 26 September.

Pieter de Hooch (1629-1684): genre paintings
Dulwich Picture Gallery,
London SE21
0181-693 5254
3 September to 15 November.

Emrys Williams: recent paintings
Collins Gallery, Glasgow
0141-548 2558
5 September to 3 October.

Outsider Art in Scotland
art.tm, Inverness
01463 712240
5 September to 10 November.

On Show 11: photography
Usher Gallery, Lincoln
01522 527980
5 September to 15 November.

Christopher de Lotbinière: paintings and prints
Leighton House, London W14
0171-602 3316
7 September to 19 September.

Jerwood Prize for Applied Arts 1998: Glass
Crafts Council, London N1
0171-278 7700
9 September to 4 October.

Vessels and Voyages: ceramics and paintings by Hilary LaForce and Hugh Durnford Wood
The Orangery, Holland Park, London
0171-603 1123
10 September to 23 September.

Juan Fernando Herran: new commission
Royal Festival Hall, London SE1
0171-921 0600
10 September to 25 October.

Cindy Sherman: photographs 1970-1998
Barbican Art Gallery, London EC2
0171-638 8891
10 September to 13 December.

Native North America
Barbican Art Gallery, London EC2
0171-638 8891
10 September to 13 December.

Autumn Exhibition including Iain Ross & Walter Awlson
Atholl Gallery, Dunkeld
01350 728855
12 September to 3 October.

Ascent of Man: paintings by Bob Brown
Durham Art Gallery
0191-384 2214
12 September to 11 October.

John Taylor: paintings & prints
Glasgow Print Studio
0141-552 0704
12 September to 17 October.

The Work of Charles & Ray Eames: from architecture to movie-making and furniture design
Design Museum, London SE1
0171-403 6935
15 September '98 to 3 January '99.

Coming to Light: Birmingham photographic collection
Birmingham Museum and Art Gallery
0121-303 2834
16 September '98 to 3 January '99.

Jonathan Miller ... On Reflection: the representation and meaning of mirrors in art
National Gallery Sainsbury Wing, London WC2
0171-747 2885
16 September to 13 December.

Picasso: Sculptor and Painter in Clay
Royal Academy of Arts, London W1
0171-300 8000
17 September to 27 December.

Black Sheepet: Sex, Politics & Power – sculpture and installations by Gail D Gill
The Ice House, Holland Park, London W8
0171-603 1123
19 September to 4 October.

Pam Carter
Lillie Art Gallery, Milngavie
0141-943 3246
19 September to 10 October.

Mick Rooney RA
Portal Gallery, London W1
0171-493 0706
21 September to 10 October.

Malchair and the Oxford School
Ashmolean Museum, Oxford
01865 278000
22 September to early December.

Royal Society of British Artists
Mall Galleries, London SW1
0171-930 6844
23 September to 4 October.

Marian Leven RSW; Moira Beaty
Open Eye Gallery, Edinburgh
0131-557 1020
26 September to 15 October.

Northern Potters' Annual Exhibition
York City Art Gallery
01904 551861
26 September to 25 October.

Japanese Screens
Ashmolean Museum, Oxford
01865 278000
26 September to 30 November.

Karl Friedrich Schinkel: lithographs
Scottish National Gallery, Edinburgh
0131-556 8921
end September to end December.

OCTOBER 1998

Robert McAulay, Helen Denerley
Gallery Heinzel, Aberdeen
01224-625629
during October.

Patka: a revived Indian textile technique
British Museum, London WC1
0171-636 1555, 0171-323 8599/8299
October to December.

When Time Began to Rant and Rave
Walker Art Gallery, Liverpool
0151-207 0001
October '98 to January '99.

William Klein: New York
Scottish National Portrait Gallery, Edinburgh
0131-556 8921
October '98 to January '99.

In Search of Times Past: Ruskin and Proust
Scottish National Portrait Gallery
0131-556 8921
October '98 to January '99.

Curwen Studio 40th Anniversary Exhibition: one print from each year
New Academy Gallery and Curwen Gallery, London W1
0171-323 4700
1 October to 31 October.

Tadao Ando: recent architectural projects
Royal Academy of Arts, London W1
0171-300 8000
1 October to 1 November.

Modern Master Prints; Stanley Dove: bronze sculptures
Cambridge Contemporary Art
01223 324222
2 October to 17 October.

Hideo Furuta: sculpture
Talbot Rice Gallery, Edinburgh
0131-650 2211
3 October to 31 October.

The Art of Joan Eardley
Stranraer Museum, Stranraer
01776 705088
3 October to 7 November.

Rustic Simplicity
Djanogly Art Gallery, Nottingham
0115-951 3189
3 October to 8 November.

Catrin Webster: abstract paintings – Swansea Festival Exhibition
Glynn Vivian Art Gallery, Swansea
01792 655006
3 October to 22 November.

Dennis Thorp: 50 years of photo-journalism
The Potteries Museum, Stoke-on-Trent
01782-232323
3 October to 17 January.

Caroline Hunter: new work
Mainhill Gallery, Ancrum, Jedburgh
01835 830518
4 October to 18 October.

Design for the prospectus for The Yellow Book by Aubrey Beardsley, at the Victoria & Albert Museum, London, 8 October '98 to 10 January '99.

Jennifer Anderson: work by new graduate from Dundee Art School
Gatehouse Gallery, Glasgow
0141-620 0235
from 4 October.

Addressing the Century: 100 Years of Art and Fashion
Hayward Gallery, London SE1
0171-921 0600
8 October '98 to 3 January '99.

Aubrey Beardsley (1872-98)
Victoria and Albert Museum, London SW7
0171-938 8349/8441
8 October '98 to 10 January '99.

Changing Pages: 3D artists' books
Collins Gallery, Glasgow
0141-548 2558
10 October to 14 November.

Photographs from the Yemen by Patricia & Charles Aithie
Newport Museum & Art Gallery, Newport, Wales
01633 840064
10 October to 21 November.

Henry Moore
Sainsbury Centre for Visual Arts, Norwich
01603 456161
13 October to 13 December.

Roy Freer & Ken Paine
Linda Blackstone Gallery, Middlesex
0181-868 5765
14 October to 31 October.

Sporting & Natural History Paintings
Malcolm Innes Gallery, Edinburgh
0131-558 9544/5
14 October to 31 October.

Satellites of Fashion: accessories
Crafts Council, London N1
0171-278 7700
15 October to 6 December.

British Sporting Heroes
National Portrait Gallery
London WC2
0171-306 0055
16 October '98 to 31 January '99.

Karen McIntyre
The Edinburgh Gallery
0131-557 5227
17 October to 3 November.

Glasgow Society of Women Artists
Lillie Art Gallery, Milngavie
0141-943 3246
17 October to 14 November.

New Work for the Towner: work commissioned in response to the 18th building & its collections
Towner Art Gallery, Eastbourne
01323 417961/725112
17 October '98 to January '99.

Burne-Jones (1833-98)
The Gas Hall, Birmingham Museum and Art Gallery
0121-303 2834
17 October '98 to 17 January '98.

Regency
Cecil Higgins Art Gallery, Bedford
01234 211222
20 October '98 to 6 February '99.

CALENDAR OF EXHIBITIONS

Life? Or Theatre? – gouaches by Charlotte Salomon, created whilst in hiding from the Nazis
Royal Academy of Arts,
London W1
0171-300 8000
22 October to 17 January.

Grinling Gibbons (1648-1721) and the Art of Carving
Victoria and Albert Museum
London SW7
0171-938 8349/8441
22 October '98 to 24 January '99.

Arturo Di Stefano
Purdy Hicks Gallery, London SE1
0171-401 9229
23 October to 28 November.

Contemporary British Glass
City Art Centre, Edinburgh
0131-529 3993
23 October 98 to 9 January 99.

Salvador Dali: A Mythology
Tate Gallery, Liverpool
0151-709 3223
24 October '98 to 31 January '99.

The Society of Scottish Artists Annual Exhibition
Royal Scottish Academy, Edinburgh
0131-225 6671
26 October to 14 November.

Will Maclean: new work
Art First, London W1
0171-734 0386
27 October to 19 November.

Graham H. D. McKean
The Leith Gallery, Edinburgh
0131-553 5255
27 October to 21 November.

John Kobal Photographic Portrait Award 1998
National Portrait Gallery, London WC2
0171-306 0055
30 October '98 to 24 January '99.

Mark Catesby's *Natural History of America*: the Watercolours from the Royal Library, Windsor Castle
The Queen's Gallery, Buckingham Palace, London SW1
0171-839 1377
30 October '98 to 10 January '99.

NOVEMBER 1998

Brian Fojcik
Thackeray Gallery, London W8
0171-937 5883
during November.

Duncan Shanks
Roger Billcliffe Fine Art, Glasgow
0141-332 4027
during November.

Sarah Raphael
Marlborough Fine Art, London W1
0171-629 5161
during November.

Steve McQueen: first major solo show
Institute of Contemporary Arts, London
0171-930 3647
November and December.

John Maxwell (1905-1962)
Scottish National Gallery of Modern Art, Edinburgh
0131-556 8921
November '98 to February '99.

Glasgow in the 1840s: watercolours by William Simpson
The People's Palace, Glasgow
0141-550 0892
November '98 to June '99.

The Silver Show: contemporary silverware
Leighton House, London W14
0171-602 3316
2 November to 14 November.

Graham Ward
Portal Gallery, London W1
0171-493 0706
2 November to 21 November.

Jane Corsellis: new paintings
New Academy Gallery, London W1
0171-323 4700
5 November to 27 November.

New English Art Club
Mall Galleries, London SW1
0171-930 6844
6 November to 16 November.

Andrew Fitzpatrick
The Edinburgh Gallery
0131-557 5227
7 November to 24 November.

Beryl Cook
The Potteries Museum & Art Gallery, Stoke-on-Trent
01782-232323
7 November to 20 December.

Michael Scott
Portland Gallery, London SW1
0171-321 0422
11 November to 27 November.

Debra Manifold: first solo show
Linda Blackstone Gallery, Middlesex
0181-868 5765
11 November to 28 November.

Signorelli (c.1440-1523) in British Collections
National Gallery, London WC2
0171-747 2885
11 November '98 to 31 January '99.

Helen McAllister: new paintings
Talbot Rice Gallery, Edinburgh
0131-650 2211
14 November to 12 December.

Book: four new artists' books
Djanogly Art Gallery, Nottingham
0115-951 3189
14 November to 20 December.

Lincolnshire Artists
Usher Gallery, Lincoln
01522 527980
15 November to 20 December.

Modern Drawings 1910-1920
Whitworth Art Gallery, Manchester
0161-275 7450
mid-November '98 to mid-January '99.

Winter Exhibition: Scottish Paintings
Calton Gallery, Edinburgh
0131-556 1010
19 November to 23 December.

Crafts; British contemporary automata
Collins Gallery, Glasgow
0141-548 2558
21 November to 23 December.

Barbara Rae and Gwen O'Dowd
Art First, London
0171-734 0386
24 November to 23 December.

Henri Cartier-Bresson: Elsewhere – photographs from the Americas
Victoria and Albert Museum
London SW7
0171-938 8349/8441
26 November '98 to 12 April '99.

The History of Photography: selection from the collection
Victoria and Albert Museum, London SW7
0171-938 8349 for recorded information, 0171-938 8441 for general enquiries
26 November '98 to August '99.

Christmas Show: On A Small Scale
Open Eye Gallery, Edinburgh
0131-557 1020
28 November to 24 December.

Lincolnshire Contemporary Crafts 10th Anniversary Exhibition
Usher Gallery, Lincoln
01522 527980
28 November to 31 December.

Paul Peter Piech Retrospective: posters
Glynn Vivian Art Gallery, Swansea
01792 655006
28 November '98 to 10 January '99.

DECEMBER 1998

Victor Pasmore 90th Birthday Retrospective
Marlborough Fine Art, London W1
0171-629 5161
December '98 to January '99.

George Devlin
Portland Gallery, London SW1
0171-321 0422
4 December to 23 December.

Medieval ceramics and tilework from Islamic Syria
Ashmolean Museum, Oxford
01865 278000
4 December '98 to 1 February '99.

Lionel Aggett: pastels of France, Italy & Spain
Llewellyn Alexander, London SE1
0171-620 1322
10 December '98 to 2 January '99.

Boundary Lines: basketmaking
Crafts Council, London N1
0171-278 7700
16 December '98 to 14 March '99.

Across Moor and Down Dale: the Yorkshire landscape
York City Art Gallery
01904 551861
19 December '98 to 31 January '99.

JANUARY 1999

June Redfern: new paintings
The Scottish Gallery, Edinburgh
0131-558 1200
during January '99.

Archetype: advertising and the persuasive power of type
Harris Museum & Art Gallery, Preston
01772 258248
January '99 to March '99.

Coming of Age: new sculpture, textiles, drawings & virtual reality by Heather Connelly
Djanogly Art Gallery, Nottingham
0115-951 3189
January '99 to March '99.

Edward Falkener: A Victorian Orientalist
British Museum, London WC1
0171-636 1555, 0171-323 8599/8299
January '99 to April '99.

Julie Brooks: painting, sculpture & film
Collins Gallery, Glasgow
0141-548 2558
16 January to 13 February '99.

Hilda Carline
Usher Gallery, Lincoln
01522 527980
16 January '99 to 7 March '99.

Monet in the 20th Century
Royal Academy of Arts, London W1
0171-300 8000
21 January '99 to 18 April '99.

Peter Prendergast: paintings & drawings
Newport Museum & Art Gallery
01633 840064
23 January '99 to 6 March '99.

Ingres (1780-1867): Portraits
National Gallery Sainsbury Wing, London WC2
0171-747 2885
27 January '99 to 25 April '99.

FEBRUARY 1999

The Pleasures of Peace: Craft, Art and Design in Britain from the '40s to the '70s
Sainsbury Centre for Visual Arts, Norwich
01603 456161
February '99 to April '99.

Julia Carter Preston
Walker Art Gallery, Liverpool
0151-207 0001
February '99 to May '99.

MARCH 1999

Charlotte Cornish: paintings & prints
Cambridge Contemporary Art, Cambridge
01223 324222
during March '99.

A Sense of History: landscape and figurative subjects from 1850
Mainhill Gallery, Ancrum, Jedburgh
01835 830518
throughout March '99.

Willie Barns-Graham
Art First, London W1
0171-734 0386
mid-March to mid-April '99.

Philip Mead and Alan Rogers
Glynn Vivian Art Gallery, Swansea
01792 655006
20 March '99 to 9 May '99.

The Arts of the Sikh Kingdoms
Victoria and Albert Museum, London SW7
0171-938 8349/8441
25 March '99 to 25 July '99.

Ethel Walker
Thackeray Gallery, London W8
0171-937 5883
end-March to end-April '99.

THE 20th CENTURY BRITISH ART FAIR

The only fair for BRITISH ART from 1900 to the present day

Royal College of Art

Kensington Gore, London SW7

23 – 27 September 1998

11am – 8pm, 7pm last two days
Admission £7

Information and lecture programme: 0181 742 1611

FAIRS & FESTIVALS

Battersea Contemporary Art Fair, next to be held in Spring 1999.

THE FOLLOWING IS A SELECTION OF FINE ART AND CRAFT FAIRS AND ARTS FESTIVALS TAKING PLACE IN THE COMING YEAR.

FOR A FREE LEAFLET COVERING 50 LEADING ARTS FESTIVALS, INCLUDING SOME OF THOSE LISTED HERE, SEND AN A5 SAE TO:
BRITISH ARTS FESTIVALS ASSOCIATION,
3RD FLOOR,
WHITECHAPEL LIBRARY,
77 WHITECHAPEL HIGH ST,
LONDON E1 7QX.

APRIL 1998

Glasgow Art Fair
George Square, Glasgow.
Call 0141-227 5511 for details and tickets).
Fair now in its third year (admission £3 adults, £2 concessions; season tickets £5, family tickets £6). Over 40 of Britain's finest art dealers selling original works of art by both celebrated and lesser-known artists, with prices starting at around £50.
16 April to 19 April.

Lovebytes Digital Arts Festival
Showroom Media and Exhibition Centre, Sheffield.
Call 0114-221 0393 for further information.
Exhibition, seminars, workshops, film screenings, performance and live music events exploring the cultural aspects of new technology.
23 April to 25 April.

Chelsea Art Fair
Chelsea Old Town Hall, Kings Road, London.
Call Penman Art Fairs, 01444 482514 for details.
Old Master to contemporary (mostly 20th-century and post-war) paintings, sculptures and studio pottery.
23 April to 26 April.

FAIRS & FESTIVALS

The Solihull Antiques Fair
Solihull Conference Centre. Call 0121-782 2899/780 4999 for details.
This fine art and antiques fair replaces the former Kenilworth Antiques fair. Deadlines of 1860 for furniture, 1898 for European ceramics, glass and prints, and 1930 for silver, jewellery, Oriental art, paintings and sculpture.
23 April to 26 April.

The Craft Movement Contemporary Craft Fair
Battersea Town Hall, London. Call 01373 813333 for details.
High quality contemporary crafts chosen by a rigorous selection procedure. Ceramics, textiles, jewellery, glassware, metal, wood & furniture.
24 April to 26 April.

London Original Print Fair
Royal Academy of Arts, London. Call 0171-300 8000 for details.
Now in its 13th year, this is Europe's only specialist print fair to span the five centuries of printmaking from the earliest medieval woodcuts to the most recent work by contemporary artists. 24 dealers of the highest calibre.
30 April to 3 May.

MAY 1998

Brighton Festival
Various venues in Brighton. Call 01273 292950 for details, or 01273 292961 for a brochure.
England's biggest arts festival.
2 May to 24 May.

Chelmsford Cathedral Festival
Chelmsford. Call 01245 359890 for details.
Concerts, exhibitions and a Fringe festival.
6 May to 16 May.

Living Crafts
Hatfield House, Hatfield, Hertfordshire AL9 5NQ. Call 01582 761235 or 01707 262823 for details.
Around 500 of Britain's top craftsmen and women demonstrating and selling a wide range of crafts from rural to highly sophisticated and traditional to state-of-the-art, in 12 giant marquees (admission £6.20 adults, £2.80 children). This year there will also be a special area dedicated to displays and demonstrations of Tudor crafts, to celebrate the 500th anniversary of the Old Palace.
7 May to 10 May (10am to 6pm).

Bury St. Edmunds Festival
Bury St. Edmunds, Suffolk. Call 01284 757099 for brochure and booking details.
Mixed arts festival.
8 May to 24 May.

Perth Festival of the Arts
Perth, Scotland. Call 01738 475295 for details.
Performing and visual arts festival.
21 May to 31 May.

Swaledale Festival
Swaledale, Yorkshire. Call 01969 622217 for details.
Music, dance, theatre, art, craft, walks and talks.
22 May to 7 June.

The Craft Movement Contemporary Craft Fair
The Queen Charlotte Hall, Richmond-upon-Thames. Call 01373 813333 for details.
High quality contemporary crafts chosen by a rigorous selection procedure. Ceramics, textiles, jewellery, glassware, metal, wood & furniture.
23 May to 25 May.

JUNE 1998

The Summer Fine Art and Antiques Fair
Olympia, London. Call 0171-370 8212/8234 for details.
This prestigious fair (catalogues £5; admission £5 from 5 June, £15 including catalogue on 4 June) celebrates its 25th anniversary with high quality paintings, prints, watercolours, pottery, porcelain, silver, glass, books, manuscripts, textiles, carpets, furniture and statuary on offer. Careful vetting of exhibits by a panel of experts ensures accuracy of identification, so the public can buy with confidence. Prices range from the affordable to the exclusive.
4 June to 14 June.

The Art of Living Fair
Eastnor Castle, Ledbury, Herefordshire HR8 1RL. Contact the Kilvert Gallery, Ashbrook House, Clyro, Herefordshire HR3 5RZ (tel/fax 01497 820831) for details.
A celebration of the best in decorative arts for home and garden, housed in canvas pavilions in the Castle grounds (admission £5 adults, £3 children). Original jewellery, fashion, art, furniture, textiles, wood and ceramics for commission and sale. Specialist advice in interior design. Books, prints and presents. Exhibition of contemporary painting and sculpture. Live music, workshops and demonstrations. Christie's valuation of small decorative antiques and works of art. Restaurant and coffee shop. Charity gala evening in aid of Marie Curie Cancer Care on 11 June, opened by Henry Sandon of Antiques Roadshow.
11 June to 14 June (11am to 5.30pm).

FAIRS & FESTIVALS

The Grosvenor House Art & Antiques Fair

Great Room, Grosvenor House, Park Lane, London W1A 3AA (0171-495 8743).
Britain's pre-eminent fair in the international world of art and antiques, now in its 64th year (admission plus handbook £15 single, £25 double, with reductions if booked in advance; £8 single ticket during final two hours each day). The world's leading dealers exhibiting works of art from antiquity to the 20th C, with quality assured by the vetting of every exhibit. Prices from £100 to over £1 million. Charity gala evening in aid of the British Red Cross, June 11 – call 0171-235 5454 for details.
11 June to 20 June (opens 11am; closes 5pm on 11 June, 8pm other weekdays, 6pm weekends).

The International Ceramics Fair and Seminar

The Park Lane Hotel, Piccadilly, London. Call 0171-734 5491 for details.
A synthesis of academia and commerce, now in its 17th year. Organised in three sections, the event comprises: a loan exhibition of contemporary ceramics from British collections, organised by the Crafts Council; a series of 15 lectures presenting the latest discoveries of museum and other academics from 8 countries; and a fair of contemporary work with 47 exhibitors from 8 countries.
12 June to 15 June.

Stoke Newington Midsummer Festival

Stoke Newington, London. Call 0171-923 1599 for details.
Performance and visual arts events.
14 June to 20 June.

Islington International Festival

Islington, London. Call 0171-637 2994 for details.
A two-week multidisciplinary arts festival.
15 June to 27 June.

The Kensington Contemporary Art & Design Show

Kensington Town Hall, London. Call Penman Art Fairs, 01444 482514 for details.
Paintings, pottery, glass, furniture, jewellery etc. by well-known and budding artists (admission £5).
19 June to 21 June (Fri 11-8, Sat 11-6, Sun 11-5).

Ludlow Festival

Ludlow, Shropshire. Details: large SAE to Ludlow Festival Box Office, Castle Square, Ludlow, Shropshire SY8 1AY (01584 875070).
Theatre, music, dance, lectures and exhibitions.
20 June to 5 July.

City of London Festival

Call 0171-377 0540 for a free brochure (available from April).
Over 100 events in 35 stunning heritage venues, many of which are not normally open to the public. Programme includes concerts, opera, dance, theatre, comedy, exhibitions, cinema, architectural and garden walks, readings and children's workshops.
23 June to 16 July.

JULY 1998

Chichester Festivities

Various venues in and around Chichester. Call 01243 785718 for details.
Music, theatre, opera, films, talks and exhibitions.
2 July to 14 July.

Henley Festival of Music and the Arts

Henley-on-Thames, Oxfordshire. Call 01491 410414 for details.
Varied programme of events taking place on the banks of the Thames.
8 July to 11 July.

Art in Action

Waterperry House, nr. Wheatley, Oxford OX33 9JZ Details: SAE to 96 Sedelscombe Road, London SW6 1RB (0171-381 3192).
Open-air event attracting approximately 25,000 visitors over four days. Over 200 artists and craftsmen of the highest quality will be selling and demonstrating their work, with examples from both western and non-western cultures. Practical classes are available: book on the day. Excellent food, plus live music and dance performances.
16 July to 19 July.

Gallery Week '98

Nationwide. Contact Engage, National Association for Gallery Education, 1 Herbal Hill, Clerkenwell, London EC1R 5EJ (0171-278 8382) for details and regional leaflets.
Over 400 galleries and museums, from local establishments to national institutions, will be hosting a variety of events to attract a wider audience to the world of contemporary art.
18 July to 26 July.

Sussex Art & Antiques Fair

Barkham Manor Vineyard, Piltdown, Nr. Uckfield. Call Penman Art Fairs, 01444 482514 for details.
Over 50 stands selling art (mostly 20th-century traditional) and antiques, plus food and wines (admission £4).
23 July to 26 July (Fri & Sat 11-6, Sun 11-5).

FAIRS & FESTIVALS

AUGUST 1998

National Eisteddfod of Wales
Pencoad, Bridge End, near Cardiff. Contact Robyn Tomos, National Eisteddfod of Wales Arts & Crafts Officer on 01222 763777 for details.
Exhibition of contemporary art, crafts, sculpture, installation, video, photography, fashion etc. by contributors who are of Welsh descent, are based in Wales or speak or write Welsh.
1 August to 8 August.

Edinburgh International Festival
Various venues throughout Edinburgh. Details from Edinburgh International Festival, 21 Market Street, Edinburgh EH1 1BW (0131-473 2001).
Cultural feast featuring some of the world's greatest artists and companies.
16 August to 5 September.

The Craft Movement Contemporary Craft Fair
The Guildhall, Winchester. Call 01373 813333 for details.
High quality contemporary crafts chosen by a rigorous selection procedure. Ceramics, textiles, jewellery, glassware, metal, wood and furniture.
29 August to 31 August.

SEPTEMBER 1998

The Contemporary Print Fair
Concourse Gallery, Barbican Centre, London. Contact Clive Jennings, 6a Goodge Place, London W1P (0171-436 4007) for details or free catalogue.
The best of printmaking today: over 1,000 original prints by around 250 artists, on sale from dealers and publishers. All the major print media, with prices

from under £50 to over £5,000.
Autumn – call or write to Clive Jennings for exact dates (address above).

Dulwich Festival
Dulwich, London. Call 0181-299 1011 for details.
A weekend of arts activities and events.
12 September to 13 September.

The Craft Movement Contemporary Craft Fair
The Assembly Rooms, Edinburgh. Call 01373 813333 for details.
High quality contemporary crafts chosen by a rigorous selection procedure. Ceramics, textiles, jewellery, glassware, metal, wood and furniture.
18 September to 20 September.

The 20th Century Art Fair
Royal College of Art, London. Contact Gay Hutson, 0181-742 1611 for details.
Founded in 1988, this is the only fair for British art covering the period 1900 to the present day, and is held at the Royal College of Art, a venue associated internationally with the best in British art. Some 60 leading galleries and dealers will be participating.
23 September to 27 September.

The Art of Living Fair
Hever Castle, Hever, Edenbridge, Kent. Contact the Kilvert Gallery, Ashbrook House, Clyro, Herefordshire HR3 5RZ (tel/fax 01497 820831) for details.
A celebration of the best in decorative arts for home and garden, housed in canvas pavilions in the

Castle grounds (admission £6.50 adults, £4 children). Original jewellery, fashion, art, furniture, textiles, wood and ceramics for commission and sale. Specialist advice in interior design. Books, prints and presents. Exhibition of contemporary painting and sculpture. Live music, workshops and demonstrations. Christie's valuation of small decorative antiques and works of art. Coffee shop and restaurant. Charity gala evening in aid of Marie Curie Cancer Care on September 25.
25 September to 27 September (11am to 5.30pm).

The Craft Movement Contemporary Craft Fair
Kensington Town Hall, London. Call 01373 813333 for details.
High quality contemporary crafts chosen by a rigorous selection procedure. Ceramics, textiles, jewellery, glassware, metal, wood and furniture.
25 September to 27 September.

OCTOBER 1998

Canterbury Festival
Various venues throughout Canterbury. Programme available from July, from Canterbury Festival Office, Christ Church Gate, The Precincts, Canterbury, Kent CT1 2EE (01227 452853).
Mixed arts festival.
10 October to 24 October.

Southwark Festival
Southwark, London. Call 0171-403 7474 for details.
Exhibitions, classes, lectures, workshops, concerts and other events with a European flavour.
10 October to 9 November.

Chelsea Crafts Fair

The Old Town Hall, Kings Road, London. Call the Crafts Council on 0171-278 7700 for details.

The 19th annual fair, organised by the Crafts Council (admission charge to be decided). Around 230 makers selling high quality work including jewellery, ceramics, furniture, textiles, glass, wood, toys, fashion and accessories.

13 October to 20 October (closed Monday 19 October).

The City of London Art Fair

Honourable Artillery Company, Armoury House, 39 City Road, London EC1. Call Penman Art Fairs, 01444 482514 for details.

Art fair in a unique setting: a 1738 palladian house in 7 acres of grass in the heart of the City of London, not normally open to the public (admission £6). 37 stands selling mainly 20th-century paintings, some sculpture, studio pottery and jewellery.

15 October to 18 October (Thursday & Friday 11am to 8pm, Saturday 11am to 6pm, Sunday 11am to 5pm.

Kensington Antiques & Fine Art Fair

Kensington Town Hall, London. Call Penman Art Fairs, 01444 482514 for details.

Strictly vetted show comprising 85 stands, including fifteen stalls selling paintings dated before 1930.

29 October to 1 November.

NOVEMBER 1998

The Craft Movement Contemporary Craft Fair

The Concert Halls, Blackheath. Call 01373 813333 for details.

High quality contemporary crafts chosen by a rigorous selection procedure.
Ceramics, textiles, jewellery, glassware, metal, wood and furniture.

7 November to 8 November.

The Winter Fine Art and Antiques Fair

Olympia, London. Call 0171-370 8234 for details.

230 leading dealers exhibiting and selling high quality antiques and outstanding works of art. Careful vetting of exhibits by a panel of experts ensures accuracy of identification, so the public can buy with confidence.

16 November to 22 November.

The Craft Movement Contemporary Craft Fair

Cheltenham Town Hall. Call 01373 813333 for details.

High quality contemporary crafts chosen by a rigorous selection procedure.
Ceramics, textiles, jewellery, glassware, metal, wood and furniture.

27 November to29 November.

DECEMBER 1998

The Craft Movement Contemporary Craft Fair

The Queen Charlotte Hall, Richmond-upon-Thames. Call 01373 813333 for details.

High quality contemporary crafts chosen by a rigorous selection procedure.
Ceramics, textiles, jewellery, glassware, metal, wood and furniture.

4 December to 6 December.

JANUARY 1999

West London Antiques & Fine Art Fair

Kensington Town Hall, London. Call Penman Art Fairs, 01444 482514 for details.

80 exhibitors, including around 15 for pre-1930 paintings, sculpture etc. (admission £5).

14 January to 17 January (Thursday & Friday 11am to 8pm, Saturday 11am to 6pm, Sunday 11am to 5pm).

ART99

Business Design Centre, Islington, London. Call 0171-359 3535 for details.

The London Contemporary Art Fair, with many of the foremost dealers selling work by leading contemporary artists as well as promising recent graduates.

20 January to 24 January.

FEBRUARY 1999

Chester Antiques & Fine Art Show

County Grandstand, Chester Racecourse. Call Penman Art Fairs, 01444 482514 for details.

Show in its 10th year, comprising 50 stands, including around 15 of pre-1930 paintings & sculpture.

11 February to 14 February.

The Spring Fine Art and Antiques Fair

Olympia, London. Call 0171-370 8234 for details.

160 of the world's leading dealers exhibiting and selling high quality antiques and 20th-century works of art. Careful vetting of exhibits by a panel of experts ensures accuracy of identification.

23 February to 28 February.

MARCH 1999

The Contemporary Print Show

Concourse Gallery, Barbican Centre, London EC2.
Contact Clive Jennings, 6a Goodge Place, London W1P (0171-436 4007) for details or free catalogue.
The best of printmaking today: over 1,000 original prints by around 250 artists, presented in exhibition format by 20 galleries and publishers. All the major print media, with prices from under £50 to over £5,000.
Spring 1999 – call or write to Clive Jennings for exact dates (address above).

Battersea Contemporary Art Fair

Battersea Old Town Hall, London SW11.
Call 0171-228 0741 or 0171-642 5318 for details.
The largest artists' art fair in the UK, with artists selling their own work direct to the public at truly affordable prices (no commission goes to the organisers). Paintings, sculptures, limited edition prints and photographs from highly traditional to cutting edge.
March or April 1999.

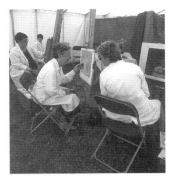

Practical classes for all ages at Art in Action, Waterperry House, 16 to 19 July.

COMPETITIONS

COMPETITIONS

This is only a selection of the awards, bursaries and competitions available, ranging from cash prizes and travel scholarships to opportunities for exhibitions and publishing. Further information can be obtained through art colleges, regional arts boards, local artists' groups and libraries. It is advisable to check before submitting work or sending money.

ALASTAIR SALVESEN ART SCHOLARSHIP

This is an enablement scholarship, offered by the Royal Scottish Academy, which comprises £8,000 in travel funds and a three-week exhibition, for an artist aged 25-35 who trained at a Scottish college of art.
Details: SAE in December to Alastair Salvesen Scholarship, Royal Scottish Academy, The Mound, Edinburgh EH2 2EL.

BANKERS TRUST PYRAMID AWARDS

Made annually to visual and performing artists from the Royal College of Art and the Guildhall School of Music & Drama, who are embarking on a freelance career. These awards comprise cash and professional assistance and involvement in Bankers Trust's community programme in the inner-London area.
Details: contact Graça Tavares de Almeida, Royal College of Art, Kensington Gore, London SW7, or Candy Blackham, Guildhall School, Barbican, London EC2.

BG WILDLIFE PHOTOGRAPHER OF THE YEAR

SUBMISSIONS BY 15 MAY
Competition organised by BBC Wildlife Magazine aiming to find the best wildlife pictures taken by photographers worldwide. Winning and commended photographs appear in a Natural History Museum exhibition from late October to February before touring worldwide, and are published in a commemorative book. Adult and junior categories are available; prizes total £14,000.
Details: call 0171-938 8714.

BRITISH DESIGN AND ART DIRECTION AWARDS

APPLICATIONS BY JANUARY
Submissions from individuals and companies are invited for printed works produced during the previous year. Presentations are made annually in May.
Details: Alex Adie, 0171-582 6487.

BRITISH SCHOOL AT ROME

APPLICATIONS BY DECEMBER
This residential centre for research in the humanities and the practice of fine arts and architecture offers scholarships ranging from 3 to 9 months, including the 9-month Abbey Scholarship in Painting, the Rome Scholarships in the Fine Arts, the Arts Council of England Helen Chadwick Fellowship, the Henry Moore Sculpture Fellowship at the BSR, the RIBA Rome Scholarship in Architecture and Urbanism and the Sargant Fellowship for Fine Arts.
Details: SA label to Registrar, The British School at Rome, Piazzale Winston Churchill 5 (gia via Gramsci 61), 00197 Rome, Italy.

COUTTS CONTEMPORARY ART FOUNDATION AWARDS

Established in 1992 as part of the bank's 300th anniversary celebrations, the awards are made biennially (the next year being 2000) at the discretion of the Foundation's Art Advisory Committee. Submissions are not required and winners tend to be artists of international standing.
Details: Sabina R. Korfmann-Bodenmann, Manager, Coutts Contemporary Art Foundation, Talsrasse 59, CH-8022 Zürich, Switzerland.

DALER-ROWNEY AWARDS

Daler-Rowney make various awards at national and regional exhibitions. See The Art Paper, available free of charge only from art stores in March, June and October, for competitions.
Details: Brenda Howley, Editor and PR Manager, Daler-Rowney, PO Box 10, Bracknell RG12 8ST.

DELFINA STUDIO TRUST

APPLICATIONS BY JANUARY
The Trust provides 18 free studio spaces: British artists are awarded two years' space and others one year with accommodation.
Details: The Administrator, The Delfina Studio Trust, 50 Bermondsey Street, Southwark, London SE1 3UD.

THE DISCERNING EYE

Works not larger than 20" in any direction are invited from artists 'not yet household names'. Prizes and an exhibition are available.

Details: A4 SAE to Exhibition/Competition Organisers and PR, Parker Harris & Company, PO Box 279, Esher, Surrey KT10 8YZ.

EUROPEAN PUBLISHERS AWARD FOR PHOTOGRAPHY

An open competition for an unpublished book project by a photographer. Open to photographers world-wide. The winning book is published in five European countries.
Details: SAE to
European Publishers Award,
Dewi Lewis Publishing,
8 Broomfield Road, Heaton Moor,
Stockport SK4 4ND.

FINE ART TRADE GUILD BUSINESS AWARDS SCHEME

Winners in several nominated art and trade categories are presented with an artist-designed trophy in the spring.
Details: SAE to Vanessa Giles,
Fine Art Trade Guild, 16 Empress Place, London SW6 1TT
(tel 0171-381 6616, fax 0171-381 2596).

FULBRIGHT POSTGRADUATE AWARDS

APPLICATIONS BY NOVEMBER
Graduate students may apply for a year's postgraduate study in the USA with a maintenance grant.
Details: A4 SAE (39p) to the British Programme Administrator, Fulbright Commission,
62 Doughty Street,
London WC1N 2LS
(tel: 0171-404 6880, website http://www.fulbright.co.uk).

FULBRIGHT SCHOLARSHIPS

APPLICATIONS BY MARCH
Awards to the value of £1,750 are available to candidates who can demonstrate academic or artistic excellence and who have an invitation to lecture or research from a US institution of higher education.
Details: A4 SAE (39p) to the British Programme Administrator, Fulbright Commission,
62 Doughty Street,
London WC1N 2LS
(tel: 0171-404 6880,
website http://www.fulbright.co.uk)

THE HUNTING ART PRIZES

Over 1,000 artists annually enter this prestigious competition which offers generous cash prizes and an exhibition at the RCA, followed by a tour.
Details: A4 SAE to Exhibition/Competition Organisers and PR, Parker Harris & Company,
PO Box 279,
Esher,
Surrey KT10 8YZ.

Below: *What if? A Portrait* by Jennifer McRae, winner of last year's Hunting Art Prize

JERWOOD PAINTING PRIZE

This major award is given for excellence in painting, with an exhibition of the shortlisted prizewinners' work in London.
Details: A4 SAE to Exhibition/Competition Organisers and PR, Parker Harris & Company, PO Box 279, Esher, Surrey KT10 8YZ.

THE JOHN KINROSS MEMORIAL FUND

APPLICATIONS BY APRIL
Students at Scottish colleges studying painting, sculpture and architecture are eligible to apply for a three-month scholarship to Florence in memory of the late John Kinross.
Details: SAE to The Secretary, Royal Scottish Academy, The Mound, Edinburgh EH2 2EL.

JOHN KOBAL PHOTOGRAPHIC PORTRAIT AWARD

APPLICATIONS BY JUNE
This annual award with exhibitions at the National Portrait Gallery and various regional galleries, prize money and publication of winning work is open to anyone over the age of 18 submitting any portrait (to be interpreted in its loosest sense).
Details: SAE to The Award Administrator, John Kobal Foundation, PO Box 3838, London NW1 3JF.

JOHN MOORES LIVERPOOL EXHIBITION

This is a leading biennale of contemporary painting. There is a £20,000 purchase prize, 10 prizes of £1,000 and an exhibition at the Walker Art Gallery, for works in any medium except traditional watercolour and no larger than 10ft by 12ft in any direction.
Next exhibition: autumn 1999.
Details: available from spring 1999 – SAE to The Exhibition Secretary, Walker Art Gallery, William Brown Street, Liverpool L3 8EL.

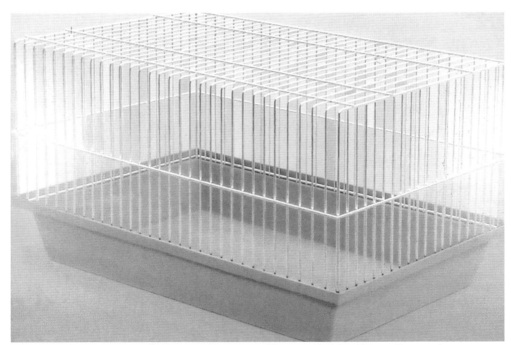

Above: *Harmony in Green* by Dan Hays, winner of last year's John Moores Liverpool

JULIET GOMPERTS MEMORIAL SCHOLARSHIPS

APPLICATIONS BY END FEBRUARY

Young artists, aged over 18 and under 40, are invited to apply for scholarships to attend courses (two weeks) at the Verrocchio Arts Centre in Tuscany. Also, the Janet Konstam Travelling Fellowship is awarded to the best applicant for travel in Italy after the tenure of the Juliet Gomperts Scholarship.
Details: SAE to
The Memorial Scholarships,
31 Addison Avenue,
London W11 4QS.

KRASZNA-KRAUSZ BOOK AWARDS

These international awards are made annually to encourage and recognise outstanding achievements in the publishing and writing of books on photography and the moving image (film, television and video). Prize money totalling more than £20,000 is awarded in January.
Details: Andrea Livingstone,
122 Fawnbrake Avenue,
London SE24 0BZ.

LAING ART COMPETITION

In this major annual competition, thousands of pounds worth of prizes are given for landscapes or seascapes, with an exhibition in London and at various regional centres, starting in the spring.
Details:
The Laing Art Competition,
John Laing plc, Maxted House,
13 Maxted Road,
Hemel Hempstead,
Herts. HP2 7DX.

THE LINBURY PRIZE FOR STAGE DESIGN

Commissions and cash awards, sponsored by one of the Sainsbury family charitable trusts, are made biennially to final-year graduate and post-graduate theatre design students from selected colleges. Finalists will exhibit in the autumn. Next entry period: 1999.
Details: Liz Martell, Kallaway, 0171-221 7883.

THE MACMILLAN PRIZE FOR A CHILDREN'S PICTURE BOOK

Art students in higher education are eligible to enter works that are original and will provide children with much enjoyment in this annual competition.
Details: SAE to
Marketing Department,
Macmillan Children's Books,
25 Eccleston Place,
London SW1W 9NF.

THE MORRISON SCOTTISH PORTRAIT AWARD

This biennial award will next be given in 1999.
Details: SAE to
Royal Scottish Academy,
The Mound, Edinburgh EH2 2EL.

THE NATIONAL ART LIBRARY ILLUSTRATION AWARDS

SUBMISSIONS BY JULY

Organised by the National Art Library and sponsored by the Enid Linder Foundation, these annual awards are for book and magazine illustrations published in the calendar year preceding the date of the award (ie. 1999 awards for 1998 books and magazines). Overall winner (£2,000), two second prizewinners (one for book and one for magazine illustration) and four distinguished mention awards. December-February exhibition.
Details: Dr. Leo Defreitas, National Art Library,
The Victoria & Albert Museum,
South Kensington,
London SW7 2RL.

NATIONAL EISTEDDFOD OF WALES

SUBMISSIONS BY 14 FEBRUARY

The Eisteddfod hosts a large contemporary exhibition of art, crafts, sculpture, installation, photography, video, fashion etc.. Gold medals and prizes awarded. Any person born in Wales, of Welsh parentage, who has lived or worked in Wales for the last three years, or able to speak or write the Welsh language is eligible.
Details: SAE to Eisteddfod Office,
40 Parc Ty Glas, Llanishen,
Cardiff CF4 5WU
(01222-763777).

NATIONAL PRINT EXHIBITION

SUBMISSIONS BY DECEMBER

February open exhibition offering 18 prizes for outstanding printmakers.
Details: SAE to FBA,
17 Carlton House Terrace,
London SW1Y 5BD.

NEW ART AWARD

Founded with the intention of recognising and helping young artists in their final year of postgraduate study this award offers cash prizes and a London exhibition. Not occurring in 1998. Details: SAE to Lynne Stern and Linnet Fielding, c/o 107 Hartfield Road, London SW19 3TJ.

NEW DESIGNERS AWARDS

This is part of the New Designers Exhibition held annually in July at the Business Design Centre, Islington. Business and sponsors from throughout the UK select winners from the show representing the best graduates from British design courses.
Details: contact Lucy Field, 0171-359 3535.

NEW ENGLISH ART CLUB

SUBMISSIONS BY OCTOBER
November open exhibition offering a number of awards plus Marks & Spencer subsidies for entries by recent art students.
Details: SAE to FBA, 17 Carlton House Terrace, London SW1Y 5BD.

NORTHERN ARTS

APPLICATIONS THROUGHOUT THE YEAR
Northern Arts invites artists from the region to submit applications for schemes covering the visual arts, crafts, photography, commissions and exhibitions. Awards include the Artists Award Prize (£3,000) for an outstanding contribution to any area of the arts; Arts Promoters' Prize (£3,000); and Arts Event of the Year Prize (£5,000). Two runners up for each prize each receive £500. Application details will be announced in May.
Details: SAE to Northern Arts, 9-10 Osborne Terrace, Jesmond, Newcastle Upon Tyne NE2 1NZ.

THE OPEN DRAWING COMPETITION, CHELTENHAM

This is a competition for professional artists which awards cash prizes every year during an exhibition held at Cheltenham & Gloucester College of Higher Education.
Details: large SAE to Sara Neish-Barker, Exhibition Administrator, Department of Arts, Cheltenham & Gloucester College of Higher Education, Albert Road, Cheltenham, Glos GL52 3JG.

PASTEL SOCIETY

SUBMISSIONS BY JANUARY
March open exhibition for members and non-members, with 12 awards.
Details: SAE to FBA, 17 Carlton House Terrace, London SW1Y 5BD.

QUEEN ELIZABETH SCHOLARSHIP TRUST

APPLICATIONS BY 15 JANUARY
Aimed at furthering education in crafts and trades, scholarships are granted (ranging from £2,500 to £12,000) every June. Application forms available from September.
Details: SAE to the Secretary, The Queen Elizabeth Scholarship Trust, 7 Buckingham Gate, London SW1E 6JY.

ROYAL ACADEMY SUMMER EXHIBITION

SUBMISSIONS BY THE SPRING
An annual open exhibition sponsored by Diageo, which usually attracts around 12,000 paintings, sculptures, prints and architectural designs, of which about ten per cent are hung. Over sixty per cent of the works hung are sold during the course of the exhibition. Awards and prizes include: the Charles Wollaston Award

(£25,000); the Korn Ferry Picture of the Year Award (£10,000); the Bovis/Architects Journal Awards (£7,500); the Jack Goldhill Award for Sculpture (£7,000); the Diageo Award for First Time Exhibitors (£5,000); the M & G Group PLC Awards (3 purchase prizes of £5,000 each); the Dupree Family Award for a Woman Artist (£2,500).
Details: send SAE to Summer Exhibition Office, The Royal Academy of Arts, Piccadilly, London W1V 0DS.

ROYAL BATH & WEST OF ENGLAND SOCIETY 99/2000

£2,000 is awarded biannually to a professional artist aged between 22 and 35 for a landscape of British rural life, which is hung in the Academy's offices and in the annual exhibition.
Details: SAE to The Administrator, Royal Bath & West of England Society, The Show Ground, Shepton Mallet, Somerset BA4 6QN.

ROYAL INSTITUTE OF OIL PAINTERS

SUBMISSIONS BY OCTOBER
Open exhibition in late December for members and non-members, with a number of prizes awarded.
Details: SAE to FBA, 17 Carlton House Terrace, London SW1Y 5BD.

ROYAL INSTITUTE OF PAINTERS IN WATERCOLOURS OPEN EXHIBITION

SUBMISSIONS BY FEBRUARY
Open exhibition at the Mall Galleries, London in the spring.

Many prizes on offer.
Details: SAE to FBA,
17 Carlton House Terrace,
London SW1Y 5BD.

ROYAL OVER-SEAS LEAGUE ANNUAL OPEN EXHIBITION

Around £6,000 worth of prizes are awarded in an exhibition of works chosen from artists from UK, Commonwealth and former Commonwealth countries, aged 35 or under in their year of submission.
Details: Department of Cultural Affairs, Royal Over-Seas League, Over-Seas House, Park Place, St. James's Street, London SW1A 1LR.

ROYAL SCOTTISH ACADEMY

SUBMISSIONS BY MARCH
The annual exhibition takes place April 25 to July 5 and is sponsored by Maclay Murray & Spens, Solicitors. It includes painting, printmaking, architecture and sculpture, with numerous awards in all categories including the McGrigor Donald Sculpture Award and the M. S. Macfarlane Charitable Trust prizes for painting and sculpture.
Details: SAE to
The Administrative Secretary,
The Royal Scottish Academy,
The Mound,
Edinburgh EH2 2EL.

ROYAL SOCIETY OF BRITISH ARTISTS

SUBMISSIONS BY AUGUST
Autumn open exhibition, with nine awards on offer.
Details: SAE to FBA,
17 Carlton House Terrace,
London SW1Y 5BD.

ROYAL SOCIETY OF MARINE ARTISTS

SUBMISSIONS BY SEPTEMBER
Open exhibition in October of works featuring the sea.
Three prizes on offer.
Details: SAE to FBA, 17 Carlton House Terrace, London SW1Y 5BD.

ROYAL SOCIETY OF PORTRAIT PAINTERS

SUBMISSIONS BY MARCH
Open exhibition held in May, offering five awards for portraiture.
Details: SAE to FBA, 17 Carlton House Terrace, London SW1Y 5BD.

ROYAL WATERCOLOUR SOCIETY

There will not be an open exhibition this year, but a new competition is being planned for 1999.
Details: contact The Royal Watercolour Society, 48 Hopton Street, Blackfriars, London SE1 9JH.

RSA ART FOR ARCHITECTURE

APPLICATIONS FOUR TIMES A YEAR
Grants are available to those involved in building or landscape projects to appoint, at the outset of a project, artists as part of the design team.
Details: Project Manager, RSA Art for Architecture, 8 John Adam Street, London WC2N 6EZ.

RSA STUDENT DESIGN AWARDS

SUBMISSIONS BY NOVEMBER.
Awards in the form of Attachment or Travel awards are made to students submitting winning designs in response to the briefs offered in the Projects Book,

which is published in September.
Details: contact RSA Design,
8 John Adam Street,
London WC2N 6EZ.

SCOTTISH ARTS COUNCIL

The Scottish Arts Council funds various projects covering the visual arts, combined arts, placements and travel, crafts and photography and commissions. There are also exhibition schemes.
Details: The Scottish Arts Council, 12 Manor Place, Edinburgh EH3 7DD (Help Desk 0131-240 2443/ 2444 – Mon-Fri 10-2 & 2-4, answering machine outwith hours).

SINGER & FRIEDLANDER/ *SUNDAY TIMES* WATERCOLOUR COMPETITION

SUBMISSIONS IN JUNE
A competition and selected exhibition for works "upholding the finest traditions of contemporary British watercolour painting." Finalists' exhibitions are held at the Mall Galleries and in several regional centres, and prizes are worth a total of around £25,000.
Details: A4 SAE to Exhibition/ Competition Organisers and PR, Parker Harris & Company, PO Box 279, Esher, Surrey KT10 8YZ.

SOCIETY OF WILDLIFE ARTISTS

SUBMISSIONS BY JUNE
Summer open exhibition of work depicting wildlife, with six prizes on offer.
Details: SAE to FBA, 17 Carlton House Terrace, London SW1Y 5BD.

SOUTH EAST ARTS

Information services and funding schemes covering the visual arts, crafts and photography.
Details: contact The Administrative Assistant, Visual & Media Arts, South East Arts, 10 Mount Ephraim, Tunbridge Wells, Kent TN4 8AS.

SOUTH WEST ARTS

SUBMISSIONS THROUGHOUT THE YEAR
Like most regional arts boards this invites artists from the region to submit applications for various schemes.
Details: Bradninch Place, Gandy Street, Exeter EX4 3LS

STOCKPORT OPEN EXHIBITION

SUBMISSIONS BY JULY
Works made by artists in the North West are exhibited annually and merit awards are made.
Details: SAE to Exhibitions Officer, Stockport Art Gallery, Wellington Road South, Stockport SK3 8AB.

THE TURNER PRIZE

This annual prize, supported by the Patrons of New Art, is usually sponsored by Channel 4. Nominations from the public are invited and four British contemporary artists under 50 are chosen by a selection panel for a popular finalists' exhibition at the end of each year on the strength of the previous year's exhibitions. A large cash prize is awarded (£20,000) at the Tate Gallery.
Details: The Turner Prize, Tate Gallery, Millbank, London SW1P 4RG.

WINSOR & NEWTON AWARDS

Winsor & Newton sponsor several awards including the ROI Young Artists' Award and the Royal Institute of Painters in Watercolours Award. The prizes consist of art materials up to the value of £750. Both award winners are shown at an exhibition in London.
Details: UK Marketing Dept., Winsor & Newton, Whitefriars Avenue, Harrow, Middlesex HA3 5RH.

YORKSHIRE & HUMBERSIDE ARTS

SUBMISSIONS THROUGHOUT THE YEAR
Artists from the region are invited to submit applications for various schemes covering the visual arts, crafts, photography, film-making, multimedia and broadcasting.
Details: Visual & Media Arts Unit, Yorkshire & Humberside Arts Board, 21 Bond Street, Dewsbury, West Yorkshire WF13 1AX.

LONDON COMMERCIAL GALLERIES

All entries in this section are sorted alphabetically by gallery.

THE ART WORLD
DIRECTORY
1998/99 25TH EDITION

11 DUKE STREET LTD
11 Duke Street, London SW1Y.
Fax: *0171-976 2733.*

180 GALLERY
*182 Westbourne Grove, London
W11 2RH.* **Tel:** *0171-229 9309.*
Fax: *0171-243 7215.*

20TH CENTURY GALLERY
821 Fulham Road, London SW6 5HG.
Tel: *071-731 5888.* **Fax:** *071-731 5888.*
Opening times: *Mon-Fri 10-6, Sat 10-1.*
Nearest Underground: *Parsons Green.*
Personnel: Hilary Chapman.
Specialist print dealer in late nineteenth and
early twentieth century British prints. Stock
includes etchings, engravings, lithographs,
wood-engravings and colour prints by major
and minor artists of the period up to the
1950's. At least two exhibitions

are held each year and illustrated lists issued
periodically. Please send details to the gallery
to be included on the mailing list.
Exhibitions for 1998 include 'Printed in
Colours' - original colour prints 1920-1950
(March/April), exhibition of wood engravings
(Oct/Nov).
Services and Facilities:
Art for Offices. Framing. Shop. Valuation.
Work Stocked and Sold:
Pr.
Price range: £50 - £1,000.

A.D. FINE ART
85 Sheen Lane, Sheen, London SW14 8AD.
Tel: *0181-878 8800.*
Fax: *081 878 8800.*

A.R.K.S. GALLERY
16 North Audley Street, London W1Y 1WE.
Tel: *0171-491 4600.*
Fax: *0171-491 4640.*

AARON GALLERY
34 Bruton Street, London W1X.
Tel: *0171-499 9434.*

ABBOTT & HOLDER
30 Museum Street, London WC1A 1LH.
Tel: *0171-637 3981.* **Fax:** *0171-631 0575.*
Email *abbott.holder@virgin.net*

Ws *http://www.artefact.co.uk/AaH.html*
Opening times: *Mon-Sat 9.30-6,
Thurs 9.30-7.*
Nearest Underground: *Tottenham Court
Road.*
Personnel: *Partners:* Phillip Athill,
John Abbott.
Over 1000 English watercolours,,
drawings and prints (with some oils) 1780-
1990 displayed on three gallery floors.
Founded in 1936 our policy has always been to
sell pictures that can be bought from income
and our price range is from £50-£5,000. We
have an in-house conservator and are happy to
give free advice of cleaning, restoring and
framing. Every seven weeks we issue a LIST
introducing 300 works to stock and announcing any particular exhibition we are featuring.
Our LISTS are free and
will be sent in application.
Services and Facilities:
*Art Consultancy. Framing. Gallery space for
hire. Restoration. Valuation.*
Work Stocked and Sold:
Pr.
Price range: £50 - £5,000.

ACKERMANN & JOHNSON
*Lowndes Lodge Gallery, 27 Lowndes Street,
London SW1X 9H7.* **Tel:** *071-235 6464.*
Fax: *0171-823 1057.*
Opening times: *Mon-Fri 9-5,
Sat by appointment only.*
Nearest Underground: *Knightsbridge, Sloane
Square.*
Personnel: Peter Johnson. Hugh Nixon.
Claire Lauf.
Eighteenth, nineteenth and early twentieth
century British landscapes (Norwich School),
portraits and sporting oil
paintings, drawings and watercolours.

Contemporary works by Ken Howard RA and
Douglas Anderson RP.
*Commissioning Service. Framing. Restoration.
Valuation.*
Work Stocked and Sold:
Dr. Pa. Sc.

ACTAEON GALLERY
15 Motcomb Street, London SW1X 8LB.
Tel: *0171-259 5095.* **Fax:** *071 259 5069.*

ADAM GALLERY
62 Walcot Square, London SE11.
Tel: *0171-582 1260.*

ADDISON ROSS GALLERY
40 Eaton Terrace, London SW1 W8TS.
Tel: *0171-730 1536, 0171-730 6353.*
Fax: *0171-823 5081.*

ADONIS ART
1B Coleherne Road, London SW10.
Tel: *0171-460 3888.*

ADRIAN SASSOON
14 Rutland Gate, London SW7 1BB.
Tel: *0171-581 9888.* **Fax:** *0171-823 8473.*

AGNEW'S
43 Old Bond Street, London W1X 4AB.
Tel: *0171-629 6176.* **Fax:** *0171-629 4359.*

AINSCOUGH CONTEMPORARY ART
Drayton Gardens, London SW10 9QS.
Tel: *0171-341 9442.*

THE AIR GALLERY
32 Dover Street, London W1X 3RA.
Tel: *0171-409 1255 / 1516 / 1395.*
Fax: *0171-409 1856.*

THE AKEHURST GALLERY
1a Rede Place, London W2 4TU.
Tel: *0171-243 8855.* **Fax:** *071 243 3099.*

AKEL MINOTT ELIA GALLERY
26 Britton Street, London EC1M 5NQ.
Tel: *0171-336 7808.*

ALAN CRISTEA GALLERY
31 Cork Street, London W1X 2NU.
Tel: *0171-439 1866.* **Fax:** *0171-734 1549.*
Opening times: *Mon-Fri 10-5.30,
Sat 10-1.*
Nearest Underground: *Green Park.*
Personnel: *Director:* Alan Cristea.

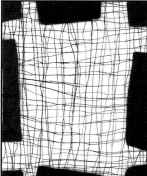

Dealers in top-rate 20th Century Master
Graphics including Braque, Gabo, Léger,
Matisse, Miró, Nicholson and Picasso.
Dealers in important contemporary artists
including Ayres, Baldessari, Baselitz, Bochner,
Buckley, Chillida, Close, Flanagan,
Frankenthaler, Guston, Hockney, Johns, Judd,
Kirkeby, Lichtenstein, Mangold, Mansen,
Manser, Nauman, Oldenburg, Pasmore,
Penck, Rainer, Rauschenberg, Rosenquist,
Scully, Self, Stella, Tapies, Turnbull, Warhol
and Winters. Publishers of major contempo-
rary artists including Blake, Caulfield, Craig-
Martin, Davey, Dibbets, Dine, Fulton,
Hamilton, Hodgkin, Hoyland, Inshaw, Jones,

Ab *Artist's Books* **App** *Applied Art* **Cer** *Ceramics* **Cra** *Crafts*
Dec *Decorative* **Dr** *Drawing* **Fur** *Furniture*

McKeever, Milroy, Moon, Motherwell, Paladino, Salle, Sultan, Tilson, Walker and Woodrow. Exhibitions about once a month including, for 1998, one-man exhibitions of Matthias Mansen, Lisa Milroy, Richard Hamilton and Ian McKeever.
Services and Facilities:
Art Consultancy. Art for Offices. Disabled Access.
Work Stocked and Sold:
Ab. Pr.
Price range: £150 - £150,000.

ALBANY GALLERY
1 Bury Street, London SW1Y.
Tel: *0171-839 6119.*

ALBEMARLE GALLERY
49 Albemarle Street, London W1X 3FE.
Tel: *0171-499 1616.*
Fax: *0171-499 1717.*
Ws *www.artnet.com/albemarle.html*
Opening times: *Mon-Fri 9.30-5.30. Sat 10-4.*
Nearest Underground: *Green Park*
Personnel: *Managing Director:* Tony Pontone. *Manager:* Kate Daniel. *Gallery Assistant:* Mayumi Bolton.
Specialising in contemporary figurative European, British and American artists, with particular emphasis on Spain.
The gallery has a reputation for lively and exciting one man and group shows, supported by full colour illustrated cataloguesw, and also for introducing artists hitherto never seen before in the UK. The gallery's activities has attracted the attention of international collectors and boasts a mailing list in excess of 6,000, growing daily. The '98 exhibition programme comprises 16 major exhibitions. Enquires should be directed to Tony Pontone, Managing Director or Kate Daniel, Gallery Manager.
Services and Facilities:
Art Consultancy. Art for Offices. Commissioning Service.
Work Stocked and Sold:
Pa.
Price range: £1,000 - £50,000.

ALCHEMY GALLERY
157 Farringdon Road, London EC1R 3AD.
Tel: *0171-278 5666.*
Fax: *0171-278 9666.*

ALEX WENGRAF
The Old Knoll, Eliot Hill, London SE13 7EB.
Tel: *0181-852 4552.*
Fax: *0181-852 4554.*

ALEXANDER GOTZ
35 Connaught Square, London W2.
Tel: *0171-724 4435.*
Fax: *0171-262 9891.*

ALEXANDRA GALLERY
Alexandra Palace Garden Centre, London N22 4BB.
Tel: *0181-444 2674.*
Email *udy@alexandragallery.demon.co.uk*

Ws *http://www.alexandragallery.demon.co.uk*
Opening times: *Mon-Sat 10-5, Sun 10.30-4.30.*
Nearest Underground: *Wood Green.*
Personnel: *Gallery Owner:* Judy Morell.
Exhibitions, crafts: pottery, sculpture, jewellery, cards, silk painting: scarves etc.
Painting and photographs restoration, in-house picture framing.
Saturday workshops: Batik, silk painting, mosaic, papermache, dried flowers arrangement. Evening classes: stained glass, mosaic, life drawing, picture framing, calligraphy.
Services and Facilities:
Art Consultancy. Art for Offices. Commissioning Service. Craftshop. Framing. Parking. Restoration. Workshop Facilities.
Work Stocked and Sold:
Ab. App. Cer. Cra. Dec. Dr. Gla. Jew. Pa. Ph. Pr. Sc.
Price range: £3 - £5,000.

ALTERNATIVE ART MARKET
47a Bushfield Street, Spitalfields, London E1 6AA.
Tel: *0171-375 0441.*
Fax: *0171-375 0484.*
Opening times: *Sundays 10-5.*
Nearest Underground: *Liverpool Street.*
Personnel: *Director:* Maggie Pinhorn. The Alternative Art Market is held every Sunday from April to December in the Old Spitalfields Market in the East End of London.
We exhibit work by contemporary artists who sell directly to the public. Each artist is allocated their own 3 sided unit.
Work in all media is accepted.
Submit to Alternative Arts who select.
Send in slides/photos and CV.
Services and Facilities:
Art Consultancy. Art for Offices. Commissioning Service. Disabled Access.

THE ALTON GALLERY
72 Church Road, Barnes, London, SW13 0DR.
Tel: *0181-748 0606.*

ALWIN GALLERY
9-10 Grafton Street, Bond Street, London W1.
Tel: *0171-499 0314.*

AMALGAM GALLERY
3 Barnes High Street, London SW13 9LB.
Tel: *0181-878 1279.*

ANDREW EDMUNDS PRINTS & DRAWINGS
44 Lexington Street, London W1R 3LH.
Tel: *0171-437 8594.*

ANDREW MUMMERY GALLERY
38 Great Sutton Street, London EC1V 0DX.
Tel: *0171-251 6265.*
Fax: *0171-251 6265.*
Opening times: *Tues-Sat 11-6.*
Nearest Underground: *Barbican, Farringdon.*

Personnel: Andrew Mummery.
Exhibiting international contemporary art.
Services and Facilities:
Art Consultancy. Art for Offices.
Work Stocked and Sold:
Pa. Ph.
Price range: £500 - £5,000.

ANIMATION ART GALLERY
13-14 Great Castle Street, London W1X.
Tel: *0171-255 1456.*

THE ANIMATION GALLERY
Gray's Antique Market, London W1Y 1AR.
Tel: *0171-493 3779.*

ANNA BORNHOLT GALLERY
3-5 Weighhouse Street, London W1Y 1YL.
Tel: *0171-499 6114.*

ANNA-MEI CHADWICK
64 New King's Road Parson's Green, London SW6 4LT.
Tel: *0171-736 1928.*

ANNE FAGGIONATO
Fourth Floor, 20 Dering Street, London W1R.
Tel: *0171-493 6732.*
Fax: *0171-493 9693.*
Opening times: *Mon-Fri 10-6.*
Nearest Underground: *Bond Street, Oxford Circus.*
Personnel: *Director:* Anne Faggionato. Lucy Diamond.
Dealers in impressionist, modern and contemporary paintings, sculpture and works on paper.
Services and Facilities:
Art Consultancy.
Work Stocked and Sold:
Dr. Pa. Ph. Sc.

ANNELY JUDA FINE ART
23 Dering Street, (off New Bond Street), London W1R 9AA.
Tel: *0171-629 7578.*
Fax: *0171-491 2139.*
Opening times: *Mon-Fri 10-6, Sat 10-1.*
Nearest Underground: *Bond Street*
Contemporary British and international artists including: Roger Ackling, Anthony Caro, Chillida, Christo, Alan Charlton, Prunella Clough, Nathan Cohen, Gloria Friedmann, Hamish Fulton, Funakoshi, Alan Green, Nigel Hall, David Hockney, Christine Hatt, Werner Haypeter, Al Held, Honegger, Malcolm Hughes, Iida, Kadishman, Kawamata, Darren Lago, Edwina Leapman, Catherine Lee, Estate of Kenneth and Mary Martin, John McLaughlin, Michaeledes, Morellet, David Nash, Saito. Also specialising in Russian Constructivism, Bauhaus, de Stijl, etc., Arp, Gabo, Kliun, Lissitzky, Malevich, Moholy Nagy, Mondrian, Rodchenko, Schwitters, Vantongerloo, Vordemberge-Gildewart.
Services and Facilities:
Art Consultancy. Art for Offices. Commissioning Service. Valuation.
Work Stocked and Sold:
Dr. Pa. Sc.

Gla Glass *Jew* Jewellery *Pa* Paintings *Ph* Photography *Pr* Prints
Sc Sculpture *Tx* Textiles *Wd* Wood

ANTHONY D'OFFAY GALLERY
9, 21 & 23 & 24 Dering Street, off New Bond Street, London W1R 9AA.
Tel: *0171-499 4100.* **Fax:** *0171-493 4443.*

ANTHONY MOULD LTD
173 New Bond Street, London W1.
Tel: *0171-491 4627.*

ANTHONY REYNOLDS
5 Dering Street, London W1R 9AB.
Tel: *0171-491 0621.*

ANTHONY WILKINSON FINE ART
242 Cambridge Heath Road, London E2 9DA.
Tel: *0181-980 2662.* **Fax:** *0181-980 0028.*

ARGENTA GALLERY
82 Fulham Road, London, SW3 6HR.
Tel: *0171-584 4480.* **Fax:** *0171-584 3119.*

ARKS GALLERY
16 North Audley Street, London W1.
Tel: *0171-491 4600.* **Fax:** *0171-491 4640.*

ART CONNOISSEUR GALLERY
95-97 Crawford Street, London W1H 1AN.
Tel: *0171-258 3835.* **Fax:** *0171-258 3532.*
Opening times: Mon-Fri 10-6, Sat 10-4.
Nearest Underground: *Baker Street, Edgware Road, Marylebone.*
Personnel: *Manager/Art Consultant:* Clare Grossman.

One of the largest galleries in London, Art Connoisseur gallery comprises of two levels of prime exhibition space in the W1 area. We specialise in a combination of Modern, European and Russian Painting from early 20th Century through to Contemporary Painting, Sculpture and Limited Edition Prints by young British artists. Gallery size over 3,000 square footage also available for hire.
Services and Facilities:
Art Consultancy. Commissioning Service. Framing. Gallery space for hire.
Work Stocked and Sold:
Cer. Pa. Sc.
Price range: £50 - £2,500.

ART & CRAFT EMPORIUM
Unit 6, 44 Grove End Road, London NW8.

ART FIRST
First Floor, 9 Cork Street, London W1X 1PD.
Tel: *0171-734 0386.* **Fax:** *0171-734 3964.*
Email *artfirst@dircon.co.uk*
Opening times: Mon-Fri 10-6.
Nearest Underground: *Green Park/Piccadilly Circus.*

Personnel: Clare Stracey. Geoffrey Bertram. Gillian Adam.
Art First is a first-floor contemporary art gallery exhibiting British and International artists. Alongside established figures we introduce younger artists. The gallery focuses on Scottish art and art from South Africa, bringing new names and exciting new imagery to London. Exhibitions take place monthly. The 1988 programme includes Luke Elwes (February), Margaret Hunter (April), Eileen Cooper (May), Jake Harvey (September), Will Maclean (November). Works by gallery artists are always available as is a collection of prints. Prices start at £100.
Services and Facilities:
Art Consultancy. Art for Offices. Valuation.
Work Stocked and Sold:
Dr. Pa. Pr. Sc.
Price range: £100 - £20,000.

ART FOR OFFICES
International Art Consultants, The Galleries, 15 Dock Street, London E1 8JL. **Tel:** *0171-481 1337.*
Fax: *0171-481 3425.*
Email *art@artservs.demon.co.uk*
Opening times: *Open Mon-Fri 9.30-6.*
Nearest Underground: *Tower Hill, Aldgate, Aldgate East.*
Personnel: *Directors:* Andrew Hutchinson. Peter Harris.
Amanda Basker.
We have 20 years experience advising architects, designers and corporate clients on the planning and implementation of art programmes.
Our 10,000 square foot galleries provide a central source of art, enabling clients and specifiers to view a comprehensive range of art on a single visit to one location. We deal directly with over 800 artists and have a large visual reference library covering art in all media which is cross referenced by style and price. This makes it possible to research works of art, or artists for commission quickly and effectively.
Art can be purchased, commissioned or acquired on a flexible rental basis.
Services and Facilities:
Art Consultancy. Art for Offices. Commissioning Service. Framing. Parking.
Work Stocked and Sold:
Cer. Cra. Dr. Gla. Pa. Ph. Pr. Sc. Tx. Wd.
Price range: £100 - £50,000.

ART SPACE GALLERY
84 St. Peter's Street, London N1 8JS.
Tel: *0171-359 7002.* **Fax:** *0171-359 7002.*

THE ART SUPERMARKET
Harvey Nichols, The Fifth Floor, Knightsbridge, London
Tel: *0171-359 2750.*

ARTEMIS FINE ARTS LIMITED
15 Duke Street, St James's, London SW1Y 6DB. **Tel:** *0171-930 8733.*
Fax: *0171-839 5009.*

ARTHAUS
Old School House, 12 Pop Street, London SE1 3PR. **Tel:** *0171-232 1097.*

ARTHOUSE
140 Lewisham Way, London SE14.
Tel: *0181-694 9011.*

ARTHUR TOOTH & SONS
13 Dover Street, London W1X.
Tel: *0171-499 6753.*

ATELIER ONE
4 Goodge Place, London W1P 1FL.
Tel: *0171-323 3350.* **Fax:** *0171-636 5282.*

ATTWELL GALLERIES
124 Lower Richmond Road, Putney, London, SW15 1LN. **Tel:** *0181-785 9559.*

AUDLEY ART
20 The Mall, Upper Street, Islington, London N1. **Tel:** *0171-704 9507.*

AUSTIN DESMOND FINE ART
Pied Bull Yard, 68-69 Great Russell Street, London WC1B 3BN. **Tel:** *0171-242 4443.*

BADA@
Tel: *0171-480 5952.*
Email *bada@ndirectdirect.co.uk*
Opening times: *By appointment and invitation.*
Personnel: *Chairman:* Terry Duffy.
This is a project based space that exhibits and promotes paintings, photography, performance, installation, new technology, media as well as design, architecture, poetry, music and film. It is also a centre for research into the development of quality, excellence and innovation in the Arts.

All the exhibitions/projects are developmental, progressive and challenging.
Its programme is irregular, proactive and unpredictable and therefore is only accessible by appointment or invitation. It promotes the work of many artists across all artforms including established artists such as Terry Duffy and younger artists such as Robin Blackledge, the performance artist.
Art Consultancy. Art for Offices. Commissioning Service. Friends/Society. Gallery

Ab *Artist's Books* **App** *Applied Art* **Cer** *Ceramics* **Cra** *Crafts*
Dec *Decorative* **Dr** *Drawing* **Fur** *Furniture*

space for hire. Restoration. Workshop Facilities.
Ab. Dr. Pa. Ph. Pr. Sc.
Price range: £200 - £5,000.

BALLANTYNE & DATE
38 Museum Street, London WC1A.
Tel: *0171-242 4249.*

BANDARY GALLERY
98 Bandary Road, London NW8.
Tel: *0171-624 1126.*

THE BARNES GALLERY
51 Church Road, Barnes, London,
SW13 9HH. **Tel:** *0181-741 1277.*

BARRY DAVIES ORIENTAL ART
1 Davies Street, London W1Y.
Tel: *0171-408 0207.*

BARTLEY DREY GALLERY
62 Old Church Street, Chelsea, London, SW3
6DP. **Tel:** *0171-352 8686.*
Fax: *0171-351 2921.*

BATTERSEA ARTS CENTRE
176 Lavender Hill, London SW11 5QF.
Tel: *0711-223 6557.*

BAUMKOTTER GALLERY
63a Kensington Church Street, London, W8
4BA. **Tel:** *0171-937 5171.*
Fax: *0171-938 2312.*
Opening times: *Mon-Fri 9.30-6.*
Nearest Underground: *High Street*
Kensington, Notting Hill Gate.
Personnel: *Proprietor:* Lore Baumkotter.
Manager: John Guy.
Fine 16th to 19th century English and
European oil paintings specialising in 17th
and 18th century Dutch and Flemish masters.
Services and Facilities:
Parking. Restoration.
Work Stocked and Sold:
Pa.
Price range: £500 - £60,000.

BCA BOUKAMEL CONTEMPORARY ART
9 Cork Street, London W1X 1PD.
Tel: *0171-734 6444.* **Fax:** *0171-287 1740.*
Email *art@bca-gallery.com*
Ws *http://www.bca-gallery.com*
Opening times: *Mon-Fri 10-6, Sat 10-2.*
Nearest Underground: *Green Park.*
Personnel: *Director:* B. Boukamel.

Contemporary British and European Art - representing: Philip Braham, Ernesto Tatafiore, Rainer Fetting, Ken Currie, Markus Lupertz, Luciano Castelli, Gerard Garouste, Joumana Mourad, Daniel Spoerri, A.R. Penck, Elvira Bach, Pierre et Gilles, Eugene Leroy, Gerard Traquandi, E.R. Nele, Helene Delprat.
Work Stocked and Sold:
Dr. Pa. Ph. Sc.
Price range: £500 - £50,000.

BEARDSMORE GALLERY
22-24 Prince Of Wales Road, Kentish Town,
London NW5 3LG. **Tel:** *0171-485 0923.*
Fax: *0171-267 0824.*

BEAUX ARTS LONDON
22 Cork Street, London W1X 1HB.
Tel: *0171-437 5799.* **Fax:** *0171-437 5798.*
Opening times: *Mon-Fri 10-6, Sat 10-2.*
Nearest Underground: *Green Park.*
Personnel: *Directors:* Reg Singh, Patricia Singh.
20th century British art including Norman Adams, Craigie Aitchison, Kenneth Armitage, Michael Ayrton, Lynn Chadwick, Elisabeth Frink, John Bellany, Roger Hilton, Ivon Hitchens, Peter Lanyon, John Piper, William Scott, Graham Sutherland, Keith Vaughan.

BEAUX ARTS
Regular shows of younger artists including Ricardo Cinalli, Philip Harris, Nicholas Jolly, Jonathan Leaman, Donna McLean, John Monks and Ray Richardson.
Services and Facilities:
Art for Offices. Commissioning Service.
Work Stocked and Sold:
Dr. Pa. Pr. Sc.
Price range: £4.000 - £100,000.

BELDAM GALLERY
Brunel University, Wilfred Brown Building,
Cleveland Road, Uxbridge,
UB8 3PH. **Tel:** *01895-273482.*
Fax: *01895-203250.*

BELGRAVE GALLERY
53 England's Lane, London NW3 4YD.
Tel: *0171-722 5150.*
Fax: *0171-722 0858.*

BENJAMIN HARGREAVES
90 Kenyon Street, London SW6 6LB.
Tel: *0171-385 7757.*

BERKELEY SQUARE GALLERY
23a Bruton Street, London W1X 8JJ.
Tel: *0171-493 7939.*
Fax: *0171-493 7798.*

BERNARD JACOBSON GALLERY
14a Clifford Street, London W1X 1RF.
Tel: *0171-495 8575.* **Fax:** *0171-495 6210.*

BLACKHEATH GALLERY
34a Tranquil Vale, Blackheath, London, SE3
0AX.
Tel: *0181-852 1802.*

BLACKMAN'S PLACE
14 All Saints Road, London W11.
Tel: *0171-243 4372.*

THE BLOOMSBURY WORKSHOP LTD
12 Galen Place, off Bury Place, London, WC1A
2JR. **Tel:** *0171-405 0632.*

THE BLUE GALLERY
93 Walton Street, London SW3 2HP.
Tel: *0171-589 4690.* **Fax:** *0171-589 4729.*

BOB LAWRENCE GALLERY
93 Sloane Street, London SW1W.
Tel: *0171-730 5900.*

BOUNDARY GALLERY, AGI KATZ FINE ART
98 Boundary Road, London NW8 0RH.
Tel: *0171-624 1126.* **Fax:** *0171-681 7663 or*
0171-624 1126.
Opening times: *Wed- Sat 11-6 and by appointment.*
Personnel: *Director & Owner:* Agi Katz.
Gallery Assistant: Louise Homes.
The gallery specialises in figurative art with emphasis on good draughtsmanship and strong use of colour. There are two periods of specialisation. 1. Modern British (1910 - 1950) including Bomberg, Brodzky, Dubsky, Epstein, Gotlib, Kramer Meninsky, Wolmark. Specialised knowledge of Anglo-Jewish artists - works in stock (available for sale) and will show by request. 2. Contemporary artists include

Phillipa Clayden, Josef Herman, Morris Kestelman, Sonia Lawson, Albert Louden, Ana Maria Pacheco, Neil MacPherson, Peter Prendergast, David Tress. Eight thematic or solo exhibitions a year. Catalogues published 3-4 times a year.
Services and Facilities:
Art Consultancy. Art for Offices. Commissioning Service. Framing. Restoration. Valuation.
Work Stocked and Sold:
Pa. Pr.
Price range: £300 - £6,000.

THE BOW HOUSE GALLERY
35 Wood Street, Barnet, EN5 4BE.
Tel: *0181-441 5841.* **Fax:** *0181-441 5841.*
Opening times: *Thurs-Sat 10-5, Sun 2-5*
(during exhibitions).
Nearest Underground: *High Barnet*
Personnel: John Brown. Pauline Brown.
We aim to present a wide range of paintings and sculpture by professional artists and to provide affordable art for home or work place

Gla *Glass* **Jew** *Jewellery* **Pa** *Paintings* **Ph** *Photography* **Pr** *Prints*
Sc *Sculpture* **Tx** *Textiles* **Wd** *Wood*

THE ARTWORLD
DIRECTORY 1998/99 **63**

through a series of exhibitions, which includes Sculpture in the Garden shows in spring and summer.

Services and Facilities:
Art Consultancy. Commissioning Service.
Work Stocked and Sold:
Cer. Pa. Sc.
Price range: £150 - £5,000.

BRIAN LEMESLE ADAMS OPEN STUDIO
St. Peter's Cottage, Hammersmith Terrace, London W6 9UD.
Tel: *0181-741 3772.*

BRITART.COM
Tel: *0181-809 5127.* **Fax:** *0181-809 5354.*
Email *info@britart.com*
Ws *http://www.britart.com*
Personnel: *Director:* David Tregunna. *Co-Director:* Mark Ellery.

The British Art Gallery on the Net. Britain's foremost virtual contemporary art gallery purely on the Net. Representing top names in British painting of both established and

emerging reputation, including: Fred Crayk, Chris Gollon, Maggi Hambling, Jim Kavanagh, Tory Lawrence, Richard Libby, Ian Welsh. We also stock works by Peter Howson. We sell to private collectors, corporate & public collections world-wide. We offer a user-friendly information service on each artist represented, providing reviews, c.v.'s, brief biographies and details on forthcoming exhibitions. We also publish catalogues, and help arrange packing, shipping, and insurance for clients buying directly from our web site.
Services and Facilities:
Art Consultancy. Art for Offices. Commissioning Service. Restoration.

BRIXTON ART GALLERY
35 Brixton Station Road, London SW9 8PB. **Tel:** *0171-733 6957.*

BROWSE AND DARBY GALLERY
19 Cork Street, London W1X 1HB.
Tel: *0171-734 7984.* **Fax:** *0171-437 0750.*

THE BRUTON STREET GALLERY
28 Bruton Street, London W1X 7DB.
Tel: *0171-499 9747.* **Fax:** *0171-409 7867.*
Ws *http://www.artnet.com/bruton.html.*
Opening times: *Mon-Fri 10-6, Sat 12-4 out of hours by appointment.*
Nearest Underground: *Green Park.*
Contemporary exhibitions every month in Galleries 1 and 2, featuring paintings and sculpture by European Contemporary artists. One-man shows by young British artists in Gallery 3. Art consultants to architects, designers, and corporate buyers. Paintings for investment portfolios and first-time collectors. On-site presentation given. Commissions for painting and sculpture undertaken.
Services and Facilities:
Commissioning Service.
Work Stocked and Sold:
Pa. Sc.
Price range: £1,000 - £40,000.

BURLINGTON GALLERIES
10/12 Burlington Gardens, London W1X 1LG.
Tel: *0171-734 9984/9228/4221.*
Fax: *0171-494 3770.*

BURLINGTON NEW GALLERY
4 New Burlington Street, London, W1X 1FE. **Tel:** *0171-437 2172.*

BURLINGTON PAINTINGS
12 Burlington Gardens, London W1X.
Tel: *0171-734 9984.*

THE CABLE STREET GALLERY
Thames House, 566 Cable Street, Limehouse, London E1 9HB.
Tel: *0171-790 1309.* **Fax:** *0171-790 1309.*

CADOGAN CONTEMPORARY ART
108 Draycott Avenue, South Avenue, London, SW3 3AE. **Tel:** *0171-581 5451.* **Fax:** *0171-589 9120.* **Email** *artcad@dircon.co.uk*
Ws *www.dircon.co.uk/cadogan-contemporary*
Opening times: *Mon-Wed 10-7,*

Thurs-Sat 10-6.
Nearest Underground: *South Kensington.*
Modern contemporary art.

CAMBERWELL GALLERY
169 Camberwell Road, London SE5.
Tel: *0171-740 6161.*

CAMDEN ART GALLERY
22 Church Street, London NW8.
Tel: *0171-262 3613.*
Fax: *0171-723 2333.*

CAMERAWORK: GALLERY AND DARKROOM
121 Roman Road, London, E2 0QN.
Tel: *0181-980 6256.*

CASSIEN DE VERE COLE FINE ARTS
50 Elgin Crescent, London W11 2JJ.
Tel: *0171-221 9161.* **Fax:** *0171-221 1082.*

CATO MILES WYNN
60 Lower Sloane Street, London SW1W.
Tel: *0171-259 0306.*

CATTO GALLERY
100 Heath Street, Hampstead, London NW3 1DP. **Tel:** *0171-435 6660.*
Fax: *0171-431 5620.*

CCA GALLERIES LTD
8 Dover Street, London W1X 3PJ.
Tel: *0171-499 6701.* **Fax:** *0171-409 3555.*

CENTAUR GALLERY
82 Highgate High Street, Highgate, London, N6.
Tel: *0181-340 0087.*

CENTRE 181 GALLERY
181 King Street, London W6.
Tel: *0181-748 3020.* **Fax:** *0181-741 3869.*

CHAUCER FINE ARTS
45 Pimlico Road, London SW1W.
Tel: *0171-730 2972.*

CHINESE CONTEMPORARY
11 New Burlington Place, London W1X 1FA. **Tel:** *0171-734 9808.*
Fax: *0171-734 9818.*

CHRIS BEETLES
8 & 10 Ryder Street, St. James's, London SW1Y 6QB. **Tel:** *0171-839 7551.*
Fax: *0171-839 1603.*
Opening times: *Mon-Sat 10-5.30.*
Nearest Underground: *Green Park.*

Specialist in 19th & 20th century watercolours, and additional specialisation in cartoons & book illustrations of the last 200

Ab Artist's Books *App* Applied Art *Cer* Ceramics *Cra* Crafts
Dec Decorative *Dr* Drawing *Fur* Furniture

years.

Services and Facilities:
Art Consultancy. Bookshop. Commissioning
Service. Framing. Restoration. Valuation.
Work Stocked and Sold:
Dr. Pa. Sc.
Price range: £150 - £100,000.

CHRISTOPHER DRAKE
Flat 1, 19 Mason's Yard, Duke Street, St.
James's, London SW1Y 6BU.
Tel: 0171-839 1198.

CHRISTOPHER HULL GALLERY
17 Motcomb Street, London SW1X 8LB.
Tel: 0171-235 0500. **Fax:** 0171-235 7912.

CINEGRAFIX GALLERY
4 Copper Row, Tower Bridge Piazza, London
SE1. **Tel:** 0171-234 0566.

THE CITY GALLERY
26 Copthall Avenue, London EC2R 7DN.
Tel: 0171-256 5815. **Fax:** 0171-256 6002.

CLARGES GALLERY
1st Floor, 158 Walton Street, London
SW3 2JZ. **Tel:** 0171-584 3022.
Opening times: Mon-Fri 2.30-5.30. Periodic
full time shows as advertised.
Nearest Underground: South Kensington.
English watercolours from 1800 to present
day, 20th century British School oils (includ-
ing living painters in oils and watercolours).
Limited edition 20th century prints. Samuel
Owen, David Cox, Samuel Prout, Harry
Watson, Menzies Marshall, Cecil Hunt,
Robert Bevan, Terrick Williams, John Piper,
G.Denholm Armour, Egerton Cooper,
Lucy Kemp-Welch, Bernard Dunstan, Diana
Armfield.
Services and Facilities:
Framing. Restoration.
Work Stocked and Sold:
Dr. Pa. Pr.
Price range: £250 - £6,000.

CLINK WHARF GALLERY
Clink Street, London SE1 9DG.
Tel: 0171-357 8355.

COLIN J. DENNY LTD
18 Cale Street, Chelsea Green, London SW3
3QU. **Tel:** 0171-584 0240.

THE COLLECTION GALLERY
264 Brompton Road, London, SW3 2AS.
Tel: 0171-225 1212.

COLLINS & HASTIE LTD
5 Park Walk, London SW10 0AJ.
Tel: 0171-351 4292.
Fax: 0171-351 7929.

COLNAGHI
15 Old Bond Street, London W1X 4LJ.
Tel: 0171-491 7408.
Fax: 0171-491 8851.

COLVILLE PLACE GALLERY
1 Colville Place, London W1P 1HN.
Tel: 0171-436 1330 / 1339.

THE COMMERCIAL GALLERY
109 Commercial Street, London E1 6BG.
Tel: 0171-392 9031. **Fax:** 0171-377 8915.

THE CONINGSBY GALLERY
30 Tottenham Street, London W1 9PN.
Tel: 0171-636 7478.
 Fax: 0171-580 7017.
Opening times: Mon-Fri 11-6.
Nearest Underground: Goodge Street
Personnel: Andrew Coningsby.
Specialists in the exhibition and marketing of
contemporary art photographers, illustrators
and fine artists who work, or are interested in
working, in the applied

the coningsby gallery

arts markets of advertising, design and pub-
lishing. Wide variety of hire and promotional
options.
Services and Facilities:
Art Consultancy. Art for Offices. Gallery space
for hire.
Work Stocked and Sold:
App. Cra. Dr. Pa. Ph. Pr. Sc.
Price range: £200 - £8,000.

CONNAUGHT BROWN
2 Albemarle Street, London
W1X 3HF. **Tel:** 0171-408 0362.
Fax: 0171-495 3137.
Opening times: Mon-Fri 10-6,
Sat 10-12.30.
Nearest Underground: Green Park
Personnel: Director: Anthony Brown.

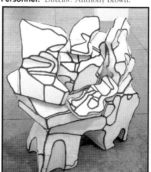

Post-Impressionist, Scandinavian, Modern
and Contemporary painting, drawing, sculp-
ture and graphics: Calder, Chagall, Dubuffet,
Dufy, Hockney, Holsoe, Matisse, Miró,
Moore, Picasso, Pissarro, Warhol,
Wesselmann. Gallery artists: Paul Richards,
Oleg Tselkov, Dennis Creffield, Derek
Boshier.
Work Stocked and Sold:
Dr. Pa. Pr. Sc.

CONNOISSEUR GALLERY
14 Holland Street, London W8.
Tel: 0171-937 0788.

CONTEMPORARY APPLIED ARTS
43 Earlham Street, Covent Garden, London
WC2H 9LD. **Tel:** 0171-836 6993.
**THE CONTEMPORARY ART
GALLERY/GROUP**
59 Ebury Street, London SW1W 0NZ.
Tel: 0171-730 6407. **Fax:** 0171-823 6521.

CONTEMPORARY CERAMICS
William Blake House, 7 Marshall Street,
London, W1V 1LP. **Tel:** 0171-437 7605.
Fax: 0171-287 9954 / 437 7605.

CONTEMPORARY TEXTILES GALLERY
6A Vigo Street, London, W1X 1AH.
Tel: 0171-439 6971.

COOMBS CONTEMPORARY
Tower Bridge Piazza, 1a Copper Row, Butlers
Wharf, London SE1 2LH.
Tel: 0171-403 6866.

**CORBALLY STOURTON CONTEMPORARY
ART**
160 New Bond Street, London W1Y 9PA.
Tel: 0171-629 7227. **Fax:** 0171-629 4494.

COSKUN & CO. LTD.
56a Walton Street, London SW3 1RB.
Tel: 0171-581 9056. **Fax:** 0171-581 1336.
Opening times: Tues-Sat 2-7 or by appoint-
ment.
Nearest Underground: Knightsbridge.
Personnel: Director: Gul Coskun.

Showing master prints in a home setting,
Coskun & Co. Ltd. specialises in Original
prints and drawings by 20th Century masters
including Braque, Chagall, Dali, Dine,
Giacometti, Leger, Matisse, Miro, Picasso and
Warhol. Forthcoming highlights include the
following exhibitions: Andy Warhol: Icons -
16 March-28 April 1998, The London
Original Print Fair - 30 April-3 May, Matisse
and the Orient - 6 May-30 May 1988, Picasso
His Contemporaries - 1 June-25 July 1998.

Services and Facilities:
Art Consultancy. Art for Offices.
Work Stocked and Sold:
Dr. Pr.

CRAFTS COUNCIL SHOP
Victoria and Albert Museum, South Kensington, London SW7 2RL.
Tel: *0171-589 5070.*

CRANE KALMAN GALLERY
178 Brompton Road, London SW3 1HQ.
Tel: *0171-584 7566/225 1931.*
Fax: *0171-584 3843.*
Opening times: *Mon-Fri 10-6, Sat 10-4.*
Nearest Underground: *Knightsbridge.*
Personnel: *Directors:* Andras Kalman.
Andrew Kalman. Sally Kalman. Robin Light.
Modern British, European, contemporary and
International paintings of merit.
Works available by: David Bomberg, Calder,
Dubuffet, Jenny Franklin, S.W.Hayter, Hans
Hofmann, Ra'anan Levy, L.S. Lowry, Alan
Lowndes, Henry Moore, Ben Nicholson,
Winifred Nicholson, Mary Newcomb, Picasso,
Rouault, Sir Matthew Smith, Ruskin Spear,
Theodoros Stamos, Graham Sutherland,
Alfred Wallis,
Christopher Wood.
Services and Facilities:
Art Consultancy. Art for Offices.
Work Stocked and Sold:
Pa.

CUBITT GALLERY
2-4 Caledonia Street, London N1.
Tel: *0171-278 8226.*

CURWEN GALLERY
4 Windmill Street, Fitzrovia, London W1P 1HF.
Tel: *0171-636 1459.*
Fax: *0171-436 3059.*
Opening times: *Mon-Fri 10-6, Sat 11-5
(closed Bank Holiday Weekends).*
Nearest Underground: *Goodge
Street/Tottenham Court Road.*
Personnel: *Directors:* Jill Hutchings, John
Hutchings. *Contact:* Caroline Brown.

Exhibition programme features Contemporary
British Art, Modern Masters & International
Graphics. Artists include: Kenneth
Blackburn, Glyn Boyd Harte, Phoebe
Dingwall, Jonathan Gibbs, Stanley Jones,
Thirza Kotzen, Ruth Martin, Laimonis
Mierins, Yuji Oki, Robin Richmond, Paul
Ryan, Johannes von Stumm, Peter Symonds,
Marjan Woulda. Master prints include
Gillian Ayres, Basil Beattie, Prunella Clough,
Elizabeth Frink RA, Barbara Hepworth, Josef
Herman RA, John Hoyland RA, Albert Irvin,

Henry Moore, Heinz-Dieter Pietsch, John
Piper, Ceri Richards, William Scott and Yuko
Shiraishi.
Services and Facilities:
*Art Consultancy. Art for Offices. Commissioning
Service. Framing.*
Work Stocked and Sold:
Dr. Pa. Pr. Sc.
Price range: £50 - £15,000.

THE CUT GALLERY
82 The Cut, London SE1 8LW.
Tel: *0171-207 8388.* **Fax:** *0171-207 8390.*

CYNTHIA BOURNE GALLERY
16 Clifford Street, London W1X 1RG.
Tel: *0171-439 0007.* **Fax:** *0171-439 2181.*

DAGGETT GALLERY
153 Portobello Road, London, W11 2DV.
Tel: *0171-229 2248.*

DANIEL HUNT
60 Lower Sloane Street, London SW1W.
Tel: *0171-259 0304.*

DANIEL KATZ LTD
*59 Jermyn Street, St. James's, London SW1Y
6LX.* **Tel:** *0171-493 0688.*
Fax: *0171-499 7493.*
Email *danny@katz.co.uk*
Ws *http://www.katz.co.uk*
Opening times: *Mon-Fri 9-6.*
Nearest Underground: *Green Park.*
Personnel: *Director:* Daniel Katz. Stuart
Lochhead. Rebecca Bailey.
European sculpture and works of art from the
Renaissance 17th and 18th centuries includ-
ing bronze statuettes, marble and terracotta
figures and old master paintings. Sales to all
major museums worldwide plus collectors and
private clients.
Art Consultancy. Restoration.
Work Stocked and Sold:
Pa. Sc.
Price range: From £5,000.

DANIELLE ARNAUD CONTEMPORARY ARTS
123 Kennington Road, London SE11 6SF.
Tel: *0171-735 8292.* **Fax:** *0171-735 8292.*

DANUSHA FINE ARTS
30 Warrington Crescent, London W9 1EL.
Tel: *0171-286 4832.* **Fax:** *0171-266 1639.*
Opening times: *Viewing by appointment all
year.*
Personnel: *Managing Director:* Tamara Bassi.
Realism & Impressionism from Ukraine. The
names of such artists as Malevitch, Tatlin,
Archipenko, Buriiuk, Ermolov, Exter - pio-
neers of Avant-gard Art - are well known to
art specialists. However, not everyone knows
that these artists were all born in Ukraine,
where they lived and worked at different
times. Their creativity had an important
influence on the development of Ukrainian
art. Even during the period of socialist realism
their ideas produced a new generation of talented artists like Tetyana Yablonska, Grygoriy
Shyshko, Evgeniy Volobuev,

Tetyana Holimbievska, Andriy Yalanskyi,
Petro Magro, Gayane Atayan, Volodymyr
Zhugan, Valentin Znoba.
Services and Facilities:
Art Consultancy. Commissioning Service.
Work Stocked and Sold:
Pa.
Price range: £200 - £5,000.

DAVID GILL GALLERY
60 Fulham Road, London, SW3.
Tel: *0171-371 8115 / 0171-589 5946.*

DAVID MESSUM FINE ART
8 Cork Street, London W1X 1PB.
Tel: *0171-408 0243/0171-437 5545.*
Fax: *0171-491 3162/0171-734 7018.*

DAVIES & TOOTH
*The Air Gallery, 32 Dover Street, London W1X
3RA.* **Tel:** *0171-409 1516.*
Fax: *0171-409 1856.*

DOUWES FINE ART
*38 Duke Street, St. James's, London, SW1Y
6DF.* **Tel:** *0171-839 5795.*
Fax: *0171-839 5904.*

DOVER STREET GALLERY
*13 Dover Street, Green Park, London W1X
3PH.* **Tel:** *0171-409 1540.*
Fax: *0171-409 1565.*

DUNCAN CAMPBELL CONTEMPORARY ART
*15 Thackeray Street, Kensington, London W8
5ET.* **Tel:** *0171-937 8665.*

DUNCAN R. MILLER FINE ARTS
*17 Flask Walk, Hampstead, London
NW3 1HJ.* **Tel:** *0171-435 5462.*
Fax: *0171-431 5352.*

E M ARTS
36 Tregunter Road, London SW10.
Tel: *0171-373 3856.*

EALING GALLERY
78 St Mary s Road, London, W5 5EX.
Tel: *0181-567 0414.*

EAST WEST
8 Blenheim Crescent, London W11 1NN.
Tel: *0171-229 7981.* **Fax:** *0171-221 0741.*

EASTERN ART GALLERY
40 Bloomsbury Way, London, WC1A 2SE.
Tel: *0171-430 1072.*

Ab Artist's Books **App** Applied Art **Cer** Ceramics **Cra** Crafts
Dec Decorative **Dr** Drawing **Fur** Furniture

EDITH GROVE GALLERY
10a Edith Grove, London, SW10 OJZ.
Tel: *0171-376 3127.* **Fax:** *0171-376 3127.*
Opening times: *Mon-Fri 2-6, and by appointment.*
Nearest Underground: *South Kensington/Earls Court.*
Personnel: *Director:* Catherine Tappenden.
The Edith Grove Gallery organises solo and small group exhibitions of work by contemporary artists which often include sculpture and ceramics. There are two large mixed shows a year at Christmas and in the Summer at which new artists are also given an opportunity to show their work. The exhibitions are changed every two or three weeks and there is a varying range of work on show with an emphasis that is realistic rather than abstract. The Gallery space is also available for hire subject to availability.
Work Stocked and Sold:
Cer. Dr. Gla. Pa. Ph. Pr. Sc. Wd.
Price range: £20 - £6,000.

EDITIONS GRAPHIQUES
3 Clifford Street, London, W1X 1RA.
Tel: *0171-734 3944.* **Fax:** *0171-437 1859.*

EDWARD COHEN
40 Duke Street, London SW1Y.
Tel: *0171-839 5180.*

ELECTRUM GALLERY
21 South Molton Street, London, W1Y 1DD.
Tel: *0171-629 6325.*

ENGLAND AND CO.
14 Needham Road, Westbourne Grove, London, W11 2RP. **Tel:** *0171-221 0417.* **Fax:** *0171-221 4499.*

ENID LAWSON GALLERY
36a Kensington Church Street, London W8 4BX. **Tel:** *0171-937 8444.*
Fax: *0171-376 0552.*
Email *0171-938 4786*
Opening times: *Mon-Sat 10-6.*
Nearest Underground: *High Street Kensington or Notting Hill Gate.*
Ours is a small, unpretentious gallery specialising in contemporary fine art and studio ceramics.
The majority of our gallery artists are already well respected in their field (most of our painters have exhibited at the Royal Academy while many of our potters' work has been shown in the V&A) but their prices are still very affordable.
Paintings range between £200-£2,000 with the majority being under £750. Ceramics range from £20 to £600, most of them selling for under £100. We hold several exhibitions each year and also exhibit at Penman Art Fairs. Come to visit and prepare to be enchanted!
Services and Facilities:
Art for Offices. Commissioning Service.
Work Stocked and Sold:
Cer. Pa.
Price range: £20 - £2,000.

ENTWISTLE
6 Cork Street, London W1X 2EE.
Tel: *0171-734 6440.* **Fax:** *0171-734 7966.*

ERMITAGE
14 Hay Hill, London W1X.
Tel: *0171-499 5459.*

FIELDBORNE GALLERIES
63 Queens Grove, London NW8 6ER.
Tel: *0171-586 3600.*

FINCHLEY FINE ART GALLERIES
983 High Road, North Finchley, London N12 8QR. **Tel:** *0181-446 4848.*
Opening times: *Mon, Tues, Thurs, Fri, Sat, Sun 12.30-7. Wed by appt.*
Nearest Underground: *Woodside Park.*
Personnel: *Director:* S. Greenman.

200 plus 18th-20th century English watercolours and paintings displayed in four galleries together with good quality Georgian, Victorian and Edwardian furniture, pottery, porcelain, smalls etc. Services: Valuations, Insurance/Probate. Restoration watercolours, paintings, cleaning, relining, framing and mounting.
Services and Facilities:
Framing. Restoration. Shop. Valuation.
Work Stocked and Sold:
Cer. Dec. Dr. Fur. Gla. Pa. Pr. Sc. Tx. Wd.
Price range: £50 - £10,000.

FINE ART SOCIETY
148 New Bond Street, London, W1Y OJT.
Tel: *0171-629 5116.*

FIONA BARCLAY FINE ART
29 Conduit Street, London W1R 9TA.
Tel: *0171-355 1433.*

FISCHER FINE ART
49 Carlton Hill, London NW8 OEL.
Tel: *0171-328 6502.* **Fax:** *0171-625 8341.*

FITCH'S ARK
6 Clifton Road, Little Venice, London W9 1SS. **Tel:** *0171-266 0202.*

FLEUR DE LYS GALLERY
227a Westbourne Grove, London W11 2SE. **Tel:** *0171-727 8595.*
Fax: *0171-722 8595.*
Email *fleur@art-connection.com*
Ws *http://www.fleur-de-lys.com*
Opening times: *Mon-Sat 10.30-5.30.*
Nearest Underground: *Notting Hill Gate.*
Personnel: Henri S. Coronel.
The gallery was established in 1967 and specialises in decorative 19th Century oil paintings - mostly British - some Dutch and Continental schools. Paintings supplied with photocopies of artbook references between £1,000 and £6,000. Prices include VAT or delivery abroad door to door. We hold NO exhibitions, issue NO catalogues, do not attend fairs but our policy is low margins with high turnover.
Services and Facilities:
Commissioning Service. Shop.
Work Stocked and Sold:
Pa.
Price range: £1.000 - £6,000.

FLORENCE TRUST STUDIOS
St. Saviour's, Aberdeen Park, Highbury, London N5 2AR. **Tel:** *0171-354 4771.* **Fax:** *0171-354 4771.*
Nearest Underground: *Highbury & Islington.*
Personnel: *Director:* Rod McIntosh.
The Florence Trust is based at St. Saviour's, Aberdeen Park, a Grade 1 listed 1866 Victorian Gothic church. The Studios offer visual artists studio awards, from 2-9 months, in an open plan environment where they can work intensively and engage in critical exchange. Regular exhibitions are held at the Trust and we have "Open Studio" events with invited guest artists exhibiting. Studio talks and slide presentations are also planned throughout the year. We have a comprehensive slide index of the artists we support, available for view by appointment. The studios and exhibition area are available for outside hire.
Services and Facilities:
Commissioning Service. Friends/Society. Gallery space for hire. Lectures. Workshop Facilities.
Work Stocked and Sold:
Dr. Pa. Sc.
Price range: £100 - £6,000.

FLOWERS EAST
199-205 Richmond Road, London E8 3NJ.
Tel: *0181-985 3333.*
Fax: *0181-985 0067.*
Email *100672.1003@compuserve.com*
Opening times: *Tues-Sun 10-6*
Nearest Underground: *Bethnal Green, then 253 or 106 bus.*
Personnel: *Directors:* Angela Flowers, Matthew Flowers, Robert Heller, David Cargill, Edgar Astaire, Sir Kit McMahon, Marian Naggar, Karen Demuth, Huei Flowers.
Also Flowers East at London Fields, 282 Richmond Road, London E8. Monthly solo exhibitions of gallery artists and group exhibitions.
Artists represented: Glenys Barton,

Gla Glass **Jew** Jewellery **Pa** Paintings **Ph** Photography **Pr** Prints
Sc Sculpture **Tx** Textiles **Wd** Wood

THE ARTWORLD
DIRECTORY 1998/99 **67**

John Bellany, Boyd & Evans, Stephen
Chambers, Bernard Cohen, Anthony Daley,
Amanda Faulkner, John Gibbons, Friedemann
Hahn, David Hepher, Nicola Hicks, Derek
Hirst, Carole Hodgson, Peter Howson, Patrick
Hughes, Neil Jeffries, Lucy Jones, Trevor
Jones, John Keane, John Kirby, Henry
Kondracki, Tim Lewis, John Loker, Tim Mara,
Michael Rothenstein, Tai-Shan Schierenberg,
Kevin Sinnott, Jack Smith, Andrew Stahl,
Trevor Sutton, Renny Tait, Alison Watt,
Gary Wragg.
Services and Facilities:
*Art Consultancy. Art for Offices. Bookshop.
Commissioning Service. Parking.*
Work Stocked and Sold:
Ab. Dr. Pa. Ph. Pr. Sc.
Price range: £100 - £50,000.

FLOWERS GRAPHICS
199/205 Richmond Road, London E8 3NJ.
Tel: *0181-985 3333.* **Fax:** *0181-985 0067.*

FLYING COLOURS GALLERY
PO Box 9361, Chelsea, London SW3 3ZJ.
Tel: *0171-351 5558.* **Fax:** *0171-351 5548.*

FRANCIS GRAHAM-DIXON GALLERY
*17-18 Great Sutton Street, London
EC1V 0DN.*
Tel: *0171-250 1962.*
Fax: *0171-490 1069.*

FRANCIS KYLE GALLERY
9 Maddox Street, London, W1R 9LE.
Tel: *0171-499 6870.*

FRANCK FINE ART
7 Victoria Square, London SW1W 0QY.

FREDERICK MULDER
*83 Belsize Park Gardens, London
NW3 4NJ.* **Tel:** *0171-722 2105.*

FRIVOLI
7a Devonshire Road, London W4 2EU.
Tel: *0171-742 3255.*
Fax: *0171-994 7372.*

FROST & REED
*2-4 King Street St. James's London
Sw1Y 6QP.* **Tel:** *0171-839 4645.*
Fax: *0171-839 1166.*

GAGLIARDI GALLERY
*509 Kings Road, Chelsea, London
SW10 0TX.*
Tel: *0171-352 3663.*
Fax: *0171-351 6283.*

GALERIE BESSON
*15 Royal Arcade, 28 Old Bond Street, Green
Park, London, W1X 3HB.*
Tel: *0171-491 1706.* **Fax:** *0171-495 3203.*

**GALERIE MODERNE LE PAVILLON DE
SEVRES / LE STYLE HALIQUE**
*9-10 Halkin Arcade, Motcomb Street, Belgravia,
London SW1X 8JT.*
Tel: *0171-245 6907.*
Fax: *0171-245 6341.*

GALERIE VALERIE KNIGHTSBRIDGE
215 Brompton Road, London SW3 2EJ.
Tel: *0171-823 9971 or 0956-310780.*

GALLERIA ENTERPRISE
606 King's Road. London SW6 2DX.
Tel: *0171-371 9940.* **Fax:** *0171-371 9950.*
Email *info@galleria-art.co.uk*
Ws *http://www.galleria-art.co.uk*
Opening times: *Mon-Sat 10.30-5.30.*
Nearest Underground: *Fulham Broadway.*
Bus Routes: 22, 11 & 14.
Personnel: *Owner:* P. Vazifdar. *Sales:*
R. Churchward-Viggers.
Fine Replicas of Old Master Paintings.
Customised Commissions, Complete Art
Program. Antique & Bespoke Frames and
Mounting. Prints, Engravings, Maps,
Photography.
Specialising in hand painted oils on canvas in
the traditional "Old Master" technique. This
gallery handles a large selection of paintings
from landscapes to portraits, still life to
seascapes.
They also create paintings of your own chosen
subject matter, from adapting a theme to
adjusting the canvas size along with sourcing
and supplying suitable illustrations for Art and
Interior Consultants for the hotel, leisure and
decorating industry.
A unique factor is that the canvasses are com-
petitively priced on size and not per subject no
matter how intricate the work. Allow up-to 6
weeks for delivery.
Services and Facilities:
*Art Consultancy. Art for Offices. Commissioning
Service. Framing.*
Work Stocked and Sold:
Dec. Fur. Pa. Ph. Pr.

GALLERY DIFFERENTIATE
*45 Shad Thames, Tower Bridge Piazza, London
SE1 2NJ.*
Tel: *0171-357 8909/403 9050.*
Fax: *0171-357 8909.*

GALLERY DUNCAN TERRACE
24 Duncan Terrace, London N1 8BS.
Tel: *0171-837 5856.*
Fax: *0171-278 2140.*
Opening times: *Phone for opening times*
Nearest Underground: *Angel*
Personnel: *Maureen O'Donoughue.*
Work Stocked and Sold:
Cer. Dr. Pa. Sc. Wd.
Price range: £100 - £10,000.

GALLERY K
101-103 Heath Street, London NW3 6SS.
Tel: *0171-794 4949.*
Fax: *0171-431 4833.*

GALLERY LINGARD
*Walpole House, 35 Walpole Street, London SW3
4QS.* **Tel:** *0171-730 9233.*
Fax: *0171-730 9152.*

GALLERY M
*London Fields, 282 Richmond Road, London E8
3QS.* **Tel:** *0181-986 9922.* **Fax:** *0181-985
0067.*

THE GALLERY OF ARCHITECTURE
6 Turnpin Lane, Greenwich, London SE10 9JA.
Tel: *0181-293 3617.*
Fax: *0181-305 2064.*

GALLERY OF MODERN ART
9 Barmouth Road, London SW18 2DT.
Tel: *0181-875 1481.* **Fax:** *0181-875 1481.*
Opening times: *Mon-Thurs 10-4, and by
appointment.*
Nearest Underground: *BR: Wandsworth
Town.*
Personnel: *Art Director:* Bea Newbery.
Commercial Gallery almost exclusively
abstract art. Full range of sizes, prices, new
and established artists. App. 4-5 exhibitions
per year. Widely known for very high standards and very reasonable prices. Also act as
agents for modern art, prints, graphic work,
large and small paintings, sculpture, also
ceramic and glass sculpture. Suppliers to interior designers, architects, institutions and general public. Available of above number at all
times for enquiries.
The gallery has a national and
international list of painters, sculptors and
graphic artists of very high standards and also
include new artists in their four yearly exhibitions.
Work Stocked and Sold:
Cer. Dr. Gla. Pa. Pr. Sc.
Price range: £50 - £5,000.

THE GALLERY
74 South Audley Street, London W1.
Tel: *0171-409 3164.*

GAVIN GRAHAM GALLERY
47 Ledbury Road, London W11 2AA.
Tel: *0171-229 4848.* **Fax:** *0171-792 9697.*

GIMPEL FILS
30 Davies Street, London W1Y 1LG.
Tel: *0171-493 2488.* **Fax:** *0171-629 5732.*

GLADWELL & CO.
69 Queen Victoria Street, London EC4N.
Tel: *0171-248 3824.*
THE GREENHOUSE AT THE DRILL HALL
16 Chenies Street, London WC1E 7EX.
Tel: *0171-631 1353.*

GROSVENOR GALLERY
18 Albemarle Street, London W1X 3HA.
Tel: *0171-629 0891.* **Fax:** *0171-491 4391.*
Opening times: *Mon-Fri 10-5.*
Nearest Underground: *Green Park.*
Personnel: *Director:* Mr Ray Perman.
20th century painting and sculpture.
Services and Facilities:
Art for Offices.
Work Stocked and Sold:
Pa. Sc.

GROSVENOR PRINTS
*28-32 Shelton Street, London,
WC2H 9HP.* **Tel:** *0171-836 1979.*

GULBENKIAN FOUNDATION
98 Portland Place, London, W1N 4ET.
Tel: *0171-636 5313.*

Ab Artist's Books   **App** Applied Art   **Cer** Ceramics   **Cra** Crafts
Dec Decorative   **Dr** Drawing   **Fur** Furniture

GUY MORRISON
91a Jermyn Street, London, SW1Y.
Tel: *0171-839 1454.*

HALES GALLERY
70 Deptford High Street, London SE8 4RT.
Tel: *0181-694 1194.* **Fax:** *0181-692 0471.*
Opening times: *Mon-Sat 10-5.*
Nearest Underground: *Deptford, New Cross.*
Personnel: Paul Hedge. Paul Maslin.

halesgallery

Hales Gallery was co-founded 7 years ago by former goldsmiths' graduate Paul Hedge. It has provided a platform for many young British artists. The Chapman Brothers had their first joint show here in 1994. It was here that John Frankland first showed his Golden Lift Shaft, "You Can't Touch This", before it was sold to Charles Saatchi. Hales Gallery artists include David Leapman, winner of the 1995 John Moores Painting Prize and Tomoko Takahashi, winner of the East International '97 Prize.
Services and Facilities:
Café.
Work Stocked and Sold:
Dr. Pa. Ph. Pr. Sc.
Price range: £150 - £10,000.

HALL & KNIGHT
15 Duke Street, St. James's,
London SW1Y 6DB. **Tel:** *0171-839 4090.*
Fax: *0171-839 4091.*

HAMILTON FORBES FINE ART
The Garden Market, Chelsea, London, SW10 OXE. **Tel:** *0171-937 2577.*
HAMILTON'S GALLERY
13 Carlos Place, London W1Y 5AG.
Tel: *0171-499 9493.* **Fax:** *0171-629 9919.*

HANINA GALLERY
180 Westbourne Grove, London
W11 2RH. **Tel:** *0171-243 8877.*
Fax: *0171-243 0132.*

HARDWARE GALLERY
162 Archway Road, Highgate, London
N6 5BB. **Tel:** *0181-341 6415.*
Fax: *0181-348 0561.*

HARRIET GREEN GALLERY
5 Silver Place, Lexington Street, Soho, London
W1R 3LJ. **Tel:** *0171-287 8328.*
Fax: *0171-287 8328.*

HART GALLERY
113 Upper Street, Islington, London N1 1QN.
Tel: *0171-704 1131.*
Fax: *0171-704 1707.*
Opening times: *Tues, Wed, Thurs, Fri 11-7.*
Sat 11-6. Sun 2-6.
Nearest Underground: *Angel.*
Personnel: Directors: John Hart, Katherine Hart.

Hart Gallery exhibits and promotes a range of contemporary painting, sculpture and ceramics.
Established in Nottingham (0115-963 8707) in 1989 and opened in London in 1994. To promote the gallery artists the gallery has forged links with other private and public galleries both in the UK and abroad and regularly exhibits at Art Fairs. A range of artist's monographs have been published including Kenneth Draper, Tom Wood and David Blackburn.
Exhibitions change monthly both in the downstairs painting/sculpture gallery and in the upstairs ceramics gallery.
Services and Facilities:
Art Consultancy. Art for Offices. Disabled Access. Lectures.
Work Stocked and Sold:
Cer. Dr. Pa. Ph. Pr. Sc.
Price range: £100 - £20,000.

HAZLITT, GOODEN & FOX
38 Bury Street, St. James's, London,
SW1Y 6BB. **Tel:** *0171-930 6422.*
Fax: *0171-839 5984.*

HICKS GALLERY
2 Leopold Road, Wimbledon, London SW19
7BD. **Tel:** *0181-944 7171.*

HIGHGATE FINE ART
26 Highgate High Street, London N6 5JG.
Tel: *0181-340 7564.* **Fax:** *0181-340 7564.*
Opening times: *Tue-Sat 10-6.*
Nearest Underground: *Archway*
Personnel: Noël Oddy. Fiona Hutson.
Contemporary paintings, drawings and prints. Monthly changing one person and group exhibitions. Permanent stock of paintings and original prints by established and young artists. A small stock of bronzes by Richard Robbins, Jonathan Wylder, Karin Jonzen, Gwynneth Holt. Exhibition tours organised.
Services and Facilities:
Art Consultancy. Commissioning Service. Framing. Valuation.
Work Stocked and Sold:
Dr. Pa. Pr. Sc.
Price range: £50 - £20,000.

HILDEGARD FRITZ-DENNEVILLE FINE ARTS
31 New Bond Street, London, W1Y 9HD.
Tel: *0171-629 2466.* **Fax:** *0171-408 0604.*
Nearest Underground: *Bond Street.*
Personnel: Mrs Fritz-Denneville.
Hildegard Fritz-Denneville Fine Arts has been established for 25 years and is a member of the Society of London Art Dealers. The gallery has developed expertise in German and Austrian art, and specialises in German Romantics, Nazarenes and Expressionists, as well as in French Impressionists.
Work Stocked and Sold:
Dr. Pa. Pr.

HIRSCHL CONTEMPORARY ART
Suite 3, 7 Sheffield Terrace, London
W8 7NG. **Tel:** *0171-727 4401.*
Fax: *0171-792 9173.*

HONOR OAK GALLERY
52 Honor Oak Park, London SE23 1DY.
Tel: *0181-291 6094.*
Opening times: *Tues-Fri 9.30-6,*
Sat 9.30-5.
Personnel: Director: John Broad.

Prints, drawings, watercolours and paintings by 20th century artists: Norman Ackroyd, Rosemary Benson, June Berry, Paul Bisson, Elizabeth Blackadder, Graham Crowley, Gill Day, Jenny Devereux, Roy Freer, Margareta Hamerschlag, A.S. Hartrick, Thomas Hennell, John Houston, Rudolph Kortokraks, Karolina Larusdottir, Clare Leighton, Vincent Lines, Charles Lloyd, Phyllis Mahon, George Mayer-Marton, Tiffany McNab, Terence Millington, Donald Myall, Charlotte Novitz, John O'Connor, Trevor Price, Gwen Raverat, Edward Stamp, Robin Tanner, Erich Wagner, Gerd Winner, Adrian Wiszniewski, etc. Agent for Glasgow Print Studio.
Services and Facilities:
Commissioning Service. Framing. Restoration.
Work Stocked and Sold:
Dr. Pa. Pr.
Price range: £12 - £2,000.

HOULDSWORTH FINE ART
The Pall Mall Deposit, 124-128 Barlby Road,
London W10 6BL.
Tel: *0181-969 8197.* **Fax:** *0181-964 3595.*
Ws *http://www.art-connection.com*
Opening times: *By appointment.*
Personnel: Pippy Houldsworth.
Sarah Tooley.

Contemporary British and international artists. Representing Richard Bray, Robin

Connelly, Gavin Lockheart, Paul McPhail,
Alastair Michie, Matthew Radford, Peter
Randall-Page, Jason Spirak. Works in stock
by Jake & Dinos Chapman, Matt Collishaw,
Ian Davenport, Anya Gallacio, John Kirby,
Georgina Starr, Sam Taylor Wood, Alison
Watt, Alison Wilding, Adrian Wisznijewski,
Catherine Yass.
Work Stocked and Sold:
Dr. Pa. Ph. Pr. Sc.
Price range: £300 - £20,000.

HYBRID
98 Columbia Road, London E2.
Tel: *0171-613 2628.*

HYDE PARK GALLERY
16 Craven Terrace, London W2 3QD.
Tel: *0171-402 2904.*

INDEPENDENT ART SPACE
23a Smith Street, London SW3.
Tel: *0171-259 9232.*

INSTITUTE OF FINE ART
5 Kirby Street, Hatton Garden, London EC1N.
Tel: *0171-831 4048.*

INTERNATIONAL ART GALLERY
*106-108 Marylebone High Street, London
W1M.* **Tel:** *0171-486 1412.*

INTERNATIONAL ART PROJECT
57 Moreton Street, London SW1V.
Tel: *0171-976 6200.*

IONA ANTIQUES
PO Box 285, London E8 4RE.
Tel: *0171-602 1193.* **Fax:** *0171-371 2843.*

JAMES COLMAN FINE ARTS
*The Tower, 28 Mossbury Road, London SW11
2PB.* **Tel:** *0171-924 3860.*
Fax: *0171-924 3860.*

JAMES ROUNDELL
58 Jermyn Street, London SW1Y.
Tel: *0171-499 0722.*

JAMES WEST FINE ART
28 Islington Park Street, London N1 1PX.

JAPAN PRINT GALLERY
43 Pembridge Road, London W11.
Tel: *0171-221 0927.*

JASON & RHODES
*4 New Burlington Place, London
W1F 1XB.* **Tel:** *0171-434 1768.*
Fax: *0171-287 8841.*
Opening times: *Mon-Fri 10-6,
Sat 10.30-1.30.*
Nearest Underground: *Oxford Circus.*
Personnel: *Directors:* Gillian Jason,
Benjamin Rhodes.
Contemporary British art. Regular exhibition
programme.
Services and Facilities:
Art Consultancy. Commissioning Service.
Work Stocked and Sold:
Dr. Pa. Ph. Sc.

JAY JOPLING
*White Cube, 44 Duke Street, St. James's,
London SW1Y 6DD.*
Tel: *0171-930 5373.*
Fax: *0171-930 9973.*
Opening times: *Fri & Sat 12-6 or by appoint-
ment.*
Nearest Underground: *Piccadilly Circus,
Green Park.*
Personnel: *Directors:* Jay Jopling,
Julia Royse. Daniela Gareh.

JEREMY HUNT FINE ART
32 Dover Street, London W1X 3RA.
Tel: *0171-409 1165/0171-629 3748.*
Fax: *0171-409 1856.*

JIBBY BEANE LIMITED
66 St John Street, London, EC1M 4DT.
Tel: *0171-689 7689, Club Membership: 0171-
689 7666.*
Fax: *0171-689 7688.*
Email *info@jibbybeane.com*
Ws *http://www.jibbybeane.com*
Opening times: *Gallery: Mon-Fri 8-8, Sat &
Sun 11-6. Art Club: Mon-Sat 8pm-1am.*
Nearest Underground: *Farringdon,
Barbican.*
Personnel: *Directors:* Jibby Beane, Jonathan
Goslan.
Jibby Beane Ltd, an impressive 8,000 foot
space in London's new art destination
Clerkenwell, provides a unique art experience
for the 21st century.
The space presents a fusion of art and cutting
edge technology with music, fashion, perfor-
mance, debate and literature. Six annual
exhibitions of contemporary art - all free of
charge - a café, shop and members art club
and bar complete the hospitable environment
for visitors.
A different kind of social interaction is facili-
tated, the web-site forming the nerve-centre
of Jibby Beane Ltd.
Services and Facilities:
*Art for Offices. Bar. Bookshop. Café.
Commissioning Service. Disabled Access.
Framing. Friends/Society. Guided Tours.
Lectures. Shop.*
Work Stocked and Sold:
*Ab. App. Cer. Cra. Dec. Dr. Fur. Gla.
Jew. Pa. Ph. Sc. Tx.*
Price range: £50 - £10,000.

JILL GEORGE GALLERY
*38 Lexington Street, Soho, London
W1R 3HR.* **Tel:** *0171-439 7319 / 439 7343.*
Fax: *0171-287 0478.*
Ws *http://www.easynet.co.uk/banca/geojills.htm*
Opening times: *Mon-Fri 10-6, Sat 11-5.*
Nearest Underground: *Piccadilly/ Oxford
Circus.*
Personnel: *Director:* Jill George.
British contemporary art. Paintings, drawings,
watercolours, limited edition prints and
monoprints from the established artist to the
recent graduate.
The gallery handles both figurative and
abstract originals and prints. Participates in
national and international art fairs. Art
Consultancy and commissions organised on

behalf of the artists. Exhibition every five
weeks throughout the year.
Services and Facilities:
*Art Consultancy. Art for Offices.
Commissioning Service.*
Work Stocked and Sold:
Dr. Pa. Pr.
Price range: £100 - £20,000.

JOANNA BARNES FINE ARTS
*14 Mason s Yard, Duke Street, St James's,
London SW1Y 6BU.*
Tel: *0171-930 4215.*
Fax: *0171-839 8307.*

JOHN DENHAM GALLERY
*50 Mill Lane, West Hampstead, London NW6
1NJ.* **Tel:** *0171-794 2635.*
Fax: *0171-794 2635.*

JOHN HUNT
*15 King Street, St. James's, London
SW1Y 6QU.*
Tel: *0171-839 2643.*
Fax: *0171-839 2643.*

JOHN MARTIN OF LONDON
38 Albemarle Street, London W1X 3FB.
Tel: *0171-499 1314.*
Fax: *0171-493 2842.*
Email *jmlondon@dircon.co.uk*
Opening times: *Mon-Fri 10-6, Sat 10-3.*
Nearest Underground: *Green Park.*
Personnel: John Martin.
Fine Art from the British Isles. John Martin of
London holds regular exhibitions of work by
contemporary figurative artists from Great
Britain and Ireland and also 20th Century
painters. We are currently purchasing work in
the following areas: Danish 19th-century
painting, Irish 20th-century painting.
Services and Facilities:
Art for Offices.
Work Stocked and Sold:
Dr. Pa. Sc.
Price range: £300 - £15,000.

JOHN MITCHELL & SON
160 Bond Street, London W1Y 9PA.
Tel: *0171-493 7567.*

JONATHAN COOPER
*Park Walk Gallery, 20 Park Walk, London,
SW10 OAQ.* **Tel:** *0171-351 0410.*
Fax: *0171-351 0410.*
Opening times: *Mon-Fri 10-6.30,
Sat 11-4.*
Nearest Underground: *South Kensington.*
Personnel: *Director:* Jonathan Cooper.
Henrietta Dudley.
19th and 20th century English and European
paintings and watercolours. Modern British
and contemporary. Sole agents for Jay
Kirkman, William Newton, Kate Nessier,
Michael Austin.
Services and Facilities:
*Art Consultancy. Framing. Restoration.
Valuation.*
Work Stocked and Sold:
Pa. Ph.
Price range: £120 - £25,000.

Ab Artist's Books **App** *Applied Art* **Cer** *Ceramics* **Cra** *Crafts*
Dec *Decorative* **Dr** *Drawing* **Fur** *Furniture*

THE JONATHAN WYLDER GALLERY AND STUDIO
2 Motcomb Street, Belgravia, London SW1X.
Tel: *0171-245 9949.* **Fax:** *0171-245 9949.*

JULIAN HARTNOLL
14 Masons Yard, off Duke Street, St. James's, London SW1Y 6BU.
Tel: *0171-839 3842.* **Fax:** *0171-930 8234.*
Ws *http://www.art-on-line.com\hartnoll*
Opening times: *Weekdays 10-12.30, 2.30-5, Sat 10-12.30.*
Nearest Underground: *Green Park & Piccadilly Circus.*
Personnel: *Director:* Julian Hartnoll. *Assistant:* Rowena Williams.
Julian Hartnoll has been dealing in Victorian and Pre-Raphaelite paintings, drawings and prints since 1968. A selection of Pre-Raphaelite drawings is always in stock, as well as some major works currently by Lord Leighton and J. W. Waterhouse. The gallery also handles

works by the Kitchen Sink artists: Bratby, Smith, Coker, Middleditch and Greaves. Occasional contemporary exhibitions.
Services and Facilities:
Art Consultancy. Art for Offices.
Work Stocked and Sold:
Cer. Dr. Pa. Pr.
Price range: £100 - £500,000.

JULIAN LAX FINE ORIGINAL PRINTS
Flat J, 37-39 Arkwright Road, London NW3 6BJ. **Tel:** *0171-794 9933.*
Fax: *0171-431 5845.*
Opening times: *By appointment.*
Nearest Underground: *Hampstead, Finchley Road.*
Personnel: *Director:* Julian Lax.

Julian Lax - Modern European Prints, Modern and Contemporary British Prints, Modern

British Paintings, Drawings and Sculpture. Original prints by European artists including Buffet, Chagall, Léger, Matisse, Miró, Picasso and Rouault; and by British artists including Colquhoun, Frink, Heron, Hockney, Hodgkin, Moore, Nevinson, Nicholson, Pasmore, Piper, Scott and Sutherland. Modern British paintings, drawings and sculpture by artists including Avezbach, Blake, Frink, Heron, Kossoff, Moore, Piper, Roberts, Scott, Sutherland and Vaughan.
Services and Facilities:
Art Consultancy. Art for Offices. Restoration. Valuation.
Work Stocked and Sold:
Dr. Pa. Pr. Sc.
Price range: £100 - £30,000.

JULIAN SIMON FINE ART
70 Pimlico Road, London SW1W 8LS.
Tel: *0171-730 8673.* **Fax:** *0171-823 6116.*

KALEIDOSCOPE
64 Willesden Lane, London, NW6 7SX.
Tel: *0171-328 5833.*

KAREN GRIFFITHS
Chenil Galleries, 181-183 Kings Road, London SW3 5EB. **Tel:** *0171-352 8002.*

KARSTEN SCHUBERT CONTEMPORARY ART
41-42 Foley Street, London W1P 7LD.
Tel: *0171-631 0031.* **Fax:** *0171-436 9255.*

KATHRYN BELL/FINE ART CONSULTANCY
Studio 123D, Canalot Production Studios, 222 Kensal Road, London W10 5BN.
Tel: *0181-960 0070.* **Fax:** *0181-960 0209.*
Opening times: *By appt.*
Nearest Underground: *Westbourne Park.*
Personnel: *Director:* Kathryn Bell.
Our art consultancy and exhibition programme are now established in London and Tokyo.
We represent British and Japanese based artists and try to encourage a true cultural exchange; by bringing artists to work, exhibit and teach in the 'opposite' culture and then by including these artists in exhibitions and site specific commissions.
Our approach is independent and unique and appeals to both private and corporate collectors.
The artists we have recently worked with include the sculptors Noe Aoki, Danny Lane and Vanessa Pooley, the textile artists Shelley Goldsmith and Marta Rogoyska, and the painters James Brook, Chikako Mori and Fraser Taylor.
Services and Facilities:
Art Consultancy. Art for Offices. Commissioning Service. Lectures. Valuation.
Work Stocked and Sold:
App. Dr. Gla. Pa. Ph. Pr. Sc. Tx. Wd.
Price range: £500 - £40,000.

L'ACQUAFORTE
49a Ledbury Road, London, W11.
Tel: *0171-221 3388.*

L'ART ABSTRAIT
18a The Circle, Queen Elizabeth Street, London SE1. **Tel:** *0171-403 9360.*

LA GALERIE
225 Ebury Street, London, SW1W.
Tel: *0171-730 9210.*

LAMONT GALLERY
67 Roman Road, Bethnal Green, London E2 0QN. **Tel:** *0181-981 6332.*
Fax: *0181-983 0144.*
Ws *http://www.lamontart.com*
Opening times: *Tues-Sat 11-6.*
Nearest Underground: *Bethnal Green.*
Personnel: *Director:* Andrew Lamont.
Gallery Manager: Sigrid Williams.

The first commercial art gallery to open in London's East End, Lamont Gallery has been a leading representative of contemporary British art for over ten years. The gallery shows at the UK's major art fairs and past exhibitions have toured to museums and abroad. Specialists in collection management, Lamont Gallery has a viewing room for private and corporate collectors. Also work by Cutting Edge Ceramicists.
Services and Facilities:
Art Consultancy. Art for Offices.
Work Stocked and Sold:
Cer. Pa. Pr. Sc.
Price range: £200 - £10,000.

LAURE GENILLARD GALLERY
First Floor, 82-84 Clerkenwell Road, London EC1M 5RJ.
Tel: *0171-490 8853.*
Fax: *0171-490 8854.*
Email *101357,2012@compuserve.com*
Ws *URL:http//ourworld.compuserve. comhome-pages/laure-genillard*
Opening times: *Tue-Sat 11-6.*
Nearest Underground: *Farringdon Road, Barbican.*
Personnel: *Director:* Laure Genillard.
The Laure Genillard Gallery is now located on a first floor in Clerkenwell at the North-West junction with St. John Street. The gallery presents paintings, sculptures and installations by a current generation of British, European and American artists. Its direction

LONDON COMMERCIAL GALLERIES

stems from late 20th century modernistic developments such as 70's minimal and conceptual art. These autonomous, formalistic and site-specific approaches, using mediums such as photography, text and video, engage the gallery in further research towards todays new forms of artistic expression. Our increasingly visual and technological (global) culture leads

artists to unlock strategies of current communication with their personal language.
Services and Facilities:
Art Consultancy. Art for Offices. Commissioning Service.
Work Stocked and Sold:
Ab. Dr. Pa. Ph. Pr. Sc.
Price range: £800 - £7,000.

LE CHAT NOIR GALLERY
35 Albemarle Street, Mayfair, London W1X 3FB. **Tel:** *0171-495 6710.*

LEFEVRE GALLERY
30 Bruton Street, London, W1X 8JD.
Tel: *0171-493 2107.* **Fax:** *0171-499 9088.*

THE LEGER GALLERIES LTD
13 Old Bond Street, London, W1X 3DB.

LENA BOYLE FINE ART
40 Drayton Gardens, London SW10 9SA.
Tel: *0171-373 8247.* **Fax:** *0171-370 7460.*
Opening times: *By appointment only.*
Nearest Underground: *Gloucester Road, South Kensington.*
Personnel: *Proprietor:* Lena Boyle. John Boyle.

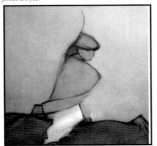

Modern British and contemporary paintings, drawings, watercolours and original Limited Edition Prints. Sculpture, boxes, ceramics.
Services and Facilities:
Art Consultancy. Art for Offices. Commissioning Service.
Work Stocked and Sold:
Cer. Dec. Dr. Pa. Pr. Wd.
Price range: £75 - £6,000.

LESLEY CRAZE GALLERY
34 Clerkenwell Green, London EC1R 0DU.
Tel: *0171-608 0393.*
Fax: *0171-251 9200.*

LINDA BLACKSTONE GALLERY
The Old Slaughterhouse, R/O 13 High Street, Pinner, HA5 5QQ.
Tel: *0181-868 5765.* **Fax:** *01923-897153 or 0181-868 4465.*
Opening times: *Wed-Sat 10-6.*
Nearest Underground: *Pinner.*
Established 1985. High quality representational paintings, ceramics and sculpture by contemporary British artists.
Continually changing exhibition punctuated by 6 major exhibitions a year. Subjects include: landscape, marine, wildlife and the figure.
Gallery artists include: Richard Bolton, Michael Cadman RI ARCA, Ashton Cannell RSMA, Patrick Cullen PS, NEAC, Pamela Davis RMS, Jackie Simmonds, Janet Ledger, Stephanie Harrison RMS, Ken Paine PS, J. Richard Plincke RI, Jacquie Turner, Debra Manifold PS, Leo McDowell RI, Colin Kent RI, Mat Barber Kennedy RI, Catherine Brennand RI, Patrick Cullen PS.
Fine art framing and restoration.
Services and Facilities:
Art for Offices. Framing. Parking. Restoration.
Work Stocked and Sold:
Ab. Cer. Pa. Pr. Sc.
Price range: £100 - £5,000.

LISSON GALLERY
67 Lisson Street and 52-54 Bell Street, London NW1 5DA. **Tel:** *0171-724 2739.* **Fax:** *0171-724 7124.*

LLEWELLYN ALEXANDER (FINE PAINTINGS) LTD
124-126 The Cut, Waterloo, London SE1 8LN. **Tel:** *0171-620 1322/1324.*
Fax: *0171-928 9469.*

LOGGIA
15 Buckingham Gate, London SW1E 6LB.
Tel: *0171-828 5963.*

LOGOS ART GALLERY
20 Barter Street, London, WC1A 2AH.
Tel: *0171-404 7091.*

LONDON CONTEMPORARY ART LTD
132 Lots Road, Chelsea, London, SW10 0RJ. **Tel:** *0171-351 7696.*
Personnel: *Piers Johnstone.*
Work Stocked and Sold:
Pr.

LONDON PRINT WORKSHOP
421 Harrow Road, London W10 4RD.
Tel: *0181-969 3247.* **Fax:** *0181-964 0008.*

LONG & RYLE ART INTERNATIONAL
4 John Islip Street, London, SW1P 4PX.
Tel: *0171-834 1434.* **Fax:** *0171-821 9409.*

LUCY B. CAMPBELL GALLERY
123 Kensington Church Street, London, W8 7LP. **Tel:** *0171-727 2205.*

LUMLEY CAZALET
33 Davies Street, London W1Y 1FN.
Tel: *0171-491 4767.*
Fax: *0171-493 8644.*
Opening times: *Mon-Fri 10-6.*
Nearest Underground: *Bond Street.*
Personnel: *Directors:* Camilla Cazalet, Caroline Lumley, Catherine Hodgkinson.
Contact: Victoria Tarry.

Original prints by 20th C. European masters including Braque, Chagall, Frink, Hockney, Matisse, Miró, Picasso. Late 19th Century.prints, including Belleroche, Helleu, Tissot. Drawings by Matisse. Sculpture and drawings by Frink.
Work Stocked and Sold:
Dr. Pr. Sc.
Price range: £50 - £300,000.

LUTZ RIESTER
P.O. Box 2769, London W2 6ZJ.
Tel: *0171-258 3467.*

M.J. PUTMAN
151 Lavender Hill, London, SW11 5QJ.
Tel: *0171-228 9087.*

THE MAAS GALLERY
15a Clifford Street, London W1X 1RF.
Tel: *0171-734 2302.* **Fax:** *0171-287 4836.*
Opening times: *Open daily 10-5.30.*
Nearest Underground: *Green Park.*
Personnel: *Directors:* Rupert Maas, Fiona Halpin.
British paintings, water-colours, drawings and sculpture from 1840 to 1940. Victorian engravings. Contemporary artists: James Lynch, Tobit Roche.
Work Stocked and Sold:
Dr. Pa. Pr. Sc.
Price range: £200 - £2,000,000.

Ab *Artist's Books* **App** *Applied Art* **Cer** *Ceramics* **Cra** *Crafts*
Dec *Decorative* **Dr** *Drawing* **Fur** *Furniture*

MALCOLM INNES GALLERY
*7 Bury Street, St. James's, London
SW7Y 6AL.*
Tel: *0171-839 8083/4.*
Fax: *0171-839 8085.*

MALL ARCADE
Camden Passage, Islington, London N1.
Tel: *0171-930 1904.* **Fax:** *0171-839 7509.*

MALL GALLERIES
*Federation of British Artists, 17 Carlton House
Terrace, London SW1Y 5BD.*
Tel: *0171-930 6844.*
Fax: *0171-839 7830.*
Opening times: *Daily 10-5.*
Nearest Underground:
Charing Cross/Piccadilly Circus.
The Mall Galleries is home to the Federation
of British Artists, the umbrella organisation
for nine of Britain's leading Art Societies.
Besides the annual exhibitions held by each
society, the FBA hosts a varied and exciting
programme of exhibitions and events through-
out the year. These include The National
Print Exhibition which is an open exhibition
featuring the work of invited artists, and
members of the Royal Society of Painter-
Printmakers, together with selected work from
the open submission.
Lectures, demonstrations and workshops are
held throughout the year to complement the
exhibitions. In addition, two major art com-
petitions are held at the Mall Galleries: The
Singer & Friedlander/ Sunday Times
Watercolour Competition and the Laing
Painting Competition. Artists' prizes and
awards are offered by many of the societies.
The FBA also operates a Fine Art and Portrait
Commissions and Advisory Service. For
details on any of the above, please contact the
administrative address.
Please see also entry under Gallery Space for
Hire and entries under Art Consultants and
Art Societies.
Services and Facilities:
*Art Consultancy. Friends/Society. Guided
Tours. Lectures. Workshop Facilities.*
Work Stocked and Sold:
Dr. Pa. Pr. Sc.
Price range: £200 - £20,000.

MANYA IGEL FINE ARTS
*21-22 Peter's Court, Porchester Road, London
W2 5DR.*
Tel: *0171-229 1669/8429.*
Fax: *0171-229 6770.*

MARBLE ARCH ART GALLERY
14 Old Quebec Street, London, W1H.
Tel: *0171-629 5159.*

MARINA HENDERSON GALLERY
11 Langton Street, London, SW10.
Tel: *0171-352 1667.*

THE MARK GALLERY
*9 Porchester Place, Marble Arch, London W2
2BS.*
Tel: *0171-262 4906.*
Fax: *0171-224 9416.*

MARKOVITCH GALLERY
*108A Boundary Road, St. Johns Wood, London
NW8 0RH.* **Tel:** *0171-372 1333.*

MARLBOROUGH FINE ART
6 Albemarle Street, London W1X 4BY.
Tel: *0171-629 5161.*
Fax: *0171-629 6338/0171-495 0641.*

MARLBOROUGH GRAPHICS
6 Albemarle Street, London W1X 4BY.
Tel: *0171-629 5161.* **Fax:** *0171-495 0641.*
Email *Marlborough@slad.org*
Opening times: *Mon-Fri 10-5.30,
Sat 10-12.30.*
Nearest Underground: *Green Park.*
Personnel: *Chairman:* The Duke of
Beaufort. *Director:* David Case. *Contact:*
Sarah Staughton. *Contact:* Nicola Togneri.
The leading dealers in Freud etchings.
Contemporary publications and prints avail-
able by the following gallery artists: Arikha,
Auerbach, Conroy, Davies, Hambling,
Jacklin, Kiff, Kitaj, Le Brun, Oulton, Pasmore,
Paul, Rego & Piper. Modern Master Prints
available by: Hepworth, Kokoschka, Matisse,
Miro, Nicholson, Picasso and Sutherland.
Recent publications include Stephen Conroy's
first lithographs, and new etchings from R.B.
Kitaj. Proposed exhibitions of prints for 1998,
Christopher Le Brun, German Expressionists,
Thérèse Oulton and Victor Pasmore.
Services and Facilities:
*Art Consultancy. Art for Offices. Framing.
Valuation.*
Work Stocked and Sold:
Ab. Dr. Ph. Pr.
Price range: £300 - £60,000.

MARLENE ELEINI - #12,
69 Westbourne Terrace, London, W2.
Tel: *0171-706 0373.* **Fax:** *0171-706 1241.*
Opening times: *By appointment.*
Nearest Underground: *Lancaster Gate,
Paddington.*
Personnel: *Director:* Marlene Eleini.
Contemporary and modern art.
Services and Facilities:
*Art Consultancy. Art for Offices.
Commissioning Service. Framing.*
Work Stocked and Sold:
Dr. Pa. Ph. Pr. Sc.
Price range: £300 - £30,000.

MARSDEN CONTEMPORARY ART
21 Dulwich Village, London SE21 7BT.
Tel: *0181-488 4169.*
Fax: *0181-693 2700.*

MARTYN GREGORY
*34 Bury Street, St. James's, London
SW1Y 6AU.* **Tel:** *0171-839 3731.*
Fax: *0171-930 0812.*

MATTHIESEN FINE ART LIMITED
7/8 Mason's Yard, Duke Street, London SW1Y.
Tel: *0171-930 2437.*
Fax: *0171-930 1387.*
Email *OldMastersLondon@ Compuserve.com*
Ws *http://www.Europeanpaintings.com*
Opening times: *Mon-Fri 10-6.*

Personnel: *Director:* Patrick Matthiesen.
Museum quality Italian, French and Spanish
Old Master paintings 1330-1848. Specialising
in Italian painting in London and French
painting in New York. Exhibition catalogues
available. In association with Stair Sainty
Matthiesen Inc., 22 E. 80th St., New York,
NY 10021, USA. Tel (212) 288 1088,
fax (212) 628 2449.
Work Stocked and Sold:
Pa.

MATTS GALLERY
42-44 Copperfield Road, London E3 4RR.
Tel: *0181-983 1771.* **Fax:** *0181-983 1435.*

MAYOR GALLERY
22a Cork Street, London W1X 1HB.
Tel: *0171-734 3558.* **Fax:** *0171-494 1377.*

MCHARDY SCULPTURE
*Cardamomm Building, 31 Shad Thames, London
SE1 2YR.* **Tel:** *0171-403 7555.*

MEDICI GALLERIES
7 Grafton Street, London W1X 3LA.
Tel: *0171-629 5675.* **Fax:** *0171-495 2997.*
Opening times: *Mon-Fri 9-5.30.*
Nearest Underground: *Green Park.*
Personnel: Ian Lewis. Jonathan Blackwell.
Jenny Kerr.

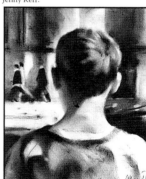

Offering a rare combination of services, The
Medici Galleries have been a West End land-
mark since 1910. The upper gallery has a
changing display of original contemporary art
- oils, watercolours, miniatures and craft - with
exhibitions several times a year. Signed limited edition, reproduction and children's prints
are available in the lower gallery, as is a framing service offering a wide choice of mounts
and frames. Rooms in the lower gallery are
devoted to displaying Fine Art Greeting
Cards, postcards, stationary, carved book ends
and art and children's books. A Personalised
Christmas Card service is available from
August.
Services and Facilities:
*Art Consultancy. Art for Offices. Commissioning
Service. Framing. Gallery space for hire. Shop.*
Work Stocked and Sold:
Cra. Pa. Pr.

MEGHRAJ GALLERY
*Meghraj Court, 18 Jockey's Fields, London
WC1R 4BW.* **Tel:** *0171-831 6881.*
Fax: *0171-404 8288.*

MERCURY GALLERY
26 Cork Street, London W1X 1HB.
Tel: *0171-734 7800.* **Fax:** *0171-287 9809.*
Email *mercury@netcomuk.co.uk*
Ws *http://www.mercury-gallery.co.uk*
Opening times: *Mon-Fri 10-5.30, Sat 10-
12.30 (except during Summer Show).*
Nearest Underground: *Green Park,
Piccadilly.*
Personnel: *Directors:* Gillian Raffles,
Gordon Samuel. *Assistant:* Sheila Donald.
Large stock of Modern British Art,
including: Burra, Eardley,
Gaudier-Brzeska, Redpath, Spencer, Vaughan,
Wallis, Wyndham Lewis
and Wood. Contemporary gallery
artists exhibiting: Samira Abbassy, Elizabeth
Blackadder RA,RSA, Janet Boulton, Robert
Callender, David Gentleman, John Houston,
Barry Hirst, Michael Kenny, RA, Simon
Laurie, David Remfry, Mick Rooney, RA, Eric
Rimmington, Carol Ann Sutherland. Young
painters' work during mixed shows.
Services and Facilities:
Art Consultancy. Art for Offices.
Work Stocked and Sold:
Ab. Cer. Dr. Pa. Pr. Sc.
Price range: £100 - £100,000.

MERRIFIELD STUDIOS
*112 Heath Street, Hampstead, London NW3
1AA.*
Tel: *0171-794 0343/0171-431 0794.*
Fax: *0171-435 8039.*

MICHAEL ELCKE
2 Old Bond Street, London, W1X.
Tel: *0171-495 2687.*

MICHAEL PARKIN FINE ART
11 Motcomb Street, London SW1X 8LB.
Tel: *0171-235 8144/1845.*
Fax: *0171-245 9846.*

MILNE & MOLLER
35 Colville Terrace, London W11 2BU.
Tel: *0171-727 1679.*

MINA RENTON FINE ART
*50 Eresby House, Rutland Gate, London SW7
1BG.* **Tel:** *0171-584 1907.*
Fax: *0171-584 1907.*

MISTRAL GALLERIES
10 Dover Street, London W1X 3PY.
Tel: *0171-499 4701/2.*
Fax: *0171-499 0618.*

MODERN AFRICAN GALLERY
102 Park Street, London, W1Y.
Tel: *0171-629 7528.*

MOMTAZ ISLAMIC ART
*79A Albany Street, Regent's Park, London
NW1 4BT.* **Tel:** *0171-486 5411, Mobile 0973-
405428.* **Fax:** *0171-487 5250.*

MONTPELIER SANDELSON
4 Montpelier Street, London SW7 1EZ.
Tel: *0171-584 0667.* **Fax:** *0171-225 2280.*

MORLEY GALLERY
*61 Westminster Bridge Road, London
SE1 7HT.* **Tel:** *0171-450 9226.*
Fax: *0171-928 4074.*
Opening times: *Mon 1-6, Tues, Thurs, Fri
10-6, Wed 10-8, closed Bank Holidays; please con-
tact gallery for details of Sat openings.*
Nearest Underground: *Lambeth North,
Waterloo BR.*
Personnel: *Exhibitions Organiser:* Jane
Hartwell.
Exhibitions of contemporary art every 3-6
weeks. Annual programme includes: painting,
drawing, prints, sculpture, photography,
ceramics and textiles. Work selected annually
by committee. Details of exhibitions listed in
Art Review.
Work Stocked and Sold:
Cer. Cra. Dr. Pa. Ph. Pr. Sc. Tx.
Price range: £50 - £10,000.

THE MUSEUM OF LONDON
150 London Wall, London, EC2Y 5HN.
Tel: *0171-600 3699.*

NAIRI SAHAKIAN CONTEMPORARY ART
*34 Burton Court, Franklin's Row, London SW3
4SZ.* **Tel:** *0171-730 0432.*
Fax: *0171-831 9489.*
Opening times: *By appointment only.*
Nearest Underground: *Sloane Square.*
Personnel: *Director:* Nairi Sahakian.
Presenting a wide range of contemporary art
practice with special emphasis on artists
whose work reflects cross-cultural elements.
Promoting young British artists and makers as
well as introducing international emerging
artists in Britain. Specialists for contemporary
art from Armenia. Exclusive representatives
for Hana Sakuma and Sarkis Hamalbashian,
with an extensive selection of his paintings
and works on paper available to view

Advise and undertake sight specific
commissions and independent curatorial ser-
vices.
Services and Facilities:
Art Consultancy. Commissioning Service.
Work Stocked and Sold:
Cra. Dr. Pa. Ph. Pr. Sc.

NARWHAL INUIT ART GALLERY
*55 Linden Gardens, Chiswick, London
W4 2EH.* **Tel:** *0181-747 1575.*
Fax: *0181-742 1268.*
Opening times: *By appointment seven days a
week.*
Nearest Underground: *Turnham Green.*
Personnel: *Directors:* Ken Mantel,
Tija Mantel.

Permanent exhibition specialising in Inuit
(Eskimo) art from Canada and Greenland.
Carvings in soapstone, jadeite, relic bone,
caribou horn and musk ox horn. Plus original
drawings and editioned graphics from 1955 to
present day. Reference books, videos, audio
tapes, touring educational exhibitions and
slide-based lectures. Museum and corporate
clients welcome. Teacher education packs 6-
18 year olds, plus in service assistance.
Currently registering NIAEF (Narwhal Inuit
Art Education Foundation) as a charity to
promote the understanding on Inuit life and
tradition through contemporary issues.
Services and Facilities:
Art for Offices. Lectures. Valuation.
Work Stocked and Sold:
Ab. Dr. Pr. Sc.
Price range: £50 - £2,500.

NEFFE-DEGANDT
32a, St. George Street, London W1R 9FA.
Tel: *0171-493 2630, 0171-629 9788.*
Fax: *0171-493 1379.*

**NEW ACADEMY GALLERY AND
BUSINESS ART GALLERIES**
*34 Windmill Street, Fitzrovia, London W1P
1HH.* **Tel:** *0171-323 4700.*
Fax: *0171-436 3059.*
Ws *http://www.screenpages.co.uk/ ac/newacad-
emy/index.html*
Opening times: *Mon-Fri 10-6, Thurs until 8,
Sat 11-5. Closed Sun and Bank Holiday weekends.*
Nearest Underground: *Goodge
St/Tottenham Court Road.*
Personnel: *Directors:* John Hutchings, Jill
Hutchings. *Contact:* Pryle Behrman.
Exhibits and promotes a wide range of con-
temporary British painting, sculpture, original
prints. Regular exhibiting artists include:
Barry Atherton, Clare Bigger, Clive
Blackmore, John Brokenshire, Roger Cecil,
Jane Corsellis, Peter Dover, Bernard Dunstan
RA, Frederick Gore RA, Alistair Grant,
Donald Hamilton Fraser RA, Brenda Hartill,
Susan-Jayne Hocking, Sarah Holliday,
Lallitha Jawahirilal, Andrew Macara, Padraig

Ab *Artist's Books* **App** *Applied Art* **Cer** *Ceramics* **Cra** *Crafts*
Dec *Decorative* **Dr** *Drawing* **Fur** *Furniture*

Macmiadhachain, Anita Mandl, Michele Noach, John Piper, Jacqueline Rizvi, Hans Schwarz, Keith Roberts, Zoe Rubens, Richard Walker and Peter Wray.

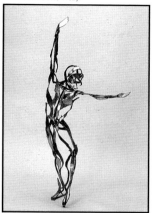

We offer a comprehensive service to businesses including free advice on purchases, a flexible hire scheme and on-site presentations; and undertake commissions (painting of portraits, houses, Christmas cards etc.) for both business and private individuals.
Services and Facilities:
Art Consultancy. Art for Offices. Commissioning Service. Framing.
Work Stocked and Sold:
Dr. Pa. Pr. Sc.
Price range: £20 - £20,000.

NEW ART CENTRE
168 Sloane Street, London, SW1X.
Tel: *0171-235 5844.*

NEW GRAFTON GALLERY
49 Church Road, Barnes, London SW13 9HH. **Tel:** *0181-748 8850.*
Fax: *0181-748 9818.*
Opening times: *Tues-Sat 10-5.30.*
Founded 1968. Mainly figurative English painting and drawing by living artists; also English painting 1900-40 and permanent Portrait Centre. Mark Adlington, Julian Bailey, Jason Bowyer, Oliver Campion, Sue Campion, Tom Coates, Anthea Craigmyl, Fred Cuming, Jane Dowling, Fred Dubery, Mary Fedden, Christa Gaa, Reg Gammon, Peter Greenham, Christopher Hall, Colin Hayes, Josef Herman, Susan-Jayne Hocking, Ken Howard, John Nash, Paul Newland, Richard Pikesley, Mick Rooney, Liam Spencer, Sarah Spencer, Ruth Stage, Pip Todd Warmoth, Josephine Trotter, Carel Weight, Jacqueline Williams.
Services and Facilities:
Art Consultancy. Commissioning Service. Disabled Access. Parking. Valuation.
Work Stocked and Sold:
Dr. Pa.
Price range: £100 - £10,000.

NICHOLAS TREADWELL GALLERY
Upstairs at 326-328 Old Street, London, EC1V 9DR. **Tel:** *0171-613 3600.*
Fax: *0171-613 3700.*

NIELSEN UK
Unit 7, Frogmore Estate, Acton, London, NW10 7NQ. **Tel:** *0181-965 5949.*

THE NORTHCOTE GALLERY
110 Northcote Road, Battersea, London, SW11 6QP. **Tel:** *0171-924 6741.*

O'SHEA GALLERY
120a Mount Street, London W1Y 5HB.
Tel: *0171-629 1122.*

THE OCTOBER GALLERY
24 Old Gloucester Street, London WC1N 3AL. **Tel:** *0171-242 7367.*
Fax: *0171-405 1851.*
Email *octobergallery@compuserve.com*
Ws *http://www.ecotechnics.edu/ ogallery.htm*
Opening times: *Tues-Sat 12.30-5.30.*
Nearest Underground: *Holborn/Russell Square.*
Personnel: *Artistic Director:* Elisabeth Lalouschek. *Director:* Chili Hawes.
The October Gallery represents a range of artists from the international avant-garde. The gallery offers an extensive selection of contemporary paintings, drawings, prints, photographs and sculpture by artists from Africa, the Americas, Asia and Europe. Artists include El Anatsui, Andrey Bartenev, Carol Beckwith, William S. Burroughs, Leroy Clarke, Ira Cohen, Sokari Douglas Camp, Ablade Glover, Emmanuel Taiwo Jegede, Elisabeth Lalouschek, Manuel Mendive, John Minihan, Z. O. Oloruntoba, Julieta Rubio, Mickael Bethe-Selassie, Laila Shawa, Wijdan, Gerald Wilde, Aubrey Williams and Xu Zhong Min. The October Gallery café serves food from around the world and is open at lunch time, Tues-Sat 12.30-2.30. Education Programme.
Services and Facilities:
Art Consultancy. Art for Offices. Bookshop. Café. Craftshop. Friends/Society. Gallery space for hire. Workshop Facilities.
Work Stocked and Sold:
Dr. Pa. Ph. Pr. Sc.
Price range: £100 - £10,000.

OFFER WATERMAN & CO. FINE ART LTD
20 Park Walk, London SW10 0AQ.
Tel: *0171-351 0068.*
Fax: *0171-351 2269.*

OLIVER HOARE
Flat 3 7 Onslow Gardens, London SW7 3LY. **Tel:** *0171-835 1600.*
Fax: *0171-373 5787.*
Islamic Art.

ORANGERY AND ICE HOUSE
Central Library, Phillimore Walk, London W8 7RX. **Tel:** *0171-361 2295.*

ORIEL CONTEMPORARY ART
25 Princess Road, Regents Park, London NW1 8JR. **Tel:** *0171-483 1375.*
Fax: *0171-483 1363.*

OSBOURNE STUDIO GALLERY
13 Motcomb Street, London SW7X 8LB.
Tel: *0171-235 9667/8.*

PAISNEL GALLERY
22 Mason's Yard, Duke Street, St. James's, London SW1Y 6BU.
Tel: *0171-930 9293.* **Fax:** *0171-930 7282.*

PARK GALLERY
26 Connaught Street, London W2 2AF.
Tel: *0171-262 2588.* **Fax:** *0171-262 2587.*

PARK WALK GALLERY
20 Park Walk, London SW10 0AQ.
Tel: *0171-351 0410.*

PARKER GALLERY
28 Pimlico Road, Chelsea, London, SW1W 8LJ. **Tel:** *0171-730 6768.*
Fax: *0171-259 9180.*

PARTRIDGE FINE ARTS
144 New Bond Street, London, W1Y.
Tel: *0171-629 0834.*

PATON GALLERY
London Fields, 282 Richmond Road, London E8 3QS. **Tel:** *0181-986 3409.* **Fax:** *0181-986 0811.*
Opening times: *Tues-Sat 11-6, Sunday 12-6.*
Nearest Underground: *Bethnal Green.*
Personnel: *Director:* Graham Paton. Emma Vial.
From its inception in 1981, Paton Gallery saw its role as a platform for a new generation of British painters' (Arts Review). This is still the gallery's policy in the 90's, testament to its success is that, over the years, the Metropolitan Museum, N.Y. has bought work by 13 Paton artists. Gallery artists include Jake Clark, Derrick Guild, Alexander Guy, Nicholas Hatton, Judy Inglis, Mary Mabbutt, Julie Major, Tim Ollivier, Kate Palmer, Shani Rhys James, Rosie Sell, Cecilia Vargas, Alex Veness.
Services and Facilities:
Art Consultancy. Art for Offices. Commissioning Service. Disabled Access.
Work Stocked and Sold:
Dr. Pa. Sc.
Price range: £450 - £14,000.

PAUL HAWKINS GALLERY
4 Davies Street, London W1Y 1LY.
Tel: *0171-499 7009.* **Fax:** *0171-499 2265.*

PAUL MASON GALLERY
149 Sloane Street, London, SW1X 9BZ. **Tel:** *0171-730 3683/7359.*

PAUL SMITH/R. NEWBOLD GALLERY
Paul Smith Press Office, 33 Longacre, London WC2E 9LA.
Tel: *0171-240 0009/32.*

PHILIP GRAHAM CONTEMPORARY ART
9a-11 Bonhill Street, London, EC2A.
Tel: *0171-920 0350.*

PIANO NOBILE
129 Portland Road, Holland Park, London W11 4LW.
Tel: *0171-229 1099.*

PICCADILLY GALLERY
16 Cork Street, London W1X 1PF.
Tel: *0171-629 2875, 0171-499 4632.*
Fax: *0171-499 0431.*

PIERS FEETHAM GALLERY
475 Fulham Road, London SW6 1HL.
Tel: *0171-381 5958.* **Fax:** *0171-381 3031.*
Opening times: *Tues-Fri 10-1, 2-6, Sat 10-1.*
Nearest Underground: *Fulham Broadway.*
Personnel: Piers Feetham. Caroline McAdam Clark.

The gallery holds eight to nine mixed and solo exhibitions a year, by contemporary British artists - with a special emphasis on drawings. Regular Xmas mixed show! "The Artist as Decorator", small and large decorated and decorative items. The gallery also comprises a long-established and comprehensive framing business, specialising in conservation framing; also paper conservation, oil restoration and antique frame restoration services.
Services and Facilities:
Framing. Restoration.
Work Stocked and Sold:
Dr.

THE PIKE GALLERY
145 St John's Hill, London, SW11 1TQ.
Tel: *0171-223 6741.*

PLANTATION HOUSE
31-35 Fenchurch Street, London, EC3M 3DX. **Tel:** *0171-623 2935.*

PLAZZOTTA LTD
10 Shalcomb Street, London SW10 0HY.
Tel: *0171-352 7493.*
Fax: *0171-352 7493.*
Opening times: *The office and storeroom are open by appointment.*
Nearest Underground: *Sloane Square, Earls Court.*
Personnel: *Director:* Richard S. O'Conor.
We are a small family run company specialising in the work of the late Italian sculptor Enzo Plazzotta (1921-1981). There remains a considerable and varied stock of sculpture within the artist's declared editions. The fully illustrated hardback catalogue raisonné is for sale at £15 plus postage and our current price list of available sculpture can be sent on request. Subjects range from mythology, ballet, horses, human form and Christian themes. With sizes from 8 inches to monumental. The office and storeroom are open by appointment.
Services and Facilities:
Valuation.
Work Stocked and Sold:
Sc.
Price range: £400 - £40,000.

POLAK GALLERY
21 King Street, St James's, London, SW1Y 6QY. **Tel:** *0171-839 2871.*

PORTAL GALLERY
43 Dover Street, Piccadilly, London W1X 3RE. **Tel:** *0171-493 0706 & 0171-629 3506.* **Fax:** *0171-493 2667.*
Email *portalgallery@btinternet.com*
Ws *http://www.portal-gallery.com*
Opening times: *Mon-Fri 10-5.30, Sat 10-4.*
Nearest Underground: *Green Park.*
Personnel: *Directors:* Lionel Levy, Jess Wilder.

The gallery specialises in idiosyncratic, figurative painting by contemporary British artists. Started in 1959, Portal has long been a venue for the work of quirky and imaginative artists such as John Byrne, Beryl Cook, Haydn Cornner, Nick Cudworth, Steve Easby, Jane Lewis, Lizzie Riches, Mick Rooney and many others.
The gallery has eight solo exhibitions each year, theme shows and a permanent exhibition of Portal painters.
Services and Facilities:
Shop.
Work Stocked and Sold:
Pa. Pr.
Price range: £500 - £20,000.

PORTLAND GALLERY
9 Bury Street, St. James's, London, SW1Y 6AB. **Tel:** *0171-321 0422.*
Fax: *0171-321 0230.*

POSK GALLERY
238 King Street, London, W6 0RF.
Tel: *0181-741 1940.* **Fax:** *0181-746 3798.*
Nearest Underground: *Ravenscourt Park*
Personnel: *Director:* J. Baranowska.
The POSK Gallery provides exhibitions of works (al kinds of media) from artists of all nationalities. The price of hiring the gallery is £36 plus VAT (£42.30) per week for the members of POSK - and £48 plus VAT (£56.40) for non-members plus 15% commission from the price of sold exhibits. The POSK Gallery will advertise all exhibitions free of charge in art magazines "Galleries" and "Art Review", also in papers of the Polish Social and Cultural Association Ltd., and in the Polish Cultural Institute. Artists who wish to

exhibit should send a short curriculum vitae and five colour photographs of their work. Exhibitors are solely responsible for printed material, advertising and invitations. Exhibitions are changed fortnightly.
Services and Facilities:
Bar. Café. Disabled Access. Gallery space for hire. Restaurant.
Work Stocked and Sold:
Cer. Cra. Dr. Jew. Pa. Ph. Pr. Sc.
Price range: £100 - £1,800.

PRIMROSE HILL GALLERY
81 Regents Park Road, London NW1 8UY.
Tel: *0171-586 3533.*

PROUD GALLERIES
5 Buckingham Street, London WC2N 6BS.
Tel: *0171-839 4942.* **Fax:** *0171-839 4947.*

PUMP HOUSE GALLERY
Battersea Park, London SW11.
Tel: *0181-871 7380 /7572.*
Fax: *0181-871 7630.*
Opening times: *Oct-Mar: Wed-Fri 11-3, Sat & Sun 11-4; April-Sept.: Wed-Fri 11-4, Sat & Sun 11-6.*
Nearest Underground: *Sloane Square. BR: Battersea Park Station (one stop from Victoria or Waterloo). Buses: 19, 39, 44, 45, 137, 170.*
Personnel: Charlie Catling.
The Pump House Gallery is situated beside the boating lakes in Battersea Park, just south of the Thames over Chelsea Bridge. The gallery runs an annual programme of about 20

Ab *Artist's Books* **App** *Applied Art* **Cer** *Ceramics* **Cra** *Crafts*
Dec *Decorative* **Dr** *Drawing* **Fur** *Furniture*

exhibitions by contemporary artists, which
emphasises variety in media and style. Hire
rates are currently £100 per week April -
September, £75 per week October - March.
20% commission on sales.
Services and Facilities:
Gallery space for hire. Shop.
Work Stocked and Sold:
Cra. Pa. Ph. Pr. Sc.
Price range: £50 - £5,000.

PYMS GALLERY
*9 Mount Street, Mayfair, London
W1Y 5AD.* **Tel:** *0171-629 2020.*
Fax: *0171-629 2060.*
Opening times: *Mon-Fri 10-6 and by appoint-
ment.*
Nearest Underground: *Green Park,
Bond Street.*
Personnel: *Alan Hobart. Mary Hobart.*

Specialising in British and Irish 18th, 19th
and 20th century paintings and 19th century
French paintings. Regular exhibitions, cata-
logues available. Requests for information and
for notification of exhibitions and events wel-
come.
Insurance valuations of single works and col-
lections. Advice on commission purchases and
cleaning and restoration of paintings.
Members of British Antique Dealers
Association. Exhibitors at Grosvenor House
Art and Antiques Fair. Members Society of
London Art Dealers.
Work Stocked and Sold:
Dr. Pa.
Price range: £200 - £1,000,000.

QUAKER GALLERY
52 St Martin's Lane, London WC2.
Tel: *0171-372 3303.*

QUANTUM CONTEMPORARY ART
*The Old Imperial Laundry, 71 Warriner
Gardens, London SW11 4XW.*
Tel: *0171-498 6868.*
Fax: *0171-498 7878.*

R. K. GALLERY
*65 Sheen Lane, Sheen, London
SW14 8AD.* **Tel:** *0181-878 8800.*

RAFAEL VALLS GALLERY
6 Ryder Street, London, SW1Y.
Tel: *0171-930 0029.*

RAILINGS GALLERY
*5 New Cavendish Street, London
W1M 7RP.* **Tel:** *0171-935 1114.*
Fax: *0171-486 9250.*

REBECCA HOSSACK GALLERY
*Fitzrovia, 35 Windmill Street, London W1P
1HH.* **Tel:** *0171-436 4899.*
Fax: *0171-323 3182.*
Email *rhg@artewisdom.com*
Ws *http://www.artewisdom.com*
Opening times: *Mon-Sat 10-6.*
Nearest Underground: *Goodge Street.*
Personnel: *Director: Rebecca Hossack.
Contact: Tom Greatrex.*
The Rebecca Hossack Gallery is one of the
most innovative galleries in Central London
with a reputation for showing top quality non-
European art as well as the best of British
Contemporary artists.
The leading European gallery for Australian
Aboriginal art and for the art of the Kalahari
Bushmen, The Rebecca Hossack Gallery has a
full range of Aboriginal and Bushman work -
both paintings and prints - always in stock
including pieces by Clifford Possum, Jimmy
Pike, Gertie Huddlestone, Emily Kngwarreye,
and Mathias Kauage.
British Contemporary art shown includes
painting (figurative and abstract), sculpture,
ceramics (Bill McCulloch, Ann Stokes) and
furniture (Camilla Meddings).
Services and Facilities:
*Art Consultancy. Art for Offices.
Commissioning Service. Framing. Gallery space
for hire. Valuation.*
Work Stocked and Sold:
Ab. Cer. Cra. Dec. Dr. Fur. Pa. Ph. Pr.
Sc.

THE RED DOT
*22b Bellevue Road, Wandsworth Common,
London SW17 7EB.*
Tel: *0181-672 6086/0181-675 8110.*
Fax: *0181-673 5066.*

REDCHURCH GALLERIES
(JOHN HUNT GALLERIES)
47-49 Redchurch Street, London E2 7DJ.
Tel: *0171-739 7333.*
Fax: *0171-739 7333.*

REDFERN GALLERY
*20 Cork Street, Burlington Gardens, London,
W1X 2HB.*
Tel: *0171-734 1732/0578.*
Fax: *0171-494 2908.*

REEL POSTER GALLERY
*First Floor, 22 Great Marlborough Street,
London W1V 1AF.*
Tel: *0171-734 4303.*
Fax: *0171-734 4260.*

RICHARD DAY
173 New Bond Street, London, W1Y.
Tel: *0171-629 2991.*

RICHARD PHILIP
59 Ledbury Road, London, W11 2AA.
Tel: *0171-727 7915.*

RICHARD SALMON LTD
*Studio 4, 54 South Edwards Square, London,
W8 6HW.*
Tel: *0171-602 9494.* **Fax:** *0171-371 6617.*

RIVERSIDE ROOM
*Old Town Hall, Whittaker Avenue, Richmond,
TW9 1TP.*
Tel: *0181-332 0534.*
Fax: *0181-940 7568.*

RONA GALLERY
1/2 Weighhouse Street, London W1Y 1YL.
Tel: *0171-491 3718.*
Fax: *0171-491 4171.*

ROPNER GALLERY
*136 Wandsworth Bridge Road, London SW16
2UL.* **Tel:** *0171-736 2524.*

ROWLEY GALLERY CONTEMPORARY
ARTS
*115 Kensington Church Street, London W8
7LN.* **Tel:** *01420-542 885.*

ROY MILES GALLERY
*29 Bruton Street, Mayfair, London
W1X 7DB.* **Tel:** *0171-495 4747.*
Fax: *0171-495 6232.*
Opening times: *Mon-Fri 9.30-5.30.*
Personnel: *Matthew Floris.*
Fine paintings. Major art from Russia. Also
British works.

THE ROYAL COLLECTION TRUST
*Stable Yard House, St. James's Palace, London
SW1A 1JR.* **Tel:** *0171-930 4832.* **Fax:** *0171-
839 8168.*

ROYAL COLLEGE OF ART
Kensington Gore, London SW7 2EU.
Tel: *0171-584 5020 / 0171-590 4444.*
Fax: *0171-584 8217.*

ROYAL EXCHANGE ART GALLERY
14 Royal Exchange, London EC3V 3LL.
Tel: *0171-283 4400.*

ROYAL OVER-SEAS LEAGUE
*Over-Seas House, Park Place, St James's Street,
London SW1A 1LR.*
Tel: *0171-408 0214 x219.*
Fax: *0171-499 6738.*
Opening times: *Open daily 10-6.*
Nearest Underground: *Green Park.*
Personnel: *Director-General: Mr R.F.
Newell. Director of Cultural Affairs: Roderick
Lakin. Promotions Officer, Cultural Affairs:
Dominic Gregory.*
Provides an established platform in Central
London for young artists from the UK and
Commonwealth. The ROSL Annual Open
Exhibition, now in its fifteenth year, is held in
September at Over-Seas House. As well as
over £7,500 in prizes, this discerning showcase
is unique in bringing together young British
artists with their contemporaries from around
the world. Regular solo exhibitions featuring
past exhibitors from the annual open exhibition are held throughout the year in the handsome setting of the Grade 1 listed 1732 recep-

tion room and staircase by architect James Gibb. Programme of literary and musical events.
Services and Facilities:
Bar. Café. Lectures. Restaurant.
Work Stocked and Sold:
Dr. Pa.
Price range: £100 - £5,000.

RUSSIAN ARTS GALLERY - GZHEL (UK)
257 High Street, Acton, London W3 9BY.
Tel: *0181-993 9096.*
Fax: *0181-993 5989.*

SABIN GALLERIES
Campden Lodge, 82 Campden Hill Road, London W8 7AA. **Tel:** *0171-937 0471.*

SACKVILLE GALLERY
26 Sackville Street, London W1X 1DA.
Tel: *0171-734 8104.* **Fax:** *0171-734 8104.*

SALLY HUNTER FINE ART
11 Halkin Arcade, Motcomb Street, London SW1X 8JT. **Tel:** *0171-235 0934.*
Fax: *0171-245 0056.*
Opening times: *Mon-Fri 10-6.*
Nearest Underground: *Knightsbridge.*
Personnel: *Director:* Nicola Blaxall.
Personnel: *Director:* Sally Hunter. *Assistant Director:* Nicola Blaxall.
Fourteen exhibitions annually of British figurative art since 1920.
Services and Facilities:
Art Consultancy. Art for Offices. Shop.
Work Stocked and Sold:
Cer. Dr. Pa. Pr.
Price range: £100 - £3,000.

SANDRA LUMMIS FINE ART
Flat 7, 17 Haslemere Road, London N8 9QP. **Tel:** *0181-340 2293.*

SARA DAVENPORT GALLERY
206 Walton Street, London, SW3 3JG.
Tel: *0171-225 2223.*

THE SCHUSTER GALLERY
14 Maddox Street, Mayfair, London, W1R 9PL. **Tel:** *0171-491 2208.*
Fax: *0171-491 9872.*

SCOLAR FINE ART
Mecklenburgh House, 11 Mecklenburgh Square, London WC1N 2AD.
Tel: *0171-837 6300.* **Fax:** *0171-837 6322.*

SHENDA AMERY STUDIO
25A Edith Grove, London SW10 0LB.
Tel: *0171-351 1775.* **Fax:** *0171-351 1775.*
Opening times: *Daily 10-6.*
Personnel: *Sculptress:* Shenda Amery ARBS.
Shenda Amery Sculptures on Exhibition : Animals, Nudes, Portrait Busts in Bronze. Commissions have included Prime Ministers : Margaret Thatcher and John Major, King Hussein of Jordon, The Lord Mayor of London, Queen Noor, The Earl of Bessborough, etc. The Ambika Fountain Regents Park, London, and Monumental

Sculpture showing the state of humanity at the end of the twentieth century - the Cutting Edge - Visitors by appointment only - Commissions undertaken. The studio is the only purpose built sculptor's studio built in Chelsea this century. It was designed by Nezam Khazal Amery who worked and studied with Frank Lloyd Wright.
Services and Facilities:
Art for Offices. Commissioning Service. Parking.
Work Stocked and Sold:
Sc.

SIMMONS GALLERY
53 Lambs Conduit Street, London WC1N 3NB. **Tel:** *0171-831 2080.*
Fax: *0171-831 2090.*
Opening times: *Mon-Fri 10.30-5.30 or by appointment.*
Nearest Underground: *Russell Square or Holborn.*
Personnel: *Directors:* Howard Simmons, Frances Simmons.

Sculpture, medals and coins - the only specialist gallery for contemporary medals in the UK. Apart from solo and group exhibitions, we always have exciting international work for sale in a relaxed setting. Visitors are warmly encouraged to touch and handle the small sculpture. We also offer a commissioning service.
Services and Facilities:
Art Consultancy. Art for Offices. Commissioning Service. Valuation.
Work Stocked and Sold:
Dec. Jew. Sc.
Price range: £5 - £5,000.

SIMON CAPSTICK-DALE FINE ART
23a St. James Street, London SW1A 1HA.
Tel: *0171-839 4070.* **Fax:** *0171-839 4077.*
Opening times: *Mon-Fri 10-6.*
Nearest Underground: *Green Park.*

Simon Capstick-Dale Fine Art Ltd, London and 128 East 72nd Street, New York, NY

10021, Tel: 001-212 628 2067. Art dealers and gallery buying , selling and exhibiting 20th century works of art including impressionist, modern and contemporary paintings, watercolours, drawings and sculpture.
Work Stocked and Sold:
Dr. Pa. Pr. Sc.

SIMON DICKINSON
58 Jermyn Street, London SW1Y 6LX.
Tel: *0171-493 0340.* **Fax:** *0171-493 0796.*

SIMS REED
43a Duke Street, St. James's, London SW1Y 6DD. **Tel:** *0171-493 5660.*

THE SPECIAL PHOTOGRAPHER'S COMPANY
21 Kensington Park Road, London W11 2EU. **Tel:** *0171-221 3489.*
Fax: *0171-792 9112.*
Email *info@specialphoto.co.uk*
Ws *http://www.specialphoto.co.uk*
Opening times: *Mon-Fri 10-6, Sat 11-5.*
Nearest Underground: *Notting Hill Gate and Westbourne Grove.*
Personnel: *Directors:* Catherine Turner, Chris Kewbank.
Exhibitions change monthly. Contemporary Fine Art photography from around the world. Photographers available for commission, and library of over 4,000 images available for usage. Representing: William Claxton, Eddie Dayan, Ewan Fraser, Lois Greenfield, Ouka Lele, Herman Leonard, Simon Marsden, Terry O'Neill, Edward S. Curtis, Joyce Tenneson and Laura Wilson.
Services and Facilities:
Art for Offices. Bookshop. Framing. Gallery space for hire. Valuation.
Work Stocked and Sold:
Ph.
Price range: £80 - £2,000.

SPINK-LEGER
5 King Street, St James's, London SW1Y 6QS. **Tel:** *0171-930 7888.*
Fax: *0171-839 4853, 4850.*

SPINK-LEGER PICTURES
13 Old Bond Street, London W1X 3DB.
Tel: *0171-629 3538/9.*

ST. JAMES'S FINE ARTS
72 New Bond Street, London W1Y 9DD.
Tel: *0171-355 1096.* **Fax:** *0171-495 3017.*

ST. JAMES'S PRINTS
15 Piccadilly Arcade, London SW1Y 6NH.
Tel: *0171-495 6487.*

ST. MARTINS GALLERY
St. Martins-in-the-Fields, Trafalgar Square. London WC2N 4JJ.
Tel: *0171-839 4342.*
Fax: *0171-839 5163.*

STABLES GALLERY
Gladstone Park, Dollis Hill Lane, Cricklewood, London NW2 6HT.
Tel: *0181-452 8655.*

Ab *Artist's Books* **App** *Applied Art* **Cer** *Ceramics* **Cra** *Crafts* **Dec** *Decorative* **Dr** *Drawing* **Fur** *Furniture*

STEPHANIE HOPPEN
17 Walton Street, London SW3.
Tel: *0171-589 3678.*
Fax: *0171-581 5744.*

STEPHEN FRIEDMAN GALLERY
25-28 Old Burlington Street, London
W1X 1LN. **Tel:** *0171-494 1434.*
Fax: *0171-494 1431.*

STEPHEN SOMERVILLE LTD
14 Old Bond Street, London W1X 3DB.
Tel: *0171-493 8363.* **Fax:** *0171-738 5995.*

STERN ART DEALERS
46 Ledbury Road, London W11 2AB.
Tel: *0171-229 6187.*
Fax: *0171-229 6187, 7016.*
Opening times: *Mon-Sat 10-6.*
Nearest Underground: *Notting Hill Gate.*
Personnel: *Director: David Stern.*

The gallery displays on its two floors over 400
19th and 20th century paintings. The ground
floor is dedicated entirely to 19th century
Victorian & European oil paintings covering a
wide range of subjects. The lower gallery
exhibits works by Camille Pissarro and his
descendants covering eight artists from four
generations. Works on display include oil
paintings and works on paper.
Services and Facilities:
Art Consultancy. Framing. Restoration.
Valuation.
Work Stocked and Sold:
Dr. Pa. Sc.
Price range: *£500 - £15,000.*

STOPPENBACH & DELESTRE
25 Cork Street, London, W1X 1HB.
Tel: *0171-734 3534, 0171-437 0568.*
Fax: *0171-494 3578.*

STRATEGIC ART
21 Douglas Street, London SW1P.
Tel: *0171-416 0173.*

STUDIO 3 GALLERY
75 Leonard Street, London EC2A 4QJ.
Tel: *0171-739 2024.*

STUDIO NINE
9 Marylands Road, London W9 2DU.
Tel: *0171-266 3729.*
Fax: *0171-286-2305.*

STUDIO SIENKO
57a Lant Street, London SE1 1QN.
Tel: *0171-403 1353.*
Fax: *0171-357 6976.*

SWAN FINE ART
120 Islington High Street, London N1.
Tel: *0171-226 5335, 0171-359 2225.*

TADEMA GALLERY
10 Charlton Place, Camden Passage, London N1
8AJ. **Tel:** *0171-359 1055.*
Fax: *0171-359 1055.*
Opening times: *Wed & Sat 10-5 or by*
appointment.
Nearest Underground: *Angel.*
Personnel: *Directors:* Sonya Newell-Smith,
David Newell-Smith.
Tadema Gallery, established 1979, is unusual,
specialising in both 20th century Abstract Art
- concentrating on the 1960's & 20th century
Jewellery - Art Nouveau, Art Deco, Arts &
Crafts through to artist designed Jewels of the
1960's.
Work Stocked and Sold:
Jew. Pa.

TALISMAN FINE ARTS
82 Mill Lane, West Hampstead, London NW6
1NL. **Tel:** *0171-794 4266.*
Fax: *0171-435 65.*

TAYLOR GALLERIES
1 Bolney Gate, London SW7.
Tel: *0171-581 0253.*

THACKEREY GALLERY
18 Thackerey Street, Kensington Square, London
W8 5ET.
Tel: *0171-937 5883.* **Fax:** *0171-937 6965.*

THAMESIDE STUDIO
109 Oxo Tower Wharf, Barge House, London
SE1. **Tel:** *0171-928 7411.*

THE GALLERY
168 Pentonville Road, London N1.
Tel: *0171-837 8490.*

THE STRONG PRINT ROOM
University College London, Gower Street,
London WC1E 6BT. **Tel:** *0171-387 7050.*

THEO WADDINGTON FINE ART
5a Cork Street, London W1X 1PB.
Tel: *0171-494 1584.*
Fax: *0171-287 0926.*

THIRD FLOOR ART GALLERY,
WHITELEYS
London W2.

THOMAS HENEAGE
42 Duke Street, St James's, London,
SW1Y 6DJ. **Tel:** *0171-930 9223.*

THOMPSON'S GALLERY
18 Dover Street, London W1X 3PB.
Tel: *0171-629 6878.*
Fax: *0171-629 6181.*

THORNTON BEVAN ARTS
130 Percy Road, London W12 9QL.
Tel: *0181-740 8084.*
Fax: *0181-740 8084.*
Opening times:

By appointment Wed-Sun.
Thornton Bevan Arts is a home based gallery
in Hammersmith established 1995 specialising
in emerging artists; many are graduates of the
Royal College of Art and the Royal Academy
Schools.
Price range: *£40 - £3,000.*

THROSSELLS
13 Broad Street, Teddington, TW11 8QZ.
Tel: *0181-943 4248.*
Nearest Station: *Teddington.*
Personnel: *Nola Throssell.*
Contemporary Art Gallery and separate exhi-
bition room (also available for hire). Café
within Art Gallery.
Services and Facilities:
Art Consultancy. Art for Offices. Café.
Commissioning Service. Craftshop. Disabled
Access. Gallery space for hire. Restaurant. Shop.
Work Stocked and Sold:
Cer. Cra. Fur. Gla. Pa. Pr.
Price range: *£25 - £500.*

TIAN ART
36 Beauchamp Place, London SW3.
Tel: *0171-823 8088.*

THE TIMOTHY TAYLOR GALLERY
1 Bruton Place, London W1.
Tel: *0171-409 3344.*

TODD GALLERY
1-5 Needham Road, London W11 2RP.
Tel: *0171-792 1404.* **Fax:** *0171-792 1505.*

THE TOM BLAU GALLERY
21 Queen Elizabeth Street, London,
SE1 2PD. **Tel:** *0171-378 1300.*

TOM TEMPEST RADFORD
16 Devonshire Row, London EC2M.
Tel: *0171-377 8004.*

THE TOWER/JAMES COLMAN
FINE ART
The Tower, 28 Mossbury Road, London, SW11
2PB. **Tel:** *0171-924 3860.*
Fax: *0171-924 3860.*

TRICYCLE GALLERY
Tricycle Theatre, 269 Kilburn High Road,
London NW6 7JR.
Tel: *0171-372 6611.*
Fax: *0171-328 0795.*

TROWBRIDGE GALLERY
555 Kings Road, London SW6.
Tel: *0171-371 8733.*

TRYON & SWANN GALLERY
23-24 Cork Street, London W1X 1HB.
Tel: *0171-634 6961, 0171-734 2256.*

VICTORIA GALLERY
158 Hermon Hill, London, E18 1QH.
Tel: *0181-989 1195.*

VICTORIA MIRO LONDON
21 Cork Street, London W1X.
Tel: *0171-734 5082.*

Gla Glass Jew Jewellery Pa Paintings Ph Photography Pr Prints
Sc Sculpture Tx Textiles Wd Wood

VYVYAN ROBINSON & CO.
235 Regent Street, London W1R.
Tel: *0171-495 6642.*

W.H. PATTERSON FINE ARTS
19 Albemarle Street, London, W1X.
Tel: *0171-629 4119.*

WADDINGTON GALLERIES
*11,12 & 34 Cork Street, London
W1X 2LT.*
Tel: *0171-437 8611, 0171-439 6262.*
Fax: *0171-734 4146.*
Opening times: *Mon-Fri 10-5.30, Sat 10-1,
(closed Sat from 18 July-29 August).*
Nearest Underground: *Green Park.*
Personnel: *Directors:* Leslie Waddington,
Thomas Lighton, Stephen Saunders,
Ms Hester van Roijen.

Exhibitions monthly. Artists represented:
The Estate of Josef Albers, Blake, Caulfield,
Craig-Martin, Davenport, Flanagan, Heron,
The Estate of Ivon Hitchens, Zebedee Jones,
Milroy, Paladino, Rae, Tàpies, Turnbull.
Works in stock by: Arp, Avery, Calder,
Chamberlain, Chia, Degas, de Kooning,
Dubuffet, Ernst, Flavin, Francis, Hepworth,
Hockney, Hodgkin, Judd, Klee, Landy, Léger,
Lichtenstein, Lim, Lipchitz, Magritte, Matisse,
Miró, Moore, Nicholson, Picabia, Picasso,
Rauschenberg, Samaras, Schnabel, Spencer,
Warhol, Wesselmann, Westermann, Yeats.
Founded 1966.
Work Stocked and Sold:
Dr. Pa. Sc.

THE WALK
23 King Edward Walk, London SE1 7PR.
Tel: *0171-928 3786.* **Fax:** *0171-261 1541.*
Opening times: *Tues-Sun 1.30-6 during exhi-
bitions. By appointment at other times.*
Nearest Underground: *Lambeth North.*
Personnel: *Directors:* Ranabir Chanda,
Gillian Salmon.

Situated in a street opposite the Imperial War
Museum, about 10 minutes walk from the
Hayward Gallery and conveniently located for
Lambeth North and Waterloo stations, this
private gallery opened in March 1997. Group
and solo shows are held in the attractive exhibition area. The Walk has a policy of encouraging relatively unknown, contemporary
artists whose work uses a range of media.
Their approaches can be traditional as well as
experimental, exploratory and challenging.
The Walk proposes to make original art
affordable to a very wide range of people.
Prices are within the range £275-£6,000. A
full programme of exhibitions is planned for
1998/89. Details of forthcoming events are
available on request. Forthcoming events:
1988: 21st April-10th May - Nick Banks : Oils
& Sculpture, 2nd-20th June - Moz Walsh :
Multi-Media Happenings, 14th July-23rd
August - Mid-Summer Festival, 8th-27th
September - David Hogan : Sculptures, 13th
October-8th November - Vincent Milne -
Recent Work, 20th November-19th
December - Sophie Mortimer - Pen Ink &
Wash. 1999: 9th February-7th March - Sue
Morris - Recent Work.
Services and Facilities:
*Art Consultancy. Art for Offices. Commissioning
Service. Gallery space
for hire.*
Work Stocked and Sold:
App. Dr. Pa. Ph. Sc.
Price range: £275 - £6,000.

WALPOLE GALLERY
38 Dover Street, London, W1X 3RB.
Tel: *0171-499 6626.*

WALTON CONTEMPORARY ART
188 Walton Street, London SW3 2JL.
Tel: *0171-581 9011.* **Fax:** *0171-581 0585.*
Personnel: Michael Potter.

Walton Contemporary Art's retail gallery is
based in the popular shopping area of Walton
Street and alongside some of the best names
in design retailing from Joseph, Conran and
Andrew Martin. The gallery exhibits work
which compliments the modern home or
office. Prices for framed, signed prints start at
around £150 and rise to £5000 for works on
canvas or sculpture. Art consultancy to private clients and firms together with it's limited edition publishing activities are run from
it's own studios close by. All enquiries to
Michael Potter.
Services and Facilities:
Art Consultancy.
Work Stocked and Sold:
Pa. Pr. Sc.
Price range: £100 - £5,000.

WATERHOUSE & DODD
110 New Bond Street, London, W1Y 9AA.
Tel: *0171-491 9293.*

WATERMAN FINE ART
*74a Jerymn Street, St. James's, London SW1Y
6NP.* **Tel:** *0171-839 5203.*
Fax: *0171-321 0212.*

WATERSIDE WORKSHOPS
99 Rotherhithe Street, London, SE16 4NF.
Tel: *0171-237 0017.*

WEISS GALLERY
1b Albemarle Street, London W1X.
Tel: *0171-409 0035.*

WELL HUNG GALLERY
*39 Ledbury Road, Notting Hill, London W11
2AA.*

WELLINGTON GALLERY
1 St. Johns Wood High Street, London, NW8.
Tel: *0171-586 2620.*

WHITE CUBE
*44 Duke Street, St. James's, London
SW1Y 6DD.* **Tel:** *0171-930 5373.*
: 0171-930 9973.

WHITFIELD FINE ART
180 New Bond Street, London W1Y.
Tel: *0171-499 3592.*

WHITFORD FINE ART
*6 Duke Street, St James's, London
SW1Y 6BN.* **Tel:** *0171-930 9332.*
Fax: *0171-930 5577.*

WIGMORE FINE ART
104 Wigmore Street, London W1H 9DR.
Tel: *0171-224 1962.* **Fax:** *0171-224 1965.*

WILKINS & WILKINS
1 Barrett Street, London W1M.
Tel: *0171-935 9613.*

WILL'S ART WAREHOUSE
*Unit 3, Heathmans Road, Parsons Green,
Fulham, London SW6 4TJ.*
Tel: *0171-371 8787.* **Fax:** *0171-371 0044.*
Ws *http://www.willsart.demon.co.uk*
Opening times: *Mon-Thur 10.30-8, Fri, Sat
& Sun 10.30-6.*
Nearest Underground: *Parsons Green.*
Personnel: *Director:* Will Ramsay.

WILL'S ART WAREHOUSE

Paintings, Prints, Sculpture, Business Art
Consultants. £50-£2,000. Contemporary Art.
Monthly exhibitions. Over 200 works by 15-
20 artists. Informed
atmosphere. "The Oddbins of the Art
World", Marie Claire; ".....making original
work accessible to all", Museums & Galleries
Magazine; "......wide scope and democratic
price range", Independent; "High & light &

Ab *Artist's Books* **App** *Applied Art* **Cer** *Ceramics* **Cra** *Crafts*
Dec *Decorative* **Dr** *Drawing* **Fur** *Furniture*

informal", Daily Telegraph.
Services and Facilities:
Art Consultancy. Art for Offices.
Commissioning Service. Disabled Access. Gallery
space for hire. Parking.
Work Stocked and Sold:
Pa. Pr. Sc.
Price range: £50 - £2,000.

WILLIAM BEADLESTON INCORPORATED
13 Masons Yard, St James's, London, SW1Y.
Tel: *0171-321 0495.*

WILLIAM HARDIE GALLERY
15a Blythswood Square, Glasgow
G2 2BG.

WILLIAM WESTON GALLERY
7 Royal Arcade, Albemarle Street, London,
W1X 4JN.
Tel: *0171-493 0722.*

WILLIAMS & SON
2 Grafton Street, London W1X.
Tel: *0171-493 5751, 0171-493 4985.*

WILSON STEPHENS FINE ART
11 Cavendish Road, London NW6 7XT.
Tel: *0181-459 0760.*
Fax: *0181-459 0760.*

WISEMAN ORIGINALS
34 West Square, Lambeth, London
SE11 4SP. **Tel:** *0171-587 0747.*
Fax: *0171-793 8817 / 9917.*
Email *100611.3631@compuserve.com*
Ws *http://www.artplanet.com/ pages/global/*
Opening times: *Any time by appointment.*
Nearest Underground: *Lambeth North.*
Personnel: *Director:* Caroline Wiseman.
Garth Wiseman.

Specialises in affordable art by modern mas-
ters. Deals from home which is used as gallery
space.
Good selection of original prints by modern
European masters including Buffet, Calder,
Chagall, Matisse, Miró, Picasso and modern
and contemporary British including
Auerbach, Frink, Hodgkin, Hockney, Frost,

Hepworth, Nicholson, McLean, Pasmore,
Piper, Moore, Sutherland, Bellany and Scott.
Services and Facilities:
Art Consultancy. Art for Offices.
Commissioning Service. Framing. Valuation.
Work Stocked and Sold:
Dr. Pa. Pr.
Price range: £100 - £10,000.

WOLSELEY FINE ARTS
12 Needham Road, Notting Hill, London W11
2RP. **Tel:** *0171-792 2788.*
Fax: *0171-792 2988.*
Email *WolseleyFineArts@btinternet.com*
Opening times: *Open during exhibitions at*
least Tues-Sat 2-5. Otherwise by appointment.
Nearest Underground: *Notting Hill.*
Personnel: *Director:* Rupert Otten.
Director: Hannene van der Werf.

Dealers in 20th century works on paper by
British and European masters from France,
Belgium, and Holland.
Specialist in all works by Eric Gill, David
Jones, Edgar Holloway, John Buckland,
Wright and Eugeen van Mieghem. Wolseley
Contemporary represents Gretta, Brian Yale,
Paul Klemann and exhibits carved lettering
and calligraphy. Fairs include: the European
Fine Art Fair, British 20th Century and Fine
Art and Antiques Fair, Works on Paper, New
York.
Services and Facilities:
Art Consultancy. Commissioning Service.
Valuation.
Work Stocked and Sold:
Dr. Pa. Pr. Sc.
Price range: £50 - £30,000.
WOODLANDS ART GALLERY
90 Mycenae Road, Blackheath, London SE3
7SE. **Tel:** *0181-858 5847.*
Fax: *0181-858 5847.*

THE WYKEHAM GALLERIES
51 Church Road, Barnes, London,
SW13 9HH. **Tel:** *0171-351 4449.*

ZELDA CHEATLE GALLERY
8 Cecil Court, London WC2N 4HE.
Tel: *0171-836 0506.* **Fax:** *0171-497 8911.*

ZELLA GALLERY
2 Park Walk, Fulham Road, London
SW10 0AD. **Tel:** *0171-351 0588.*
Fax: *0171-352 4752.*
Opening times: Mon-Sat 9.30-6,
Sun 11.30-5.30.
Personnel: Mrs M. Gore.
Well known gallery, established 1971, that
specialises in finding and promoting young
inspired artists who work in a mainly
Contemporary Figurative and Abstract way on
canvas and on paper.
40 Gallery Artists' work on exhibit all year in
our lower gallery and in portfolios. (Gallery
Artists are mostly British and European print-
makers). Programme of one man exhibitions
throughout the year on the ground floor.
Works from as little as £50 up to around
£1,000 though most are in the £200 to £600
region.
Services and Facilities:
Art Consultancy. Art for Offices. Framing.
Work Stocked and Sold:
Pa. Pr.
Price range: £50 - £1,200.

ZENITH GALLERY
41 Balham High Road, London,
SW12 9AN. **Tel:** *0181-675 7570.*

Gla *Glass* **Jew** *Jewellery* **Pa** *Paintings* **Ph** *Photography* **Pr** *Prints*
Sc *Sculpture* **Tx** *Textiles* **Wd** *Wood*

YOU ARE HERE?

A full listing in the Art World Directory including full text description, image and cross-referencing puts you in front of thousands of potential clients for an entire year.

To ensure you appear in the 1999/2000 edition simply register below. You will receive entry forms and material for completion as soon as compilation for the new edition begins.

ART WORLD DIRECTORY 1999/2000 REGISTRATION FORM

Please register me for the next edition of the Art World Directory. I understand I do not need to send any payment now, nor is this registration binding in any way.

Name (Mr/Mrs/Ms) _____

Job Title _____

Company/Establishment Name _____

Address _____

_____ Postcode _____

Tel: _____ Fax _____ email _____

Nature of Business (see our contents page for headings) _____

Please complete this form and return to: Art Review. AWD Registrations, Freepost, London EC1B 1DE.

LONDON PUBLIC GALLERIES

All entries in this section are sorted alphabetically by gallery.
Where this information has been provided, entries are designated
'P' for public gallery or museum or 'PS' for a public gallery or
museum holding selling shows.

THE ART WORLD
DIRECTORY
1998/99 25TH EDITION

Open: Mon - Sat
10.00 - 18.00
Sun 12.00 - 18.00
Closed:
1 Jan, Good Friday,
May Day Bank Holiday,
24 – 26 Dec

St Martin's Place
London WC2H OHE
Tel 0171 306 0055
⊖ Leicester Square
or Charing Cross

NATIONAL
PORTRAIT
GALLERY

Bobby Charlton by Peter Edwards 1991

198 GALLERY PS

194-198 Railton Road, Herne Hill, London SE24 0LU. **Tel:** *0171-978 8309.*
Fax: *0171-652 1418.* **Email** *198gallery@globalnet.co.uk*
Ws *http:www.globalnet.co.uk/~198gallery*
Opening times: Mon-Sat 11-7.
Nearest Underground: *BR Thameslink Herne Hill 92 mins).* Buses 3, 37, 68, 196, 332.
Personnel: *Administration:* Zoe Linsley-Thomas. *Press/Marketing:* Sonia Mackintosh. *Education:* Paul Howard. *Exhibitions:* Godfried Donkor.

198 Gallery, education and training resource. Contemporary art by artists from diverse cultural backgrounds, wide range of media including new technologies. Education centre offers programmes for schools/colleges/training for adults in arts/new technologies, agency for artists in schools/hospitals/public commissions. Eight exhibitions per annum, shop offers original paintings, prints, ceramics, sculpture, stools, Benin bronzes, from around the world.
Services and Facilities:
Commissioning Service. Disabled Access. Friends/Society. Museum Shop. Parking. Shop. Workshop Facilities.
Work Stocked and Sold:
Cer. Pa. Pr. Sc. Tx.
Price range: £50 - £5,000.

ARCHITECTURE FOUNDATION P

30 Bury Street, London SW1Y.
Tel: *0171-839 9389.*

THE ARK (MUSEUM OF GARDEN HISTORY) P

220 Lambeth Road, London SE7 7JY.
Tel: *0171-582 890.*

BANK OF ENGLAND MUSEUM P

Bank of England, Threadneedle Street, (public entrance Bartholomew Lane), London EC2R 8AH. **Tel:** *0171-601 5545 (information desk; Minicom 0171-601 5140).* **Fax:** *0171-601 5808.* **Email** *museum@bankofengland.co.uk*
Ws *http://www.bankofengland.co.uk*
Opening times: *10-5 all year. Closed weekends and Public and Bank Holidays. Open on the day of the Lord Mayor's Show.*
Nearest Underground: *Bank (Northern, Central, Docklands Light Railway, Waterloo and City). BR: Liverpool Street, Fenchurch Street, Cannon Street.*
Personnel: *Assistant Curator:* June Greenhalf.
The Museum is housed within the Bank of England right at the heart of the City of London. It traces the history of the Bank from its foundation by Royal Charter in 1694 to its role today as the nation's central bank. Displays include: gold; banknotes; 18th century banking hall and state of the art interactive

video systems on the Bank and its roles, as well as foreign exchange dealing games.
Services and Facilities:
Disabled Access. Guided Tours. Museum Shop.

BANKSIDE GALLERY PS

48 Hopton Street, Blackfriars, London SE1 9JH.
Tel: *0171-928 7521.* **Fax:** *0171-928 2820.*
Email *RE&RWS@banksidegallery.demon.co.uk*
Opening times: *During exhibitions Tues 10-8, Wed-Fri 10-5, Sun 1-5. Outside exhibition times the bookshop remains open Tues-Fri*
Nearest Underground: *Blackfriars.*

Bankside Gallery is the home of the Royal Watercolour Society and the Royal Society of Painter-Printmakers. This friendly gallery runs a changing programme of exhibitions of contemporary watercolours and artists prints. Members of the two societies are elected by their peers and represent a tradition of excellence reaching back two hundred years. Their work embraces both established and experimental practices and the exhibitions balance these different approaches. Informal 'Artists Perspectives' take place every Tuesday evening during the course of an exhibition. A range of practical courses and tutorials are held every year by artist members of the two societies. Full details are available from the Gallery. Admission: £3.50, concessions £2. Free admission to Friends.
Services and Facilities:
Art for Offices. Bookshop. Commissioning Service. Friends/Society. Gallery space for hire. Lectures. Shop.
Work Stocked and Sold:
Pa. Pr.
Price range: £40 - £2,000.

BARBICAN ART GALLERY P

Gallery Floor, Level 3, Barbican Centre, London EC2Y 8DS. **Tel:** *0171-588 9023.* **Fax:** *0171-628 0364.* **Ws** *http://www.uk-calling.co.uk*
Opening times: *Mon, Thur-Sat 10-6.45, Tues 10-5.45, Wed 10-7.45, Sun + Public Hols 12-6.45.*
Nearest Underground: *Moorgate, Barbican, St.Pauls, Liverpool Street.*
Personnel: *Curator:* John Hoole.
Barbican Art Gallery, a leading international art exhibition venue located in the heart of the City, presents an annual programme of up to six shows covering a diverse range of subjects including Impressionist painting, interactive new media, photography, sculpture and fashion. 1998 exhibitions focus on American culture and include The Warhol Look, on Andy Warhol and fashion (28 May-16 August), Cindy Sherman whose work explores female identity through art and film (10 Sep-13 Dec), and The Native North American, a

look at past and present representation of Native Americans. Admissions £5.00/£3.00 reductions.
Services and Facilities:
Bar. Bookshop. Disabled Access. Guided Tours. Lectures. Parking. Restaurant. Workshop Facilities.

BARBICAN CONCOURSE GALLERY P

Gallery Floor, Level 3, Barbican Centre, London EC2Y 8DS. **Tel:** *0171-638 7515.*
Nearest Underground: *Moorgate, Barbican, St.Pauls, Liverpool Street.*

BEN URI ART SOCIETY PS

126 Albert Street, London NW1 7NE.
Tel: *0171-482 1234.* **Fax:** *0171-482 1414.*
Email *benuri@ort.org*
Ws *http://www.ort.org/benuri/*
Opening times: *Closed Jewish Holy days and Bank Holidays, otherwise by arrangement.*
Nearest Underground: *Camden Town.*
Personnel: *Director:* Jo Velleman.
The aim of the society, which is a registered charity founded in 1915, is to promote Jewish art as part of the Jewish cultural heritage. The Gallery provides a showcase for contemporary exhibitions, as well as works from the Society's own permanent collection of over 800 works by Jewish artists including Auerbach, Bomberg, Epstein, Gertler, Kossoff, Kramer and Pissarro.
A new catalogue of the Collection was published in 1994 and all works are accessible on CD ROM. The Society is presently in temporary office accommodation, pending the building of a new Jewish Arts and Cultural Centre in Camden Town.
Services and Facilities:
Art for Offices. Café. Disabled Access. Friends/Society. Gallery space for hire. Lectures.

BETHNAL GREEN MUSEUM OF CHILDHOOD P

Cambridge Heath Road, London E2 9PA.
Tel: *0181-983 5200, recorded info. 0181-980 2415.*
Fax: *0181-983 5225.*

BHOWNAGREE AND TODAY GALLERIES PS

The Commonwealth Experience, Commonwealth Institute, Kensington High Street, London W8 6NQ. **Tel:** *0171-603 4535.*
Fax: *0171-602 7374.*
Email *info@commonwealth.org.uk*
Ws *http://www.commonwealth.org.uk*
Opening times: *Daily 10-5. Admission fee, phone for details.*
Nearest Underground: *High Street Kensington, Earl's Court.*
Personnel: *Director General:* David French.
As part of the visitor attraction The Commonwealth Experience, these two established galleries present a rolling programme of Commonwealth art and craft with work for sale.
Acrylic paintings of birds of Trinidad and Tobago and powerful figurative work in a mix of oil paint and sand are on view until 22 March 1998, followed by mixed media works on hand-made paper from India and water-

Ab *Artist's Books* **App** *Applied Art* **Cer** *Ceramics* **Cra** *Crafts* **Dec** *Decorative* **Dr** *Drawing*
Fur *Furniture* **Gla** *Glass* **Jew** *Jewellery* **Pa** *Paintings* **Ph** *Photography* **Pr** *Prints*
Sc *Sculpture* **Tx** *Textiles* **Wd** *Wood*

THE ARTWORLD
DIRECTORY 1998/99   **85**

programme to June 1999 features life-size sculptures from Nigeria, photographs from India and New Zealand, oil paintings from

Bangladesh and the Falkland Islands and work by artists from Ghana, Zimbabwe and Nigeria resident in Britain.
Services and Facilities:
Café. Friends/Society. Gallery space for hire. Shop.

BOLIVAR HALL *P*
Venezuelan Embassy, 54 Crafton Way, London W1P 5LB. **Tel:** *0171-388 5788.*
Fax: *0171-383 3253.*

BRITISH ARCHITECTURAL LIBRARY DRAWINGS COLLECTION/RIBA HEINZ GALLERY *P*
21 Portman Square, London, W1H 9HF.
Tel: *0171-580 5533.*
Fax: *0171-486 3793.*

BRITISH MUSEUM *P*
Great Russell Street, London WC1B 3DG.
Tel: *0171-636 1555.*

CAFE GALLERY *P*
By The Pool, Southward Park, Bermondsey, London, SE16 2TY. **Tel:** *0171-266 4665/0171-237 1230/0171-232 2170.*
Fax: *0171-232 2170.*
CAMDEN ARTS CENTRE *P*
Arkwright Road, London, NW3 6DG.
Tel: *0171-435 2643 / 5224.* **Fax:** *0171-794 3371.*

CARLYLE'S HOUSE *P*
24 Cheyne Row, London SW3 5HL.
Tel: *0171-352 7087.*

CHALK FARM GALLERY *P*
20 Chalk Farm Road, London NW1 8AG.
Tel: *0171-267 3300.*

CHISENHALE GALLERY *P*
64 Chisenhale Road, London E3 5QZ.
Tel: *0181-981 4518.*
Fax: *0181-980 7169.*

CHISWICK HOUSE *P*
Burlington Lane, London W4 2RP.
Tel: *0181-995 0508.*
Fax: *0181-742 3104.*
COMMONWEALTH INSTITUTE *P*

Kensington High Street, London W8 6NQ.
Tel: *0171-603 4535.* **Fax:** *0171-602 7374.*

COURTAULD INSTITUTE GALLERIES *P*
Somerset House, Strand, London WC2R 0RN.
Tel: *0171-837 2526 .* **Fax:** *0171-873 2589.*

CRYSTAL PALACE MUSEUM *P*
Anerley Hill, SE19 2BA. **Tel:** *0181-676 0700.*

DELFINA STUDIOS *P*
50 Bermondsey Street, London SE1 3UD.
Tel: *0171-357 6600.* **Fax:** *0171-357 0250.*
Personnel: David Gilmour.
Temporary exhibitions of modern and contemporary art.

DESIGN MUSEUM *P*
Butler's Wharf, Shad Thames, London SE1 2YD.
Tel: *0171-403 6933, 0171-378 6055 (recorded info.).* **Fax:** *0171-378 6540.*
Opening times: *Mon-Fri 11.30-6, Sat-Sun 12-6. Admission £5.25 and £4.00 concessions.*
Personnel: *Director:* Paul Thompson.

Desigmuseum

Visitors can rediscover the excitement of classic design from the past hundred years in the panoramic top floor Collection Gallery. State-of-the-art innovations from around the globe can be found in the Review Gallery. Also offers a programme of critically acclaimed special exhibitions on design and architecture.
Services and Facilities:
Café. Disabled Access. Gallery space for hire. Guided Tours. Lectures. Museum Shop. Shop.

DULWICH PICTURE GALLERY *P*
College Road, London SE21 7AD. **Tel:** *0181-693 5254.* **Fax:** *0181-693 0923.*
Opening times: *Tue-Fri 10-5, Sat & Bank Holiday Monday 11-5,*
Nearest Underground: *British Rail: Victoria to West Dulwich.*
Personnel: *Director:* Desmond Shawe-Taylor.
"London's most perfect gallery" - The Guardian. Britain's oldest purpose-built gallery, Dulwich was founded in 1811 and designed by the Regency architect Sir John Soane.
The collection contains some remarkable works, including Rembrandt's Girl at Window, important works by Poussin and Claude, Rubens, Van Dyck and Murillo. Watteau's dreamy Le Bal Champêtre and works by Hogarth, Gainsborough, Reynolds are among 18th Century paintings. The earliest painting is Piero di Cosimo's Portrait of a Young Man. Refreshments - less than five minutes' walk away in Dulwich Village.
Exhibitions in 1998: 4 March-24 May - Italy in the Age of Turner, 17 June-19 July - Paula Rego, September-November - Pieter de Hooch.
Services and Facilities:
Bookshop. Disabled Access. Friends/Society. Guided Tours. Lectures. Museum Shop. Parking. Shop.

ESTORICK COLLECTION OF

MODERN ITALIAN ART *P*
Northampton Lodge, 39A Cannonbury Square, London N1 2AN. **Tel:** *0171-704 9522.*
Fax: *0171-704 9531.*
Opening times: *Tues-Sat 11-6.*
Nearest Underground: *Highbury & Islington.*
Personnel: *Curator:* Alexandra Noble.
A new museum which opened in January 1998 in a handsome, Grade II, Georgian villa showing a permanent collection of early 20th century Italian art including world famous works by the Futurists, Boccioni, Balla, Carra, Severini and Russolo.
Other artists represented include de Chirico, Modigliani, and Morandi and sculptors Medardo Rosso, Giacomo Manzu and Marino Marini. There is a changing exhibition and education programme in development. Group and school visits are always welcome, but must book in advance.
Art reference library by appointment. Access for wheelchair users on two floors only.
Zwemmers gallery shop and Cafe Panini open museum hours.
Services and Facilities:
Café. Guided Tours. Shop.

GEFFRYE MUSEUM *P*
Kingsland Road, London, E2 8EA.
Tel: *0171-739 9893.* **Fax:** *0171-729 5647.*

GOETHE-INSTITUT LONDON *P*
50 Princes Gate, Exhibition Road, London SW7 2PH. **Tel:** *0171-411 3445.*
Fax: *0171-581 0974.*

GOLDSMITHS' HALL *P*
Foster Lane, London EC2V 6BN. **Tel:** *0171-606 7010.* **Fax:** *0171-606 1511.*

GOVERNMENT ART COLLECTION *P*
c/o Dept of Culture, Media and Sport, 2-4 Cockspur Street, London SW1Y 5DH. **Tel:** *0171-287 2877.* **Fax:** *0171-287 1181.*

GUILDHALL ART GALLERY *P*
Aldermanbury, London EC2P 2EJ. **Tel:** *0171-606 3030 /332 1632 / 332 1856 (direct line).*
Fax: *0171-600 3384.*

HAYWARD GALLERY *P*
South Bank Centre, Belvedere Road, London SE1 8XZ. **Tel:** *0171-928 3144.* **Fax:** *0171-401 2664.*
Ws *http://www.hayward-gallery.org.uk*
Opening times: *10-6 daily, Tues-Wed 10-8.*
Nearest Underground: *Waterloo.*
Personnel: *Director:* Susan Ferleger Brades.
Exhibitions of international stature are the hallmark of the Hayward Gallery, with a programme featuring the works of modern masters, thought-provoking historical shows and the most exciting names in contemporary art. Exhibitions for 1998: Francis Bacon: The Human Body and Henri Cartier - Bresson Europeans (5th February - 5th April), Anish Kapoor (30th April - 14th June), Bruce Nauman (16th July - 6th September). Admissions: £5, £3.50. Concessions. Further information on 0171-928 3144.

Ab *Artist's Books* **App** *Applied Art* **Cer** *Ceramics* **Cra** *Crafts*
Dec *Decorative* **Dr** *Drawing* **Fur** *Furniture*

Services and Facilities:
Bookshop. Café. Disabled Access. Lectures. Parking.

HOGARTH'S HOUSE FOUNDATION *P*
Hogarth's House, Hogarth Lane, Great West Road, London W4 2QN. **Tel:** *0181-994 6757/570 0622.* **Fax:** *0181-862 7602.*

THE HORNIMAN MUSEUM AND GARDENS *P*
100 London Road, Forest Hill, London SE23 3PQ. **Tel:** *0181-699 1872.* **Fax:** *0181-291 5506.* **Email** *enquiry@horniman.demon.co.uk* **Ws** *http://www.horniman.demon.co.uk*
Opening times: *Mon-Sat 10.30-5.30, Sun 2-5.30 (except over Christmas).*
Nearest Underground: *Forest Hill (from London Bridge).*
Personnel: *Director:* Michael Houlihan. *Head of Public Services:* Janet Vitmayer.
A popular museum with world famous ethnographic collections from all world cultures. The Music Room houses a nationally important collection of musical instruments and the National History Gallery includes The Living Waters Aquarium. There are autumn and spring series of concerts. Events, workshops and courses are held throughout the year for both children and adults. Admission Free.
Services and Facilities:
Café. Disabled Access. Friends/Society. Gallery space for hire. Lectures. Museum Shop.

IMPERIAL WAR MUSEUM *P*
Lambeth Road, London SE1 6HZ. **Tel:** *0171-416 5000.* **Fax:** *0171-416 5374.* **Email** *art@iwm.org.uk* **Ws** *http://www.iwm.org.uk*
Opening times: *Daily 10-6, free after 4.30.*
Nearest Underground: *Lambeth North, Elephant and Castle.*
Personnel: *Director:* Robert Crawford.

The main temporary exhibition gallery will remain closed throughout 1998 (re-opens officially November 1999 with major C R W Nevinson show) but the following exhibitions are planned in what are normally the permanent collection galleries in 1998: Rodrigo Moynihan: The End of the Picnic; Paul Vézelay: Permit Declined both 4 June-31 August; Art of the First World War (permanent collection), January-November 1998. Forewarning: John Singer Sargent's 'Gassed' will be on loan to the Tate Gallery's Sargent exhibition and tour to the USA for a year from October 1998. Small temporary exhibitions are planned for this space.

Services and Facilities:
Café. Disabled Access. Friends/Society. Museum Shop.

INSTITUTE OF CONTEMPORARY ARTS *P*
The Mall, London SW1Y 5AH. **Tel:** *0171-839 6751, 873 0061, box office 0171-930 3647.* **Fax:** *0171-873 0051.*

KENSINGTON PALACE *P*
Kensington Gardens, London W8 4PX.
Tel: *0171-937 7079.* **Fax:** *0171-376 0198.*
Nearest Underground: *High Street Kensington, Gloucester Road, Queensway.*
Kensington Palace opens 1 May 1998. Please telephone 0171-937 7079 or fax 0171-376 0198 for further details. Adult admission is £7.00.
Services and Facilities:
Café. Guided Tours. Museum Shop.

KENWOOD HOUSE *P*
The Iveagh Bequest, Hampstead Lane, London NW3 7JR. **Tel:** *0171-973 3891.*

KINGSGATE GALLERY *PS*
114 Kingsgate Road, London NW6 2JG.
Tel: *0171-328 7878.* **Fax:** *0171-328 7878.*
Opening times: *Sat & Sun 12-6 and by appointment.*
Nearest Underground: *West Hampstead.*
Personnel: *Administrator:* Stephen Williams.

Contemporary work shown in a split level space. Monthly exhibitions. The exhibition programme is decided by a panel at quarterly meetings and is particularly interested in group proposals. It is part of the charitable organisation Kingsgate Workshops Trust. In 1997 exhibitions included works by: Mark Rawley, Tasha Amini, Neil Chapman, Julia Spicer, Michael Weinkove, Andre Bannister, Nikki Kyriakidou, Derek Osbourne, James Swinson, Rachel Withers, Jim Forster, Debbie Humphrey, Magda Segal, Eugenia Vronskaya, Peter Jeffrey, Michael Geyersbach, Paul Eachus, Holly Lynton, Josie Taylor, Tina Gallifent, Kasia Morawska, Ken Butler, Martin Appleton, Fiona Banner, Nicola & Natasha Hood, Mark Harrison, Langlands & Bell, Hadrian Piggott.
Services and Facilities:
Art Consultancy. Commissioning Service. Framing.

KUFA GALLERY *PS*
26 Westbourne Grove, London W2 5RH.
Tel: *0171-229 1928.* **Fax:** *0171-243 8513.*
Email *kufa@dircon.co.uk*
Opening times: *Tues-Sat 10-6.*
Nearest Underground: *Bayswater, Queensway.*
Personnel: *Manager:* Walid Atiyeh.
A non-profit making organisation, specialising in Islamic/Middle Eastern Art and Architecture, including art exhibitions, poetry & musical evenings and cultural lectures and talks. The gallery hall is available for hire for similar events.
Services and Facilities:
Gallery space for hire. Lectures.
Work Stocked and Sold:
Ab. App. Cer. Cra. Dec. Dr. Pa. Ph. Pr. Tx.

LAUDERDALE HOUSE COMMUNITY ARTS CENTRE *P*
Waterlow Park, Highgate Hill, London N6 5HG. **Tel:** *0181-348 8716/341 2332.* **Fax:** *0181-3484293.*

LEIGHTON HOUSE MUSEUM *PS*
12 Holland Park Road, London W14 8LZ.
Tel: *0171-602 3316.* **Fax:** *0171-371 2467.*
Opening times: *Mon-Sat 11-5.30.*
Nearest Underground: *High St. Kensington.*

Leighton House was the home of, Frederic, Lord Leighton (1830-1896) The great classical painter and president of the Royal Academy. The house was built between 1867-1879 to designs by George Aitchison and is the expression of Leighton's vision of a private palace devoted to art. The Arab Hall is the centrepiece of Leighton House with dazzling gilt mosaics and authentic Isnik tiles. The opulent fantasy extends throughout the other rooms of the house, culminating in Leighton's studio, the heart and purpose of the house. Leighton House contains a fine collection of Victorian art and may be booked for concerts, lectures, receptions and private functions. The galleries adjoining Leighton House may be

hired for exhibitions. They are recently refurbished and work should be submitted to the curator. Wide and extensive exhibition programme.
Services and Facilities:
Gallery space for hire. Lectures.

LONDON INSTITUTE *P*
65 Davies Street, London W1Y 2DA.
Tel: *0171-514 6129.* **Fax:** *0171-514 6131.*
Email *marcom@linst.ac.uk*
Opening times: *Mon-Fri.*
Nearest Underground: *Bond Street.*
Personnel: *Rachel Hudson.*
The London Institute Gallery acts as a focal point for the work of the Institute's staff and students.
There is a regular programme of exhibitions throughout the year which reflect the diversity of the Institute's Colleges. Camberwell College of Arts. Central Saint Martins College of Art and Design. Chelsea College of Art and Design. London College of Fashion. London College of Printing.

LOTHBURY GALLERY *PS*
41 Lothbury, London EC2P 2BP.
Tel: *0171-726 1642/1643.*
Opening times: *Mon-Fri 10-4.*
Nearest Underground: *Bank underground, Moorgate, Liverpool Street (BR), Cannon Street.*
Personnel: *Curator:* Rosemary Harris.
Assistant: Lynne Richards. *Office Administrator:* Daksha Patel.
The Lothbury Gallery displays works from the Nat West Group Art Collection and a series of changing exhibitions. This important corporate art collection has been established over many years for display in our offices. It includes work from the seventeenth century to the present day with a focus on twentieth century post-war British art. The Collection includes work by such artists as Frank Auerbach, Adrian Berg, David Hockney, Albert Irvin, Patrick Caulfield, Gillian Ayres, Jason Martin and Mark Francis. Nat West also holds an annual major painting competition which is open to all artists under 35 who are living, working or studying in Britain.

MARBLE HILL HOUSE *P*
(English Heritage) Richmond Road, Twickenham, TW1 2NL. **Tel:** *0181-892 5115.*

MUSEUM OF INSTALLATION *P*
175 Deptford High Street, London SE8 3NU.
Tel: *0181-692 8778.* **Fax:** *0181-692 8122.*
Opening times: *Tue-Fri 12-5, Sat 2-5.*
Nearest Underground: *Deptford.*
Personnel: *Directors:* Nicola Oxley, Nicolas de Oliveira, Michael Petry. *Assistant Director:* Jeremy Wood. *Administrator:* Calan Stanley. *Project Assistants:* David Howells, Jane Matthews.
The Museum of Installation is an artist led organisation and registered charity set up in 1990 as a unique institution dedicated to the research, production and dissemination of installation. MOI has initiated 60 exhibitions and projects at sites in the UK, Europe and the United States. At its base in London MOI has

begun to compile the first major archive of installation and the book "Installation Art" has been published by Thames and Hudson. MOI is committed to the cross fertilisation of

theory and practice, and to encourage new artists and new audiences to engage with contemporary art practice.
Services and Facilities:
Art Consultancy. Commissioning Service. Guided Tours. Lectures. Workshop Facilities.

MUSEUM OF MANKIND *P*
The Ethnography Dept. of the British Museum, Burlington Gardens, London W1.
Tel: *0171-437 2224.*

MUSEUM OF WOMEN'S ART *P*
Correspondence: 2nd Floor North, 55-63 Goswell Road, London EC1V 7EN. **Tel:** *0171-251 4881.* **Fax:** *0171-251 4882.*

NATIONAL ARMY MUSEUM *P*
Royal Hospital Road, Chelsea, London SW3 4HT. **Tel:** *0171-730 0717.*
Fax: *0171-823 6573.*

NATIONAL GALLERY *P*
Trafalgar Square, London WC2N 5DN.
Tel: *0171-747 2885.*
Email *information@ng-london.org.uk*
Opening times: *Mon-Sat 10-6, Sun 12-6, Weds until 8pm. Closed New Year's Day, Good Friday, 24-26 Dec.*
Nearest Underground: *Charing Cross, Leicester Square, Embankment. All buses to Trafalgar Square.*
Personnel: *Director:* Neil MacGregor.

The Collection numbers over 2,200 works and covers Western European painting from 1260 to 1900, including works by Leonardo, Titian, Rubens, Rembrandt, Turner, Constable, and the Impressionists.
Exhibitions and displays; many educational events: quizzes for children, lectures, audio-visuals and guided tours. Admission free, except for some major exhibitions.
Micro Gallery computer information room. Gallery Guide Soundtrack (CD Audio commentary on the collection for hire).
Services and Facilities:
Bookshop. Café. Disabled Access. Guided Tours. Lectures. Museum Shop. Restaurant. Shop.

NATIONAL MARITIME MUSEUM, QUEEN'S HOUSE AND OLD ROYAL OBSERVATORY *P*
Romney Road, Greenwich, London SE10 9NF.
Tel: *0181-858 4422.* **Fax:** *0181-312 6632.*

NATIONAL PORTRAIT GALLERY *PS*
St. Martin's Place, London WC2H 0HE.
Tel: *0171-306 0055.* **Fax:** *0171-306 00 56.* **Ws** *http://www.npg.org.uk*
Opening times: *Mon-Sat 10-6, Sun 12-6.*
Nearest Underground: *Charing Cross, Leicester Square.*
Personnel: *Director:* Dr Charles Saumarez Smith. The National Portrait Gallery was founded in 1856 to collect the likenesses of famous British men and women. Today the collection is the most comprehensive of its kind and constitutes a unique record of men and women who created (and are still creating) the history and culture of the nation.

The gallery houses over 9,000 works, as well as an immense archive. There are oil paintings, watercolours, drawings, sculptures, caricatures and photographs.
The gallery continues to develop its role through changing displays, a programme of temporary exhibitions and an annual portrait competition for young artists.
Services and Facilities:
Bookshop. Disabled Access. Friends/Society. Gallery space for hire. Guided Tours. Lectures. Museum Shop. Shop. Workshop Facilities.

ORLEANS HOUSE GALLERY *PS*
Riverside, Twickenham, TW1 3DJ.
Tel: *0181-892 0221.* **Fax:** *0181-744 0501.*
Email *jane.dalton@virgin.net*
Ws *http://www.guidetorichmond.co.uk/orleans.html*
Opening times: *Apr-Sept Tues-Sat 1-5.30, Sun 2-5.30, (Oct-Mar closes at 4.30). Bank Holidays as for Sundays, closed Christmas Eve,*

Ab Artist's Books **App** Applied Art **Cer** Ceramics **Cra** Crafts
Dec Decorative **Dr** Drawing **Fur** Furniture

Christmas Day, Boxing Day, Dec 31.
Nearest Station: *St. Margaret's from Waterloo.*
Personnel: *Curator:* Jane Dalton. *Assistant Curator:* Rachel Tranter.
Overlooking the Thames, Orleans House Gallery resides in preserved natural woodland less than half hour from central London. The gallery comprises the Octagon Room and 2 surviving wings of the 18th century Orleans House. Exhibitions for 1998 draw on the permanent collection of topographical fine art as well as contemporary fine and applied arts of natural significance. Admissions: £1 adult, under 16's free.
Services and Facilities:
Craftshop. Disabled Access. Lectures. Parking. Workshop Facilities.
Work Stocked and Sold:
Cra.
Price range: £10 - £200.

PERCIVAL DAVID FOUNDATION P
53 Gordon Square, London WC1H 0PD.
Tel: *0171-387 3909.* **Fax:** *0171-383 5163.*

PHOTOGRAPHERS' GALLERY P
5-8 Great Newport Street, London WC2H 7HY.
Tel: *0171-831 1772 minicom.* **Fax:** *0171-836 9704.*

POLISH CULTURAL INSTITUTION P
34 Portland Place, London W1N 4HQ.
Tel: *0171-636 6032.* **Fax:** *0171-637 2190.*
Opening times: *Mon-Fri 10-4, Thurs 10-8.*
Personnel: *Director:* Mrs Aleksandra Czapiewska. *Deputy Director:* Ms Elzbieta Lyszkowska.
Exhibitions including Polish paintings, graphics, photography, posters, tapestry and folk art. Space available for hire for events connected with Poland and Polish art.
Services and Facilities:
Gallery space for hire. Lectures.

QUEEN'S GALLERY P
Buckingham Palace. London SW1A 1AA.
Tel: *0171-799 2331 / 0171-839 1377.*

RIBA HEINZ GALLERY P
21 Portman Square, London W1H 9HF.
Tel: *0171-307 3628.* **Fax:** *0171-486 3797.*
Email *dwgs@inst.riba.org*
Ws *http://www.riba.org/*
Opening times: *Mon-Fri 11-5, Sat 11-2.*
Nearest Underground: *Marble Arch.*
Personnel: *Curator:* Charles Hind.

The Heinz Gallery has five exhibitions each year based on architectural drawings from the collection. For a brochure with details of forthcoming exhibitions, please contact Philippa Martin on 0171-307 3628.

The Gallery also sells posters, postcards, books and catalogues relating to current exhibitions.
Services and Facilities:
Bookshop. Disabled Access. Guided Tours.

ROYAL ACADEMY OF ARTS P
Burlington House, Piccadilly, London W1V 0DS.
Tel: *0171-300 8000.* **Fax:** *0171-300 8001.*
Ws *http://www.RoyalAcademy.org.uk*
Opening times: *Mon-Sun 10-6.*
Nearest Underground: *Piccadilly Circus/Green Park.*
Personnel: *Press & Promotions Officer:* Katharine Jones.
Founded in 1768, The Royal Academy is the oldest arts institution in the UK, governed by its artist members. Its exhibition programme includes the annual Summer Exhibition of work by living artists and internationally acclaimed travelling exhibitions.
Services and Facilities:
Bookshop. Café. Disabled Access. Framing. Friends/Society. Guided Tours. Lectures. Museum Shop. Restaurant. Shop.

SAATCHI COLLECTION P
98a Boundary Road, London NW8 0RH.
Tel: *0171-624 8299.*
Fax: *0171-624 3798.*

SERPENTINE GALLERY P
Kensington Gardens, London W2 3XA.
Tel: *0171-402 6075/0343 / 0171-823 9727.*
Fax: *0171-402 4103.*

SIR JOHN SOANE'S MUSEUM P
13 Lincoln's Inn Fields, London WC2A 3BP.
Tel: *0171-430 0175.* **Fax:** *0171-831 3957.*

THE SLADMORE GALLERY - 19TH AND 20TH CENTURY BRONZE SCULPTURE. P
32 Bruton Place, Berkeley Square, London W1X 7AA. **Tel:** *0171-499 0365.* **Fax:** *0171-409 1381.*

SMALL MANSION ARTS CENTRE PS
Gunnersbury Park, Popes Lane, Acton, London, W3 8IQ. **Tel:** *0181-993 8312.*
Opening times: *11-6.*
Nearest Underground: *Acton Town.*
Personnel: *Maureen Adiloglu.* The Small Mansion Arts Centre is an artist run organisation that provides:- studio space for artists (currently six), art classes and workshops and study trips abroad (currently four evening classes and one Saturday morning), exhibitions of interest to local community as well as London-wide audience.
The gallery is for hire at £195 per week. The Small Mansion Arts Centre was established in 1985.

It is a non profit making limited company and a registered charity.
Services and Facilities:
Disabled Access. Gallery space for hire. Parking.
Work Stocked and Sold:
Dr. Pa. Pr.
Price range: £50 - £5,000.

ST. MARYLEBONE CRYPT GALLERY P
St. Marylebone Parish Church, 17 Marylebone Road, London NW1 5LT.
Tel: *0171-935 6374.* **Fax:** *0171-935 6374.*

STRANG PRINT ROOM P
University College London, London WC1E 6BT.
Tel: *0171-387 7050 ext 2540.* **Fax:** *0171-813 2803.*

STUDIO GLASS GALLERY P
63 Connaught Street, London W2.
Tel: *0171-706 3013, 3069.*

TATE GALLERY P
Millbank, London SW1P 4RG. **Tel:** *0171-887 8000/8008.* **Fax:** *0171-887 8007.*
Opening times: *Mon-Sun 10-5.50.*
Nearest Underground: *Pimlico.*
Personnel: *Director:* Nicholas Serota. *Press Office:* Kate Burvill. *Press Office:* Tiffany Vignoles.
The gallery houses the national collection of British painting from the 16th century to the present day. It is also the national gallery for international modern art. In addition the collection includes substantial holdings of works on paper. The Clore Gallery added in 1987 houses the Turner Bequest. Changing exhibitions and display programme.
Services and Facilities:
Bookshop. Café. Disabled Access. Friends/Society. Guided Tours. Lectures. Museum Shop. Restaurant. Shop.

TWO10 GALLERY P
The Wellcome Trust, 210 Euston Road, London NW1 2BE. **Tel:** *0171-611 8888.* **Fax:** *0171-611 8562.*
Email *k.arnold@wellcome.ac.uk*
Ws *http://www.wellcome.ac.uk*
Opening times: *Mon-Fri 9-6 (closed weekends and public holidays).*
Nearest Underground: *Euston.*
Personnel: *Exhibitions Unit Manager:* Dr Ken Arnold. *Exhibitions Unit Assistant:* Denna Jones.

The TWO10 Gallery presents temporary exhibitions on the interaction between contemporary medical science and art. Recent exhibitions have included 'Inside Information: imag-

Gla Glass **Jew** Jewellery **Pa** Paintings **Ph** Photography **Pr** Prints
Sc Sculpture **Tx** Textiles **Wd** Wood

THE ARTWORLD
DIRECTORY 1998/99 **89**

ing the human body' (1996) and 'Look Hear: art and science of the ear' (1995). TWO10 exhibitions are available for loan to other museums. Admission free. Limited disabled access.

VICTORIA & ALBERT MUSEUM
THE NATIONAL MUSEUM OF ART AND DESIGN *P*
Cromwell Road, South Kensington, London SW7 2RL. **Tel:** *0171-938 8500.* **Fax:** *0171-938 8341.*
Ws *http://www.vam.ac.uk*
Opening times: *Mon 12-5.45, Tue-Sun 10-5.45, Wed late view (seasonal) 6.30-9.30pm. Open every day except 24, 25 & 26 December.*
Nearest Underground: *South Kensington.*
The V&A is the world's greatest museum of art and design. Founded in 1852, the 145 galleries of furniture, fashion, textiles, paintings, silver, glass, ceramics, sculpture, jewellery, books, prints and photographs, reflect centuries of artistic achievement from all over the world.

The exciting programme of exhibitions for 1998 include; The Power of the Poster, 2 April-26 July; Aubrey Beardsley, 8 October-10 January 1999; Grinling Gibbons and the Art of Carving, 22 October 1998-24 January 1999; and The Canon Photography Gallery at the V&A, a superb new gallery opening 21 May. Museum Admission: Full £5.00, senior citizens £3.00. V&A annual season ticket £15.00, senior citizens £9.00. Admission is free for those under 18, students, pre-booked educational groups, disabled people with carer, ES40 holders, V&A Friends, Patrons and American and International Friends and season ticket holders. Entry if free daily between 16.30 and 17.50.
Services and Facilities:
Café. Disabled Access. Friends/Society. Gallery space for hire. Guided Tours. Lectures. Museum Shop. Restaurant. Shop.

WALLACE COLLECTION *P*
Hertford House, Manchester Square, London W1M 6BN. **Tel:** *0171-935 0687.*

WESTMINSTER GALLERY *P*
Central Hall, Storey's Gate, London SW1 9NH. **Tel:** *0171-222 2723, 0171-222 8010.* **Fax:** *0171-222 6883.*

WHITECHAPEL ART GALLERY *P*
Whitechapel High Street, London E1 7QX. **Tel:** *Recorded information: 0171-522 7878, other enquiries, 0171-522 7888.*

WILLIAM MORRIS GALLERY *P*
Lloyd Park, Forrest Road, Walthamstow, London, E17 4PP. **Tel:** *0181-527 3782.*

NOTES

Ab Artist's Books **App** Applied Art **Cer** Ceramics **Cra** Crafts **Dec** Decorative **Dr** Drawing **Fur** Furniture **Gla** Glass **Jew** Jewellery **Pa** Paintings **Ph** Photography **Pr** Prints **Sc** Sculpture **Tx** Textiles **Wd** Wood

ENGLISH REGIONAL GALLERIES

The regional galleries section is sorted by region, starting with the South West and finishing with the North. On the following pages you will find indices by Region/County/Town and Town/County/Region.

Where this information has been provided, galleries are designated 'C' for commercial, 'P' for public gallery or museum or 'PS' for a public gallery or museum holding selling shows.

THE ART WORLD
DIRECTORY
1998/99 25TH EDITION

REGION/ COUNTY/ TOWN INDEX

SOUTH WEST

Bath & North East Somerset
Bath

Bristol
Bristol

Cornwall
Camelford
Falmouth
Helston
Marazion
Par
Penzance
Polperro
Saltash
St. Ives
Truro

Devon
Appledore
Bideford
Bovey Tracey
Buckfastleigh
Budleigh Salterton
Dartmouth
Exeter
Plymouth
Tiverton
Topsham
Torrington
Totnes

Dorset
Abbotsbury
Beaminster
Bridport
Dorchester
Sherborne
Swanage

Gloucestershire
Bourton on the Water
Chalford
Cheltenham
Cirencester
Gloucester
Lechlade
Nailsworth
Painswick
Stow-on-the-Wold
Stroud

South Gloucestershire
Chipping Sodbury

Somerset
Frome
Montacute
Taunton
Wedmore
Wells
Yeovil

North Somerset
Weston Super Mare

SOUTHERN

Berkshire
Bracknell
Cookham
Eton
Maidenhead
Newbury
Reading
Windsor

Bournemouth
Bournemouth

Buckinghamshire
Aylesbury
Milton Keynes

Hampshire
Alresford
Alton
Andover
Basingstoke
Christchurch
Eastleigh
Gosport
Havant
New Alresford
Portsmouth
Ringwood
Selbourne
Southsea
Stockbridge
Winchester

Isle of Wight
Newport
Ryde

Oxfordshire
Bampton
Banbury
Chipping Norton
Henley-on-Thames
Oxford
Wallingford

Poole
Poole

Southampton
Southampton

Swindon
Swindon

Wiltshire
Calne
Devizes
Lacock
Marlborough
Salisbury

SOUTH EAST

Brighton & Hove
Brighton
Hove

Kent
Canterbury
Folkestone
Gillingham
Maidstone
Ramsgate
Rochester
Sandwich
Sevenoaks
Tunbridge Wells
Whitstable

Surrey
Chobham
East Molesey
Farnham
Godalming
Gomshall
Guildford
Kingston upon Thames
New Malden
Redhill
Reigate
Richmond
Virginia Water
West Byfleet
Woking

East Sussex
Eastbourne
Hassocks
Hastings
Lewes
Rye

West Sussex
Arundel
Billingshurst
Chichester
East Grinstead
Haywards Heath
Horsham
Midhurst
Worthing

EASTERN

Bedfordshire
Bedford
Biggleswade
Bromham
Leighton Buzzard
Luton

Cambridgeshire
Bourn
Cambridge
Ely
Peterborough

REGIONAL GALLERIES

Essex
Brentwood
Buckhurst Hill
Chelmsford
Coggeshall
Colchester
Harlow
Saffron Walden
Southend-on-Sea
Westcliff-on-Sea

Hertfordshire
Barnet
Berkhamsted
Hitchin
Letchworth
Much Hadham
Royston
Sawbridgeworth
St. Albans
Stevenage
Ware
Watford

Lincolnshire
Boston
Gainsborough
Lincoln
Spalding
Stamford

North Lincolnshire
Scunthorpe

Norfolk
Aylsham
Castle Acre
Diss
Gorleston on Sea
Great Yarmouth
Hunstanton
King's Lynn
Mundesley
Norwich
Wells-next-the-Sea

Suffolk
Aldeburgh
Bury St. Edmunds
Cransford
East Bergholt
Felixstowe
Hadleigh
Halesworth
Ipswich
Lowestoft
Newmarket
Saxmundham
Southwold
Sudbury
Woodbridge

EAST MIDLANDS

Derby
Derby

Derbyshire
Buxton
Chesterfield

Ilkeston
Wirksworth

Leicester
Leicester

Leicestershire
Ashby de-la-Zouch
Lutterworth
Market Harborough

Northamptonshire
Kettering
Northampton
Towcester
Wellingborough

Nottinghamshire
Newark
Nottingham
Ravenshead
Worksop

Rutland
Uppingham

WEST MIDLANDS

Birmingham
Birmingham

Coventry
Coventry

Dudley
Dudley
Kingswinford

Hereford & Worcester
Bewdley
Broadway
Bromsgrove
Cradley
Great Malvern
Hereford
Kidderminster
Leominster
Malvern
Ombersley
Worcester

Sandwell
Wednesbury

Shropshire
Bishops Castle
Bridgnorth
Ellesmere
Ludlow
Shrewsbury
Telford

Staffordshire
Burton upon Trent
Leek
Newcastle-under-Lyme
Stafford

Stoke-on-Trent
Stoke-on-Trent

Warwickshire
Alcester
Henley-in-Arden
Leamington Spa
Rugby
Stratford-upon-Avon
Warwick

Wolverhampton
Wolverhampton

NORTH WEST

Bolton
Bolton

Cheshire
Northwich
Prestbury
Warrington
Winsford

Lancashire
Accrington
Blackburn
Blackpool
Burnley
Chorley
Lancaster
Preston

Liverpool
Liverpool

Manchester
Manchester

Oldham
Oldham

Rochdale
Rochdale

Salford
Salford

Sefton
Southport

St. Helens
St. Helens

Stockport
Stockport

Tameside
Stalybridge

Wigan
Leigh

Wirral
Bebington
Birkenhead
Heswall

YORKSHIRE & HUMBERSIDE

Bradford
Bradford
Keighley

Calderdale
Halifax
Todmorden

Doncaster
Doncaster

Hull
Hull

Kirklees
Batley
Dewsbury
Huddersfield
Mirfield

Leeds
Leeds

Rotherham
Rotherham

Sheffield
Sheffield

Wakefield
Wakefield

York
York

East Riding of Yorkshire
Beverley
Bridlington
Goole

North Yorkshire
Harrogate
Helmsley
Knaresborough
Richmond
Scarborough
Settle
Thirsk
Whitby

NORTHERN

Cumbria
Alston
Ambleside
Carlisle
Cockermouth
Coniston
Egremont
Kendal
Keswick
Penrith
Whitehaven
Workington

Durham
Barnard Castle
Castle Eden
Darlington
Durham

Hartlepool
Hartlepool

Middlesbrough
Middlesbrough

Newcastle-upon-Tyne
Gateshead
Newcastle-upon-Tyne

North Tyneside
Wallsend

Northumberland
Alnwick
Belford
Berwick Upon Tweed
Cramlington
Hexham
Rothbury
Stamfordham
Warkworth

Redcar and Cleveland
Guisborough
Redcar
Saltburn By The Sea

Stockton on Tees
Billingham
Stockton on Tees

Sunderland
Sunderland
Washington

North Tyneside
North Shields

South Tyneside
Jarrow
South Shields

TOWN/ COUNTY/ REGION INDEX

A

Abbotsbury *(Dorset)*
South West
Accrington *(Lancashire)*
North West
Alcester *(Warwickshire)*
West Midlands
Aldeburgh *(Suffolk)*
Eastern
Alnwick *(Northumberland)*
Northern
Alresford *(Hampshire)*
Southern
Alston *(Cumbria)*
Northern
Alton *(Hampshire)*
Southern
Ambleside *(Cumbria)*
Northern
Andover *(Hampshire)*
Southern
Appledore *(Devon)*
South West
Arundel *(West Sussex)*
South East
Ashby de-la-Zouch *(Leicestershire)*
East Midlands
Aylesbury *(Buckinghamshire)*
Southern
Aylsham *(Norfolk)*
Eastern

B

Bampton *(Oxfordshire)*
Southern
Banbury *(Oxfordshire)*
Southern
Barnard Castle *(Durham)*
Northern
Barnet *(Hertfordshire)*
Eastern
Basingstoke *(Hampshire)*
Southern
Bath *(Bath & North East Somerset)*
South West
Batley *(Kirklees)*
Yorkshire & Humberside
Beaminster *(Dorset)*
South West
Bebington *(Wirral)*
North West
Bedford *(Bedfordshire)*
Eastern
Belford *(Northumberland)*
Northern
Berkhamsted *(Hertfordshire)*
Eastern

REGIONAL GALLERIES

Berwick Upon Tweed *(Northumberland)*
Northern
Beverley *(East Riding of Yorkshire)*
Yorkshire & Humberside
Bewdley *(Hereford & Worcester)*
West Midlands
Bideford *(Devon)*
South West
Biggleswade *(Bedfordshire)*
Eastern
Billingham *(Stockton on Tees)*
Northern
Billingshurst *(West Sussex)*
South East
Birkenhead *(Wirral)*
North West
Birmingham *(Birmingham)*
West Midlands
Bishops Castle *(Shropshire)*
West Midlands
Blackburn *(Lancashire)*
North West
Blackpool *(Lancashire)*
North West
Bolton *(Bolton)*
North West
Boston *(Lincolnshire)*
Eastern
Bourn *(Cambridgeshire)*
Eastern
Bournemouth *(Bournemouth)*
Southern
Bourton on the Water *(Gloucestershire)*
South West
Bovey Tracey *(Devon)*
South West
Bracknell *(Berkshire)*
Southern
Bradford *(Bradford)*
Yorkshire & Humberside
Brentwood *(Essex)*
Eastern
Bridgnorth *(Shropshire)*
West Midlands
Bridlington *(East Riding of Yorkshire)*
Yorkshire & Humberside
Bridport *(Dorset)*
South West
Brighton *(Brighton & Hove)*
South East
Bristol *(Bristol)*
South West
Broadway *(Hereford & Worcester)*
West Midlands
Bromham *(Bedfordshire)*
Eastern
Bromsgrove *(Hereford & Worcester)*
West Midlands
Buckfastleigh *(Devon)*
South West
Buckhurst Hill *(Essex)*
Eastern
Budleigh Salterton *(Devon)*
South West
Burnley *(Lancashire)*
North West
Burton upon Trent *(Staffordshire)*
West Midlands
Bury St. Edmunds *(Suffolk)*
Eastern
Buxton *(Derbyshire)*
East Midlands

C

Calne *(Wiltshire)*
Southern
Cambridge *(Cambridgeshire)*
Eastern
Camelford *(Cornwall)*
South West
Canterbury *(Kent)*
South East
Carlisle *(Cumbria)*
Northern
Castle Acre *(Norfolk)*
Eastern
Castle Eden *(Durham)*
Northern
Chalford *(Gloucestershire)*
South West
Chelmsford *(Essex)*
Eastern
Cheltenham *(Gloucestershire)*
South West
Chesterfield *(Derbyshire)*
East Midlands
Chichester *(West Sussex)*
South East
Chipping Norton *(Oxfordshire)*
Southern
Chipping Sodbury *(South Gloucestershire)*
South West
Chobham *(Surrey)*
South East
Chorley *(Lancashire)*
North West
Christchurch *(Hampshire)*
Southern
Cirencester *(Gloucestershire)*
South West
Cockermouth *(Cumbria)*
Northern
Coggeshall *(Essex)*
Eastern
Colchester *(Essex)*
Eastern
Coniston *(Cumbria)*
Northern
Cookham *(Berkshire)*
Southern
Coventry *(Coventry)*
West Midlands
Cradley *(Hereford & Worcester)*
West Midlands
Cramlington *(Northumberland)*
Northern
Cransford *(Suffolk)*
Eastern

D

Darlington *(Durham)*
Northern
Dartmouth *(Devon)*
South West
Derby *(Derby)*
East Midlands
Devizes *(Wiltshire)*
Southern
Dewsbury *(Kirklees)*
Yorkshire & Humberside
Diss *(Norfolk)*
Eastern

Doncaster *(Doncaster)*
Yorkshire & Humberside
Dorchester *(Dorset)*
South West
Dudley *(Dudley)*
West Midlands
Durham *(Durham)*
Northern

E

East Bergholt *(Suffolk)*
Eastern
East Grinstead *(West Sussex)*
South East
East Molesey *(Surrey)*
South East
Eastbourne *(East Sussex)*
South East
Eastleigh *(Hampshire)*
Southern
Egremont *(Cumbria)*
Northern
Ellesmere *(Shropshire)*
West Midlands
Ely *(Cambridgeshire)*
Eastern
Eton *(Berkshire)*
Southern
Exeter *(Devon)*
South West

F/G

Falmouth *(Cornwall)*
South West
Farnham *(Surrey)*
South East
Felixstowe *(Suffolk)*
Eastern
Folkestone *(Kent)*
South East
Frome *(Somerset)*
South West
Gainsborough *(Lincolnshire)*
Eastern
Gateshead *(Newcastle-upon-Tyne)*
Northern
Gillingham *(Kent)*
South East
Gloucester *(Gloucestershire)*
South West
Godalming *(Surrey)*
South East
Gomshall *(Surrey)*
South East
Goole *(East Riding of Yorkshire)*
Yorkshire & Humberside
Gorleston on Sea *(Norfolk)*
Eastern
Gosport *(Hampshire)*
Southern
Great Malvern *(Hereford & Worcester)*
West Midlands
Great Yarmouth *(Norfolk)*
Eastern
Guildford *(Surrey)*
South East
Guisborough *(Redcar and Cleveland)*
Northern

H

Hadleigh (*Suffolk*)
Eastern
Halesworth (*Suffolk*)
Eastern
Halifax (*Calderdale*)
Yorkshire & Humberside
Harlow (*Essex*)
Eastern
Harrogate (*North Yorkshire*)
Yorkshire & Humberside
Hartlepool (*Hartlepool*)
Northern
Hassocks (*East Sussex*)
South East
Hastings (*East Sussex*)
South East
Havant (*Hampshire*)
Southern
Haywards Heath (*West Sussex*)
South East
Helmsley (*North Yorkshire*)
Yorkshire & Humberside
Helston (*Cornwall*)
South West
Henley-in-Arden (*Warwickshire*)
West Midlands
Henley-on-Thames (*Oxfordshire*)
Southern
Hereford (*Hereford & Worcester*)
West Midlands
Heswall (*Wirral*)
North West
Hexham (*Northumberland*)
Northern
Hitchin (*Hertfordshire*)
Eastern
Horsham (*West Sussex*)
South East
Hove (*Brighton & Hove*)
South East
Huddersfield (*Kirklees*)
Yorkshire & Humberside
Hull (*Hull*)
Yorkshire & Humberside
Hunstanton (*Norfolk*)
Eastern

I/J/K

Ilkeston (*Derbyshire*)
East Midlands
Ipswich (*Suffolk*)
Eastern
Jarrow (*South Tyneside*)
Northern
Keighley (*Bradford*)
Yorkshire & Humberside
Kendal (*Cumbria*)
Northern
Keswick (*Cumbria*)
Northern
Kettering (*Northamptonshire*)
East Midlands
Kidderminster (*Hereford & Worcester*)
West Midlands
King's Lynn (*Norfolk*)
Eastern
Kingston upon Thames (*Surrey*)

South East
Kingswinford (*Dudley*)
West Midlands
Knaresborough (*North Yorkshire*)
Yorkshire & Humberside

L/M

Lacock (*Wiltshire*)
Southern
Lancaster (*Lancashire*)
North West
Leamington Spa (*Warwickshire*)
West Midlands
Lechlade (*Gloucestershire*)
South West
Leeds (*Leeds*)
Yorkshire & Humberside
Leek (*Staffordshire*)
West Midlands
Leicester (*Leicester*)
East Midlands
Leigh (*Wigan*)
North West
Leighton Buzzard (*Bedfordshire*)
Eastern
Leominster (*Hereford & Worcester*)
West Midlands
Letchworth (*Hertfordshire*)
Eastern
Lewes (*East Sussex*)
South East
Lincoln (*Lincolnshire*)
Eastern
Liverpool (*Liverpool*)
North West
Lowestoft (*Suffolk*)
Eastern
Ludlow (*Shropshire*)
West Midlands
Luton (*Bedfordshire*)
Eastern
Lutterworth (*Leicestershire*)
East Midlands
Maidenhead (*Berkshire*)
Southern
Maidstone (*Kent*)
South East
Malvern (*Hereford & Worcester*)
West Midlands
Manchester (*Manchester*)
North West
Marazion (*Cornwall*)
South West
Market Harborough (*Leicestershire*)
East Midlands
Marlborough (*Wiltshire*)
Southern
Middlesbrough (*Middlesbrough*)
Northern
Midhurst (*West Sussex*)
South East
Milton Keynes (*Buckinghamshire*)
Southern
Mirfield (*Kirklees*)
Yorkshire & Humberside
Montacute (*Somerset*)
South West
Much Hadham (*Hertfordshire*)
Eastern

Mundesley (*Norfolk*)
Eastern

N/O/P

Nailsworth (*Gloucestershire*)
South West
New Alresford (*Hampshire*)
Southern
New Malden (*Surrey*)
South East
Newark (*Nottinghamshire*)
East Midlands
Newbury (*Berkshire*)
Southern
Newcastle-under-Lyme (*Staffordshire*)
West Midlands
Newcastle-upon-Tyne (*Newcastle-upon-Tyne*)
Northern
Newmarket (*Suffolk*)
Eastern
Newport (*Isle of Wight*)
Southern
North Shields (*North Tyneside*)
Northern
Northampton (*Northamptonshire*)
East Midlands
Northwich (*Cheshire*)
North West
Norwich (*Norfolk*)
Eastern
Nottingham (*Nottinghamshire*)
East Midlands
Oldham (*Oldham*)
North West
Ombersley (*Hereford & Worcester*)
West Midlands
Oxford (*Oxfordshire*)
Southern
Painswick (*Gloucestershire*)
South West
Par (*Cornwall*)
South West
Penrith (*Cumbria*)
Northern
Penzance (*Cornwall*)
South West
Peterborough (*Cambridgeshire*)
Eastern
Plymouth (*Devon*)
South West
Polperro (*Cornwall*)
South West
Poole (*Poole*)
Southern
Portsmouth (*Hampshire*)
Southern
Prestbury (*Cheshire*)
North West
Preston (*Lancashire*)
North West

R/S

Ramsgate (*Kent*)
South East
Ravenshead (*Nottinghamshire*)
East Midlands
Reading (*Berkshire*)
Southern

Redcar (*Redcar and Cleveland*)
Northern
Redhill (*Surrey*)
South East
Reigate (*Surrey*)
South East
Richmond (*North Yorkshire*)
Yorkshire & Humberside
Ringwood (*Hampshire*)
Southern
Rochdale (*Rochdale*)
North West
Rochester (*Kent*)
South East
Rothbury (*Northumberland*)
Northern
Rotherham (*Rotherham*)
Yorkshire & Humberside
Royston (*Hertfordshire*)
Eastern
Rugby (*Warwickshire*)
West Midlands
Ryde (*Isle of Wight*)
Southern
Rye (*East Sussex*)
South East
Saffron Walden (*Essex*)
Eastern
Salford (*Salford*)
North West
Salisbury (*Wiltshire*)
Southern
Saltash (*Cornwall*)
South West
Saltburn By The Sea (*Redcar and Cleveland*)
Northern
Sandwich (*Kent*)
South East
Sawbridgeworth (*Hertfordshire*)
Eastern
Saxmundham (*Suffolk*)
Eastern
Scarborough (*North Yorkshire*)
Yorkshire & Humberside
Scunthorpe (*North Lincolnshire*)
Eastern
Selbourne (*Hampshire*)
Southern
Settle (*North Yorkshire*)
Yorkshire & Humberside
Sevenoaks (*Kent*)
South East
Sheffield (*Sheffield*)
Yorkshire & Humberside
Sherborne (*Dorset*)
South West
Shrewsbury (*Shropshire*)
West Midlands
South Shields (*South Tyneside*)
Northern
Southampton (*Southampton*)
Southern
Southend-on-Sea (*Essex*)
Eastern
Southport (*Sefton*)
North West
Southsea (*Hampshire*)
Southern
Southwold (*Suffolk*)
Eastern

Spalding (*Lincolnshire*)
Eastern
St. Albans (*Hertfordshire*)
Eastern
St. Helens (*St. Helens*)
North West
St. Ives (*Cornwall*)
South West
Stafford (*Staffordshire*)
West Midlands
Stalybridge (*Tameside*)
North West
Stamford (*Lincolnshire*)
Eastern
Stamfordham (*Northumberland*)
Northern
Stevenage (*Hertfordshire*)
Eastern
Stockbridge (*Hampshire*)
Southern
Stockport (*Stockport*)
North West
Stockton on Tees (*Stockton on Tees*)
Northern
Stoke-on-Trent (*Stoke-on-Trent*)
West Midlands
Stow-on-the-Wold (*Gloucestershire*)
South West
Stratford-upon-Avon (*Warwickshire*)
West Midlands
Stroud (*Gloucestershire*)
South West
Sudbury (*Suffolk*)
Eastern
Sunderland (*Sunderland*)
Northern
Swanage (*Dorset*)
South West
Swindon (*Swindon*)
Southern

T

Taunton (*Somerset*)
South West
Telford (*Shropshire*)
West Midlands
Thirsk (*North Yorkshire*)
Yorkshire & Humberside
Tiverton (*Devon*)
South West
Todmorden (*Calderdale*)
Yorkshire & Humberside
Topsham (*Devon*)
South West
Torrington (*Devon*)
South West
Totnes (*Devon*)
South West
Towcester (*Northamptonshire*)
East Midlands
Truro (*Cornwall*)
South West
Tunbridge Wells (*Kent*)
South East

U/V/W/Y

Uppingham (*Rutland*)
East Midlands
Virginia Water (*Surrey*)
South East

Wakefield (*Wakefield*)
Yorkshire & Humberside
Wallingford (*Oxfordshire*)
Southern
Wallsend (*North Tyneside*)
Northern
Ware (*Hertfordshire*)
Eastern
Warkworth (*Northumberland*)
Northern
Warrington (*Cheshire*)
North West
Warwick (*Warwickshire*)
West Midlands
Washington (*Sunderland*)
Northern
Watford (*Hertfordshire*)
Eastern
Wedmore (*Somerset*)
South West
Wednesbury (*Sandwell*)
West Midlands
Wellingborough (*Northamptonshire*)
East Midlands
Wells (*Somerset*)
South West
Wells-next-the-Sea (*Norfolk*)
Eastern
West Byfleet (*Surrey*)
South East
Westcliff-on-Sea (*Essex*)
Eastern
Weston Super Mare (*North Somerset*)
South West
Whitby (*North Yorkshire*)
Yorkshire & Humberside
Whitehaven (*Cumbria*)
Northern
Whitstable (*Kent*)
South East
Winchester (*Hampshire*)
Southern
Windsor (*Berkshire*)
Southern
Winsford (*Cheshire*)
North West
Wirksworth (*Derbyshire*)
East Midlands
Woking (*Surrey*)
South East
Wolverhampton (*Wolverhampton*)
West Midlands
Woodbridge (*Suffolk*)
Eastern
Worcester (*Hereford & Worcester*)
West Midlands
Workington (*Cumbria*)
Northern
Worksop (*Nottinghamshire*)
East Midlands
Worthing (*West Sussex*)
South East
Yeovil (*Somerset*)
South West
York (*York*)
Yorkshire & Humberside

South West

BATH & N E SOMERSET

BATH

ADAM GALLERY C
13 John Street, Bath, BA1 2JL. **Tel:** *01225-480406.* **Fax:** *01225-480406.*
Email *adamgallery@clara.net*
Opening times: *Mon-Sat 9.30-5.30.*
Personnel: *Directors:* Paul Dye, Philip Dye.
James McDonagh, Vanessa Yeomans.
20th Century British Art including Ben
Nicholson, Patrick Heron, William Scott,
Roger Hilton, John Piper, Henry Moore, Sir
Robin Philipson, Algernon Newton, David
Hockney, Terry Frost and Alan Davie. Also
large stock of work by leading contemporary
artists including Susan Foord, William Selby,
Marj Bond, Melita Denaro, Gail Harvey,
Richard Cartwright, Colin Kent and Padraig
Macmiadhachain.
Services and Facilities:
*Art Consultancy. Art for Offices. Framing.
Restoration. Valuation.*
Work Stocked and Sold:
Dr. Pa. Pr. Sc.

AMERICAN MUSEUM IN BRITAIN P
Claverton Manor, Bath, BA2 7BD.
Tel: *01225-460503.*
Fax: *01225-480726.*

**ANTHONY HEPWORTH FINE ART
GALLERY**
*Ivy House, Cavendish Road, Sion Hill, Bath,
BA1 2UE.* **Tel:** *01225-442917.* **Fax:** *01225-442917.*

BEAUX ARTS C
12/13 York Street, Bath, BA1 1NG.
Tel: *01225-464850.* **Fax:** *01225-422256.*
Opening times: *Mon-Sat 10-5.*
Personnel: *Directors:* Reg Singh, Patricia
Singh.

Beaux Arts is the longest established commer-
cial gallery in Bath and the sister gallery of
Beaux Arts in London. It is situated near the
Abbey. The gallery specialises in the work of
major 20th century British painters, sculptors
and young contemporaries, as well as leading
modern ceramicists.
Services and Facilities:
*Art Consultancy. Art for Offices. Commissioning
Service.*
Work Stocked and Sold:
Cer. Dr. Pa. Pr. Sc.
Price range: **£50 - £10,000.**

BECKFORD'S TOWER AND MUSEUM P
Lansdown, Bath, BA1 9BH. **Tel:** *01225-422212.*

BOUGH & LIME
Crossleaze Farm, Nr Woolley, Bath, BA1 8AU.
Tel: *01225-859772.* **Fax:** *01225-859088.*

BRUTON GALLERY
35 Gay Street, Queen Square, Bath, BA1 2NT.
Tel: *01225-466292.*

CCA GALLERIES
5 George Street, Bath, BA1 2EH. **Tel:** *01225-448121.*

FACADE C
5-8 Saville Row, Bath. **Tel:** *01225-723636.*

HITCHCOCK'S C
10 Chapel Row, Bath, BA1 1HN. **Tel:** *01225-330646.*

**HOLBURNE MUSEUM AND CRAFTS STUDY
CENTRE** PS
Great Pulteney Street, Bath, BA2 4DB.
Tel: *01225-466669.* **Fax:** *01225-333121.*
Opening times: *6 Mar-11 Dec 11-5 week-
days, Sun 2-5.30 (including bank holidays).
Closed Mondays, Nov to Easter. Group bookings
by appointment.*
Nearest Station: *Bath Spa.*
Personnel: *Directors:* Barley Roscoe, Barbara
Milner .

Historic building named after Sir William Holburne (1793-1874) whose collections form
nucleus of 17/18th century British and continental paintings by Gainsborough, Ramsay,
Stubbs, Turner, Guardi and others: superb silver, porcelain, sculpture, glass, maiolica, portrait miniatures, furniture and other fine and
decorative art. Also work by leading British
20th century artist-craftspeople includes
woven/printed textiles, ceramics (including
Bernard Leach), exquisite calligraphy and furniture. Leaflet available listing exhibitions,
events, lectures. Licensed Teahouse/Restau-

rant, Garden. Crafts Study Centre. Research,
workshop/library facilities, guided tours, by
appointment. Space for 2 coaches.
Services and Facilities:
*Art Consultancy. Bookshop. Café. Disabled
Access. Friends/Society. Gallery space for hire.
Guided Tours. Lectures. Museum Shop. Parking.
Restaurant. Workshop Facilities.*

KELSTON FINE ARTS C
*Kelston House, College Road, Lansdown, Bath,
BA1 5RY.* **Tel:** *01225-424224.*

LARKHALL FINE ART C
9 Cambridge Mews, Bath, BA1 6QE.
Tel: *01225-329030.*

MUSEUM OF EAST ASIAN ART P
12 Bennett Street, Bath, BA1 2QL.
Tel: *01225-464640.* **Fax:** *01225-461718.*

**PETER HAYES CONTEMPORARY
ART**
2 Cleveland Bridge, Bath, BA1 5DH.
Tel: *01225-466215.*

ROOKSMOOR GALLERY
31 Brock Street, Bath, BA1 2LN.
Tel: *01225-420495.*

THE ROYAL PHOTOGRAPHIC SOCIETY
*The Octagon Galleries, Milsom Street, Bath,
BA1 1DN.* **Tel:** *01225-462841.*
Fax: *01225-448688.*

SIX CHAPEL ROW CONTEMPORARY ART
Six Chapel Row, Bath, BA1 1HN.
Tel: *01225-337900.* **Fax:** *01225-336577.*

ST. JAMES'S GALLERY, C
9b Margaret's Buildings, Bath, BA1 2LP.
Tel: *01225-319197.*

TRIMBRIDGE GALLERIES
2 Trimbridge, Bath, BA1 1HD.

VICTORIA ART GALLERY P
Bridge Street, Pulteney Bridge, Bath, BA2 4AT.
Tel: *01225-477772.* **Fax:** *01225-477231.*

BRISTOL

BRISTOL

3D GALLERY
13 Perry Road, Bristol BS1 5BG. **Tel:** *0117-929 1363.*

ALEXANDER GALLERY C
122 Whiteladies Road, Clifton, Bristol BS8 2RP.
Tel: *0117-973 4692.* **Fax:** *0117-940 6991.*

ARNOLFINI GALLERY C
16 Narrow Quay, Bristol BS1 4QA.
Tel: *0117-929 9191.* **Fax:** *0117-925 3876.*
Email *publicity@arnolfini.demon.co.uk*
http://www.channel.org.uk/channel/arnolfini
Opening times: *Mon-Sat 10-7, Sun 12-6.*
Nearest Station: *Bristol Temple Meads.*

Ab *Artist's Books* **App** *Applied Art* **Cer** *Ceramics* **Cra** *Crafts*
Dec *Decorative* **Dr** *Drawing* **Fur** *Furniture*

Nearest Station: *Bristol Temple Meads.*
Personnel: *Director:* Tessa Jackson. *Deputy Director:* Una McCarthy. *Exhibitions Officer:* Josephine Lanyon. *Head of Artistic Programme:* Denise Robinson. *Education Officer:* Lindsey Fryer. *Marketing & Publicity Officer:* Tim Martienssen.

Arnolfini is one of Europe's leading centres for the contemporary arts with a national and international reputation for presenting new and innovative work in the visual arts, performance, film and music. Ten to twelve exhibitions are mounted annually and recent showings have included Dominique Blain, Rhapsodies in Black: Art of the Harlem Renaissance, Nick Stewart, Bob and Roberta Smith, Supastore. Exhibitions for '98 include Voiceover, Select, Kenny Hunter. Arnolfini welcomes over 450,000 visitors a year. For a full list of Arnolfini publications please contact the Exhibitions Officer at Arnolfini. Also Café/Bar and specialist Art Bookshop.
Services and Facilities:
Bar. Bookshop. Café. Disabled Access. Friends/Society. Lectures.

BRISTOL MUSEUM AND ART GALLERY P
Queen's Road, Bristol BS8 1RL. **Tel:** *0117-922 3571.* **Fax:** *0117-922 2047.*

CROFT GALLERY
26 Stokes Croft, Bristol BS1 3QD. **Tel:** *0117-942 2213.* **Fax:** *0117-942 3016.*

DAVID CROSS GALLERY
7 Boyces Avenue, Clifton, Bristol BS8 4AA. **Tel:** *0117-973 2614.*

EMPIRE AND COMMONWEALTH MUSEUM P
Clock Tower Yard, Temple Meads, Bristol BS1 6QH. **Tel:** *0117-925 4980/292688.*

GUILD GALLERY C
68 Park Street, Bristol BS1 5JY. **Tel:** *0117-926 5548.*
Opening times: *Mon-Sat 9.30-5 except Sun and Bank Hols.*
Personnel: *Gallery Organiser:* John Stops.

A large and well-lit gallery on the second floor of the Bristol Guild of Applied Art. It is rented by exhibitors and no commission is charged on sales. There are monthly exhibitions by mainly, but not exclusively, West Country artists and craftspeople, individually or in small groups. A large multi-media exhibition is held every Christmas. There is now a small gallery next to our craft dept. which holds occasional exhibitions by craftsmen.
Services and Facilities:
Café. Craftshop. Gallery space for hire. Restaurant. Shop.
Work Stocked and Sold:
App. Cer. Cra. Dr. Pa. Sc.
Price range: £100 - £500.

INNOCENT FINE ART C
7a Boyces Avenue, Clifton, Bristol BS8 4AA
Tel: *0117-973 2614.* **Fax:** *0117-974 1425.*
Opening times: *Mon-Sat 10-5.30.*
Nearest Station: *Bristol Temple Meads.*
Personnel: Carole Innocent. Diedre Hardwick.
New gallery opened this year in heart of Clifton, near Brunel's suspension bridge. Gallery stocks a large selection of contemporary painting and sculpture including Sir Terry Frost, RA, Rose Hilton, Sylvia Edwards, Jeremy Le Grice etc. The Lower gallery shows a collection of 19th century oils and watercolours with an emphasis on south west artists and subject matter.
Services and Facilities:
Art Consultancy. Art for Offices. Commissioning Service. Framing. Restoration. Valuation.
Work Stocked and Sold:
Pa. Sc.
Price range: £60 - £18,000.

MICHAEL STEWART GALLERIES
24 The Mall, Clifton, Bristol BS8 4DS.
Tel: *0272-706265.* **Fax:** *0272-706268.*

PARKVIEW FINE PAINTINGS C
24 The Mall, Clifton, Bristol BS8 4DS.
Tel: *0117-970 6265.* **Fax:** *0117-970 6268.*

ROYAL WEST OF ENGLAND ACADEMY C
Queen's Road, Clifton, Bristol BS8 1PX.
Tel: *0117-973 5129.* **Fax:** *0117-923 7874.*
Opening times: *Mon-Sat:10-5.30, Sun 2-5 during exhibitions. Office open 9-5.*
Nearest Station: *Temple Meads.*
Personnel: *Academy Secretary:* Rachel Fear.
Exhibitions mainly by practising artists, representing a "broad church" are shown throughout the year in the RWA's beautiful Victorian toplit galleries, arranged by RWA Council.

Royal West of England Academy

Annual open Autumn Exhibition attracts thousands of submissions, with approximately 700 selected and hung, the majority for sale. Open Print and Sculpture Exhibitions are held triennially. Several student bursaries are awarded annually. Galleries are available for hire for evening functions. Friends' association organises lectures, visits and holidays. Coffee available during exhibitions.
Services and Facilities:
Disabled Access. Friends/Society. Gallery space for hire. Lectures. Shop.
Work Stocked and Sold:
Pa. Pr. Sc.

SIR WILLIAM RUSSELL FLINT GALLERY
Broad Street, Wrington, Bristol BS18 7LA.
Tel: *0117-940 5440.*

WATERSHED GALLERY
Watershed Media Centre, 1 Canons Road, Bristol BS1 5TX. **Tel:** *0117-927 6444, 925 3845.*
Fax: *0117-921 3958.*

CAMELFORD

NORTH CORNWALL MUSEUM & GALLERY P
The Clease, Camelford, **Tel:** *01840-212954.*

FALMOUTH

FALMOUTH ART GALLERY PS
Municipal Buildings, The Moor, Falmouth, TR11 2RT. **Tel:** *01326-313863.* **Fax:** *01326-312662.*
Opening times: *Open all year (except Bank Holidays) Mon-Fri 10-5, Sat 10-1.*
Personnel: *Curator:* Catherine Wallace. *Assistant:* Alix Hooper. *Assistant:* Shelley Brett.
Permanent collection includes 200 works of art from Maritime prints and paintings (1600 - 1950) to Victorian and Edwardian paintings by artists like Burne-Jones, Munnings, Waterhouse, Laura Knight and H.S. Tuke. The display of the collection is rotated every six months. The gallery holds 10 temporary exhibitions per year including contemporary solo and group shows and historic, general, local artistic subjects plus two touring. Now open after major renovation and expansion of exhibiting space providing disabled access via new lift. Also new shop selling local artists' work on permanent basis and books, postcards and posters. Admission Free.
Services and Facilities:
Disabled Access. Guided Tours. Lectures. Shop.
Work Stocked and Sold:
Ab.

FALMOUTH ARTS CENTRE
24 Church Street, Falmouth, TR11 3EG.
Tel: *01326-314566.* **Fax:** *01326-211078.*

HELSTON

CREFTOW GALLERY C
6 Church Street, Helston, TR13 8TE.
Tel: *01326-572848.*
Opening times: *Mon-Sat 10-5.*
The Creftow Gallery is a co-operative of artists and craftspeople living and working in West

Cornwall. The Gallery provides an on-going exhibition of all that is best in contemporary arts and crafts. It has a unique character well suited to the high quality of the work displayed. The Creftow artists are producing a variety of styles which are now attracting attention both in this country and abroad.

The work of the potters and ceramicists is of a professional standard and imaginatively designed. This Helston Gallery is forward looking and well worth a visit.
Services and Facilities:
Craftshop.
Work Stocked and Sold:
Cer. Cra. Dec. Dr. Jew. Pa. Ph. Pr. Sc. Tx. Wd.
Price range: £5 - £1,000.

MULLION GALLERY
Nansmellyon Road, Mullion, Helston, TR12 7DQ. **Tel:** *01326-241170.*

MARAZION

AVALON ART
West End, Marazion, TR17 0EL.
Tel: *01736-710161/711737.*

PAR

MID-CORNWALL GALLERIES
Discovery, Par, PL24 2EG. **Tel:** *01726-812131.*

PENZANCE

THE BAKEHOUSE GALLERY C
Old Bakehouse Lane, Chapel Street, Penzance,
Tel: *01736-332223, 369979.*

CONTEMPORARY GALLERY
The Art & Design Building, 46 Queen Street, Penzance, TR18 4BQ. **Tel:** *01736-62396.*

NEWLYN ART GALLERY PS
New Road, Newlyn, Penzance, TR18 5PZ.
Tel: *01736-363715.* **Fax:** *01736-331578.*
Opening times: *Mon-Sat 10-5.*
Personnel: *Director: Emily Ash. Shop Manager: Blair Todd.*
Founded 1974 Newlyn Art Gallery has been established as a venue for exhibiting contemporary art for over 100 years, showing the best work by local, national and international artists. To compliment the exhibitions programme we organise talks, lectures, workshops and educational activities for schools and colleges. The gallery also presents a programme of events including music concerts, live arts, festival activities, art classes and a Summer Art Week of children's workshops. The gallery shop stocks a wide range of art books and mag-

azines, greetings cards, ceramics, jewellery, prints and small paintings.
Services and Facilities:
Bookshop. Disabled Access. Friends/Society. Lectures. Shop. Workshop Facilities.
Work Stocked and Sold:
Ab. App. Cer. Cra. Dec. Dr. Jew. Pa. Ph. Pr. Sc. Tx. Wd.
Price range: £3 - £3,000.

ROUND HOUSE GALLERY
Sennen Cove, Lands End, Penzance, TR19 7DF.
Tel: *01736-871859.*

SHEARS FINE ART
58 Chapel Street, Penzance, TR18 4AW.
Tel: *01736-50501.*

TONY SANDERS PENZANCE GALLERY
14 Chapel Street, Penzance, TR18 4AW.
Tel: *01736-66620.*

VICTORIA STUDIOS
Morrab Road, Penzance, **Tel:** *01736-62228.*

POLPERRO

PEAK ROCK ARTIST'S STUDIO & GALLERY
Peak Rock Art Studio, The Harbour, Polperro,
PL13 2QY. **Tel:** *01503-72490.*

SALTASH

THE NATIONAL TRUST FOR PLACES OF HISTORIC INTEREST OR NATURAL BEAUTY P
36 Queen Anne's Gate, London SW1H 9AS.
Tel: *0171-222 9251.* **Fax:** *0171-222 5097.*
Personnel: *President: H.M The Queen Mother. Director General: Mr M. Drury. Historic Buildings Secretary: Mr S. Jervis. Director of Public Affairs: Mr M. Taylor.*
To preserve places of historic interest or natural beauty in England, Wales and Northern Ireland, for people to enjoy now and in the future.
The Cotehele Quay Gallery, St. Dominick, Saltash, Cornwall, PL12 6TA. Contact: *Rebecca Coombes - 01579-351494.*
The gallery shows a wide range of contemporary crafts, paintings and prints by artists and craftspeople living in the South-West. It occupies a beautiful riverside position with parking nearby. Open daily 12 noon-5pm April-November.
The Chapel Gallery, Saltram, Plympton, Devon, PL7 3UH Contact: *Rebecca Coombes - 01752-336546.* The Chapel was renovated in the 1970s and now provides an elegant space for selling exhibitions of fine art and sculpture. The gallery shop sells books, cards and prints. Open 10.30am-5pm April-November, Sunday-Thursday. Limited Christmas opening.
The Trelissick Gallery, Trelissick Garden, Feock, Cornwall, TR3 6QL. Contact: *Tony Crosby - 01872-864084.* The National Trust in partnership with Cornwall's Craft Association presents at Trelissick Gallery a showcase for Cornwall's creativity, featuring contemporary work from leading artists and craftspeople. Changing exhibitions run from 1st March to end December. Open 7 days a week, all work

is for sale.
Services and Facilities:
Commissioning Service.

ST. IVES

BARBARA HEPWORTH MUSEUM P
Barnoon Hill, St. Ives, **Tel:** *01736-796226.*

THE BOOK GALLERY
2a & 2b Bedford Road, St. Ives, TR26 1SP.
Tel: *01736-793545.*

JUDI EMMANUEL
30 Fore Street, St. Ives, TR26 1HE.
Tel: *01736-797303/798448.*

MOSAIC GALLERY
8 St. Andrews Street, St. Ives, TR26 1AH.
Tel: *01736-793459.*

NEW CRAFTSMAN C
24 Fore Street, St. Ives, TR26 1HE.
Tel: *01736-795652.*

THE NEW MILLENIUM GALLERY
Street-An-Pol, St. Ives, TR26 2DS.
Tel: *01736-793121.*

PENHAVEN GALLERY
4 St. Peters Street, St. Ives, **Tel:** *01736-798147.*

PENWITH GALLERIES
Back Road West, St. Ives, TR26 1NL.
Tel: *01736-795579.*
Opening times: *Tues-Sat 10-1, 2.30-5.*
Admission: 50p.
Nearest Station: *St. Ives.*
Personnel: *Director:* Kathleen Watkins.
The Penwith Society was founded in 1949 by a group of notable contemporary artists in St. Ives and its seasonal exhibitions became a national showing place for contemporary work. The Society has an elected membership, limited to fifty and an unlimited associated membership. Its aims are to encourage practising artists and craftsmen in Cornwall and foster public interest in the arts.
The gallery has charity status. It is a unique complex of buildings including public galleries, print workshop, book shop, artists' studios and workshops. Continuous exhibitions of paintings sculpture and ceramics throughout the year.
Services and Facilities:
Art for Offices. Bookshop. Commissioning Service. Friends/Society. Shop. Workshop Facilities.
Work Stocked and Sold:
Ab. Cer. Cra. Dr. Jew. Pa. Pr. Sc.

PICTURE HOUSE GALLERIES C
Island Square, St. Ives, TR26 1NT.
Tel: *01736-794423.*
Opening times: *Mon-Sun 10.30-5.*
Personnel: Roger Gadwallader.
Also at: The Quay, St. Mawes, Cornwall. Tel: 01326 270495 and Commercial Road, Penryn, Cornwall. Tel: 01326 378248.
Opening times: St. Ives, Easter to November 7 days 10.30-5.30. Winter, Thurs-Sat, 10.30-4.

Ab *Artist's Books* **App** *Applied Art* **Cer** *Ceramics* **Cra** *Crafts* **Dec** *Decorative* **Dr** *Drawing* **Fur** *Furniture*

Opening times: St. Ives, Easter to November 7 days 10.30-5.30. Winter, Thurs-Sat, 10.30-4. Sun 12-4.

St. Mawes, Easter to October 7 days 10.30-5.30. Closed Winter.

Penryn, Open all year, Mon-Sat, 9-5.30.

The galleries are commercial and have a Mediterranean feel, with abright and decorative mixed exhibition of local and national artists. During the year the gallery also houses several one man exhibitions.

Services and Facilities:
Framing.

Work Stocked and Sold:
Cer. Gla. Pa. Pr.

PLUMBLINE GALLERY C
2 Barnoon Hill, St. Ives, TR26 1AD.
Tel: *01736-797771.*

PORTHMEOR GALLERY
Porthmeor Road, St. Ives, TR26 1NP.
Tel: *01736-798412.*

SALTHOUSE GALLERY
Norway Square, St. Ives, TR26 1NA.
Tel: *01736-795003.*

SIMS GALLERY
22 Fore Street, St. Ives, TR26 1HE.
Tel: *01736-797148.* **Fax:** *01736-797148.*

ST. IVES SOCIETY OF ARTISTS
Norway Gallery, Norway Square, St. Ives, TR26 1NA. **Tel:** *01736-795582.*

TATE GALLERY ST. IVES P
Porthmeor Beach, St. Ives, TR26 1TG.
Tel: *01736-796226.* **Fax:** *01736-794480.*
Opening times: *1 Apr-31 Sep, Mon-Sat 11-7, Sun 11-5, Bank Hols 11-5. 1 Oct-31 Mar closed Mon, Tues-Sun 11-5. Closed 24/25 Dec.*
Personnel: *Curator:* Michael Tooby. *Press & Information:* Ina Cole. *Education:* Susan Lamb.

The Tate Gallery St. Ives opened in 1993 and presents changing displays of 20th century art from the Tate Gallery's collections, focusing on the post-war modern movement St. Ives is so famous for. Key artists represented in the collection include Alfred Wallis, Ben Nicholson, Barbara Hepworth, Naum Gabo, John Wells, Patrick Heron, Terry Frost and Wilhelmina Barns-Graham.

The displays are complemented by a series of exhibitions and artists' projects and residencies, which explore the diversity of working methods in art today. The Barbara Hepworth Museum and Sculpture Garden in St. Ives is

run by Tate Gallery St. Ives.
Services and Facilities:
Bookshop. Café. Disabled Access. Friends/Society. Guided Tours. Lectures. Museum Shop. Restaurant. Shop. Workshop Facilities.

WILLS LANE GALLERY
Wills Lane, St. Ives, TR26 1AF.
Tel: *01736-795723.*

TRURO

THE GALLERY PORTSCATHO
Portscatho, Nr St Mawes, Truro, TR2 5HQ.
Tel: *01872-580719.* **Fax:** *01872-580719.*

ROYAL CORNWALL MUSEUM P
River Street, Truro, TR1 2SJ. **Tel:** *01872-72205.*

DEVON

APPLEDORE

GALLERIE MARIN
31 Market Street, Appledore, EX39 1PP.
Tel: *01237-473679.*

BIDEFORD

THE APPLEDORE CRAFTS COMPANY
5 Bude Street, Appledore, Bideford, EX32 1PS.
Tel: *01237-423547.*

BURTON ART GALLERY & MUSEUM P
Kingsley Road, Bideford, EX39 2QQ.
Tel: *01237-471455.* **Fax:** *01237-471455.*

COOPER GALLERY C
Cooper Street, Bideford, EX39 2DA.
Tel: *01237-477370.* **Fax:** *01237-423415.*

BOVEY TRACEY

DEVON GUILD OF CRAFTSMEN C
Riverside Mill, Bovey Tracey, TQ13 9AF.
Tel: *01626-832223.* **Fax:** *01626-834220.*
Opening times: *Daily 10-5.30 (except Winter Bank Holidays), Café 10-5.*
Nearest Station: *Newton Abbot.*
Personnel: *Director:* Francis Bung. *Contact:* Tess Coulson.

The picturesque Riverside Mill, a grade II listed building, has a shop, Exhibition Gallery and café. The shop, selected for quality by the Crafts Council, displays a wide variety of contemporary crafts including ceramics, jewellery, furniture, textiles, prints and woodwork by

members of the Devon Guild. The Exhibition gallery holds a regularly changing programme of themed exhibitions featuring work by Guild members and invited contributors. The café is Egon Ronay recommended and serves delicious homemade food. Educational work with schools. Free adjacent parking.

Services and Facilities:
Café. Commissioning Service. Craftshop. Friends/Society. Lectures. Shop.

Work Stocked and Sold:
Cer. Cra. Dr. Fur. Gla. Jew. Pr. Sc. Tx. Wd.

Price range: £5 - £5,000.

BUCKFASTLEIGH

BUCKFAST ABBEY P
Buckfastleigh, TQ11 0EE. **Tel:** *01364-642519.* **Fax:** *01364-643891.*

BUDLEIGH SALTERTON

OTTERTON MILL GALLERY C
Budleigh Salterton, EX9 7HG. **Tel:** *01395-568521.* **Fax:** *01395-568521.*
Opening times: *Daily 10.30-5.30 daily mid March-end October, 11.00-4.00 daily Nov-Mid March.*
Nearest Station: *Exmouth.*
Personnel: *Director:* Desna Greenhow.

Otterton Mill Gallery has an annual programme of fine arts and crafts exhibitions. The annual exhibition of furniture design is normally held in October. Frequent exhibitions include sculpture, both inside the gallery and in the courtyard, and the work of West Country craftspeople. Five studio-workshops include a pottery, stained glass workshop, painting studio and wood turning and framing workshop. A co-operative craft shop is run by local craftspeople.

Services and Facilities:
Bookshop. Café. Craftshop. Framing. Parking. Workshop Facilities.

Work Stocked and Sold:
Cer. Cra. Fur. Pa. Ph. Pr. Sc. Tx. Wd.

Price range: £10 - £1,500.

DARTMOUTH

COOMBE FARM GALLERY C
Dittisham, Dartmouth, TQ6 0JA.
Tel: *01803-722352.* **Fax:** *01803-722275.*
Email *Rileyarts@AOL.com*
Opening times: *Daily 10-5. Sundays by appointment.*
Nearest Station: *Totnes.*
Personnel: *Gallery Owner:* Tina Riley. *Gallery Director:* Mark Riley. *P.R Admin.:* Gina Carter.

A contemporary art and craft gallery featuring the work of artists and makers mainly from the West Country. The gallery shows ceramics, paintings, prints, jewellery, glass, wood and papier maché. Two or three exhibitions annually feature the work of specific artists and new young designers. Coombe Farm Studios is the educational part of the gallery where we run a variety of Fine Art and Craft courses in Devon

and painting holidays abroad tutored by Paul Riley.

Services and Facilities:
Art for Offices. Craftshop. Parking. Workshop Facilities.
Work Stocked and Sold:
App. Cer. Cra. Dec. Dr. Fur. Gla. Jew. Pa. Ph. Pr. Sc. Tx. Wd.
Price range: £10 - £5,000.

FACETS C
14 Broadstone, Dartmouth, TQ9 9NR.
Tel: *01803-833534.*

HIGHER STREET GALLERY C
1 Higher Street, Dartmouth, TQ6 9RB.
Tel: *01803-833157.*

SIMON DREW GALLERY C
13 Foss Street, Dartmouth, TQ6 9DR.
Tel: *01803-832832.* **Fax:** *01803-833040.*

EXETER

VINCENT GALLERY C
15 Magdalen Road, Exeter, EX2 4TA.
Tel: *01392-430082.*

BOATYARD STUDIOS
76 Haven Road, St. Thomas, Exeter, EX2 8DP.
Tel: *01392-218704.*

GORDON HEPWORTH GALLERY
Hayne Farm, Sandowne Lane, Newton St. Cyres, Exeter, EX5 5DE. **Tel:** *01392-851351.*

LAUREL KEELEY GALLERY
4 St. David's Hill, Exeter, **Tel:** *01392-428128.*

THE LOOK C
53 Queen Street, Exeter, **Tel:** *01392-219855.*
Opening times: *Mon-Sat 9.15-5.30.*
Nearest Station: *Exeter Central.*
Personnel: *Proprietor:* Jeff Goodwin.
Commercial gallery specialising in contempo-

rary art including painting, photography, ceramics, drawings, sculpture. Mostly 'one person' shows lasting six weeks. No entry fee. Browsing encouraged. Relaxed atmosphere. Refreshments on request (free!). New work by young professionals encouraged, especially South West based artists.

THE·L·O·O·K
Gallery

Gallery ajoins one of the South West top hair salons. Guaranteed viewing by 200 people every week. Regular private views. Ring us if you would like to go on our mailing list. Ring us if you would like to exhibit.
Work Stocked and Sold:
Cer. Cra. Dr. Fur. Gla. Pa. Ph. Sc. Tx. Wd.
Price range: £50 - £500.

ROYAL ALBERT MEMORIAL MUSEUM & ART GALLERY PS
Queen Street, Exeter, EX4 3RX.
Tel: *01392-265858.* **Fax:** *01392-421252.*
Email *rerandall@pop.ex.ac.uk*
Ws *http://www.eter.ac.uk/projects/ALBERT/*
Opening times: *Mon-Sat 10-5.*
Nearest Station: *Exeter Central.*
Personnel: *Head of Museums:* Katherine Chant. *Exhibitions Administrator:* Fay Squire. *Curator of Decorative Art:* John Madin. *Assistant Curator of Art:* Caroline Worthington. *Press & Events Officer:* Ruth Randall. Large regional museum with collections of regional, national and international importance. Fine Art collection, Decorative Art collection, art from peoples around the world in the Ethnography collection, a programme of temporary exhibitions, workshops, lectures and children's activities.
Important exhibitions 1998: Going Modern and Being British, Art, Architecture and Design in Devon c1910-1960 - 4th April-30th May 1998. An exhibition which reveals Devon's lace in twentieth century British art, architecture and design; Fire and Ice, Watercolour diaries of volcanoes by Tony Foster - 15th June-31st August 1998. Volcanoes of the Americas painted by Tony Foster on his travels from Alaska to Chile; The Oppé Collection of British Drawings and Watercolours - 19th September-7th November 1998. A selection from one of the finest private collections of British watercolours and drawings.
Services and Facilities:
Café. Friends/Society. Lectures. Museum Shop. Shop. Workshop Facilities.

SPACEX GALLERY
45 Preston Street, Exeter, EX1 1DF.
Tel: *01392-431786.*

PLYMOUTH

ATLANTIC GALLERY C
Armada Centre, Plymouth, **Tel:** *01752-221600.*
PLYMOUTH ARTS CENTRE PS

38 Looe Street, Plymouth, PL4 0EB.
Tel: *01752-206114.* **Fax:** *01752-206118.*
Opening times: *Mon 10-5, Tues-Sat 10-8, Sun 5.30-7.30. Group bookings by appointment.*
Nearest Station: *Plymouth.*
Personnel: Jeremy Davies. *Curator:* Miranda Gardiner. *House Manager:* Stefan Aloszko.

Plymouth Arts Centre shows a range of new and innovative contemporary work. It promotes the work of regional/national and international artists.
A changing programme of exhibitions represent painting, sculpture, photography, film, video, and new media works. Recent shows include; 'Witness' by photographic installation artists Lindsay Seers, prints by Barbara Rae, Elizabeth Blackadder, John Bellany, and 'Surfing the Net', works using new media and technology. Facilities; 3 galleries, 100-seat arthouse cinema, book/gift shop, café/restaurant. Free admission to exhibitions. Occasional lectures. Founded 1947.
Services and Facilities:
Bookshop. Café. Restaurant. Shop.
Work Stocked and Sold:
Cer. Dr. Pa. Ph. Pr. Sc. Tx.
Price range: £20 - £3,500.

PLYMOUTH CITY MUSEUM & ART GALLERY P
Drake Circus, Plymouth, PL4 8AJ.
Tel: *01752-264878.*
Fax: *01752-264959.*

WHITE LANE GALLERY C
1 White Lane, The Barbican, Plymouth, PL1 2LP. **Tel:** *01752-221450.*

TIVERTON

ANGEL GALLERY
1 Angel Terrace, Tiverton, EX16 6PD.
Tel: *01994-254778.*

TOPSHAM

THE SHIP AGROUND GALLERY
36 Fore Street, Topsham, EX3 0HQ.

TORRINGTON

PLOUGH GALLERY
Plough Arts Centre, The High Street, Torrington, EX38 8HQ. **Tel:** *01805-622552.* **Fax:** *01805-624624.*

Ab *Artist's Books* **App** *Applied Art* **Cer** *Ceramics* **Cra** *Crafts*
Dec *Decorative* **Dr** *Drawing* **Fur** *Furniture*

TOTNES

DARTINGTON ARTS GALLERY PS
Dartington Hall, Totnes, TQ9 6DE.
Tel: 01803-867068. **Fax:** 01803-868108.
Opening times: Mon-Fri 10.30-1, 2-5, Sat 2-5.
Personnel: *Gallery Co-ordinator:* Lisa Warren.
Dartington Arts Gallery is situated on the 900-acre medieval Dartington Hall Estate and has a wall space of 77.8 m2.
It is constantly invigilated during opening hours and has a Nacoss approved intruder alarm system. The gallery has a programme of innovative exhibitions supporting both local and national/international artists. The Gallery is part of the overall activities at Dartington Arts.
Services and Facilities:
Bar. Craftshop. Disabled Access. Gallery space for hire. Lectures. Parking. Restaurant. Workshop Facilities.

HIGH CROSS HOUSE
Dartington Hall, Totnes, TQ9 6ED.
Tel: 01803-864114.
Fax: 01803-867057.

MARSHALL ARTS GALLERY
3 Warland, The Plains, Totnes, TQ9 5EL.
Tel: 01803-863533.

SEYMOUR GALLERY
10 High Street, Totnes, TQ9 5RY. **Tel:** 01803-864200.

DORSET

ABBOTSBURY

DANSEL GALLERY C
Rodden Row, Abbotsbury, Weymouth, DT3 4JL.
Tel: 01305-871515.
Fax: 01305-871518. **Email** dansel@wdi.co.uk
Ws http://www.wdi.co.uk/dansel
Opening times: Every day 10-5 including weekends.
Nearest Station: Dorchester South.
Personnel: *Partners:* Danielle Holmes, Selwyn Holmes.
Gallery with emphasis on contemporary design and quality specialising in wood products only. One-off bowls, boxes and cabinets are featured, as well as a range of kitchen, desk and domestic ware.
Commissions can be taken for pieces of furniture designed by Dansel as well as by other craftsmen. There is a toy section including handmade wooden toys, jigsaws and automata and a area devoted to books about trees, woodworking and design.
Services and Facilities:
Bookshop. Commissioning Service. Craftshop. Parking. Workshop Facilities.
Work Stocked and Sold:
Fur. Wd.
Price range: £1 - £3,000.

BEAMINSTER

PARNHAM HOUSE PS
Beaminster, DT8 3NA. **Tel:** 01308-862204.
Fax: 01308-863494.
Opening times: House, Workshops and Gardens open Tues, Weds, Thurs, Suns and Bank Hols.
28 Mar-30 Oct; 10-5.
Nearest Station: Crewkerne.
Personnel: Bruce Hunter-Inglis.
Parnham is a 16thC manor surrounded by 14 acres beautiful gardens. Furniture by John Makepeace. Quality British craftshop; licensed buttery. The Parnham Trust runs Parnham College (two-year course), one-week residential summer courses, and lively arts programme of events. Further details on request. Also, visit Hooke Park and see the award-winning buildings, the entrance by Andy Goldsworthy; and the Woodland Trail. Open Wednesdays and Sundays only 2-5pm. 01308-862204. Group visits to both Parnham and Hooke Park welcome by appointment only. Dorset Art Week 1998 - 23rd-31st May. Special exhibitions: 1) Craft Gallery 1998 - leading craft galleries showing at Parnham; 2) "Selected works and west country classics paintings from the Machaidhachains private collection" including Hilton, Scott, Wallace, Pearce, Fedden and McClure until end June 1998.
Services and Facilities:
Bar. Bookshop. Café. Commissioning Service. Craftshop. Disabled Access. Friends/Society. Guided Tours. Lectures. Parking. Restaurant. Shop.
Work Stocked and Sold:
Ab. App. Cer. Fur. Tx. Wd.
Price range: £5 - £50,000.

BRIDPORT

BRIDPORT ARTS CENTRE
South Street, Bridport, DT6 3NR.
Tel: 01308-424204.

BRIDPORT MUSEUM P
South Street, Bridport, DT6 3NR.
Tel: 01308-422116.
Fax: 01308-420659.

GROSVENOR GALLERY
Grosvenor House, Gundry Lane, Bridport, DT6 3RL. **Tel:** 01308-458787.

DORCHESTER

GALLERY GILBERT C
48 High West Street, Dorchester, DT1 1UT.
Tel: 01305-263740.

THE GALLERY C
20 Durngate Street, Dorchester DT1 1JP.
Tel: 01305-267408. **Fax:** 01305-251429.
Email john.pearson1@virgin.net.uk
Opening times: Tues-Sat, 10-5.
Nearest Station: Dorchester South.
Personnel: *Directors:* John Pearson, Susie Pearson.
Found in Dorchester's ancient Durngate

Street, this gallery is on the ground floor of a 16th century building. Previously well known for representing established watercolourists, the owners now exhibit and promote original printmakers. Artists represented include: Jo Barry, Stephen Brown, Michael Cadman, Katie Clemson, Ros and David Cuthbert, Anne Desmet, Edwina Ellis, Jason Hicklin, Ron Jesty, Peter Toms, Alan Simpson and others. Four to five exhibitions a year. Bespoke conservation. Framing.
Services and Facilities:
Disabled Access. Framing. Restoration.
Work Stocked and Sold:
Dr. Pa. Pr.
Price range: £100 - £1,000.

THOMAS HENRY FINE ART C
The Old Warehouse, Durngate Street, Dorchester, DT1 1JP. **Tel:** 01305-250388.

SHERBORNE

ALPHA HOUSE GALLERY C
Alpha House, South Street, Sherborne, DT9 3LU. **Tel:** 01935-814944/850511.

SWANAGE

ALPHA GALLERY
21A Commercial Road, Swanage, **Tel:** 01929-423692.

WHITE YARD STUDIO
3 Arcade Terrace, Swanage, BH19 1DE.
Tel: 01929-426621/426578.

GLOUCESTERSHIRE

BOURTON ON THE WATER

CHESTNUT GALLERY
High Street, Bourton on the Water,

CHALFORD

GALLERY PANGOLIN C
Unit 9, Chalford Industrial Estate, Chalford, GL6 8NT. **Tel:** 01453-886527. **Fax:** 01453-731499.
Opening times: Opening hours by appointment.
Nearest Station: Stroud.
Personnel: Jane Buck. Claude Koenig.
Gallery Pangolin has an established reputation for selling high quality bronze sculpture by contemporary artists. The gallery revives the traditional association between foundry and gallery, showing a selection of bronzes cast by Pangolin Editions.

The proximity of the foundry allows gallery visitors the opportunity to tour the workshops and to gain an insight into casting processes. The gallery works with a wide range of sculptors and is ideally placed to coordinate a broad spectrum of commissions ranging in scale from monumental to intimate.

Enquiries are welcomed from individuals, public bodies and corporate clients.

Services and Facilities:
Art Consultancy. Art for Offices. Commissioning Service. Parking. Restoration. Valuation.
Work Stocked and Sold:
Dr. Sc.

CHELTENHAM

AXIOM CENTRE FOR THE ARTS *PS*
57-59 Winchcombe Street, Cheltenham, GL52 2NE. **Tel:** *01242-253183.*
Fax: *01242-253183.*
Email *arts@axiomcentre.u-net.com*
Opening times: *Mon-Sat 10-6, Sun 12-4.*
Personnel: *Visual Arts Co-ordinator:* Helen Lawson.

The Axiom Centre for the Arts contains not only the largest gallery space in Gloucestershire, but workshops, theatre. A music venue and studios; which inhibit some of Cheltenhams most cutting-edge artists.

The main gallery exhibits 12 shows a year, consisting of painting, sculpture and prints by local and national artists. The bar contains a photographic gallery exhibiting local up and coming photographers. All gallery spaces are available to rent.
Services and Facilities:
Bar. Café. Friends/Society. Gallery space for hire. Lectures. Workshop Facilities.
Work Stocked and Sold:
Dr. Pa. Ph. Pr. Sc.
Price range: £10 - £4,000.

CHELTENHAM ART GALLERY & MUSEUM *P*
Clarence Street, Cheltenham, GL50 3JT.
Tel: *01242-237431.*
Fax: *01242-262334.*

HOLST BIRTHPLACE MUSEUM *P*
4 Clarence Road, Cheltenham, GL52 2AY.
Tel: *01242-524846.*

JONATHAN POOLE *C*
Compton Cassey Gallery, Nr. Withington, Cheltenham, GL54 4DE.
Tel: *01242-890224.*
Fax: *01242-890479.*
Personnel: Jonathan Poole.
European representatives for John Lennon and Miles Davis Estates. Exhibition organisers with venues in Europe and the Middle East. Contemporary Sculpture, Paintings and Sculpture by Jonathan Poole and Bobby

Plisnier.
Services and Facilities:
Art Consultancy. Valuation.
Work Stocked and Sold:
Dr. Pa. Pr. Sc.
Price range: £50 - £15,000.

MANOR HOUSE GALLERY
16 Royal Parade, Bayshill Road, Cheltenham, GL50 3AY. **Tel:** *01242-228330.* **Fax:** *01242-228328.*

MONTPELLIER GALLERY *C*
27 The Courtyard, Montpellier Street, Cheltenham, GL50 1SR. **Tel:** *01242-515165.* **Fax:** *01242-515165.*
Opening times: *Mon-Sat 9.30-5.30.*
Personnel: *Proprietor:* Peter Burridge.
Located in Regency Cheltenham, Montpellier Gallery is set in an elegant courtyard in Montpellier Street. Established in 1990, we have built a reputation for contemporary paintings and handmade printmaking, alongside fine British Crafts, including ceramics, studio glass, contemporary jewellery and sculpture.

A series of approximately 4 exhibitions, either group or solo, are held during the year. In between exhibitions we have a varied display of work selected from the 400+ artists and makers that we represent. This display is changed from week to week, giving a constantly diverse and stimulating exhibition.
Services and Facilities:
Art Consultancy. Art for Offices. Commissioning Service. Craftshop. Disabled Access. Framing.
Work Stocked and Sold:
Cer. Cra. Gla. Jew. Pa. Pr. Wd.
Price range: £20 - £1,500.

THE NORTHLEACH GALLERY
The Green, Northleach, Cheltenham, GL54 3EX. **Tel:** *01451-860519.*

CIRENCESTER

BREWERY ARTS CENTRE *C*
Brewery Court, Cirencester, GL7 1JH.
Tel: *01285-657181.*
Fax: *01285 644060.*

GLOUCESTER

GLOUCESTER CITY MUSEUM & ART GALLERY *P*
Brunswick Road, Gloucester, GL1 1HP.
Tel: *01452-524131.* **Fax:** *01452-410898.*

ROBERT OPIE COLLECTION MUSEUM OF ADVERTISING
Albert Warehouse, Gloucester Docks, Gloucester.. **Tel:** *01452-302309.* •

LECHLADE

FILKINS GALLERY & STUDIO
Cross Tree, Filkins, Lechlade, GL7 3JL.
Tel: *01367-850385 (evenings).*

KELMSCOTT MANOR *P*
Kelmscott, Lechlade, GL7 3HJ.
Tel: *01367-252486.*
Fax: *01367-253754.*

NAILSWORTH

HAND PRINTS & WATERCOLOUR GALLERY
3 Bridge Street, Nailsworth, GL6 0AA.
Tel: *01453-834967.*

PAINSWICK

NINA ZBOROWSKA *C*
Damsels Mill, Paradise, Painswick, GL6 6UD.
Tel: *01452-812460.* **Fax:** *01452-812912.*

STOW-ON-THE-WOLD

FOSSE GALLERY
The Square, Stow-on-the-Wold, GL54 1AF.
Tel: *01451-831319.*

THE JOHN DAVIES GALLERY *C*
Church Street, Stow-on-the-Wold, GL54 1BB.
Tel: *01451-831698.* **Fax:** *01451-832477.*
Opening times: *Mon-Sat 9.30-1.30, 2.30-5.30.*
Nearest Station: *Moreton in Marsh.*
Personnel: John Davies. Tony Retallack. Jeffrey Garrington.
Established 1977. A fresh, spacious and welcoming gallery offering contemporary and earlier 20th Century works from the traditional to the more progressive. Artists include David Prentice, Lionel Aggett, Peter Evans, Keith Dunkley, Brian Peacock, Tanya Short. Bronzes by Richard Cowdy, Kate Denton, Deborah Scaldwell and Adrian Sorrell. Restoration in all media to museum level. Regular Exhibitions. Artists invited to send photographs.
Services and Facilities:
Restoration.
Work Stocked and Sold:
Cer. Dr. Pa. Pr. Sc.

TRAFFORDS *C*
Digbeth Street, Stow-on-the-Wold, GL54 1BN.
Tel: *01451-830424.*

STROUD

YEW TREE GALLERY C
Steanbridge Lane, Nr. Stroud, Slad, GL6 7QE.
Tel: *01452-813601.*

SOUTH GLOUCESTERSHIRE

CHIPPING SODBURY

CAROUSEL GALLERY
21a High Street, Chipping Sodbury, BS17 6AE.
Tel: *01454-312622.*

SOMERSET

FROME

THE BLACK SWAN GUILD
2 Bridge Street, Frome, BA11 1BB.
Tel: *01373-473980.*

MONTACUTE

NATIONAL TRUST MONTACUTE HOUSE P
Montacute, TA15 6XP. **Tel:** *01935-823289.*
Fax: *01935-823289.*

TAUNTON

ALBERMARLE CENTRE GALLERY
Albermarle Centre, Taunton, TA1 1BA.
Tel: *01823-252945.*
Opening times: *Mon-Fri 8.30-5.*
Personnel: *Centre Manager: Cleve Lott.*

BREWHOUSE THEATRE & ARTS CENTRE C
Coal Orchard, Taunton, TA1 1JL. **Tel:** *01823-274608.* **Fax:** *01823-323116.*
Opening times: *Mon 12.15-5.30, Tues-Sat 10-5.30. Performance evenings till 9.30.*
Personnel: *Arts Assistant: Kim Hoar.*
Services and Facilities:
Bar. Café. Disabled Access. Gallery space for hire. Lectures. Parking. Restaurant. Workshop Facilities.
Work Stocked and Sold:
Dr. Pa.
Price range: £5 - £1,000.

BYRAM GALLERY
Somerset College of Art & Technology, Wellington Road, Taunton, TA1 5AX.
Tel: *01823-283403.*

WEDMORE

THE STUDIO GALLERY
Poolbridge, Blackford, Wedmore, BS28 4PD.
Tel: *01934-713380.*
Fax: *01934-712511.*

WELLS

SADLER STREET GALLERY C
7a Sadler Street, Wells, BA5 2RR. **Tel:** *01749-670220.*

WELLS MUSEUM P
8 Cathedral Green, Wells, BA5 2UE.
Tel: *01749-673477.* **Fax:** *01749-676013.*

YEOVIL

80 SOUTH STREET GALLERY
Yeovil Community Arts Centre, 80 South Street, Yeovil, BA20 1QH.
Tel: *01935-32123.*

NORTH SOMERSET

WESTON SUPER MARE

HANS PRICE GALLERY
Weston Super Mare College, Creative Arts and Design, Knightstone Road, Weston-super-Mare, BS23 2AL.

THE TIME MACHINE
North Somerset Museum Service, Burlington Street, Weston-super-Mare, BS23 1PR.
Tel: *01934-621028.* **Fax:** *01934-612526.*

Southern

BERKSHIRE

BRACKNELL

SOUTH HILL PARK ARTS CENTRE PS
Bracknell, RG12 7PA.
Tel: *01344-427272.*
Fax: *01344-411427.*
Email *visual.art@southhillpark.org.uk*
Opening times: *Bracknell Gallery:- Wed-Fri 1-5 & 7-9.30pm, Sat 1-10pm, Sun 1-5. Mansion House:- Mon-Sat 9-11pm, Sun & Bank Holidays 12 noon-10.30pm.*
Nearest Station: *Bracknell.*
Personnel: *Exhibitions Officer: Mark Segal. Visual Arts Co-ordinator: Denise Keegans.*

Mansion building and the purpose built Bracknell Gallery hosting a lively range of temporary fine art and craft exhibitions.
The Bracknell Gallery programme ranges across major solo exhibitions to group exhibitions and historical shows. Further spaces in the Mansion building present exhibitions by local artists, young artists and groups both formal and informal.
Craft cabinets feature a range of work both by national and local makers. Also printmaking

studio, jewellery studio and ceramics studio.
Services and Facilities:
Bar. Café. Disabled Access. Gallery space for hire. Parking. Restaurant. Workshop Facilities.
Work Stocked and Sold:
Cer. Cra. Jew. Pa. Ph. Sc.

COOKHAM

STANLEY SPENCER GALLERY P
Kings Hall, High Street, Cookham, SL6 9JF.
Tel: *01628-520890 / 523484.*

ETON

CONTEMPORARY FINE ART GALLERY & SCULPTURE PARK C
31 High Street, Eton, SL4 6AX. **Tel:** *01753-854315, after 7pm 01753-830731.*

MAIDENHEAD

ROYAL BOROUGH COLLECTION P
c/o Royal Borough of Windsor and Maidenhead, Town Hall, St. Ives Road, Maidenhead, SL6 1QS. **Tel:** *01628-798888.*

NEWBURY

ARTS WORKSHOP
Northcroft Lane, Newbury, RG13 1BU.
Tel: *01635-47851.*

NEWBURY MUSEUM P
The Wharf, Newbury, RG1 5AS.
Tel: *01635-3051.*

READING

BLAKES LOCK MUSEUM P
Gasworks Road, Reading, **Tel:** *01734-390918.*

BLOND FINE ART C
Barnat Works, 1A Upper Redlands Road, Reading RG1 5JJ.
Tel: *0118-926 0880.* **Fax:** *0118-926 9101.*
Opening times: *By appointment.*
Nearest Station: *Reading.*
Personnel: *Jonathon Blond.*

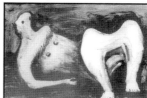

British original prints 1920-80.
Services and Facilities:
Art Consultancy. Art for Offices.
Work Stocked and Sold:
Pr.
Price range: £50 - £2,500.

READING MUSEUM AND ART GALLERY P
Blagrave Street, Reading, RG1 1QH.
Tel: *0118-939 9800/9898.*

Gla *Glass* **Jew** *Jewellery* **Pa** *Paintings* **Ph** *Photography* **Pr** *Prints*
Sc *Sculpture* **Tx** *Textiles* **Wd** *Wood*

THE ARTWORLD
DIRECTORY 1998/99 **107**

RISING SUN INSTITUTE
30 Silver Street, Reading, RG1 2ST.
Tel: *01734-866788.*

WINDSOR

CENTURY GALLERY DATCHET
*The Shop on the Green, Datchet, Windsor, SL3
9JH.* **Tel:** *01753-581284.*

**THE CONTEMPORARY FINE ART GALLERY,
ETON** C
31 High Street, Eton, Windsor, SL4 6AX.
Tel: *01753-854315, after 7pm 01753-830731.*
Fax: *01753-620390.*

ETON APPLIED ARTS C
81 High Street, Windsor, SL4 6AF.
Tel: *01753-860771.*

THE PEMBROKE GALLERY C
*15A The Arches, Goswell Hill, Windsor, SL4
1RH.* **Tel:** *01753-868844.* **Fax:** *01344-
876546.*

WINDSOR ARTS CENTRE
*The Old Court, St. Leonard's Road, Windsor,
SL4 3DB.* **Tel:** *01753-859421.*

BOURNEMOUTH

BOURNEMOUTH

RIDDETTS OF BOURNEMOUTH
26 Richmond Hill, Bournemouth BH2 6EJ.
Tel: *01202-555686.*

**RUSSELL-COTES ART GALLERY AND
MUSEUM** P
East Cliff, Bournemouth BH1 3AA.
Tel: *01202-451800.* **Fax:** *01202-451851.*
Email *enquiries@russell-cotes.demon.co.uk*
Opening times: *Tues-Sun 10-5.*
Personnel: *Director:* Simon Olding. *Visual
Arts Officer:* Mark Bills.

The Russell-Cotes Art Gallery and Museum
houses an important collection of Victorian,
Edwardian, Modern and Contemporary British
and European fine art, and excellent decorative art, sculpture and ethnographic collections relevant to the original Victorian and
Edwardian buildings. A distinguished group of
contemporary craft and sculpture commissions
is housed in the award-winning new museum
extension and beautifully restored gardens. A
highly regarded exhibition programme of con-

temporary and 19th Century fine art, and
crafts is also held throughout the year. The
Museum is closed for building work until
Autumn 1998 when the new extension re-
opens with the launch of the Craft Café and
1999 for East Cliff Hall and the Art Galleries.
Services and Facilities:
*Art Consultancy. Art for Offices. Café. Commis-
sioning Service. Friends/Society. Guided Tours.
Lectures. Museum Shop. Workshop Facilities.*

TZB SOUTHBOURNE GALLERY C
*2 Carbery Row, (Southbourne Road),
Bournemouth BH6 3QR.*
Tel: *01202-426967.*

BUCKINGHAMSHIRE

AYLESBURY

**BUCKINGHAMSHIRE ART GALLERY
COUNTY MUSEUM** PS
Church Street, Aylesbury, HP20 2QP.
Tel: *01296-331441.* **Fax:** *01296-334884.*
Email *sanderegg@buckscc.gov.uk*
Opening times: *Mon-Sat 10-5, Sun & Bank
Holidays 2-5.*
Nearest Station: *BR: Aylesbury.*
Personnel: *Director:* Colin V. Dawes. *Keep-
er of Art & Exhibitions:* Post vacant.~
Voted Joint Museum of the Year, 1996. The
new Buckinghamshire County Museum
opened in October 1995.

As part of a multi-million pound redevelop-
ment, a suite of exhibition galleries were added
to show the best in regional, national and
international art, craft, design and photography.
A range of major exhibitions is held supplemented by a series of small, theme-based shows
occasionally focusing on works from the collections. Educational events include workshops, lectures and talks - school packs and
teacher oriented events are organised regularly.
Entrance to the museum is free. The gallery
holds selling exhibitions of Buckinghamshire
artists.
Services and Facilities:
*Bookshop. Café. Disabled Access. Friends/Soci-
ety. Guided Tours. Lectures. Museum Shop.
Workshop Facilities.*
Work Stocked and Sold:
App. Cer. Cra. Jew. Pa. Pr.
Price range: £50 - £3,500.
QUEEN PARK ARTS CENTRE GALLERY

Queens Park Road, Aylesbury, HP21 7RT.
Tel: *01296-243325.*

**WADDESDON MANOR - THE ROTH-
SCHILD COLLECTION** P
Waddesdon, Aylesbury, HP18 0JH.
Tel: *01296-651226.* **Fax:** *01296-651293.*
Opening times: *Gardens, Aviary, Restau-
rant and Shops: Sun 1 Mar-Sun 20 Dec, Wed-
Sun and Bank Holiday Mondays 10-5. House
(including Wine Cellars) Thur 2 April-Sun 1
Nov, Thurs-Sun, Bank Holiday Mondays and
Wednesday in July & August 11-4. Bachelors'
Wing open Thurs only (access cannot be guaran-
teed.)*

Waddesdon Manor won the Museum of the
Year and Best National Trust Property awards
in 1997. This French Renaissance-style
château was built (1874-89) for Baron Ferdinand de Rothschild to display his vast collection of works of art. The Collection includes
French Royal furniture, Savonnerie carpets
and Sèvres porcelain as well as important portraits by Gainsborough and Reynolds and
works by Dutch and Flemish masters of the
17th century. The formal gardens, parkland,
Rococo-style aviary, wine cellars, shops and
fully licensed restaurant are also open to the
public. Lectures, garden workshops and special
events take place throughout the year.
Services and Facilities:
*Disabled Access. Guided Tours. Lectures. Muse-
um Shop. Parking. Restaurant. Shop.*

MILTON KEYNES

ARTS WORKSHOP TRUST LTD
*The Barn Office, The Courtyard, Milton Keynes,
MK14 5DZ.* **Tel:** *01908-663966.*

FENNY LODGE GALLERY C
*Simpson Road, Fenny Stratford, Bletchley, Milton
Keynes, MK1 1BD.*

MILTON KEYNES CRAFT GUILD C
*CBX2, 380 Midsummer Boulevard, Central Mil-
ton Keynes,* **Tel:** *01908-694764.*

STANTONBURY GALLERY
Stantonbury Campus, Milton Keynes,
Tel: *01908-605536.*

HAMPSHIRE

ALRESFORD

ALRESFORD GALLERY C
36 West Street, Alresford, SO24 9AU
Tel: *01962-735286.* **Fax:** *01962-735295.*
Opening times: *Tue-Sat 10-5. Closed 1-*

Opening times: *Tue-Sat 10-5. Closed 1-1.30.*
Nearest Station: *Winchester.*
Personnel: *Director: Brian Knowler RI.*

ALRESFORD GALLERY

Services and Facilities:
Art Consultancy. Art for Offices. Commissioning Service.
Work Stocked and Sold:
Cer. Dr. Pa. Sc.
Price range: £100 - £10,000.

CANDOVER GALLERY *C*
22 West Street, Alresford, SO24 9AE.
Tel: *01962-733200.*

ALTON

ALLEN GALLERY *C*
(Hampshire County Museums Service), 10-12 Church Street, Alton, GU34 2BW.
Tel: *01420-82802.*

ANDOVER

ANDOVER MUSEUM *P*
(Hampshire County Museums Service), 6 Church Close, Andover, SP10 1DP.
Tel: *01264-366283.*

BASINGSTOKE

WILLIS MUSEUM AND ART GALLERY *P*
Market Place, Basingstoke, RG21 1QD.
Tel: *01256-465902.*

CHRISTCHURCH

RED HOUSE MUSEUM AND ART GALLERY *P*
(Hampshire County Museums Service), Quay Road, Christchurch, BH23 1BU. **Tel:** *01202-482860.*

EASTLEIGH

EASTLEIGH MUSEUM *P*
25 High Street, Eastleigh, SO5 5LF.
Tel: *01703-643026.*

GOSPORT

GOSPORT MUSEUM *P*
Walpole Road, Gosport, PO12 1LQ.
Tel: *01705-588035.*

HAVANT

HAVANT MUSEUM *P*
East Street, Havant, PO9 1BS.
Tel: *01705-451155.*

OLD TOWN HALL ARTS CENTRE
East Street, Havant,

NEW ALRESFORD

HITCHCOCKS
11 East Street, New Alresford,
Tel: *01962-734762.*

PORTSMOUTH

ASPEX GALLERY
27 Brougham Road, Southsea, Portsmouth, PO5 4PA.
Tel: *01705-812121.*

MOUNTBATTEN GALLERY
Guildhall Square, Portsmouth, PO1 2AD.
Tel: *01705-827261.*

PORTSMOUTH CITY MUSEUM AND RECORDS OFFICE *P*
Museum Road, Portsmouth, PO1 2LJ.
Tel: *01705-827261.*

RINGWOOD

BETTLES GALLERY *C*
80 Christchurch Road, Ringwood, BH24 1DR.
Tel: *01425-470410.*
Fax: *01425-479002.*
Opening times: *Tues-Fri 10-5, Sat 10-1.*
Personnel: *Directors: Gill Bettle, Roger Bettle.*
A small privately owned gallery specialising in the exhibition and sale of contemporary ceramics and paintings in a 300-year-old building on the outskirts of Ringwood, which borders the New Forest.

The work of leading potters and artists from around the British Isles is shown in nine annual exhibitions in addition to the comprehensive stock which is constantly changing. The gallery actively promotes the work of new makers alongside that of established craftsmen and artists and is pleased to arrange temporary displays for business venues etc.
Services and Facilities:
Commissioning Service. Parking.
Work Stocked and Sold:
Cer. Jew. Pa.
Price range: £10 - £1,000.

SELBOURNE

COURTYARD GALLERY *C*
The Plestor, High Street, Selbourne, GU34 3JQ.
Tel: *01420-511334.* **Fax:** *01420-346822.*

SOUTHSEA

THE RED GALLERY *C*
98 Marmion Road, Southsea, PO5 2BB.
Tel: *01705-793924.*

STOCKBRIDGE

COURCOUX & COURCOUX CONTEMPORARY ART LTD *C*
Nomads House, High Street, Stockbridge, SO20 6HE.
Tel: *01264-810717.* **Fax:** *01264-810481.*
Email *ianorrichard@courcoux.demon.co.uk*
Opening times: *Tues to Sat 10-5.*
Nearest Station: *Andover.*
Personnel: *Director:* Ian Courcoux. Richard Courcoux.

Specialising in figurative but non-realistic sculpture and paintings by contemporary artists, the gallery has eight local exhibitions annually and a mixed summer show.
Always in stock are works by Elisabeth Frink and Sophie Ryder. We exhibit at London Contemporary Art Fair and Glasgow Art Fair. There is an attractive garden at the rear of the premises and the 1,200 sq. ft. exhibitions space flows through premises dating back to the 18th century. Stockbridge, situated on the River Test, is an attractive market town on the A30, readily accessible from London.
There is unrestricted parking in the wide High Street.
Services and Facilities:
Art Consultancy. Commissioning Service. Shop. Valuation.
Work Stocked and Sold:
Cer. Pa. Sc.
Price range: £300 - £25,000.

WYKEHAM GALLERIES
Stockbridge, **Tel:** *01962-846304.*

WINCHESTER

ANGELUS GALLERY
Winchester College, Winchester,
Tel: *01962-864242.*

GUILDHALL GALLERY
The Broadway, Winchester,
Tel: *01962-840222.*

Gla Glass Jew Jewellery Pa Paintings Ph Photography Pr Prints
Sc Sculpture Tx Textiles Wd Wood

WINCHESTER CONTEMPORARY ART
3a Minster Street, Winchester, SO23 9HA.
Tel: *01962-877601.*

THE WINCHESTER GALLERY
Park Avenue, Winchester, SO23 8DL.
Tel: *01962-852500.*

ISLE OF WIGHT

NEWPORT

THE QUAY ARTS CENTRE
Sea Street, Newport, PO30 5BD.
Tel: *01983-528825.*

SEELY GALLERY
Lord Louis Library, Newport, PO30 1LL.
Tel: *01983-527655.*

RYDE

RYDE LIBRARY GALLERY
George Street, Ryde, PO33 2JE. **Tel:** *01983-62170.*

OXFORDSHIRE

BAMPTON

BAMPTON ARTS CENTRE
(West Oxfordshire Arts Association), Town Hall, Bampton,
Tel: *01993-850137.*

BANBURY

BANBURY MUSEUM P
8 Horsefair, Banbury, OX16 0AA.
Tel: *01295-259855.*

CHIPPING NORTON

COMPTON CASSEY
Lyneham Farmhouse, Lyneham, Chipping Norton, OX7 6QL. **Tel:** *01993-830886.*
Fax: *01993-830707.*

MANOR HOUSE GALLERY C
West Street, Chipping Norton, OX7 5LH.
Tel: *01608-642620.* **Fax:** *01608-642240.*

THE THEATRE GALLERY
2 Spring Street, Chipping Norton, OX7 4NL.
Tel: *01608-2349.*

HENLEY-ON-THAMES

BOHUN GALLERY C
15 Reading Road, Henley-on-Thames, RG9 1AB. **Tel:** *01491-576228.* **Fax:** *01491-576228.*
Opening times: *Mon-Sat 9.30-5.30 (closed Weds).*
Nearest Station: *Henley.*
Personnel: *Director: Patricia Jordan Evans.*
Bohun Gallery celebrates its 25th Anniversary

in 1988. Monthly exhibitions of contemporary figurative paintings and sculpture.

Artists include: Charles Bartlett, Marj Bond, Mary Fedden, Donald Hamilton Fraser, Elizabeth Frink, Maggi Hambling, John Houston, William Littlejohn, Jennifer McRae, Edward Piper, John Piper, David Remfry, June Redfern, Julian Trevelyan, Louis Turpin. Wendy Ramshaw jewellery each December. Room devoted to original prints. The gallery handles the Estate of Julian Trevelyan etchings.
Services and Facilities:
Art for Offices. Commissioning Service.
Work Stocked and Sold:
Pa. Pr. Sc.

LUXTERS FINE ART
Old Luxters, Hamleden, Henley-on-Thames, RG9 6JW. **Tel:** *01491-638816.*

OXFORD

ASHMOLEAN MUSEUM OF ART AND ARCHAEOLOGY P
Beaumont Street, Oxford, OX1 2PH.
Tel: *01865-278000.* **Fax:** *01865-278018.*
Email *jonathan.moffett@ashmus.ox.ac.uk*
Ws *http://www.ashmol.ox.ac.uk/*
Opening times: *Tue-Sat 10-4, Sun 2-4. Admission Free.*
Nearest Station: *Oxford.*
Personnel: *Acting Director:* Dr P.R.S. Moorey.

Founded 1683. The oldest Museum in the UK and the largest Gallery in Oxfordshire. Houses the University of Oxford's collections of European and Oriental fine and applied art; artifacts from Ancient Egypt, Greece and Rome, and northern Europe from the Dark Ages up to the end of the Middle Ages; and Numismatics. Paintings range from the early Italian Masters through to the Pre-Raphaelites and French Impressionists. Major collections of Majolica, English Ceramics, European Silver. Temporary exhibitions and loan exhibitions. Education Service.
Services and Facilities:
Bookshop. Café. Disabled Access. Friends/Society. Guided Tours. Lectures. Museum Shop. Shop.
Work Stocked and Sold:
Pr.

BRAMPTON ARTS CENTRE
West Oxfordshire Arts Association, Town Hall,

Brampton, Oxford, **Tel:** *01973-85013??.*

CHRIST CHURCH PICTURE GALLERY PS
Christ Church, Oxford, OX1 1DP.
Tel: *01865-276172.* **Fax:** *01865-202429.*
Email *dennis.harrington@christ-church.ox.ac.uk*
Ws *http://www.chch.ox.ac.uk*
Opening times: *Mon-Fri 10.30-1 and 2-4.30, Sun 1-4.30, open until 5.30 Easter to Sept.*
Personnel: Christopher Baker. Brigid Cleaver.
Collection of Old Master paintings and drawings displayed in a modern gallery. Quattrocento Masters; works by Tintoretto, Veronese, the Carracci, Frans Hals and Van Dyck. Changing displays in the print room of works selected from over 2000 Old Master drawings and prints. Special temporary exhibitions. Guided tours each Thursday 2.15-3 and by advance request.
Services and Facilities:
Guided Tours. Museum Shop.

ELIZABETH HARVEY-LEE - ORIGINAL PRINTS c.1490 - c.1940. C
1 West Cottages, Middle Aston Road, North Aston, Oxford, OX6 3QB. **Tel:** *01869-347164.* **Fax:** *01869-347956.*
Opening times: *By appointment.*
Personnel: *Proprietor:* Elizabeth Harvey-Lee.
Private printdealer, offering a large range of fine etchings and engravings. Interesting and unusual old masters and 19th & 20th century British & European artists; both major and minor masters of printmaking from five centuries.

Two fully illustrated new stock catalogues each year (annual subscription £12 or U.S.$25). Previous reference catalogues still available:- LASTING IMPRESSIONS - A Survey of the Techniques & History of Printmaking c.1490-c.1940, (£15 + pp). MISTRESSES OF THE GRAPHIC ARTS - Famous & Forgotten Women Printmakers c.1550-c.1950, (£13.50 + pp). Regular exhibitor at the London Original Print Fair at the Royal Academy and at the June and November Olympia Fine Art & Antiques Fairs.
Services and Facilities:
Lectures.
Work Stocked and Sold:
Pr.
Price range: £100 - £6,000.

MUSEUM OF MODERN ART P
30 Pembroke Street, Oxford, OX1 1BP.

Ab Artist's Books *App Applied Art* *Cer Ceramics* *Cra Crafts*
Dec Decorative *Dr Drawing* *Fur Furniture*

MUSEUM OF MODERN ART P
30 Pembroke Street, Oxford, OX1 1BP.
Tel: Recorded information : 01865-728608,
Office 01865-722733.
Fax: Office: 01865-722573.
Opening times: Tues-Sat 11-6, Thurs 11-9,
Sun 2-6. Closed Monday.
Nearest Station: Oxford.
Personnel: Press & Publicity Officer: Tiffany
Black.
Founded 1965. The Museum of Modern Art is
internationally acclaimed as a centre for the
display of 20th c. visual culture. Its constantly
changing exhibition programme includes
painting, sculpture, photography, film, video,
installations, design, crafts and performance.
Supporting schedule of lectures, guided tours,
debates and an education programme of workshops and other activities. Full disabled access
to all public areas. Hire of gallery space and
museum facilities available (including functions and conferences). Disabled WC. Baby
change unit. Registered Charity No. 313035.
Services and Facilities:
Bookshop. Café. Disabled Access. Friends/Soci-
ety. Gallery space for hire. Guided Tours. Lectures. Restaurant.

MUSEUM OF OXFORD P
St. Aldates, Oxford, **Tel:** 01865-815539.

OXFORD GALLERY C
23 High Street, Oxford. **Tel:** 01865-242731.

STABLES GALLERY
Green College, Woodstock Road, Oxford, OX2
6HG. **Tel:** 01865-274770.

WALLINGFORD

JULIUS GOTTLIEB GALLERY
Carmel College, Wallingford, OX10 8BT.
Tel: 01491-837505.
Fax: 01491-825305.

WALLINGFORD ARTS CENTRE
Kinecroft, Goldsmith Lane, Wallingford,
Tel: 01753-859336.

POOLE

POOLE

POOLE ARTS CENTRE
Kingland Road, Poole BH15 1UG.
Tel: 01202-685222.

WATERFRONT MUSEUM P
High Street, Old Town, Poole BH15 1BW.
Tel: 01202-683138.

SOUTHAMPTON

SOUTHAMPTON

BEATRICE ROYAL ART GALLERY,
Nightingale Avenue, Eastleigh. SO5 3JJ. **Tel:**

THE FIRST GALLERY
1 Burnham Chase, Bitterne, Southampton SO18
5DG. **Tel:** 01703-462723.

ON LINE GALLERY C
76 Bedford Place, Southampton SO15 2DF.
Tel: 01703-330660. **Fax:** 1703-330660.

SWINDON

SWINDON

SWINDON MUSEUM & ART GALLERY P
Bath Road, Swindon SN1 4BA.
Tel: 01793-493181. **Fax:** 01793-541685.

WILTSHIRE

CALNE

BOWOOD HOUSE
Calne, SN11 0LZ. **Tel:** 01249-812102.

DEVIZES

THE GALLERY
Handel House, Sidmouth Street, Devizes, SN8
1JQ. **Tel:** 01672-52860.

GARTON & CO. C
Roundway House, Devizes, SN10 2EG.
Tel: 01380-729624.

LACOCK

FOX TALBOT MUSEUM OF PHOTOGRAPHY PS
Lacock, SN15 2LG.
Tel: 01249-730459. **Fax:** 01249-830472.
Email m.w.gray@bath.ac.uk
Ws http://www.Fox-Talbot.org.uk
Opening times: 11-5 Daily, March-October,
closed Good Friday. 11-4 Weekends only,
November-February. Closed Christmas week.
Personnel: Curator: Michael Grey.
Dedicated to the life and work of William
Henry Fox Talbot (1800-1877) Scientist,
Philosopher, Philologist and Botanist. In 1835
he made, what is now recognised as being the
first photographic negative. The museum is
located within a mediaeval barn at the
entrance to Lacock Abbey Estate.
On the first floor is located the Upper Gallery,
a space dedicated to showing at least 3 exhibi-
tions per year.
Bookshop. Disabled Access. Gallery space for
hire. Lectures. Museum Shop. Parking.
Work Stocked and Sold:
Ph. Pr.
Price range: £5 - £100.

MARLBOROUGH

THE ANTIQUE & BOOK COLLECTOR C
Katharine House, The Parade, Marlborough,
SN8 1NE. **Tel:** 01672-514040.
Opening times: Mon-Sat 9.45-5.30.
Nearest Station: Swindon.

Personnel: Director: Christopher Gange.
Modern British prints and drawings always in
stock:
Eric Gill, David Jones, Laura Knight, Clare
Leighton, F.L. Griggs, Vanessa Bell, H. Gaudi-
er-Brzeska, Graham Sutherland, Elyse Lord,
Orovida Pissarro, Stanley Spencer, Augustus
John, Frank Dobson and others.
Exhibitions twice a year in this field. We also
deal in good quality unusual antiques and
antiquities, as well as fine second hand and
rare books.
Services and Facilities:
Bookshop.
Work Stocked and Sold:
Ab. Dr. Pa. Pr.
Price range: £75 - £2,000.

BAJAZZO GALLERY
8 St. Martins, Marlborough, SN8 1AR.
Tel: 01672-512860.

MARLBOROUGH STUDIO ART GALLERY
4 Hughenden Yard, High Street, Marlborough,
SN8 1LT. **Tel:** 01672-514848.

SALISBURY

THE JERRAM GALLERY
7 St. John Street, Salisbury, SP1 2SB.
Tel: 01722-412310.

MARGARET TURNER GALLERY
15 St. Ann's Street, Salisbury, SP1 2DP.
Tel: 01722-333501.

SALISBURY ARTS CENTRE
Bedwin Street, Salisbury, SP1 3UT.
Tel: 01722-321744.

South East

BRIGHTON & HOVE

BRIGHTON

BARLOW COLLECTION OF CHINESE ART P
University Library, University of Sussex, Falmer,
Brighton, BN1 9QE. **Tel:** 01273-606755.

BRIGHTON MUSEUM AND ART GALLERY PS
Church Street, Brighton, BN1 1UE.
Tel: 01273-603005/202900/290900.
Fax: 01273-779108.
Opening times: Mon, Tues, Thurs-Sat 10-5,
Sun 2-5.
Personnel: Head of Libraries and Museums:
Jessica Rutherford . Exhibitions Section: Nicola
Coleby. Exhibitions Section: Helen Grundy.
Brighton Museum and Art Gallery has an
exciting range of collections of both local and
national importance.
The museum has recently undertaken an
extensive programme of gallery refurbishment.
The collections include arts from Asia, Africa,
the Pacific and the Americas, fashion from the
18th Century to the 1980s 20th Century and

The local history gallery houses a multi-media computer exhibit, "My Brighton", and the archaeology gallery includes a hands-on discovery area. Continual temporary exhibitions. Education Programme.
Services and Facilities:
Café. Friends/Society. Guided Tours. Lectures. Museum Shop. Shop.

FIRST LIGHT
3 Nile Street, Brighton, BN1 1HW.
Tel: *01273-327344.*

GARDNER CENTRE GALLERY C
University of Sussex, Falmer, Brighton, BN1 9RA. **Tel:** *01273-685447.* **Fax:** *01273-678551.*

HUGO BARCLAY C
7 East Street, Brighton, BN1 1HP
Tel: *01273-321694.* **Fax:** *01273-725959.*

PHOENIX GALLERY
10-14 Waterloo Place, Brighton, BN2 2NB.
Tel: *01273-603700.*

PRESTON MANOR P
Preston Park, Brighton, BN1 6SD.
Tel: *01273-292770.*

ROYAL PAVILION P
Pavilion Buildings, Brighton, BN1 1EE.
Tel: *01273-290900.* **Fax:** *01273-292871.*

UNIVERSITY OF BRIGHTON GALLERY
Grand Parade, Brighton, BN2 2JU.
Tel: *01273-643012.*
Fax: *01273-643128.*

HOVE

HOVE MUSEUM & ART GALLERY P
19 New Church Road, Hove, BN3 4AB.
Tel: *01273-290200.*
Fax: *01273-292827.*

KENT

CANTERBURY

DREW GALLERY
16 Best Lane, Canterbury, CT1 2JB.
Tel: *01227-458759.*

THE HERBERT READ GALLERY
KIAD at Canterbury, New Dover Road, Canterbury, CT1 3AN.
Tel: *01227-769371 ext 240.* **Fax:** *01227-451320.*

NEVILL GALLERY C
43 St. Peters Street, Canterbury, CT1 2BG.
Tel: *01303-248403 / 01227-765291.*

ROYAL MUSEUM & ART GALLERY P
High Street, Canterbury, CT1 2JE.
Tel: *01227-452747.*

FOLKESTONE

FOLKESTONE MUSEUM P
2 Grace Hill, Folkestone, CT20 1HD.
Tel: *01303-850123.* **Fax:** *01303-242907.*

METROPOLE ARTS CENTRE PS
The Leas, Folkestone, CT20 2LS.
Tel: *01303-255070.* **Fax:** *01303-244706.*
Opening times: *Apr-Oct: Mon-Sat 10-5, Sun 2.30-5;*
Nov-Mar: Tue-Sat 10-4, Sun 2.30-5.
Personnel: *Director: Ann Fearey.*
10 major exhibitions per year with an emphasis on contemporary painting, photography and sculpture (admission free). The Arts Centre programmes include a Children's Festival (April), Kent Literature Festival (September), Classical Concert Series, Annual Short Story Writing Competition (send SAE for entry form from Feb '98), Art History Lectures and one-off events throughout the year. Sales area and coffee shop. Free parking on The Leas.
Services and Facilities:
Café. Craftshop. Friends/Society. Lectures. Parking.
Work Stocked and Sold:
Cer. Pa.
Price range: £5 - £3,000.

GILLINGHAM

GILLINGHAM LIBRARY GALLERY
High Street, Gillingham, ME7 1BG.
Tel: *01634-281066.* **Fax:** *01634-855814.*

SPACE FRAME GALLERY C
Gillingham Adult Education Centre Green Street, Gillingham, ME7 1XA. **Tel:** *01634-856439.*

MAIDSTONE

BEARSTED GALLERY
The Green, Bearsted, Maidstone, ME14 4DN.
Tel: *01622-744130.*

THE GALLERY
KIAD at Maidstone, Oakwood Park, Maidstone, ME16 8AG. **Tel:** *01622-757286.*
Fax: *01622-692003.*

GRAHAM CLARKE C
White Cottage, Green Lane, Boughton Monchelsea, Maidstone, ME17 4LF.
Tel: *01622 743938.* **Fax:** *01622 747229.*
Opening times: *Open by appointment.*
Personnel: *Dawn Masters.*

Graham Clarke

Graham Clarke's 'Up The Garden Studio' is open by appointment. Graham Clarke the artist, writer and humorist, one of Britain's most popular and best-selling printmakers, has created some five hundred images of English rural life and history, and of the Englishman's view of Europe. He has been widely exhibited in Britain and abroad, examples of his work being held by royal, public and private collections in addition to those hanging on the walls of homes all over the world. His original etch-

ings which are produced entirely by hand using traditional processes in strictly limited editions are available together with his watercolours, books, and greetings cards. Price lists and illustrations of recent images will be sent on request.
Work Stocked and Sold:
Ab. Dr. Pa. Pr.
Price range: £50 - £2,000.

MAIDSTONE LIBRARY GALLERY
St. Faith's Street, Maidstone, ME14 1LH.
Tel: *01622-752344.* **Fax:** *01622-754980.*

RAMSGATE

ADDINGTON STREET STUDIO & GALLERY
49 Addington Street, Ramsgate, CT11 9JJ.
Tel: *084-359 7405.*

RAMSGATE LIBRARY GALLERY
Guildford Lawn, Ramsgate, CT11 9AY.
Tel: *01843-593532.* **Fax:** *01843-293015.*

ROCHESTER

THE GALLERY
KIAD at Rochester, Fort Pitt, Rochester, ME1 1DZ. **Tel:** *01634-830022.*
Fax: *01634-829461.*

MEDWAY TOWNS GALLERIES PS
c/o Head of Arts, Civic Centre, Strood, Rochester, ME20 4AW. **Tel:** *01634-727777.*
Opening times: *Phone for details.*
The new Medway Towns unitary authority comprises the former borough of Gillingham and City of Rochester upon Medway.
A wide-ranging visual arts programme is presented in a variety of places throughout the Medway area. The principal gallery spaces are Gillingham Library Gallery, Lordswood Art Space, Rochester Art Gallery and Strood Library Gallery. Smaller displays are shown in the branch libraries.
The Royal Engineers Museum, Brompton Barracks, and the Guildhall Museum, Rochester, have permanent displays including historical art and occasionally show contemporary art.
A high quality programme of contemporary art residencies, interventions and installations in non-gallery spaces is leading up to the major visual arts Biennale centred on Chatham Historic Dockyard in 2001.
Services and Facilities:
Disabled Access. Lectures.

STROOD LIBRARY GALLERY
32 Bryant Road, Strood, Rochester, ME2 3EP.
Tel: *01634-718161.* **Fax:** *01634-718161.*

SANDWICH

THE HUNT GALLERY C
33 Strand Street, Sandwich, CT13 9DS.
Tel: *01304-612792 or 01227-722287.*
Fax: *01227-721969.*
Opening times: *By appointment.*
Personnel: *Director: Rosemary Hunt.*

We have a permanent but constantly changing exhibition of work by the contemporary English painter Michael John Hunt. Topographical, architectural and interior paintings with an emphasis on accurate draughtsmanship.
Work Stocked and Sold:
Pa.
Price range: £100 - £10,000.

SEVENOAKS

BANK STREET GALLERY
3-5 Bank Street, Sevenoaks, TN13 1UW.
Tel: 01732-458063.

PRATT CONTEMPORARY ART/PRATT EDITIONS C
The Gallery, Ightham, Sevenoaks, TN15 9HH.
Tel: 01732-882326/884417.
Fax: 01732-885502.
Opening times: *Gallery open seven days a week by appointment.*
Nearest Station: *Charing Cross to Sevenoaks or Victoria to Borough Green.*
Personnel: *Directors:* Bernard Pratt, Susan Pratt.

Established 1976. Printers and publishers of original limited edition prints (see Print Publishers and Dealers) working directly with artists: screenprints, etchings, drypoints, woodcuts, monotypes, artists' books.
Proofing and editioning service. Sculpture, Paintings and Drawings by artists represented. Artists include: Ana Maria Pacheco, Seyed Edalatpour, Julian Grater, Akram Rahmanzadeh, Susan Adams, Kristian Krokfors, Mick Rooney RA, Michael Kenny RA, Marcus Rees Roberts, Denise Walker, Leonam Nogueira Fleury, Richard Davies. Print Studios.
Services and Facilities:
Art Consultancy. Commissioning Service. Framing.

Work Stocked and Sold:
Ab. Dr. Pa. Pr. Sc.
Price range: £50 - £150,000.

TUNBRIDGE WELLS

FAIRFAX GALLERY C
23 The Pantiles, Tunbridge Wells, TN2 5TD.
Tel: 01892-525525.
Fax: 01892-525525.
Opening times: *Tue-Sat 10-6, Sun 11-4.*
Personnel: *Directors:* Andrew Scrutton, Lucy Scrutton, Tonia Bates.
The gallery provides a striking juxtaposition of contemporary art with its setting in the heart of the historic Pantiles. Its spacious listed building offers two floors of gallery space the monthly exhibitions of Contemporary British Art.

Both Thematic and solo exhibitions are held, in addition to a large and changing display of works by gallery artists including: David Armitage, David Atkins, Theo Matoff, Charles Newington, Alan Rankle, Alice Scrutton, Helen Sinclair, Sara Wicks.
Services and Facilities:
Art for Offices.
Work Stocked and Sold:
Cer. Dr. Pa. Sc.

NICHOLAS BOWLBY
9 Castle Street, Tunbridge Wells, TN1 1XJ.
Tel: 01892-510880.
Fax: 01892-510880.

SQUEAKY DOOR
1 The Pantiles, Tunbridge Wells, TN2 5TD.
Tel: 01892-518024.

TRINITY GALLERY
Church Road, Tunbridge Wells, TN1 1JP.
Tel: 01892-525111. **Fax:** 01892-525112.

TUNBRIDGE WELLS MUSEUM & ART GALLERY P
Civic Centre, Mount Pleasant, Tunbridge Wells, TN1 1JN.
Tel: 01892-526121 / 547221.
Fax: 01892-534227.

WHITSTABLE

WHITSTABLE MUSEUM & ART GALLERY P
Oxford Street, Whitstable, CT5 1DB.
Tel: 01227-276998.
Fax: 01227-772379.

CHOBHAM

THE BANK GALLERY C
73-75 High Street, Chobham, GU24 8AF.
Tel: 01276-857369.

EAST MOLESEY

THE MOLESEY GALLERY C
46 Walton Road, East Molesey, KT8 0DQ.
Tel: 0181-979 6464 or 0181-941 2706.

FARNHAM

ANDREW LLOYD GALLERY
17 Castle Street, Farnham, GU9 7AJ.
Tel: 01252-724333.

CCA GALLERIES C
13 Lion and Lamb Yard, West Street, Farnham, GU9 7LL. **Tel:** 01252-722231. **Fax:** 01252-733336.

FARNHAM MALTINGS GALLERY
Bridge Square, Farnham, GU9 7QR.
Tel: 01252-713637. **Fax:** 01252-718177.

JAMES HOCKEY GALLERY AND FOYER GALLERY PS
Surrey Institute of Art and Design, Falkner Road, Farnham, GU9 7DS.
Tel: 01252-892668. **Fax:** 01252-892667.
Email ckapteijn@surrart.ac.uk
Ws *http://www.surrart.ac.uk*
Opening times: *Mon-Fri 10-4.30, Sat 10-4, Sun closed.*
Nearest Station: *Farnham.*
Personnel: *Galleries Co-ordinator:* Christine Kapteijn.

THE SURREY INSTITUTE OF ART & DESIGN
The James Hockey Gallery and Foyer Gallery are operated as public galleries. They are committed to the accessibility of the visual arts to all, including those with special needs. The Galleries show a wide range of exhibitions, including art, craft, design and related media, both from Britain and from abroad. They aim to promote work of lasting importance, which will contribute to the public and professional debate. Many of the educational events organised in conjunction with the exhibitions programme, are open to a broad audience from the community, fostering the audience and arts professionals of the future.
Services and Facilities:
Art for Offices. Disabled Access. Guided Tours. Lectures. Parking. Restaurant.

NEW ASHGATE GALLERY C
Wagon Yard, Lower Church Lane, Downing Street, Farnham, GU9 7PS. **Tel:** 01252-713208. **Fax:** 01252-737398.
Opening times: *Mon-Sat 10-5.*
Nearest Station: *Farnham.*
Personnel: *Director:* Susan Szabanowicz. *Manager:* Joanne Barber.

Gla *Glass* **Jew** *Jewellery* **Pa** *Paintings* **Ph** *Photography* **Pr** *Prints*
Sc *Sculpture* **Tx** *Textiles* **Wd** *Wood*

THE ARTWORLD
DIRECTORY 1998/99 **113**

The gallery exhibits work by well-established professional contemporary artists and crafts people, whilst also promoting emerging younger talents.

New Ashgate Gallery

Monthly changing exhibitions, and a large stock of paintings, prints, sculpture, ceramics, jewellery, glass, wood textiles.
Services and Facilities:
Art Consultancy. Art for Offices. Commissioning Service. Craftshop. Disabled Access. Framing. Friends/Society. Lectures. Parking. Restoration.
Work Stocked and Sold:
App. Cer. Cra. Dr. Fur. Gla. Jew. Pa. Pr. Sc. Tx. Wd.
Price range: £30 - £5,000.

GODALMING

GODALMING MUSEUM *P*
109a High Street, Godalming, GU7 1AQ.
Tel: *01483-426510.*

GOMSHALL

GOMSHALL GALLERY *PS*
Station Road, Gomshall, GU5 9LB.
Tel: *01483-203795.* **Fax:** *01483-203282.*
Opening times: *Mon-Sat 10-5.30.*
Nearest Station: *Gomshall (Guildford/Dorking).*
Gomshall Gallery is an Art Gallery selling work of the highest quality. We specialise in hand crafted tables showing the beauty of the patterns of English hardwoods. We also sell handblown glass, ceramics, woodcarvings and a large selection of older pictures with a few contemporary water-colours. We hold a major exhibition each year, in October. The Gallery is situated on the A25, in the beautiful Surrey hills along the banks of the

Tillingbourne, less than an hour's drive from central London.
Services and Facilities:
Craftshop. Parking. Shop.
Work Stocked and Sold:
Cer. Cra. Dec. Fur. Gla. Pa. Wd.
Price range: £20 - £1,500.

GUILDFORD

GUILDFORD HOUSE GALLERY
155 High Street, Guildford, GU1 3AJ.
Tel: *01483-444740.* **Fax:** *01483-444742.*

JONLEIGH GALLERY
The Street, Wonersh, Guildford, GU5 0PF.
Tel: *01483-893177.*

KINGSTON UPON THAMES

THE STANLEY PICKER GALLERY FOR THE ARTS *P*
Kingston University, Middle Mill Island, Knights Park, Kingston upon Thames, KT1 2QJ.
Tel: *0181-547 8074.*
Fax: *0181-547 8068.*

NEW MALDEN

GALLERY FOCUS *C*
Unit 2 Apex Tower, 9 High Street, New Malden, KT3 3DQ.
Tel: *0181-336 0761 / 942 9914.* **Fax:** *0181-336 2674.*

REDHILL

THE CIDER HOUSE GALLERY *C*
Norfolk House, 80 High Street, Bletchingly, Redhill, RH1 4PA.
Tel: *01883-742198.*
Fax: *01883-744014.*

REIGATE

BOURNE GALLERY *C*
31-33 Lesbourne Road, Reigate, RH2 7JS.
Tel: *01737-241614.*
Fax: *01737-223291.*
Opening times: *Tue-Sat 10-5. Closed Mondays & Lunch 1-2pm.*
Nearest Station: *Redhill*
Personnel: *Directors:* John Robertson, Ian Read, Linda Read.
25,000 paintings... that's how many Victorian and traditional pictures we have sold in the past twenty-six years. A remarkable achievement for a gallery tucked away in a quiet side street of a market town.
Today, we continue to stock original works priced from under £200 to over £20,000. If you are looking for a particular artist or would like to join us for a glass of champagne at our next exhibition please write for our brochure now or call in (phone for directions).
Services and Facilities:
Art Consultancy. Art for Offices. Commissioning Service. Restoration. Valuation.
Work Stocked and Sold:
Dr. Pa.
Price range: £150 - £50,000.

RICHMOND

HENRY BOXER
98 Stuart Court, Richmond Hill, Richmond, TW10 6RJ.
Tel: *0181-948 1633.*
Fax: *0181-948 1633.*

PIANO NOBILE *C*
26 Richmond Hill, Richmond, TW10 6QX.
Tel: *0181-940 2435.*

VIRGINIA WATER

THE GALLERY *C*
13 Station Approach, Virginia Water, GU25 4DP.
Tel: *01344-844460.*
Fax: *01344-844785.*
Email *Carpathian@btinternet.com*
Ws *http://www.1.btwebworld.com/carpathian/*
Opening times: *Wed-Fri 10-5, Sat 10-6 or later, Sun 12-6.*
Nearest Station: *Virginia Water.*
Personnel: *Directors:* Bryan Forbes, Richard Dolinski, Andrew Dolinski, Peter Nagy, Nanette Forbes.
We cater for traditional and contemporary art in mixed media. Artists can be seen at work in the gallery and commissions are accepted.
Regular exhi-

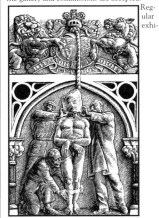

bitions by both local and international artists hosted in a unique atmosphere. The Rostrum Library contains rare and limited edition books, art books and fine prints. A bespoke framing service is available. The gallery boasts a working private press producing our own fine limited edition books. Enquiries for commissions are welcomed.
Services and Facilities:
Art for Offices. Bookshop. Commissioning Service. Disabled Access. Framing. Gallery space for hire. Parking. Restoration. Shop. Workshop Facilities.
Work Stocked and Sold:
Ab. Cer. Dec. Dr. Pa. Ph. Pr. Sc.
Price range: £50 - £6,000.

WEST BYFLEET

T. P. I. GALLERY
32 Station Approach, West Byfleet, KT14 6NF.
Tel: *01932-351733.*
Fax: *01932-341472.*

WOKING

GALLERY KNAPHILL
40 High Street, Knaphill, Woking, GU21 2PY.
Tel: *01483-476230.*

Ab *Artist's Books* **App** *Applied Art* **Cer** *Ceramics* **Cra** *Crafts*
Dec *Decorative* **Dr** *Drawing* **Fur** *Furniture*

EAST SUSSEX

EASTBOURNE

TOWNER ART GALLERY AND LOCAL MUSEUM PS
Manor Gardens, High Street, Old Town, Eastbourne, BN20 8BB. **Tel:** 01323-417961 (Admin.) & 411688 (Info. Service).
Fax: 01323-648182.
Opening times: Tues-Sat 12-5 (closes at 4 Nov-March).
Personnel: Curator: Fiona Robertson. Administrator: Sarah Blessington.
Housed in an elegant 18th Century building, the Towner is set in delightful gardens.
There is a lively and innovative programme of exhibitions from historical to contemporary art in all media, accompanied by education projects. The art collection includes works by: Joseph Wright of Derby, Picasso, Christopher Wood, Frances Hodgkins, Ivon Hitchens, John Virtue, Estelle Thompson and Karen Knorr, a selection of which is always on show and there is a gallery devoted to Eric Ravilious.
The South East Arts Collection of Contemporary Art is housed at the Towner.
Services and Facilities:
Disabled Access. Friends/Society. Gallery space for hire. Guided Tours. Lectures. Shop.

HASSOCKS

DITCHLING MUSEUM P
Church Lane, Ditchling, Hassocks, BN6 8TB. **Tel:** 01273-844744.

HASTINGS

HASTINGS MUSEUM AND ART GALLERY P
Johns Place, Cambridge Road, Hastings, TN38 1ET.
Tel: 01424-721202 / 781155. **Fax:** 01424-781165.

RIVIERA GALLERY
6 Pelham Arcade, Hastings, TN34 3AE.
Tel: 01424-427088.

LEWES

CHARLESTON GALLERY C
Charleston Farmhouse, Nr. Firle, Lewes, BN8 6LL. **Tel:** 01323-811265/811626.
Fax: 01323-811628.

FIRLE PLACE
Lewes, BN8 6LP. **Tel:** 01273-858188.

STAR GALLERY C
Castle Ditch Lane, Lewes, BN7 1YJ.
Tel: 01273-480218. **Fax:** 01273-488241.
Opening times: Mon-Sat 10.30-5.30, closed Suns and Bank Holidays.
Nearest Station: Close to the castle and railway station, just off the High Street.
Personnel: Director: Patricia Cooper.
Popular gallery with a reputation for showing British and International contemporary art. The gallery enthusiastically encourages the work of new artists with talent.

Six major exhibitions a year plus group shows and summer craft exhibition. Artists showing in 1998 include Henrietta Dubrey, Tom Hammick, Mary Fedden, Mick Rooney RA, William Bowyer RA, Michael Cooper,

Anthony Whishaw RA, Harold Mockford, Peter Messer, John Blight, Anne de Geus.
Star Gallery is set on the ground floor of the Victorian Star Brewery building amidst artists' and designers' workshops and studios, many of which are open to the public.
Services and Facilities:
Disabled Access. Framing. Gallery space for hire. Restoration. Workshop Facilities.
Work Stocked and Sold:
Cer. Cra. Dr. Gla. Pa. Pr. Sc.
Price range: £50 - £5,000.

THE WORKSHOP C
164 The High Street, Lewes, BN7 1XU.
Tel: 01273-474207.

RYE

RYE ART GALLERY C
Stormont Studio, Ockman Lane, Rye, TN31 7JY. **Tel:** 01797-223218.
Fax: 01797-225376.

WEST SUSSEX

ARUNDEL

TRINITY ART GALLERY
18B Tarrant Street, Arundel, BN18 9DJ.
Tel: 01903-883689. **Fax:** 01903-884309.

BILLINGSHURST

LANARDS GALLERY C
Okehurst Lane, Billingshurst, RH14 9HR.
Tel: 01403-782692.

CHICHESTER

MITRE GALLERY
Chichester College of Higher Education, College Lane, Chichester, PO19 1PE. **Tel:** 01243-816000. **Fax:** 01243-536011.

PALLANT HOUSE GALLERY TRUST
9 North Pallant, Chichester, PO19 1TJ.
Tel: 01243-774557. **Fax:** 01243-536038.

EAST GRINSTEAD

THE ANTIQUE PRINT SHOP C
11 Middle Row, High Street, East Grinstead, RH19 3AX. **Tel:** 01342-410501.

HAYWARDS HEATH

ASHDOWN GALLERY C
49-53 Sussex Road, Haywards Heath,
Tel: 01444-412827.

HORSHAM

CAUFOLD GALLERY C
Caufold, Horsham, RH **Tel:** 01403-864237.

CHRIST'S HOSPITAL THEATRE FOYER PS
Christ's Hospital, Horsham, RH13 7LE.
Tel: 01403-267005. **Fax:** 01403-211580.
Opening times: During working hours of school and theatre.
Nearest Station: Christ's Hospital.
Personnel: Director of Drama: Duncan Noel-Paton.
The Theatre Foyer of the award-winning, courtyard-style Christ's Hospital Theatre, both the centre of a prestigious drama department and a busy and successful professional touring house for Drama, Dance and Physical Theatre.

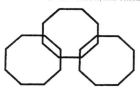

The foyer houses regular visiting exhibitions of paintings and other work that can be hung and welcomes inquiries from artists, preferably accompanied by photographs of recent work. There are no gallery charges. Our objective is to fill our simple white-painted brick walls with live art as a stimulating welcome both to our students and our public audiences and hopefully, sell them as well!
Services and Facilities:
Bar. Disabled Access. Friends/Society. Gallery space for hire. Guided Tours.

HORSHAM ARTS CENTRE PS
North Street, Horsham, RH12 1RL.
Tel: 01403-259708 / 268689. **Fax:** 01403-211502.
Opening times: Mon-Sat 10-7, Sun 5-7.
Nearest Station: Horsham.
Personnel: Visual Art Co-ordinator: Belinda Holden.

HORSHAM
ArtsCENTRE

Contemporary art work shown in two exhibition spaces. The programme is made up of invited artists, touring shows, opens and group proposals. Exhibitions run for 3-4 weeks with 15-20 shows a year. An Education Outreach

Programme linked to the exhibitions runs for children and adults. In 1997 shows included the following artists, Parm Rai, Gerry Walden, Patrick Caulfield, Anthony Moffet, Roland Fiddy Pop Prints, Mark Harris, Geoff Hands, Mike Walker and Liz Allen.
Services and Facilities:
Bar. Café. Commissioning Service. Parking. Workshop Facilities.
Work Stocked and Sold:
Dr. Pa. Ph. Pr.
Price range: £50 - £5,000.

MIDHURST

PETERS BARN GALLERY C
South Ambersham, Midhurst, GU29 0BX.
Tel: *01798-861388.* **Fax:** *01798-861581.*
Opening times: *By appointment Nov-May 1st, May-Oct Tue-Fri 2-6, Sat, Sun & Bank Hols 11-6.*
Nearest Station: *Chichester, Petersfield, Pulborough, Haslemere - then taxi or bus.*
Personnel: *Directors: Gabrielle & Annabel.*
Small very attractive gallery within a large wild garden. Wooded walks by stream and pond. Very peaceful setting. Showing work by known, established and up & coming artists, both inside the barn and out. Deaf interpreting. From the A272 - 3m. East of Midhurst & 3m. West of Petworth, take road opposite the Half Way Bridge Pub. Sign posted to South Ambersham, Graffham & Selham. After 1 mile take first right to South Ambersham & Selham Church. Continue 1 mile, turn right at T-junction in South Ambersham. Peters Barn is 200 yards on the left. From Chichester take A286. Turn right 1/2m out of Cocking to Heyshoff & Graffham. 2m on turn left to Ambersham at the cross roads. Peters Barn on left after 1 mile.
Services and Facilities:
Disabled Access. Parking.
Work Stocked and Sold:
Ab. App. Cer. Dr. Gla. Jew. Pa. Pr. Sc.
Price range: £10 - £7,000.

WORTHING

WORTHING MUSEUM & ART GALLERY P
Chapel Road, Worthing, BN11 1HP. **Tel:**
10903-236552 ext 2526. **Fax:** *01903-236552.*

Eastern

BEDFORDSHIRE

BEDFORD

BEDFORD CENTRAL LIBRARY GALLERY
Harpur Street, Bedford, MK40 1PG.
Tel: *01234-350931.*

BEDFORD MUSEUM P
Castle Lane, Bedford, MK40 3XD. **Tel:** *01234-353323.* **Fax:** *01234-214599.*

CECIL HIGGINS ART GALLERY AND MUSEUM P
Castle Close, Castle Lane, Bedford, MK40 3RP.
Tel: *01234-211222.* **Fax:** *01234-327149.*
Opening times: *Tue-Sat 11-5, Sun 2-5.*
Nearest Station: *Midland Road (Thameslink).*
Personnel: *Curator: Amanda Beresford.*
Housed in an elegantly converted and extended Victorian Mansion, original home of the Higgins family of wealthy Bedford brewers, is one of the most outstanding fine and decorative art collections outside London. Offering: British and European watercolours from 18th-20thC and International prints from Impressionism to present. Includes works by Rembrandt, Turner, Blake, Cotman, Rossetti, Burne-Jones, Whistler, Renoir, Picasso, Dali, Moore, Warhol, Hockney.

Exhibitions changes regularly; ceramics and glass from Renaissance to 20th century; Authentically reconstructed Victorian room settings in the Victorian Mansion; The William Burges room: a complete Arts and Crafts experience. Free admission, but variable charges for guided tours etc.
Services and Facilities:
Disabled Access. Friends/Society. Guided Tours. Lectures. Museum Shop.
Work Stocked and Sold:
Jew. Pr.

THE GATEHOUSE
Foster Hill Road, Bedford, MK41 7TD.
Tel: *01234-355870.*

BIGGLESWADE

FAIRFIELD GALLERY
Fairfield House, Biggleswade, SG18 0AA.
Tel: *01767-312176.*

BROMHAM

BROMHAM MILL ART GALLERY PS
Bromham Mill, Bridge End, Bromham, MK43 8LP. **Tel:** *01234-824330.* **Fax:** *01234-228315.*
Opening times: *Mar-Oct, Wed-Sun 12-4. Sun and Bank Holidays 10.30-5.*
Nearest Station: *Midland Road, Bedford*
Changing programme of contemporary art and craft work, including much textile work. '98 Crafts Council new glass exhibition, innovative materials from schools loan collection including Michael Brennard - wood, ceramics including studio and functional work and The Book Project.
Café. Craftshop. Guided Tours. Parking. Shop.
App. Cer. Cra. Dr. Fur. Gla. Jew. Pa. Ph. Sc. Tx. Wd.
Price range: £5 - £5,000.

LEIGHTON BUZZARD

LEIGHTON BUZZARD THEATRE
Lake Street, Leighton Buzzard, LU7 8RX.
Tel: *01525-371788.*

LUTON

33 ARTS CENTRE GALLERY
33-35 Guildford Street, Luton, LU1 2NQ.
Tel: *01582-419584.*

THE GALLERY, LUTON CENTRAL LIBRARY
St. George's Square, Luton, LU1 2NG.
Tel: *01582-30161.*
Fax: *01582-24638.*

LUTON MUSEUM AND ART GALLERY P
Wardown Park, Luton,
Tel: *01582-746722.*

CAMBRIDGESHIRE

BOURN

WYSING ARTS P
Fox Road, Bourn, CB3 7TX.
Tel: *01954-718881.*
Fax: *01954-718500.*
Email *info@wysing.demon.co.uk*
Ws *http://www.wysing.demon.co.uk*
Opening times: *7 days a week. Phone for details.*
Nearest Station: *Cambridge/Royston.*
Personnel: *Director: Trystan Hawkins.*
Wysing Arts is based nine miles south-west of Cambridge. Resources - 22 studios, large performance studio, fully equipped darkroom, ceramics studio, café and meeting rooms. On-site residential accommodation. Situated in eleven acres of open farm land, comprising three fields, Wysing commissions/exhibits sculpture and 'site specific' sculpture, alongside a programme of exhibitions in our spacious Gallery.
Open throughout the year please phone for details of our programme of exhibitions, workshops and space hire information. Four dead-

Ab Artist's Books **App** *Applied Art* **Cer** *Ceramics* **Cra** *Crafts*
Dec *Decorative* **Dr** *Drawing* **Fur** *Furniture*

Commissions for sculpture advertised in arts press or send details to join our mailing list. Charity Number 1039555.

Services and Facilities:
Commissioning Service. Disabled Access. Gallery space for hire. Guided Tours. Parking. Workshop Facilities.

CAMBRIDGE

ARCHITECTURE GALLERY
6 Kings Parade, Cambridge, **Tel:** *01223-324157.*

BROUGHTON HOUSE GALLERY *C*
98 King Street, Cambridge, CB1 1LN.
Tel: *01223-314960.* **Fax:** *01223-314960.*
Opening times: *Mar-Dec Tues-Sat 10.30-5.30.*
Personnel: *Director:* Rosemary Davidson.

This modern gallery has been built into the ground floor of an 18th century house, opening onto a walled garden, in the centre of Cambridge.

There are monthly exhibitions from March to December, each lasting three weeks (both one-man/woman and theme shows).

Contemporary paintings and prints, also sculpture, from British and European, artists. A wide variety of paintings and prints always in stock (including Gwen Raverat wood engravings). Friends of the Broughton House Gallery scheme. Consultancy for private and business clients.

Services and Facilities:
Art Consultancy. Disabled Access. Friends/Society.

Work Stocked and Sold:
Pa. Pr. Sc.

CAMBRIDGE ARTS *C*
Willowhurst, Station Road, Fordham, Nr. Ely, Cambridge, CM7 5LW. **Tel:** *01638-721884.*
Fax: *01638-721885.*

CAMBRIDGE CONTEMPORARY ART *C*
6 Trinity Street, Cambridge, CB2 1SU.
Tel: *01223-324222.* **Fax:** *01223-315606.*
Email *cam.cont.art@dial.pipex.com*
Opening times: *Mon-Sat 9-5.30.*
Nearest Station: *Cambridge.*
Personnel: *Director:* Denise Collins. *Gallery Manager:* Rosy Gounaris.
Situated just a stone's throw from King's College in the heart of this beautiful and historic city, Cambridge Contemporary Art is the largest commercial art gallery in Cambridge, specialising in paintings, sculptures, crafts, master graphics and original prints.

Since opening in 1990 the gallery has gained a reputation for the extensive range of its high quality exhibits and innovative exhibition programme. Artists include: Karolina Larusdottir, Charlotte Cornish, Anita Klein, Jonathon Clarke, Stanley Dove, Eoghan Bridge, Aliisa Spence, Jane Poulton, Donald Hamilton Fraser, Dorothy Stirling, June Carey, Marj Bond, Sheila McInnes, Elisabeth Frink, Bert Irvin and John Piper.

Services and Facilities:
Art Consultancy. Art for Offices. Commissioning Service. Craftshop. Disabled Access. Framing. Friends/Society. Restoration. Shop.

Work Stocked and Sold:
Ab. App. Cer. Cra. Dec. Fur. Gla. Pa. Pr. Sc. Tx. Wd.
Price range: £50 - £5,000.

CAMBRIDGE DARKROOM
Dales Brewery, Gwydir Street, Cambridge, CB1 2LJ. **Tel:** *01223-312188 (01223-566725, 01223-350725).*

CONSERVATORY GALLERY *C*
6 Hills Avenue, Cambridge, CB1 4XA.
Tel: *01233-211311.* **Fax:** *01233-214588.*

CURWEN CHILFORD PRINTS *C*
Chilford Hall, Linton, Cambridge, CB1 6LE.
Tel: *01223-893544.* **Fax:** *01223-893544.*

Opening times: *Mon-Fri 9-5.30.*
Nearest Station: *Cambridge.*
Personnel: *Directors:* Stanley Jones, Sam Alper, Simon Alper, Mary Grace.
Fine art printing studio established in 1958 by the Curwen Press for the production of limited edition artists' prints.
Specialists in continuous tone lithography with facilities for direct and offset printing from stone and plate.
Silkscreen printer for hand drawn and photographic process work. Technical expertise offered to painters and sculptors in all forms of experimental printmaking.
Publishers of limited edition prints. Recent artists who have worked at the studio include: Gillian Ayres, Prunella Clough, Bernard Dunstan, Kitaj, Eduardo Paolozzi, Ken Kiff, Paul Hogarth, Chloe Cheese, John Hoyland, Albert Irvin, Ana Maria Pacheco, Josef Herman, Patrick Heron, Jane Corsellis and Richard Deacon.

Services and Facilities:
Art for Offices. Café. Commissioning Service. Disabled Access. Parking.
Work Stocked and Sold:
Pr. Sc.
Price range: £65 - £2,000.

FITZWILLIAM MUSEUM *P*
Trumpington Street, Cambridge, CB2 1RB.
Tel: *01223-332900.* **Fax:** *01223-332923.*
Opening times: *Tues-Sat 10-5; Sun 2.15-5. Closed Mon (except Easter Mon, Spring and Summer Bank Hols). Closed Good Friday, May Day Holiday and 24 Dec-1Jan inclusive.*
Personnel: *Director:* Duncan Robinson. *Education Officer:* Frances Sword.

Antiquities from Egypt, Greece, Rome, refurbished Western Asiatic displays; Applied arts including: ceramics, furniture, textiles; coins and medals; manuscripts and rare printed books; paintings, including masterpieces by Titian, Veronese, Brueghel, Rubens, Canaletto, Monet, Renoir, Cézanne; drawing, prints.

Varied temporary exhibition programme, concerts, gallery talks. Disabled Access, preferably by arrangement. Guided tours Sun 2.30 and by arrangement. Admission Free.

Services and Facilities:
Café. Disabled Access. Friends/Society. Guided Tours. Lectures. Museum Shop. Shop.

THE GALLERY
23 High Street, Fen Ditton, Cambridge, CB5 8ST.
Tel: *012205-5264.*

THE HEFFER GALLERY C
19 Sidney Street, Cambridge, CB2 3HL.
Tel: *01223-568491.* **Fax:** *01223-568410.*
Email *heffers@heffers.co.uk*
Ws *http://www.heffers.co.uk*
Opening times: *Mon-Sat 9-5.30.*
Nearest Station: *Cambridge.*
Personnel: *Gallery Manager:* Christopher
Witchall.
The Heffer Gallery is an elegant glass roofed
exhibition area, situated on the fourth floor of
Heffers, Sidney Street store in the heart of
Cambridge.
The gallery has gained a reputation over many
years for showing popular, interesting and
innovative art, and we continue to offer an
exciting programme of exhibitions representing a broad spectrum of lively contemporary
art, from the traditional to the new, more challenging work.
A long tradition of showing work by local
artists remains an important part of our programme, drawing upon the wealth of artistic
talent around Cambridge and East Anglia.
Services and Facilities:
Framing. Shop.
Work Stocked and Sold:
Dr. Pa. Ph. Pr.
Price range: £50 - £5,000.

KETTLE'S YARD
Castle Street, Cambridge, CB3 0AQ.
Tel: *01223-352124.*
Fax: *01223-324377.*

LYNNE STROVER GALLERY C
*23 High Street, Fen Ditton, Cambridge, CB5
8ST.* **Tel:** *01223-295264.*
Fax: *01223-295264.*

THE PETER MCMILLEN GALLERY
168 Mill Road, Cambridge, **Tel:** *01223-
242037.* **Fax:** *01223-211275.*

PRIMAVERA C
10 King's Parade, Cambridge, CB2 1SJ.
Tel: *01223-357708.* **Fax:** *01223-576920.*
Opening times: *Mon-Sat 9.30-5.30.*
Personnel: *Director:* Ronald Pile.
Situated opposite Kings College in Cambridge,
Primavera has long been associated with the
best in British craft and design. Ceramics
(both functional and "one-off"), furniture and
paintings always on show in the basement galleries, alongside changing exhibitions throughout the year. Studio glass, metalwork and textiles on the ground floor, which also features
an extensive range of contemporary British
jewellery.
Services and Facilities:
Commissioning Service. Craftshop. Shop.
Work Stocked and Sold:
*App. Cer. Cra. Fur. Gla. Jew. Pa. Sc.
Tx. Wd.*
Price range: £10 - £5,000.

ELY

KERAMIKOS
37 Mildenhall, Fordham, Ely, CB7 5NW.
Tel: *01638-721371.* **Fax:** *01638-720375.*

THE STAINED GLASS MUSEUM P
*North Triforium, Ely Cathedral, Ely, CB7
4DN.* **Tel:** *01353-667735.* **Fax:** *01223-
327367.*

PETERBOROUGH

ANNAKIN FINE ARTS
Owlburn, Church Lane, Helpston, Peterborough,
Tel: *01733-252555.*

**PETERBOROUGH MUSEUM & ART
GALLERY** P
Priestgate, Peterborough, PE1 1LF.
Tel: *01733-343329.*

YARROW GALLERY
*Art Department, Oundle School, Glapthorn
Road, Oundle, Peterborough, PE8 4EN.*
Tel: *01832-274034.*
Fax: *01832-274034.*
Opening times: *Mon-Fri 10.30-1 & 2.30-5,
Sun 2.30-5.*
Nearest Station: *Peterborough.*
Personnel: *Director:* Roger Page.
School-sponsored exhibitions and available for
hire. See Gallery Space for Hire.
Services and Facilities:
Gallery space for hire.

ESSEX

BRENTWOOD

BRANDLER GALLERIES C
1 Coptfold Road, Brentwood, CM14 4BM.
Tel: *01277-222269.*
Fax: *01277-222786.*
Email *art.british@dial.pipex.com*
Ws *http://www.brandler-galleries.com*
Opening times: *Tues-Sat 10-5.30.*
Nearest Station: *Brentwood 400 yds, Shenfield 1 mile.*
Personnel: *Director:* John Brandler. Linda
Rodrigues.

Brandler Galleries

A friendly gallery just 2 miles from exit 28 on
the M25 with free parking. A wide selection
of prints and paintings by British old and modern masters.
As we purchase virtually all our stock we have
to choose the best examples. Without the
London overheads our clients know they get a
much better deal on the same artists, without
having to fight to get into London with all its
problems. We are happy to send photographs
or E-Mail images before your trip. Clients
include banks, insurance companies and collectors all wanting the best art at realistic
prices.
Services and Facilities:
*Art Consultancy. Art for Offices. Commissioning
Service. Framing. Parking. Restoration. Valuation.*
Work Stocked and Sold:
Cer. Dr. Pa. Pr. Sc.
Price range: £50 - £65,000.

BUCKHURST HILL

REYNOLDS FINE ART C
59 Queens Road, Buckhurst Hill, IG9 5BU.
Tel: *0181-504 2244.*
Opening times: *Tues-Sat 10-6.*
Nearest Station: *Buckhurst Hill.*
Personnel: *Proprietor:* Michael R. Reynolds.
Small, friendly suburban gallery offering a varied selection of modern British and contemporary art. Established and new artists.
Services and Facilities:
Restoration.
Work Stocked and Sold:
Dr. Pa.
Price range: £150 - £5,000.

CHELMSFORD

**CHELMSFORD AND ESSEX REGIMENTAL
MUSEUMS** P
*Oaklands Park, Moulsham Street, Chelmsford,
CM2 9AQ.* **Tel:** *01245-353066.*

CHELMSFORD MUSEUM P
Old Cemetry Lodge, 1 Writtle Road, Chelmsford,
Tel: *01245-281660.*

COGGESHALL

ADAM GALLERY
7 East Street, Coggeshall, CO6 1SH.
Tel: *01376-62803.*

COLCHESTER

CHAPPEL GALLERIES
*15 Colchester Road, Chappel, Colchester, CO6
2DE.*
Tel: *01206-240326.*

DRAGONFLY
*The Old Bakery, Fordstreet, Aldham, Colchester,
CO6 3PH.* **Tel:** *01206-241043.*

FIRSTSITE C
*The Minories, 74 High Street, Colchester, CO1
1UE.*
Tel: *01206-577067.*
Fax: *01206-577161.*

PRINTWORKS C
45 Sir Isaac's Walk, Colchester, CO1 1JJ.
Tel: *01206-562049.*

SIR ALFRED MUNNINGS ART MUSEUM P
Castle House, Dedham, Colchester, CO7 6AZ.
Tel: *01206-322127.* **Fax:** *01206-322127.*
Opening times: *1998 - 3 May - 4 Oct, Wed,
Sun, Bank Holiday Mons. Also Thurs & Sats
Aug 2-5.*
Nearest Station: *Colchester, Manningtree,
Ipswich.*
Personnel: *Chairman of Trustees:* Mr J. D.
Short. *Administrator:* Mrs C. Woodage.
The home, studios and grounds where Sir
Alfred Munnings, KCVO, President of the
Royal Academy 1944-1949, lived and painted
for 40 years.
A large collection of his paintings and other
works. Castle House, lying east of Dedham

Ab *Artist's Books* **App** *Applied Art* **Cer** *Ceramics* **Cra** *Crafts*
Dec *Decorative* **Dr** *Drawing* **Fur** *Furniture*

Village is 6 miles from Colchester and approximately 1 mile from village centre on corner of East Lane, Castle Hill.
Special Exhibition for 1998 season: 29 World War I Pictures on loan from The Canadian War Museum, Ottawa. Greetings cards. Postcards and prints, books.
Services and Facilities:
Disabled Access. Museum Shop. Parking.
Work Stocked and Sold:
Ab. Pr.

UNIVERSITY OF ESSEX GALLERY P
Wivenhoe Park, Colchester, CO4 3SQ.
Tel: *01206-284100 / 873333 / 872074 / 873260.* **Fax:** *01206-873598 / 873702.*

HARLOW

ADDISON WESLEY LONGMAN
Edinburgh Gate, Harlow, CM20 2JE.
Tel: *01279-623260.*

JOHN GRAHAM FINE ARTS
19 The Rows, Stonecross, Harlow, CM20 1DD.
Tel: *01279-26672.*

SAFFRON WALDEN

THE CHURCH STREET GALLERY
17 Church Street, Saffron Walden,
Tel: *01799-24422.*

FRY PUBLIC ART GALLERY
Bridge End Gardens, Castle Street, Saffron Walden, CB10 1BD.
Tel: *01799-513779.*

NEWPORT GALLERY
High Street, Newport, Saffron Walden, CB11 3QZ. **Tel:** *01799-40623.*

SAFFRON WALDEN MUSEUM P
Museum Street, Saffron Walden, CB10 1LL.
Tel: *01799-22494.*

SOUTHEND-ON-SEA

FOCAL POINT GALLERY P
Southend Central Library, Victoria Avenue, Southend-on-Sea, SS2 6EX.
Tel: *01702-612621 ext 207.* **Fax:** *01702-469241.*

WESTCLIFF-ON-SEA

BEECROFT ART GALLERY PS
Station Road, Westcliff-on-Sea, SS0 7RA.
Tel: *01702-347418.*
Opening times: *Tues-Sat 9.30-5 (closed between 1-2).*
Nearest Station: *Westcliff (Fenchurch Street line).*
Personnel: *Curator: Arthur C Wright AMA. Assistant Keeper of Art: Miss C. Furlong.*
The gallery has some 2,000 works in its permanent collections, including works by Constable, Molenaer, Bright, Epstein, Weight, Lear and Seago. A selection is normally on view. There is a programme of temporary

exhibitions with many works for sale at reasonable prices.
Art groups and classes meet at the Beecroft on a regular basis and rooms and galleries may be hired for exhibitions, tutorial, etc.
Home of the Annual Essex Open Exhibition.
Services and Facilities:
Friends/Society. Gallery space for hire.

HERTFORDSHIRE

BARNET

CONTEMPORARY CERAMICS C
Whalebones, Wood Street, Barnet, EN5 48Z.
Tel: *0181-449 5288.*

OLD BULL ARTS CENTRE
68 High Street, Barnet, EN5 5SJ.
Tel: *0181-449 5189.*

BERKHAMSTED

DOWER HOUSE GALLERY
108 High Street, Berkhamsted, HP4 2BL.
Tel: *014427-2562.*

HITCHIN

THE GROSVENOR ART GALLERY
11 Bridge Street, Hitchin, **Tel:** *01462-33663.*

HITCHIN MUSEUM & ART GALLERY P
Paynes Park, Hitchin, SG5 1EQ.
Tel: *01462-434476.*

LETCHWORTH

LETCHWORTH MUSEUM AND ART GALLERY P
Broadway, Letchworth, SG6 3PF.
Tel: *01462-685647.*

VILAS FINE ARTS C
8-10 Leys Avenue, Letchworth, SG6 3EU.
Tel: *01462-677455.* **Fax:** *01462-677455.*

MUCH HADHAM

THE HENRY MOORE FOUNDATION
Dane Tree House, Perry Green, Much Hadham, SG10 6EE. **Tel:** *01279-843333.* **Fax:** *01279-843647.*

ROYSTON

THE MALTINGS STUDIO
99 North End, Meldreth, Royston, SG8 6NY.
Tel: *01763-261615.*

MANOR GALLERY
13 Angel Pavement, Royston, SG8 9AS.
Tel: *01763-45518.*

SAWBRIDGEWORTH

THE GOWAN GALLERY C
3 Bell Street, Sawbridgeworth, CM21 9AR.
Tel: *01279-600004.*

ST. ALBANS

ARTE - GALLERY
26 George Street, St. Albans **Tel:** *01920-469620.*

MARGARET HARVEY GALLERY PS
University of Hertfordshire, 7 Hatfield Road, St. Albans, AL1 3RS. **Tel:** *01707-285376.*
Fax: *01707-285312.*
Email *m.shaul@herts.ac.uk*
Ws *http://www.herts.ac.uk/artdes/*
Opening times: *Wed-Sat 11-5.*
Nearest Station: *St. Albans.*
Personnel: *Exhibitions Officer: M. Shaul.*

MARGARET HARVEY
GALLERY

Purpose built gallery showcasing work by artists, craftspeople and designers of a national and international standard. Operated by University of Herts Faculty of Art & Design.
Services and Facilities:
Café. Commissioning Service. Gallery space for hire. Lectures.
Work Stocked and Sold:
Ab. App. Cer. Cra. Dec. Dr. Pa. Ph.

MUSEUM OF ST. ALBANS P
Hatfield Road, St. Albans, AL1 3RR.
Tel: *01727-56679.*

STEVENAGE

BOXFIELD GALLERY PS
Stevenage Arts & Leisure Centre, Stevenage, SG1 1LZ. **Tel:** *01438-766644.* **Fax:** *01438-766675.*
Opening times: *Mon-Sun 9.30-10.*
Personnel: *Director: George Cass.*
Boxfield Gallery, run by contract to Stevenage Borough Council, runs a varied programme of temporary exhibitions. Duration one month each, about four a year are contemporary shows, the remainder are mixed theme exhibitions. The gallery aims to increase public awareness and appreciation of art in general and to make the art gallery a welcoming and popular place. Gallery space 36 linear metres, height 3 metres. Gallery pays for preview, and hire cost. At present work sold not a priority. Craft Cabinets.
Services and Facilities:
Bar. Café. Craftshop. Disabled Access. Gallery space for hire. Restaurant.
Work Stocked and Sold:
Cer. Wd.

WARE

LOFT GALLERY
63 Cappell Lane, Stanstead Abbotts, Ware, SG12 8BX. **Tel:** *01920-870013.*

TRADING PLACES GALLERY
11 New Road, Ware, SG12 7BS.
Tel: *01920-469620.* **Fax:** *01920-463003.*

Gla Glass *Jew* Jewellery *Pa* Paintings *Ph* Photography *Pr* Prints
Sc Sculpture *Tx* Textiles *Wd* Wood

WATFORD

JOHN HARSFIELD
25 Valley Rise, Watford,
WD2 7EY.
Tel: 01923-675671/463123/226642.

WATFORD MUSEUM P
194 High Street, Watford, WD1 2HG.
Tel: 01923-32297.

LINCOLNSHIRE

BOSTON

BLACKFRIARS ART CENTRE
Spain Lane, Boston, PE21 6HP.
Tel: 01205-363108.

THE GUILDHALL MUSEUM P
South Street, Boston, PE21 6HT.
Tel: 01205-365954.

GAINSBOROUGH

GAINSBOROUGH OLD HALL P
Parnell Street, Gainsborough, DN21 2NB.
Tel: 01427-612669. **Fax:** 01427-612779.

LINCOLN

DODDINGTON HALL P
Doddington, Lincoln, LN6 4RU.
Tel: 01522-694308. **Fax:** 01522-682584.

USHER GALLERY PS
Lindum Road, Lincoln, LN2 1NN. **Tel:** 01522-527980. **Fax:** 01522-560165.
Opening times: Mon-Sat 10-5.30, Sun 2.30-5. Admission charge.
Nearest Station: Lincoln.
Personnel: Curator and Manager: Richard H. Wood. Assistant Curator: Rosalyn Thomas. Assistant Curator: Judith Robinson. Exhibitions Officer & Education Officer: Janita Elton & Pauline Roberts.
This regional gallery houses collections of clocks and watches, miniatures, ceramics, silver and English glass. There are important collections of paintings by Peter de Wint (1784-1849), topographical paintings of Lincolnshire, the Alfred Lord Tennyson collection and English coins. As well as 20th c. works there is an inspiring programme of special exhibitions. The Gallery organises various educational activities and workshops based on the permanent collections and the temporary exhibitions programme. Further details are available from the Education Officer. Baby Changing facilities, Café (light refreshments). Founded 1927.
Services and Facilities:
Café. Disabled Access. Friends/Society. Guided Tours. Shop.

SPALDING

WOODBINE COTTAGE GALLERY C
Back Bank, Whaplode Drove, Spalding, PE12 0TT. **Tel:** 01406-330693.

Opening times: Sat, Sun, Mon 10.30-5.30 or by appt.
Nearest Station: Spalding or Peterborough.
Personnel: Artist/Gallery Owner: Liz Yorath. Artist/Gallery Owner: Rowan Yorath.

Woodbine Cottage Gallery is an old Fenland cottage, which until its renovation and conservation to a gallery had stood empty for sixteen years. It is situated in the village of Whaplode Drove, 10 miles from Spalding and 14 miles from Peterborough, in the South Holland area of Lincolnshire.
Owned and run by Liz and Rowen Yorath, the gallery features changing exhibitions of high quality contemporary art at accessible prices. The wide range of media shown include wood engraving, etching, ceramics, bronze and glass sculptures, painting and drawing.
For details of current and forthcoming exhibitions please telephone. Limited disabled access.
Services and Facilities:
Art for Offices. Commissioning Service. Parking.
Work Stocked and Sold:
Cer. Dr. Pa. Ph. Pr. Sc.
Price range: £50 - £1,000.

STAMFORD

BURGHLEY HOUSE
Stamford, PE9 3JY.
Tel: 01780-65262.

TORKINGTON GALLERY
38 St. Peters Street, Stamford, PE9 2PF.
Tel: 01780-62281.

NORTH LINCOLNSHIRE

SCUNTHORPE

NORMANBY HALL COUNTRY PARK
Normanby, Scunthorpe, DN15 9HU.
Tel: 01724-720226.

SCUNTHORPE MUSEUM & ART GALLERY P
Oswald Road, Scunthorpe, DN15 7BD.
Tel: 01724-843533.

NORFOLK

AYLSHAM

RED LION GALLERY
Holman House, Market Place, Aylsham, NR11 6EJ. **Tel:** 0263-732115. **Fax:** 0263-732115.

CASTLE ACRE

THE OLD RED LION
Bailey Street, Castle Acre, PE32 2AG.
Tel: 017605-557.

DISS

PALGRAVE GALLERY
The Old Rectory, Rose Lane, Palgrave, Diss, IP22 1AP. **Tel:** 01379-652056.

GORLESTON ON SEA

HARDIES GALLERY AND ART SHOP
205/6 High Street, Gorleston on Sea, NR31 6RR. **Tel:** 01493-668003.

GREAT YARMOUTH

MUSEUMS GALLERIES P
Central Library, Tolhouse Street, Great Yarmouth, NR30 2SH. **Tel:** 01493-858900 / 745526. **Fax:** 01493-745459.

HUNSTANTON

RINGSTEAD GALLERY
Ringstead, Hunstanton, PE36 5JZ.
Tel: 01485-525316.

KING'S LYNN

DEEPDALE EXHIBITIONS
The Old Plough House,
Burnham, Deepdale, Nr Brancaster, King's Lynn, PE31 8DD. **Tel:** 01485-210801.

GALERIA REFLEXIONS
56 Norfolk Street, King's Lynn, PE30 1AG.
Tel: 01553-760766.

HOUGHTON HALL
Estate Office, Houghton, King's Lynn, PE31 6UE. **Tel:** 01485-528569.

KING'S LYNN ARTS CENTRE PS
27-29 King Street, King's Lynn, PE30 1HA.
Tel: 01553-774725. **Fax:** 01553-770591.
Opening times: Nov 1-Mar 31, Tues-Sat 11-4. Apr 1-Oct 31, 10-5.
Personnel: Visual Arts Manager: Liz Falconbridge.
Founded 1963. Varied programme of contemporary exhibitions in three gallery spaces. A regular series of crafts showcases, annual Eastern Open exhibition, and Christmas Crafts Fair, range of workshops and residencies, plus children's Art Club. Prospective candidates for subsidised exhibitions are encouraged to submit proposals. Arts Centre brochure avail-

Ab Artist's Books **App** Applied Art **Cer** Ceramics **Cra** Crafts
Dec Decorative **Dr** Drawing **Fur** Furniture

able. Free admission. Gardens and grounds.
Services and Facilities:
*Café. Disabled Access. Gallery space for hire.
Restaurant. Workshop Facilities.*
Work Stocked and Sold:
App. Cer. Cra. Dec. Dr. Jew. Pa. Sc. Tx.
Wd.
Price range: £10 - £5,000.

MUNDESLEY

ST. BRANNOCK'S GALLERY C
7 Cromer Road, Mundesley, NR11 8BE.
Tel: *01263-722622.* **Fax:** *01692-650330.*
Opening times: *Suns & Mons 11-8 or by
appointment.*
Nearest Station: *North Walsham.*
Personnel: *Curator:* Jonathan Plumb.
St. Brannock's Gallery has been established
(since 1996) to exhibit and promote the Barrington Farm artists, from Walcott, Norfolk,
all of whom are adults with learning difficul-
ties.

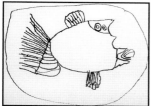

We are the only gallery in East Anglia to offer
art works by self taught/outsider artists, either
those from Barrington or otherwise.
Services and Facilities:
Gallery space for hire. Parking.
Work Stocked and Sold:
Cer. Cra. Dr. Fur. Pa. Pr. Sc. Tx.
Price range: £1,50 - £400.

NORWICH

CONTACT GALLERY C
56 St. Benedicts Street, Norwich, NR2 4AR.
Tel: *01603-760219.*

FREDERICK GALLERY C
*The Raveningham Centre, Beccles Road, Raven-
ingham, Norwich, NR14 6NU.*
Tel: *01508-548688.* **Fax:** *01508-548958.*
Opening times: *Mon-Sun 11-5. Closed
Tuesdays.*
Personnel: *Directors:* Adrian Woodard,
Janet Woodard.
Rural location on the Norfolk/Suffolk border 3
miles north of Beccles off the B1140, close to
A143/A146.
The Gallery specialises in contemporary East
Anglian artists and sculptors with over 200
exhibits permanently on display. Wide range
of styles from traditional to modern impres-
sionism and abstract. Regular special exhibi-
tions.
Gallery artists include John Burman, Paul Dar-
ley, Margaret Glass, Andrew King, Raymond
Leech, Ross Loveday, John Patchett, David
Quantrill, Tony Stocker, Kevin

Thompson, Adrian Woodard and sculptors
Andrew Campbell, Louise Richardson, Ann
Richardson and Madeline Smith. Studio
Pottery.
Services and Facilities:
*Commissioning Service. Disabled Access. Park-
ing.*
Work Stocked and Sold:
Cer. Dr. Pa. Sc. Wd.
Price range: £25 - £3,000.

JUDY HINES PAINTINGS
*Coach House, Townhouse Road, Old Costessey,
Norwich, NR8 5BX.*
Tel: *01603-742977/0378-281821.*

THE KING OF HEARTS
13-15 Fye Bridge Street, Norwich, NR3 1LJ.
Tel: *01603-766129.*

MANDELL'S GALLERY
Elm Hill, Norwich, NR3 1HN.
Tel: *01603-629180.*

NORWICH CASTLE MUSEUM P
Norwich, NR1 3JU. **Tel:** *01603-493624.*
Fax: *01603-765651.*
Opening times: *Mon-Sat 10-5, Sun 2-5.*
Nearest Station: *Thorpe, Norwich.*
Personnel: *Director:* Catherine M. Wilson.
Curator: Andrew W. Moore.
Headquarters of the Norfolk Museums Service.
Sited prominently in the City centre, the
museum houses an important collection of the
Norwich School featuring works by John
Crome and John Sell Cotman. Other major
attractions include The Annual Tate Gallery
Collection Exhibition and its lively
programme of events. Other attractions
are: archaeology and natural history displays,
battlements and dungeons tours daily,
lively education programme. Also provide:
Guided Tours on request.
Services and Facilities:
*Art Consultancy. Art for Offices. Bookshop.
Café. Craftshop. Disabled Access. Friends/Soci-
ety. Guided Tours. Lectures. Museum Shop.*

NORWICH GALLERY
*Norwich School of Art and Design, St. George
Street, Norwich, NR3 1BB.* **Tel:** *01603-
610561.* **Fax:** *01603-615728.*

SAINSBURY CENTRE FOR VISUAL ARTS P
University of East Anglia, Norwich, NR4 7TJ.
Tel: *01603-456060 (Galleries), 01603-593199
(Enquiries).* **Fax:** *01603-259401.*
Email *scva@uea.ac.uk*
Opening times: *Tue-Sun 11-5. Admission
£2 (£1 concs.).*
Nearest Station: *Norwich.*
Personnel: *Director:* Nichola Johnson. *Head
of Admin. & Services:* Kate Carreno. *Curator,
Exhibitions:* Dr William Jeffett. *Head of
Education:* Dr Veronica Sekules. *Head of
Conservation & Collection Management:* Don
Sale.
The museum and gallery of the University of
East Anglia, designed by world famous
architect Sir Norman Foster to house the
Robert

and Lisa Sainsbury Collection, which was
given to the University in the 1970's. Modern
European sculpture and painting, including
works by Bacon, Degas, Epstein, Giacometti,
Moore and Picasso are displayed alongside one
of the finest collections of non-Western art
outside London.
The centre also has a lively programme of spe-
cial exhibitions, events and education work.
Exhibition highlights for 1998 include "Woven
Images: Tapestries designed by major 20th
Century Artists", "Light", curated by UEA's
Museology students, "Pop Art in Spain",
"Henry Moore: Friendships and Influences"
and "Moore in Mexico".
The Centre has a coffee bar and gallery shop
and offers facilities for special functions, meet-
ings and conferences.
Services and Facilities:
*Art for Offices. Bar. Bookshop. Café.
Friends/Society. Guided Tours. Lectures. Muse-
um Shop. Parking. Restaurant. Shop.*

WELLS-NEXT-THE-SEA

HOLKHAM PICTURE GALLERY
*The Ancient House, Holkham, Wells-next-the-
Sea.*

SCHOOL HOUSE GALLERY C
Wighton, Nr. Wells-next-the-Sea, NR23 1AL.
Tel: *01328-820457.*
Opening times: *11.30-5.30 inclusive Sat,
Sun and Bank Holidays. Closed Monday.*
Personnel: *Director:* Diana Cohen.

Contemporary paintings, watercolours, drawings, limited edition prints and sculpture
shown in an attractive space that was once the
Wighton village school. 20th century British
and European art of the highest quality, also
work by foremost East Anglian artists. Four
major exhibitions a year interspersed with constantly changing mixed shows. Situated two
miles from Wells and the North Norfolk coast.
Large car park.
Services and Facilities:
Parking.
Work Stocked and Sold:
Cer. Dr. Pa. Pr. Sc.
Price range: £100 - £3,000.

SUFFOLK

ALDEBURGH

THOMPSON'S GALLERY
175 High Street, Aldeburgh, IP15 5AN.
Tel: *01728-453743.* **Fax:** *01728-452488.*

BURY ST. EDMUNDS

CHIMNEY MILL GALLERIES
Chimney Mill, West Stow, Bury St. Edmunds,
Tel: *01284-778234.*

MANOR HOUSE MUSEUM P
Honey Hill, Angel Corner, Bury St. Edmunds,
IP33 1UZ. **Tel:** *01284-757074.*

MOYSES HALL MUSEUM P
Cornhill, Bury St. Edmunds, **Tel:** *01284-769834.*

OTTEWELL ART GALLERY
50 St. Andrew's Street South, Bury St. Edmunds,
IP33 3PH. **Tel:** *01284-61172.*

CRANSFORD

BOUNDARY GALLERY
Boundary House, Cransford, **Tel:** *01728-723862.*

EAST BERGHOLT

WOODGATES GALLERY
Woodgates Road, East Bergholt, CO7 6RE..

FELIXSTOWE

ARTWORKS
Victoria Street, Felixstowe, **Tel:** *01502-583521.*

HADLEIGH

BRETT GALLERY
105 High Street, Hadleigh, IP7 5EJ.
Tel: *01473-822132.*

HALESWORTH

HALESWORTH GALLERY
Steeple End, Halesworth, **Tel:** *01986-872409.*

IPSWICH

CHRISTCHURCH MANSION PS
Christchurch Park, (Ipswich Museums and Galleries: Ipswich Borough Council). Ipswich, IP4
2BE. **Tel:** *01473-253246.* **Fax:** *01473-210328.*
Opening times: *Tue-Sat 10-5, Sun 2.30-4.30 or dusk in winter. Open Bank Hol. Mons.*
Personnel: *Exhibitions Officer: Rebecca Weaver.*
Grade I listed mansion with period rooms from Tudor to Victorian, which houses paintings by Gainsborough, Constable and Suffolk Artists. Incorporating gallery spaces with a lively exhibitions programme: The Wolsey Art Gallery

and "The Room Upstairs".
Services and Facilities:
Art for Offices. Disabled Access. Friends/Society. Guided Tours. Lectures. Workshop Facilities.
FIRST FLOOR GALLERY
at M. F. Frames Ltd, 10 St. Helens Street, Ipswich, **Tel:** *01473-225544.*

IPSWICH MUSEUMS & GALLERIES CHRIST CHURCH MANSION PS
(including Wolsey Art Gallery), Soane Street, Ipswich, IP4 5NB. **Tel:** *01473-253246.*
Fax: *01473-210328.*
Opening times: *Tues-Sat 10-5, Sun 2.30-4.30. Closes at dusk in Winter.*
Personnel: *Senior Assistant Curator: Jane Sedge. Exhibitions Organiser: Rebecca Weaver.*
Christchurch Mansion is a 16th century Manor house in an historic 100 acre park, opened in 1896 as a free Museum. The rooms are furnished in various period styles from Tudor to Victorian. It houses a fine collection of work by Suffolk artists including the best collection of the work of Constable and Gainsborough outside London. There is a lively programme of exhibitions in the Wolsey Art Gallery and The Room Upstairs and Sculpture in the Park during the summer.
Services and Facilities:
Disabled Access. Friends/Society. Gallery space for hire. Lectures. Museum Shop. Shop.

JOHN RUSSELL GALLERY
4-6 Wherry Lane, Ipswich, IP4 1LG.
Tel: *01473-212051.* **Fax:** *01473-212051.*

SHELLEY PRIORY
Hadleigh, Ipswich, **Tel:** *01206-337220.*

LOWESTOFT

THE ART CENTRE GALLERY
Regent Road, Lowestoft, NR32 1PA.
Tel: *01502-583521 ext 281.*

NEWMARKET

THE BRIDGE STREET GALLERY
8 Bridge Street, Moulton, Newmarket,

EQUUS ART GALLERY
Sun Lane, Newmarket, CB8 8EW.
Tel: *01638-560445.*

NEWMARKET FINE ART GALLERY
Nell Gwynn Studio, Palace Street, Newmarket,
Tel: *94-660065.*

SAXMUNDHAM

SNAPE MALTINGS GALLERY C
Snape Maltings Riverside Centre, Saxmundham,
IP17 1SR.
Tel: *01728-688305.* **Fax:** *01728-688930.*
Email *snapemalt@aol.com*
Opening times: *Mon-Sun all year round ,*
10-5 (6 during the summer).
Nearest Station: *Saxmundham.*
Personnel: *Julia Pipe.*
Housed in a collection of 19th century maltings on the River Alde. Continuing mixed

exhibition of paintings, artists' prints and British craft. Painting and craft courses in summer. Also six interesting shops, tea shop and pub. Additional space available to hire for exhibitions.
Services and Facilities:
Bar. Café. Craftshop. Gallery space for hire. Parking. Shop.
Work Stocked and Sold:
Ab. Cer. Cra. Dr. Pa. Pr.

SOUTHWOLD

NEW GALLERY
10 Market Place, Southwold, **Tel:** *01728-724269.*

PORTLAND STUDIO
Portland House, High Street, Southwold, IP18 6AB. **Tel:** *01502-723652.*

SUDBURY

GAINSBOROUGH'S HOUSE P
46 Gainsborough Street, Sudbury, CO10 6EU.
Tel: *01787-372958.*
Fax: *01787-376991.*
Opening times: *Tues-Sat 10-5, Sun 2-5. (closes at 4 Nov-March).*
Nearest Station: *Sudbury.*
Personnel: *Curator: Hugh Belsey. Assistant Curator: Andrew Hunter.* Georgian-fronted town house, the birthplace of Thomas Gainsborough, displays a substantial collection of paintings, drawings and prints from throughout the artist's career and houses a library and study collection of works on paper.

Lively contemporary and historical exhibitions of regional and national interest are shown in galleries overlooking the charming garden. The open-access print workshop is available to individual artists and for summer courses. Disabled Access ground floor only.
Services and Facilities:
Friends/Society. Guided Tours. Lectures. Museum Shop. Workshop Facilities.
Work Stocked and Sold: **Pr.**

THE PHOENIX GALLERY
97 High Street, Lavenham, Sudbury, CO10 9PZ.
Tel: *01787-247356.*

Ab *Artist's Books* **App** *Applied Art* **Cer** *Ceramics* **Cra** *Crafts*
Dec *Decorative* **Dr** *Drawing* **Fur** *Furniture*

WOODBRIDGE

THE BARN GALLERY
Mill Lane, Butley, Woodbridge, IP12 3PA.
Tel: *01394-450843.* **Fax:** *01394-450843.*

THE DEBEN GALLERY
26 Market Hill, Woodbridge, IP12 4LU.
Tel: *013943-3216.*

THE FRASER GALLERY
62a New Street, Woodbridge, IP12 1DX.
Tel: *01394-387535.*

East Midlands

DERBY

DERBY

THE ARBOR DARKROOMS & GALLERY *C*
Arboretum Lodge, Arboretum Square, Derby DE23 8FN. **Tel:** *01332-299049.*

ART FOR ALL
Derby City General Hospital, Uttoxeter Road, Derby DE22 3NE. **Tel:** *01332-340131.*

THE ATRIUM GALLERY
The Derwent Business Centre, Clarke Street, Derby DE1 2BU.

DERBY MUSEUM AND ART GALLERY *P*
The Strand, Derby DE1 1BS. **Tel:** *01332-255586.* **Fax:** *01332-255804.*

ROYAL CROWN DERBY MUSEUM *P*
Royal Crown Derby Porcelain Co. Ltd., 194 Osmaston Road, Derby DE3 8JZ.
Tel: *01332-712800.* **Fax:** *01332-712899.*

DERBYSHIRE

BUXTON

BUXTON MUSEUM & ART GALLERY *P*
Terrace Road, Buxton, SK17 6DJ.

CHESTERFIELD

CHESTERFIELD MUSEUM & ART GALLERY *P*
St Mary's Gate, Chesterfield, S41 7TY. **Tel:** *01246-559727.* **Fax:** *01246-206667.*

UNO GALLERY *C*
5 South Street, Chesterfield, S40 1QX.

ILKESTON

BOTTLE KILN GALLERY
High Lane East, West Hallam, Ilkeston, DE7 6HP. **Tel:** *0115-932 9442.*

CHARLES STONE GALLERY OF CONTEMPORARY PAINTING
Bottle Kiln Gallery, High Lane East, West Hallam, Ilkeston, DE7 6HP. **Tel:** *0115-932 9442.*

EREWASH MUSEUM *P*
Ilkeston, DE7 5JA. **Tel:** *01602 440440 ext 331.*

WIRKSWORTH

MODERN PRINT GALLERY
25 Market Place, Wirksworth, DE4 4ET.
Tel: *01629-824525.*

LEICESTER

LEICESTER

THE CITY GALLERY *PS*
90 Granby Street, Leicester LE1 1DJ.
Tel: *0116-254 0595.* **Fax:** *0116-254 0593.*
Opening times: *Tue-Fri 11-6, Sat 10-5.*
Nearest Station: *Leicester.*
Personnel: *Manager: Sylvia Wright.*
The City Gallery promotes the very best in contemporary art and craft, through a dynamic and accessible programme of changing exhibitions and events. There are three gallery spaces: The Main Gallery, Craft Gallery and Gallery Upstairs which is available for hire at competitive rates. The Crafts Council - recommended shop is stocked with work by new makers and famous names. The Gallery runs an active education programme and a touring exhibitions scheme. The City Gallery is directly managed by Leicester City Council. Admission is free. There is level access from the street and a chairlift to the Upstairs Gallery.
Services and Facilities:
Art for Offices. Commissioning Service. Craftshop. Disabled Access. Friends/Society. Gallery space for hire. Shop.
Work Stocked and Sold:
Cer. Cra. Dr. Gla. Jew. Pa. Ph. Pr. Sc. Tx.
Price range: £5 - £10,000.

GADSBY GALLERY
22 Market Place, Leicester LE1 5GF.
Tel: *0116-262 2410.*

LEICESTERSHIRE

ASHBY DE-LA-ZOUCH

FERRERS GALLERY *C*
Staunton Harold, Ashby de-la-Zouch, LE6 5RU. **Tel:** *01332-863337.*

LUTTERWORTH

CEDAR HOUSE CRAFT SHOP & GALLERY
Main Street, Peatling Pava, Lutterworth, LE17 5QA. **Tel:** *0116-273 0482.*

MARKET HARBOROUGH

COUGHTON GALLERIES *C*
The Old Manor, Arthingworth, Market Harborough, LE6 8JD. **Tel:** *01858-525436.* **Fax:** *01858-525535.*

THE FRANK HAYNES GALLERY
50 Station Road, Great Bowden, Market Harborough, LE16 7HN. **Tel:** *01858-464862.*

NORTHAMPTONSHIRE

KETTERING

ALFRED EAST ART GALLERY *PS*
c/o, The Coach House, Sheep Street, Kettering, NN16 8AN. **Tel:** *01536-534274/534381/534394.* **Fax:** *01536-410795/534370.*
Opening times: *Mon-Sat 9.30-5, not BH.*
Nearest Station: *Kettering (5 mins walk).*
Personnel: *Heritage Manager: Su Davies. Assistant Museum & Gallery Manager: Catherine Nisbet.*

A constantly changing programme of exhibitions ensures that there will always be something new for you to see at the Alfred East Art Gallery. You may even decide to take an original work home - Fine Arts, Crafts and Photography can all be found on display and are often for sale. The gallery's permanent collections are based on a foundation collection of works by Sir Alfred East, RA, as well as featuring local artists such as Thomas Cooper Gotch and William Bounder Gash. A new gallery room, dedicated to the permanent collections, will be opening in 1999.
Services and Facilities:
Friends/Society. Lectures. Parking. Shop.

NORTHAMPTON

CENTRAL MUSEUM AND ART GALLERY *PS*
Guildhall Road, Northampton, NN1 1DP.
Tel: *01604-39415.* **Fax:** *01604-238720.*
Opening times: *Mon-Sat 10-5, Sun 2-5.*
Nearest Station: *Northampton.*
Personnel: *Curator: S. Stone.*
Central Museum, Northampton houses an

Gla Glass Jew Jewellery Pa Paintings Ph Photography Pr Prints
Sc Sculpture Tx Textiles Wd Wood

unexpectedly fine collection of 15th-18th century art, including works by Guardi and Giordano.

The rich British collection features early watercolours, and Norwich School and Pre-Raphaelite works. Modern and contemporary strands are represented by Sickert, John Nash, Sutherland, Moore and Hockney amongst others, and our print collection includes works by Pasmore and Nolan.

Our outstanding ceramics collections comprise comprehensive ranges of both British and Oriental pottery and porcelain. The small collection of studio ceramics includes pieces by Ewen Henderson and Gordon Baldwin.

Services and Facilities:
Bookshop. Friends/Society. Gallery space for hire. Guided Tours.
Museum Shop.

FOUR SEASONS GALLERY
39 St Giles Street, Northampton,
Tel: *01604-32287.*

ONSIGHT GALLERY
The Roadmender, 1 Lady's Lane, Northampton,
NN1 3AH.

WESTON FAVELL LIBRARY
Weston Favell Shopping Centre, Northampton,
Tel: *01604-413327.*

TOWCESTER

BLAKESLEY GALLERY C
Barton House, High Street, Blakesley, Towcester,
NN12 8RE. **Tel:** *01327-860282.* **Fax:** *01327-860282.*

TOWCESTER LIBRARY
Richmond Road, Towcester, NN12 7EX.
Tel: *01327-50794.*

WELLINGBOROUGH

THE GALLERY
108 Midland Road, Wellingborough, NN8 1NB.
Tel: *01933-274215.*

RAUNDS LIBRARY
High Street, Raunds, Wellingborough, NN9
6HT. **Tel:** *01933-623671.*

WELLINGBOROUGH LIBRARY
Pebble Lane, Wellingborough, NN8 1AS.
Tel: *01933-225365.* **Fax:** *01933-44060.*

NOTTINGHAMSHIRE

NEWARK

MILLGATE MUSEUM P
48 Millgate, Newark, NG24 4TS.
Tel: *01636-79403.*

PIERREPONT GALLERY
Thoresby Park, Nr Ollerton, Newark,
Tel: *01623-822365.* **Fax:** *01623-822301.*

NOTTINGHAM

ANGEL ROW GALLERY PS
Central Library Building, 3 Angel Row, Nottingham, NG1 6HP. **Tel:** *0115-947 6334.* **Fax:** *0115-947 6335.*
Opening times: *Mon-Sat 11-6, Wed 11-7.*
Personnel: *Exhibitions Officer:* Deborah Dean.
Situated in central Nottingham, Angel Row Gallery shows an exciting and diverse programme of contemporary visual arts. A large gallery with three exhibitions spaces it promotes regional, national and international artists. An extensive programme of events and activities is organised in conjunction with the exhibitions. Bookshop stocks a wide range of art magazines, catalogues, postcards and greetings cards.
Services and Facilities:
Bookshop. Disabled Access. Friends/Society. Lectures.

ARNOLD LIBRARY
Front Street, Arnold, Nottingham, NG5 7EE.
Tel: *0115-920 2247.*

THE BONINGTON ART GALLERY
The Nottingham Trent University, Dryden Street, Nottingham, NG1 4FX. **Tel:** *0115-948 6443 (office), 0115-941 8418 (gallery).*

BYARD GALLERY
9 Byard Lane, Nottingham, **Tel:** *0115-950 0434.*

DJANOGLY ART GALLERY
The University of Nottingham Arts Centre, University Park, Nottingham, NG27 2RD.
Tel: *0115-951 3192.* **Fax:** *0115-951 3194.*
Email *liz.oneill@nottingham.ac.uk*
Ws *http://www.nottingham.ac.uk/artscentre/*
Opening times: *Mon-Sat 11-5, Sun & Bank Hols 2-5.*
Nearest Station: *Nottingham.*
Personnel: *Director:* Joanne Wright. *Exhibitions Officer:* Neil Walker. *Marketing Officer:* Liz O'Neill. *Exhibitions Secretary:* Tracey Isgar.
The Djanogly Art Gallery originates historical and contemporary exhibitions and also hosts a wide range of touring shows. Foyer exhibitions and craft cabinets extend the range of work shown and the gallery also has an artist in residence - Heather Connelly (until September 1998).
Services and Facilities:
Bookshop. Café. Craftshop. Disabled Access. Lectures. Parking.

FOCUS GALLERY
108 Derby Road, Nottingham, NG1 5FB.
Tel: *0115-953 7575.*

THE HART GALLERY C
23 Main Street, Linby, Nottingham, NG15 8AE. **Tel:** *0115-963 8707.*

NOTTINGHAM PLAYHOUSE GALLERY
Wellington Circus, Nottingham, NG1 5AF.
Tel: *0115-941 9419.*
THE WEST END GALLERY C

St. Mary's Church, High Pavement, The Lace Market, Nottingham, NG1 1HF.
Tel: *0115-947 2476.* **Fax:** *0115-947 2476.*
Email *stmary@john316.com.*
Opening times: *Tues-Sat 9-4.30.*
Nearest Station: *Nottingham.*
Personnel: *Artist in Residence:* Sophie Hacker.
'The West End Gallery' is situated within the nave of the ancient parish church of St. Mary in Nottinghams historic Lace Market.
The gallery holds monthly group and solo shows of contemporary works by young local artists, community organisations, and more established national and international painters, photographers and sculptors. The gallery also supports students from the two local universities and holds degree shows. Workshops and talks take place throughout the year. 'The West End Gallery' is a non profit making organisation run by a volunteer Artist in Residence. The gallery shows all works that are in keeping with the setting of the space. We especially welcome visual arts dealing with issues of faith.
Services and Facilities:
Disabled Access. Gallery space for hire. Lectures.
Work Stocked and Sold:
Pa. Ph. Sc.
Price range: *£20 - £1,000.*

RAVENSHEAD

LONGDALE GALLERY
Longdale Craft Centre, Museum and Restaurant, Longdale Lane, Ravenshead, NG15 9AH.
Tel: *01623-794858.*

WORKSOP

HARLEY GALLERY C
Welbeck, Worksop, S80 3LW. **Tel:** *01909-501700.* **Fax:** *01909-488747.*

RUTLAND

UPPINGHAM

THE GOLDMARK GALLERY C
Orange Street, Uppingham, LE15 9SQ.
Tel: *01572-821424.* **Fax:** *01572-821503.*

West Midlands

BIRMINGHAM

BIRMINGHAM

THE ANGLE GALLERY
Dakota Buildings, James Street, Birmingham B3 1SD. **Tel:** *0121-233 9260.*
ASTON HALL P

Ab *Artist's Books* **App** *Applied Art* **Cer** *Ceramics* **Cra** *Crafts*
Dec *Decorative* **Dr** *Drawing* **Fur** *Furniture*

ASTON HALL P

Trinity Road, Aston, Birmingham B6 6JD.
Tel: *0121-327 0062.* **Fax:** *0121-327 7162.*

THE BARBER INSTITUTE OF FINE ARTS P

*The University of Birmingham, Birmingham B15
2TS.* **Tel:** *0121-414 7333.* **Fax:** *0121-414
3370.*
Opening times: *Mon-Sat 10-5, Sun 2-5.*
Nearest Station: *New Street (Main line),
University (Cross City Line).*
Personnel: *Director:* Professor Richard
Verdi. *Curator:* Paul Spencer-Longhurst.
Administrator: Sophie Wilson.

One of the finest small picture galleries in the
world housing an outstanding collection of old
masters and modern paintings including masterpieces by Bellini, Rubens, Poussin, Murillo,
Gainsborough, Rossetti, Whistler and
Magritte. Among the Impressionist pictures
are major works by Manet, Monet, Renoir,
Degas, Gauguin and Van Gogh.
The Institute regularly holds concerts, lectures
and recitals - all of which are open to the pub-
lic. It is also available for hire for seminars,
receptions, concerts and private views.
Services and Facilities:
*Disabled Access. Friends/Society. Gallery space
for hire. Guided Tours. Lectures. Museum Shop.
Parking.*
Work Stocked and Sold:
Pa.

BIRMINGHAM & MIDLAND INSTITUTE

9 Margaret Street, Birmingham B3 3BS.
Tel: *0121-236 3591.*

BIRMINGHAM MUSEUM AND ART GALLERY, INCLUDING THE GAS HALL EXHIBITION GALLERY PS

Chamberlain Square, Birmingham B3 3DH.
Tel: *0121-303 2834/1966.*
Fax: *0121-303 1394.*
Opening times: *Mon-Thurs & Sat 10-5, Fri
10.30-5, Sun 12.30-5.*
Nearest Station: *Birmingham New Street.*
A spectacular Victorian building housing one
of the world's finest collections of Pre-
Raphaelite paintings. Older schools are repre-
sented by Dutch, Italian and French artists and
other works from the 14th century to the pre-
sent day. The museum has displays of ceramics

and fine silver, and a new sculpture gallery.
Other sections include Greek and Roman
antiquities, objects from the Near East, Mexico
and Peru and a life-size dinosaur in the natural
history gallery.
The Edwardian tea room offers a varied menu
in elegant surroundings. The highlight of the
years's programme is the Burne-Jones cente-
nary exhibition, held in collaboration with the
Metropolitan Museum of Art, New York, and
Musee d'Orsay, Paris.
Other exhibitions in 1998 include: 7 March-
25 May, Pre-Raphaelite Women Artists. 28
March-31 May, Birmingham Arts Lab. 16
May-6 September, Dinosaurs. 13 June-30
August, Jim Malone: Artist Potter. 22 June-6
September, William Blake and His Circle. 16
September 1998-3 January 1999, Coming to
Light. 17 October 1998-17 January 1999,
Burne-Jones.
Services and Facilities:
*Café. Disabled Access. Friends/Society. Gallery
space for hire. Guided Tours. Museum Shop.
Restaurant.*

THE BOND GALLERY

*Design & Studio Centre, The Bond Warehouse,
180-182 Fazeley Street, Birmingham B5 5SP.*
Tel: *0121-753 2065.*

CARLETON GALLERY

*91 Vivian Road, Harborne, Birmingham B17
0DR.* **Tel:** *0121-427 2487.*

DANFORD COLLECTION OF WEST AFRICAN ART AND ARTEFACTS P

*Centre for West African Studies, University of
Birmingham, Birmingham B15 2TT.* **Tel:** *0121-
414 5128.* **Fax:** *0121-414 3228.*

GOATE GALLERY

*First Floor, Birmingham Chambers, New Street,
Birmingham B2 4JH.* **Tel:** *0121-643 2624.*

HELIOS GALLERY

*25 Valentine Road, Kings Heath, Birmingham
B14 7AN.* **Tel:** *0121-444 1585.*

IKON GALLERY C

58-72 John Bright Street, Birmingham B1 1BN.
Tel: *0121-643 0708.* **Fax:** *0121-643 2254.*

MAC (MIDLANDS ARTS CENTRE) P

Cannon Hill Park, Birmingham B12 9HQ.
Tel: *0121-440 4221.* **Fax:** *0121-446 4372.*
Opening times: *Daily 9.30-11*
Personnel: *Director:* Geoff Sims. *Marketing
Manager:* Shirley Kirk. *Exhibition Programmer:*
Judy Dames.

40 exhibitions a year, of which 20 originated
and 20 touring. Two stewarded galleries plus
three public spaces, with 194 lin. m. hanging

space and 300 sq. m. floor space. Shows contemporary fine art, craft and photography from
both artists of known stature and those in the
early stages of a promising career. Visited by
12,000 people a week. Extensive programme of
live performance, cinema, education and exhibitions.
Has bar, restaurant and bookshop and set in a
large park. Only one space does not have disabled access. Applications from individual
artists and touring organisations welcomed.
MAC is funded by Birmingham City Council
and West Midlands Arts.
Services and Facilities:
Bar. Bookshop. Disabled Access. Restaurant.

THE MINE FINE ART GALLERY

24 Temple Street, Birmingham B2 5DB.
Tel: *0121-643 8424.*

COVENTRY

COVENTRY

HERBERT ART GALLERY AND MUSEUM P

Jordan Well, Coventry CV1 5QP. **Tel:** *01203-
832381 / 832386; Minicom: 01203-83240.*
Fax: *01203-832410.*
Email *coventry.museums@dial.pipex.com*
Opening times: *Mon-Sat 10-5, Sun 12-5.*
Nearest Station: *Coventry.*

Coventry is associated with outstanding manu-
facturing skills, post war reconstruction and
the legend of Lady Godiva. As a focus for the
city's heritage, the Herbert Art Gallery &
Museum offers a fascinating visit with international appeal.
The 'Godiva City' exhibition is a lively interpretation of one thousand years of Coventry's
history. Here, the tale is told through historical treasures, interactive games, archive films
and objects to handle. An optional audiotape
tour is available. You can see Graham Sutherland's working drawings for the famous Coventry Cathedral Tapestry, portraits of Lady Godiva through the centuries, sculpture by Henry
Moore and Jacob Epstein and paintings by L.S.
Lowry, John Collier and David Cox. Please
telephone for details of our lively temporary
exhibition programme, workshops, lectures and
children's activities. The Herbert Art Gallery
& Museum has a tea room, gift shop, toilets for
people with disabilities, baby changing facilities and parking for orange badge holders.
Admission is free.
Services and Facilities:
*Café. Disabled Access. Friends/Society. Gallery
space for hire. Lectures. Museum Shop.*

MEAD GALLERY, WARWICK ARTS CENTRE

University of Warwick, Coventry CV4 7AL
Tel: *01203-22589.* **Fax:** *01203-523883.*

DUDLEY

DUDLEY

DUDLEY MUSEUM AND ART GALLERY P
St. James's Road, Dudley DY1 1HU.
Tel: 01384-815575. **Fax:** 01384-815576.

HIMLEY HALL PS
Himley Park, Dudley DY3 4DF.
Tel: 01902-326665. **Fax:** 01902-894163.
Opening times: 21 March - 4 October.
Nearest Station: Wolverhampton.
Personnel: Director: Charles Hajdamach.
Keeper: Jane Carney.

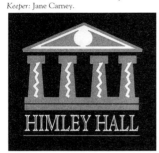

Himley Hall is a Grade II* listed building set
amongst 180 acres of 'Capability' Brown landscaped parkland.
Once the home to the family of the Earls of
Dudley, the Hall currently houses temporary
exhibitions from March to October. Contemporary art and sculpture, fairground art and
carvings, models and studio glass are included
in the 1998 programme. Dudley MBC have
embarked on a development project to create a
Glass Museum of national significance at Himley Hall.
Services and Facilities:
Disabled Access. Guided Tours. Museum Shop.
Parking. Workshop Facilities.

KINGSWINFORD

BROADFIELD HOUSE GLASS MUSEUM P
Compton Drive, Kingswinford, DY6 9QA.
Tel: 01384-812745.

HEREFORD & WORCESTER

BEWDLEY

BEWDLEY MUSEUM P
The Shambles, Load Street, Bewdley, DY12
2AE. **Tel:** 01299-403573.

BROADWAY

ANDERSON GALLERY C
96 High Street, Broadway, WR12 7AJ.
Tel: 01386-858086.
Fax: 01386-858086.

BROMSGROVE

THE JINNEY RING CRAFT CENTRE C
Old House Farm, Hanbury, Bromsgrove, B60
4BU. **Tel:** 01527-821272. **Fax:** 01527-
821869.
Opening times: Tues-Sat 10.30-5, Sun
11.30-5.30.
Personnel: Richard Greatwood.
Take a step back in time and absorb the
charming rural surroundings of The Jinney
Ring Craft Centre. Beautiful old timbered
barns have been lovingly restored by Richard
and Jenny Greatwood and now house twelve
individual Craft Studios, Craft Gallery - with
local artist work on display, Farmhouse
Kitchen Gift Shop and a specialist needlework
department. Free admission. Open all year.
Services and Facilities:
Café. Commissioning Service. Framing. Parking.
Restaurant. Shop. Workshop Facilities.

CRADLEY

THE LOWER NUPEND GALLERY C
Nr. Malvern, Cradley, WR13 5NP.
Tel: 01886-880500/334. **Fax:** 01886-880848.

GREAT MALVERN

MALVERN ART GALLERY
Malvern Library, Graham Road, Great Malvern,
WR14 2HW. **Tel:** 016845-61223.

HEREFORD

BROOK STREET POTTERY C
Brook Street, Hay-on-Wye, Hereford, HR3
5BQ. **Tel:** 01497-821026.

HATTON ART GALLERY
Churchill House Museum, 3 Venns Lane, Here-
ford, **Tel:** 01432-267409.
Fax: 01432-342492.

HEREFORD CITY ART GALLERY
City Museums & Art Gallery, Broad Street,
Hereford, HR1 9AU. **Tel:** 01432-268121, ext
207.

**HEREFORD CITY MUSEUM AND ART
GALLERY** P
Broad Street, Hereford, HR4 9AU.
Tel: 01432-364691. **Fax:** 01432-342492.

JOHN MCKELLER C
23 Church Street, Hereford, HR1 2LR.
Tel: 01432-354460.

MAPPA MUNDI AND CHAINED LIBRARY P
5 College Cloisters, Cathedral Close, Hereford,
HR1 2NG. **Tel:** 01432-359880. **Fax:** 01432-
355929.

MERIDIAN CONTEMPORARY ARTS C
13 High Town, Hay-on-Wye, Hereford, HR3
5AE. **Tel:** 01497-821633.

OLD CHAPEL GALLERY C
East Street, Pembridge, Nr Leominster, Hereford,
HR6 9HB. **Tel:** 01544-388842.

KIDDERMINSTER

**HEREFORD & WORCESTER COUNTY
MUSEUM** P
Hartlebury Castle, Hartlebury, Kidderminster,
DY11 7XZ. **Tel:** 01299-250416.

LEOMINSTER

LION GALLERY C
15b Broad Street, Leominster, HR6 8BT.
Tel: 01568-611898. **Fax:** 01568-614644.
Ws http://www.cogent-comms.co.uk/lion.htm
Opening times: Mon-Sat 10-5.
Nearest Station: Leominster.
Personnel: Chairman: Blake Mackinnon.
Administrator: Rozie Keogh. Publicity Officer:
Chris Noble.

This lively gallery promotes principally the
artists and makers of the area, many of whom
have national reputations. It is run as a non-
profit making venture by many of the artists
themselves who have control over selection
and display. The gallery shows exhibitions of
Fine Art and contemporary craftwork in mixed
shows or built around special themes. A broad
range of work is covered from paintings, original prints and photographs, to studio ceramics
and kiln formed and blown glass. The work of
over thirty jewellers is always on display, com-
plimented by selections of textiles and items in
wood including furniture.
Services and Facilities:
Commissioning Service. Craftshop. Disabled
Access. Framing.
Work Stocked and Sold:
Ab. App. Cer. Cra. Dr. Fur. Gla. Jew.
Pa. Ph. Pr. Sc. Tx. Wd.
Price range: £5 - £2,000.

MALVERN

MALVERN ARTS WORKSHOP
90 Worcester Road, Link Top, Malvern, WR14
1NY. **Tel:** 01684-568993.

Ab Artist's Books App Applied Art Cer Ceramics Cra Crafts
Dec Decorative Dr Drawing Fur Furniture

OMBERSLEY

OMBERSLEY GALLERY C
Church Terrace, Nr Droitwich, Ombersley, WR9 0EP. **Tel:** *01905-620655.*

WORCESTER

CITY MUSEUM & ART GALLERY P
Foregate Street, Worcester,
Tel: *01905-25371.*

REGENT GALLERIES C
22 Reindeer Court, Worcester, WR1 2DS.
Tel: *01905-21300.*

WORCESTER CITY ART GALLERY & MUSEUM P
Foregate Street, Worcester, WR1 1DT.
Tel: *01905-25371.*

SANDWELL

WEDNESBURY

WEDNESBURY MUSEUM & ART GALLERY P
Holyhead Road, Wednesbury, WS10 7DF.
Tel: *0121-556 0683.*
Fax: *0121-505 1625.*

SHROPSHIRE

BISHOPS CASTLE

LONGHOUSE GALLERY
25 The High Street, Bishops Castle, **Tel:** *01588-638147.*

BRIDGNORTH

CLODE GALLERY
New Market Building, Listley Street, Bridgnorth, WV16 4AW.
Tel: *01746-768338.*

ELLESMERE

ELLESMERE ARTS CENTRE
Ellesmere College, Ellesmere, SY12 9AB.
Tel: *01691-622828.*

LUDLOW

FEATHERS GALLERY
20 The Bull Ring, Ludlow, SY8 1AA.
Tel: *01584-875390.*

SILK TOP HAT GALLERY
4 Quality Square, Ludlow, SY8 1AR.
Tel: *01584-875363.*

SHREWSBURY

ARTIFEX C
Porch House, Swan Hill, Shrewsbury, SY1 1NQ.
Tel: *01743-241031.*

GATEWAY GALLERIES GATEWAY EDUCATION & ARTS CENTRE
Chester Street, Shrewsbury, SY1 1NB.
Tel: *01743-55159.*

GROVE CONTEMPORARY ARTS C
Ruyton XI Towns, Shrewsbury, SY4 1LA.
Tel: *01939-260377.*
Opening times: *11-5 During major exhibitions - other times by appointment.*
Nearest Station: *Shrewsbury.*
Personnel: *Proprietor:* Yvonne Cooper.
Grove Contemporary Arts has as its primary intent the exhibiting of quality work in a part of the world where there is little opportunity to view or to purchase contemporary art. The policy of staging a limited number of exhibitions prevents the pressure felt by many galleries to be always open and selling. Grove Contemporary Arts is in the enviable position of being able to concentrate on displaying work for its artistic merit rather than its immediate commercial viability, and seen in the conjunction of the proprietor's 'home-gallery' (Victorian elegance grafted on the traditional timbered cottage) - contemporary work works.
Services and Facilities:
Parking.
Work Stocked and Sold:
Dr. Pa. Sc.
Price range: £50 - £3,000.

TELFORD

ELTON GALLERY
Ironbridge Gorge Museum, Coalbrookedale, Telford, TF8 7DG. **Tel:** *01952-433522.*

THE GALLERY
Spout Farm House, Telford Town Park, Telford,
Tel: *01952-290240.*

STAFFORDSHIRE

BURTON UPON TRENT

BREWHOUSE
Union Street, Burton upon Trent, DE14 1EB.
Tel: *01283-67720.*

ROUND HOUSE GALLERY C
38 High Street, Tutbury, Burton upon Trent, DE13 9LS. **Tel:** *01238-814964.*

LEEK

LEEK ART GALLERY
Nicholson Institute, Stockwell Street, Leek, ST13 6HQ. **Tel:** *01538-399181.*

NEWCASTLE-UNDER-LYME

HOOD & BROOMFIELD FINE ART
29 Albert Street, Newcastle-under-Lyme, ST5 1JP. **Tel:** *01782-626859.*

NEWCASTLE-UNDER-LYME MUSEUM & ART GALLERY P
Brampton Park, Newcastle-under-Lyme.

WAVERTREE GALLERY
Berkeley Co, Borough Road, Newcastle-under-Lyme, ST5 1TT. **Tel:** *01782-715555.*

STAFFORD

THE SHIRE HALL GALLERY P
Market Square, Stafford, ST16 2LD.
Tel: *01785-278345.* **Fax:** *01785-278327.*

SHUGBOROUGH
Ancestral home of the Earls of Milford, Stafford, ST17 0XB. **Tel:** *01889-881388.*

STOKE-ON-TRENT

STOKE-ON-TRENT

CITY MUSEUM AND ART GALLERY, STOKE ON TRENT P
Bethesda Street, Hanley, Stoke-on-Trent ST1 3DW. **Tel:** *01782-232323.* **Fax:** *01782-205033.*

WEDGWOOD MUSEUM P
Barlaston, Stoke-on-Trent ST12 9ES.
Tel: *01782-204141.* **Fax:** *01782-204666.*

WARWICKSHIRE

ALCESTER

COUGHTON COURT P
Alcester, B49 5JA. **Tel:** *01789-400777, Visitor info:* 01789-762435. **Fax:** *01789-765544.*

HENLEY-IN-ARDEN

THE GALLERY UPSTAIRS C
Torquil, 81 High Street, Henley-in-Arden,
Tel: *01564-792174.*

LEAMINGTON SPA

LEAMINGTON SPA ART GALLERY AND MUSEUM P
Avenue Road, Leamington Spa, CV31 3PP.
Tel: *01926-426559.* **Fax:** *01926-317867.*

RUGBY

RUGBY ART GALLERY & MUSEUM P
St. Matthews Street, Rugby, CV21 3BZ.
Tel: *01788-542687.*

STRATFORD-UPON-AVON

MONTPELLIER GALLERY C
8 Chapel Street, Stratford-upon-Avon, CV37 3EP. **Tel:** *01789-261161.* **Fax:** *01789-261161.*
Opening times: *Mon-Sat 9.30-5.30.*
Personnel: *Proprietor:* Peter Burridge.
Montpellier Gallery is Crafts Council selected, specialising in contemporary paintings, printmaking, studio ceramics, designer glass, jewellery and sculpture. Annual exhibition pro-

Gla Glass **Jew** Jewellery **Pa** Paintings **Ph** Photography **Pr** Prints
Sc Sculpture **Tx** Textiles **Wd** Wood

THE ARTWORLD
DIRECTORY 1998/99 **127**

grammes feature groups of artists or solo exhibitions. The Gallery is established since 1991 in the heart of Stratford, but 3 minutes walk from the RSC Theatre.

We have built a reputation for high quality fine British crafts and contemporary art - figurative and semi-abstract - with a strong emphasis on hand-made printmaking. Established names are shown alongside emerging talent, giving an inspiring, progressive feel to the Gallery, which we believe is important for a sense of creative vitality.
Services and Facilities:
Art Consultancy. Art for Offices. Commissioning Service. Craftshop. Disabled Access. Framing.
Work Stocked and Sold:
Cer. Cra. Gla. Jew. Pa. Pr. Sc. Wd.
Price range: £20 - £1,500.

WARWICK

CHURCH STREET GALLERY
5 Church Street, Warwick, CV34 4AB.

MASON WATTS FINE ART
60 Smith Street, Warwick, CV34 4HU.

WARWICK GALLERY C
14 Smith Street, Warwick, CV34 4HH.
Tel: 01926-495880.
Ws *http://members.aol.com/ukgallery*
Opening times: Mon-Sat 9.30-5.30.
Nearest Station: *Warwick or Leamington Spa.*
Personnel: Peter.

A craft and design gallery specialising in contemporary design of individual work by established and emerging British artist craftsmen.

Comprehensive range of English original etchings, silk screenprints and watercolours, embroidered pictures, studio and one-off ceramics. Permanent exhibition of sculpture by Deborah Scaldwell. Original etchings by Terence Millington, John Brunsdon, Graham Evernden, Julian Williams, Michael Richecoeur, Donald Wilkinson, Jan Dingle, Liz Elmhirst; silk screen prints by Clive Harris, Chris Noble, Fairchild. We offer a full framing service. Also available on request, selections of suitable work for corporate clients. Designer jewellery, glass.
Services and Facilities:
Art Consultancy. Art for Offices. Commissioning Service. Craftshop. Framing. Shop.
Work Stocked and Sold:
Cer. Cra. Dec. Dr. Gla. Jew. Pa. Pr. Sc. Tx. Wd.
Price range: £1 - £2,000.

WOLVERHAMPTON

WOLVERHAMPTON

BILSTON ART GALLERY AND MUSEUM PS
Mount Pleasant, Bilston, Wolverhampton WV14 7LU. **Tel:** 01902-552507. **Fax:** 01902-552504.
Opening times: Mon-Thur 10-4, Fri group bookings only. Sat 11-4.
Nearest Station: *Wolverhampton, Coseley. Bilston Metro.*
Personnel: Arts Officer: Carol MacGregor. Four temporary exhibitions a year on the theme of contemporary crafts and popular culture. Local history exhibition, 18th century enamels gallery and sculpture garden make up the permanent collection.
Services and Facilities:
Commissioning Service. Craftshop. Disabled Access. Lectures.
Work Stocked and Sold:
Cer. Cra. Gla. Jew. Tx.
Price range: £10 - £200.

WOLVERHAMPTON ART GALLERY AND MUSEUM PS
Lichfield Street, Wolverhampton WV1 1DU.
Tel: 01902-552055. **Fax:** 01902-552053.
Opening times: Mon-Sat 10-5. Admission free.
Nearest Station: *Wolverhampton.*
Personnel: Head of Arts & Museums: Nicholas Dodd BA AMA.
Wolverhampton has the largest collection of Contemporary Art in the region. Beautiful Victorian galleries show 18th and 19th Century paintings. We also have one of the best public collections of Pop Art in the country. An exciting programme of exhibitions, from international to local, is planned for 1998, and will be accompanied by a range of workshops and activities. We are pleased to have won the 1997 Interpret Britain Award in the Access for Visitors with Disabilities Special Category. A pre-visit pack and audio tape guide is available. "Ways of Seeing", offers new and hands-on ways of looking at art.

Don't miss our tempting Tearoom and excellent Gallery Shop.
Services and Facilities:
Café. Craftshop. Disabled Access. Friends/Society. Shop. Workshop Facilities.
Work Stocked and Sold:
Cer. Cra. Jew.
Price range: £10 - £100.

North West

BOLTON

BOLTON

BOLTON MUSEUM, ART GALLERY AND AQUARIUM P
Le Mans Crescent, Bolton BL1 1SE. **Tel:** 01204-522311 ext 2191. **Fax:** 01204-391352.

CHESHIRE

NORTHWICH

WEAVER GALLERY
12 High Street, Weaverham, Northwich, CW8 3HB. **Tel:** 01606-853585.

PRESTBURY

ARTIZANA C
The Village, Prestbury, SK10 4DG.
Tel: 01625-827582. **Fax:** 01625-827582.

WARRINGTON

CASTLE PARK ARTS CENTRE
Off Fountain Lane, Frodsham, Warrington, WA6 6SE. **Tel:** 01928-35832.

WARRINGTON MUSEUM & ART GALLERY P
Bold Street, Warrington, WA1 1JG.
Tel: 01925-630550/444400.

WINSFORD

CHESHIRE VISUAL ARTS
Woodford Lodge, Woodford Lane, Winsford, CW7 4EH. **Tel:** 01606-557328.

WOODFORD VISUAL ART CENTRE
Woodford Lane West, Winsford, CW7 4EH.
Tel: 01606-557328. **Fax:** 01606-862113.

LANCASHIRE

ACCRINGTON

HAWORTH ART GALLERY P
Haworth Park, Manchester Road, Accrington, BB5 2JS. **Tel:** 01254-233782.

Ab Artist's Books **App** Applied Art **Cer** Ceramics **Cra** Crafts
Dec Decorative **Dr** Drawing **Fur** Furniture

BLACKBURN

BLACKBURN MUSEUM AND ART GALLERY P
Museum Street, Blackburn, BB1 7AJ.
Tel: *01254-667130.* **Fax:** *01254-680870.*

LEWIS TEXTILE MUSEUM P
Exchange Street, Blackburn, BB1 7JN.
Tel: *01254-667130.*

THE STREET
Blackburn Central Library, Town Hall Street,
Blackburn, BB2 1AH. **Tel:** *01254-661221.*
Fax: *01254-690539.*

WITTON COUNTRY PARK VISITOR CEN-
TRE
Preston Old Road, Blackburn, BB2 2TP.
Tel: *01254-55423.*

BLACKPOOL

GRUNDY ART GALLERY P
Queen Street, Blackpool, FY1 1PX.
Tel: *01253-751701.* **Fax:** *01253-26370.*

BURNLEY

TOWNELEY HALL ART GALLERY AND
MUSEUMS P
Burnley, BB11 3RQ. **Tel:** *01282-424213.*
Fax: *01282-424213.*

WHEATLEY LANE LIBRARY
Wheatley Lane, Burnley, BB12 9QH.
Tel: *01282-693160.*

CHORLEY

ASTLEY HALL MUSEUM AND ART
GALLERY P
Astley Park, Chorley, PR7 1NP. **Tel:** *01257-*
515555. **Fax:** *01257-515556.*

LANCASTER

CITY MUSEUM P
Market Square, Lancaster, LA1 1HT.
Tel: *01524-64637.* **Fax:** *01524-841692.*

PETER SCOTT GALLERY P
University of Lancaster, Lancaster, LA1 4YW.
Tel: *01524-593057/593056.* **Fax:** *01524-*
592603/593056.

PRESTON

COUNTY & REGIMENTAL MUSEUM P
Stanley Street, Preston, PR1 4YP. **Tel:** *01772-*
264075.

HARRIS MUSEUM & ART GALLERY P
Market Square, Preston, PR1 2PP.
Tel: *01772-258248.* **Fax:** *01772-886764.*
Email *harris@pbch.demon.co.uk*
Opening times: *Mon-Sat 10-5.*
Personnel: *Museum & Art Officer: Alexan-*
dra Walker.
Fine Art collections mainly British 18th-20th
century paintings, drawings and prints.
Includes works by the Devis family, Newsham

bequest of 19th century paintings and sculpture. A collection of British ceramics, glass and
costume includes Cedric Houghton bequest of
ceramics. A lively and varied programme of
temporary exhibitions. No Parking. Lift.
Chairlifts to Mezzanine Galleries. Wheelchair
Ramp. Audio Guide. Tactile Guide to Interior.
Refreshments. Guided tours are available and
an education service to complement the permanent collection and exhibitions.
Services and Facilities:
Café. Disabled Access. Friends/Society. Guided
Tours. Shop.

SAMLESBURY HALL
Preston New Road, Samlesbury, Preston, PR5
OUP. **Tel:** *01254-812010.*

VERNON GALLERY
Moor Lane, Preston, PR1 3PQ. **Tel:** *01772-*
59383. **Fax:** *01772-201378.*

LIVERPOOL

LIVERPOOL

ACORN GALLERY
16-18 Newington, Liverpool, L1 4ED
Tel: *0151-709 5423.* **Fax:** *0151-709 0759.*

ARTREACH LTD
Unit B61, Brunswick Enterprise, Liverpool, L3
4BD. **Tel:** *0151-708 7620.*

BLUECOAT DISPLAY CENTRE C
Bluecoat Chambers, School Lane, Liverpool, L1
3BX. **Tel:** *0151-709 4014.* **Fax:** *0151-707*
0048.

LIVERPOOL MUSEUM P
William Brown Street, Liverpool, L3 8EN.
Tel: *0151-478 4399.* **Fax:** *0151-478 4390.*

LIVERPOOL UNIVERSITY EXHIBITION
Abercromby Square, P.O. Box.147, Liverpool,
L69 3BX. **Tel:** *0151-794 2000.*

OPEN EYE GALLERY P
110 Bold Street, Liverpool, OL1 4HY.
Tel: *0151-709 9460.* **Fax:** *0151-709 3059.*
Email *info@openeye.u-net.com*
Opening times: *Tues-Fri 10-5.30, Sat*
10.30-5.
Nearest Station: *Liverpool Central.*
Personnel: *Director: Paul Mellor.*

THE OPEN EYE GALLERY

Open Eye is an organisation which develops,
promotes, enables, celebrates, challenges and
contextualises contemporary and historical art
practices which uses or acknowledges a photographic language or technology for Merseyside
and the greater North West region. The aims

of the organisation are to:- Develop: new
artists, existing artists, informal educational
programmes, formal educational programmes,
training opportunities, bridges to new and
existing audiences, curatorial skills and awareness, collaboration; Create: opportunities for
new work, exhibitions (external, internal and
virtual), technical support services, pathways
to facilities; Disseminate: touring exhibitions,
publications (both image and text), archived
resources, the mission.
Services and Facilities:
Commissioning Service. Disabled Access. Gallery
space for hire.

OPEN-EYE PHOTOGRAPHY GALLERY
28-32 Wood Street, Liverpool, L1 4AQ.
Tel: *0151-709 9460/709 2439.* **Fax:** *0151-709*
3050.
Personnel: *Catrina Henderson. Paul Mel-*
lor.

SUDLEY ART GALLERY P
Mossley Hill Road, Aigburth, Liverpool, L18
8BX. **Tel:** *0151-724 3245.* **Fax:** *0151-478*
4190.
Opening times: *Mon-Sat 10-5, Sun 12-5.*
Nearest Station: *Aigburth.*
Personnel: *Keeper of Art Galleries: Julian*
Treuherz.
Sudley is undoubtedly one of Merseyside's
gems. Situated in the leafy suburb of Mossley
Hill, it was the home of George Holt (1825-
1896) a founder of Lamport and Holt Shipping
line. On display is a fine collection of late
18th and 19th century British paintings
including two of Turner's most ambitious and
dazzling works. There are superb paintings by
Gainsborough, Bonnington and the Pre-
Raphaelites and a group of 19th century sculp-
tures ranging from Neo-classical marbles to
decorative bronzes.
Services and Facilities:
Café. Disabled Access. Friends/Society. Lectures.
Parking.

TATE GALLERY LIVERPOOL P
Albert Dock, Liverpool, L3 4BB.
Tel: *0151-709 3223.* **Fax:** *0151-709 3122.*
Email *liverpoolinfo@tate.org.uk*
Opening times: *Tues-Sun 10-6, closed Mon,*
except Bank Holidays.
Personnel: *Curator: Lewis Biggs.*
Opened in May 1988, Tate Gallery Liverpool
is housed in a Victorian warehouse converted
by the distinguished architect James Stirling.
Attracting more than half a million visitors a
year, the gallery offers a unique opportunity to
see the best of the national collection of 20th
c. art through a changing programme of displays, as well as special loan exhibitions.
Audience development is central to the
gallery's aim, and the education programme,
comprising workshops, talks, study days and
outreach projects, is recognised as among the
most innovative in the country.
Tate Gallery Liverpool re-opens on 23 May
1998, its tenth anniversary. The £6.96 million
development scheme has transformed previously undeveloped spaces of the Grade I listed
building into new galleries on the top floor

Gla Glass **Jew** *Jewellery* **Pa** *Paintings* **Ph** *Photography* **Pr** *Prints*
Sc Sculpture **Tx** *Textiles* **Wd** *Wood*

THE ARTWORLD
DIRECTORY 1998/99 **129**

which will allow more of the national collection of modern art to be shown in Liverpool. An auditorium, seminar room, education suite, audio-visual room and information area will also be provided with disabled access substantially improved.

The ground floor development includes the re-design of the entrance as well as a new dock-side shop and cafe-bar with views across the Albert Dock. Group Talks.

Services and Facilities:
Bookshop. Café. Disabled Access. Friends/Society. Guided Tours. Lectures. Shop. Workshop Facilities.

University of Liverpool Art Gallery PS
3 Abercromby Square, Liverpool L69 3BX.
Tel: 0151-794 2348. **Fax:** 0151-794 2343.
Opening times: Mon, Tues, Thurs 12-2, Wed, Fri 12-4. Closed: Weekends, Bank Holidays and August. Admission free.
Nearest Station: Lime Street.
Personnel: Curator: Ann Compton. Assistant Curator: Matthew H. Clough.

The art gallery displays a selection of the finest works of art belonging to the University of Liverpool. Among the highlights are a representative group of English watercolours, paintings by Joseph Wright of Derby and J.M.W. Turner, rare oil paintings by the wild-life artist J.J. Audubon, a rare selection of early English porcelain, stained glass cartoons by Edward Burne-Jones, portraits by August John, sculpture by John Foley and Lord Leighton and important works by leading twentieth century artists, including Sir Jacob Epstein, Lucian Freud and Dame Elizabeth Frink.

The collection has grown up over the last hundred years through the generosity of local benefactors, supplemented more recently by purchases. These gifts and acquisitions of paintings, watercolours, sculpture, medals, silver, ceramics, furniture and textiles are both a fine collection of British art and an integral part of the University's history since its foundation in 1881.

The presentation of the Art Gallery complements the elegant Georgian terrace house in Abercromby Square it occupies. A fine selection of clocks, furniture, carpets and tapestries lends a domestic atmosphere to this charming gallery. Only a small part of the University's substantial collection is on display in the Art Gallery; a tour of art around the Precinct is available from the Curator.

Postcards and publications are on sale at the entrance to the Art Gallery. Coffee and light refreshments are available in Staff House next door to the Art Gallery at 4-5 Abercromby Square. Free lunchtime gallery talks are organised in term time, please telephone for details. No prior booking necessary.

Services and Facilities:
Café. Gallery space for hire. Lectures. Museum Shop.

Walker Art Gallery P
William Brown Street, Liverpool, L3 8EL. **Tel:**
0151-207 0001/0151-478 4199. **Fax:** 0151-478 4190.
Opening times: Mon-Sat 10-5, Sun 12-5.

Nearest Station: Lime Street.
Personnel: Director: Mr R Foster. Keeper: Mr J B Treuherz.

Founded in 1877, the gallery exhibits an internationally important collection of art from the 14th to the 20th century. It is especially rich in European Old Masters, Victorian and Pre-Raphaelite pictures and modern British works. Includes the award-winning Sculpture Gallery, Medieval and Renaissance, eighteenth century and High Victorian galleries.

There is an exciting exhibitions programme, including Britain's premier painting biennial, the John Moores Liverpool exhibitions. The John Moores is the only national, open submission exhibition of British painting besides the Royal Academy and the first prize-winning painting becomes part of the Walker's outstanding collection of contemporary art.

Services and Facilities:
Café. Disabled Access. Friends/Society. Lectures. Parking. Shop.

MANCHESTER

MANCHESTER

Beech Road Gallery
70 Beech Road, Chorlton, Manchester M21.
Tel: 0161-881 4912.

Castlefield Gallery
5 Campfield Avenue Arcade, Manchester.
Tel: 0161-832 8034.

Colin Jellicoe Gallery C
82 Portland Street, Manchester M1 4QX.
Tel: 0161-236 2716.
Opening times: Tue-Fri 11-5, Sats 1-5.
Nearest Station: Piccadilly or Oxford Road.
Personnel: Directors: Colin Jellicoe, Alan Behar.

Sixty gallery artists including Colin Jellicoe (pictured) exhibiting drawings, paintings and graphics in three major mixed collections: 35th Anniversary Exhibitions April-June; 35th Summer Ex. July-Oct; 35th Winter Ex. Nov-March 99. Most works priced £50-£250. Founded 1963.
Services and Facilities:
Framing. Gallery space for hire.
Work Stocked and Sold:
Dr. Pa. Pr.
Price range: £50 - £250.

Cornerhouse PS
70 Oxford Street, Manchester M1 5NH.
Tel: 0161-228 7621. **Fax:** 0161-236 7323.
Opening times: Tues-Sat 11-6, Sun 2-6.
Nearest Station: Oxford Road.
Personnel: Exhibitions Director: Paul Bayley.

Cornerhouse offers the best of contemporary visual arts, exhibiting work of international significance, initiating and receiving touring shows, while also identifying opportunities to support and promote artists from the North West.

The programme also includes occasional exhibitions on architecture and design. The education programme which complements the exhibitions presents a wide variety of events including evening lecture programmes, artists' tours and schools workshops.

Services and Facilities:
Bar. Bookshop. Café. Disabled Access. Guided Tours. Lectures.

The Gallery, Manchester's Art House C
131 Portland Street, Manchester M1 4PY.
Tel: 0161-237 3551. **Fax:** 0161-228 3621.
Opening times: Mon-Fri 10-5, Thurs 10-7, Sat 10-4, Sun closed.
Nearest Station: Oxford Road/Piccadilly.
Personnel: Proprietor: Elaine Mather. Manager: Simeon Wardle.

The Gallery, Manchester's Art House, based on two floors, is the largest independent gallery in the NW.
Services and Facilities:
Art Consultancy. Art for Offices. Commissioning Service. Disabled Access. Framing. Friends/Society. Gallery space for hire. Restoration. Valuation.
Work Stocked and Sold:
Ab. App. Cer. Cra. Dec. Dr. Fur. Jew. Pa. Pr. Sc. Tx.
Price range: £10 - £10,000.

Manchester Central Library
St. Peter's Square, Manchester M2 5PD.
Tel: 0161-234 1900.

Manchester City Art Gallery PS
Mosley Street/Princess Street, Manchester M2 3JL. **Tel:** 0161-236 5244.
Fax: 0161-236 7369.

Ab Artist's Books App Applied Art Cer Ceramics Cra Crafts
Dec Decorative Dr Drawing Fur Furniture

Email *cityart@mcr1.poptel.org.uk*
Ws *http://www.u-net.com/set/mcag/cag.html*
Opening times: *Mon 11-5.30, Tue-Sat 10-5.30, Sun 2-5.30. Free admission.*
Nearest Station: *Piccadilly, Oxford Road.*
Personnel: *Director:* Virginia Tandy. *Press Officer:* Kate Farmery. *Senior Keeper, Exhibitions:* Howard Smith. *Senior Keeper, Collections:* Lesley Jackson.
Manchester City Art Gallery, the largest gallery in the region, spans two striking listed buildings in the centre of Manchester. It was established in 1882 and houses works by Stubbs, Gainsborough and Turner as well as a world-renowned collection of Pre-Raphaelites. There is a lively and innovative programme of temporary exhibitions and a fine display of decorative arts.
In 1998, work begins on a major expansion project which will double the amount of display space available and greatly improve visitor facilities. Visitors should therefore call ahead for details of gallery closures.
Government Designated Status. Good Food Guide recommended café. Gallery shop.
Services and Facilities:
Café. Friends/Society. Gallery space for hire. Guided Tours. Lectures. Shop.
Work Stocked and Sold:
Cer. Fur. Pa. Sc.

MANCHESTER CRAFT CENTRE
17 Oak Street, Smithfield, Manchester M4 5JD.
Tel: *0161-832 4274.*
Fax: *0161-832 3416.*

MANCHESTER METROPOLITAN UNIVERSITY (HOLDEN GALLERY) *P*
Grosvenor Building, Manchester Metropolitan University, Cavendish, All Saints, Manchester M15 6BR.
Tel: *0161-247 1708, 0161-247 2000.*
Fax: *0161-236 0820, 0161-247 6393.*

THE MUSEUM OF SCIENCE & INDUSTRY IN MANCHESTER
Liverpool Road, Castlefield, Manchester M3 4FP.
Tel: *0161-832 2244.* **Fax:** *0161-833 2184.*

PHILIPS CONTEMPORARY ART *C*
37, Ducie Street Piccadilly, Manchester
Tel: *0161-236 2707.*

RAINMAKER GALLERY OF CONTEMPORARY NATIVE AMERICAN INDIAN ART *C*
41 Lapwing Lane, West Didsbury, Manchester M20 2NT. **Tel:** *0161-4480 1495.* **Fax:** *0161-4480 1495.*

TIB LANE GALLERY *C*
14a Tib Lane (off Cross Street), Manchester M2 4JA. **Tel:** *0161-834 6928.*
Opening times: *Open during exhibitions 11-2, 3-5, Sat 11-1; closed Sun.*
Personnel: *Director:* J.M. Green.
Founded in 1959, Tib Lane Gallery continues to exhibit British, mainly figurative 20th Century paintings, watercolours, drawings etc. and some sculpture, particularly bronzes by Adrian Sorrell. Solo and mixed exhibitions between September and the end of June each

year show the work of well-established artists (Frink, Herman, Sutherland, Valette, Vaughan etc.) as well as that by many artists whose work, though distinguished, is less widely known. Conservation and Framing.
Services and Facilities:
Art Consultancy. Art for Offices. Commissioning Service. Framing. Restoration. Valuation.
Work Stocked and Sold:
Dr. Pa. Sc.
Price range: From £100.

THE WHITWORTH ART GALLERY *P*
University of Manchester, Oxford Road, Manchester M15 6ER. **Tel:** *0161-275 7450.* **Fax:** *0161-275 7451.*
Opening times: *Mon-Sat 10-5, Sun 2-5. Free admission.*
Personnel: *Director:* Alistair Smith. *Marketing Officer:* Emma Marshall.

The Whitworth Art Gallery

Founded in 1889, the Whitworth is famous for its collections of British watercolours, prints, drawings, modern art, sculpture and the largest textile and wallpaper holdings outside London. A lively programme of temporary exhibitions and changing displays from the gallery's collections runs throughout the year. Works not currently on show can be seen by appointment in the Study Rooms. Gallery Bistro.
Services and Facilities:
Disabled Access. Friends/Society. Guided Tours. Lectures. Parking. Restaurant. Shop.
Work Stocked and Sold:
Dr. Pa. Pr. Sc. Tx.

OLDHAM

OLDHAM

ARTISAN
3 King Street, Delph, Oldham OL3 5DL.
Tel: *01457-874506.*

OLDHAM ART GALLERY *P*
Union Street, Oldham OL1 1DN.
Tel: *0161-911 4653 / 4650.* **Fax:** *0161-627 1025.*

SADDLEWORTH MUSEUM AND ART GALLERY *P*
High Street, Uppermill, Oldham OL3 6HS.
Tel: *01457-874093/870336.*

ROCHDALE

ROCHDALE

ROCHDALE ART GALLERY *P*
Esplanade Arts & Heritage Centre, Esplanade, Rochdale OL16 1AQ.
Tel: *01706-342154.*
Fax: *01706-342154.*

SALFORD

SALFORD

CHAPMAN GALLERY
University of Salford, The Crescent, Salford M5 4WT. **Tel:** *0161-745 5000 ext 3219.*

SALFORD MUSEUM & ART GALLERY *PS*
Peel Park, Salford M5 4WU.
Tel: *0161-736 2649.*
Fax: *0161-745 9490.*
Opening times: *Mon-Fri 10-4.45, Sat & Sun 1-5. Admission Free.*
Nearest Station: *Salford Crescent.*
L S Lowry Gallery displaying over 100 of the best paintings and drawings from the City's vast collection of work by the artist.
In addition, there is a gallery of fine Victorian paintings and decorative arts and temporary exhibitions of contemporary art, craft, social history and photography.
Also a reconstruction of a cobbled Victorian Street complete with carriages and authentic sounds.
Services and Facilities:
Café. Disabled Access. Friends/Society. Gallery space for hire. Museum Shop. Parking. Workshop Facilities.

VIEWPOINT PHOTOGRAPHY GALLERY
Fire Station Square, The Crescent, Salford M5 4NZ.
Tel: *0161-737 1040, 0161-736 9448.*
Fax: *0161-737 1091.*

SEFTON

SOUTHPORT

ATKINSON ART GALLERY
Lord Street, Southport, PR8 1DH.
Tel: *01704-533133 Ext. 2111.*
Fax: *0151-934 2107.*

Gla Glass **Jew** Jewellery **Pa** Paintings **Ph** Photography **Pr** Prints
Sc Sculpture **Tx** Textiles **Wd** Wood

THE ARTWORLD
DIRECTORY 1998/99 **131**

ST. HELENS

ST. HELENS

PILKINGTON GLASS MUSEUM *P*
Prescot Road, St. Helens, WA10 3TT.
Tel: *01744-28882, 692499, 692014.*
Fax: *01744-30569.*

ST. HELENS MUSEUM & ART GALLERY *P*
College Street, St. Helens, WA10 1TW.
Tel: *01744-616614, 24061 ext 2961.*

STOCKPORT

STOCKPORT

STOCKPORT ART GALLERY *C*
Wellington Road South, Stockport SK3 8AB.
Tel: *0161-474 4453.* **Fax:** *0161-480 4960.*

TAMESIDE

STALYBRIDGE

ASTLEY CHEETHAM ART GALLERY *PS*
Trinity Street, Stalybridge, SK15 2BN.
Tel: *0161-338 2708.*
Opening times: *Mon-Fri 1-7.30pm, Thurs closed, Sat 9-4.*
Nearest Station: *Stalybridge.*
Personnel: *Director:* Dr Alan Wilson.
Astley Cheetham Art Gallery opened in 1901, founded by local mill-owner, John Frederick Cheetham.

The permanent collection comprises of the Cheetham bequest of fourteenth and fifteenth century Italian paintings and nineteenth century watercolours by Prout, Cox, Callow and Bonnington. Later additions include work by Edward Burne-Jones, G.F. Watts, Duncan Grant and Eduardo Paolozzi. The gallery also

collects work by local artists such as Harry Rutherford and Stanley Royle. Each year, the gallery hosts a varied programme of exhibitions and events featuring selections from the permanent collection, works by contemporary artists of the region and hosts several national touring exhibitions.
Services and Facilities:
Friends/Society. Gallery space for hire. Lectures. Museum Shop.
Work Stocked and Sold:
Ab. App. Cra. Dr. Pa. Pr.
Price range: £10 - £200.

WIGAN

LEIGH

TURNPIKE GALLERY *P*
Civic Square, Leigh WN7 1EB.
Tel: *01942-404469.*
Fax: *01942-404447.*
Email *tmgal@globalnet.co.uk*
Opening times: *Mon,Thur,Fri 9.30-5.30, Tues 10-5.30, Wed 9.30-5, Sat 10-3.*
Nearest Station: *Atherton.*
Personnel: *Gallery Officer:* Andrea Hawkins.
The Turnpike Gallery is a modern purpose built gallery 3200 sq. feet in size situated on the first floor of the Turnpike Centre. The temporary exhibitions programme reflects a variety of visual arts practices, and promotes contemporary art by regional, national and international artists.
There is an Arts Education service for schools and exciting Outreach activities for the public organised throughout the year. Small changing display of prints from the permanent collection include work by Patrick Caulfield and Andy Warhol. Free admission, large print guides and toilets.
Services and Facilities:
Disabled Access. Guided Tours. Lectures. Parking. Workshop Facilities.

WIRRAL

BEBINGTON

LADY LEVER ART GALLERY *P*
Port Sunlight, Bebington, L62 5EQ.
Tel: *0151-478 4136.*
Fax: *0151-478 4140.*
Opening times: *Mon-Sat 10-5, Sun 12-5.*
Nearest Station: *Bebington.*
Personnel: *Curator:* Julian Treuherz.
Opened in 1922. The gallery was founded and built by Philanthropist and soap manufacturer William Hesketh Lever, later the first Viscount Leverhulme, and houses his personal collection of works of art. These include Pre-Raphaelites, 18th and 19th century paintings, 18th century furniture, Chinese ceramics, Wedgwood, sculpture, embroideries and tapestries.
The Lady Lever Art Gallery is named in memory of Lever's wife and forms the centre piece

of the garden village Lever built for his workforce. Of special note is a series of superb carved or inlaid cabinets, some by Chippendale and paintings by Reynolds, Wilson, Sargent, Burne - Jones and Leighton.
Services and Facilities:
Café. Disabled Access. Friends/Society. Parking. Shop.

BIRKENHEAD

BLACKTHORN GALLERIES *C*
Della Robbia Building, 2a Price Street, Hamilton Quarter, Birkenhead, L41 6JN.
Tel: *0151-649 0099.*
Fax: *0151-649 0088.*
Email *ogilvie@galleries.u-net.com*
Ws *http://www.galleries.u-net.com*
Opening times: *Mon-Sat 9.30-5.30.*
Nearest Station: *Hamilton Square (Mersey Rail).*
Personnel: *Director (M.D.):* Iain Ogilvie.
Arts Director: Chris Wells.

The Blackthorn galleries exists to promote the work of its stable of artists/designers in the UK and further afield, to raise the awareness of fine art and contemporary design in its locale and to provide a platform for artists and designers to show their work in a professional and creative environment.
We have a world-wide vision and plans are progressing to open 4 "twin" galleries in Europe, 1 in Georgia USA and another in Romania.
We exhibit and sell an exciting combination of work; fine art paintings, sculpture, photography, ceramics, glass and contemporary jewellery. See Internet - http://www.galleries.u-net.com for more details.
Services and Facilities:
Art for Offices. Café. Craftshop. Gallery space for hire. Shop. Workshop Facilities.
Work Stocked and Sold:
Cer. Gla. Jew.
Price range: £15 - £2,500.

WILLIAMSON ART GALLERY AND MUSEUM *P*
Slatey Road, Birkenhead, L43 4UE.
Tel: *0151-652 4177.*
Fax: *0151-670 0253.*

HESWALL

DEE FINE ARTS
182 Telegraph Road, Heswall, L60 0AJ.
Tel: *0151-342 6657.*

Ab *Artist's Books* **App** *Applied Art* **Cer** *Ceramics* **Cra** *Crafts*
Dec *Decorative* **Dr** *Drawing* **Fur** *Furniture*

Yorkshire & Humberside

BRADFORD

BRADFORD

BRADFORD ART GALLERIES AND MUSEUMS *P*
*Headquarters, Cartwright Hall, Lister Park,
Bradford BD9 4NS.* **Tel:** *01274-493313.*
Fax: *01274-481045.*

CARTWRIGHT HALL ART GALLERY *PS*
*(Bradford Metropolitan Council), Lister Park,
Bradford BD9 4NS.* **Tel:** *01274-493313.*
Fax: *01274-481045.*
Opening times: *Tues-Sat 10-5, Sun 1-5.
Closed Mondays except Bank Holidays.*
Nearest Station: *Frizinghall/Bradford.*
Personnel: *City Arts, Museums and Libraries
Officer: P. Lawson.*

Situated in the heart of Lister Park, Cartwright
Hall opened in 1904 as Bradford's civic art
gallery. Collections of 19th and 20th century
British works, 19th century predominating in
permanent display. Reserve collections of
international works including contemporary
prints acquired from the British International
Print Biennale. Permanent display of works by
artists of South Asian origin or descent. Lively
exhibitions programme.
Services and Facilities:
*Café. Disabled Access. Friends/Society. Lectures.
Museum Shop. Parking.*

THE COLOUR MUSEUM *PS*
*Perkin House, PO Box 244, 1 Providence Street,
Bradford BD1 2PW.* **Tel:** *01274-390955.*
Fax: *01274-392888.*
Opening times: *Tues-Fri 2-5, Sat 10-4 and
to pre-booked parties on Tues-Fri mornings.
Admission: Adults £1.50, Concessions £1, Family Group £3.75.*
Nearest Station: *Forster Square.*
Personnel: *Curator: Sarah Burge.*
Britain's only museum of colour consists of two

galleries, both or which are packed with visitor
operated exhibits.
The World of Colour Gallery looks at the concept of colour and how it is perceived. You
can see how the world looks to other animals.
Mix coloured lights and experience colour illusions.
In the Colour and Textiles gallery you can discover the fascinating story of dyeing and textile printing from ancient Egypt to the present
day. You can also use computerised technology to take charge of a dye making factory or try
your hand at interior design.
Exhibitions/Events:- Annual programme of
temporary exhibitions, many accompanied by
a lecture. Two photographic exhibitions will
be held during 1998 as part of the Year of Photography and the Electronic Image. School
and holidays workshops. Free programme
available from the above address. (An Educational Activity of the Society of Dyers and
Colourists).
Services and Facilities:
*Disabled Access. Gallery space for hire. Lectures.
Museum Shop. Workshop Facilities.*

**NATIONAL MUSEUM OF PHOTOGRAPHY,
FILM AND TELEVISION** *P*
Temporary Address: The Art Mill, Upper Parkgate, Little Germany, Bradford BD1 5BJ. **Tel:**
01274-72748. **Fax:** *01274-394540.*
Opening times: *Tues-Sun 10-5. Open
Mondays during main holidays.*

Postal address: *National Museum of Photography, Film and Television, Pictureville, Bradford,
BD1 1NQ.*
Whilst the National Museum is undergoing
major refurbishment, temporary photography
exhibitions and events will continue at our
temporary site. The main museum will re-open bigger and better than ever in early 1999.
Services and Facilities:
*Café. Disabled Access. Guided Tours. Museum
Shop. Restaurant. Shop.*

SOUTH SQUARE GALLERY *C*
Thornton Road, Bradford BD13 3LD.
Tel: *01274-834747.*

TREADWELL'S ART MILL
*Upper Park Gate, Little German, Bradford BD1
5DW.* **Tel:** *01274-306065.*

UNIVERSITY OF BRADFORD
*Gallery II, University of Bradford, Chesham
Building, (off Great Horton Road), Bradford
BD7 1DP.* **Tel:** *01274-383365.*

KEIGHLEY

BRONTE PARSONAGE MUSEUM *P*
Haworth, Keighley, BD22 8DR. **Tel:** *01535-
642323.* **Fax:** *01535-647131.*

CLIFFE CASTLE ART GALLERY
*Spring Gardens Lane, Keighley,
BD20 6LH.*
Tel: *01535-606593.*

CALDERDALE

HALIFAX

THE DEAN CLOUGH GALLERIES *P*
Halifax, HX3 5AX.
Tel: *01422-250250.*
Fax: *01422-341148.*

PIECE HALL ART GALLERY *P*
The Piece Hall, Halifax, HX1 1RE.
Tel: *01422-358087.*
Fax: *01422-349310.*

TODMORDEN

TODMORDEN FINE ART
27 Water Street, Todmorden, OL14 5AB.
Tel: *01706-814723.*

DONCASTER

DONCASTER

**DONCASTER MUSEUM AND
ART GALLERY** *P*
Chequer Road, Doncaster DN1 2AE.
Tel: *01302-734222 / 734293.*
Fax: *01302-735409.*

HULL

HULL

**UNIVERSITY OF HULL ART
COLLECTION** *PS*
*University of Hull, Cottingham Road, Hull HU6
7RX.*
Tel: *01482-465192 / 465035.*
Fax: *01482-465192.*
Email *j.g.bernasconi@hist.hull.ac.uk*
Ws *http://www.hull.ac.uk*
Opening times: *Mon-Fri 2-4, Wed 12.30-4
(except Public Hols.).*
Personnel: *Director:* John G. Bernasconi.
The Hull University Art Collection specialises
in paintings, sculpture, drawings and prints
produced in Britain 1890-1940.
It includes works by Beardsley, Sickert, Steer,
Lucien Pissarro, Augustus John, Stanley
Spencer, Wyndham Lewis and Ben Nicholson,
as well as sculpture by Epstein, Gill, Gaudier-Brzeska and Henry Moore. The Camden
Town Group and Bloomsbury artists are particularly well represented.
Also on display are the Thompson Collections
of Chinese ceramics on long-term loan. Regular loan exhibitions are shown.
Services and Facilities:
Disabled Access. Friends/Society. Lectures.

YORKSHIRE & HUMBERSIDE

KIRKLEES

BATLEY

BAGSHAW MUSEUM P
Wilton Park, Batley, WF17 OAS.
Tel: 01924-326156.

BATLEY ART GALLERY
Market Place, Batley, WF17 5DA.
Tel: 01924-326090.
Fax: 01924-326308.

DEWSBURY

DEWSBURY EXHIBITION GALLERY
Wellington Road, Dewsbury, WF13.
Tel: 0113-233 6107.

HUDDERSFIELD

THE ARK C
113 North Road, Kirkburton, Huddersfield, HD8 0RL. **Tel:** 01484-605055.

HUDDERSFIELD ART GALLERY P
Princess Alexandra Walk, Huddersfield, HD1 2SU. **Tel:** 01484-221964 / 221962.
Fax: 01484-221952.

LUPTON SQUARE GALLERY C
1 & 2 Lupton Square (off Westgate), Honley, Huddersfield, HD7 2AA.
Tel: 01484-666144.
Fax: 01484-661221. **Email** *Luptonsquare-gallery@btinternet.com*
Opening times: *Fri, Sat Sun and Bank Holidays 10-5, or by appointment.*
Nearest Station: *Huddersfield.*
Personnel: Geoffrey S. Harrop.

Lupton Square Gallery

Housed in an 18th century cottage, grade II listed building, the gallery has 3 floors of exhibition space.
A wide selection of contemporary art works including metal sculpture and ceramics on show. Paintings are mainly of artists working in and around Yorkshire. A good selection of prints are available including some interesting ones from the 50's & 70's. Exhibitions are mounted periodically, please contact the gallery for details.
Services and Facilities:
Art for Offices. Commissioning Service. Framing. Parking.
Work Stocked and Sold:
Cer. Pa. Pr. Sc.
Price range: £15 - £3,000.

MIRFIELD

EASTTHORPE GALLERY
Huddersfield Road, Mirfield, WF14 8AT.
Tel: 01924-497646.

LEEDS

LEEDS

ABBEY HOUSE MUSEUM P
Kirkstall Road, Leeds LS5 3EH.
Tel: 01532-755821.

CITY ART GALLERY
The Headrow, Leeds LS1 3AA. **Tel:** 0113-2478248. **Fax:** 0113-2449689.

THE CRAFT CENTRE AND DESIGN GALLERY C
City Art Gallery, The Headrow, Leeds LS1 3AB.
Tel: 0113-247 8241.
Opening times: *Tues-Fri 10-5, Sat 10-4.*
Nearest Station: *Leeds.*
Personnel: *Director:* Hayley Walker.
The Craft Centre and Design Gallery aims to provide 'Art for Everyone' by showing contemporary fine craft from established and new designers. A lively exhibition programme features two main exhibitions a year, jewellery and ceramics showcases, limited edition print exhibitions and a new works section. In addition displays of contemporary jewellery, studio ceramics and domesticware, textiles, limited edition prints and applied arts provide a permanent feature. All year round approximately two hundred designers show their work, making it an excellent venue to browse, to learn or to buy.
Services and Facilities:
Commissioning Service. Craftshop. Disabled Access.
Work Stocked and Sold:
App. Cer. Cra. Gla. Jew. Pr. Tx. Wd.
Price range: £10 - £3,000.

THE HENRY MOORE INSTITUTE P
74 The Headrow, Leeds LS1 3AA. **Tel:** 0113-234 3158 (Information line). **Fax:** 0113-246 1481.
Opening times: *Open daily 10-5.30, Weds 10-9pm.*
Nearest Station: *Leeds City.*
Personnel: Helen Pearson.

The Henry Moore Institute, formerly a neglected group of early victorian merchants offices, has been transformed into a unique building devoted to the exhibition, study and promotion of sculpture. Situated in the heart of Leeds, the Institute houses four sculpture galleries for temporary exhibitions, also a sculpture reference library, archive and slide

library. The Institute organises talks, seminars and lectures. Please call our information line for further details: 0113-234 3158.
Services and Facilities:
Guided Tours. Lectures. Shop.

LEEDS METROPOLITAN UNIVERSITY GALLERY P
Woodhouse Lane, Leeds LS1 3HE.
Tel: 0113-283 3130. **Fax:** 0113-283 5999.
Email *c.slattery@lmu.ac.uk*
Ws *http://www.lmu.ac.uk/arts*
Opening times: *Mon-Fri 11-5, late night Wed until 9pm. Sat 11-4.*
Personnel: *Gallery Development Officer:* Claire Slattery.

Leeds Metropolitan University Gallery is one of the major contemporary arts venues in the city of Leeds. It is a public gallery specialising in commissioning contemporary art exhibitions and hosting touring exhibitions by artists of national and international significance. The main programme is interjected with seasonal shows by staff and students of the University. All exhibitions are temporary - there is no permanent collection. Our exhibitions policy covers the visual arts in its widest sense. In 1998 the gallery programme includes three commissioned shows for PHOTO 98 - the UK Year of Photography and the Electronic Image.
Services and Facilities:
Bar. Disabled Access. Lectures. Restaurant. Workshop Facilities.

THE PAVILLION PHOTOGRAPHY CENTRE
235 Woodhouse Lane, Leeds LS2 3AP.
Tel: 0113-275 1347.

TERRACE GALLERY P
Harewood House Harewood, Leeds LS17 9LQ.
Tel: 0113-288 6331. **Fax:** 0113-288 6467.
Email *business@harewood.org*
Ws *http://www.harewood.org*
Opening times: *Open daily, 17 March-25 October, 11-5. (Last admission 4.30pm).*
Nearest Station: *Leeds.*
Personnel: *Visual Arts Administrator:* Philippa Brough.

Contemporary Art Gallery in country house. One of the only galleries of its kind in UK. 3-4 temporary exhibitions a year. 1988: 17

Ab *Artist's Books* **App** *Applied Art* **Cer** *Ceramics* **Cra** *Crafts*
Dec *Decorative* **Dr** *Drawing* **Fur** *Furniture*

4 temporary exhibitions a year. 1988: 17 March-14 April 'Seeing is Believing' interactive/hands on exhibition investigating origins of photography in camera obscura A contrasting with new digital imaging techniques. 18 April-19 July Zarina Bhimji - photographic installation exploring Europe through formal gardens. 25 July-25 October 'Halo' by Simon Biggs, interactive artwork using video projection and realtime computing. Educational events for adults and children accompany all exhibitions.

Services and Facilities:
Bookshop. Café. Disabled Access. Guided Tours. Lectures. Parking. Shop.

UNIVERSITY GALLERY LEEDS PS
Parkinson Building, Woodhouse Lane, Leeds LS2 9JT.
Tel: 0113-233 2777.
Email H.M.Diaper@leeds.ac.uk
Ws http://www.leeds.ac.uk/library/gall/exhibs.html
Opening times: Exhibitions Mon-Fri 10-5, Thurs 10-7.
Nearest Station: Leeds City.
Personnel: Keeper: Dr Hilary Diaper.

Changing programme of exhibitions during each academic year, covering a wide range of historic and contemporary works in a variety of media. A room dedicated to the display of the University's permanent collection of mainly 19th & 20th century British paintings, drawings and prints, is due to open in September 1998. Wheelchair Access at north end of Parkinson Building.
Services and Facilities:
Disabled Access. Friends/Society.

ROTHERHAM

ROTHERHAM

ART GALLERY P
Rotherham Arts Centre, Walker Place, Rotherham S65 1JH. **Tel:** 01709-382121 ext 3624.
Fax: 01709-823650.

SHEFFIELD

SHEFFIELD

SHEFFIELD GALLERIES AND MUSEUMS TRUST
MAPPIN, GRAVES, RUSKIN GALLERIES

CITY MUSEUM AND MAPPIN ART GALLERY P
Weston Park, Western Bank, Sheffield S10 2TP.
Tel: 0114-2768588.
Fax: 0114-2750957.
Opening times: Wed-Sat 10-5, Sun 11-5, closed Mon & Tues.
Personnel: Senior Principal Keeper: Janet Barnes. Contact: Keeper of Mappin Art Gallery: Julie Milne.
Situated in Weston Park near the University of Sheffield, the City Museum and Mappin Art Gallery house and display the city's collections of fine and applied art, archaeology and ethnography and natural history.
There is a continuous changing programme of temporary exhibitions, largely reflecting the strengths of the 19th and 20th c., visual arts collections, but with a commitment to contemporary work.
Educational activities include a full schools programme plus workshops and art classes organised by the Mappin Art Workshops. Gallery and museum shop and Mappin café.
Services and Facilities:
Café. Museum Shop. Shop. Workshop Facilities.

GRAVES ART GALLERY P
Surrey Street, Sheffield S1 1XZ.
Tel: 0114-273 5158.
Fax: 0114-273 4705.
Opening times: Tues-Sat 10-5. Closed Sundays.
Nearest Station: Sheffield. Midland.
Personnel: Keeper: Anne Goodchild.
Founded 1934. Collection of 16th to 20th century British Art, European Old Masters, French painting and Oriental art. Regular exhibitions.
Services and Facilities:
Café. Lectures. Museum Shop. Shop.

RUSKIN GALLERY P
101 Norfolk Street, Sheffield S1 2JE.
Tel: 0114-273 5299.
Fax: 0114-273 5994.
Opening times: Tues-Sat 10-5, closed Sun.
Personnel: Principal Keeper: Camilla Hampshire.
The Ruskin Gallery was founded by John Ruskin (1819-1900) in Sheffield in 1875. It houses the collection of the Guild of St. George which comprises paintings, watercolours, prints, photographers, minerals, plaster casts, mediaeval illuminated manuscripts and a library.
This extensive collection is presented in a series of temporary exhibitions. Ruskin Craft Gallery has exhibitions of contemporary crafts.
Services and Facilities:
Gallery space for hire. Museum Shop. Shop.

UNTITLED PHOTOGRAPHIC GALLERY & WORKSHOP
1 Brown Street, Sheffield S1 2BS.

WAKEFIELD

WAKEFIELD

WAKEFIELD ART GALLERIES AND MUSEUMS P
Wakefield Art Gallery, Wentworth Terrace, Wakefield WF1 3QW. **Tel:** 01924-305796, Minicom 01924- 305769. **Fax:** 01924-305770.
Opening times: Tues-Sat 10.30-4.30, Sun 2-4.
Two of the most outstanding British sculptors of the 20th Century, Henry Moore and Barbara Hepworth, were born within a few miles of Wakefield Art Gallery and not surprisingly, the Gallery has acquired some significant early sculpture and drawings by these now internationally celebrated artists. These, and work from other major British modern artists, including David Bomberg, Anthony Caro, Patrick Heron, Maggi Hambling, David Hockney, Ben Nicholson, William Scott and Sir Matthew Smith, form the core of the collection. Works from other periods and European Schools are also on display.
There is a changing programme of touring exhibitions and displays from the permanent collections. Educational and community outreach service. Sculpture garden and family summer garden trail. Services and facilities: Family activities, INSET. We regret there is no wheelchair access.
Services and Facilities:
Friends/Society. Shop.

YORK

YORK

CASTLE HOWARD
York YO6 7DA. **Tel:** 01653-648333.

KENTMERE HOUSE GALLERY C
53 Scarcroft Hill, York YO2 1DF. **Tel:** 01904-656507. **Fax:** 01904-433949.
Opening times: Open every Thursday evening 6-9, first weekend of every month, each day 11-5 and any other time by appointment.
Personnel: Director: Ann Petherick.
A gallery within the owners' home which aims to banish elitism and expand the market for the work of professional living artists. The work is predominantly figurative, contemporary without being avant garde. Exhibitions change approximately every 6 weeks, and there is also a changing display of stock. Prices range from under £100 - £3,000+
Services and Facilities:
Art Consultancy. Art for Offices. Commissioning Service. Framing. Parking.
Work Stocked and Sold:
Cer. Pa. Pr.
Price range: £50 - £3,000.

PYRAMID GALLERY C
43 Stonegate, York YO1 2AW. **Tel:** *01904-641187.*

ROBERT FEATHER JEWELLERY GALLERY C
10 Gillygate, York YO3 7EQ. **Tel:** *01904-632025.*

YORK CITY ART GALLERY PS
Exhibition Square, York YO1 2EW.
Tel: *01904-551861.*
Fax: *01904-551866.*
Opening times: *Open to the public: Mon-Sat 10-5, Sun 2.30-5, last admission each day 4.30. The Gallery is closed on 1 January, Good Friday and 25 & 26 December.*
Nearest Station: *York.*
Personnel: *Curator: Richard Green.*

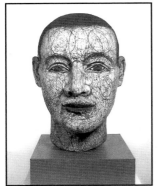

Six hundred years of painting, from early Italian gold-ground panels to the art of the 20th century.
Exceptional in its range and interest, the collection includes pictures by Parmigianino and Bellotto, Lely and Reynolds, Frith and Boudin, Lowry and Nash, and nudes by York-born Etty. Outstanding collection of studio pottery. Varied and exciting programme of temporary exhibitions and events. Gallery Shop. Admission free.
Services and Facilities:
Bookshop. Disabled Access. Friends/Society. Guided Tours. Lectures. Shop.

EAST RIDING OF YORKSHIRE

BEVERLEY

BEVERLEY ART GALLERY & MUSEUM P
Champney Road, Beverley, HU17 9BQ.
Tel: *01482-883903 / 884956.*

BRIDLINGTON

SEWERBY HALL ART GALLERY AND MUSEUM (MUSEUM OF EAST YORKSHIRE) P
Sewerby Hall, Bridlington, YO15 1EA.
Tel: *01262-677874.*
Fax: *01262-674265.*

GOOLE

GOOLE MUSEUM & ART GALLERY P
Carlisle Street, Goole, DN14 5AA.
Tel: *01405-768329.* **Fax:** *01405-768329.*

NORTH YORKSHIRE

HARROGATE

ANSTEY GALLERIES C
33 Swan Road, Harrogate, HG1 2SA.
Tel: *01423-500102.* **Fax:** *01423-500102.*

CHANTRY HOUSE GALLERY C
Ripley, Harrogate, HG3 3AY.
Tel: *01423-771011.*
Opening times: *Apr-Sept Tues-Sat 10-5, Sun 12-5. Oct-Mar Wed-Sat 10-4, Sun 12-4.*
Personnel: *Directors: Terry Logan, Georgina Logan.*

The Chantry House Gallery is situated in the beautiful and historic village of Ripley Castle, 3 miles north of Harrogate. Established in 1980, the gallery provides a show space for established artists working in a variety of media. Several exhibitions are arranged but the gallery maintains a mixed show of work by gallery artists which is ever-changing throughout the year. The Chantry House Gallery strives to provide high quality work whilst catering for a wide variety of tastes and interests.
Services and Facilities:
Art Consultancy. Art for Offices. Commissioning Service. Disabled Access. Framing.
Work Stocked and Sold:
Dr. Pa. Pr.
Price range: *£10 - £1,000.*

HARROGATE MUSEUMS AND ARTS P
Royal Pump Room Museum, Crown Place, Harrogate, HG1 2RY. **Tel:** *01423-503340.*

MERCER ART GALLERY P
Swan Road, Harrogate, HG1 2SA.
Tel: *01423-503340.* **Fax:** *01423-840026.*

RIPLEY CASTLE P
Ripley, Harrogate, HG3 3AY. **Tel:** *01423-770152.* **Fax:** *01423-771745.*

HELMSLEY

LOOK GALLERY C
20 Castlegate, Helmsley, YO6 5AB.
Tel: *01439-770545.*
Opening times: *Mon-Sat 10.30-5, Sun 2-5.*

Personnel: *Director: Nicholas Coombes.*
Contemporary painting, sculpture, ceramics and glass. The gallery shows a wide variety of contemporary work from living British artists. The policy of the gallery is to maintain throughout the year a mixed show of work by gallery artists. Artists represented include: Caroline Bailey, Edna Bizon, David Greenwood, Janet Skea, Robert Tilling and Simon Turvey.
Work Stocked and Sold:
Cer. Gla. Pa. Sc.
Price range: *£100 - £1,000.*

KNARESBOROUGH

EUROPEAN CERAMICS C
The Warehouse, Breakers Yard, Finkle Street, Knaresborough, HG5 8AA.
Tel: *01423-867401.* **Fax:** *01423-867401.*
Opening times: *Daily 11-5, Sun 2-5. Closed Thurs.*
Nearest Station: *Knaresborough, 5 ins walk (connecting to York & Leeds).*
Personnel: *Director: Maggie Barnes.*
European Ceramics is firmly established as one of the UK's leaders in its chosen specialisation; showing the work of the finest makers in mainland Europe and Britain. Regular solo exhibitions and occasional thematic shows are supported by the gallery's superb reserve collection where the serious collector has the unique opportunity to acquire items of premier quality by leading makers.
Services and Facilities:
Art Consultancy. Art for Offices. Bookshop. Commissioning Service. Lectures.
Work Stocked and Sold:
Ab. Cer. Cra. Gla. Sc. Tx.
Price range: *£25 - £2,500.*

GORDON REECE GALLERY C
Finkle Street, Knaresborough, HG5 8AA.
Tel: *01423-866219.* **Fax:** *01423-868165.*

OLD COURTHOUSE MUSEUM P
Castle Grounds, Knaresborough,
Tel: *01423-503340.* **Fax:** *01423-840026.*

RICHMOND

RICHMONDSHIRE MUSEUM P
Ryder's Wynd, Richmond, DL10 4JA.
Tel: *01748-825611.*

SCARBOROUGH

CRESCENT ARTS WORKSHOP P
The Crescent, Scarborough, YO11 2PW.
Tel: *01723-351461.*

SCARBOROUGH ART GALLERY
The Crescent, Scarborough, YO11 2PW.
Tel: *01723-374553.* **Fax:** *01723-376941.*

SETTLE

LINTON COURT GALLERY C
Duke Street, Settle, BD24 9DW.
Tel: *01729-822695.*
Opening times: *Please phone for information*

Ab *Artist's Books* **App** *Applied Art* **Cer** *Ceramics* **Cra** *Crafts* **Dec** *Decorative* **Dr** *Drawing* **Fur** *Furniture*

about exhibitions and opening times.
Nearest Station: *Settle.*
Personnel: *Director:* Ann Carr.
The Gallery started in 1980 and is in a 200-year-old converted hay loft. During the year there are a wide variety of exhibitions showing work of young as well as nationally known artists. Ceramics and original prints are always available.
Work Stocked and Sold:
Cer. Pa. Pr.
Price range: £100 - £3,000.

THIRSK

SION HILL HALL MUSEUM *P*
Kirby Wiske, Thirsk, YO7 4EU. **Tel:** *01845-587206.*

WHITBY

SUTCLIFFE GALLERY
1 Flowergate, Whitby, YO21 3BA. **Tel:** *01947-602239.*

Northern

CUMBRIA

ALSTON

GOSSIPGATE GALLERY *C*
The Butts, Alston, CA9 3JU.
Tel: *01434-381806.*
Opening times: *10-5 daily including Sundays Easter-October and winter weekends. Winter weekdays - telephone for details (closed 4 Jan-mid Feb).*
Personnel: *Proprietor:* Sonia Kempsey.
Gossipgate Gallery, the first and foremost art and craft venue in the North Pennines Area of Outstanding Natural Beauty, lies in a quiet back-lane of Alston, a picturesque town with cobbled streets situated in the heart of the North Pennines. The gallery specialises in displaying the work of contemporary artists and crafts-people from the North of England and the emphasis each season is on showing quality and originality from within this region. A programme of exhibitions displaying the work of well-established and aspiring young artists and craftspeople is complemented by a permanent selection of northern work in the gallery shop.
Services and Facilities:
Art Consultancy. Café. Craftshop. Disabled Access. Friends/Society. Parking. Shop.
Work Stocked and Sold:
Cer. Cra. Gla. Jew. Pa. Pr. Sc. Tx. Wd.
Price range: £0,25 - £500.

AMBLESIDE

DEXTERITY *C*
Kelsick Road, Ambleside, LA22 OBZ.
Tel: *015394-34045.*

Opening times: *7 days 9.30-6, not 25/26 Dec.*
Nearest Station: *Windermere.*
Personnel: *Directors:* Gillean Bell, Roger Bell.

Set in the heart of the Lake District, Dexterity has been open since 1989 selling the work of living British based artists and craftspeople including those based locally. We sell to holidaymakers but our main customers are within a two to three hours journey (Glasgow, Newcastle, Manchester, Liverpool). The Gallery style is contemporary and we are particularly strong on ceramics and limited edition prints but also have a good selection of jewellery, paintings, studio glass and sculpture. Framing commissions welcomed.
Services and Facilities:
Art for Offices. Commissioning Service. Craftshop. Disabled Access. Framing.
Work Stocked and Sold:
Ab. Cer. Cra. Gla. Jew. Pa. Pr. Sc. Wd.
Price range: £5 - £500.

CARLISLE

TULLIE HOUSE, CITY MUSEUM & ART GALLERY *PS*
Castle Street, Carlisle, CA3 8TP. **Tel:** *01228-534781.* **Fax:** *01228-5810249.*
Opening times: *Mon-Sun 10-5, Sun 12-5.*
Personnel: *Director:* N.W. Winterbotham.
Major new museum and art gallery development opened 1991. Continuous programme of contemporary visual arts and crafts. Exhibitions also drawn from the Fine and Decorative Art collections of 19th and 20th century British art including the Bottomley Bequest of Pre-Raphaelites and an outstanding collection of porcelain from the major English factories. Lecture theatre and restaurant available for evening hire. Grounds and gardens.
Services and Facilities:
Bookshop. Café. Disabled Access. Friends/Society. Museum Shop. Restaurant. Shop. Workshop Facilities.

COCKERMOUTH

CASTLEGATE HOUSE
Cockermouth, CA13 9HA.
Tel: *01900-822149.*

CONISTON

BRANTWOOD *P*
Brantwood, Coniston, LA21 8AD.
Tel: *015394-41396.* **Fax:** *015394-41263.*

EGREMONT

LOWES COURT GALLERY
12 Main Street, Egremont, CA22 2DW.
Tel: *01946-820693.*

KENDAL

ABBOT HALL ART GALLERY
Kendal, LA9 5AL. **Tel:** *01539-722464.*
Fax: *01539-722494.*
Opening times: *Open 7 days a weeks 12 February 98 - 31 January 99, 10.30-5 (reduced hours in winter). Admission: Adult £2.80 (concessions available).*
Personnel: *Director:* Mr Edward King.
This elegant Georgian building provides a superb setting for its collection of fine art. Paintings by George Romney fill the walls of rooms furnished by Gillows of Lancaster.

Touring exhibitions complement the permanent collection of 18th, 19th and 20th century British art.
1998 Temporary Exhibition Programme: 12 Feb-19 April - John Swannell - Photographic Portraits and Landscapes; 14 March-13 April - Histoire Naturelle - Etchings by Picasso; 28 April-31 May - Amanda Faulkner - Recent Paintings; 10 June-13 Sept - Head First - Portraits from the Arts Council Collection; 2 Sept-1 Nov - Kitty North - Landscape Paintings; 10 Nov-1988-31 Jan 1999 - Bridget Riley - A Major Retrospective. Coffee Shop, Gift Shop, Free Parking, Picnic Area.
Services and Facilities:
Bookshop. Café. Commissioning Service. Disabled Access. Friends/Society. Guided Tours. Lectures. Museum Shop. Parking.

BREWERY ARTS CENTRE
Warehouse Gallery, 122a Highgate, Kendal, LA9 4HE. **Tel:** *01539-725133.* **Fax:** *01539-730257.*

ODDFELLOWS GALLERY
Highgate, Kendal,
Tel: *01539-734669.*

KESWICK

KESWICK MUSEUM & ART GALLERY P
Fitz Park, Station Road, Keswick, CA12 4NF.
Tel: *017687-73263.*

THORNTHWAITE GALLERY
Thornthwaite, Keswick, CA12.
Tel: *017687-78248.*

PENRITH

BECK MILL GALLERY
Langwathby, Penrith, CA10 1NY.
Tel: *01768-881371.*

LABURNUM CERAMICS
Yanwath, Penrith, CA10 2LF.
Tel: *01768-864842.*
Fax: *01768-863518.*

PENRITH MUSEUM P
*Robinson's School, Middlegate, Penrith, CA11
7PT.* **Tel:** *01768-64671.*

WHITEHAVEN

THE HARBOUR GALLERY
The Beacon, Whitehaven,
Tel: *01946-592302.*

**WHITEHAVEN MUSEUM &
ART GALLERY** P
Civic Hall, Lowther Street, Whitehaven,
Tel: *01946-3111307.*
Fax: *01946-693373.*

WORKINGTON

CARNEGIE ARTS CENTRE
Finkle Street, Workington, CA14 2B.
Tel: *01900-602122.* **Fax:** *01900-604351.*

GREENHOUSE
Curwen Park, Workington, CA14 3YJ.
Tel: *01900-602986.*

DURHAM

BARNARD CASTLE

THE BOWES MUSEUM P
Barnard Castle, DL12 8NP. **Tel:** *0183-369
0606.* **Fax:** *0183-637 163.*

CASTLE GALLERY
*Witham Hall, Horsemarket, Barnard Castle,
DL12.*

CASTLE EDEN

CASTLE EDEN GALLERY
Castle Eden, TS27 4SD.

DARLINGTON

BERNHARDT GALLERY
60 Coniscliffe Road, Darlington, DL3 7RN.
Tel: *01325-356633.*

DARLINGTON ART GALLERY P
Crown Street, Darlington, DL1 1ND.
Tel: *01325-462034 / 469858.*

DURHAM

DURHAM ART GALLERY P
Aykley Heads, Durham, DH1 5TU.
Tel: *0191-384 2214.*
Fax: *0191-386 1770.*
Opening times: *Tues-Sat 10-5, Sun 2-5.
Closed Mondays.*
Nearest Station: *Durham (5 mins walk).*
Personnel: Arts Development Manager: Zoe
Channing. Art Gallery Assistant: Dennis Hard-
ingham.
Situated in parkland on the northern edge of
the city, the Art Gallery features a changing
programme of temporary exhibitions related to
all aspects of the visual arts, plus illustrated
talks, films, workshops, demonstrations,
lunchtime concerts and other events aimed at
a wide range of visitors and special interest
groups.

The gallery provides a secure venue for high
quality displays, including national touring
exhibitions, and the 1998 programme includes
jewellery by Wally Gilbert, Art Textiles, satiri-
cal art from Private Eye, the Society of Wood
Engravers, Mayan costumes, Beryl Cook,
Emrys Williams, Disasters of War (South Bank
Centre) and Andy Capp.
Services and Facilities:
*Café. Disabled Access. Framing. Friends/Society.
Museum Shop. Parking.*

**DURHAM UNIVERSITY ORIENTAL MUSE-
UM** PS
Elvet Hill, Durham, DH1 3TH.
Tel: *0191-374 7911.*
Fax: *0191-374 3242.*
Email *oriental.museum@durham.ac.uk*
Ws *http://www.dur.ac.uk/~dcm0www/omuseum.htm*
Opening times: *Weekdays 9.30-1 & 2-5.
Weekends 2-5.*
Personnel: *Keeper:* John Ruffle.
The Oriental Museum is a major resource for
anyone in the North East who is interested in
the visual arts.
Its collections range from ancient Egypt to
modern Japan and the major cultures of the
Orient are well represented.
The Museum runs a programme of lectures,
day-schools and other events. Events
planned for 1998 include S.E. Asian ceramics
and Japanese prints. Details from the Oriental
Museum.
Services and Facilities:
*Bookshop. Friends/Society. Lectures. Museum
Shop. Parking. Shop.*

HARTLEPOOL

HARTLEPOOL

GRAY ART GALLERY AND MUSEUM P
Clarence Road, Hartlepool TS24 8BT.
Tel: *01429-266522.*

HARTLEPOOL ART GALLERY P
Church Square, Hartlepool TS24 8EQ.
Tel: *01429-869706.* **Fax:** *01429-523408.*

MIDDLESBROUGH

MIDDLESBROUGH

CLEVELAND COUNTY MUSEUMS SERVICE P
*County Leisure Services, PO Box 41, Middles-
brough TS3 0YZ.* **Tel:** *01642-248155.*

CLEVELAND CRAFT CENTRE C
57 Gilkes Street, Middlesbrough TS1 5EL.
Tel: *01642-262376 / 226351.* **Fax:** *01642-
226351.*

CLEVELAND GALLERY P
Victoria Road, Middlesbrough TS1 3QS.
Tel: *01692-262375.* **Fax:** *01692-253661.*

DORMAN MUSEUM P
Linthorpe Road, Middlesbrough TS5 6LA.
Tel: *01642-813781.* **Fax:** *01642-813781.*

MIDDLESBROUGH ART GALLERY P
320 Linthorpe Road, Middlesbrough TS1 4AW.
Tel: *01642-247445.* **Fax:** *01642-813781.*

NEWCASTLE-UPON-TYNE

GATESHEAD

DESIGN WORKS
William Street, Gateshead, NE10 0PJ.
Tel: *0191-495 0066.*

**THE GALLERY, GATESHEAD CENTRAL
LIBRARY**
Prince Consort Road, Gateshead, NE8 4LN.
Tel: *0191-477 3478.* **Fax:** *0191-477 7454.*

PORTCULLIS CRAFT GALLERY
*7 The Arcade, Metro Centre, Gateshead, NE11
9YL.* **Tel:** *0191-460 6345.* **Fax:** *0191-460
4285.*

SHIPLEY ART GALLERY
Prince Consort Road, Gateshead, NE8 4JB.
Tel: *0191-477 1495.*
Fax: *0191-477 1495.*

NEWCASTLE-UPON-TYNE

BROWNS
*First Floor, 15 Acorn Road, Jesmond, Newcastle-
upon-Tyne NE2 2DJ.* **Tel:** *0191-281 1315.*

Ab *Artist's Books* **App** *Applied Art* **Cer** *Ceramics* **Cra** *Crafts*
Dec *Decorative* **Dr** *Drawing* **Fur** *Furniture*

CHAMELEON GALLERY
Milburn House, Dean Street, Newcastle-upon-Tyne NE1 1PQ. **Tel:** *0191-232 2819.*

CORRYMELLA SCOTT GALLERY C
5 Tankerville Terrace, Jesmond, Newcastle-upon-Tyne NE2 3AH. **Tel:** *0191-281 8284, 0191-401 7513.* **Fax:** *0191-281 5434.*

GULBENKIAN GALLERY
c/o 72 Moor Road North, Newcastle-upon-Tyne NE3 1AB.

HATTON GALLERY PS
Newcastle University, Newcastle-upon-Tyne NE1 7RU.
Tel: *0191-222 6057.* **Fax:** *0191-222 6057.*
Opening times: *Mon-Fri 10-5.30, Sat 10-4.30.*
Personnel: *Director:* Andrew Burton.
The Hatton Gallery was founded in 1926 and is attached to the Fine Art Department of Newcastle University. The Hatton gallery hosts a varied programme of temporary art exhibitions of both a historical and contemporary nature. As a registered museum, the Hatton Gallery possesses an extensive collection of paintings, prints, drawings and sculptures from Renaissance to Modern periods. In addition the gallery houses a splendid collection of African sculptures donated by Fred & Diana Uhlman as well as the famous Elterwater Merzbarn, a unique installation by the German Dada artist Kurt Schwitters. Both of these are on permanent display. The gallery is funded by the university and is supported by the Friends of the Hatton.
Services and Facilities:
Bookshop. Friends/Society. Gallery space for hire. Guided Tours. Lectures.

LAING ART GALLERY
Higham Place, Newcastle-upon-Tyne.
Tel: *0191-232 7734.*

NEWCASTLE ARTS CENTRE
67-69 Westgate Road, Newcastle-upon-Tyne NE1 1SG. **Tel:** *0191-261 5618.*

SIDE GALLERY
5/9 Side, Newcastle-upon-Tyne NE1 3JE.
Tel: *0191-232 2000.*

SQUIRES GALLERY
University of Northumbria at Newcastle, Sandyford Road, Newcastle-upon-Tyne NE1 8ST.

THE UNIVERSITY GALLERY PS
University of Northumbria, Sandyford Road, Newcastle-upon-Tyne NE1 8ST.
Tel: *0191-227 4424.* **Fax:** *0191-227 4718.*
Email *mara-helen.wood@unn.ac.uk*
Opening times: *Mon-Thu 10-5, Fri-Sat 10-4. Closed Sundays and Bank Holidays throughout the year and Saturdays during vacations.*
Personnel: *Director:* Mara-Helen Wood.
The University Gallery is recognised as a public gallery with an annual average attendance of 80,000 visitors. It presents a programme of temporary exhibitions by artists of national and international reputation, as well as exhibitions by lesser known, promising artists. Since its inception in 1977, the gallery has presented over 600 exhibitions which have ranged in character from group shows to one-man shows; thematic exhibitions of historical or topical interest; major touring exhibitions for museums and schools and an extensive programme of lectures, seminars, literary events and art classes for adults and children.
The gallery is responsible for the Permanent Collection comprising over 200 paintings, drawings and prints by leading contemporary British artists including, for example, Norman Adams, Peter Greenham, Sean Scully, Albert Irvin and Victor Pasmore.
Services and Facilities:
Bookshop. Lectures.
Work Stocked and Sold:
Dr. Pa.
Price range: £50 - £5,000.

NORTH TYNESIDE

WALLSEND

BUDDLE ARTS CENTRE PS
258b Station Road, Wallsend, NE28 8RH.
Tel: *0191-200 7132.* **Fax:** *0191-200 7142.*
Email *buddle@ntynearts.demon.co.uk*
Opening times: *Tues-Thurs 1-5, Fri 10-5, Sat 2-5.*
Nearest Station: *BR: Newcastle, Metro: Wallsend.*
Personnel: *Principal Arts Officer:* Mike Campbell.
Mixed use arts centre including gallery space (46.5m linear hanging space) showing a range of exhibitions in various media. Two or three professional shows per year, including annual North Tyneside Open Exhibition; other shows by schools, community groups and amateur art clubs. Also occasional temporary installations and commissioned work. Outlet for new prints supplied by Northern Print Studio. Digital artist residency based in facility during 1998. The Buddle Arts Centre is managed by North Tyneside Arts.
Services and Facilities:
Bar. Commissioning Service. Disabled Access. Gallery space for hire. Parking. Workshop Facilities.
Work Stocked and Sold:
Pr.
Price range: £50 - £500.

NORTHUMBERLAND

ALNWICK

BONDGATE GALLERY P
22 Narrowgate, Alnwick, NE66 3JG.
Tel: *01665-576450.*

THE CHATTON GALLERY C
Church House, New Road, Chatton, Alnwick, NE66 5PU. **Tel:** *01668-215494.*

BELFORD

NORSELANDS GALLERY C
The Old School, Warenford, Belford, NE70 7HY.
Tel: *01668-213465.*
Opening times: *Winter: 9-5, Summer: 9-9. Closed two weeks over Christmas/New Year.,*
Nearest Station: *Berwick-Upon-Tweed.*
Personnel: *Directors:* Barrie Rawlinson, Veronica Rawlinson.
Home to Studio Two Ceramics, Norselands Gallery is situated in an old school in the hamlet of Warenford in rural North Northumberland. Set against a backdrop of glazed victorian tiles, is a fine collection of original paintings, etchings and quality crafts with emphasis on ceramics.
Artists featured include Barbara Gormar-Stone, Julian Williams, Collin Kellam, Diana Worthy and Veronica Rawlinson, resident ceramic artist. Childrens play area.
Services and Facilities:
Café. Craftshop. Disabled Access. Parking. Workshop Facilities.
Work Stocked and Sold:
Cer. Cra. Dr. Gla. Pa. Pr.
Price range: £15 - £250.

BERWICK UPON TWEED

BERWICK UPON TWEED BOROUGH MUSEUM AND ART GALLERY P
The Clock Block, Berwick Barracks, Ravensdowne, Berwick Upon Tweed, TD15 1DQ.
Tel: *01289-330933 (Curator), 01289-330044 (Council).*
Fax: *01289-330540 (Council).*

SALLYPORT GALLERY
48 Bridge Street, Berwick Upon Tweed, TD15 1AQ.

THREE FEATHERS GALLERY
83c Mary Gate, Berwick Upon Tweed, TD15 1BA.
Tel: *01289-307642.*

CRAMLINGTON

CRAMLINGTON LIBRARY
Forum Way, Civic Precinct, Cramlington, NE23 6QE.
Tel: *01670-714371.*

FORUM GALLERY
Cramlington Library, Forum Way, Civic Precinct, Cramlington,
Tel: *0167-071 4371.*

HEXHAM

MOOT HALL
Market Place, Hexham,

QUEENS HALL ART CENTRE
Beaumont Street, Hexham, NE46 3LS.
Tel: *01434-606787/8.*
Fax: *01434-606043.*

Gla Glass *Jew* Jewellery *Pa* Paintings *Ph* Photography *Pr* Prints
Sc Sculpture *Tx* Textiles *Wd* Wood

ROTHBURY

ALEXANDRA HOUSE GALLERY
High Street, Rothbury, NE65 7TE.
Tel: *01669-621463.*

ROTHBURY LIBRARY AND ART GALLERY
Front Street, Rothbury,
Tel: *01669-620428.*

SMITH & WATSON STAINED GLASS
The Rothbury Gallery, Townfoot, Rothbury,
NE65 7SL.
Tel: *01669-621156.*

STAMFORDHAM

STAMFORDHAM GALLERY
23 North Side, Stamfordham,

WARKWORTH

DIAL GALLERY C
5 Dial Place, Warkworth, NE65 0UR.
Tel: *01665-710822.*

REDCAR AND CLEVELAND

GUISBOROUGH

WALTON GALLERIES
Walton Terrace, Guisborough, TS14 6QG.
Tel: *01287-638639.*

REDCAR

KIRKLEATHAM OLD HALL MUSEUM P
Kirkleatham Village, Redcar, TS10 5NW.
Tel: *01642-479500.*

SALTBURN BY THE SEA

SALTBURN GALLERY
21 Milton Street, Saltburn By The Sea, TS12
1DJ. **Tel:** *01287-622245.*

STOCKTON ON TEES

BILLINGHAM

BILLINGHAM ART GALLERY P
Queensway, Billingham, TS23 2LN.
Tel: *01642-397590.* **Fax:** *01642-397590.*

STOCKTON ON TEES

DOVECOT ARTS CENTRE
Dovecot Street, Stockton on Tees TS18 1LL.
Tel: *01642-611625.*

GREEN DRAGON GALLERY
6 Finkle Street, Stockton on Tees TS18 1AT.
Tel: *01642-617600.*

PRESTON HALL MUSEUM P
Yarm Road, Stockton on Tees TS18 3RH.
Tel: *01642-791424.*

SUNDERLAND

SUNDERLAND

NORTHERN GALLERY FOR CONTEMPO-
RARY ART P
City Library and Arts Centre, Fawcett Street,
Sunderland SR1 1RE. **Tel:** *0191-514 1235.*
Fax: *0191-514 8444.* **Email**
ngca@Sund2.unity.libris.co.uk
Opening times: *Mon/Wed 9.30-7.30,*
Tues/Thurs/Fri 9.30-5, Sat 9.30-4. Closed Sun-
days/Bank Holidays.
Nearest Station: *Sunderland*
Personnel: *Principal Curator:* Louise Wirz.
Exhibitions Officer: Ele Carpenter.
Located in the heart of the city, this exciting,
new gallery complex has been established as a
leading centre for the very best international
contemporary visual art. Year-round pro-
gramme of events, education and outreach.
Telephone above number for current informa-
tion about exhibitions and events. WC.
Services and Facilities:
Craftshop. Disabled Access. Friends/Society.
Guided Tours. Lectures.
Work Stocked and Sold:
Cer. Cra. Dec. Gla. Jew. Pr. Sc. Tx.
Wd.
Price range: £5 - £500.

SUNDERLAND MUSEUM &
ART GALLERY P
Fine and Applied Arts, Borough Road, Sunder-
land SR1 1PP. **Tel:** *0191-565 0723.* **Fax:**
0191-510 0675.

WASHINGTON

ARTS CENTRE PS
Biddick Lane, Fatfield, District 7, Washington,
NE38 8AB.
Tel: *0191-219 3455.* **Fax:** *0191-219 3466.*
Opening times: *Mon-Sat 9-7.30.*
Personnel: *Manager:* Marie Kirbyshaw.
The Arts Centre, Washington is a former 19th
Century farm building which now offers space
for arts events and activities throughout the
year. Open to visitors are six studios occupied
by artists and designers, a craft shop, gallery
and public bar.
Exhibitions in the Gallery change monthly,
providing a variety of art, craft and design.
The Arts Centre, Washington has a craft fayre
on the first Saturday of each month with over
70 stalls of unique hand crafted items. In addition there is free parking, a 120 seat theatre
and many classes open to the public throughout the week.
Services and Facilities:
Bar. Café. Craftshop. Disabled Access. Parking.
Shop. Workshop Facilities.
Work Stocked and Sold:
Cer. Cra. Dec. Gla. Jew.
Price range: £3 - £75.

SUN ARTS
Biddick Farm, Fat Field, Washington, NE38
8AB.

NORTH TYNESIDE

NORTH SHIELDS

GLOBE GALLERY
97 Howard Street, North Shields, NE30 1NA.
Tel: *0191-259 2614.*

SOUTH TYNESIDE

JARROW

BEDE GALLERY
Springwell Park, Butchersbridge Road, Jarrow,
NE32 5QA. **Tel:** *0191-489 1807/420 0585.*
Fax: *0191-420 0585.*

SOUTH SHIELDS

SOUTH SHIELDS MUSEUM & ART
GALLERY P
Ocean Road, South Shields, NE33 2AU.
Tel: *0191-456 8740.*

Regional
Focus –

What
to see,
where
to go.

A different region
every month in Art
review magazine.

Ab *Artist's Books* **App** *Applied Art* **Cer** *Ceramics* **Cra** *Crafts* **Dec** *Decorative* **Dr** *Drawing*
Fur *Furniture* **Gla** *Glass* **Jew** *Jewellery* **Pa** *Paintings* **Ph** *Photography* **Pr** *Prints*
Sc *Sculpture* **Tx** *Textiles* **Wd** *Wood*

SCOTTISH GALLERIES

Town/County index. Main listings.

Where this information has been provided, galleries are designated 'C' for commercial, 'P' for public gallery or museum or 'PS' for a public gallery or museum holding selling shows.

THE ART WORLD
DIRECTORY
1998/99 25TH EDITION

TOWN/ COUNTY INDEX

A

Aberdeen *(Aberdeen)*
Alford *(Aberdeenshire)*
Alloa *(Clackmannanshire)*
Anstruther *(Fife)*
Ayr *(South Ayrshire)*

B

Ballater *(Aberdeenshire)*
Banff *(Aberdeenshire)*
Broughton *(North Lanarkshire)*

C

Caithness *(Highland)*
Cardenden *(Fife)*
Cleland *(South Lanarkshire)*
Coatbridge *(North Lanarkshire)*
Crail *(Fife)*
Crieff *(Perth and Kinross)*
Culloden *(Highland)*
Cumnock *(East Ayrshire)*
(See Glasgow & Edinburgh)

D

Dumbarton *(West Dunbartonshire)*
Dumfries *(Dumfries & Galloway)*
Dundee *(Dundee)*
Dunfermline *(Fife)*
Dunkeld *(Perth and Kinross)*

E/F/G

Edinburgh *(Edinburgh)*
(See Glasgow & Edinburgh)
Elgin *(Moray)*
Ellon *(Aberdeenshire)*
Falkirk *(Falkirk)*
(See Glasgow and Edinburgh)
Forfar *(Angus)*
Forres *(Moray)*
Glasgow *(Glasgow)*
(See Glasgow & Edinburgh)
Glenrothes *(Fife)*
Greenock *(Inverclyde)*
(See Glasgow & Edinburgh)
Gullane *(East Lothian)*

H/I/J

Haddington *(East Lothian)*
Helensburgh *(Argyll and Bute)*
Inverness *(Highland)*
Irvine *(North Ayrshire)*
(See Glasgow & Edinburgh)
Jedburgh *(Scottish Borders)*

K/L/M

Kilmarnock *(East Ayrshire)*
(See Glasgow & Edinburgh)
Kirkcaldy *(Fife)*
Kirkcudbright *(Dumfries & Galloway)*
Kirkintilloch *(East Dunbartonshire)*
(See Glasgow & Edinburgh)
Kirkwall *(Orkney Islands)*
Leven *(Fife)*
Livingston *(West Lothian)*
(See Glasgow & Edinburgh)
Loanhead *(Midlothian)*
Macduff *(Aberdeenshire)*

N/O/P

Paisley *(Renfrewshire)*
(See Glasgow & Edinburgh)
Peebles *(Scottish Borders)*
Perth *(Perth and Kinross)*
Portree *(Isle of Skye)*

Q/R/S

Selkirk *(Scottish Borders)*
St. Andrews *(Fife)*
Stirling *(Stirling)*
Stonehaven *(Aberdeenshire)*
Stornoway *(Western Isles)*
Stranraer *(Dumfries & Galloway)*
Strathdon *(Aberdeenshire)*
Stromness *(Orkney Islands)*

V/W

Viewforth *(Stirling)*
Waternish *(Isle of Skye)*
Weisdale *(Shetland Islands)*

ABERDEEN

ABERDEEN

ABERDEEN ART GALLERY AND MUSEUM *P*
Schoolhill, Aberdeen AB9 1FQ.
Tel: *01224-646333.* **Fax:** *01224-632133.*

ABERDEEN ARTS CENTRE *P*
33 King Street, Aberdeen AB2 3AA.
Tel: *01224-635208.*

GALLERY HEINZEL *C*
21 Spa Street, Aberdeen AB1 1PU.
Tel: *01224-625629.*

GRAYS SCHOOL OF ART *P*
*Faculty of Design, The Robert Gordon
University, Garthdee Road, Aberdeen AB9
2QD.* **Tel:** *01224-263506 / 01224-263600.*

HODDO ARTS TRUST
*The Hale, Hoddo Estate, Tarves, Aberdeen
AB41 0ER.* **Tel:** *01651-851770.*

THE LEMON TREE *C*
5 West North Street, Aberdeen AB2 3AT.

Tel: *01224-642230.*

PEACOCK PRINTMAKERS GALLERY *C*
21 Castle Street, Aberdeen AB1 1AJ.
Tel: *01224-627094 / 639539.*

THE RENDEZVOUS GALLERY *C*
100 Forest Avenue, Aberdeen AB15 6TL.
Tel: *01224-323247.*

ABERDEENSHIRE

ALFORD

SYLLAVETHY GALLERY *C*
Montgarrie, Alford, AB33 8AQ.
Tel: *019755-62273.*
Fax: *019755-63173.*

BALLATER

McEWAN GALLERY
Glengarden, Ballater, AB35 5UB.
Tel: *013397-55429.*

BANFF

WAREHOUSE GALLERY
7 Quayside, Banff Harbour, Banff, AB45 1HQ.
Tel: *01261-818048.*

ELLON

TOLQUHON GALLERY *C*
Tolquhon, Tarves, Ellon AB41 0LP.
Tel: *01651-842343.*

MACDUFF

MACDUFF ARTS CENTRE
*c/o Aberdeenshire Council, 1 Church Street,
Macduff..* **Tel:** *01261-813384.*

STONEHAVEN

RIVERSIDE GALLERY
30a David Street, Stonehaven, AB3 2AL.
Tel: *01569-63931.*

STRATHDON

THE LOST GALLERY *C*
Strathdon, AB36 8UJ.
Tel: *019756-51287.*

ANGUS

FORFAR

FORFAR MUSEUM AND ART GALLERY *P*
*Meffan Institute, 20 West High Street, Forfar,
DD8 1BB.* **Tel:** *01307-464123.*

THE MEFFAN INSTITUTE
20 West High Street, Forfar, DD8 1DD.
Tel: *01307-464123.*

Ab Artist's Books **App** Applied Art **Cer** Ceramics **Cra** Crafts **Dec** Decorative
Dr Drawing **Fur** Furniture **Gla** Glass **Jew** Jewellery **Pa** Paintings
Ph Photography **Pr** Prints **Sc** Sculpture **Tx** Textiles **Wd** Wood

ARGYLL AND BUTE

HELENSBURGH

THE HILL HOUSE P
Upper Colquhoun Street, Helensburgh, G84 9AJ.
Tel: *01436-673900.*
Fax: *01436-674685.*

SOUTH AYRSHIRE

AYR

MACLAURIN ART GALLERY C
Rozelle Park, Monument Road, Ayr, KA7 4NQ.
Tel: *01292-443708 / 445447.*

ROZELLE HOUSE GALLERY C
Rozelle Park, Monument Road, Ayr, KA7 4NQ.
Tel: *01292-445447.*

SCOTTISH BORDERS

JEDBURGH

MAINHILL GALLERY C
Ancrum, Jedburgh, TD8 6XA. **Tel:** *01835-830518.*
Opening times: *Mon-Sat 10-5.*
Personnel: *Director: Diana Bruce.*

Paintings, drawings, etchings, sculpture.
Artists include; Tom Scott, H.W. Kerr, John
Blair, Frank Wood, Philipson and many more.
Contemporary; The Earl Haig, Caroline
Hunter, Michael Gibbison, Brent Millar,
David Sinclair, Andrew Walker and others.
Sculpture; Ayrton, Schotz, Frink, Lorna
Graves, John Coen. A strong tradition in
Borders landscape and figurative subjects; Tom
Scott and H.W. Kerr.
Several exhibitions per year. Large stock.
Situated in the village of Ancrum, just off the
A68, 2 miles north of Jedburgh.
Easy parking at gallery.
Prior 'phone call advisable as opening times
may vary.
Work Stocked and Sold:
Dr. Pa. Pr. Sc.

PEEBLES

PICTURE GALLERY/TWEEDDALE
MUSEUM P
High Street, Peebles, EH45 8AP. **Tel:** *01721-723123.*

TWEEDDALE MUSEUM & ART
GALLERY P
*Chambers Institute, High Street, Peebles, EH45
8AP.* **Tel:** *01721-720123.*

SELKIRK

PEEBLES PICTURE GALLERY
*c/o Municipal Buildings, High Street, Selkirk,
TD7 4JX.* **Tel:** *01750-20096.*

ROBSON GALLERY P
*c/o Municipal Buildings, High Street, Selkirk,
TD7 4JX.* **Tel:** *01750-20096.*

THE SCOTT GALLERY
*Municipal Buildings, High Street, Selkirk, TD7
4JX.* **Tel:** *01750-20096.*

CLACKMANNANSHIRE

ALLOA

ABERDONA GALLERY P
Aberdona Mains, Alloa, FK10 3QP.
Tel: *01259-752721.* **Fax:** *01259-750276.*

ALLOA MUSEUM AND GALLERY P
*Speirs Centre, 29 Primrose Street, Alloa, FK10
1JJ.* **Tel:** *01259-213131.*
Fax: *01259-721313.*

DUMFRIES & GALLOWAY

DUMFRIES

GRACEFIELD ARTS CENTRE
28 Edinburgh Road, Dumfries, DG1 1JQ.
Tel: *01387-262084.* **Fax:** *01387-60453.*

ROBERT BURNS CENTRE P
*c/o Dumfries Museum, The Observatory,
Dumfries, DG2 7SW.*
Tel: *01387-253374.*

KIRKCUDBRIGHT

CASTLE DOUGLAS ART GALLERY
Council Offices, Kirkcudbright, DG6 4JG.
Tel: *01557-331643.*

TOLBOOTH ART CENTRE
c/o Council Offices, Kirkcudbright, DG6 4JG.
Tel: *01557-331643.*

STRANRAER

STRANRAER MUSEUM P
55 George Street, Stranraer, DG9 7JP.
Tel: *01776-705088.*

DUNDEE

DUNDEE

BONAR HALL P
*The University of Dundee, Park Place, Dundee
DD1 4HN.* **Tel:** *01382-345466.*

DUNCAN OF JORDANSTONE COLLEGE
OF ART AND DESIGN PS
*A Faculty of the University of Dundee, Perth
Road, Dundee DD1 4HT.*
Tel: *01382-345330.* **Fax:** *01382-345192.*
Email *djcexhib@dundee.ac.uk*
Ws *http://www.dundee.ac.uk/*
Opening times: *Mon-Fri 9.30-8.30, Sat
9.30-4.30. Closed Sun.*
Nearest Station: *Dundee.*
Personnel: *Curator of Exhibitions: Deirdre
MacKenna.*
Continually changing programme in six exhi-
bition spaces; four in Duncan of Jordanstone
College of Art and Design, and two in the
University of Dundee. The programme ranges
from student and graduate work, to national
and international exhibitions in Fine Art,
Design, Television and Imaging, Performance,
Time Based Art, Architecture and Planning.
Traditional and contemporary lectures and
seminars. All exhibitions and events are free
and open to the public.
Services and Facilities:
*Bar. Disabled Access. Lectures. Parking.
Restaurant.*

DUNDEE ART GALLERIES AND
MUSEUMS P
Albert Square, Dundee. **Tel:** *01382-223141.*

McMANUS GALLERIES P
*Dundee Art Galleries & Museums, Albert
Square, Dundee DD1 1DA.* **Tel:** *01382-432020 / 01382 432028.*

McMANN'S GALLERIES
*Dundee Art Gallaries & Museums,
Albert Square, Dundee DD1 1DA.*
Tel: *01382-432020.*

SEAGATE GALLERY
36-40 Seagate, Dundee DD1 2EJ. **Tel:** *01382-226331.*

FIFE

ANSTRUTHER

KELLIE CASTLE P
by Pittenweem, Anstruther, KY10 2RF.
Tel: *01333-720271.* **Fax:** *01333-720326.*

CARDENDEN

ARTS IN FIFE
*Fife Council, Tower Block, ASDARC, Woodend
Road, Cardenden, KY5 0NE.* **Tel:** *01592-414714 / 414727.*

Ab *Artist's Books* **App** *Applied Art* **Cer** *Ceramics* **Cra** *Crafts*
Dec *Decorative* **Dr** *Drawing* **Fur** *Furniture*

CRAIL

THE COURTYARD GALLERY C
42 Marketgate South, Crail, KY10 3TL.
Tel: 01333-450797.

DUNFERMLINE

DUNFERMLINE MUSEUM P
The Small Gallery, Viewfield Terrace,
Dunfermline, KY12 7HY. **Tel:** 01383-721814.

GLENROTHES

CORRIDOR GALLERY
Fife Institute, Viewfield Road, Glenrothes, KR6
2RA. **Tel:** 01592-771700.

KIRKCALDY

KIRKCALDY MUSEUM & ART GALLERY P
War Memorial Gardens, Kirkcaldy, KY1 1YG.
Tel: 01592-412860. **Fax:** 01592-412870.

LEVEN

LOOMSHOP GALLERY
126 Main Street, Lower Largo, Leven, KY8 6BP.
Tel: 01333-320330.

ST. ANDREWS

CRAWFORD ARTS CENTRE PS
93 North Street, St. Andrews, KY16 9AL.
Tel: 01334-474610. **Fax:** 01334-479880.
Opening times: *Mon-Sat 10-5, Sun 2-5.*
Nearest Station: *Leuchars.*
Personnel: *Director:* Diana Sykes.
Exhibitions Officer: Susan Davis. *Gallery*
Assistant: Lucy Portchmouth.

CRAWFORD
A R T S
C E N T R E

Founded 1977. Monthly changing exhibitions
with contemporary emphasis; several touring.
Partially equipped studio theatre available for
hire. Workshops and classes for young people
and adults organised regularly.
Some Lectures and guided Tours of exhibi-
tions. Admission free.
Services and Facilities:
Craftshop. Disabled Access. Friends/Society.
Guided Tours. Lectures. Shop. Workshop
Facilities.
Work Stocked and Sold:
App. Cer. Cra. Dr. Jew. Pa. Ph. Pr. Sc.
Tx. Wd.
Price range: £5 - £1,500.

GLASGOW & EDINBURGH

EAST AYRSHIRE

CUMNOCK

BAIRD INSTITUTE P
East Ayrshire Council, 3 Lugar Street, Cumnock,
KA18 1AD. **Tel:** 01290-421701.

KILMARNOCK

DEAN CASTLE
c/o Kilmarnock & London
District Museums, Dick Institute, Kilmarnock,
KA1 3BU. **Tel:** 01563-26401.

DICK INSTITUTE PS
Elmbank Avenue, Kilmarnock KA1 3BU.
Tel: *01563-526401.* **Fax:** *01563-529661.*
Opening times: *Mon-Fri 10-8, Wed & Sat*
10-5, closed Sundays.
Nearest Station: *Kilmarnock.*
One of Ayrshire's major arts venues, The Dick
Institute combines an art gallery and museum
spaces.
The art gallery provides a continuous pro-
gramme of temporary exhibitions featuring
work by artists of both local and international
standing. Artists' residencies and public arts
projects are also commissioned.
The gallery's permanent collection includes
work by Hornel, Millais, Leighton and
Raeburn. The museum presents semi-perma-
nent displays of social history, natural history,
ethnography and geology.
The museum service also incorporates the
Baird Institute, a local studies centre and
museum in Cumnock, and Cathcartson Visitor
Centre in Dalmellington, Dean Castle in
Kilmarnock, housing significant displays of
European arms & armour, tapestries and the
Van Raalte collection of early musical instru-
ments.
Services and Facilities:
Craftshop. Disabled Access. Museum Shop.
Parking. Shop. Workshop Facilities.

NORTH AYRSHIRE

IRVINE

GLASGOW VENNEL ART GALLERY PS
10 Glasgow Vennel, Irvine, KA12 0BD.
Tel: *01294-275059.* **Fax:** *01294-275059.*
Opening times: *October-May: Tue, Thur,*
Fri & Sat: 10-1 & 2-5.
June-September: Mon-Sat: 10-1 & 2-5, Sun: 2-
5. (Closed Wednesdays).
Nearest Station: *Irvine.*

Personnel: *Museums Curator:* Martin
Bellamy. *Senior Museum Assistant:* John Gray.

The gallery has a varied programme of exhibi-
tions.
Exhibitions tend to concentrate on contempo-
rary Scottish fine and applied art but also
include some historical shows and artists from
outside Scotland.
Artists on show in 1998 include Jamie O'Dea,
Peter Russell and Picasso.
The gallery is situated in a restored 18th centu-
ry street, and includes the Heckling Shop
where Robert Burns worked.
There is also an audio visual display in the
Lodging House where Burns lived in 1781.
Services and Facilities:
Craftshop. Disabled Access. Museum Shop.

EAST DUNBARTONSHIRE

KIRKINTILLOCH

AULD KIRK MUSEUM P
c/o East Dumbartonshire Museum, Auld Kirk
Museum, The Cross, Kirkintilloch, G66 1AB.
Tel: 0141-775 1185.

WEST DUNBARTONSHIRE

DUMBARTON

DUMBARTON PUBLIC LIBRARY
Strathleven Place, Dumbarton, G82 1BD.
Tel: 01389-763129.

EDINBURGH

EDINBURGH

369 GALLERY
233 Cowgate, Edinburgh EH1 1NQ.
Tel: 0131-225 3013.

BOURNE FINE ART C
4 Dundas Street, Edinburgh EH3 6HZ.
Tel: 0131-557 4050. **Fax:** 0131-557 8382.

CALTON GALLERY C
10 Royal Terrace, Edinburgh EH7 5AB.
Tel: 0131-556 1010.
Fax: 0131-558 1150.

Gla *Glass* **Jew** *Jewellery* **Pa** *Paintings* **Ph** *Photography* **Pr** *Prints*
Sc *Sculpture* **Tx** *Textiles* **Wd** *Wood*

THE ARTWORLD
DIRECTORY 1998/99 **145**

CAMEO CINEMA
38 Home Street, Tolcross, Edinburgh EH3 9LZ.
Tel: *0131-228 4141.*

CARLYLE'S GALLERY C
North Bridge, Edinburgh EH1 1SO.
Tel: *0131-557 5068.*

CHESSEL GALLERY C
Moray House College, Holyrood Campus,
Edinburgh EH8 8AQ. **Tel:** *0131-556 8455.*

CITY ART CENTRE P
2 Market Street, Edinburgh EH1 1DE.
Tel: *0131-529 3993.* **Fax:** *0131-529 3977.*
Opening times: Mon-Sat 10-5, Sundays during the Festival 2-5.
Personnel: *Keeper, Fine Art Collections:* Ian
O'Riordan.
Located next to Waverley Station and built as
a warehouse in the 1890s, the City Art Centre
has six floors of gallery space, served by escala-
tors and a lift. It is a major temporary exhibition space, with an active and diverse programme showing a wide range of material from
contemporary culture to historical antiquities.
Contemporary art and design - Scottish,
British and International - is an important feature of the programme. The gallery is also
home to the City's collection of 19th and 20th
Century Scottish art, which is displayed regularly as a series of thematic temporary exhibitions. Admission free except for special exhibitions.
Services and Facilities:
Bar. Café. Disabled Access. Friends/Society.
Lectures. Shop.

COLLECTIVE GALLERY
22-28 Cockburn Street, Edinburgh EH1 1NY.
Tel: *0131-220 1260.*

CONTACT GALLERY C
Grindlay Court Centre, Crindlay Street Court,
Edinburgh EH3 9AR. **Tel:** *0131-229 7941.*

DANISH CULTURAL INSTITUTE
3 Doune Terrace Edinburgh EH3 6DY.
Tel: *0131-225 7189.* **Fax:** *0131-220 6162.*
Email *fa@dancult.demon.co.uk*
Opening times: Mon-Fri 10-5.
Personnel: *Director:* Mette Bligaard.
Exhibitions of Danish paintings, prints, pho-
tography and craft.

THE DIGNON COLLECTIVE C
46 Dundas Street, Edinburgh EH3 6JN.
Tel: *0131-556 1820.*

THE DUNDAS STREET GALLERY C
6a Dundas Street, Edinburgh EH3 6HZ.
Tel: *0131-557 4050.*
Fax: *0131-557 8382.*

EASTERN GENERAL HOSPITAL (EAST AND
MIDLOTHIAN UNIT ART FUND)
Seafield Street, Edinburgh EH6 7LN.

EDINBURGH GALLERY
18a Dundas Street, Edinburgh EH3 6HZ.
Tel: *0131-557 5227.*

EDINBURGH PRINTMAKERS C
23 Union Street, Edinburgh EH1 3LR.
Tel: *0131-557 2479.* **Fax:** *0131-558 8418.*
Email *printmakers@ednet.co.uk*
Opening times: Tues-Sat 10-6.
Personnel: *Director:* Robert Adam.
Edinburgh's foremost gallery devoted to contemporary prints and printmaking. Large
friendly open access studio with excellent
facilities for acrylic resist etching, water-based
screenprinting, lithography and relief printing.
Studio actively used by artists from Scotland,
the UK and all over the world. Specialist
courses and seminars running regularly.
Lively print-publishing programme including
thematic print folios. Fine print gallery with
changing exhibitions and large stock of studio
prints. Also studio viewing window allowing
visitors to see artists at work.
Prints recently published include work by John
Bellany, Mary Newcombe, Barbara Rae,
Graham Dean and Victoria Crowe and many
more.
Services and Facilities:
Art Consultancy. Art for Offices. Framing.
Workshop Facilities.
Work Stocked and Sold:
Pr.

EDINBURGH SCULPTURE WORKSHOP C
25 Hawthornvale, Newhaven, Edinburgh EH6
4JT. **Tel:** *0131-551 4490.* **Fax:** *0131-551*
4491.

ESU GALLERY
23 Atholl Crescent, Edinburgh EH3 8HQ.
Tel: *0131-229 1528.*

FIRTH GALLERY C
35 William Street, Edinburgh EH3 7LW.
Tel: *0131-225 2196.*
Fax: *0131-225 2196.*
FRENCH INSTITUTE
13 Randolph Crescent, Edinburgh EH3 7TT.
Tel: *0131-225 5366.*

FRUITMARKET GALLERY P
45 Market Street, Edinburgh EH1 1DF.
Tel: *0131-225 2383.* **Fax:** *0131-220 3130.*

HANOVER FINE ARTS C
22A Dundas Street, Edinburgh EH3 6JN.
Tel: *0131-556 2181.* **Fax:** *0131-556 2181.*
Opening times: Tue-Fri 10.30-6; Sat 10-4,
Jan-Dec.
Nearest Station: Waverley.
Personnel: *Proprietor:* Richard Ireland.

Independent owner-run commercial gallery sit-

uated in Dundas Street, right at the heart of
the New Town galleries. The present policy of
exhibitions (12 per year) features some established Scottish contemporary artists along with
lesser-known ones, but concentrating on good
quality accessible work at affordable prices.
The majority of artists live or work in
Scotland, but a number come from abroad, inc.
Belgium, Brazil, China, Germany, India,
Romania, Russia, Ukraine and the USA.
Works exhibited are: oils, watercolours,
original prints, ceramics, wood and stone
sculpture, jewellery, wooden boxes, tiles, tex-
tiles and original/printed cards.
Services and Facilities:
Framing.
Work Stocked and Sold:
Cer. Cra. Dr. Gla. Jew. Pa. Pr. Sc. Tx.
Wd.
Price range: £5 - £1,500.

INGLEBY GALLERY C
6 Carlton Terrace, Edinburgh EH7 5DD.
Tel: *0131-556 4441.* **Fax:** *0131-556 4441.*
Opening times: Wed-Sat 10-5 and by
appointment at all other times. Closed through
January.
Nearest Station: *10 minutes from Edinburgh*
Waverley.
The Ingleby Gallery opens in July 1998 on the
ground floor of a Georgian house overlooking
the Palace of Holyrood and the site of the new
Scottish Parliament. We specialise in 20th
century British art, predominantly in the work
of leading contemporary painters, sculptors,
photographers and ceramicists. 1 July-1
August - Opening Exhibition, 5 August-12
September - Howard Hodgkin, 30 September-
31 October - Photo 98, Susan Derges &
Patricia MacDonald, 11 November-19
December - Andy Goldsworthy, 10 February-
20 March - Margaret Mellis, 3 April-9 May -
Jeffrey Blondes, 19 May-27 June - Sculpture for
the Home & Garden.
Work Stocked and Sold:
Cer. Pa. Ph. Pr. Sc.
Price range: £50 - £50,000.

INSTITUTO ITALIANO DI CULTURA
82 Nicholson Street, Edinburgh EH8 9EW.
Tel: *0131-668 2232.*

JOHN STEPHENS FINE ART C
2A St Vincent Street, Edinburgh **Tel:** *0131-557*
6474.

KINGFISHER GALLERY C
5 Northumberland Street, North West Lane,
Edinburgh EH3 6JL. **Tel:** *0131-557 5454.*
Fax: *0131-557 5454.*
Opening times: Tue-Sat 11-4.30 or by
appointment.
Personnel: *Director:* Lena McGregor.
Director: Ronnie McGregor. *Manager:* Loura
Brooks.
Established in 1987, the Kingfisher's main
focus is on presenting the very best in contemporary Scottish art to public, private and corporate clients. Over the past ten years we
have introduced many artists to the Edinburgh
art scene, and will continue to present a blend

Ab *Artist's Books* **App** *Applied Art* **Cer** *Ceramics* **Cra** *Crafts*
Dec *Decorative* **Dr** *Drawing* **Fur** *Furniture*

of both established and new talent.
Our Gallery is on two levels, both benefiting
from natural light. We are able to present a
variety of works: paintings, sculpture, ceramics,
tapestry and jewellery.
There is disabled access to the ground floor
only, however, provision can be made to allow
as many as possible to view works here.
We are easily reached from the city centre, at
the heart of the New Town Gallery district.
Services and Facilities:
*Art Consultancy. Art for Offices. Disabled
Access.*
Work Stocked and Sold:
Cer. Cra. Gla. Jew. Pa. Pr. Sc.
Price range: £150 - £10,000.

THE LEITH GALLERY
93 Giles Street, Edinburgh EH6 6BZ.
Tel: *0131-553 5255.*

LOTHIAN FINE ART
155 Dalry Road, Edinburgh EH11 2EA.
Tel: *0131-337 2055.*

MALCOLM INNES GALLERY C
4 Dundas Street, Edinburgh EH3 6HZ.
Tel: *0131-558 9544/5.* **Fax:** *0131-558 9525.*

NATIONAL GALLERIES OF SCOTLAND P
*Department of Administration, 13 Herriot Row,
Edinburgh EH3 6HP.* **Tel:** *0131-556 8921.*

NATIONAL GALLERY OF SCOTLAND P
The Mound, Edinburgh EH2 2EL.
Tel: *0131-624 6200.* **Fax:** *0131-220 0917.*
Opening times: *Mon-Sat 10-5, Sun 2-5.*
Nearest Station: *Waverley.*
Personnel: *Director:* Timothy Clifford.
An outstanding collection of paintings, draw-
ings and prints by the greatest artists from the
Renaissance to Post-Impressionism, including
Velázquez, El Greco, Rembrandt, Vermeer,
Turner, Monet, Constable and Van Gogh;
shown alongside the National Collection of
Scottish Art - Ramsay, Raeburn, Wilkie and
McTaggart. Department of Prints & Drawings
is open by arrangement at Gallery front desk,
Mon-Fri 10am-12.30pm and 2-4.30pm.
Services and Facilities:
*Bookshop. Disabled Access. Gallery space for
hire. Museum Shop. Shop.*

NATIONAL LIBRARY OF SCOTLAND P
George IV Bridge, Edinburgh EH1 1EW.
Tel: *0131-226 4531.*

NETHERBROW ART CENTRE
43-45 High Street, Edinburgh EH1 1SR.
Tel: *0131-556 9579.*

OPEN EYE GALLERY C
75/79 Cumberland Street, Edinburgh EH3 6RD.
Tel: *0131-557 1020.*
Opening times: *Mon-Fri 10-6, Sat 10-4.*
The Open Eye Gallery situated in the heart of
Edinburgh's Historic Georgian New Town,
equidistant between the Gallery of Modern
Art and The National Gallery of Scotland.
An ambitious programme of 15 exhibitions per
year is organised, covering both contemporary

and fine art, ranging from the work of the
young contemporary to that of the established
school.

In addition to paintings the gallery specialises
in early 20th c. prints, sculpture and contem-
porary crafts covering ceramics, glass, wood
and jewellery.
Services and Facilities:
*Art Consultancy. Art for Offices. Commissioning
Service. Disabled Access. Framing. Restoration.
Valuation.*
Work Stocked and Sold:
Cer. Cra. Dr. Gla. Jew. Pa. Pr. Sc. Wd.

PORTFOLIO GALLERY C
43 Candlemaker Row, Edinburgh EH1 2QB.
Tel: *0131-220 1911.*
Fax: *0131-226 4287.*
Opening times: *Tue-Sat 12-5.30.*
Personnel: *Director:* Gloria Chalmers.
Portfolio Gallery was established in 1988 since
which time it has become one of the UK's
leading galleries which exhibits and promotes
contemporary photographic art.

The gallery is an intimate space, with a programme of eight solo exhibitions a year from
leading British, European and American photographic artists.
Portfolio Gallery also regularly commissions
work by British photographers and publishes
the bi-annual PORTFOLIO - The Catalogue
of Contemporary Photography in Britain -
which features new work by both established
photographic artists and young emerging talent.
An education programme of talks and seminars compliments the exhibitions programme.
Services and Facilities:
*Commissioning Service. Gallery space for hire.
Lectures.*
Work Stocked and Sold:
Ph.
Price range: £500 - £5,000.

QUEEN'S HALL
Clerk Street, Edinburgh EH8 9JG. **Tel:** *0131-
668 3456.*

RIAS GALLERY
*15 Rutland Square, off West End Princes Street,
Edinburgh EH1 2BE.* **Tel:** *0131-229 7545.*

ROYAL INCORPORATION OF ARCHITECTS IN SCOTLAND GALLERY
15 Rutland Square, Edinburgh EH1 2BE.
Tel: *0131-229 7545.*

ROYAL MUSEUM OF SCOTLAND P
Chambers Street, Edinburgh EH1 1JF.
Tel: *0131-225 7534.* **Fax:** *0131-220 4819.*

LANDINGS GALLERY, ROYAL OVER-SEAS LEAGUE C
*Over-Seas House, 100 Princes Street, Edinburgh
EH2 3AB.* **Tel:** *0131-225 1501.* **Fax:** *0131-
225 3936 / 226 3936.*
Opening times: *Open daily 10-6.*
Personnel: *Contact:* Dominic Gregory.
Situated in the heart of Edinburgh, the
Landings Gallery provides a unique opportuni-
ty for young artists up to the age of 35 from the
UK and Commonwealth to display their work
in Scotland. All artists have been chosen
through the ROSL Annual Open Exhibition,
an established showcase now in its 15th year
which tours to the Edinburgh College of Art
each autumn after its London opening. Bi-
monthly exhibitions compliment similar solo
shows held at Over-Seas, London. Number of
Fringe events.
Services and Facilities:
Bar. Café. Restaurant.
Work Stocked and Sold:
Dr. Pa.
Price range: £100 - £5,000.

ROYAL SCOTTISH ACADEMY PS
The Mound, Edinburgh EH2 2EL.
Tel: *0131-225 6671.* **Fax:** *0131-225 2349.*
Opening times: *During exhibitions:* Mon-Sat
10-5, Sun 2-5.
Personnel: Bruce Laidlaw. Margaret
Wilson.
Founded in 1826. The Royal Scottish
Academy is widely acknowledged as one of the
foremost promoters of contemporary art in
Scotland. Covering the disciplines of painting,
sculpture, architecture and printmaking. The
Annual Exhibition (25th April - 5th July) is a
key event in the Scottish Arts calendar. This
year the Academy is organising the 'Gillies
Centenary' Exhibition (1st August - 11th
October). In addition, the RSA plays an
important educational role with its unique
Students' Exhibition (7th March - 18th
March) together with awards and travelling
scholarships.
Services and Facilities:
*Art for Offices. Disabled Access. Friends/Society.
Shop.*

SCOTTISH GALLERY (AITKEN DOTT LTD) C
16 Dundas Street, Edinburgh EH3 6HZ.
Tel: *0131-558 1200.* **Fax:** *0131-558 3900.*
Email *mail@scottish-gallery.co.uk*
Ws *http://www.scottish-gallery.co.uk*
Opening times: *Mon-Fri 10-6, Sat 10-4.*
Personnel: *Director:* Iain Barnet.

Gla Glass *Jew* Jewellery *Pa* Paintings *Ph* Photography *Pr* Prints
Sc Sculpture *Tx* Textiles *Wd* Wood

The Scottish Gallery, founded in 1842, specialises in 20th c. and contemporary Scottish art.

The gallery has had close relationships with all the major Scottish painters of this century - The Scottish Colourists, 'The Edinburgh School' - Gillies, Redpath, MacTaggart, etc and others such as Joan Eardley. Recently we have held major shows by Blackadder, Houston, McLaren, Morrocco, Philipson, Redpath, Rae, Morrison, Michie, McClure. An exciting and varied monthly exhibition programme is supplemented by extensive stocks of paintings. In addition we have the most prestigious selection of British Crafts in Scotland.
Services and Facilities:
Art Consultancy. Commissioning Service. Craftshop. Valuation.
Work Stocked and Sold:
App. Cer. Cra. Dr. Gla. Jew. Pa. Pr. Sc. Tx. Wd.
Price range: £20 - £20,000.

SCOTTISH NATIONAL GALLERY OF MODERN ART *P*
Belford Road, Edinburgh EH4 3DR.
Tel: *0131-624 6200.* **Fax:** *0131-343 3250.*
Opening times: *Mon-Sat 10-5, Sun 2-5.*
Nearest Station: *Haymarket.*
Personnel: *Keeper:* Richard Calvocoressi.
Scotland's finest collection of 20th century painting, sculpture and graphic art. Includes work by Bacon, Hockney, Miro, Matisse, Moore, Paolozzi, Peploe and Picasso. Prints and drawings study room open by prior appointment, Mon-Fri 10am-12 noon, 2-4.30pm.
Services and Facilities:
Bookshop. Café. Disabled Access. Gallery space for hire. Museum Shop. Parking. Shop.

SCOTTISH NATIONAL PORTRAIT GALLERY *P*
1 Queen Street, Edinburgh EH2 1JD.
Tel: *0131-624 6200.*
Fax: *0131-558 3691.*
Opening times: *Mon-Sat 10-5, Sun 2-5.*
Nearest Station: *Waverley.*
Personnel: *Keeper:* James Holloway.
Portraits in all media of people who have played a significant role in Scottish history from the 16th century to the present.
Also houses the National Photography Collection with regular photography exhibitions.
The Print Room and Reference Archive are open by arrangement at the Gallery front desk,

Mon-Fri 10am-12.30pm and 2-4pm.
Services and Facilities:
Bookshop. Café. Disabled Access. Gallery space for hire. Museum Shop. Shop.

STILLS GALLERY
23 Cockburn Street, Edinburgh EH1 1BP.
Tel: *0131-225 9876.*

TALBOT RICE GALLERY *C*
University of Edinburgh,
Old College, South Bridge, Edinburgh EH8 9YL.
Tel: *0131-650 2210-2085.* **Fax:** *0131-650 2213.* **Email** *val.fiddes@ed.ac.uk*
Opening times: *Tues-Sat 10-5.*
Personnel: Valerie Fiddes.
A university gallery which houses a permanent collection of old master paintings and bronzes, as well as operating a busy temporary exhibition programme. Founded in 1970, the gallery's commitment to the visual arts in Scotland is to provide a platform for more mature (mainly Scottish) artists to mount major solo exhibitions. Exhibitions of work from Europe and elsewhere are also shown. Education programme. Limited Disabled Access.
Services and Facilities:
Friends/Society. Lectures.
Work Stocked and Sold:
Pa.

THEATRE WORKSHOP
34 Hamilton Place, Edinburgh EH3 5AX.

TORRANCE GALLERY *C*
29b Dundas Street, Edinburgh EH3 6QQ.
Tel: *0131-556 6366.*

VINCENT KOSMAN FINE ART *C*
8 Burgess Terrace, Newington, Edinburgh EH9 2BD. **Tel:** *0131-662 9990.* **Fax:** *0131-662 9990.*
Opening times: *By appointment.*
Nearest Station: *Central Edinburgh.*
Personnel: Louise Kosman.
Vincent Kosman Fine Art is a small family company of art dealers and consultants established thirty years ago. We offer modern British pictures, painted 1900 to contemporary. Our stock is constantly changing, and on request we will send photographs. Viewing of our stock is by appointment only, but we are available most of the time. We also provide advice on restoration, framing, and the art market. Our prices are very competitive.
Services and Facilities:
Art Consultancy. Commissioning Service. Valuation.
Work Stocked and Sold:
Dr. Pa. Sc.
Price range: £500 - £50,000.

FALKIRK

FALKIRK

CALLENDER HOUSE *P*
Callender Park, Falkirk. **Tel:** *01324-503770.*

GLASGOW

GLASGOW

90S GALLERY
12 Otago Street, Kelvinbridge, Glasgow G12 8HJ. **Tel:** *041-339 3158.*

ART EXPOSURE GALLERY *C*
19 Parnie Street, Glasgow G1 5RJ.
Tel: *0141-552 7779.*

ARTBANK
24 Cleveden Road, Glasgow G12 0PX.
Tel: *0141-334 6180.*

BARCLAY LENNIE FINE ART *C*
203 Bath Street, Glasgow G2 4HZ. **Tel:** *0141-226 5413.*

THE BURRELL COLLECTION *P*
2060 Pollokshaws Road, Pollock Country Park, Glasgow G43 1AT. **Tel:** *0141-649 7151.*
Fax: *0141-636 0086.*
Opening times: *Mon, Wed-Sat 10-5, Sun 11-5, closed Tues.*
Nearest Station: *Pollokshaws West.*
Personnel: *Director:* Julian Spalding.
Sir William Burrell's collection of art objects from ancient civilisations of the East and Medieval Europe and painting and drawing from 15-19 century, housed in a specially designed award-winning building.
Services and Facilities:
Bar. Café. Disabled Access. Friends/Society. Guided Tours. Lectures. Museum Shop. Parking. Restaurant.
Work Stocked and Sold:
App. Cer. Cra. Dec. Dr. Gla. Jew. Ph. Pr.
Price range: £5 - £100.

COLLINS GALLERY *PS*
University of Strathclyde, 22 Richmond Street, Glasgow G1 1XQ. **Tel:** *0141-553 4145.*
Fax: *0141-552 4053.*
Opening times: *Mon-Fri 10-5, Sat 12-4.*
Cl. public holidays and during exhibitions changeovers.
Nearest Station: *Queen Street.*
Personnel: *Curator:* Laura Hamilton.
Exhibitions Organiser: Morag Davidson.

Ab *Artist's Books* **App** *Applied Art* **Cer** *Ceramics* **Cra** *Crafts*
Dec *Decorative* **Dr** *Drawing* **Fur** *Furniture*

Monthly programme of temporary exhibitions ranging from contemporary Fine and Applied Art, Photography and Design, and multi-media installations to social history. Most exhibition are complemented by educational workshops, videos, performances or lectures. Plus activities for special need's groups. Permanent collection: Historic and contemporary Fine Art and Scientific Instruments.

Services and Facilities:
Disabled Access. Friends/Society. Gallery space for hire. Lectures. Parking. Workshop Facilities.

COMPASS GALLERY
178 West Regent Street, Glasgow G2 4RL.
Tel: *0141-221 6370.* **Fax:** *0141-248 1322.*
Opening times: *Mon-Sat: 10-5.30.*
Personnel: *Cyril Gerber.*
Glasgow's oldest established contemporary gallery with emphasis on young and mid-career artists. Changing monthly exhibitions of paintings, drawings, prints and ceramics by Scottish and international artists.
Also each July and August, "New Generation Artists", selected new graduates from Glasgow, Edinburgh, Dundee and Aberdeen Art Colleges.

CYRIL GERBER FINE ART C
148 West Regent Street, Glasgow G2 2RQ.
Tel: *0141-221 3095.* **Fax:** *0141-248 1322.*
Opening times: *Mon-Sat 9.30-5.30.*
Personnel: *Cyril Gerber. Jill Gerber. Stephanie Hand.*
Regularly in stock: D Y Cameron, Cowie, Gaudier-Brzeska, Cadell, Eardley, Fergusson, Gillies, Peploe, Hunter, Herman, Hilton, Kay, Lanyon, Redpath, Sehilsky, McCanee, Vaughn, Gill, "Glasgow Boys" - Paterson, Wingate, Melville, Lavery, McGregor.
 Contemporary: Knox, Morrocco, Shanks, Banks, Herman Bellany, Howson. Plus several catalogued shows per year.

DUNCAN R. MILLER FINE ARTS
144 West Regent Steet, Glasgow G2 2RQ.
Tel: *0141-204 0708.*

EASTWOOD HOUSE P
Eastwood Park, Giffnock, Glasgow G46 6UG.
Tel: *0141-638 1101.*

EWAN MUNDY FINE ART
211 West George Street, Glasgow G2 2LW.
Tel: *0141-248 9755.* **Fax:** *0141-248 9744.*

FOSSIL GROVE P
Victoria Park, Glasgow G14 1BN.
Tel: *0141-950 1448 / 287 2000.*

GALLERY OF MODERN ART P
Queen Street, Glasgow G1 3AZ.
Tel: *0141-229 1996.* **Fax:** *0141-204 5316.*
Opening times: *Mon, Wed-Sat 10-5, Sun 11-5, closed Tues.*
Nearest Station: *Queen Street.*
Personnel: *Director: Julian Spalding.*
Housed in a specially refurbished neo-classical Georgian building in the heart of Glasgow, the eclectic collection is displayed on four floors themed on the natural elements of fire, earth,

water and air. The roof-top café has been uniquely designed by acclaimed Scottish artist Adrian Wiszniewski.
Services and Facilities:
Café. Disabled Access. Friends/Society. Museum Shop.
Work Stocked and Sold:
App. Cra. Dr. Jew. Ph.
Price range: £5 - £100.

GATEHOUSE GALLERY C
Rouken Glen Road, Giffnock, Glasgow G46 7UG. **Tel:** *0141-620 0235.*

GLASGOW PRINT STUDIO GALLERY C
22 King Street, Glasgow G1 5QP. **Tel:** *0141-552 0704.* **Fax:** *0141-552 2919.*

GLASGOW SCHOOL OF ART P
167 Renfrew Street, Glasgow G3 6RQ.
Tel: *0141-353 4500.* **Fax:** *0141-353 4746.*

GLASGOW TOURIST BOARD
39 St Vincent Place, Glasgow G1 2ER.
Tel: *0141-204 4480.*

HILLHEAD UNDERGROUND GALLERY
2 Creswell Lane, Glasgow G12 8AA.
Tel: *0141-339 0968.*

HUNTERIAN ART GALLERY P
University of Glasgow, 82 Hillhead Street, Glasgow G12 8QQ. **Tel:** *0141-330 5431.*
Fax: *0141-330 3618.*
Email *J.E.Barrie@museum.gla.ac.uk*
Ws *http://www.gla.ac.uk/museum/*
Opening times: *Mon-Sat 9.30-5,*
(Mackintosh House closed 12.30-1.30).
Nearest Station: *Patrick (rail), Hillhead (underground).*
Personnel: *Administrator: June Barrie.*
This award-winning gallery houses the University of Glasgow's outstanding art collections.
In the Main Gallery there are paintings by Rembrandt, Stubbs and Chardin, 18th century British portraits, some fine Scottish 19th and 20th century paintings, and the Estate of the American painter, J.M. Whistler, making this the largest display of his works anywhere. The Mackintosh House comprises the principal rooms from the Glasgow home of the architect Charles Rennie Mackintosh, with changing displays of his work in the Gallery above the House. Contemporary sculpture is displayed in The Sculpture Courtyard and here are temporary exhibitions from the print collection.
Services and Facilities:
Bookshop. Disabled Access. Gallery space for hire.
Work Stocked and Sold:
Pr.

JOHN GREEN FINE ART C
203 Bath Street, Glasgow G2 4HJ.
Tel: *0141-221 6025.*

THE KELLY GALLERY
118 Douglas Street, Glasgow G2 4ET.
Tel: *0141-248 6386.*

KELVINGROVE ART GALLERY AND MUSEUM P
Kelvingrove, Glasgow G3 8AG. **Tel:** *0141-221 9600 / 287 2000.* **Fax:** *0141-305 2690 / 287 2690.*
Paintings by major artists from Botticelli to Picasso, magnificent armour, furniture, ceramics, silver and glass; the natural history of Scotland from prehistoric time to the present day. The headquarters of Glasgow Museums.

LILLIE ART GALLERY
Station Road, Milngavie, Glasgow G62 8BZ.
Tel: *0141-943 3247.*
Fax: *0141-943 3246.*

LLOYD JEROME GALLERY C
At The Dental Practice, 200 Bath Street, Glasgow G2 4HG.
Tel: *0141-331 0722.*
Fax: *0131-331 0733.*

McLELLAN GALLERIES P
270 Sauchiehall Street, Glasgow G2 3EH.
Tel: *0141-331 1854.*
Fax: *0141-332 9957.*
Opening times: *Opening dates depend upon exhibition schedule. Please call to check.*
Nearest Station: *Queen Street,*
Personnel: *Director: Julian Spalding.*
Purpose-built in 1854 as exhibition galleries, now completely refurbished. Major temporary and touring exhibitions from all over the world.
Services and Facilities:
Disabled Access. Museum Shop.
Work Stocked and Sold:
Cra.
Price range: £3 - £60.

MICHAEL MAIN GALLERY
34 Gibson Street, Kelvinbridge, Glasgow G12 8NX. **Tel:** *0141-334 8858.*

MITCHELL LIBRARY P
North Street, Glasgow G3 7DN. **Tel:** *0141-305 2803.*

MUSEUM OF TRANSPORT P
1 Bunhouse Road, Kelvinhall, Glasgow G3 8DP.
Tel: *0141-287 2000 / 287 2698.*
Fax: *0141-287 2692.*
Opening times: *Mon, Wed-Sat 10-5, Sun 11-5, closed Tues.*
Nearest Station: *Queen Street.*
Personnel: *Director: Julian Spalding.*
The history of transport especially in Scotland with thematic displays of bicycles, motor cycles, horse drawn vehicles, buses, trams, trains, fire engines and cars and including a specially reconstructed 1930's Glasgow street.
Services and Facilities:
Disabled Access. Guided Tours. Lectures. Museum Shop. Parking. Restaurant.

THE NS GALLERY
53 Cresswell Street, Glasgow G12 9AE.
Tel: *0141-334 4240*

PEARCE INSITUTE
840 Govan Road, Glasgow G51 3UT.

Gla Glass *Jew* Jewellery *Pa* Paintings *Ph* Photography *Pr* Prints
Sc Sculpture *Tx* Textiles *Wd* Wood

PEOPLE'S PALACE *P*
Glasgow Green, Glasgow G40 1AT. **Tel:**
0141-554 0223. **Fax:** *0141-550 0892.*
Opening times: *Mon, Wed-Sat 10-5, Sun
11-5, closed Tues.*
Nearest Station: *Central Station.*
Personnel: *Director:* Julian Spalding.
The story of Glasgow from 1175 to the present
day with a series of temporary exhibitions
highlighting the collection against social his-
torical background.
Services and Facilities:
Café. Museum Shop. Parking.
Work Stocked and Sold:
Cra. Dr. Jew.
Price range: £3 - £30.

POLLOK HOUSE *P*
*2060 Pollokshaws Road, Pollok Country Park,
Glasgow G43 1AT.*
Tel: *0141-632 0274.*
Fax: *0141-649 0823.*
Opening times: *Open from Easter weekend
to September weekend every year. Mon, Wed-Sat
10-5, Sun 11-5, closed Tues.*
Nearest Station: *Pollokshaws West.*
Personnel: *Director:* Julian Spalding.
The ancestral home of the Maxwell family
built c1750, set in beautiful gardens in the
heart of 361 acres of park and woodland, it
contains some of the finest Spanish paintings
in Britain.
Services and Facilities:
*Café. Disabled Access. Friends/Society. Lectures.
Museum Shop. Parking. Shop.*
Work Stocked and Sold:
App. Cer. Dec. Dr. Gla. Jew. Ph. Sc.
Price range: £5 - £50.

THE PRACTICE GALLERY *C*
58 Virginia Street, Glasgow G1 TX. **Tel:** *0141-
552 7722.*

PROVAND'S LORDSHIP *P*
3 Castle Street, Glasgow G4 0RB. **Tel:** *0141-
552 8819.*
Opening times: *Mon, Wed-Sat 10-5, Sun
11-5, closed Tues.*
Nearest Station: *Queen Street.*
Personnel: *Director:* Julian Spalding.
The oldest house in Glasgow, built in 1471 as
the Manse for St. Nicholas Hospital, it contains period displays including relics of the
original ground floor sweet shop.
Services and Facilities:
Museum Shop.

ROGER BILLCLIFFE FINE ART *C*
134 Blythswood Street, Glasgow G2 4EL.
Tel: *0141-332 4027.*
Fax: *0141-332 6573.*

ROWAN GALLERY *C*
36 Main Street, Drymen, Glasgow G63 0BG.
Tel: *01360-660996.*

**ROYAL GLASGOW INSTITUTE OF THE
FINE ARTS**
5 Oswald Street, Glasgow G1 4QR.
Tel: *0141-248 7411.*
Fax: *0141-221 0417.*

RUTHERGLEN MUSEUM *P*
King Street, Rutherglen, Glasgow G73 1DQ.
Tel: *0141-647 0837.*

**SCOTLAND STREET SCHOOL, MUSEUM
OF EDUCATION** *P*
*(Opposite Shields Road Underground Station),
225 Scotland Street, Glasgow G5 8QB.*
Tel: *0141-429 1202.*

SPRINGBURN MUSEUM *P*
Atlas Square, Ayr Street, Glasgow G21 4BW.
Tel: *0141-557 1405.*

**ST. MUNGO MUSEUM OF RELIGIOUS
LIFE AND ART** *P*
2 Castle Street, Glasgow G4 0RH. **Tel:** *0141-
553 2557.* **Fax:** *0141-552 4744.*
Opening times: *Mon-Sat 10-5, Sun 1-5,
closed Tues.*
Nearest Station: *Queen Street.*
Personnel: *Director:* Julian Spalding.
Opened 1993, the only museum anywhere to
look at all the world's major religions together.
Three galleries focus on religious art, life and
religion in Scotland. Among its many attrac-
tions are Salvador Dali's Christ of St. John of
the Cross and Britain's only authentic
Buddhist Zen Garden.
Services and Facilities:
*Disabled Access. Friends/Society. Guided Tours.
Lectures. Museum Shop. Parking. Restaurant.*
Work Stocked and Sold:
Dec. Dr. Gla. Jew. Pa.
Price range: £5 - £50.

STRATHCLYDE ARTS CENTRE
12 Washington Street, Glasgow G12 8PD.
Tel: *0141-221 4526.*

**STREET LEVEL PHOTOGRAPHY GALLERY
AND WORKSHOP** *C*
26 King Street, Glasgow G1 5QP.
Tel: *0141-552 2151.* **Fax:** *0141-552 2323.*

T. GARNER GALLERY
4 Parnie Street, Glasgow G1 5LR. **Tel:** *0141-
552 4585.*

T & R ANNAN & SONS LTD
*The Annan Gallery, 164 Woodlands Road,
Glasgow G3 6LL.*
Tel: *0141-332 0028.*

TRAMWAY
25 Albert Drive, Glasgow G41 2PE.
Tel: *0141-422 2023.*

TRANSMISSION GALLERY *C*
28 King Street, Transgate, Glasgow G1 5QP
Tel: *0141-552 4813.*

INVERCLYDE

GREENOCK

McLEAN MUSEUM AND ART GALLERY *P*
15 Kelly Street, Greenock, PA16 8JX.
Tel: *01475-723741.*

EAST LOTHIAN

GULLANE

NORRIE TOCH STUDIOS
St Peters, Main Street, Gullane.

HADDINGTON

PETER POTTER GALLERY *C*
10 The Sands, Haddington, EH41 3EY.
Tel: *01875-320010 / 01620-822080.*
Opening times: *Mon-Sat, 10-4.30.*
This gallery, which is beautifully situated on
the bank of the River Tyne in Haddington
with views toward St. Mary's Church was
established in 1976 with the objective of
increasing knowledge, understanding and practice of art.
The gallery today still operates against that
background. Regular exhibitions of paintings,
prints and craftwork by established and new
artists are held throughout the year. There is
also a permanent display of high quality contemporary craft for sale. A range of artists'
materials and cards is available. Tea, coffee
and light lunches are served daily.
Work Stocked and Sold:
Cra. Pa. Pr.

WEST LOTHIAN

LIVINGSTON

BALBARDIE GALLERY *P*
*West Lothian Council,
Almondbank Campus, The Mall, Craigshill,
Livingston, EH54 5BJ.* **Tel:** *01506-442765.*

MIDLOTHIAN

LOANHEAD

DALKEITH ARTS CENTRE *P*
*Midlothian Council, Library HQ, 2 Clerk Street,
Loanhead, EH20 9DR.* **Tel:** *0131-440 2210 /
0131-663 6986*

RENFREWSHIRE

PAISLEY

PAISLEY ARTS CENTRE
New Street, Paisley, PA1 1EZ.
Tel: *0141-887 1010.*

**PAISLEY MUSEUM, ART GALLERIES AND
COATS OBSERVATORY** *PS*
High Street, Paisley, PA1 2BA.
Tel: *0141-889 3151.* **Fax:** *0141-889 9240.*
Email *renlib7@cqm.co.uk*
Wshttp://www.cqm.co.uk/www/sdc/leisurestart.h
tml

Ab *Artist's Books* **App** *Applied Art* **Cer** *Ceramics* **Cra** *Crafts*
Dec *Decorative* **Dr** *Drawing* **Fur** *Furniture*

Opening times: *Mon-Sat 10-5.*
Personnel: *Keeper of Art:* Jane Kidd MA AMA. *Assistant Keeper of Art:* Andrea Kusel. Paisley Museum and Art Galleries, Lavery, Guthrie, Hornel, Kennedy, Scottish Colourists, Eardley, Redpath, Gillies and Byrne.
Large collection of British studio pottery from Leach onwards includes Rie, Coper, Cardew, Hamada, Fritsch, Britton, Lowndes. Selection of exhibitions from Permanent Collection, local art societies etc.
Please check availability of all above before visiting. Also large collection of Paisley Shawls. Gift Shop.
Services and Facilities:
Disabled Access. Shop.
Work Stocked and Sold:
Pa.
Price range: £50 - £5,000.

HIGHLAND

CAITHNESS

LYTH ARTS CENTRE
by Wick, Caithness, KW1 4UD. **Tel:** *01955-641270.*

CULLODEN

CULLODEN LIBRARY MINI GALLERY
Culloden Library, Kappoch Road, Culloden, IV1 2LL. **Tel:** *01463-792531.*

INVERNESS

HIGHLAND ARTS
Inverness Museum & Art Gallery, Castle Wynd, Inverness, IV2 3ED. **Tel:** *01463-237114.*
Fax: *01463-225293.*

INVERNESS MUSEUM & ART GALLERY P
Castle Wynd, Inverness, IV2 3ED.
Tel: *01463-237114.*

IONA GALLERY C
c/c Inverness Museum & Art Gallery, Castle Wynd, Inverness, IV2 3ED.
Tel: *01463-237114.*

RHUE STUDIO C
Rhue, Ullapool, IV26 2TJ.
Tel: *01854-612460*

SCOTTISH FINE ARTS GROUP
57 Church Street, Inverness, IV1 1DR.
Tel: *01463-243575.*

ISLE OF SKYE

PORTREE

AN TUIREANN ARTS CENTRE
Struan Road, Portree, IV15 9ES. **Tel:** *01478-613306.*

WATERNISH

ARTIZANIA
Captains House, Stein, Waternish, IV55 8GA.
Tel: *01470-592361.*

NORTH LANARKSHIRE

BROUGHTON

BROUGHTON GALLERY C
Broughton Place, Nr Biggar, Broughton, ML12 6HJ. **Tel:** *01899-830234.*

COATBRIDGE

IRONWORKS GALLERY
Summerlee Heritage Trust, West Canal Street, Coatbridge, ML5 1QD. **Tel:** *01236-431261.*

SOUTH LANARKSHIRE

CLELAND

CLELAND ARTS SCHOOLHOUSE
24 Main Street, Cleland, **Tel:** *01698-861740.*

MORAY

ELGIN

ELGIN MUSEUM P
1 High Street, Elgin, IV30 1EQ. **Tel:** *01343-543675.*

FORRES

LOGIE STEADING ART GALLERY C
Logie, Forres, IV36 0QN. **Tel:** *01309-611378/278.* **Fax:** *01309-611300.*
Email *Panny@logie.co.uk*
Opening times: *Tues-Fri 11-5, Sat & Sun 12-5, April-Nov.*
Personnel: *Mrs A. Laing.*

LOGIE
STEADING
ART GALLERY

The Art Gallery is in the Logie Steading which is converted store farm buildings. Throughout the season there is an ever changing exhibition of individual work by predominantly Scottish artists, oils, watercolours, textiles, ceramics, sculpture, wood, cards etc. Also in the complex is an engraver, silversmith and tea-room. Gardens are open and

plants are for sale.
Services and Facilities:
Café. Craftshop. Disabled Access. Gallery space for hire. Parking. Restaurant. Shop.
Work Stocked and Sold:
App. Cer. Cra. Dec. Dr. Fur. Gla. Jew. Pa. Pr. Sc. Tx. Wd.
Price range: £5 - £1,500.

ORKNEY ISLANDS

KIRKWALL

TAUKERNESS HOUSE MUSEUM P
Broad Street, Kirkwall, KW15 1DH.

STROMNESS

PIER ARTS CENTRE P
Victoria Street, Stromness, KW16 3AA. **Tel:** *01856-850209.*

PERTH AND KINROSS

CRIEFF

STRATHEARN GALLERY AND POTTERY C
32 West High Street, Crieff, PH7 4DL.
Tel: *01764-656100.*
Email *info@strathearn-gallery.com*
Ws *http://www.strathearn-gallery.com*
Opening times: *Mon-Sat 10-5, Sun 1-5.*
Nearest Station: *Perth.*
Personnel: *Directors:* Edith Maguire, Owen Maguire. *Contact:* Fiona Maguire.
Opened in March 1994, one of 5 Scottish galleries selected for quality by the Craft Council. We exhibit work by artists and craftspeople based in Scotland. Our annual graduates show is selected from Glasgow, Edinburgh, Dundee and Aberdeen Colleges of Art to encourage and promote new emerging talent. The Strathearn Pottery which is located in the basement of the gallery, opened in December 1995, and is run by John Maguire. You can be assured of a warm welcome in the bright and friendly atmosphere of our family run gallery.
Services and Facilities:
Commissioning Service. Disabled Access.
Work Stocked and Sold:
App. Cer. Cra. Dr. Fur. Gla. Jew. Pa. Ph. Pr. Sc. Wd.
Price range: £15 - £1,000.

DUNKELD

ATHOLL GALLERY C
6 Atholl Street, Dunkeld, PH8 0AR.
Tel: *01350-728855.* **Fax:** *01577-840636.*
Opening times: *Mar-Oct: Mon-Sat 11-5, Dec-Jan: Wed, Fri-Sun 11-4.*
Personnel: *Proprietor:* Edward Mackay.
Group and changing exhibitions monthly of contemporary Scottish paintings and crafts with National Provenance. 110 sq. m. of wall space. Scenically situated on the A9 North of Perth (10 mins) Dundee (30 mins) and

Glasgow and Edinburgh (1 hour).
Services and Facilities:
*Commissioning Service. Craftshop. Disabled
Access. Framing. Gallery space for hire.
Valuation.*
Work Stocked and Sold:
Cer. Cra. Dr. Jew. Pa. Pr. Sc.
Price range: £100 - £2,000.

PERTH

THE FERGUSSON GALLERY P
Marshall Place, Perth, PH2 8NU, **Tel:** *01738 -
441944.* **Fax:** *01738-443505.*
Opening times: *Mon-Sat 10-5. Closed
Christmas/New Year.*
Nearest Station: *Perth Bus & Rail stations -
Leonard St (5 mins walk from Gallery).*
Personnel: *Fine & Applied Art Officer:*
Kirsten Simister.
Opened in 1992. Dedicated gallery to the life
and work of the Scottish Colourist John
Duncan Fergusson (1874-1961), housing the
largest collection of his work in existence.
Temporary exhibition programme. Archive
available for consultation by appointment.
MGC registered. Disabled Access (Ground
Floor)/WC.
Services and Facilities:
Disabled Access. Parking. Shop.

FRAMES CONTEMPORARY GALLERY C
10 Victoria Street, Perth, PH2 8LW.
Tel: *01738-631085.* **Fax:** *01738-631085.*

PERTH MUSEUM AND ART GALLERY PS
George Street, Perth, PH1 5LB. **Tel:** *01738-
632488.* **Fax:** *01738-443505.*
Opening times: *Mon-Sat 10-5. Closed
Christmas/New Year.*
Nearest Station: *Perth (Rail & Bus).*
Personnel: *Head of Arts & Heritage:* Michael
A. Taylor.
Collections of Scottish and local paintings,
prints and drawings, 17th to 20th century.
Temporary exhibitions programme. Catalogue
paintings and drawings (1981). Appointments
necessary to view material not on display.
MGC registered. Galleries opened 1935.
Services and Facilities:
*Disabled Access. Lectures. Museum Shop.
Parking. Workshop Facilities.*

SHETLAND ISLANDS

WEISDALE

BONHOGA GALLERY C
Weisdale Mill, Weisdale, ZE2 9LW.
Tel: *01595-830400.*

STIRLING

STIRLING

MACROBERT ARTS CENTRE P
University of Stirling, Stirling FK9 4LA.

Tel: *01786-467159.*

SMITH ART GALLERY & MUSEUM P
Dumbarton Road, Stirling FK8 2RQ.
Tel: *01786-471917.*
Fax: *01786-449523.*

VIEWFORTH

COWANE GALLERY
*c/o Stirling District Council, Community Services,
Room 634, Ground Floor West, Viewforth,*
Tel: *01786-443128.*

WESTERN ISLES

STORNOWAY

AN LANNTAIR PS
*Town Hall, South Beach, Stornoway,
HS1 2BX.*
Tel: *01851-703307.*
Fax: *01851-703307.*
Email *lanntair@sol.co.uk*
Ws *http://www.lanntair.com*
Personnel: *Director:* Roddy Murray.

An Lanntair is the main public arts facility in
the Western Isles.
Among its many roles the centre promotes a
monthly contemporary exhibitions programme
and tours self-generated exhibitions, nationally
and internationally.
These have included Steve Dilworth (featured
above) and Calanais: the Atlantic Stones.
The accent is on local or locally-relevant work
in the summer and on "imported" shows from
the touring circuit in the winter.
Gaelic is a key part of its cultural identity and
it actively supports the language through a bi-
lingual policy.
An Lanntair also promotes an active and
diverse events programme which includes
drama, folk, classical, jazz and Scottish tradi-
tional music.
Services and Facilities:
*Bar. Bookshop. Café. Disabled Access.
Friends/Society. Gallery space for hire. Guided
Tours. Museum Shop. Parking. Restaurant.*
Work Stocked and Sold:
Dr.

Ab *Artist's Books* **App** *Applied Art* **Cer** *Ceramics* **Cra** *Crafts* **Dec** *Decorative* **Dr** *Drawing* **Fur**
Furniture **Gla** *Glass* **Jew** *Jewellery* **Pa** *Paintings* **Ph** *Photography* **Pr** *Prints*
Sc *Sculpture* **Tx** *Textiles* **Wd** *Wood*

WELSH GALLERIES

Town/County index. Main listings.

Where this information has been provided, galleries are
designated 'C' for commercial, 'P' for public gallery or museum
or 'PS' for a public gallery or museum holding selling shows.

THE ART WORLD
DIRECTORY
1998/99 25TH EDITION

The Gallery
Ruthin Craft Centre

A Craft Council Selected Gallery housed within a purpose built Craft Centre in the picturesque Vale of Clwyd. The Gallery shows the best of fine crafts by contemporary designer-makers form all over the British Isles. We run an exciting programme of regularly changing exhibitions which aim through a stimulating and diverse view of contemporary work, to show the breadth of excellence in the field of the applied arts.

OPENING TIMES
Summer: 10.00–5.30 daily
Winter: Monday–Saturday 10.00–5.00, Sunday: 12.00–5.00.

Free admission

FACILITIES
10 Independent Craft Studios • Restaurant
Car Park • Level access and disabled toilet facilities.

Ruthin Craft Centre, Park Road, Ruthin, Denbighshire LL15 1BB Tel: 01824 704774

Ruthin Craft Centre is part of the Directorate of Planning and Economic Development of Denbighshire County Council. The Gallery Exhibition Programme is supported by the Arts Council of Wales.

Sir Ddinbych
Denbighshire

TOWN/ COUNTY INDEX

ANGLESEY

ANGLESEY

MICHAEL WEBB FINE ART C
Llangristiolus, Bodorgan, Anglesey LL62 5DN.
Tel: 01407-840336.
Opening times: *Available 7 days a week - by appointment.*
Nearest Station: *Bangor, Gwynedd.*
Personnel: Proprietor: Michael Webb.

Michael Webb buys and sells Victorian oil paintings, water-colours and etchings. The list of artists given are artists I have handled in recent months; I cannot guarantee to have any particular one in stock at any one time because we do have a continuous turnover of pictures. However, we are always pleased to help you find a particular artist. We also have a collection of water-colours by the living wild life artist Owen Williams.
Services and Facilities:
Art Consultancy. Restoration. Valuation.
Work Stocked and Sold:
Dr. Pa.
Price range: £100 - £25,000.

BRIDGEND

BRIDGEND

NOLTON GALLERY
66 Nolton Street, Bridgend CF31 3BP.
Tel: 01656-663278.

PETER WILLS CERAMICS
Pottery and Gallery, 44 Newcastle Hill, Bridgend CF31 4EY. **Tel:** 01656-662902.

CAERPHILLY

BLACKWOOD

THE GALLERY
Blackwood Miners' Institute, High Street, Blackwood, NP2 1BB. **Tel:** 01495-224425.
Fax: 01495-226457.

CARDIFF

CARDIFF

ALBANY GALLERY C
74B Albany Road, Cardiff CF2 3RS.
Tel: 01222-487158. **Fax:** 01222-489158.

CARDIFF BAY ART TRUST
Pilotage House, Stuart Street, Cardiff CF1 6BW.
Tel: 01222-488772. **Fax:** 01222-472439.

CARDIFF CENTRAL LIBRARY
St David's Link, Frederick Street, Cardiff CF1 4DT. **Tel:** 01222-382116.

CHAPTER GALLERY
Market Road, Canton, Cardiff CF5 1QE.
Tel: 01222-396061.

THE COLLECTORS GALLERY
1st Floor, Cardiff Antiques Market, Morgan Arcade, Cardiff. **Tel:** 01446-773324.

HOWARD GARDENS GALLERY PS
University of Wales Institute Cardiff, Howard Gardens, Cardiff CF2 1SP. **Tel:** 01222-506678. **Fax:** 01222-506678.
Email *wwarrilow@uwic.ac.uk*
Opening times: *Mon-Thur 9.30-8, Fri 9.30-5.*
Personnel: Director: Walt Warrilow.

Purpose-built gallery of 264 sqm within the Faculty of Art, Design & Engineering. It has a

Ab *Artist's Books* **App** *Applied Art* **Cer** *Ceramics* **Cra** *Crafts* **Dec** *Decorative* **Dr** *Drawing* **Fur** *Furniture*

continuous programme throughout the year which spans not only the visual and applied arts, but also other related disciplines including architecture, design, historical and cultural studies. There are complementary events, lectures, workshops etc. The gallery hosts the Faculty's final BA and MA Degree exhibitions.
Services and Facilities:
Disabled Access. Lectures. Parking. Workshop Facilities.

MANOR HOUSE FINE ARTS C
73 Pontcanna Street, Pontcanna, Cardiff CF1 9HS. **Tel:** *01222-227787.*

MARTIN TINNEY GALLERY C
6 Windsor Place, Cardiff CF1 3BX.
Tel: *01222-641411.* **Fax:** *01222-665051.*
Email *mtg@artwales.com*
Ws *http://www.ARTWALES.COM*
Opening times: *Mon-Fri 10-6, Sat 10-5.*
Personnel: Martin Tinney.

20th century and contemporary artists with a strong emphasis on Welsh artists and artists who have worked in Wales. Monthly exhibitions and large stock of work by both established and emerging artists including: Leonard Beard, Neil Canning, Roger Cecil, George Chapman, Evan Charlton, Michael Crowther, Ivor Davies, John Elwyn, Merlyn Evans, Mary Griffiths, Josef Herman, Harry Holland, J.D. Innes, Augustus John, Gwen John, David Jones, Edward Morland Lewis, Mary Lloyd Jones, John Macfarlane, Sally Moore, John Piper, Edward Povey, Peter Prendergast, Gwilym Prichard, Shani Rhys James, Ceri Richards, Mark Samuel, Kevin Sinnott, Graham Sutherland, Claudia Williams, Emrys Williams, Kyffin Williams and Ernest Zobole.
Services and Facilities:
Art Consultancy. Art for Offices. Commissioning Service.
Work Stocked and Sold:
Dr. Pa. Pr. Sc.
Price range: £75 - £10,000.

NATIONAL MUSEUMS AND GALLERIES OF WALES P
National Museum & Gallery Cardiff, Cathays Park, Cardiff CF1 3NP. **Tel:** *01222-397951.*
Fax: *01222-577010.*
Opening times: *Tue-Sun 10-5; open Bank Holiday Mondays.*
Nearest Station: *Cardiff Queen Street.*
Personnel: *Director:* Colin Ford. *Keeper of Art:* David Alston. *Exhibitions Co-ordinator:* Deborah Spillards.

One of eight sites under the umbrella of the National Museums & Galleries of Wales, the National Museum & Gallery Cardiff is home to one of the finest collections of art treasures in Europe. The Davies collection includes works by Monet, Manet, Renoir, Van Gogh and Sisley, also bronzes by Degas and Rodin, including Rodin's Kiss. A fine collection of 18th and 19th century landscapes and important works by Welsh artists Augustus & Ewen John. Works from the museum's collection are also displayed at Turner House Gallery, Penarth, in addition to exhibitions by local art societies.
Services and Facilities:
Disabled Access. Friends/Society. Museum Shop. Parking. Restaurant.

ST. DAVID'S HALL PS
The Hayes, Cardiff CF1 2SH. **Tel:** *01222-878500.* **Fax:** *01222-878599.*
Opening times: *Mon-Sat 10-4. Also open to concert-goers.*
St. David's Hall, the National Concert Hall of Wales, is situated in the city centre. The two main galleries currently show around 25 exhibitions each year.
Exhibitions include both group and single artist shows covering a wide range of work. There is also additional space for regular photography and craft exhibitions. St. David's Hall's broad spectrum of concert hall events brings the visual arts to the attention of more than 10,000 people a week who pass through the foyers. WC.
Services and Facilities:
Bar. Café. Craftshop. Disabled Access. Friends/Society. Gallery space for hire. Restaurant. Shop.

CARMARTHENSHIRE

AMMANFORD

THE GALLERY
38 Quay Street, Ammanford, SA18 2EN.
Tel: *01269-594959.*

CARMARTHEN

CARMARTHEN MUSEUM P
Abergwili, Carmarthen, SA31 2JG.
Tel: *01267-231691.*

HENRY THOMAS GALLERY
Carmarthenshire College of Technology and Art, Job's Well Road, Carmarthen, SA31 3HY.
Tel: *01554-759165 ext 4403 (Art).*
Fax: *01267-221515.*

ORIEL MYRDDIN C
Church Lane, Carmarthen, SA31 1LH.
Tel: *01267-222775.*

LAUGHARNE

THE POWERHOUSE GALLERY
Behind the Clock, Laugharne, SA33 4SB.
Tel: *01994-427580.*

LLANDEILO

FOUNTAIN FINE ART
Rhosmaen Street, Llandeilo, SA19 6EN.
Tel: *01558-823328.*

THE TRAPP ART AND CRAFT CENTRE
Llwyndewi, Trapp, Llandeilo, SA19 6TT.
Tel: *01269-850362.*

LLANELLI

NEVILL GALLERY
Llanelli Library, Vaughan Street, Llanelli, SA15 3AF. **Tel:** *01554-773538.*

PARC HOWARD MANSION P
Felinfoel Road, Llanelli, SA15 3AS.
Tel: *01554-772029, Hire details 01554-741100..*

LLANWRDA

STUDIO GALLERY C
Trebeddau, Pumpsaint, Llanwrda, SA19 8YA.
Tel: *01558-650598.*

CEREDIGION

ABERAERON

GORDON MILES GALLERY
Merrihill Press, Unit 4, Clos Pengarreg Courtyard, Panteg Road, Aberaeron, SA46 0EN.
Tel: *01545-571661.*

ABERYSTWYTH

ABERYSTWYTH ARTS CENTRE C
Penglais, Aberystwyth, SY23 3DE. **Tel:** *01970-623232 / 622895.* **Fax:** *01970-622883.*

CATHERINE LEWIS GALLERY
Hugh Owen Library, The University of Wales, Penglais, Aberystwyth, SY23 1BH. **Tel:** *01970-623339 / 622460.* **Fax:** *01970-622461.*

THE CERAMICS GALLERY
Aberystwyth Arts Centre, The University of Wales, Penglais, Aberystwyth, SY23 3DE.
Tel: *01970-622460.* **Fax:** *01970-622461.*

CEREDIGION MUSEUM P
Coliseum, Terrace Road, Aberystwyth, SY23 2AQ. **Tel:** *01970-633088.*

THE NATIONAL LIBRARY OF WALES P
Aberystwyth, SY23 3BU. **Tel:** *01970-632800.*
Fax: *01970-615709.*
Email *holi@llgc.org.uk*
Ws *http://www.llgc.org.uk*
Opening times: *Mon-Fri 10-5 except Bank Holidays and first week of October.*
Nearest Station: *Aberystwyth.*
The National Library of Wales is one of six legal deposit libraries in the British Isles. A major reference library, the Library houses a wide range of printed, manuscript, visual and sound and moving image material. A perma-

Gla *Glass* **Jew** *Jewellery* **Pa** *Paintings* **Ph** *Photography* **Pr** *Prints*
Sc *Sculpture* **Tx** *Textiles* **Wd** *Wood*

THE ARTWORLD
DIRECTORY 1998/99 **157**

nent exhibition, and a programme of temporary exhibitions, are mounted at the Library's Gregynog Gallery and Central Hall.
Services and Facilities:
Bookshop. Café. Disabled Access. Friends/Society. Gallery space for hire. Guided Tours. Parking. Shop.
Work Stocked and Sold:
Dr. Pa. Pr.

ORIEL COLISEUM GALLERY
Ceredigion Museum, Terrace Road, Aberystwyth, SY23 2AQ. **Tel:** *01970-633086.* **Fax:** *01970-633084.*
Opening times: *Mon-Sun, School Holidays 10-5.*
Personnel: *Gwenllian Ashley.*

The newly refurbished gallery exhibits the best in Welsh art be it contemporary, abstract paintings or 19th Century primitive quilts. It has an exciting programme of temporary exhibitions and is attached to the Ceredigion Museum which also holds temporary exhibitions in its auditorium area. The Museum, which is housed in in an Edwardian music hall, has a fascinating permanent display of the history of life in Cardiganshire and has been described as having possibly the most beautiful museum interior in Britain.
Services and Facilities:
Gallery space for hire. Museum Shop. Shop.

SCHOOL OF ART GALLERY & MUSEUM *PS*
University of Wales, Aberystwyth, SY23 1NE.
Tel: *01970-622460.* **Fax:** *01970-622461.*
Email *alc@aber.ac.uk*
Ws *http://www.aber.ac.uk*
Opening times: *Mon-Fri 10-1, 2-5.*
Nearest Station: *Aberystwyth.*
Personnel: *Keeper of College Collections:*

Prof. Alistair Crawford.Changing exhibitions drawn from college collections of printmaking, photography, drawing and painting and ceramics, staff and students, touring exhibitions, and invited British and international artists. Also curates the Ceramics Gallery, Aberystwyth Arts Centre and the Gregynog Gallery, Newtown and organises exhibitions for other

venues in UK and abroad. Reference collection of prints, drawings and photographs by appointment. School of Art Press publishes books, catalogues and research papers. Museum contributes to the School of Art programme in Museum and Gallery Studies.
Services and Facilities:
Guided Tours. Lectures. Parking.
Work Stocked and Sold:
Ab. Dr. Pa. Ph. Pr.
Price range: *£25 - £1,500.*

CARDIGAN

FRAME BY FRAME
11 Black Lion Mews, Cardigan, SQ43 1HJ.
Tel: *01239-615398.*

THE STUDIO *C*
3 Cambrian Quay, Cardigan, SA43 1EZ.
Tel: *01239-613711.*
Opening times: *Open all year 11-5: Easter and July-September every day; October-June closed Thursday and Sunday.*
Nearest Station: *Carmarthen.*
Personnel: *David Wilson.*

This artist-run gallery overlooking the river Teifi near the bridge is also David Wilson's studio. His paintings and prints draw their inspiration from many sources, but especially from the varied landscape and coast of West Wales. Examples of fine furniture designed by Guy Wilson are also on display.
Services and Facilities:
Art for Offices. Commissioning Service. Parking. Shop.
Work Stocked and Sold:
Dr. Fur. Pa. Pr.
Price range: *£10 - £3,000.*

LAMPETER

ST. DAVID'S UNIVERSITY COLLEGE
College Street, Lampeter, SA48 7ED.
Tel: *01570-422351.*

Y GALERI
2 Bridge Street, Lampeter, SA48 7HG.

CONWY

LLANDUDNO

FULMAR GALLERY
First Floor, 44 Madoc Street, Llandudno, LL30 2TL. **Tel:** *01492-879880.*

LLANDUDNO MUSEUM AND ART GALLERY *P*
Chardon House, 17-19 Gloddaeth Street, Llandudno, LL30 2DD. **Tel:** *01492-879130.*

ORIEL MOSTYN *PS*
12 Vaughan Street, Llandudno, LL30 1AB.
Tel: *01492-879201/870875.* **Fax:** *01492-878869.*
Opening times: *Mon-Sat 10-1, 1.30-5. Admission free.*
Nearest Station: *Llandudno 500 yds.*
Personnel: *Director:* Martin Barlow. *Administrator:* Mary Heathcote. *Education Officer:* Alison Lebegue.
A beautiful Victorian purpose-built gallery showing a changing programme of exhibitions of historical and contemporary fine art. The Education Unit and 10 - bay professional Dark Room offer facilities, events and activities for all ages relating to the exhibitions in the gallery. The Craft and Design Shop offers for sale the best of studio work, craft and the applied arts and there is an excellent card and specialist bookshop. Friends and membership scheme with discounts on courses and purchases.
Services and Facilities:
Bookshop. Commissioning Service. Craftshop. Disabled Access. Friends/Society. Guided Tours. Lectures. Workshop Facilities.
Work Stocked and Sold:
Ab. App. Cer. Cra. Dec. Dr. Fur. Gla. Jew. Pa. Ph. Pr. Sc. Tx. Wd.
Price range: *£6 - £6,000.*

DENBIGHSHIRE

DENBIGH

DENBIGH LIBRARY, MUSEUM AND GALLERY *P*
Hall Square, Denbigh, LL16 3AU.
Tel: *01745-816313.*

LLANGOLLEN

ECTARC
The European Centre for Traditional and Regional Cultures, Parade Street, Llangollen, LL20 8RB.

ROYAL INTERNATIONAL PAVILION
Abbey Road, Llangollen, LL20 8SW.
Tel: *01978-860111.* **Fax:** *01978-860046.*

RUTHIN

THE GALLERY, RUTHIN CRAFT CENTRE *C*
Park Road, Ruthin, LL15 1BB.
Tel: *01824-704774, 702060.*
Opening times: *Summer: 10-5.30 daily, Winter: Mon-Sat 10-5, Sun 12-5.*
Personnel: *Director:* Philip Hughes. Jane Gerrard.
A Craft Council Selected Gallery housed within a purpose built Craft Centre in the picturesque Vale of Clwyd. The Gallery shows the best of fine crafts by contemporary designer-

Ab Artist's Books *App Applied Art* *Cer Ceramics* *Cra Crafts* *Dec Decorative* *Dr Drawing* *Fur Furniture*

makers form all over the British Isles. We run an exciting programme of regularly changing exhibitions which aim through a stimulating and diverse view of contemporary work, to show the breadth of excellence in the field of the applied arts. We receive financial support from the Arts Council of Wales.
Work Stocked and Sold:
App. Cer. Cra. Gla. Jew. Tx. Wd.

FLINTSHIRE

HAWARDEN

THE BLACK SHEEP GALLERY C
The Old Stable Yard, Hawarden Castle, Hawarden, CH5 3NY. **Tel:** *01244-535505.*
Opening times: *Mon closed, Tue-Fri 10-6, Sat & Sun 10-5. Admission free.*
Nearest Station: *Hawarden.*
Personnel: *Director: Mr. F. P. Garbutt.*

An Independent commercial Gallery offering a monthly changing programme of selling exhibitions in a wide variety of styles and media. Attractively located in converted stables within the grounds of Hawarden Castle, 6 miles outside of Chester, the Gallery offers over 3000 sq. ft. of exhibition space in seven Galleries, each different in size and character. The Black Sheep Gallery has earned a reputation as a leading showcase for contemporary art in the region, attracting artists, visitors and buyers from North Wales, Cheshire, Merseyside and further afield. The Gallery also supplies artists' materials, provides a framing service and runs regular life classes and workshops.
Services and Facilities:
Commissioning Service. Framing. Gallery space for hire. Parking. Workshop Facilities.
Work Stocked and Sold:
Cer. Dr. Pa. Ph. Pr. Sc. Tx. Wd.
Price range: £75 - £2,500.

MOLD

ORIEL GALLERY PS
Theatr Clwyd, Mold, CH7 1YA. **Tel:** *01352-756331.* **Fax:** *01352-758323.*
Email *drama@celtic.co.uk*
Opening times: *Mon-Sat 10-10.*
Nearest Station: *Chester.*
Personnel: *Curator: J. Le Vay.*
Two galleries with 110 lin. m. hanging space; emphasis on exhibiting the work of new artists

in solo or group exhibitions, but work by established artists also shown.

The galleries are part of a major regional multi-media Arts Centre, with annual visitor turn-over of 350,000.
Services and Facilities:
Art Consultancy. Bar. Bookshop. Café. Craftshop. Disabled Access. Gallery space for hire. Parking. Restaurant.

VALE OF GLAMORGAN

PENARTH

TURNER HOUSE
Plymouth Road, Penarth, CF64 3DM.
Tel: *01222-708870.*

THE WASHINGTON GALLERY
1-3 Stanwell Road, Penarth, CF64 2AB.
Tel: *01222-708047.*
Fax: *01222-700310.*

GWYNEDD

ABERDOVEY

THE GALLERY
11 New Street, Aberdovey, LL35 0EH.
Tel: *01654-767319, eves. 01654-710523.*

BANGOR

BANGOR MUSEUM & ART GALLERY P
Ffordd Gwynedd, Bangor, LL57 1DT.
Tel: *01248-353368.*

DAVID WINDSOR GALLERY
201 High Street, Bangor, LL57 1NU.
Tel: *01248-364639.*

BETWS-Y-COED

THE GALLERY
Holyhead Road, Betws-y-Coed, LL24 0BW.
Tel: *01690-710432.*

CAERNARFON

ARFON GALLERY
Palace Street, Caernarfon, LL55 1RR.
Tel: *01286-672602.*
Fax: *01286-76728.*

CAERNARFON LIBRARY
Pavilion Road, Caernarfon, LL55 1AS.
Tel: *01286-675944.*

DOLGELLAU

THE LIBRARY GALLERY
Borthwog Hall, Bontddu, Dolgellau, LL40 2TT.
Tel: *01341-430271.* **Fax:** *01341-430682.*

HARLECH

THE WHITE ROOM GALLERY AT HARLECH POTTERY
Pentre Fail, Harlech, LL46 2YG. **Tel:** *01766-247397 (after 6pm in summer)..*

PWLLHELI

LLANBEDROG POTTERY AND PRINTS
The Pottery, Llanbedrog, Pwllheli, LL53 7UA.
Tel: *01758-740296.*

ORIEL PLAS GLYN-Y-WEDDW C
Llanbedrog, Pwllheli, LL53 7TT.
Tel: *01758-740763.* **Fax:** *01758-740232.*
Email *David.Jeffreys@virgin.net*
Opening times: *Winter 10-4 except Tuesdays. Summer 10-5 except Tuesdays.*
Nearest Station: *Pwllheli (Cambrian Railway) or Bangor (Main Line).*
Personnel: *Director: David Jeffreys.*
Plas Glyn y Weddw Art Gallery, under new management, is one of the oldest public art galleries in Wales.
Pictures, arts and crafts, are housed in a superb listed Victorian Gothic mansion, with fine views from the Llyn Peninsula over Cardigan Bay. There are gardens, woodland and beach walks, and a tea room in the Gallery's conservatory. Contemporary Welsh paintings form the core of the Gallery's collection, as well as changing exhibitions and a distinguished collection of porcelain. The Gallery re-opens in April 1998.
Services and Facilities:
Café. Craftshop. Disabled Access. Friends/Society. Gallery space for hire. Lectures. Parking. Workshop Facilities.
Work Stocked and Sold:
Ab. Cer. Cra. Dr. Jew. Pa. Ph. Pr. Sc. Tx. Wd.
Price range: £30 - £6,000.

ISLE OF ANGLESEY

ANGLESEY

CENTRAL GALLERY
Field Street, Llangefni, Anglesey LL77 7UR.
Tel: *01248-723527.*

ORIEL FACH
46a Castle Street, Beaumaris, Anglesey LL58 8BB. **Tel:** *01248-810445.*

ORIEL YNYS MON
Rhosmeirch, Llangefni, Anglesey LL77 7TQ.
Tel: *01248-724444.* **Fax:** *01248-750282.*

LLANGEFNI

ORIEL YNS MON
Rhosmeirch, Llangefni, LL77 7TQ.
Tel: *01248-724444.*

MERTHYR TYDFIL

MERTHYR TYDFIL

CYFARTHFA CASTLE MUSEUM *P*
Brecon Road, Merthyr Tydfil, CF47 8RE.
Tel: *01685-723112.* **Fax:** *01685-722146.*

MONMOUTHSHIRE

ABERGAVENNY

HILL COURT GALLERY
Hill Court, Pen Y Pound, Abergavenny, NP7 7RW. **Tel:** *01873-854180.*

CHEPSTOW

ART APPROACH
The Station Building, Station Road, Chepstow, NP6 5PF. **Tel:** *01291-621854.*

THE WORKSHOP GALLERY
13 Lower Church Street, Chepstow, NPH 5HJ.
Tel: *01291-624836.*

MONMOUTH

THE ART CENTRE
Monk Street, Monmouth, NP5 3NZ.
Tel: *01600-713905.*

BEAVER ART AND FRAMING CENTRE
Monk Street, Monmouth, NP5 3NZ.
Tel: *01600-713905.*

MONMOUTH MUSEUM *P*
Priory Street, Monmouth, NP5 3XA.
Tel: *01600-713519.*

RAGLAN

THE OLD VICARAGE *C*
Penrhos, Raglan, NP5 2LE. **Tel:** *01600-780239.*

USK

THE ARTHOUSE
Pen Y Parc, Llangibby, Usk, NP5 1NY.
Tel: *01633-450320.* **Fax:** *01633-450552.*

NEWPORT

NEWPORT

NEWPORT MUSEUM & ART GALLERY *P*
John Frost Square, Newport NP9 1PA.
Tel: *01633-840064.* **Fax:** *01633-222615.*

Opening times: *Mon-Thu 9.30-5, Fri 9.30-4.30, Sat 9.30-4.*
Personnel: *Keeper of Art: Roger Cucksey. Exhibitions Officer: Sandra Jackaman.*
Founded 1888. Collection of early English watercolours, oil paintings, mainly British 20th century with emphasis on Welsh artists. Extensive changing exhibition programme with related events and activities. The John Wait Teapot collection 1780-1980. WC.
Services and Facilities:
Disabled Access. Shop.

TOWER GALLERY
Caldicot Castle Museum, Caldicot, Newport NP6 4HU. **Tel:** *01291-420241.*

PEMBROKESHIRE

FISHGUARD

GALLERY ONE
West Street, Fishguard, SA65 9AE.
Tel: *01348-872707.*

ORIEL/DRAGON GALLERY
The Old Post Office, 9 West Street, Fishguard, SA65 9AE.
Tel: *01348-875175.*

WEST WALES ARTS CENTRE, *C*
Castle Hill, 16 West Street, Fishguard, SA65 9AE. **Tel:** *01348-873867.* **Fax:** *01348-873867.*
Opening times: *Mon-Sat 9-5.30, Sundays by appointment.*
Nearest Station: *Fishguard or Haverfordwest.*
Personnel: *Myles Pepper. Vicki Craven.*
The privately run West Wales Arts Centre was established in 1987 by Myles Pepper in partnership with the late William James OBE. Over the years the Centre has established a reputation for showing leading fine and contemporary applied art and is recognised by the Crafts Council for quality. Our policy is to show the work of national and international artists and craftspeople, together with encouraging and promoting emerging talent.
The Centre is also active in staging a varied Live Arts Programme of lectures and music recitals and information is available upon request.
Services and Facilities:
Art Consultancy. Art for Offices. Commissioning Service. Craftshop. Lectures.
Work Stocked and Sold:
App. Cer. Cra. Dr. Gla. Jew. Pa. Pr. Sc.
Price range: £100 - £5,000.

WORKSHOP WALES GALLERY
Lower Town, Fishguard, SA65 9LY.
Tel: *01348-872261.*

HAVERFORDWEST

THE ARTISTS STUDIO *C*
"Red Rails" Marloes, Haverfordwest, SA62 3BB.
Tel: *01646-636380.*
Opening times: *Mon-Sun 9-6.*

Personnel: *Keith M. Parsons.*
The working studio of Keith Parsons N.D.D., where there is a continually changing display of work in oil, pastel and watercolour which mainly reflect the local landscape and seascape. However there are also signed limited edition prints and greetings cards, as well as the opportunity to commission portraits and talk to the artist about his work.
The studio is open from 9-6 throughout the year, although it is advisable to phone if travelling from any distance. Painting demonstrations by arrangement.
Services and Facilities:
Commissioning Service. Parking.
Work Stocked and Sold:
Dr. Pa.
Price range: £75 - £600.

THE GALLERY
Haroldston House, Clay Lanes, Haverfordwest, SA61 1UH. **Tel:** *01437-762611.*

GILLIAN RICHARDSON
Fine Art Photography, The Gallery, Fair Winds, Spittal, Haverfordwest, SA62 5QT.
Tel: *01437-87311.*

HAMILTON HOUSE GALLERY
Caerfarchell, Solva, Haverfordwest, SA62 6XG.
Tel: *01437-721264.*

THE PINK HOUSE
Contemporary Arts, Nine Wells, Solva, Haverfordwest, SA62 6UH. **Tel:** *01437-721543.*

TREVIGAN GALLERY
Croesgoch, Haverfordwest, SA62 5JP.
Tel: *01348-831374.*

MILFORD HAVEN

TORCH THEATRE
St Peters Road, Milford Haven, SA73 2BU.
Tel: *01646-694192.*

NARBERTH

THE GALLERY AT COLBY
Colby Woodland Gardens (National Trust Property), Stepaside, Narberth, SA67 8PP.
Tel: *01834-814164.*

THE GOLDEN SHEAF GALLERY *C*
High Street, Narberth, SA67 7AR.
Tel: *01834-860407.* **Fax:** *01834-860407.*

NEWPORT

FINE ARTS GALLERY
Carningli Centre, East Street, Newport, SA42 0SY. **Tel:** *01239-820724.*

PAULINE HARRIES GALLERY
Ty Clyd, Long Street, Newport, SA42 0TL.
Tel: *01239-820404.*

THE SESSIONS HOUSE
East Street, Newport, SA42 0SY. **Tel:** *01239-820853.*

Ab *Artist's Books* **App** *Applied Art* **Cer** *Ceramics* **Cra** *Crafts*
Dec *Decorative* **Dr** *Drawing* **Fur** *Furniture*

PEMBROKE

THE GOLDEN PLOVER STUDIO
GALLERY C
Warren, Pembroke, SA17 5HR. **Tel:** *01646-661201.*
Opening times: *Telephone for details.*
Nearest Station: *Pembroke.*
Personnel: Arthur Giardelli. Bim Giardelli.
Paintings and watercolours of Pembrokeshire
and other places by Bim and Arthur Giardelli -
France, Italy and Far East.
Fabric pictures and relief sculptures exhibited
in Wales, London and abroad, including the
National Museum of Wales and the Tate
Gallery.
Services and Facilities:
Commissioning Service. Parking.
Work Stocked and Sold:
Dr. Pa. Sc.
Price range: £100 - £4,000.

ST. DAVID'S

ALBION GALLERY
41 Nun Street, St. David's, SA62 6NU.
Tel: *01437-720120.*

THE GALLERY
Peters Lane, St. David's, SQ62 6NT.
Tel: *01437-720570.*

JOHN ROBERTS GALLERY
Ti Meini 16 Cross Street, St. David's, SA62 6SE.
Tel: *01437-720220.*

TENBY

THE HARBOUR GALLERY AND ETCHING STUDIO
1 St Julian Street, Tenby, SA70 7AY.
Tel: *01834-842370.*

TENBY MUSEUM & ART GALLERY
Castle Hill, Tenby, SA70 7BP.
Tel: *01834-842809.*
Fax: *01834-842809.*
Opening times: *Easter-end September, daily
10-5. Sundays only during July & August.
October-Easter, Mon-Fri only 10-5.*
Personnel: *Honorary Curator:* Jon Beynon.
An independent, community museum since
1878, it is situated within the castle walls in a
magnificent setting, overlooking Carmarthen
Bay.
The art gallery houses a permanent collection
of works by local artists, Augustus John, Gwen
John and Niña Hamnett, and paintings of the
Tenby area by leading artists since the 18th
century.
The recently opened New Art Gallery will dis-
play a variety of temporary exhibitions. The
Local History Gallery is currently exhibiting a
history of Monasticism on the nearby Caldey
Island.
The museum has an outstanding display of
geology, archaeology, natural history and mar-
itime history of Pembrokeshire.
Services and Facilities:
Friends/Society. Museum Shop.

POWYS

BRECON

THE BEACONS POTTERY AND GALLERY
*The Old School House, Defynnog, Brecon, LD3
8SU.* **Tel:** *01874-638919, Home 015504619.*

SABLE AND HOGG GALLERIES C
15 Lion Street, Brecon, LD3 7HY. **Tel:** *01874-625901.*
Opening times: *Mon-Sat 10-5. Closed
Wed.*
Nearest Station: *Abergavenny (20 mins
away).*
Personnel: Michael Egbers.
Sales of original paintings, limited edition
prints, etchings, photographs, cards. Bespoke
picture framing, restoration, cleaning.
Photographic work, events - social - industrial
- commercial. Computer reconstruction of old
photographs, copy work. Disabled access
ground floor only.
Services and Facilities:
*Craftshop. Framing. Gallery space for hire.
Restoration. Shop. Valuation.*
Work Stocked and Sold:
Pa. Ph. Pr.
Price range: £20 - £5,000.

WATTON STUDIO
37 The Watton, Brecon, LD3 7EG.
Tel: *01874-611232.*

CRICKHOWELL

BEAUFORT GALLERY
*2 Bank Buildings, Beauford Street, Crickhowell,
NP8 1AD.* **Tel:** *01873-810025.*

HAY-ON-WYE

HAY PRINTS
9 High Town, Hay-on-Wye, HR3 5AE.
Tel: *01497-820172.*

KILVERT GALLERY C
*Ashbrook House, Clyro, Hay-on-Wye, HR3
5RZ.* **Tel:** *01497-820831.* **Fax:** *01497-820831.*
Opening times: *Closed Christmas-Easter
(except by appointment). From Easter: Open
Tues-Sun 10-5 (closed Mon). 'Phone if in doubt.*
Personnel: Elizabeth Organ. Eugene Fisk.

Contemporary Art Gallery in the former home
of the 19th century diarist the Revd. Francis
Kilvert, run by designer and painter, Elizabeth
Organ.
Showing a constantly changing selection of
paintings, sculpture, ceramics, jewellery, furni-
ture, papier mâché and more unusual three-
dimensional work by both renowned and
young and promising artists. Regular exhibi-
tions and painting courses. Art and Interior
Design consultancy. Organisers of the ART
OF LIVING
Decorative Arts Fairs; Artist in Residence:
Portrait and landscape painter, Eugene Fisk.
Services and Facilities:
*Art Consultancy. Art for Offices. Commissioning
Service. Craftshop. Lectures. Valuation.*
Work Stocked and Sold:
*Cer. Cra. Dec. Dr. Fur. Jew. Pa. Pr. Sc.
Tx. Wd.*
Price range: £10 - £6,000.

LLANDRINDOD WELLS

PORTICUS C
*1 Middleton Street, Llandrindod Wells, LD1
5ET.* **Tel:** *01597-823989.*

MACHYNLLETH

THE MUSEUM OF MODERN ART, WALES
PS
Heol Penrallt, Machynlleth, SY20 8AJ.
Tel: *01654-703355.* **Fax:** *01654-702160.*
Opening times: *Mon Sat- 10-4. Admission
free.*
Nearest Station: *Machynlleth.*
Personnel: *Chairman:* Ruth Lambert .

The Museum Of Modern Art, Wales, forms
part of a cultural centre which has grown
around a former chapel, The Tabernacle, in
the mid-Wales market town of Machynlleth.
It has a permanent collection of 20th century
British Art including works by Augustus John,
Wyndham Lewis and Stanley Spencer. A spe-
cial room is devoted to The Brotherhood of
Ruralists. Showcase Wales is a semi-permanent
exhibition featuring Wales' top artists.
MOMA,
Wales is particularly vibrant in August when
the Tabernacle Art Competition is held in
conjunction with The Machynlleth Festival.
Admission Free.
Services and Facilities:
*Bar. Disabled Access. Friends/Society. Gallery
space for hire. Parking.*
Work Stocked and Sold:
Dr. Pa. Ph. Pr. Sc.
Price range: £100 - £10,000.

Gla *Glass* **Jew** *Jewellery* **Pa** *Paintings* **Ph** *Photography* **Pr** *Prints*
Sc *Sculpture* **Tx** *Textiles* **Wd** *Wood*

THE ARTWORLD
DIRECTORY 1998/99 **161**

YR ORIEL FACH
Plas Rhiwgwreiddyn, Ceinws, Machynlleth, SY20 9EX. **Tel:** *01654-761697.*

MONTGOMERY

COUNTRY WORKS GALLERY C
Broad Street, Montgomery, SY15 6PH.
Tel: *01686-668866.*

NEWTOWN

ORIEL 31, DAVIES MEMORIAL GALLERY P
The Park, Newtown, SY16 2NZ.
Tel: *01686-625041.*
Fax: *01686-623633.*

PRESTEIGNE

THE EAGLE GALLERY
Broad Street, New Radnor, Presteigne, LD8 2SN. **Tel:** *01544-260402.*

TALGARTH

TALGARTH LIBRARY
New Street, Talgarth, LD3 0BP.
Tel: *01874-711665.*

WELSHPOOL

WELSHPOOL LIBRARY
Brook Street, Welshpool, SY21 7PH.
Tel: *01938-553001.*

RHONDDA CYNON TAF

ABERDARE

DARE VALLEY COUNTRY PARK PS
Visitor Centre, Aberdare, CF44 7RG.
Tel: *01685-874672.*
Fax: *01685-882919.*
Opening times: *Open Easter to end of September, daily 9-7. Winter period 9-4. Closed Christmas week.*
Personnel: *Manager:* David Protheroe.
The 500 acre DARE VALLEY COUNTRY PARK welcomes around 100,000 visitors each year. The Visitor Centre Complex comprises hotel, caravan and camping site, interpretive centre, cafeteria, preview theatre, schoolroom and two small galleries.
 A year-round activity programme includes musical and visual entertainment, lectures, demonstrations and sporting events. Exhibitions are invited from artists for consideration in preparing a diverse and balanced programme for each year (22 are planned for 1998).
The gallery charges a modest commission on sales. Admission to the public is free and all work must be suitable for family viewing and be appropriate to the country setting.
Services and Facilities:
Bar. Café. Disabled Access. Museum Shop. Parking.
Work Stocked and Sold:
Cra.

PONTYPRIDD

ORIEL Y BONT
University of Glamorgan, Pontypridd, CF37 1DL. **Tel:** *01443-480480 ext 2568.*
Opening times: *Term time only Mon-Fri 9-5.*
Personnel: *Exhibition Organiser:* Alan Salisbury (School of Humanities & Social Science).
Gallery in foyer of large building at front of the university campus. Space is roughly octagonal in shape with hanging surfaces 28' in length and 8' in height. Walls provide additional space of approx 20' x 8' also display cases. Sales not a priority. Intention is to provide arena for contemporary visual arts that will inform and extend students' visual and cultural awareness, acting as 'shop window' for institution establishing links with local community. Exhibitors usually give lectures/run workshops relating to exhibition.
Services and Facilities:
Lectures.
Work Stocked and Sold:
Cer. Dr. Pa. Ph. Pr.
Price range: £250 - £5,000.

SWANSEA

SWANSEA

CAFE GALLERY
Salubrious Passage, Off Wind Street, Swansea SA1 1EG **Tel:** *01792-460333.*

THE CRAFTSMAN GALLERY
58 St Helens Road, Swansea SA1 4BE.
Tel: *01792-642043.*

GALLERY 28
28 St Helen's Road, Swansea SA1 4AR.
Tel: *01792-465934.*

GLYNN VIVIAN ART GALLERY C
Alexandra Road, Swansea SA1 5DZ.
Tel: *01792-655006.* **Fax:** *01792-651713.*

MUMBLES GALLERY
618 Mumbles Road, Swansea SA3 4EA.
Tel: *01792-367102.*

THE NEW GALLERY
59 Newton Road, Mumbles, Swansea SA3 4BL.
Tel: *01792-367910.*

ORIEL CERI RICHARDS GALLERY PS
Taliesin Arts Centre, University of Wales Swansea, Singleton Park, Swansea SA2 8PZ.
Tel: *01792-295526.* **Fax:** *01792-295899.*
Email *taliesin@swan.ac.uk*
Ws *http://www.whatsonwales.com*
Opening times: *Mon 11-5, Tue 11-6, Sat 12-6.*
Personnel: *Marketing Officer:* Evaline Heinzl.
Oriel Ceri Richards Gallery hosts approximately 10 exhibitions each year. Of these, there are three mixed shows, exhibiting a range of work from local artists and crafts peo-ple. In addition to the mixed shows, the gallery stocks an excellent range of artists and

designer cards, as well as jewellery, prints, drawings, paintings, ceramics and other craft items.
Services and Facilities:
Art Consultancy. Bar. Bookshop. Café. Disabled Access. Framing. Friends/Society. Museum Shop. Parking. Shop.
Work Stocked and Sold:
Cer. Cra. Dr. Jew. Pa. Pr.

PHILIP DAVIES GALLERY
58 St Helen's Road, Swansea SA3 4EU.
Tel: *01792-642043.*
Fax: *01792-361453.*

SWANSEA ARTS WORKSHOP GALLERY
Gloucester Place, Swansea SA1 1TY.
Tel: *01792-652016.*

SWANSEA MUSEUM P
Victoria Road, Swansea SA1 1SN. **Tel:** *01792-653763.*

TY LLEN PS
The Dylan Thomas Centre, Somerset Place, Swansea SA1 1RR. **Tel:** *01792-463980.*
Fax: *01792-463993.*
Opening times: *Daily 10.30-5.*
Nearest Station: *Swansea Central.*
Personnel: *Arts & Literature Officer:* David Woolley.
Buildings Manager: Hugh Evans.
The magnificently refurbished Dylan Thomas Centre is an unique mix of public and commercial space.
The centre houses a permanent, changing exhibition, "I, in my intricate image" dedicated to the life and work of Dylan Thomas. It also hosts a regular programme of literary events and festivals, and the corridor gallery has small, changing exhibitions.
Bar, bookshop-café, gift shop, and restaurant are also open to the public when not being used for private functions, conferences etc. The centre is situated in the city's attractive marina area, close to the centre of town.
Services and Facilities:
Bar. Bookshop. Café. Disabled Access. Friends/Society. Gallery space for hire. Lectures. Restaurant. Shop.

TORFAEN

PONTYPOOL

TORFAEN GALLERY
31 Commercial Street, Pontypool, NP4 6JQ.
Tel: *01495-751518.*

Ab *Artist's Books* **App** *Applied Art* **Cer** *Ceramics* **Cra** *Crafts*
Dec *Decorative* **Dr** *Drawing* **Fur** *Furniture*

WREXHAM

WREXHAM

WREXHAM ARTS CENTRE *PS*
Rhosddu Road, Wrexham LL1 1AU.
Tel: *01978-292093.* **Fax:** *01978-292611.*
Email *gallery@wrexhamlib.u-net.com*
Opening times: *Mon-Fri 9.30-6.45, Sat 9.30-5, Sun closed.*
Nearest Station: *Wrexham.*
Personnel: *Visual Arts Officer:* Stephen West. *Cultural & Heritage Officer:* Hazel Hawarden.
Visual Arts Officer: Jonathon le Vay (temporary).
Education Officer: Dawn Parry.
Gallery Assistant: Donn Critchley.
Exhibitions Assistant: Sharon Reed.

Gallery opened 1973 to show contemporary art from Wales, Britain and International. 109 sq. metre main gallery. Foyer craft cases showing contemporary crafts for sale. Gallery 2 shows mainly local artists and groups. Exhibitions for 1998 include The Wales Drawing Biennale, Paul Davies retrospective, Roy Omade and Rose Wylie.
Services and Facilities:
Café. Craftshop. Disabled Access. Lectures. Parking.
Work Stocked and Sold:
Ph.

NOTES

Gla *Glass* **Jew** *Jewellery* **Pa** *Paintings* **Ph** *Photography* **Pr** *Prints*
Sc *Sculpture* **Tx** *Textiles* **Wd** *Wood*

SUBSCRIBE NOW

PHONE OUR CREDIT CARD HOTLINE ON 0171 236 4880 OR SIMPLY COMPLETE THE COUPON BELOW AND RETURN FREEPOST TO US

Please enrol me as an Art Review subscriber as follows:

☐ One Year Subscription @ £36.00

☐ Two Year Subscription @ £72.00 - £59.50 (save £12.50)

☐ Three Year Subscription @ £108.00 - £79.50 (save £28.50)

☐ I enclose my cheque payable to Art Review for £ _____

☐ Please debit my ☐ Visa ☐ Amex ☐ Access Card

Card No. _____

Expiry Date _____

Name on card _____

Signature _____ Date _____

Name _____

Address _____

_____

_____

Postcode _____

Send this form to: Art Review, Freepost, London EC1B 1DE

**The above offer is limited to UK subscriber addresses only.
Europe £48   USA $79   Canada $85   Rest of the World £48**

IRISH GALLERIES

Town/County index. Main listings.

Where this information has been provided, galleries are designated 'C' for commercial, 'P' for public gallery or museum or 'PS' for a public gallery or museum holding selling shows.

THE ART WORLD
DIRECTORY
1998/99 25TH EDITION

TOWN/ COUNTY INDEX

A/B

C/D

E/F/G

H/I/J

K/L/M/N

O/P/Q

R/S

T/U/V/W

ANTRIM

BELFAST

THE BELL GALLERY
13 Adelaide Park, Malone Road, Belfast, BT9 6FX. **Tel:** *01232-662998.* **Fax:** *01232-381524.*

CATALYST ARTS
5 Exchange Place, Belfast, BT1 2NA.
Tel: *01232-313303.*

CAVEHILL GALLERY
18 Old Cavehill Road, Belfast, BT15 5GT.
Tel: *01232-776784.*

CRESENT ARTS CENTRE
2-4 University Road, Belfast, BT7 1NT.
Tel: *01232-242338.*

THE FENDERESKY GALLERY AT QUEEN'S
5-6 Upper Crescent, Belfast, BT7 1NT.
Tel: *01232-235245.*

THE GALLERY
56-60 Dublin Road, Belfast, BT2 7HP.
Tel: *01232-321402.*

JOHN MAGEE LTD
455-457 Ormeau Road, Belfast, BT7 3GQ.
Tel: *01232-693830.*
Fax: *01232-491009.*

OLD MUSEUM ARTS CENTRE PS
7 College Square North, Belfast, BT1 6AR.
Tel: *01232-235053.* **Fax:** *01232-322912.*
Opening times: *Mon-Sat 10-6 during exhibitions.*
Personnel: *Director:* Anne McReynolds.
Services and Facilities:
Café. Workshop Facilities.
Work Stocked and Sold:
Ph. Pr.

ONE OXFORD STREET
1 Oxford Street, Belfast, BT1 3LA.
Tel: *01232-310400.* **Fax:** *01232-310444.*

ORMEAU BATHS GALLERY
18 A Ormeau Avenue, Belfast, BT2 8HS..
Tel: *01232-321402.* **Fax:** *01232-312232.*

ULSTER MUSEUM PS
Botanic Gardens, Belfast, BT9 5AB.
Tel: *01232-381251 / 383000.* **Fax:** *01232-665510 / 383003 / 383103.*
Opening times: *Mon-Fri 10-5, Sat 1-5, Sun 2-5.*
Nearest Station: *Botanic.*
Personnel: *Head of Fine and Applied Art:* S.B. Kennedy. *Exhibition Organiser:* Anne Stewart.
The Ulster Museum, an interdisciplinary institution whose origins go back to the Belfast Natural History Society Museum of 1831, contains a wide variety of fine and applied art of various periods and schools.
Included in the fine art holdings are works by Thomas Gainsborough, Sir Joshua Reynolds and J.M.W. Turner and by modern masters such as Francis Bacon, Henry Moore and Stanley Spencer.
Irish art from the seventeenth century to the present day is also well represented, as is modern European and American painting and sculpture.
Highlights of the applied art collection include The Kildare Silver-Gilt Toilet Set and the Bute Glass Bowl and Stand, both highly important eighteenth century Irish pieces and a pair of rare Matisse wall hangings, produced in 1947.
Services and Facilities:
Bookshop. Café. Disabled Access. Friends/Society. Guided Tours. Lectures. Museum Shop. Restaurant.

LISBURN

HARMONY HILLS ARTS CENTRE
Clonmore House, 54 Harmony Hill, Lisburn, BT27 4ES. **Tel:** *01232-678219.*

SEYMOUR GALLERIES
20 Seymour Street, Lisburn, **Tel:** *01232-662685.* **Fax:** *01232-662685.*

PORTRUSH

PORTRUSH GALLERY
93-95 Main Street, Portrush, BT56 8DA.
Tel: *01265-823739.*

RANDALSTOWN

CLOTWORTHY ARTS CENTRE
Antrim Castle Gardens, Randalstown, BT41 4LH. **Tel:** *01849-428000.* **Fax:** *01849-460360.*

ARMAGH

ARMAGH

ADAM GALLERY
28 Linenhall Street, Armagh, **Tel:** *01861-526908/523654.*

Ab *Artist's Books* **App** *Applied Art* **Cer** *Ceramics* **Cra** *Crafts*
Dec *Decorative* **Dr** *Drawing* **Fur** *Furniture*

ARMAGH COUNTY MUSEUM P
The Mall East, Armagh, BT61 9BE.
Tel: *01861-523070.*
Fax: *01861-522361.*

HAYLOFT GALLERY P
Palace Stables Heritage Centre, The Palace Demesne, Armagh, BT60 4EL.
Tel: *01861-529629.*
Fax: *01861-529630.*
Opening times: *April-Sept: Mon-Sat 10-5.30, Sun 1-6. Oct-Mar: Mon-Sat 10-5, Sun 2-5.*
Personnel: *Supervisor: Debbie Leacock.*

Located in listed Georgian stable block, the Hayloft Gallery offers exhibition hire space for art forms which will appeal to general public with interest and educational emphasis. Walls: dusty pink natural Armagh stone and some wood panelling. Floor: stained medium teak. Hanging display system. Light: Good natural light plus spotlights on track. Good disability access. Size 15.3mx5.7m plus additional area 4.25mx4m approximately. Gallery on first floor of Heritage Centre. 40,000 visitors expected annually. The Centre also houses permanent exhibition on Georgian life in Armagh.
Located beside Palace (former residence of Church of Ireland primates) and primates chapel.
Services and Facilities:
Bar. Café. Craftshop. Disabled Access. Gallery space for hire. Guided Tours. Parking. Restaurant.
Work Stocked and Sold:
Cer. Cra. Fur. Jew. Pr. Wd.
Price range: £0.50 - £100.

CRAIGAVON

THE PEACOCK GALLERY
Pinebank House Arts Centre, Tullygally Road, Craigavon, BT65 5BY. **Tel:** *01762-341618.*
Fax: *01762-342402.*

PORTADOWN

ROY EDWARDS FINE ARTS LTD`
Mahon Road, Portadown, BT62 3EH.
Tel: *01762-339116.* **Fax:** *01762-350179.*

CARLOW

CARLOW

PEMBROKE STUDIO GALLERY
1 Pembroke, Carlow, **Tel:** *00353-1-503 41562.*
Fax: *00353-1-503 41562.*

CAVAN

CAVAN

CAVAN COUNTY ARTS SERVICE
Cavan County Library, 17 Farnham Street, Cavan, **Tel:** *00353-1-493 1799.* **Fax:** *00353-1-496 1565/31384.*

CLARE

BALLYVAUGHAN

DALLAN GALLERY
Ballyvaughan, **Tel:** *00353-1-657 7156.*

ENNIS

DE VALERA LIBRARY
Harmony Row, Ennis, **Tel:** *00353-1-652 1616.*
Fax: *00353-1-652 8233.*

ENNISTYMON

ENNISTYMON BRANCH LIBRARY
The Square, Ennistymon, **Tel:** *00353-1-657 1245.*

KILSHANNY

THE ATLANTIS GALLERY
Caherkinalla, Kilshanny, **Tel:** *00353-1-657 4270.*

SHANNON

SEAN LEMASS LIBRARY
Town Centre, Shannon, **Tel:** *00353-1-613 64266.*

CORK

CORK

BLACKCOMBE ART GALLERY
44a MacCurtain Street, Cork, **Tel:** *00353-1-215 00040.* **Fax:** *00353-1-215 00040.*

CORK ARTS SOCIETY LAVITT'S GALLERY
16 Lavitt's Quay, Cork,
Tel: *00353-1-212 77749.* **Fax:** *00353-1-212 77749.*

CORK PUBLIC MUSEUM P
Fitzgerald Park, Mardyke, Cork, **Tel:** *00353-21 270679.* **Fax:** *00353-21 270931.*

CRAWFORD MUNICIPAL ART GALLERY P
Emmet Place, Cork, **Tel:** *00353-1-212 73377.*
Fax: *00353-1-212 75680 / 860 ?.*

TRISKEL ARTS CENTRE
Tobin Street, off South Main Street, Cork, **Tel:** *00353-1-212 72022/272023.* **Fax:** *00353-1-212 75945.*

MACROOM

VANGARD GALLERY
New Street, Macroom, **Tel:** *00353-1-264 1198.*

WEST CORK

THE BANDON GALLERY
83 North Main Street, Bandon, West Cork,
Tel: *00353-1-234 1360.* **Fax:** *00353-1-234 1287.*

O'KANE'S GREEN GALLERY
Glengarriff Road, Bantry, West Cork,
Tel: *00353-1-275 0003.*

WEST CORK ARTS CENTRE
Skibbereen, West Cork, **Tel:** *00353-1-282 2090.*

DERRY

COLERAINE

RIVERSIDE GALLERY
Riverside Theatre, Coleraine, BT52 1SA.
Tel: *01265-324449.* **Fax:** *01265-324160.*

TOWN HOUSE GALLERY
45 Milburn Road, Coleraine, BT52 1QT.
Tel: *01265-44869.*

DERRY

CONTEXT GALLERY
The Playhouse, 5-7 Artillery Street, Derry,
Tel: *01504-264481.* **Fax:** *01504-261884.*

GORDON GALLERIES
7 London Street, Derry, BT48 6RQ.
Tel: *01504-374044.*
Fax: *01504-374044.*

ORCHARD GALLERY
Orchard Street, Derry, BT48 6EG.
Tel: *01504-269675.* **Fax:** *01504-267273.*

PORTSTEWART

FLOWERFIELD ARTS CENTRE
185 Coleraine Road, Portstewart, BT55 7HV.
Tel: *01265-833959.*

DONEGAL

GLEANN CHOLM CILLE

FORAS CULTUIR ULADH - ULSTER CULTURAL INSTITUTE
Gleann Cholm Cille, **Tel:** *00353-1-733 0248* *(Apr-Sept).*

LETTERKENNY

DONEGAL COUNTY MUSEUM P
High Road, Letterkenny, **Tel:** *00353-1-742 4613.*

Gla Glass *Jew* Jewellery *Pa* Paintings *Ph* Photography *Pr* Prints
Sc Sculpture *Tx* Textiles *Wd* Wood

GLEBE HOUSE AND GALLERY
Church Hill, Letterkenny,
Tel: *00353-1-743 7071.* **Fax:** *00353-1-743 7072.*

PORT GALLERY
86a Upper Main Street, Letterkenny,
Tel: *00353-1-742 5073.*

DOWN

BANGOR

NORTH DOWN VISITORS AND HERITAGE CENTRE *PS*
Town Hall, Castle Park Avenue, Bangor, BT20 4BT.
Tel: *01247-270371 ext 275.*
Fax: *01247-271370.*
Opening times: *Tues-Sat 10.30-4.30, Sun 2-4 (open until 5.30 July-Aug), Bank Holiday Mons.*
Nearest Station: *Bangor.*
Personnel: *Manager: Ian Wilson.*
North Down Heritage Centre is a registered museum.
Its mission statement includes its aim to reflect all aspects of local heritage including artistic. The Centre is situated in beautifully re-furbished out-buildings of Bangor Castle, built in 1852 for local landlord R.E. Ward.
An Out-Centre (Summer only) is now located in re-furbished 17th century fishermen's cottages at Cockle Row, Groomsport, 3 miles away.
Services and Facilities:
Bookshop. Café. Commissioning Service. Disabled Access. Gallery space for hire. Restaurant.
Work Stocked and Sold:
Cra. Jew. Pr.
Price range: *£5 - £30.*

COMBER

CASTLE ESPIE GALLERY
78 Ballydrain Road, Comber, **Tel:** *01247-872517.*

SALEM GALLERY
29 Mill Street, Comber, **Tel:** *01247-874455.*

DONAGHADEE

THE CLEFT ART GALLERY
3 Market House, New Street, Donaghadee,
Tel: *01247-888502.*

DOWNPATRICK

DOWN ARTS CENTRE
2-6 Irish Street, Downpatrick, BT30 6BN.
Tel: *01396-615283.* **Fax:** *01369-616621.*

HILLSBOROUGH

SHAMBLES ART GALLERY
Dromore Road/Park Lane, Hillsborough,
Tel: *01232-667528.* **Fax:** *01232-681469.*

HOLYWOOD

PRIORY ART GALLERY
10 Shore Road, Holywood, BT18 9HX.
Tel: *01232-428173/424570.*

NEWCASTLE

GRANT FINE ART *C*
87c Bryansford Road, Newcastle,
Tel: *013967-22349.* **Fax:** *013967-22349.*
Opening times: *Mon-Sat 2-5 during exhibitions, or by appointment (phone ahead to confirm).*
Personnel: *Owner: Margaret Grant.*
Work Stocked and Sold:
Dr. Gla. Pa. Pr. Sc.

NEWCASTLE ART GALLERY
18-22 Main Street, Newcastle,
Tel: *013967-23555.*

NEWTOWNARDS

ARDS ARTS CENTRE
Townhall, Conway Square, Newtownards, BT23 4DD. **Tel:** *01247-810803.* **Fax:** *01247-823131.*

DUBLIN

DALKEY

THE JAMES GALLERY
7 Railway Road, Dalkey, **Tel:** *00353-1-285 8703.*

DUBLIN

THE ARCHITECTURE CENTRE
The Royal Institute of the Architects of Ireland, 8 Merrion Square, Dublin 2, **Tel:** *00353-1-676 1703.* **Fax:** *00353-1-661 0948.*

COMBRIDGE FINE ARTS LTD
Gainboro House, 24 Suffolk Street, Dublin 2,
Tel: *00353-1-677 4652.*

CRAFTS COUNCIL GALLERY
Powerscourt Town House, South William Street, Dublin 2, **Tel:** *00353-1-679 7368.*
Fax: *00353-1-679 9197.*

DAVIS GALLERY *C*
11 Capel Street, Dublin 1, **Tel:** *00353-1-872 6969.* **Fax:** *00353-1-872 5580.*
Opening times: *Mon-Fri 10-5, Sat 11-5.*
Personnel: *Owner: Gerald Davis.*

Dublin's longest running commercial gallery of Modern Art. Specialising in original works in all media by artists living in Ireland. Gallery also available for rent.
Services and Facilities:
Art Consultancy. Art for Offices. Gallery space for hire.
Work Stocked and Sold:
Cra. Pa. Sc.
Price range: *£50 - £3,000.*

DESIGNYARD
12 East Essex Street, Dublin 2,
Tel: *00353-1-677 8453/677 8467.*
Fax: *00353-1-677 8482.*

DOUGLAS HYDE GALLERY
Trinity College, Nassau Street, Dublin 2.
Tel: *00353-1-702 1116.* **Fax:** *00353-1-677 2694 (attn: DHG).*

THE GALLERY OF PHOTOGRAPHY
Meeting House Square, Temple Bar, Dublin 2,
Tel: *00353-1-671 4654.* **Fax:** *00353-1-671 4654.*

GORRY GALLERY
20 Molesworth Street, Dublin 2, **Tel:** *00353-1-679 5319.* **Fax:** *00353-1-679 5319.*

GRAPHIC STUDIO DUBLIN GALLERY *C*
8a Cope Street (through the Arch), Temple Bar, Dublin 2, **Tel:** *00353-1-679 8021.*

GREEN ON RED GALLERY
58 Fitzwilliam Square, Dublin 2, **Tel:** *00353-1-661 3881.* **Fax:** *00353-1-661 3881.*

GUINNESS GALLERY
Foxrock Village, Dublin 18, **Tel:** *00353-1-289 7955.*

GUINNESS HOP STORE
Crane Street, (off Thomas Street), Dublin 8,
Tel: *00353-1-453 6700.* **Fax:** *00353-1-453 3631.*

HALLWARD GALLERY
64 Merrion Square, Dublin 2, **Tel:** *00353-1-662 1482.*

HUGH LANE MUNICIPAL GALLERY OF MODERN ART *P*
Charlemont House, Parnell Square North, Dublin 1. **Tel:** *00353-1-874 1903.* **Fax:** *00353-1-872 2182.* **Email** *hughlane@iol.ie*
Opening times: *Tues-Thurs 9.30-6, Fri-Sat 9.30-5, Sun 11-5.*
Nearest Station: *Connolly.*
Personnel: *Director: Barbara Dawson.*
The gallery contains the second largest collection of fine art in Ireland, concentrating primarily from the mid 19th century to contemporary art practice. The nucleus of the collection was assembled by the late Sir Hugh Lane whose reputation as a dealer and collector in these islands was legendary. It was he who bought the now famous Renoir's Les Parapluies and Manet's Concert aux Tuileries for a Gallery of Modern Art in Dublin. Also included in the collection are works by

Ab *Artist's Books* **App** *Applied Art* **Cer** *Ceramics* **Cra** *Crafts*
Dec *Decorative* **Dr** *Drawing* **Fur** *Furniture*

Whistler, Sargent, Augustus John, Fantin-Latour, Monet, Degas, Bonnard and Vlaminck. The Gallery devotes a considerable amount of its purchasing fund to the acquisition of contemporary Irish art, as well as international art. Recent acquisitions include Sean Scully, Agnes Martin, Nikki de St. Phalle and the young Scottish landscape artist, Barbara Rae.
Services and Facilities:
Bookshop. Disabled Access. Friends/Society. Guided Tours. Lectures. Restaurant.

IRISH MUSEUM OF MODERN ART *P*
Royal Hospital, Military Road, Kilmainham, Dublin 8. **Tel:** *00353-1-612 9900.*
Fax: *00353-1-612 9999.*
Email *info@modernart.ie*
Opening times: *Tue-Sat 10-5.30, Sun 12-5.30.*
Personnel: *Director:* Declan McGonagle.
Senior Curator: Exhibitions: Brenda McParland.
Senior Curator: Collection: Catherine Marshall. *Senior Curator: Education & Community:* Helen O'Donoghue.
The Museum presents a wide cross-section of Irish and international art of the 20th century, from its own collection and through temporary exhibitions.

There is also a busy Community and Education Programme and an Artists Work Programme, based in the studio and workshop blocks at the Museum. Talks, seminars, music and other events also form part of the Museum's work. The Museum is housed in the Royal Hospital Kilmainham, a large elegant 17th century building said to be the finest of its period in Ireland. Gardens/Grounds. Heritage Video.
Services and Facilities:
Bookshop. Café. Disabled Access. Friends/Society. Guided Tours. Lectures. Parking. Workshop Facilities.

KERLIN GALLERY *C*
Anne's Lane, South Anne Street, Dublin 2, **Tel:** *00353-1-670 9093.* **Fax:** *00353-1-670 9096.* **Email** *gallery@kerlin.ie*
Opening times: *Mon-Fri 10-5.45, Sat 11-4.30.*
Personnel: *Directors:* John Kennedy, David Fitzgerald.
Work Stocked and Sold:
Pa. Ph. Pr. Sc.

MILMO-PENNY FINE ART LTD *C*
55 Ailesbury Road, Ballsbridge, Dublin 4, **Tel:** *00353-1-269 3486.* **Fax:** *00353-1-283 0414.* **Email** *finearts@indigo.ie*

Opening times: *By appointment.*
Nearest Station: *Sydney Parade.*
Personnel: *Director:* Dominic Milmo-Penny.

MILMO-PENNY FINE ART

Specialist gallery dealing mainly in premium Irish post-impressionist and early 20th century art.
An unconditional written guarantee and condition report is given with every painting sold. We have pioneered the description 'signed by the artist'. Our main activity is the formation of collections for private clients world-wide. We are interested in purchasing first class examples of European and American paintings of the period 1860 to 1940, particularly Irish, Newlyn and Breton Schools.
Our conservation, restoration and framing service is available only to our clients. We also offer expert reports on authenticity and condition.
Services and Facilities:
Art Consultancy. Art for Offices. Framing. Restoration.
Work Stocked and Sold:
Dr. Pa. Sc.
Price range: £500 - £5,000.

NATIONAL GALLERY OF IRELAND *P*
Merrion Square West, Dublin 2.
Tel: *00353-1-661 5133.* **Fax:** *00353-1-661 5372.*
Opening times: *Mon-Sat 10-5.30, Thurs 10-8.30, Sun 2-5. (closed Dec 24/25/26 and Good Friday)*
Personnel: *Director:* Raymond Keaveney.
The National Gallery of Ireland was established by an Act of Parliament in 1854 and opened to the public in 1864 (architect, Francis Fowke).
There are over 13,000 items in the Gallery's collection; 3,000 oil paintings, 5,000 watercolours and drawings, the remainder, prints and sculpture.
It houses a prestigious collection of European masterpieces dating from the 14th to the 20th Century; Fra Angelico, Mantegna, Caravaggio, Vermeer, Rembrandt, Ruysdael; Zurbarán, Goya, Picasso; Rubens, Jordaens, van Dyck; Poussin, Cézanne, Degas; Hogarth, Gainsborough, Reynolds.
It also houses an important historic collection of Irish paintings (17th to 20th Century) with works by Thomas Roberts, Nathaniel Hone the Elder and Younger, Hugh Douglas Hamilton, James Barry, Daniel Maclise, Sarah Purser, Roderic O'Conor, William Leech, Paul Henry, William Orpen, John Lavery and Jack B. Yeats. Exhibition and Education Programme, Friends of the National Gallery. Admission to the Gallery is free.
Services and Facilities:
Bookshop. Disabled Access. Friends/Society. Gallery space for hire. Guided Tours. Lectures. Restaurant.

NEW APOLLO GALLERY *C*
18 Duke Street, Dublin 2,
Tel: *00353-1-671 2609.*
Fax: *00353-1-679 7558.*

OISIN ART GALLERY
10 Marino Mart, Fairview, Dublin 3,
Tel: *00353-1-833 3456.* **Fax:** *00353-1-833 5197.*

OISIN ART GALLERY
44 Westland Row, Dublin 2, **Tel:** *00353-1-661 1315.* **Fax:** *00353-1-661 0464.*

ORIEL GALLERY
17 Clare Street, Dublin 2, **Tel:** *00353-1-676 3410.*

RHA GALLAGHER GALLERY
15 Ely Place, Dublin 2, **Tel:** *00353-1-661 2558.* **Fax:** *00353-1-661 0762.*

RUBICON GALLERY *C*
10 St. Stephens Green, Dublin 2,
Tel: *00353-1-670 8055.* **Fax:** *00353-1-670 8057.* **Email** *rubi@iol.ie*
Opening times: *Mon-Sat 11-5.30.*
Nearest Station: *Grafton St.*
Personnel: *Director:* Josephine Kelliher.

The Rubicon Gallery shows contemporary art focusing on painting, drawing and graphics and specialising in important Irish artists. The gallery programmes eight solo exhibitions per year and also hosts a number of challenging group shows.
Services and Facilities:
Art Consultancy. Art for Offices. Commissioning Service. Gallery space for hire.
Work Stocked and Sold:
Dr. Pa. Pr.
Price range: £200 - £20,000.

THE SOLOMON GALLERY *C*
Powerscourt Town House, South William Street, Dublin 2. **Tel:** *00353-1-679 4237.*
Fax: *00353-1-671 5262.*
Email *solomon@indigo.ie*
Ws *http://indigo.ie/~solomon*
Opening times: *Mon-Sat 10-5.30.*
Personnel: *Owner:* Suzanne MacDougald. *Director:* Tara Murphy.
The Solomon Gallery was established in 1980 and is situated in the original drawing-room of an 18th Century Georgian townhouse formerly owned by Lord Powerscourt.
Now considered one of Ireland's leading contemporary art galleries, the Solomon has built its reputation on representing Irish and international painters and sculptors working primarily in a figurative style. The Solomon Gallery also deals in fine Irish period paintings

and sculpture. Exhibitions are mounted every three to four weeks.

Artists include: Martin Mooney, Rowan Gillespie, Brian Ballard, Hector McDonnell, John Lessore, Sarah Spackman, Elizabeth Cope, Francis Tansey, Peter Collis RHA and Darragh Hogan. Export facilities available.
Services and Facilities:
Art Consultancy. Art for Offices. Commissioning Service. Valuation.
Work Stocked and Sold:
Dr. Gla. Pa. Sc.
Price range: £40 - £10,000.

TAYLOR GALLERIES
34 Kildare Street, Dublin 2, **Tel:** 00353-1-676 6055. **Fax:** 00353-1-676 8305.

TEMPLE BAR GALLERY & STUDIOS PS
5-9 Temple Bar, Dublin 2, **Tel:** 00353-1-671 0073. **Fax:** 00353-1-677 7527.
Email tbgs@indigo.ie
Ws http://www.paddynet.ie/tbgs
Opening times: Mon-Sat 10-6, Sun 2-6.
Personnel: Director: Norah Norton.
Administrator: Jeni Baker. Education Officer:
Vaari Claffey.
Temple Bar Gallery and Studios is located in the centre of Dublin's cultural quarter. The building contains a gallery, an atrium exhibition space on three floors and 30 artists studios. The work selected and exhibited is by emerging and established contemporary artists. Artists curated shows are regularly facilitated. Ancillary programming supports artist led initiatives inside and outside the TBGS&S space and provides a forum for artists and curators through debates and discussions on contemporary arts issues. Three studios are reserved for artists working on specific short-term projects and International residencies. Studio members are open to International studio exchanges.
Services and Facilities:
Art Consultancy. Art for Offices. Commissioning Service. Disabled Access. Friends/Society. Guided Tours. Lectures.
Work Stocked and Sold:
Dr. Pa. Ph. Sc.
Price range: £250 - £10,000.

WYVERN GALLERY
2 Temple Lane, Temple Bar, Dublin 2,
Tel: 00353-1-679 9589.

HOWTH

HOWTH HARBOUR GALLERY
6 Abbey Street, Howth, **Tel:** 00353-1-839 3366.

SKERRIES

VILLAGE ART GALLERY
Thomas Hand Street. **Tel:** 00353-1-849 2236.

GALWAY

CONNEMARA

AN DANLANN
Casla, Connemara, **Tel:** 00353-1-917 2141.

GALWAY

GALWAY ARTS CENTRE
47 Dominick Street, (also 23 Nun's Island, Galway), Galway, **Tel:** 00353-1-916 5888.

THE GRAINSTORE GALLERY
Lower Abbeygate Street, Galway, **Tel:** 00353-1-916 6620.

THE KENNY GALLERY
High Street, Galway, **Tel:** 00353-1-916 1014/61021. **Fax:** 00353-1-916 8544.

OUGHTERARD

WEST SHORE GALLERY
Camp Street, Oughterard, **Tel:** 00353-1-918 2562.

KERRY

KILLARNEY

THE FRANK LEWIS GALLERY
6 Bridewell Lane, Killarney, **Tel:** 00353-1-643 1108/34843 - after hours 00353-1-643 1734.
Fax: 00353-1-643 1570.

THE KILLARNEY ART GALLERY
52 High Street, Killarney, **Tel:** 00353-1-643 4628.

LISTOWEL

ST. JOHN'S ART & HERITAGE CENTRE PS
The Square, Listowel, **Tel:** 00353-1-682 2566.
Opening times: Mon-Fri 10-5, Sat 11-5, Sun 11.30-5 (occasionally closed for a day in low season).
Personnel: Manager: Joe Murphy.

Services and Facilities:
Café. Disabled Access. Gallery space for hire.
Workshop Facilities.

TRALEE

BIN BAN GALLERY
124 Lower Rock Street, Tralee, **Tel:** 00353-1-662 2520.

SIAMSA TIRE THEATRE/ARTS CENTRE
Tralee, **Tel:** 00353-1-662 3055. **Fax:** 00353-1-662 7276.

THE WELLSPRING GALLERY
16 Denny Street, Tralee, **Tel:** 00353-1-662 1218. **Fax:** 00353-1-662 3870.

KILDARE

KILCOCK

KILCOCK ART GALLERY
School Street, Kilcock, **Tel:** 00353-1-628 7619/628 8586/00353-1-885 78283.

KILKENNY

KILKENNY

BUTLER GALLERY
The Castle, Kilkenny, **Tel:** 00353-1-566 1106.
Fax: 00353-1-566 3448.

LEITRIM

CARRICK-ON-SHANNON

OLD BARREL STORE ARTS CENTRE
The Quays, Carrick-on-Shannon, **Tel:** 00353-1-782 0911/after hours 00353-1-784 2093.

LIMERICK

LIMERICK

CHRIS DOSWELL'S GALLERY
The Basement, 28 Mallow Street, Limerick,
Tel: 00353-1-613 18292.

DOLMEN GALLERY
Honan's Quay, Limerick, **Tel:** 00353-1-614 17929.

LIMERICK CITY GALLERY OF ART
Pery Square, Limerick, **Tel:** 00353-1-613 10633.
Fax: 00353-1-614 15266.

MUSE GALLERY
75 O'Connell Street, Limerick, **Tel:** 00353-1-613 14699.

UNIVERSITY OF LIMERICK - AV GALLERY P
University of Limerick, Limerick, **Tel:** 00353-1-61 202040. **Fax:** 00353-1-61 202938.
Email David.Lilburn@ul.ie.

Ab Artist's Books **App** Applied Art **Cer** Ceramics **Cra** Crafts
Dec Decorative **Dr** Drawing **Fur** Furniture

Opening times: *Daily 8am-10pm.*
Personnel: *Exhibition Organiser:* David Lilburn.
Policy - The gallery is best suited to exhibitions of small work. Local and national artists are promoted in approx 8 shows a year. There are also occasional touring shows of literary and scientific interest. Artists may apply to exhibit.
Services and Facilities:
Disabled Access. Parking.
Work Stocked and Sold:
Ab. Dr. Pa. Pr.
Price range: £100 - £1,000.

LONGFORD

LONFORD

CARROLL GALLERY
6 Keon's Terrace, Lonford, **Tel:** *00353-1-434 1148.*

LOUTH

CARLINGFORD

ARTISTIC LICENSE
The Old Coach House, Dundalk Street, Carlingford,
Tel: *00353-1-417 3745.*
Fax: *00353-1-427 3745.*

DUNDALK

THE BASEMENT GALLERY
The Town Hall, Dundalk,
Tel: *00353-1-423 2276.* **Fax:** *00353-1-423 6171.*

MAYO

ACHILL ISLAND

WESTERN LIGHT ART GALLERY
The Sandybanks, Keel, Achill Island,
Tel: *00353-1-984 3325.* **Fax:** *00353-1-984 3325.*

CLAREMORRIS

CLAREMORRIS GALLERY
James Street, Claremorris, **Tel:** *00353-1-947 1348.*

MONAGHAN

MONAGHAN

MARKET HOUSE GALLERY
Tourist Office, Market House, Monaghan,
Tel: *00353-1-478 1122.*

SLIGO

RIVERSTOWN

TAYLOR'S ART GALLERY
Taunagh, Riverstown, **Tel:** *00353-1-716 5138.*
Fax: *00353-1-716 5138.*

SLIGO

SLIGO ART GALLERY
Yeats Memorial Building, Hyde Bridge, Sligo,
Tel: *00353-1-714 5847.* **Fax:** *00353-1-716 2301.*

TIPPERARY

BIRDHILL

THE LUCY ERRIDGE GALLERY
Birdhill, **Tel:** *00353-1-613 79366.*
Fax: *00353-1-613 02459.*

WESTMEATH

ATHLONE

DOLAN MOORE GALLERY
33 Church Street, Athlone, **Tel:** *00353-1-902 78507.*

WEXFORD

BUNCLODY

THE CHANTRY GALLERY
Bunclody, **Tel:** *00353-1-547 7482.*

GOREY

WOODLAND ARTS & CRAFTS GALLERY
Tinnock, Gorey, **Tel:** *00353-1-402 37474.*

WICKLOW

BRAY

CRAFT ART GALLERY
74 Main Street, Bray, **Tel:** *00353-1-286 6728.*

THE HANGMAN GALLERY
2 Westbourne Terrace, Quinnsborough Road, Bray, **Tel:** *00353-1-286 6208.* **Fax:** *00353-1-286 6207.*

WICKLOW

RENAISSANCE III GALLERY
County Buildings, Wicklow,
Tel: *00353-1-404 67324.*
Fax: *00353-1-404 67792.*

ART REVIEW PRINTS SPECIALS

The guide to buying Prints.

One of the most attractive and affordable mediums to begin or enhance any collection. Art Review's special print supplement provides essential reading on contemporary, Victorian, and Old Master prints. Plus print exhibitions, collections, workshops and publishers.

Published anually with the September issue of Art Review. **FREE TO ART REVIEW SUBSCRIBERS** (still only £36.00).

Call our subscription line now on **0171 236 4880** or complete the subscription form on page 194.

PRINTS AND PRINTMAKING

Print workshops, Print publishers/dealers/galleries, fine press printers/publishers.

PRINTS & PRINTMAKING

PRINT WORKSHOPS

ABACUS (COLOUR PRINTERS) LTD C
Lowick Green, Lowick, Ulverston, LA12 8DX.
Tel: *01229-885361.* **Fax:** *01229 -885348.*
Opening times: Mon-Sat 9-5.
Personnel: *Directors:* John Sutcliffe, Vicki
Sutcliffe.
Specialist printers to the art world - nation-
wide! Mail order postcards, greetings cards,
posters, catalogues from your own art work.
All work is in house to ensure maximum print
quality and accuracy of colour to the original
art work. Print members of the Fine Art Trade
Guild for 10 years.
Services and Facilities:
Parking.

ACTIVE GRAPHICS
Unit 12, Eastmead Trading Estate, Lavant,
Chichester, PO18 0DB.
Tel: *01243-787230.* **Fax:** *01243-787258.*
Email *actives.demon.co.uk*
Personnel: John Bradford. Avril Bradford.
Screen process print studio offers a complete
service to artists and publishers for the production of artists original screenprints.
Working closely with the artist in our informal, relaxed studio on the south coast we are
able to produce prints up to a maximum
48"x34" image, using a combination of traditional and more modern and experimental
techniques. Prints can be produced on paper,
plastic, glass, metal and textiles. Why not ring
John or Avril to discuss any forthcoming projects?

ART HOUSE EDITIONS C
25 Bruton Street, London W1X 7AB.
Tel: *0171-491 3337.*

ARTICHOKE PRINT WORKSHOP C
Unit 51, Shakespeare Business Centre, 245
Coldharbour Lane, London SW9 8RR.
Tel: *0171-924 0600.*

BATH ARTIST PRINTMAKERS C
7 Lower Borough Walls, Bath, BA1 1QS.
Tel: *01225-446136.*

BELFAST PRINT WORKSHOP C
185 Stranmillis Road, Belfast, BT9 5DU.
Tel: *01232-687223.* **Fax:** *01232-661715.*
Opening times: *Mon, Wed, Fri 10-5, Tues*
& Thurs 10-9.
Personnel: *Director:* James Allen.
Open access workshop for artists/printmakers
offering facilities for etching, screenprinting,
stone lithography and relief printing. A darkroom is also available with black-and-white
enlarger and process camera.

BOND ART C
P.O. Box 647, London E3 5UB.
Tel: *01225-892009.*

BOOKWORKS C
19 Holywell Row, London EC2A 4JB.
Tel: *0171-247 2536.*

BRISTOL PRINTMAKER'S WORKSHOP C
MacArthur Building, Cross Ferry Road, Bristol
BS1. **Tel:** *0117-924 9167.*

CORIANDER C
56 Kings Bridge Crescent, Southall, UB1 2DL.
Tel: *0181-893 6888.*

CURWEN CHILFORD PRINTS C
Chilford Hall, Linton, Cambridge, CB1 6LE.
Tel: *01223-893544.* **Fax:** *01223-893544.*
Opening times: Mon-Fri 9-5.30.
Nearest Station: *Cambridge.*
Personnel: *Directors:* Stanley Jones, Sam
Alper, Simon Alper, Mary Grace.
Fine art printing studio established in 1958 by
the Curwen Press for the production of limited
edition artists' prints. Specialists in continuous
tone lithography with facilities for direct and
offset printing from stone and plate. Silkscreen
printer for hand drawn and photographic
process work.
Technical expertise offered to painters and
sculptors in all forms of experimental print-
making. Publishers of limited edition prints.
Recent artists who have worked at the studio
include: Gillian Ayres, Prunella Clough,
Bernard Dunstan, Kitaj, Eduardo Paolozzi, Ken
Kiff, Paul Hogarth, Chloe Cheese, John
Hoyland, Albert Irvin, Ana Maria Pacheco,
Josef Herman, Patrick Heron, Richard Deacon
and Jane Corsellis.
Services and Facilities:
Art for Offices. Café. Commissioning Service.
Disabled Access. Parking. **Pr. Sc.**
Price range: £65 - £2,000.

EDINBURGH PRINTMAKERS C
23 Union Street, Edinburgh EH1 3LR.
Tel: *0131-557 2479.* **Fax:** *0131-558 8418.*
Email *printmakers@ednet.co.uk*
Opening times: Tues-Sat 10-6.
Personnel: *Director:* Robert Adam.
Large, friendly open-access printmaking studio.
A focus on acrylic resist etching, and water-
based screenprinting within the UK. Also the
finest facilities for stone lithography, relief and
monoprinting. Used actively by artists from
Scotland, the UK, and all over the world.
Regular intensive courses in all media as well
as specialist acrylic resist etching seminars for
professional printmakers and educators.
Our studio is one of the most attractive and
well equipped printmaking workshops in
Britain. Up to thirty artists work here each
day as artist-members, and we run a continuous print-publishing programme involving collaborative projects with many artists of international standing, such as Sir Eduardo Paolozzi
and Barbara Rae.
We have successfully pioneered the use of
exciting techniques within water-based screenprinting and acrylic-based etching, which offer
a whole new range of possibilities to artists,
together with a considerable increase in user-
and environment-friendliness.
Services and Facilities:
Art Consultancy. Art for Offices. Framing.
Workshop Facilities.
Work Stocked and Sold:
Pr.

ENITHARMON PRESS C
38 St. George Avenue, London N7 0HD.
Tel: *0171-607 7144.*

FOUR IMPRESSIONS C
Cherry Tree Cottage, 12 Bassetsbury Lane, High
Wycombe, HP11 1QU. **Tel:** *01494-443607.*

GLASGOW PRINT STUDIO WORKSHOP C
22 King Street, Glasgow G1 5QP.
Tel: *0141-552 0704.* **Fax:** *0141-552 2919.*
Email *gallery@gpsart.co.uk*
Ws *http://www.gpsart.co.uk*
Opening times: Tue/Wed/Thur 10-9;
Fri/Sat 10-6.
Nearest Station: *Glasgow Queen Street or*
Glasgow Central.
Personnel: *Manager:* Stuart Duffin.
Development Officer: Leona Stewart.
Glasgow Print Studio, Workshop, Gallery and
Print Shop. In the workshop, the high stan-
dard of printmaking is encouraged by the range
and versatility of the facilities.
The studio attracts artists from the UK and
worldwide, creating a lively atmosphere and
friendly environment. Access is open to all
members of the public with printmaking expe-
rience. Regular classes for those who wish to
learn new skills. There are facilities for all
printmaking media, with expert advice on
hand from the staff. Editioning facilities
include studio co-publications by Blackadder,
Howson, Wiszniewski and John Byrne among
others.
Services and Facilities:
Art Consultancy. Art for Offices. Bookshop.
Commissioning Service. Craftshop. Framing.
Friends/Society. Gallery space for hire. Guided
Tours. Lectures. Workshop Facilities.
Work Stocked and Sold:
Ab. Cer. Cra. Dec. Jew. Pa. Ph. Pr.
Price range: £50 - £5,000.

HALF MOON PRINTMAKERS C
10 Beckwith Road, London SE24 9LG.
Tel: *0171-733 9166.*

HARWOOD KING FINE ART C
Euro Business Park, New Road, Newhaven,
BN9. **Tel:** *01273-512554.*

MILTON KEYNES PRINTMAKERS C
South Pavilion, Courtyard Arts Centre,
Parklands, Great Linford, MK14 5DZ.
Tel: *01908-583845.*

NORTHERN PRINT STUDIOS C
42-47 Fish Quay, North Shields, NE30 1JA.
Tel: *0191-259 1996.*

OXFORD GUILD OF PRINTMAKERS C
The Stoke House, Shipton Oliffe, GL54 4JF.
Tel: *01242-820073.*

OXFORD PRINTMAKERS' COOP C
Christadelphian Hall, Tyndale Road, Oxford,
OX4 1JL **Tel:** *01865-726472.*

THE PRINTMAKERS COUNCIL C
Clerkenwell Workshop, 31, Clerkenwell Close,
London EC1R 0AT. **Tel:** *0171-250 1927.*

Ab *Artist's Books* **App** *Applied Art* **Cer** *Ceramics* **Cra** *Crafts*
Dec *Decorative* **Dr** *Drawing* **Fur** *Furniture*

Opening times: *Wed & Thurs 2-6.*
Personnel: *President:* Mr Stanley Jones.
Administrator: Helen Ward.

Printmakers
COUNCIL

The Printmakers Council is a non-profitmak-ing artist-run group. Their objectives are to promote the use of both traditional and innov-ative printmaking techniques by:- holding exhibitions of prints, providing information on prints and printmaking to both its membership and the public, encouraging co-operation and exchanges between members, other associa-tions and interested individuals. Exhibitions in major London venues and throughout the UK. Exchange shows recently in Paris, Landau Germany and Fremantle Australia. A slide index of members work is held in the London office for consultation. Membership is open to all printmakers.

POOLE PRINTMAKERS *C*
5 Bowling Green Alley, Poole BH15 1AG.
Tel: *01202-393776.*
PORTHMEOR PRINTMAKERS WORKSHOP
Penwith Galleries, Back Road West, St. Ives,
TR18 5BL. **Tel:** *01736-61125.*

SARAH JAMES PRINTMAKING *C*
32 Staple Gardens, Winchester, SO23 8SR.
Tel: *01962-877860.*

THE SHEFFIELD PRINT WORKSHOP *C*
Heeley Bank Centre, Heeley Bank Road,
Sheffield S2 3GL. **Tel:** *0114-250 8449.*

ST. BARNABAS PRESS
10b Saint Barnabas Road, Cambridge, CB1 2BY.
Tel: *01223-576221.* **Fax:** *01223-576204.*
Opening times: *Mon-Sat 10-10, additional*
hours for members.
Nearest Station: *Cambridge.*
Personnel: *James Hill.*
Editioning and proofing by contract or co-pub-lication, with Open Access facilities and Studio space, founded by James Hill in 1993.

One aim of the Press is to give experienced printmakers access to fully equipped areas of Etching, Screenprinting, Relief Printing, Stone-Lithograph and allied photo-repro-graphic facilities. Also available to those with little or no experience are evening classes, short courses & individual supervised sessions. The Press works with Artists taking an experi-mental approach to printmaking, mixing the process using Jame's 11 years experience of col-

laborating in producing High Quality, Original Prints.
Services and Facilities:
Commissioning Service. Framing. Lectures.
Parking. Restoration. Shop. Workshop Facilities.

STUDIO PRINTS
159 Queen's Crescent, London, NW5 4EA.
Tel: *0171-485 4527.* **Fax:** *0171-485 4527.*
Opening times: *Telephone for appointment.*
Nearest Underground: *Chalk Farm/Kentish*
Town.
Personnel: *Partners:* Dorothy Wright, M. Balakjian.
Editioning workshop for Intaglio and Mezzotint.
Work Stocked and Sold:
Pr.

ZINK EDITIONS *C*
33 Charlotte Road, London EC2A 3PB.
Tel: *0171-739 7207.*
Opening times: *Mon-Fri 10-6.*
Nearest Underground: *Old Street.*
Personnel: *Alan Cox.*
Fine art limited edition lithographic printing and publishing. Offset - max. sheet size 29" x 40" for art work from hand drawn plates plus 4 col; half-tone work, typographic sheets and limited edition books.

Direct Lithography - from hand drawn plates. Also capable of printing monoprints, lino and up to 0.25" thick wood-cuts from materials such as plywood and hardboard. Max. sheet size 47" x 33".
Services and Facilities:
Workshop Facilities.
Work Stocked and Sold:
Pr.
Price range: £100 - £1,000.

PUBLISHERS, DEALERS, AND GALLERIES

ADVANCED GRAPHICS LONDON *C*
C103 Faircharm, 8-12 Creekside, London SE8
3DX. **Tel:** *0181-691 1330.* **Fax:** *0181-694*
9930.
Opening times: *Mon-Fri 9.30-6, Sat by*
appointment.
Nearest Underground: *BR: Deptford.*
Personnel: *Robert Saich. Louise Peck.*
David Wood.
Printers and publishers of limited edition origi-nal prints, specialising in silkscreen and wood-block. Own publications include prints made directly with the following artists: Craigie Aitchison, Stephen Bartlett, Basil Beattie, Paul Benjamins, Donald Hamilton Fraser,

Tom Hammick, Rolf Hanson, John Hoyland, James Hugonin, Albert Irvin, Trevor Jones, Anita

Klein, John McLean, Matthew Radford, Ray Richardson and Kate Whiteford. Printing clients include Alan Cristea Gallery; CCA Galleries; Flowers Graphics and The Obsession of Dance Company.
Services and Facilities:
Art for Offices. Disabled Access. Parking.
Work Stocked and Sold:
Ab. Pr.
Price range: £180 - £1,000.

ANDERSON O'DAY GRAPHICS *C*
5 St. Quintin Avenue, London W10 6NX.
Tel: *0181-969 8085.* **Fax:** *0181-960 3641.*
Opening times: *Mon-Fri 9.30-6 by appoint-ment.*
Nearest Underground: *Ladbroke Grove.*
Personnel: *Don Anderson.*
Major publishers of contemporary limited edi-tion prints since 1971, we produce over 50 new editions each year. We are also dealers and distributors of a wide range of contemporary artists in media including etching, screenprint-ing, lithography, woodcut etc. Artists include Ackroyd, Daniels, Davey Winter, Delderfield, Irvin, I. Jones, McLean, Neiland, Neville, O'Neill, Rowe, Shave and Wilkinson. Trade catalogue on request.
Price range: £75 - £1,500.

ART FROM SCOTLAND *C*
65 The Shore, Port of Leith, Edinburgh EH6
6RA. **Tel:** *0131-555 5580.* **Fax:** *0131-553*
5655.

THE ART GROUP LTD *C*
146 Royal College Street, London NW1 0TA.
Tel: *0171-482 3206.* **Fax:** *0171-284 0435.*

BRANDLER GALLERIES *C*
1 Coptfold Road, Brentwood, CM14 4BM.
Tel: *01277-222269.* **Fax:** *01277-222786.*
Email *art.british@dial.pipex.com*
Ws *http://www.brandler-galleries.com*
Opening times: *Tues-Sat 10-5.30.*
Nearest Station: *Brentwood 400 yds,*
Shenfield 1 mile.
Personnel: *Director:* John Brandler. Linda Rodrigues.
A friendly gallery just 2 miles from exit 28 on the M25 with free parking. A wide selection of prints and paintings by British old and mod-

ern masters. As we purchase virtually all our stock we have to choose the best examples. Without the London overheads our clients

Brandler Galleries

A friendly gallery just 2 miles from exit 28 on the M25 with free parking. A wide selection of prints and paintings by British old and modern masters. As we purchase virtually all our stock we have to choose the best examples. Without the London overheads our clients know they get a much better deal on the same artists, without having to fight to get into London with all its problems. We are happy to send photographs or E-Mail images before your trip. Clients include banks, insurance companies and collectors all wanting the best art at realistic prices.

Services and Facilities:
Art Consultancy. Art for Offices. Commissioning Service. Framing. Parking. Restoration. Valuation.
Work Stocked and Sold:
Cer. Dr. Pa. Pr. Sc.
Price range: £50 - £65,000.

CAMBRIDGE CONTEMPORARY ART C
6 Trinity Street, Cambridge, CB2 1SU.
Tel: 01223-324222. **Fax:** 01223-315606.
Email cam.cont.art@dial.pipex.com
Opening times: *Mon-Sat 9-5.30.*
Nearest Station: *Cambridge.*
Personnel: *Director:* Denise Collins. *Gallery Manager:* Rosy Gounaris.

■ CAMBRIDGE ■
CONTEMPORARY
■ ART ■

Situated just a stone's throw from King's College in the heart of this beautiful and historic city, Cambridge Contemporary Art is the largest commercial art gallery in Cambridge, specialising in paintings, sculptures, crafts, master graphics and original prints. Since opening in 1990 the gallery has gained a reputation for the extensive range of its high quality exhibits and innovative exhibition programme. Artists include: Karolina Larusdottir, Charlotte Cornish, Anita Klein, Jonathon Clarke, Stanley Dove, Eoghan Bridge, Aliisa Spence, Jane Poulton, Donald Hamilton Fraser, Dorothy Stirling, June Carey, Marj Bond, Sheila McInnes, Elisabeth Frink, Bert Irvin and John Piper.
Services and Facilities:
Art Consultancy. Art for Offices. Commissioning Service. Craftshop. Disabled Access. Framing. Friends/Society. Restoration. Shop.
Work Stocked and Sold:
Ab. App. Cer. Cra. Dec. Fur. Gla. Pa. Pr. Sc. Tx. Wd.
Price range: £50 - £5,000.

CURWEN GALLERY
4 Windmill Street, (off Charlotte Street), London W1P 1HF. **Tel:** 0171-636 1459. **Fax:** 0171-436 3059.
Opening times: *Mon-Fri 10-6, (Thur 10-8), Sat 11-5.*

Nearest Underground: *Goodge Street.*
Personnel: *Directors:* John Hutchings, Jill Hutchings.
Work Stocked and Sold:
Pr.

EDITIONS ALECTO C
Head Office: The Court House, Lower Woodford, Salisbury, SP4 6NQ.
Tel: *01722-782544.*
Fax: *01722-782669.*
Email *100306.1645@compuserve.com*
Opening times: *By appointment.*
Nearest Station: *Salisbury.*
Personnel: *Director:* Joe Studholme.
London Office: 121/123 Rotherhithe Street, London SE16 4NF. Tel: 0171-237 7117, Fax: 0171-237 1163,
Email: Alectouk@aol.com.

Publishing house established 1962 now specialising in historical editions, hand printed and hand coloured, from plates and blocks and in facsimile.
New and current publications include: Mark Catesby's "Natural History of Carolina, Florida and the Bahama Islands", in association with the Royal Library, Windsor; Ferdinand Bauer's watercolours of the zoological specimens collected on the first circumnavigation of Australia by Commander Matthew Flinders in HMS Investigator 1801-1803, in association with the British Museum (Natural History); and the Millennium Edition of William the Conqueror's "Domesday Book", in association with the Public Record Office.
Stock of contemporary prints include David Hockney, Allen Jones, Tom Phillips, Patrick Procktor, George Segal and Eduardo Paolozzi. New projects usually four per annum, please enquire.
Services and Facilities:
Art Consultancy. Art for Offices. Commissioning Service.
Work Stocked and Sold:
Ab. Pr.
Price range: £50 - £100,000.

ELIZABETH HARVEY-LEE - ORIGINAL PRINTS c.1490 - c.1940. C
1 West Cottages, Middle Aston Road, North Aston, Oxford, OX6 3QB.
Tel: *01869-347164.* **Fax:** *01869-347956.*
Opening times: *By appointment.*
Personnel: *Proprietor:* Elizabeth Harvey-Lee. Private printdealer, offering a large range of fine etchings and engravings.
Interesting and unusual old masters and 19th & 20th century British & European artists; both major and minor masters of printmaking from five centuries. Two fully illustrated new stock catalogues each year (annual subscrip-

tion £12 or U.S.$25). Previous reference catalogues still available:- LASTING IMPRESSIONS - A Survey of the Techniques & History of Printmaking c.1490-c.1940, (£15 + pp). MISTRESSES OF THE GRAPHIC ARTS - Famous & Forgotten Women Printmakers c.1550-c.1950, (£13.50 + pp).

Regular exhibitor at the London Original Print Fair at the Royal Academy and at the June and November Olympia Fine Art & Antiques Fairs.
Services and Facilities:
Lectures.
Work Stocked and Sold:
Pr.
Price range: £100 - £6,000.

GRAHAM CLARKE C
White Cottage, Green Lane, Boughton Monchelsea, Maidstone, ME17 4LF.
Tel: *01622 743938.* **Fax:** *01622 747229.*
Opening times: *Open by appointment.*
Personnel: Dawn Masters.

Graham Clarke

Publisher and sole international distributor for Graham Clarke the artist, writer and humorist. His original etchings are produced entirely by hand using traditional processes in strictly limited editions; no photomechanical methods are used in their production. Watercolours, books, greetings cards and hand cut arch-topped mounts for the etchings are also available. Price lists and illustrations of recent images will be sent on request. Studio open by appointment.
Work Stocked and Sold:
Ab. Dr. Pa. Pr.
Price range: £50 - £2,000.

GREENWICH PRINTMAKERS ASSOCIATION C
1a Greenwich Market, London SE10 9HZ.
Tel: *0181-858 1569.*
Email *longtitude0.co.uk/printmakers/*
Ws *http://www.longtitude0.co.uk/printmakers/*
Opening times: *Tues-Sun 10.30-5.30.*
Nearest Underground: *Greenwich (British Rail), Island Gardens (Docklands).*
Personnel: *Manager:* John Hurley.
Founded 1979. The Greenwich Printmakers is a co-operative of 45 artists including some of the country's leading printmakers as well as recent graduates. Mixed exhibitions of etchings, lithographs, silk screen, relief prints, watercolours and drawings. Price range £25-£500. Each fortnight one artists work is spe-

Ab Artist's Books *App* Applied Art *Cer* Ceramics *Cra* Crafts
Dec Decorative *Dr* Drawing *Fur* Furniture

cially featured in a mini-exhibition.

Work not on display is in plan chests for browsing.
Services and Facilities:
Art for Offices. Commissioning Service.
Work Stocked and Sold:
Dr. Pr.
Price range: £30 - £400.

GRESHAM STUDIO
4 Chapel Street, Duxford, CB2 4RY
Tel: 01223-576558.
Fax: 01223-576559.
Email *studio@gresham.demon.co.uk*
Opening times: *NOT open to the public.*
Nearest Station: *Cambridge/Whittlesford.*
Personnel: *Studio Director:* Kip Gresham.
Ian Wilkinson. Chris Wood. Jimi Kazak.
The studio prints and publishes artist's original graphics and monotypes.
Each year about 50 collaborative projects are undertaken. Artists frequently stay for an extended period and dedicated accommodation is available.
There are full facilities for screen printing and etching. The experience of the staff is considerable and there is a long history of experimentation and innovation to support the artists in their work.
The studio has a strong international emphasis. In consequence, the studio archive is held by a foundation in the USA. A range of publications is available for sale.
Contract work is undertaken for galleries and publishers. Recent projects with W. Barns Graham, John Bellany, Elizabeth Blackadder, Peter Blake, Patrick Caulfield, Prunella Clough, Sue Coe, Alfred Cohen, Barry Flanagan, Anthony Frost, Antony Gormley, Peter Griffin, Susan Hiller, Matthew Hilton, John Hoyland, Lin Jammet, Yvonne Jaquette, Joseph Kosuth, Ellen Lanyon, Kim Lim, Richard Long, David Mach, John Mclean, Melissa Miller, Janet Nathan, Claes Oldenburg, Bryan Pearce, Bill Penney, Eduardo Paolozzi, Patrick Proctor, Cornelia Parker, Paula Rego, Kiki Smith, Jo Taylor, William Turnbull, Alison Watt, Paul Wunderlich.
Work Stocked and Sold:
Pr.
Price range: £150 - £3,500.

JONATHAN POTTER C
125 New Bond Street, London W1Y 9AF.
Tel: 0171-491 3520. **Fax:** 0171-491 9754.
Email *jpmaps@cbm.net*
Opening times: *Weekdays 10-6.*
Nearest Underground: *Bond Street.*

Our very large, fine quality, stock includes original antique maps, plans and charts of all areas of Britain and the World. Prices range from around £50 to several thousand pounds per item for museum quality pieces. Maps, city plans or sea charts can be made elegant, unusual office or restaurant decoration of genuine worth. Catalogues issued and a search service offered for items not in stock. Framing service. We are members of BADA, ABA, PBFA and LAPADA.
Services and Facilities:
Art for Offices. Framing.
Work Stocked and Sold:
Pr.
Price range: £50 - £10,000.

MARLBOROUGH GRAPHICS C
6 Albemarle Street, London W1X 4BY.
Tel: 0171-629 5161.
Fax: 0171-495 0641.
Email *Marlborough@slad.org*
Opening times: *Mon-Fri 10-5.30, Sat 10-12.30.*
Nearest Underground: *Green Park.*
Personnel: *Director:* David Case. Sarah Staughton. Nicola Togneri.
London's leading publishers of contemporary limited edition prints. Also stock European Modern Master Prints including Bacon, Hepworth, Matisse, Miro, Moore, Nicholson, Picasso and Sutherland. Gallery artists represented include Arikha, Auerbach, Conroy, Davies, Freud, Hambling, Jacklin, Kiff, Kitaj, Le Brun, Oulton, Pasmore, Paul, Rego and Piper. Recent publications include coloured etchings by Ken Kiff and Maggi Hambling. In 1998 we will be publishing Victor Pasmore's 90th Birthday Print Portfolio of etchings.
Services and Facilities:
Art Consultancy. Art for Offices. Framing. Valuation.
Work Stocked and Sold:
Ab. Ph. Pr.
Price range: £300 - £60,000.

THE MEDICI SOCIETY LIMITED
34-42 Pentonville Road, London N1 9HG.
Tel: 0171-837 7099; *Retail Enquiries Tel:* 0171-629 5675 *Jonathan Blackwell; General & Trade Enquiries Tel:* 0171-837 7099.
Fax: 0171-837 9152.
Opening times: *Mon-Fri 9-5*
Nearest Underground: *Angel.*
Established in 1908, The Medici Society was founded to publish fine art prints at reasonable prices, a tradition upheld today using the latest

methods of production. As exclusive distributors of Medici, Pallas Gallery, Ganymed Press and Modern Art Society reproductions they provide work from most periods of Art History. This range is widened even further by acting as agents for leading American and European publishing houses.

A print catalogue and price list is available on request, as are details of other Medici publications. These include: Fine Art Greeting Cards, stationary, postcards and art and children's books.
Work Stocked and Sold:
Pr.

PRATT CONTEMPORARY ART/PRATT EDITIONS C
The Gallery, Ightham, Sevenoaks, TN15 9HH.
Tel: 01732-882326/884417. **Fax:** 01732-885502.
Opening times: *Open seven days a week by appointment.*
Nearest Station: *Charing Cross to Sevenoaks or Victoria to Borough Green.*
Personnel: *Directors:* Bernard Pratt, Susan Pratt.

Established in 1976. Printers and publishers of original limited edition prints working directly with artists: screenprints, etchings, drypoints, woodcuts, monotypes, artists' books. Proofing and editioning service. Artists include: Ana Maria Pacheco, Seyed Edalatpour, Julian Grater, Akram Rahmanzadeh, Susan Adams, Kristian Krokfors, Mick Rooney RA, Michael

PRINTS & PRINTMAKING

Kenny RA, Marcus Rees Roberts, Denise Walker, Leonam Nogueira Fleury, Richard Davies. Also handles and exhibits sculpture, paintings and drawings by artists represented (see Regional Galleries).
Services and Facilities:
Art Consultancy. Commissioning Service. Framing.

St. Barnabas Press
10b Saint Barnabas Road, Cambridge, CB1 2BY.
Tel: *01223-576221.*
Fax: *01223-576204.*
Opening times: *Mon-Sat 10-10, additional hours for members.*
Nearest Station: *Cambridge.*
Personnel: James Hill.
Editioning and proofing by contract or co-publication, with Open Access facilities and Studio space, founded by James Hill in 1993. One aim of the Press is to give experienced printmakers access to fully equipped premises of Etching, Screenprinting, Relief Printing, Stone-Lithograph and allied photo-reprographic facilities.
Also available to those with little or no experience are evening classes, short courses & individual supervised sessions.
The Press works with Artists taking an experimental approach to printmaking, mixing the process using Jame's 11 years experience of collaborating in producing High Quality, Original Prints.
Services and Facilities:
Commissioning Service. Framing. Lectures. Parking. Restoration. Shop. Workshop Facilities.

Swan Gallery
Flat 2, 135 Upper Grosvenor Road, Tunbridge Wells,

The Wild Hawthorn Press
Saint Paulinus, Brough Park, Richmond, DL10 7PJ.
Tel: *01748-812127.*
Fax: *01748-812127.*
Email *TOTE@GREV.DEMON.CO.UK*
Nearest Station: *Darlington.*
The archive of the graphic work of Ian Hamilton Finlay, compiled of prints, books, multiple objects house in an important architectural 19th century chapel in the North Yorkshire Dales.
Services and Facilities:
Bookshop. Framing. Parking.
Work Stocked and Sold:
Ab. Pr. Sc.
Price range: £0.50 - £400.

University of Limerick - AV Gallery
University of Limerick, Limerick,
Tel: *00353-1-61 202040.* **Fax:** *00353-1-61 202938.*
Email *David.Lilburn@ul.ie.*
Opening times: *Daily 8am-10pm.*
Personnel: *Exhibition Organiser:* David Lilburn.
Policy - The gallery is best suited to exhibitions of small work. Local and national artists are promoted in approx 8 shows a year. There are also occasional touring shows of literary

and scientific interest. Artists may apply to exhibit.
Services and Facilities:
Disabled Access. Parking.
Work Stocked and Sold:
Ab. Dr. Pa. Pr.
Price range: £100 - £1,000.

FINE PRESS PRINTERS AND PUBLISHERS

Printers and publishers of specialist limited edition books.

Basement Press
Basement Flat, 29 Burrell Road, Ipswich, IP2 8AH.
Tel: *01473-601596.*

Circle Press C
26 St. Luke's Mews, London W11 1DF.
Tel: *0171-792 9298.*

Delos Press
11 School Road, Moseley, Birmingham B13 9ET.
Tel: *0121-449 1406.*

First Folio Cards
Hollow Cottage, Charingworth, Chipping Campden, GL55 6NY. **Tel:** *01386-593477.*

Golden Apple Press
Pebble Court Cottage, Swinbrook, Burford, OX18 4DY.
Tel: *01993-824097.*

Hayloft Press
99 Oakfield Road, Birmingham B29 7HW.
Tel: *0121-472 1768.*

Incline Press
11A Printer Street, Oldham OL1 1PN.
Tel: *0161-627 1966.*

Ken Ferguson
20 Lanercost Park, Cramlington, NE23 6RU.
Tel: *01670-733927.*

Nine Elms Press
21 Gwendolen Avenue, London SW15 6ET.
Tel: *0181-788 4029.*

Old School Press
The Old School, The Green, Hinton Charterhouse, Bath, BA3 6BJ.

Oleander Press
17 Stansgate Avenue, Cambridge, CB2 2QZ.
Tel: *01223-244688.*

Prospect Hill Press
35 Bank Street, Herne Bay, CT6 5AW.

Redlake Press
Brook House, Clun, SY7 8LY.
Tel: *01588-640524.*

Ruth Bader Gilbert
8 Portland Road, Oxford, OX2 7EY.
Tel: *01865-559176.*

Simon King Press
Ashton House, Beetham, Milthorpe, LA7 7AL.
Tel: *015395-62194.* **Fax:** *015395-62194.*

Tern Press
Saint Mary's Cottage, Great Hales Street, Market Drayton, TF9 1JN.
Tel: *01630-652153.*

Woodcraft Press
152 Hadlow Road, Tonbridge, TN9 1PB.
Tel: *01732-359206.*

The Yew Tree Press
Park Place, Aldsworth, Cheltenham, GL54 3QZ.
Tel: *01451-844487.*
Opening times: *By appointment.*
Nearest Station: *Cheltenham.*
Personnel: *Colin Honnor.*
A small press in the heart of the Cotswolds where fine printing of every description is carried out.
We employ historically researched methods, specially preparing inks from pigments and varnish, cast our types and graphics, even rollers. Everything as far as possible is made by ourselves - inks are ground and mixed in the workshop and printed on handmade papers from English mills.
We publish books and designs, bindings and printings where aesthetics are combined with traditional materials. We also undertake pamphlets, prints and occasional printing.
Services and Facilities:
Guided Tours.

INTERNET AND 'VIRTUAL GALLERIES'

'Virtual' galleries (work may only be viewed on the Internet).
Listing of all establishments in this Directory
with internet addresses.

THE ART WORLD
DIRECTORY
1998/99 25TH EDITION

INTERNET GALLERIES

ART ARENA GALLERY C
16 Crane Furlong, Highworth, SN6 7JX
Tel: 01793-766818.
Fax: 01793-766818.
Email katy@artarena.force9.co.uk
Ws www.artarena.force9.co.uk
Opening times: 24 hours a day, as it is on the internet.
Personnel: Artist & Owner: Katy Kianush-Wallace.

Art Arena is a Virtual gallery providing an exciting and comprehensive collection of original paintings, creative literature, and greeting card designs.
The artist's varied use of media and painting techniques, and the multiplicity of subjects treated encourage appreciation of her art on many levels. Original works can be reserved for purchase on line.
An interesting feature is the 'Creative Cards' section, which provides a personalised greeting card service for all occasions.
The Writers' Corner section includes works by well known and respected Iranian writers and poets. These books can also be purchases on line from the Art Arena bookstore. Bookstore on the Internet. Art Arena hosts the website of the National Acrylic Painters' Association UK.
Services and Facilities:
Bookshop. Friends/Society.
Work Stocked and Sold:
Dr. Pa.
Price range: £200 - £3,500.

BRITART.COM C
Tel: 0181-809 5127.
Fax: 0181-809 5354.
Email info@britart.com
Ws http://www.britart.com
Personnel: Director: David Tregunna. Co-Director: Mark Ellery.
The British Art Gallery on the Net. Britain's foremost virtual contemporary art gallery purely on the Net. Representing top names in British painting of both established and emerging reputation, including: Fred Crayk, Chris Gollon, Maggi Hambling, Jim Kavanagh, Tory Lawrence, Richard Libby, Ian Welsh. We also stock works by Peter Howson. We sell to private collectors, corporate & public collections world-wide. We offer a user-friendly information service on each artist represented, providing reviews, c.v.'s, brief biographies and details on forthcoming exhibitions.

We also publish catalogues, and help arrange packing, shipping, and insurance for clients buying directly from our web site.
Services and Facilities:
Art Consultancy. Art for Offices. Commissioning Service. Restoration.

NETWORK GALLERY C
9 Lower Cwrt-y-vil Road, Penarth CF64 3HQ.
Tel: 01222-350124. **Fax:** 01222-350124.
Email info@networkgallery.com
Ws networkgallery.com
Personnel: Director: Lorraine Wingert-Scheeres.
The Network Gallery exists to promote the work of established and emerging artists on an international basis by exhibiting the arts on the World Wide Web - The Internet.
Work of every genre is exhibited together with news, views and comment and the gallery is continually changing and adding to exhibits. Of particular interest to interior designers is the ability to 'download' files of hundreds of works to assist in the choice of work to be exhibited in public places such as offices and hotels, the gallery can advise and supply interior designers on 'bulk buy' purchases for such applications.
Dr. Pa. Sc. Tx.
Price range: £200 - £20,000.

PACHALAFAKA C
Freepost, Southampton SO14 0QE.
Tel: 01703-907777 (Enquiries/Sales), 01703-585539 (Accounts Dept.).
Email bis@pachalafaka.co.uk
Ws http://www.pachalafaka.co.uk/pachalafaka/
Opening times: Mon-Sat 8-8.
Personnel: UK Sales Co-ordinator: Richard Harrison. Web Master: Samuel Durkin. Research Manager: Samuel Collis.
Art Agency and Virtual Gallery. Promotion and publicity for artists, artwork and exhibition.
Extensive collection of art by leading professionals and aspiring amateurs. Painting, Sculpture, Illustration, Photography and Crafts. Artists needed to fill demand from international outlets, sales achieved through various publishing means and media exposure. No Commission Charges. International delivery and contracts arranged. Free service for Artbuyers, Publishers, Dealers, Curators. Working for commerce and individuals we endeavour to match artists to your requirements.

Participation in joint ventures with artists, magazines and gallery's.
Services and Facilities:
Art for Offices. Commissioning Service. Gallery space for hire.

OTHER INTERNET SITES

Listed below are other internet sites by establishment type.

ART BOOK PUBLISHERS

Ashgate/Scolar Press
http://www.ashgate.com
Macmillan Publishers Ltd.
The Dictionary of Art
groveartmusic.com
Oxford University Press
http://www.oup.co.uk (and specific art page), oup-usa.org/arthis/art1.html
Thames & Hudson
thttp://www.hameshudson.co.uk

ART BOOKSHOPS

Arnolfini Gallery
www.channel.org.uk/arnolfini
Arts Bibliographic
http://www.artsbib.com
Hunterian Art Gallery
gla.ac.uk/museum
Victoria & Albert Museum
vam.ac.uk

ART CONSULTANTS

Alexandra Wettstein Fine Art
http://graffiti.virgin.net/alexandra.wettstein/
Art Contact Ltd
http://www.artcontact.co.uk
Brandler Galleries
http://www.brandler-galleries.com

Ab Artist's Books **App** Applied Art **Cer** Ceramics **Cra** Crafts **Dec** Decorative **Dr** Drawing **F** Furniture **Gla** Glass **Jew** Jewellery **Pa** Paintings **Ph** Photography **Pr** Pr **Sc** Sculpture **Tx** Textiles **Wd** Wo

Business Art Galleries
http://www.screenpages.co.uk/ac/newa-cademy/index.html
Egee Art Consultancy
http://www.globebyte.co.uk/egee/egeeart
.htm OR http://www.egeeart.co.uk

ART EDUCATION

Bath Spa University College (Formerly Bath College of Higher Education)
http://www.bathspa.ac.uk/
Byam Shaw School of Art
http://www.byam-shaw.ac.uk
Cavendish College
http://www.cavendish.ac.uk
Christie's Education
http://www.christies.com
Cumbria College of Art and Design
http://www.cumbriacollart.ac.uk
Dartington College of Arts
http://www.dartington.ac.uk
Edinburgh College of Art
http://www.eca.ac.uk
Edinburgh College of Art (Heriot-Watt University)
http://www.hw.ac.uk/eca
Glasgow University
http://www.arts.gla.ac.uk/ArtHist/decarts.htm
Goldsmiths College
http://www.gold.ac.uk/
Kent Institute of Art & Design at Maidstone
http://kiad.ac.uk/kiad.htm
Lancaster University, School of Creative Arts, The Art Department
http://www.lancs.ac.uk/users/art/
Nottingham Trent University
http://www.ntu.ac.uk
Ruskin School of Drawing and Fine Art
http://www.ruskin-sch.ox.ac.uk/
The Slade School of Fine Art
http://www.ucl.ac.uk/slade/
University College of Ripon and York St. John
http://www.ucrysj.ac.uk
University of Plymouth
http://www.fae.plym.ac.uk/
Warwickshire College, School of Art and Design
http://www.warkscol.ac.uk

ART IN COUNTRY HOUSES

Harewood House,
http://www.harewood.org

ART SOCIETIES

Association of Art Historians
http://www.gold.ac.uk/aah
The British Society of Master Glass Painters
proteusweb.com/bsmgp
Public Monuments and Sculpture Association
http://www.unn.ac.uk/~hcv3

Royal Academy of Arts
http://www.royalacademy.org.uk
The Royal Photographic Society
http://www.rps.org
Society of Women Artists
http://www.nal.vam..ac.uk/.

ARTISTS MATERIALS

Alec Tiranti Ltd.
thttp://www.iranti.co.uk
Daler-Rowney
www.daler-rowney.com
E. Ploton (Sundries) Ltd
http://www.ploton.co.uk/ploton
T N Lawrence & Son Ltd
lawrence.co.uk

AUCTION HOUSES

Phillips Fine Art Auctioneers
http://www.phillips-auctions.com
Woolley & Wallis
http://www.auctions-on-line.com/wool-leywallis

CONSERVATORS AND RESTORERS

Abbott & Holder
http://www.artefact.co.uk/AaH.html

DIGITAL GRAPHICS
Rutters/Scanachrome
www.scanachrome.com/rutters

ELECTRONIC SERVICES

Thesaurus Group Ltd
thesaurus.co.uk/

FAIRS & FESTIVALS

The Contemporary Print Show & The Contemporary Print Fair
http://www.artnet.co.uk

FINE ART FOUNDERS

Bronze Age Sculpture Foundry
http://www.netcomuk.co.uk/-duncanh
Burleighfield Arts Limited
http://www.polestarltd/sculpture/
Leander Architectural
http://www.leanderarch.demon.co.uk

FINE ART MAGAZINES

Art Review
http://www.art-review.co.uk
Crafts Magazine
http://www.craftscouncil.org.uk

FINE ART PRINTERS - ART CARDS

Thought Factory
http://www.kpegroup@aol.com

FINE PRESS PRINTERS/PUBLISHERS
Old School Press
praxis.co.uk/ppuk/osp.htm

FRAMING SUPPLIES

Peak Rock
peakrock.com

GALLERY HANGING SUPPLIES

Peak Rock
http://peakrock.com

GALLERY SPACE FOR HIRE

Abbott & Holder
http://www.artefact.co.uk/AaH.html
The Air Gallery
airgallery.co.uk

INFORMATION SERVICES

Axis
http://www.lmu.ac.uk/ces/axis

INSURANCE BROKERS

Hiscox plc.
http://www.hiscox.co.uk

INTERNET GALLERIES

Art Arena Gallery
www.artarena.force9.co.uk
BritArt.com
http://www.britart.com
Network Gallery
networkgallery.com
Pachalafaka
http://www.pachalafaka.co.uk/pacha-lafaka/

IRISH GALLERIES

Crawford Municipal Art Gallery
synergy.ie/crawford
The Solomon Gallery
http://indigo.ie/~solomon
Temple Bar Gallery & Studios
http://www.paddynet.ie/tbgs

LONDON COMMERCIAL GALLERIES

Abbott & Holder
http://www.artefact.co.uk/AaH.html
The Air Gallery
airgallery.co.uk
Albemarle Gallery
www.artnet.com/albemarle.html
Alex Wengraf
wengraf.com
Alexandra Gallery
http://www.alexandragallery.demon.co.uk
BCA Boukamel Contemporary Art
http://www.bca-gallery.com
Beldam Gallery
brunel.ac.uk/depts/arts
BritArt.com
http://www.britart.com
The Bruton Street Gallery
http://www.artnet.com/bruton.html.
Cadogan Contemporary Art
www.dircon.co.uk/cadogan-contempo-rary

Catto Gallery
catto.co.uk
Daniel Katz Ltd
http://www.katz.co.uk
Davies & Tooth
art-net.co.uk/banca/toodav
Fleur de Lys Gallery
http://www.fleur-de-lys.com
Galleria Enterprise
http://www.galleria-art.co.uk
Houldsworth Fine Art
http://www.art-connection.com
Jibby Beane Limited
http://www.jibbybeane.com
Jill George Gallery
http://www.easynet.co.uk/banca/geo-jills.htm
Julian Hartnoll
http://www.art-on-line.com \hartnoll
Lamont Gallery
http://www.lamontart.com
Laure Genillard Gallery
URL:http://ourworld.compuserve.comho
mepages/laure-genillard
London Print Workshop
freeweb.nethead.co.uk/london-print-workshop
Matthiesen Fine Art Limited
http://www.Europeanpaintings.com
Mercury Gallery
http://www.mercury-gallery.co.uk
New Academy Gallery and Business Art Galleries
http://www.screenpages.co.uk/ac/newa-cademy/index.html
The October Gallery
http://www.ecotechnics.edu/ogallery.htm
Portal Gallery
http://www.portal-gallery.com
Rebecca Hossack Gallery
http://www.artewisdom.com
The Special Photographer's Company
http://www.specialphoto.co.uk
Spink-Leger
spinkandson.co.uk
Will's Art Warehouse
http://www.willsart.demon.co.uk
Wiseman Originals
http://www.artplanet.com/pages/global/

LONDON PUBLIC GALLERIES

198 Gallery
http:www.globalnet.co.uk/~198gallery
Bank of England Museum
http://www.bankofengland.co.uk
Barbican Art Gallery
http://www.uk-calling.co.uk
Ben Uri Art Society
http://www.ort.org/benuri/
Bethnal Green Museum of Childhood
vam.ac.uk/bgm/welcome.html
Bhownagree and Today Galleries
http://www.commonwealth.org.uk
British Architectural Library Drawings Collection/RIBA Heinz Gallery
riba.org

Commonwealth Institute
commonwealth.org.uk/
Geffrye Museum
lattimore.co.uk/geffrye
Goethe-Institut London
goethe.de/gr/lon/enindex.htm
Hayward Gallery
http://www.hayward-gallery.org.uk
The Horniman Museum and Gardens
http://www.horniman.demon.co.uk
Imperial War Museum
http://www.iwm.org.uk
Institute of Contemporary Arts
illumin.co.uk/ica/
National Army Museum
failte.com/nam/
National Portrait Gallery
http://www.npg.org.uk
Orleans House Gallery
http://www.guidetorichmond.co.uk/orle
ans.html
RIBA Heinz Gallery
http://www.riba.org/
Royal Academy of Arts
http://www.RoyalAcademy.org.uk
TWO10 Gallery
http://www.wellcome.ac.uk
Victoria & Albert Museum The National Museum of Art and Design
http://www.vam.ac.uk
Wallace Collection
demon.co.uk/heritage/wallace
William Morris Gallery and Brangwyn Gift
lbwf.gov.uk

MATERIALS AND EQUIPMENT

Conservation By Design
http://www.conservation-by-design.co.uk

PACKERS & SHIPPERS

Art Services Ltd
artservices@ukbusiness.com.
Oxford Exhibition Services
www.oxex.demon.co.uk

PHOTOGRAPHERS

The Photography of Art
www.books.mcmail.com/photo.htm

PRINT WORKSHOPS

Glasgow Print Studio Workshop
http://www.gpsart.co.uk

PRINT PUBLISHERS/DEALERS

Brandler Galleries
http://www.brandler-galleries.com
Greenwich Printmakers Association
http://www.longditude0.co.uk/print-makers/

REGIONAL ART BOARDS

South West Arts
http://www.swa.co.uk
West Midlands Arts
http://www.arts.org.uk
Yorkshire & Humberside Arts
http://www.arts.org.uk

REGIONAL GALLERIES

Arnolfini Gallery
http://www.channel.org.uk/channel/arn
olfini
Ashmolean Museum of Art and Archaeology
http://www.ashmol.ox.ac.uk/
Blackthorn Galleries
http://www.galleries.u-net.com
The Bonington Art Gallery
http://www.ntu.ac.uk/ppr/sp-arts.html
Brandler Galleries
http://www.brandler-galleries.com
Christ Church Picture Gallery
http://www.chch.ox.ac.uk
The Contemporary Fine Art Gallery, Eton
CFAG.co.UK
Contemporary Fine Art Gallery & Sculpture Park
CFAG.co.UK
Corrymella Scott Gallery
corymella.co.uk
Dansel Gallery
http://www.wdi.co.uk/dansel
Djanogly Art Gallery
http://www.nottingham.ac.uk/artscentre/
Durham University Oriental Museum
http://www.dur.ac.uk/~dcm0www/omu-seum.htm
Fox Talbot Museum of Photography
http://www.Fox-Talbot.org.uk
The Gallery, Gateshead Central Library
wamses.unn.ac.uk
The Gallery
http://www.1.btwebworld.com/carpathi-an/
The Heffer Gallery
http://www.heffers.co.uk
The Henry Moore Foundation
henry-moore-fdn.co.uk/hnt
Ikon Gallery
dialspace.dial.pipex.com/ikon/
James Hockey Gallery and Foyer Gallery
http://www.surrart.ac.uk
Leeds Metropolitan University Gallery
http://www.lmu.ac.uk/arts
Manchester City Art Gallery
http://www.u-net.com/set/mcag/cag.html
Margaret Harvey Gallery
http://www.herts.ac.uk/artdes/
Parkview Fine Paintings
//ourworld.compuserve.com/home-pages/parkviewpaintings

Royal Albert Memorial Museum & Art Gallery
http://www.eter.ac.uk/projects/ALBERT/
The Royal Photographic Society
http://www.rps.org
The Stanley Picker Gallery for the Arts
JPEGDESIGN.CO.UK
Terrace Gallery
http://www.harewood.org
University Gallery Leeds
http://www.leeds.ac.uk/library/gall/exhibs.html
University of Essex Gallery
essex.ac.uk
University of Hull Art Collection
http://www.hull.ac.uk
Warwick Gallery
http://members.aol.com/ukgallery
Wysing Arts
http://www.wysing.demon.co.uk

SCOTTISH GALLERIES

An Lanntair
http://www.lanntair.com
Duncan of Jordanstone College of Art and Design
http://www.dundee.ac.uk/
Frames Contemporary Gallery
users.zetnet.co.uk/hgoring
Hunterian Art Gallery
http://www.gla.ac.uk/museum/
Paisley Museum, Art Galleries and Coats Observatory
http://www.cqm.co.uk/www/sdc/leisurestart.html
Scottish Gallery (Aitken Dott Ltd)
http://www.scottish-gallery.co.uk
Strathearn Gallery and Pottery
http://www.strathearn-gallery.com

SCULPTURE PARKS

The Henry Moore Foundation
http://www.henry-moore-fdn.co.uk/hmf
Scottish Sculpture Workshop
http://www.ssw.org.uk
Sculpture at Goodwood
http://www.sculpture.org.uk

STUDIO SPACE FOR HIRE

Space
http://www.ecna.org

WELSH GALLERIES

Catherine Lewis Gallery
aber.ac.uk
The Ceramics Gallery
aber.ac.uk
Martin Tinney Gallery
http://www.ARTWALES.COM
The National Library of Wales
http://www.llgc.org.uk
Oriel Ceri Richards Gallery
http://www.whatsonwales.com
School of Art Gallery & Museum
http://www.aber.ac.uk

Additional copies of the Art World Directory.

Save more than 20%.

Use this form to buy additional copies of this edition for just £9.95 plus £2.00 p&p.

Simply complete the form below and return with your remittance to Art Review, Art World Directory, Freepost, London EC1B 1DE. *(A photocopy of the page is fine).*

Art World Directory Additional Copies Order Form.

Please send me _____ additional copy(ies) of the 1998/99 Art World Directory @ £9.95 plus £2.00 p&p each.*

I enclose my remittance for £ _____ made payable to Art Review Ltd.

Please debit my ☐ Access ☐ Visa ☐ Amex ☐ Mastercard

Card No: _____ Expiry Date _____

Signature _____ Date _____

Name _____ Address _____

_____

_____ Postcode _____

Tel _____ (in case of queries only)

Ref: AWDF1

*The postage and packing cost relates to UK orders only, European p&p £3.00, Overseas £6.00.

AUCTION HOUSES

THE ART WORLD
DIRECTORY
1998/99 25TH EDITION

A.C.J. DIXON C
121 Shepherds Bush Road, London W6 7LP.
Tel: *0171-603 8300.*

BEARNES C
Avenue Road, Torquay, TQ2 5TG.

BIDDLE & WEBB
Ladywood Middleway, Birmingham B16 0PP.

BONHAM'S C
*Montpelier Street, Knightsbridge, London SW7
1HH.* **Tel:** *0171-584 9161, 0171-393
3962/3900.* **Fax:** *0171-589 4072, 0171-393
3905.*

CHRISTIE'S
8 King Street, St James's, London SW1Y 6QT.
Tel: *0171-839 9060.*

CHRISTIE'S C
85 Old Brompton Road, London SW7 3LD.
Tel: *0171-321 3120, 0171-581 7611.* **Fax:**
0171-581 3679.

CHRISTIE'S SCOTLAND
164-166 Bath Street, Glasgow G2 4TB.

DREWEATT NEATE C
*Donnington Priory, Donnington, Newbury,
RG14 2JE.* **Tel:** *01635-31234.* **Fax:** *01635-
522639.*
Opening times: *9-5.30.*
Nearest Station: *Newbury.*
Personnel: *Partner in Charge of Fine Art
Dept.: Clive Stewart-Lockart.*

DREWEATT NEATE
FINE ART AUCTIONEERS ESTABLISHED 1759

Sales of Antique and Later Furniture and
Effects, held fortnightly, and Antique
Furniture, Works of Art, Clocks, Pictures,
Ceramics, Silver and Jewellery held every
month, at our Donnington Priory and Banbury
salerooms. Specialist sale catalogues can be
bought individually or by subscription. No
catalogues produced for Antique and Later
Furniture and Effects sales. Specialist staff
available to advise and give condition reports
during view days. Valuation work undertaken,
including insurance, probate and family division. Easy access from M4 and M40 and direct
train routes from London to Newbury and
Banbury. Extensive parking available with
good disabled access to all salerooms. Also
offices at: 49 Parsons Street, Banbury, Oxon
0X16 8PF. Tel: 01295-253197; Fax: 01295-
252642; Head of Saleroom, Tim Holloway.
Services and Facilities:
Disabled Access. Parking. Valuation.

GRAYS AUCTION ROOMS C
5-7 Buck Street, London NW1. **Tel:** *0171-284
2026.*

HENRY SPENCER & SON

20 The Square, Retford, DN22 6BX.

**LLOYDS INTERNATIONAL AUCTION
GALLERIES** C
118 Putney Road, London SW15 2NQ. **Tel:**
0181-788 7777.

MALLAMS C
St. Michael's Street, Oxford, OX1 2EB.

OUTHWAITE & LITHERLAND C
*Kingsway Galleries, Fontenoy Street, Liverpool,
L3 2BE.*

PETER FRANCIS
*Curiosity Sale Room, 19 King Street,
Carmarthen, SA31 1BH.* **Tel:** *01267-233456.*

**PHILLIPS FINE ART AUCTIONEERS AND
VALUERS** C
101 New Bond Street, London W1Y 0AS. **Tel:**
0171-629 6602. **Fax:** *0171-629 8876.* **Ws**
http://www.phillips-auctions.com
Opening times: *Mon-Fri 8.30-5 & most
Sundays for viewing 2-5.*
Nearest Underground: *Bond Street.*
Personnel: *Chairman: Christopher Weston.
Managing Director: Roger Hollest.*
Phillips hold Fine Art auctions at their Bond
Street premises throughout the year.
Established in 1796, they have 23 salerooms
in Britain, all staffed by experienced specialists
and valuers, who are happy to advise on all
aspects of buying and selling at auction. The
Bond Street salesroom specialises in Fine
Furniture, Paintings, Ceramics, Jewellery,
Silver, Clocks, Watches, Oriental Works of
Art, Textiles, Books, Musical Instruments,
Works of Art, Stamps, Medals and Decorative
Arts. The salesrooms are normally open for
viewing 2 to 3 days before an auction, and visi-
tors are always welcome.
Services and Facilities:
Art for Offices. Valuation.
Work Stocked and Sold:
Dr. Pa. Sc.

PHILLIPS WEST C
2 Salem Road, London W2. **Tel:** *0171-221
5303.*

ROSEBERY'S C
*The Old Railway Station, Crystal Palace, Station
Road, London SE19 2AZ.* **Tel:** *0181-778
4024.*

SOCIETY OF FINE ART AUCTIONEERS C
7 Blenheim Street, London W1Y. **Tel:** *0171-
629 2933.*

SOTHEBY'S C
Summers Place, Billingshurst, RH14 9AD. **Tel:**
01403-783933. **Fax:** *01403-785153.*

WOOLLEY & WALLIS C
*Salisbury Salerooms, 51-61 Castle Street,
Salisbury, SP1 3SU.* **Tel:** *01722-424500.* **Fax:**
01722-424508. **Email**
woolley@interalpha.co.uk **Ws** *http://www.auc-*

tions-on-line.com/woolleywallis
Opening times: *Mon-Fri 9-5.30, Sat 9-12
noon.*
Nearest Station: *Salisbury.*
Personnel: *Managing Director: Paul Viney.*

WOOLLEY & WALLIS

Woolley & Wallis have been holding auctions
in Salisbury since 1884 and today are one of
the leading regional fine art salerooms in the
UK. We have a full team of specialists and
hold regular auctions in the following categories: Antique Furniture : Oil Paintings &
Watercolours : Silver & Jewellery : European
& Oriental Ceramics : Rugs, Carpets &
Textiles : Books & Prints : Wine : Collectors
Items : Fortnightly General Sales. Written
valuations on behalf of professional and private clients for insurance, probate and family
division purposes. We welcome all enquiries
and look forward to hearing from you.
Services and Facilities:
Parking. Valuation.

ART IN COUNTRY HOUSES

THE ART WORLD
DIRECTORY
1998/99 25TH EDITION

ASCOTT HOUSE
Ascott Estate Office Wing, Leighton Buzzard, LU7 0PS. **Tel:** *01296-688242.* **Fax:** *01296-681904.*

BLENHEIM PALACE *P*
Woodstock, OX20 1PX. **Tel:** *01993-811091.* **Fax:** *01993-813527.*
Opening times: Mid March-End of October 10.30-5.30 *(last admission 4.45).*
Nearest Station: Oxford.
Personnel: Education Officer: Mr J. D. Forster.

BLENHEIM PALACE

Blenheim Palace was built for John Churchill, 1st Duke of Marlborough by a grateful nation after his victory over the French at the Battle of Blenheim. The Palace and 2,100 acre park are outstanding examples of the work of Sir John Vanbrugh's English Baroque architecture and of Capability Brown's landscape design. The collection includes tapestries, paintings, sculpture and fine furniture set in magnificent gilded state rooms. The 183 foot long library is particularly beautiful. As the birthplace of Sir Winston Churchill Blenheim has a special Churchill exhibition, including some of his paintings.
Services and Facilities:
Bookshop. Café. Guided Tours. Museum Shop. Parking. Restaurant. Shop.

BLICKLING HALL
Blickling, Aylsham, NR11 6NF. **Tel:** *01263-733471.* **Fax:** *01263-734924.*

BODELWYDDAN CASTLE
Bodelwyddan, Rhyl, LL18 5YA. **Tel:** *01745-583539 / 584060.* **Fax:** *01745-584563.*

BOWHILL
Selkirk,
Tel: *01750-22204.* **Fax:** *01750-22204.*
Opening times: House: public opening in July. Country Park: May-Aug. Times and dates vary annually. Educational parties by appointment throughout the year.
Nearest Station: Edinburgh Waverly 40m, Berwick 40m.
Personnel: The Duke of Buccleuch. This part of the renowned Buccleuch Collection includes Canaletto's Whitehall, a key Ruisdael, and several Guardis, works by Gainsborough, Reynolds, Claude, Vernet, Raeburn and Wilkie. French furniture 1680-1780. Porcelain includes a Sèvres set made for Madame du Barry.
Lecture theatre, arts courses, visitor centre, conference centre, audio visual. Bowhill Little Theatre (drama, music, dance).
Gardens/Grounds. Adventure Playground. Education Service.
Services and Facilities:
Café. Disabled Access. Gallery space for hire. Guided Tours. Lectures. Parking. Restaurant. Shop.

BRODIE CASTLE
Brodie, Forres, IV36 0TE. **Tel:** *01309-641371.* **Fax:** *01309-641600.*

BRYN BRAS CASTLE
Llanrug, Nr Llanberis, Caernarfon, LL55 4RE. **Tel:** *01286-870210.*

CASTLE MUSEUM AND ART GALLERY
The Castle, Nottingham, NG1 6EL. **Tel:** *0115-915 3700 (General information).* **Fax:** *0115-915 3653.*

CHIRK CASTLE
Chirk Wrexham, LL14 5AF. **Tel:** *01691-777701.* **Fax:** *01691-774706.*

DALMENY HOUSE
South Queensferry, EH30 9TQ. **Tel:** *0131-331 1888.* **Fax:** *0131-331 1788.*
Opening times: July & August: Mon-Tue 12-5.30, Sun 1-5.30 *(last admission 4.45). Closed other days except by appointment.*
Nearest Station: Dalmeny.
Personnel: Administrator: Mrs L. Morison. Family home of the Earl and Countess of Rosebery in spectacular situation on the shores of the Firth of Forth, yet only 7 miles west of Edinburgh.
Built in 1817 by William Wilkins. Contains superb collections of works of art, Rothschild French furniture, tapestries and porcelain. Rosebery collection of Napoleonic memorabilia and paintings. Early Scottish furniture and books. Fine British portraits.
Gardens/Grounds. Teashop.
Services and Facilities:
Café. Disabled Access. Guided Tours. Parking.

DRUMLANRIG CASTLE
Thornhill, DG3 4AQ. **Tel:** *01848-330248.* **Fax:** *01848-600244.*
Opening times: Please phone for details of opening times.
Personnel: Administrator/Archivist: Mr Andrew Fisher.
Renowned Buccleuch collection includes Rembrandt's Old Woman Reading, Holbein's Sir Nicholas Carew, Leonardo da Vinci's Madonna with the Yarnwinder, Merton's Countess of Dalkeith.
Cabinets made for Versailles, much French and English furniture 1680-1750 and 1670 silver chandelier. Gardens/Grounds.
Services and Facilities:
Craftshop. Disabled Access. Guided Tours. Lectures. Parking. Restaurant. Shop.

DUNROBIN CASTLE AND MUSEUM
Dunrobin Castle, Golspie, KW10 6RR. **Tel:** *01408-633177.* **Fax:** *01408-633800.*

EASTNOR CASTLE
Portcullis Office, Eastnor, Ledbury, HR8 1RN. **Tel:** *01531 633160.* **Fax:** *01531 631776.*

EUSTON HALL
Estate Office, Euston, Thetford, IP24 2QP. **Tel:** *01842-766366.*

FLOORS CASTLE
Roxburghe Estates Office, Kelso, TD5 7SF. **Tel:** *01573-223333.* **Fax:** *01573-226056.*

GLAMIS CASTLE
Glamis, DD8 1RL. **Tel:** *01307-840202.* **Fax:** *01307-840257.*

HAREWOOD HOUSE,
Harewood, Leeds LS17 9LQ. **Tel:** *0113-288 6331.* **Fax:** *0113-288 6467.* **Email** *business@harewood.org* **Ws** *http://www.harewood.org*
Opening times: Open daily: 17 March -25 October, 11-5. (Last admission 4.30pm).
Nearest Station: Leeds.
Personnel: Visual Arts Administrator: Philippa Brough.

Home of the Earl and Countess of Harewood. Important English and Italian collection of paintings as well as fine Chippendale furniture and Sevres porcelain. In 1988 retained by popular demand, 'The Yorkshire Princess', exhibition celebrating the life of Princess Mary, the Princess Royal, who lived at Harewood for 35 years. 'Off the shelf' objects in focus from the libraries collection. Both exhibitions run throughout the season. 17 March-12 Sept, exhibition of family photographs, formal and informal, recording life on a great country estate over the last century. 12 Sept-25 Oct, 'Ice and Fire' Tony Foster's watercolour studies of volcanoes, alongside 19th century photographs of volcanoes by Dr Tempest Anderson.
Services and Facilities:
Bookshop. Café. Craftshop. Disabled Access. Friends/Society. Guided Tours. Lectures. Parking. Shop.

HATFIELD HOUSE
Hatfield, AL9 5NQ. **Tel:** *01707-262823.* **Fax:** *01707-275719.*
Opening times: 25 Mar-4 Oct. Every day except Mon and Good Friday 12-4, Sun 1-4.30, Bank Holiday Mon 11-4.30.
Nearest Station: Hatfield (opposite main gates).
Personnel: The Marquess of Salisbury. Portraits of each generation of Cecil family since Wm. Cecil, Lord Burghley. Artists include Reynolds, Lawrence, Romney and Richmond. Rainbow and Ermine portraits of Queen Elizabeth I and A Fête at Bermondsey, c. 1570, by Joris Hoefnagel. Catalogue of paintings (by Erna Auerbach) available (458 entries). WC, Gardens/Grounds.
Services and Facilities:
Café. Disabled Access. Guided Tours. Parking. Restaurant. Shop.

ART IN COUNTRY HOUSES

HOPETOUN HOUSE
South Queensferry, EH30 9SL.
Tel: *0131-331 2451.*

HOUSE OF THE BINNS
Linlithgow, EH49 7NA. **Tel:** *0150683-4255.*

KNEBWORTH HOUSE
Knebworth, SG3 6PY. **Tel:** *01438-813303 / 812661.* **Fax:** *01438-811908.*

LEEDS CASTLE
Maidstone, ME17 1PL.
Tel: *01622-765400.* **Fax:** *01622-735616.*
Opening times: *Open All Year. Mar-Oct 10-5*. Castle 11-5.30*. Nov-Feb 10-3*. Castle 10.15-3.30*. (*Last admission).*
Nearest Station: *Bearsted.*
A fine collection of early English Furniture, English and Continental tapestries and pictures. Leeds Castle a Royal Palace for over three centuries has been called the 'loveliest castle in the world'. Within 500 acres of parkland other attractions include a unique Dog Collar Museum, a duckery, an aviary, maze and grotto, greenhouses and a vineyard.
Services and Facilities:
Bar. Disabled Access. Guided Tours. Parking. Restaurant. Shop.

LOSELY HOUSE
Guildford, GU3 1HS. **Tel:** *01483-304440.*
Fax: *01483-302036.*

LOTHERTON HALL
(Leeds City Art Galleries), Aberford, LS25 3EB.
Tel: *0113-281 3259.*

MANDERSTON
Duns, TD11 3PP.
Tel: *01361-883450.* **Fax:** *01361-882010.*
Opening times: *14 May-27 Sep: Thu & Sun 2-5.30, also Bank Hols 25 May and 31 Aug. Group visits anytime of year by appointment.*
Personnel: *Lord Palmer. Secretary:* Julie Bareham.
A house on which no expense was spared. Sumptuous state rooms and a wonderful silver staircase - the only one in the world. Coupled with the amazingly sophisticated domestic quarters, these give an intriguing insight into the 'upstairs and downstairs' life and the way in which people lived in a large house only ninety years ago.
Today, Manderston is still a lived-in home. Outside there are princely stables and an extravagant marble dairy, fifty-six acres of immaculate gardens with a lake. Visitors can see Britain's first privately-owned Biscuit Tin Museum. Cream teas are served. Shop selling souvenirs and home-made goods.
Services and Facilities:
Café. Shop.

MELBOURNE HALL P
Melbourne, DE73 1EN. **Tel:** *01332-862502.*
Fax: *01332-862263.*

PENSHURST PLACE AND GARDENS
Penshurst, Tonbridge, TN11 8DG. **Tel:** *01892-870307.* **Fax:** *01892-810866.*

RAGLEY HALL
Alcester, B49 5NJ. **Tel:** *01789-762090.*
Fax: *01789-764791.*

SUDELEY CASTLE
Winchcombe, **Tel:** *01242-602308.*
Fax: *01242-602959.*

TATTON PARK
Knutsford, WA16 6QN. **Tel:** *01565-654822.*
Fax: *01565-650179.*

TEMPLE NEWSAM HOUSE
Leeds City Council, Leeds LS15 0AE.
Tel: *01532-647321 or 0113-264 7321/264 1358.* **Fax:** *01532-602285 or 0113-260 2285.*

TOWNELEY HALL
Burnley, BB11 3RQ.
Tel: *01282-424213.* **Fax:** *01282-361138.*

TRAQUAIR HOUSE
Innerleithen, EH44 6PW.
Tel: *01896-830323.* **Fax:** *01896-830639.*

TREDEGAR HOUSE AND PARK P
Coedkernew, Newport NP1 9YW.
Tel: *01633-815880.* **Fax:** *01633-815895.*
Opening times: *Easter to October, Wed-Sun. Except August all week. October weekends only. Open Bank Holidays & special Halloween & Christmas openings.*
Nearest Station: *Newport.*
Personnel: *Marketing and Events Officer:* Sarah Freeman.
Set in 90 acres of award winning gardens and parkland Tredegar House is one of the architectural wonders of Wales. It is one of the best examples of 17th century, Charles II, historical house in Britain.
The earliest surviving part of the building goes back to the early 1500s. For over 500 years it was the ancestral home of the Morgans, later Lord Tredegar.
The house has been restored and on display are family portraits of the early 16th century to the early mid 20th century. A collection of marble portrait busts by Welsh sculptors - Je Thomas and Goscombe John. Also on display around the house are approx 50 pictures on loan from the Dulwich gallery 17th century Dutch landscape. Limited disabled access.
Services and Facilities:
Bookshop. Café. Craftshop. Guided Tours. Lectures. Parking. Restaurant. Shop.

TURTON TOWER P
Chapeltown Road, Turton BL7 0HG.
Tel: *01204-852203.* **Fax:** *01204-853759.*
Opening times: *May-Sept Mon-Thur 10-12 and 1-5, weekends 1-5; Mar, Oct Sat-Wed 1-4; April Sat-Wed 2-5; Nov/Feb 1-4.*
Nearest Station: *Bromley.*
Personnel: *Keeper:* M. J. Robinson Dowland.
Lancashire country house based on mediaeval stone tower with Tudor, Stuart and Victorian era extensions.
Located in the West Penine moors with its own woodland gardens, the museum comprises furnished period rooms including a major loan

from the Victoria and Albert Museum, temporary exhibitions, contemporary craft, activities, school and guided tours and a Friends organisation.
Services and Facilities:
Bookshop. Café. Craftshop. Disabled Access. Friends/Society. Guided Tours. Lectures. Museum Shop. Parking. Shop. Workshop Facilities.

WILTON HOUSE
Wilton Salisbury, SP2 0BJ.
Tel: *01722-746720.* **Fax:** *01722-744447.*
Opening times: *4 Apr-25 Oct 1988, Daily 11-6 (last admission 5).*
Nearest Station: *Salisbury.*
Personnel: *Tourism Assistant:* Sally Watkins.

Wilton House has a superb private art collection, with over 200 paintings on show to the public. These include: winter landscapes by Pieter Brueghel the Younger and Jan Brueghel, Democritus by Ribera, The Card Players by Lucas van Leyden and works by Rubens, David Teniers, Lorenzo Lotto, Andrea del Sarto, Hugo van der Goes and Gerard Ter Borch. Portrait artists featured include Mytens, Sir Peter Lely, Reynolds, Sir William Beechey, Gerrit van Honthorst, Pompeo Batoni and the nine Van Dyck's in the Double Cube Room. There are landscapes by Samuel Scott, George Lambert and Richard Wilson and a unique set of 55 paintings in gouache of the haute école riding school by the Baron d'Eisenberg. Gardens/ Grounds.
Services and Facilities:
Bar. Bookshop. Café. Disabled Access. Gallery space for hire. Parking. Restaurant. Shop.

WOBURN ABBEY
Woburn, MK43 0TP. **Tel:** *01525-290666.*
Fax: *01525-290271.*
Personnel: *Mr P. A. Gregory.*
Woburn Abbey is the home of the Marquess and Marchioness of Tavistock and their family. One of the most important private art collections in the world can be seen here, including paintings by Van Dyke, Gainsborough, Reynolds, Velazquez and Canaletto. The collection also includes French and English 18th century furniture, silver and gold. The tour of the Abbey covers three floors, including the vaults, filled with exquisite French, Japanese, German and English porcelain. There is an Antique Centre, coffee shop and gift shops. Open daily from March 22nd to September 27th, and weekends only from 3rd October - 1st November.
Services and Facilities:
Café. Guided Tours. Museum Shop. Parking.

NOTES

SCULPTURE PARKS

Sculpture Parks, sculpture trusts and sculpture workshops.

THE ART WORLD
DIRECTORY
1998/99 25TH EDITION

Barbara Hepworth Museum and Sculpture Park
Barnoon Hill, St. Ives,
Tel: *01736-792226.*

The Chilford Hall Sculpture Centre C
Linton,
Tel: *01223-892641.*
Fax: *01223-894056.*
Opening times: *11-5.30, or dusk, whichever is earlier.*
Personnel: M.D.: Simon Alper.
The Chilford Hall Sculpture Centre near Cambridge is currently home to a major international exhibition of works by the community of artists from all over the world who work in Pietrasanta, Italy.
The Chilford Hall Centre gives them the opportunity to exhibit their larger sculptures for sale in a landscaped setting which is large enough to do them justice.
Through the summer months, Chilford Hall has a varied programme of exhibitions by British based artists to complement the work from Italy.
The 40-acre estate also houses Chilford Hall Vineyard which makes award-winning English wines.
Services and Facilities:
Art Consultancy. Café. Commissioning Service. Disabled Access. Gallery space for hire. Parking. Shop.
Work Stocked and Sold:
Sc.

Chiltern Sculpture Trail
25A Cave Street, (Site location Cowlease Wood, between Stokenchurch and Watlington, Oxon), Oxford, OX4 1BA. **Tel:** *01865-723684.*

Cywaith Cymru - Artworks Wales
2 John Street, Cardiff CF1 5AE.
Tel: *01222-489543.*
Fax: *01222-465458.*

Edinburgh Sculpture
25 Hawthornvale, Edinburgh EH6 4JT.
Tel: *0131-551 4490.*
Fax: *0131-551 4490.*

The Garden Gallery
Rookery Lane, Broughton, Stockbridge, SO20 8AZ.
Tel: *01794-301144.*
Fax: *01794-301761.*

The Grizedale Society PS
Grizedale, Hawkshead, Ambleside, LA22 0QJ.
Tel: *01229-860291.*
Fax: *01229-860050.*
Opening times: *Open daily (trails) office Mon-Sat 9-4. Admission free.*
Personnel: *Director:* David Penn.
Theatre in the Forest, a truly unique, very comfortable, professional theatre presenting the best in entertainment throughout the year - set in the heart of Grizedale Forest. The Grizedale Forest sculpture trails hold over eighty sculptures inspired by the forest, and most made of local found materials. There's always something new to see as new sculptors

are working each year. The gallery tells the story of the sculptures, and shows the work of painters and craftspeople.

Admission free throughout the year. Guide maps and theatre programmes available.
Services and Facilities:
Bookshop. Café. Disabled Access. Parking. Workshop Facilities.

Hannah Peschar Gallery C
Black and White Cottage, Standon Lane, Ockley, Dorking, RH5 5QR. **Tel:** *01306-627269.*
Fax: *01306-627662.*

The Henry Moore Foundation
Dane Tree House, Perry Green, Much Hadham, SG10 6EE.
Tel: *01279-843333.*
Fax: *01279-843647.*
Email *info@henry-moore-fdn.co.uk*
Ws *http://www.henry-moore-fdn.co.uk/hmf*
Personnel: C. M. Joint.
The Foundation was established in 1997 to advance the education of the public by the promotion of their appreciation of the fine arts and in particular the works of Henry Moore. It concentrates its support on sculpture, drawing and print making.
Services and Facilities:
Guided Tours. Lectures. Parking. Restaurant. Shop.
Work Stocked and Sold:
Pr.
Price range: £500 - £5,000.

New Art Centre Sculpture Park and Gallery C
Roche Court, East Winterslow, Salisbury, SP5 1BG.
Tel: *01980-862244.*
Fax: *01980-862447.*
Opening times: *Open every day all year round, 11-4.*
Personnel: *Administrator:* Sarah Fagan.

20th Century sculpture from Europe and the USA. Works from the Estate of Barbara Hepworth, Nevelson, Gormley, Armitage, Butler, King, Kenny, Frink and others. All works for sale.
Services and Facilities:
Art Consultancy. Art for Offices. Commissioning Service. Guided Tours.
Work Stocked and Sold:
Cer. Fur. Pa. Sc. Wd.

Parc Glynllifon
Ffordd Clynnog, Caernarfon, LL54 5DY.
Tel: *01286-830222.*

Scottish Sculpture Workshop
1 Main Street, Lumsden, Huntly, AB54 4JN.
Tel: *01464-861372.*
Fax: *01464-861550.*
Email *ssw@sculptur.demon.co.uk*
Ws *http://www.ssw.org.uk*
Opening times: *Mon-Fri 9-5.*
Personnel: C. Fremantle.
The Scottish Sculpture Workshop provides facilities for artists, both professional and amateur, to make sculpture.
The Workshop also runs events such as commissions, symposia, outreach projects and exhibitions including the biennial Scottish Sculpture Open. Artists come from all over the world to work at the Workshop. The facilities include: wood and metal workshops equipped with power tools; a stone yard with pneumatic tools; a kiln.
During the summer of 1994 we inaugurated our bronze foundry which is designed so that artists can work directly in bronze and aluminium.
All of this is backed up with technical help which means refreshing old skills and imparting new skills (including the bronze casting process), driving the 2-ton forklift, ordering materials and in general ensuring you can make your sculpture. Further information and charges are available on application to the above address.

Sculpture at Goodwood PS
Hat Hill Copse, Goodwood, Chichester, PO18 0QP.
Tel: *01243-538449.*
Fax: *01243-531853.*
Email *w@sculpture.org.uk*
Ws *http://www.sculpture.org.uk*
Opening times: *Thu/Fri/Sat 10.30-4.30 March to November. Directions: 01243-771114.*
Nearest Station: *Barnham.*
Personnel: *Founder:* Wilfred Cass.
Sculpture at Goodwood is a changing collection of contemporary British sculpture set in the beautiful grounds of Hat Hill Copse, 20 acres of woodland walks, informal gardens and rides on the southern slopes of the South Downs overlooking Chichester and the Channel coast. Artists whose work can be seen at Hat Hill include: Allington, Cox, Cragg, Davey, Hamilton-Finlay, Frink, Goldsworthy, Hall, Houshiary, King, Long, O'Connell, Pacheco, Sandle, Woodrow and many more. Compact disc imaging systems

Ab *Artist's Books* **App** *Applied Art* **Cer** *Ceramics* **Cra** *Crafts*
Dec *Decorative* **Dr** *Drawing* **Fur** *Furniture*

SCULPTURE PARKS

located in the information centre show retrospective surveys of the work of artists represented in the displays. Sculpture and discs are available for sale.

A book on sculpture at Goodwood is published annually. Artists whose work can be seen at Hat Hill include: Allington, Armitage, Caro, Chadwick, Cox, Cragg, Goldsworthy, Hall, Houshiary, Jones, Kneale, Mach, De

Monchaux, Nash, Tucker, Woodrow and many more.

Services and Facilities:
Art Consultancy. Bookshop. Commissioning Service. Disabled Access. Parking.
Work Stocked and Sold:
Sc.
Price range: £10,000 - £1,000,000.

SCULPTURE PARK
Queen Mary's College, Cliddesden Road, Basingstoke, RG1 3HF.
Tel: *01256-479221.*

YORKSHIRE SCULPTURE PARK *PS*
Bretton Hall, West Bretton, Wakefield WF4 4LG.
Tel: *01924-830302.*
Fax: *01924-830044.*
Email *ysp@globalnet.co.net*
Opening times: *Summer: Grounds 10-6 daily, Galleries/Café 11-5 daily. Winter: Grounds 10-4 daily, Galleries/Café 11-4 daily.*
Nearest Station: *Wakefield Westgate.*
Personnel: *Director:* Peter Murray.
Yorkshire Sculpture Park, one of Europe's leading open-air art galleries, is set within 100 acres of beautiful 18th c. landscape, attracting over 200,000 visitors annually. It presents a programme of international open-air exhibitions alongside smaller projects, providing opportunities for the practice, understanding and enjoyment of sculpture for everyone. Two galleries and the Camellia House provide indoor space. Monumental sculptures by Henry Moore in the adjacent 96-acre Bretton Country Park is a significant collection of the

artist's work. Changing displays from the collection include sculpture by Hepworth, Frink, Bourdelle, Nash, LeWitt and Paladino.

A sensory trail has been developed for people with disabilities: audio guides and electric scooters available.
Services and Facilities:
Bookshop. Café. Craftshop. Disabled Access. Friends/Society. Lectures. Parking. Shop.

NOTES

SUBSCRIBE NOW

art REVIEW
THE ESSENTIAL MONTHLY GUIDE

R/JANUARY 1998 £3.80/$8.60

"inting will never
in the forefront
art again"
NNY SAVILLE - IN PROFILE

ainting
A case of 20th
century decline?

NEWS & COMMENT ARTIST
ARTIST'S DIARY CRITIC'S D
ART98 13 PAGES OF IST

9 770004 409031

ART SOCIETIES AND ORGANISATIONS

THE ART WORLD
DIRECTORY
1998/99 25TH EDITION

56 GROUP WALES
18 Tydfil Place, Roath Park, Cardiff CF2 5HP.
Tel: *01222-487369.*

57 ART GROUP
9 Clwyd Avenue, Prestatyn, LL19 9NG.
Tel: *01745 856565.*

ABERDEEN ARTISTS SOCIETY
Aberdeen **Tel:** *01224-322691.*

AN TAISCE - THE NATIONAL TRUST FOR IRELAND
The Tailor's Hall, Back Lane, Dublin 8.
Tel: *00353-1-454 1786.* **Fax:** *00353-1-453 3255.*

THE ANTIQUITIES DEALERS ASSOCIATION (ADA)
c/o Faustus Ancient Art and Jewellry, 41 Dover Street, London W1X 3RB. **Tel:** *0171-930 1864.* **Fax:** *0171-495 2882.*

THE ART LOSS REGISTER LTD
13 Grosvenor Place, London SW1X 7HH.
Tel: *0171-235 3393.* **Fax:** *0171-235 1652.*

ART WORKERS GUILD
6 Queen Square, Bloomsbury, London WC1N 3AR. **Tel:** *0171-837 3474.*

THE ARTANGEL TRUST (Artangel)
36 St John's Lane, London EC1M 4BJ.
Tel: *0171-336 6801.* **Fax:** *0171-336 6802.*

ARTISTS ASSOCIATION OF IRELAND (AAI)
Arthouse, Curved Street, Temple Bar, Dublin 2,
Tel: *00353-1-874 0529.* **Fax:** *00353-1-677 1585.*
Email *artists-ireland@connect.ie*
Personnel: *Chairperson: Una Walker.*
Director: Stella Coffey.
Resource for professional visual artists. Publish Art Bulletin bi-monthly ISSN 0790-5858.

ARTISTS' GENERAL BENEVOLENT INSTITUTION
Burlington House, Piccadilly, London W1V 0DJ.
Tel: *0171-734 1193.* **Fax:** *0171 734 1193.*
Personnel: *Secretary: Miss April Connett-Dance.*
A charity managed by artists to provide financial assistance for members of the profession who are in need, as result of illness, accident or old age. Widows of artists are also eligible to apply. The AGBI depends on voluntary contributions to carry out this work. There is also an Artists' Orphan Fund.

ARTISTS ORPHAN FUND
Burlington House, Piccadilly, London W1V 0DJ. **Tel:** *0171 734 1193.* **Fax:** *0171 734 1193.*

ARTS WORLD WIDE (AWW)
309a Aberdeen House, 22 Highbury Grove, London N5 2DQ. **Tel:** *0171-354 3030.*

ASPEX VISUAL ARTS TRUST
27 Brougham Road, Southsea, Portsmouth, PO5 4PA. **Tel:** *01705-812121.*

ASSOCIATION FOR ADVANCEMENT THROUGH VISUAL ART (ACAVA)
23-29 Faroe Road, London W14 0EL.
Tel: *0171-603 3039.* **Fax:** *0171-603 3278.*

ASSOCIATION FOR APPLIED ARTS (AAA)
6 Darnaway Street, Edinburgh EH3 6BG.
Tel: *0131-220 5070.* **Fax:** *0131-225 5079.*

ASSOCIATION FOR BUSINESS SPONSORSHIP OF THE ARTS (ABSA)
60 Gainsford Street, London SE1 2NY.
Tel: *0171-378 8143.* **Fax:** *0171-407 7527.*

ASSOCIATION OF ART GALLERIES IN WALES
Ffotogallery Wales, 31 Charles Street, Cardiff CF1 4EA. **Tel:** *01222-341667.* **Fax:** *01222 341672.*

ASSOCIATION OF ART HISTORIANS
77 Cowcross Street, London EC1M 6BP.
Tel: *0171-490 3211.* **Fax:** *0171-490 3277.*
Email *admin.aah@btinternet.com*
Ws *http://www.gold.ac.uk/aah*
Personnel: *Administrator: Andrew Falconer.*

Registered Charity No 282579

The Association of Art Historians represents the interests of art and design historians in all aspects of the discipline including art, design, architecture, film, media and photography, cultural studies and conservation. Members are active in museums and galleries, publishing, teaching, research and environmental work.
Among the benefits offered to members are an annual conference, a quarterly journal Art History, a quarterly magazine, The Art Book, a newsletter three times a year called, Bulletin, symposia on a great variety of subjects and periods; professional interest groups with their own programme of activities - universities and colleges, art galleries and museums, freelance, schools and students.
Membership is open to art and design historians and to those interested in the advancement of the study of history of art. Special subscription rates to students and the unwaged.

THE ASSOCIATION OF BRITISH PICTURE RESTORERS (ABPR)
Station Avenue, Kew, TW9 3QA.
Tel: *0181-948 5644.* **Fax:** *0181-948 5644.*

ASSOCIATION OF ILLUSTRATORS (AOI)
1st Floor, 32-38 Saffron Hill, London EC1N 8FH. **Tel:** *0171-831 7377.* **Fax:** *0171 831 6277.*

THE BLAKE TRUST
43 Gordon Square, London WC1H 0PD. **Tel:** *0171-388 0708.* **Fax:** *0171 388 0854.*

BRITISH AMERICAN ARTS ASSOCIATION (BAAA)
116-118 Commercial Street, London E1 6NF.
Tel: *0171-247 5385.* **Fax:** *0171-247 5256.*

BRITISH ARTISTS IN GLASS
The Glass Gallery, St. Erth, Hayle, TR27 6HT.
Tel: *01736 756577.*

BRITISH ASSOCIATION OF ART THERAPISTS (BAAT)
11a Richmond Road, Brighton, BN2 3RL.
Tel: *0118-926 5407.* **Fax:** *01273-685852.*

BRITISH COMPUTER ARTS ASSOCIATION
College Manor, Farquhar Road, London SE19 1SS. **Tel:** *0181-761 9807.*

THE BRITISH COUNCIL
Visual Arts Department, 11 Portland Place, London W1N 4EJ. **Tel:** *0171-389 3009.*
Fax: *0171-389 3101.*

BRITISH INSTITUTE OF PROFESSIONAL PHOTOGRAPHY (BIPP)
Fox Talbot House, Amwell End, Ware, SG12 9HN. **Tel:** *01920-464011.* **Fax:** *01920-487056.*

THE BRITISH SOCIETY OF MASTER GLASS PAINTERS (BSMGP)
6 Queen Square, London WC1. **Tel:** *01943-602521.* **Fax:** *01943-602521.*

THE BRITISH SPORTING ART TRUST (BSAT)
BSAT Gallery, 99 High Street, Newmarket, CB8 8JL. **Tel:** *01264-710344.* **Fax:** *01264-710114.*
Personnel: *Organising Secretary: Mrs M. Lawton.*
The Trust's objectives are the formation and display of a representative collection of British sporting art, at the Trust's Vestey Galleries of Sporting Art at the National Horseracing Museum, Newmarket, and other galleries and houses open to the public. Also to support and publish research on the subject of sporting art.

CADW: WELSH HISTORIC MONUMENTS
Crown Building, Cathays Park, Cardiff CF1 3NQ. **Tel:** *01222-500200.* **Fax:** *01222-826375.*

CARDIFF BAY ART TRUST
Pilotage House, Stuart Street, Cardiff CF1.

CHARLES RENNIE MACKINTOSH SOCIETY (CRM Society)
Queen's Cross, 870 Garscube Road, Glasgow G20 7EL. **Tel:** *0141-946 6600.* **Fax:** *0141-945 2321.*

THE CHARLESTON TRUST
Charleston Framhouse, Nr Firle, Lewes, BN8 6LL. **Tel:** *01323-811626.* **Fax:** *01323-811628.*

CONTEMPORARY ART SOCIETY (CAS)
17 Bloomsbury Square, London, WC1A 2LP.
Tel: *0171-831 7311.* **Fax:** *0171-831 7345.*

Opening times: *By appointment only.*
Nearest Underground: *Holborn.*
Personnel: *Director:* Gill Hedley. *Projects
Director:* Cat Newton-Groves. *Museum
Liaison:* Mary Doyle. *Membership Manager:*
Elizabeth Tulip.

Contemporary Art Society

The Contemporary Art Society is a charity.
We acquire paintings, sculpture, photographs,
video, installation work and applied art and
crafts by contemporary artist to give to member museums.
We have given over 4,500 works since 1910.
Date Established: 1910. Number of full members: 1,400. Membership options: Individual,
joint, student, institutional and corporate.
Membership fees (In same order): £30.00,
£35.00, £22.50, £75.00 and £500.
Membership benefits: Trips to art fairs, private
views, artist studios and private collections,
lectures by leading contemporary artists and
critics. Discounts on major events throughout
each year. Publications: Contemporary Art
Society Newsletter, Quarterly. Other information: For more information on our Corporate
Advisory service contact: Cat Newton-Groves.
Services and Facilities:
*Art Consultancy. Art for Offices. Commissioning
Service. Friends/Society. Guided Tours. Lectures.*

THE CONTEMPORARY ART SOCIETY FOR WALES (CASW)
*1 Court Cottages, Michaelston Road, St. Fagans,
Cardiff CF5 6EN.* **Tel:** *01222-595206.*

COUNCIL OF MUSEUMS IN WALES (CMW)
*The Courtyard, Letty Street, Cathays, Cardiff
CF2 4EL.* **Tel:** *01222-225432.* **Fax:** *01222-
668516.*

COUNCIL OF REGIONAL ARTS ASSOCIATIONS
*Litton Lodge, 13a Clifton Road, Winchester,
SO22 5BP.* **Tel:** *01962-51063.*

CRAFT POTTERS ASSOCIATION (CPA)
21, Carnaby Street, London W1V 1PH.
Tel: *0171-439 3377.*
Fax: *0171-287 9954.*
Personnel: *Chairman:* Jack Doherty.
Honorary Secretary: Liz Gale.
The C.P.A. was established to promote and
sell the work of its members and to educate
and interest the public in the craft. The asso-
ciation owns 'Contemporary Ceramics' the
potters gallery. Date Established: 1958.
Number of full members: 150 Fellows, 150
Professional members, 500 Associate members.
Qualification for membership: Fellows and
professional members by selection: Associate
membership open to everyone interested in
studio ceramics.
Membership options: Fellow, Professional
member, Associate. Membership fees: Fellow
£101.00, Professional member £64.75,
Associate £20.75. Membership benefits:
Fellow: Full exhibiting rights and entry in
'Potters'. Professional member: entry in

'Potters', limited exhibition rights. Associate
member: CPA News, discounts at the gallery.
Invitations to lectures and events.
Members show dates 1998: Bi-monthly exhibi-
tions in 'Contemporary Ceramics', Marshall
Street, London. Open show dates: 'Earth and
Fire', Rufford, Notts. - 27th/28th June 1998.
Publications: 'Ceramic Review' (bi-monthly),
'Potters' (bi-monthly), 'CPA News' (bi-
monthly) and technical books ie Clays and
Glazes.
The CPA is the only national organisation
representing potters. We welcome applica-
tions from potters, teachers, students and
enthusiasts in all parts of the UK.
Services and Facilities:
Lectures.

CRAFTS COUNCIL OF IRELAND
*Powerscourt Townhouse Centre, South William
Street, Dublin 2.*
Tel: *00353-1-679 7368.* **Fax:** *00353-1-679
9197.*

THE CRAFTS COUNCIL
*44a, Pentonville Road, Islington, London N1
9BY.*
Tel: *0171-278 7700.* **Fax:** *0171-837 6891.*

THE DECORATIVE ARTS SOCIETY (DAS)
*47 Combe Crescent, Bury, Pulborough, RH20
1PE.* **Tel:** *01798-831734.*

THE DESIGN AND ARTISTS COPYRIGHT SOCIETY LTD
*Parchment House, 13 Northburgh Street, London
EC1V 0AH.*
Tel: *0171-336 8811.* **Fax:** *0171-336 8822.*

THE DESIGN COUNCIL
*Haymarket House, 1, Oxendon Street, London
SW1Y 4EE.* **Tel:** *0171-208 2121.* **Fax:** *0171
839 6033.*

ENGLISH HERITAGE
429 Oxford Street London W1R 2HD.

FEDERATION OF BRITISH ARTISTS (FBA)
*Mall Galleries, 17 Carlton House Terrace,
London SW1Y 5BD.*
Tel: *0171-930 6844.*
Fax: *0171-839 7830.*
Personnel: *Acting Chairman:* Ronald
Maddox PRI Hon RWS. *Chief Executive:* John
Molony. *Company Secretary :* John Sayers.
General Manager: John Deston.
The FBA is based at the Mall Galleries in
London and is the umbrella organisation for
nine art societies including: Royal Institute of
Painters in Water Colours (RI), Royal Society
of British Artists (RBA), Royal Society of
Marine Artists (RSMA), Royal Society of
Portrait Painters (RP), Royal Institute of Oil
Painters (ROI), New English Art Club
(NEAC), Pastel Society (PS), Society of
Wildlife Artists (SWLA), Hesketh Hubbard
Art Society (HH).
Services and Facilities:
*Art Consultancy. Commissioning Service.
Friends/Society. Gallery space for hire. Guided
Tours. Workshop Facilities.*

FINE ART TRADE GUILD
16-18 Empress Place, London SW6 1TT.
Tel: *0171-381 6616.* **Fax:** *0171-381 2596.*

THE GEORGIAN GROUP
6 Fitzroy Square, London W1P 6DX.
Tel: *0171-387 1720.* **Fax:** *0171-387 1721.*

GUILD OF AVIATION ARTISTS (GAvA)
*DFC, Bondway Business Centre, 71 Bondway,
Vauxhall Cross, London SW8 1SQ.* **Tel:** *0171-
735 0634.* **Fax:** *0171-735 0634.*

THE GUILD OF GLASS ENGRAVERS
19, Wildwood Road, London NW11 6UL.
Tel: *0181-731 9352.*

THE GUILD OF RAILWAY ARTISTS (GRA)
45 Dickins Road, Warwick, CV34 5NS.
Tel: *01926-499246.*

GWELED
*Pen Roc, Rhodfa'r Môr, Aberystwyth, SY23
3DE.* **Tel:** *01970-623690.* **Fax:** *01970-
612245.*

THE HENRY MOORE FOUNDATION
*Dane Tree House, Perry Green, Much Hadham,
SG10 6EE.* **Tel:** *01279-843333.* **Fax:** *01279-
843647.*

HESKETH HUBBARD ART SOCIETY
*Mall Galleries, 17 Carlton House Terrace,
London SW1Y 5BD.* **Tel:** *0171-930 6844.*
Fax: *0171-839 7830.*
The HH is a flourishing drawing society found-
ed in 1930 by the RBA. The society meets
weekly throughout the year to draw from life
models. Members include professional and
amateur artists. Although not tutored, partici-
pants learn from the company of fellow artists.
Services and Facilities:
*Art Consultancy. Commissioning Service.
Friends/Society. Gallery space for hire. Workshop
Facilities.*

THE HILLIARD SOCIETY OF MINIATURE ARTISTS
15 Union Street, Wells, BA5 2PU. **Tel:** *01749-
674472.* **Fax:** *01749 672918.*

THE INSTITUTE OF INTERNATIONAL VISUAL ARTS (in IVA)
*Kirkham House, 12/14 Whitfield Street, London
W1P 5RD.* **Tel:** *0171-636 1930.* **Fax:** *0171-
636 1931.*

THE INTERNATIONAL ASSOCIATION OF ART, BRITISH NATIONAL COMMITTEE (IAANBC)
49 Stainton Road, Sheffield S11 7AX.
Tel: *0114-266 9889.* **Fax:** *0114-266 9298.*

INTERNATIONAL ASSOCIATION OF ART CRITICS
*91 Eton Hall, Eton College Road, London NW3
2DH.*

IRISH ASSOCIATION OF ART HISTORIANS (IAAH)
c/o National Gallery of Ireland, Merrion Square,

Dublin 2, **Tel:** 00353-1-661 5133.
Fax: 00353-1-661 5372.

IRISH GEORGIAN SOCIETY
74 Merrion Square, Dublin 2, **Tel:** 00353-1-
676 7053. **Fax:** 00353-1-662 0290.

IRISH MUSEUMS ASSOCIATION (IMA)
c/o 59 Lambard Street West, Dublin 8.
Tel: 00353-1-454 1947.

IRISH WATERCOLOUR SOCIETY (IWCS)
68 Crannagh Road, Rathfarnham, Dublin 14.
Tel: 00353-1-490 4248.

LIVE ART PRESS (LAP)
49 Stainton Road, Sheffield S11 7AX.
Tel: 0114-266 9889. **Fax:** 0114-266 9298.

THE LONDON GROUP
PO Box 447, London SE22 9LL.

MANCHESTER ACADEMY OF FINE ARTS
(MAFA)
4 Delph Greaves, Delph, Oldham OL3 5TY.
Tel: 01457-875718. **Fax:** 01422-370256.
Personnel: President: Ian Thompson NDD
DA ATC ARBS FRSA. Vice President: Glenys
Latham Dip AD CIE. Hon. Secretary: Cliff
Moorhouse TD. Hon. Treasurer: Philip
Livesey FCA.
The Academy is a society of artists which seeks
to promote the Fine Arts in general and the
work of its members in particular; initiating
exhibition and commission opportunities
whilst maintaining its long historical associa-
tion with the City Art Gallery. It actively
encourages membership applications from
committed artists, especially from the North
West and aims to attract work of the highest
quality from non-members into its Annual
Open Exhibition.
Services and Facilities:
Friends/Society. Lectures.

THE MASTERS PHOTOGRAPHERS
ASSOCIATION (MPA)
Hallmark House, 2 Beaumont Street, Darlington,
DL1 5SZ. **Tel:** 01325-356555. **Fax:** 01325-
357813.

THE MUSEUMS AND GALLERIES
COMMISSION (MGC)
16 Queen Anne's Gate, London SW1H 9AA.
Tel: 0171-233 4200. **Fax:** 0171-233 3686.

MUSEUMS ASSOCIATION
42 Clerkenwell Close, London EC1R 0PA.
Tel: 0171-250 1834. **Fax:** 0171-250 1929.

NATIONAL ART COLLECTIONS FUND
(NACF)
Millais House, 7 Cromwell Place, London SW7
2JN. **Tel:** 0171-225 4800. **Fax:** 0171-225
4848.

NATIONAL ARTISTS ASSOCIATION (NAA)
Spitalfields, 21 Steward Street, London E1 6AJ.
Tel: 0171-426 0911. **Fax:** 0171-426 0282.
Email naa@gn.apc.org
Nearest Underground: Liverpool Street.

Personnel: Chair of Management Committee:
Anya Patel. Director: Rose Anne Schoof.
National Artists Association is a representative body for practising artists in the UK.
Its aims are the advancement of the economic
situation, working condition and professional
status of visual artists and to ensure that the
views of artists are represented at regional,
national and international level.
Date established: 1985. Number of full members: approximately 3,000. Membership fees:
Individual artists - £15 per year, Artists group
£25-£45 per year, Associate £50 per year,
Student leavers £5.
Membership benefits: low premium insurance
scheme for artists; discounts on artists' materials; concessionary admission for paying exhibitions at the Tate Gallery in London, Liverpool
and St. Ives; NAA artists' helpline, providing
information and advice - including legal
advice; free copy of the NAA Bulletin, published quarterly; free copy of the NAA Code of
Practice for the Visual Arts; free copy of the
NAA Public Exhibitions Contract; discount
on life membership of DACS (the Designs and
Artists Copyright Society); voucher giving £2
off subscription to Artists Newsletter or any
AN publication (once only, except resale
books).

NATIONAL ASSOCIATION FOR FINE ART
EDUCATION
University of the West of England,
Faculty of Art, Media and Design, Clanage Road,
Bower Ashton, Bristol BS3 2JU.
Tel: 01179-660222.
Fax: 01179-763946.

THE NATIONAL ASSOCIATION OF
DECORATIVE AND FINE ARTS SOCIETIES
(NADFAS)
All enquiries to the Administrator, NADFAS, 8
Guilford Street, London WC1N 1DT.
Tel: 0171-430 0730. **Fax:** 0171-242 0686.
Personnel: Patron: HRH The Duchess of
Gloucester, GCVO. President: Mr Timothy
Clifford. Administrator: Lindley Maitland.
NADFAS is an organisation of 300 societies
dedicated to the enjoyment and care of the
visual arts.
It arose to satisfy a need to increase the aware-
ness of the history of art and the enjoyment
which this provides.
It gives active help with the problems facing
museums, country houses and historic church-
es. Many members are trained to do straight-
forward tasks, such as cleaning old books,
mending fabrics, cataloguing and learning to
guide. Instruction is provided by museum
experts and help is given by the staff of the
Victoria & Albert Museum and other museums throughout the country.
Young NADFAS exists to encourage those
aged between 8 & 18.

NATIONAL ASSOCIATION OF MEMORIAL
MASONS (NAMM)
Crown Buildings, High Street, Aylesbury, HP20
1SL.
Tel: 01296-434750.
Fax: 01296-431332.

NATIONAL CAMPAIGN FOR THE ARTS
(NCA)
Francis House, Francis Street, London SW1P
1DE. **Tel:** 0171-828 4448.

NATIONAL PORTRAITURE ASSOCIATION
59/60 Fitzjames Avenue, London W14 0RR.
Tel: 0171-602 0892. **Fax:** 0171 602 0892.

THE NATIONAL SOCIETY FOR
EDUCATION IN ART AND DESIGN
(NSEAD)
The Gatehouse, Corsham Court, Corsham,
SN13 0BZ. **Tel:** 01249-714825. **Fax:** 01249-
716138.

NATIONAL SOCIETY OF PAINTERS,
SCULPTORS AND PRINTMAKERS (National
Society)
122 Copse Hill, Wimbledon, London SW20
0NL. **Tel:** 0181-946 7878.
Personnel: President: Denis C. Baxter UA
FRSA. Vice President: Jenifer Ford FRSA.
Honorary Treasurer: Chris Spencer FCA.
Honorary Secretary: Gwen Spencer.
To meet a growing desire among artists of
every creed and outlook for an annual and
other exhibitions which would embrace all
aspects of art under one roof, without prejudice
or favour to any one.
Date Established: 1930. Affiliations: None.
Number of full members: 72. Other members:
Associated 28. Qualifications for membership:
Associate: Selected by Council. To be Full
Members: After exhibiting in 3 Annual
Exhibitions, by secret ballot of Full Members.
Membership fees: Full Member: £65.00,
Associate: £32.50.
Membership benefits: Twice yearly Newsletter,
Annual Exhibition plus occasional other exhi-
bitions. Members' show dates 1998: October 8
to 18, 1998 - Atrium Gallery, Queensway,
London W2.

THE NATIONAL TRUST FOR PLACES OF
HISTORIC INTEREST OR NATURAL BEAUTY
(National Trust)
36 Queen Anne's Gate, London SW1H 9AS.
Tel: 0171-222 9251. **Fax:** 0171-222 5097.
Personnel: President: H.M The Queen
Mother. Director General: Mr M. Drury.
Historic Buildings Secretary: Mr S. Jervis.
Director of Public Affairs: Mr M. Taylor.
To preserve places of historic interest or natur-
al beauty in England, Wales and Northern
Ireland, for people to enjoy now and in the
future. See Regional Galleries, Cornwall for main
entry.

NATIONAL TRUST FOR SCOTLAND (NTS)
5 Charlotte Square, Edinburgh EH2 4DU.
Tel: 0131-226 5922. **Fax:** 0131-243 9501.

NEW ENGLISH ART CLUB
F. B. A., Mall Galleries, 17 Carlton House
Terrace, London SW1Y 5BD.
Tel: 0171-930 6844. **Fax:** 0171-839 7830.
Personnel: Hon. Secretary: William Bowyer
RA, RP, NEAC. Keeper: Charlotte Halliday
NEAC.

The NEAC was formed in 1886. Its members then and now have been concerned with the fresh handling of paint and the direct observation of nature. The NEAC holds exhibitions at various galleries throughout the year, but their major annual open exhibition is at the Mall Galleries in November.
Services and Facilities:
Art Consultancy. Commissioning Service. Friends/Society. Gallery space for hire. Guided Tours. Lectures. Workshop Facilities.

NORTHERN IRELAND MUSEUMS COUNCIL (NIMC)
185 Stranmillis Road, Belfast, BT9 5DU.
Tel: *01232-661023.* **Fax:** *01232-683513.*

ORIENTAL CERAMIC SOCIETY (OCS)
30b Torrington Square, London WC1E 7JL.
Tel: *0171-636 7985.* **Fax:** *0171-580 6749.*

PAINTINGS IN HOSPITALS
SHERIDAN RUSSELL GALLERY PSS
16 Crawford Street, London W1H 1PF.
Tel: *0171-935 0250.* **Fax:** *0171-935 1701.*
Opening times: *Mon-Fri 10-5.*
Nearest Underground: *Baker Street.*
Personnel: *Director:* Marjorie Power.
Curator: Mary-Alice Stack.
Paintings in Hospitals (Registered Charity No. 1065963) was established in 1959 to lend modern and contemporary works of art to hospitals and healthcare establishments throughout the British Isles.
Its unique collection of paintings currently numbers over 2,500 and can be seen on display in hundreds of hospitals for the benefit of patients, staff and visitors.
Paintings in Hospitals relies on grants, donations and sponsorship to continue to provide this service which supports both the healthcare services and the arts. Its London Headquarters, The Sheridan Russell Gallery, shows work from the collection and is also available for hire.
Services and Facilities:
Gallery space for hire. Shop.
Work Stocked and Sold:
Pa. Ph. Pr.
Price range: £50 – £3,000.

PAISLEY MUSEUM & ART GALLERY (PAI)
High Street, Paisley PA1 2BA.
Tel: *0141-889 3151.* **Fax:** *0141-889 9240.*
Personnel: *President:* Joe Hargan PAI. *Vice President:* Dr. George Addis. *Secretary & Honorary Treasurer:* Margaret Duff. *Honorary Collector:* Ruth Donald.

To promote the best in Scottish painting, drawing and sculpture. The PAI also promotes an enjoyment of the arts in general through

visits to private collections of paintings, and by holding musical recitals in their galleries.
Date Established: 1876. Number of full members: 170. Other members: 150 Lay members. Qualifications for membership: Artist members are elected by a committee of management. Lay membership is open. Membership fees: £7 per year.
Membership benefits: Access to the annual exhibition, lectures, visits, musical evenings etc.
Publications: PAI Newsletter (Quarterly). Other information: We have established the PAI Scottish Open Drawing Competition with major prizes. Distinguished member artists include Mary Armour RSA, RSW, RGI, PAI, LLD; W. M. Birnie RSW, PAI; Gordon Wyllie RSW; Robert Kelsey DA.
Services and Facilities:
Lectures. Museum Shop. Parking. Workshop Facilities.

PASTEL SOCIETY (PS)
Mall Galleries, 17 Carlton House Terrace, London SW1Y 5BD. **Tel:** *0171-930 6844.*
Fax: *0171-839 7830.*

PATRONS OF BRITISH ART
Development Office, Tate Gallery, Millbank, London SW1P 4RG. **Tel:** *0171-887 8743.*
Fax: *0171 887 8755.*

PATRONS OF NEW ART
Development Office, Tate Gallery, Millbank, London SW1P 4RG. **Tel:** *0171-887 8743.*
Fax: *0171 887 8755.*

THE PRINTMAKERS COUNCIL
Clerkenwell Workshop, 31, Clerkenwell Close, London EC1R 0AT. **Tel:** *0171-250 1927.*
Opening times: *Wed & Thurs 2-6.*
Personnel: *President:* Mr Stanley Jones. *Administrator:* Helen Ward.

Printmakers
COUNCIL

The Printmakers Council is a non-profitmaking artist-run group. Their objectives are to promote the use of both traditional and innovative printmaking techniques by:- holding exhibitions of prints, providing information on prints and printmaking to both its membership and the public, encouraging co-operation and exchanges between members, other associations and interested individuals.
Exhibitions in major London venues and throughout the UK. Exchange shows recently in Paris, Landau Germany and Fremantle Australia.
A slide index of members work is held in the London office for consultation. Membership is open to all printmakers.

PUBLIC ART FORUM (PAF)
Halfpenny Wharf, Torrington Street, East-the-Water, Bideford, EX39 4DP.
Tel: *01237-470440.*
Fax: *01237-470440.*

PUBLIC MONUMENTS AND SCULPTURE ASSOCIATION (PMSA)
c/o Conway Library, Courtauld Institute, Somerset House, Strand, London WC2R 0RN.
Tel: *0171-485 0566 or 0171-873 2614/2406.*
Fax: *0171-267 1742 or 0171-873 2406.*
Email *pmsa@pemail.con*
Ws *http://www.unn.ac.uk/~hcv3*
Opening times: *N/A (Conway/Witt Libraries Mon-Fri 10-6).*
Nearest Underground: *Temple or Charing Cross.*
Personnel: *Chief Executive:* Jo Darke . *Chair holder:* Benedict Read.
Formed in 1991 to promote public enjoyment of open-air monuments and sculptures, old and new.
The National Recording Project, supported by the Heritage Lottery Fund, was set up in 1992 to survey monuments and sculptures nationwide. "The Sculpture Journal", Britain's only scholarly journal devoted to sculpture (from the 16th Century in the Western tradition) appears annually.
The Association collaborates with other groups' campaigns, conferences and events as well as its own. The PMSA Newsletter 'Circumspice' carries Association news and general news and comment on sculpture matters. Individual and corporate members include all areas of public art, plus educational and cultural institutions.
Services and Facilities:
Friends/Society. Lectures.

ROYAL ACADEMY OF ARTS (RA)
Burlington House, Piccadilly, London W1V 0DS.
Tel: *0171-300 8000.* **Fax:** *0171-300 8001.*
Ws *http://www.royalacademy.org.uk*
Opening times: *Mon-Sun 10-6.*
Nearest Underground: *Green Park & Piccadilly.*
Personnel: *Press & Promotions Officer:* Katharine Jones.
Founded in 1768, The Royal Academy is the oldest arts institution in the UK, governed by its artist members. Its exhibition programme includes the annual Summer Exhibition of work by living artists and internationally acclaimed travelling exhibitions.
Services and Facilities:
Bookshop. Café. Disabled Access. Framing. Friends/Society. Guided Tours. Lectures. Museum Shop. Restaurant. Shop.

ROYAL BIRMINGHAM SOCIETY OF ARTISTS
69a New Street, Birmingham B2 4DU.
Tel: *0121-643 3768.* **Fax:** *0121-644 5298.*
Opening times: *10.30-5.*
Nearest Station: *New Street, Snow Hill.*
Personnel: *PRBSA:* Marylane Barfield.
Curator: Roger Forbes. *Secretary:* Paul Bartlett. *Treasurer:* Andrew Matheson.
Royal status: 1868. Full timetable of activities for RBSA Friends. Members (by invitation) Full: 76; Associates: 30; Hon: 4. Encourages the practice and appreciation of Fine Arts and allied crafts by staging exhibitions, workshops, lectures, demonstrations. (Submission forms & details via RBSA Hon. Sec.)

1998 Open Exhibitions with prizes: Open Oil & Sculpture; Feb 23rd-March 14th, Sending in: 15th Feb. Open Watercolour & Craftwork; 11th-30th May, Sending in: 3rd May. £1000 Prize Competition: (Numerous substantial prizes), June 29th-July 18th, Sending in: 29th Nov.

Other 1998 exhibitions combining local & national interest:- Jan 12th-24th: RBSA Permanent Collection; Feb 2nd-14th: RBSA Friends Winter; 16th-28th March: Society of Graphic Fine Arts; 6th-18th April: RBSA Contemporary Printmakers; 20th April-2nd May: National Acrylic Painters Association; 1st-13th June: Eileen Hemsoll; 20th July-1st August: Midland Painting Group; 17th Aug-5th Sept: RBSA Friends Summer; 7th-19th Sept: Birmingham Art Circle; 20th Sept-3rd Oct: 'art pARTy' (Contemporary Art Fair); 12th-31st Oct: RBSA Members & Associates; 2nd-14th Nov: Birmingham Watercolour Society; 16th-28th Nov: Singer & Friedlander Watercolour Competition.

Services and Facilities:
Commissioning Service. Disabled Access. Friends/Society. Gallery space for hire. Lectures. Workshop Facilities.

ROYAL CAMBRIAN ACADEMY OF ART
(RCA)
Crown Lane, Conwy, LL32 8BH. **Tel:** *01492-593413.*

ROYAL COMMISSION ON THE ANCIENT AND HISTORICAL MONUMENTS OF WALES (RCAHMW)
Crown Building, Plas Crug, Aberystwyth, SY23 1NJ. **Tel:** *01970-621227.* **Fax:** *01970-627701.*

ROYAL COMMISSION ON THE ANCIENT AND HISTORICAL MONUMENTS OF SCOTLAND (RCAHMS)
John Sinclair House, 16 Bernard Terrace, Edinburgh EH8 9NX. **Tel:** *0131-662 1456.* **Fax:** *0131-662 1477.*

ROYAL COMMISSION ON THE HISTORICAL MONUMENTS OF ENGLAND/NATIONAL MONUMENTS RECORD (RCHME/NMRC)
Kemble Drive, Swindon SN2 2GZ. **Tel:** *01793-414600.* **Fax:** *01793-414606.*

ROYAL DUBLIN SOCIETY
Ballsbridge, Dublin 4, **Tel:** *00353-1-668 0866.* **Fax:** *00353-1-660 4014.*

THE ROYAL FINE ART COMMISSION FOR SCOTLAND
9 Atholl Crescent, Edinburgh EH3 8HA. **Tel:** *0131-229 1109.* **Fax:** *0131-229 6031.*

ROYAL GLASGOW INSTITUTE OF THE FINE ARTS (RGI)
5 Oswald Street, Glasgow G1 4QR. **Tel:** *0141-248 7411.* **Fax:** *0141-221 0417.* **Personnel:** *Secretary:* Gordon C. McAllister CA. Mrs Lesley Nicholl.
The Royal Glasgow Institute of the Fine Arts which was first established in 1861 with the

aim of promoting contemporary art, does so by staging its prestigious annual exhibition at the

McLellan Galleries, Glasgow, and by running a full programme of exhibitions, lectures and artists' demonstrations at the RGI Kelly Gallery, 118 Douglas Street, Glasgow G2 4ET. The RGI Kelly Gallery is available for hire to artists for solo or group exhibitions.
Services and Facilities:
Disabled Access. Gallery space for hire. Lectures.

ROYAL HIBERNIAN ACADEMY R.H.A.
15 Ely Place, Dublin 2,
Tel: *00353-1-676 6212.*
Fax: *00353-1-676 6212.*

ROYAL INSTITUTE OF BRITISH ARCHITECTS (RIBA)
66 Portland Place, London W1N 4AD.
Tel: *0171-636 4389.*
Fax: *0171-637 5775.*

ROYAL INSTITUTE OF OIL PAINTERS
Mall Galleries, 17 Carlton House Terrace, London SW1Y 5BD.
Tel: *0171-930 6844.* **Fax:** *0171-839 7830.*
Personnel: Mr Frederick Beckett PROI, Hon. RI.
Founded in 1882 the ROI is the only National Art Society devoted exclusively to oil painting. Its annual exhibitions aim to show a cross section of the highest standard of work in that medium currently being produced. The annual open exhibition is held at the Mall Galleries in December.
Services and Facilities:
Art Consultancy. Commissioning Service. Friends/Society. Gallery space for hire. Guided Tours. Lectures.

ROYAL INSTITUTE OF PAINTERS IN WATER COLOURS
Mall Galleries, 17 Carlton House Terrace, London SW1Y 5BD.
Tel: *0171-930 6884.*
Fax: *0171-839 7830.*
Personnel: *President:* Ronald Maddox PRI Hon. RWS.
Founded in 1831, the RI is a major society representing British watercolour painting, holding an annual exhibition of work by members and non-members.
Its aims are to promote the best in modern and traditional uses of the medium. The annual open exhibition is held at the Mall Galleries in March/April and includes over 500 works. Many artists' awards are on offer, including the Winsor and Newton Awards for Young Artists.
Services and Facilities:
Art Consultancy. Commissioning Service. Friends/Society. Gallery space for hire. Guided Tours. Lectures. Workshop Facilities.

THE ROYAL PHOTOGRAPHIC SOCIETY
(RPS)
The Octagon, Milson Street, Bath, BA1 1DN.
Tel: *01225-462841.* **Fax:** *01225-448688.*
Email *info@rpsbath.demon.co.uk*
Ws *http://www.rps.org*
Opening times: *Daily 9.30-5.30.*
Admission: Adults £2.50, Concessions £1.75
Nearest Station: *Bath.*
Personnel: *Secretary General:* Barry Lane. *Curator:* Pam Roberts. *Exhibitions Officer:* Carole Sartain. *Membership Officer:* Sara Beaugeard.
Four constantly changing photographic exhibitions, holography display and museum of photography. Membership and photography workshops and lectures. We welcome everyone with a real interest in photography - and that includes newcomers to photography, teachers, historians and scientists as well as dedicated amateurs and full time professionals.
Date Established: 1853. Number of full members: 10,000. Qualifications for membership: None. Membership options: Student, overseas, family, disabled. Membership fees: Ordinary UK £77 pa, Student £28. Membership benefits: Work towards internationally recognised Distinctions - Fellowship, Associateship and Licentiateship. Attend private views, free access to Octagon Galleries, clubroom, darkroom for hire. Special discounts. Members' show dates 1998: See programme. Open show dates: See current Octagon Galleries Programme. Publications: The Photographic Journal - 10/12, The Imaging Science Journal - 6/12.
Services and Facilities:
Bookshop. Disabled Access. Friends/Society. Gallery space for hire. Lectures. Museum Shop. Restaurant. Shop. Workshop Facilities.

THE ROYAL SCOTTISH ACADEMY (RSA)
The Mound, Edinburgh EH2 2EL. **Tel:** *0131-225 6671.* **Fax:** *0131-225 2349.*

ROYAL SCOTTISH SOCIETY OF PAINTERS IN WATER COLOURS (RSW)
29 Waterloo Street, Glasgow G2 6BZ.
Tel: *0141-226 3838.* **Fax:** *0141-221 1397.*

ROYAL SOCIETY OF BRITISH ARTISTS
Mall Galleries, 17 Carlton House Terrace, London SW1Y 5BD. **Tel:** *0171-930 6844.* **Fax:** *0171-839 7830.*
Founded in 1823 the society boasts many celebrated members including Whistler, Brangwyn and Sickert. The annual open exhibition at the Mall Galleries in September includes a diverse selection of painting and sculpture. Many prizes are awarded through the exhibition, including the De Laszlo medal.
Services and Facilities:
Art Consultancy. Commissioning Service. Friends/Society. Gallery space for hire. Guided Tours. Lectures. Workshop Facilities.

THE ROYAL SOCIETY OF BRITISH SCULPTORS
108 Old Brompton Road, South Kensington, London SW7 3RA. **Tel:** *0171-373 5554.*
Fax: *0171-373 9202.*

ROYAL SOCIETY OF MARINE ARTISTS
Mall Galleries, 17 Carlton House Terrace, London SW1Y 5BD.
Tel: *0171-930 6844.* **Fax:** *0171-839 7830.*
Personnel: *President:* Mark Myers F/ASMA.
Vice President: Bert Wright. *Honorary Treasurer:* Geoff Hunt. *Honorary Secretary:* Sonia Robinson SWA.
The RSMA was formed in 1939. The subject matter is broadly marine in character. Membership is in two categories: artist members and lay members who support the society through their appreciation. The society's Fine Diploma collection is housed in the Ferens Gallery in Hull. The annual open exhibition is held at the Mall Galleries in October.
Services and Facilities:
Art Consultancy. Commissioning Service. Friends/Society. Gallery space for hire. Guided Tours. Lectures.

ROYAL SOCIETY OF MINIATURE PAINTERS, SCULPTORS AND ENGRAVERS
(RMS)
1 Knapp Cottages, Wyke, Gillingham, SP8 4NQ. **Tel:** *01747-825718.* **Fax:** *01747-825718.*

ROYAL SOCIETY OF PAINTER PRINTMAKERS
The Bankside Gallery, 48 Hopton Street, London SE1 9JH. **Tel:** *0171-928 7521.* **Fax:** *0171 928 2820.*

ROYAL SOCIETY OF PORTRAIT PAINTERS
Mall Galleries, 17 Carlton House Terrace, London SW1Y 5BD. **Tel:** *0171-930 6844.*
Fax: *0171-839 7830.*
Personnel: *Patron:* Her Majesty the Queen.
Vice President: Daphne Todd. *Vice President :* Trevor Stubley. *Treasurer:* Andrew Festing.
Formed in April 1891 and achieving the Royal Patronage in 1911 the RP aims to ensure the continuance of portraiture in this country. Distinguished artists from abroad have traditionally joined the best of British artists at the Society's annual exhibition at the Mall Galleries in May, awards include the £5,000 Ondaatje prize and RP gold medal, The Carroll Foundation Award for Young Portrait Painters and The Philip Solomon Award for Portrait Drawing.
Services and Facilities:
Art Consultancy. Commissioning Service. Friends/Society. Gallery space for hire. Guided Tours.

ROYAL WATERCOLOUR SOCIETY
The Bankside Gallery, 48 Hopton Street, London SE1 9JH. **Tel:** *0171-928 7521.* **Fax:** *0171 928 2820.*

ROYAL WEST OF ENGLAND ACADEMY
Queen's Road, Clifton, Bristol BS8 1PX.
Tel: *0117-973 5129.* **Fax:** *0117-923 7874.*

RSA
The Royal Society for the Encouragement of Arts, Manufactures and Commerce, 8 John Adam Street, London WC2N 6EZ. **Tel:** *0171-930 5115.* **Fax:** *0171-839 5805.*

RUSKIN SOCIETY OF LONDON
351 Woodstock Road, Oxford, OX2 7NX.
Tel: *01865 310987 / 515962.*

SCOTTISH ARTISTS' BENEVOLENT ASSOCIATION
(SABA)
Second Floor, 5 Oswald Street, Glasgow G1 4QR. **Tel:** *0141-248 7411.* **Fax:** *0141-221 0417.*

SCOTTISH GLASS SOCIETY (SGS)
32 Farington Street, Dundee DD2 1PF.
Tel: *01382-669864.*

SCOTTISH POTTERS ASSOCIATION (SPA)
77 Spottiswood Gardens, St. Andrews, KY16 8SB. **Tel:** *01334-472303.* **Fax:** *01334-472303.*

SCOTTISH SCULPTURE TRUST (SST)
6 Darnaway Street, Edinburgh EH3 6BG.
Tel: *0131-220 4788.*
Fax: *0131-220 4787.*
Email *trust@ssta.demon.co.uk*
Personnel: *Director:* Andrew Guest.

A charitable body committed to the promotion of contemporary sculpture in Scotland, founded in 1978.
The Trust's aims are to make new opportunities for the creation and appreciation of contemporary sculpture (of the broadest definition) in Scotland. It campaigns for new space for sculpture by facilitating closer relationships between sculptors and those who make, maintain, fund and use public places.
It runs a sculpture database covering both individuals and organisations in Scotland and Britain, practitioners and patrons. It stimulates communication about sculpture through publications, meetings and debates, and advises architects and artists on sculpture projects and commissions.
Services and Facilities:
Art Consultancy. Commissioning Service.

SCOTTISH SOCIETY FOR ART HISTORY
Talbot Rice Gallery, University of Edinburgh, Old College, South Bridge, Edinburgh EH8 9YL.
Tel: *0131-650 2211.*
Fax: *0131 650 2213.*

THE SCULPTORS' SOCIETY OF IRELAND
119 Capel Street, Dublin 2, **Tel:** *00353-1-872 2296/2364.* **Fax:** *00353-1-872 2364.*

THE SCULPTURE COMPANY
108 Old Brompton Road, South Kensington, London SW7 3RA. **Tel:** *0171-373 8615/244 8431.* **Fax:** *0171-370 3721.*

SOCIETY OF AMATEUR ARTISTS (SAA)
PO Box 50, Newark, NG23 5GY.
Tel: *01949-844050.* **Fax:** *01949-844051.*

SOCIETY OF BOTANICAL ARTISTS (SBA)
1 Knapp Cottages, Wyke, Gillingham, SP8 4NQ. **Tel:** *01747-825718.* **Fax:** *01747-825718.*

SOCIETY OF CATHOLIC ARTISTS (SCA)
c/o 19 Cranford Close, West Wimbledon, London SW20 0DP. **Tel:** *0181-947 6476.*

SOCIETY OF EQUESTRIAN ARTISTS (SEA)
63 Gordon Close, Knowle Green, Staines, TW8 1AP **Tel:** *01784-889669.*
Personnel: *Secretary:* John Collins.
Chairman: Philip Gibson OBE.
To encourage the study of equine art and by mutual assistance between members promote excellence in its practice.
Services and Facilities:
Friends/Society. Workshop Facilities.

SOCIETY OF GRAPHIC FINE ART
15 Willow Way, Hatfield, AL10 9QD.
Tel: *01707-880615.*
Personnel: *President:* Jean Cantler. *Vice President:* Michael Taylor. *Vice President/Publicity:* Geraldine Jones. *Hon. Treasurer:* David Brooke. *Secretary:* Mrs Sharon Curtis.
The Society of Graphic Fine Art, founded in 1919, is a professional society that exists to promote good drawing skills.
Members are selected solely on their quality of work, and membership is open to any artist working in any drawing medium or any form of original printmaking. Oil painting or 'pure' watercolours are inadmissible.
The society holds an annual open exhibition in central London and has been increasing its out-of-town exhibitions. Members receive a newsletter and occasional visits and painting weekends are arranged.

THE SOCIETY OF LONDON ART DEALERS
(SLAD)
91 Jermyn Street, London SW1Y 6JB.
Tel: *0171-930 6137.* **Fax:** *0171-321 0685.*

SOCIETY OF SCOTTISH ARTISTS (SSA)
11a, Leslie Place, Edinburgh EH4 1NF.
Tel: *0131-332 2041.*

SOCIETY OF SCOTTISH ARTISTS AND ARTISTS CRAFTSMEN (SAAC)
10 Wellington Street, Edinburgh EH7 5ED.
Tel: *0131-556 0244.* **Fax:** *0131-556 0244.*

SOCIETY OF WILDLIFE ARTISTS
Mall Galleries, 17 Carlton House Terrace, London SW1Y 5BD. **Tel:** *0171-930 6844.*
Fax: *0171-839 7830.*
Personnel: *President:* Mr Bruce Pearson.
The SWLA was formed in 1964 to foster all forms of visual art based on or representing the world's wildlife. Through art the society actively seeks to advance the interest, education, and concerns of the public in the conservation of wildlife. The annual open exhibition is held at the Mall Galleries in July. Many

artists awards are on offer.
Services and Facilities:
Art Consultancy. Commissioning Service. Friends/Society. Gallery space for hire. Guided Tours. Lectures. Workshop Facilities.

SOCIETY OF WOMEN ARTISTS (SWA) C
Willow House, Ealing Green, Ealing, London W5 5EN. **Tel:** *(Only during Annual Exhibition)* 0171-222 2723.
Ws *http://www.nal.vam..ac.uk/.*
Opening times: *10-7 excluding Sundays, 6th-21st March 1988.*
Nearest Underground: St. James Park or Victoria.
Personnel: *President:* Barbara Tate. *Vice Presidents:* Joyce Wyatt, Muriel Owen, Susan Millis, Joyce Rogerson.
Founded in the mid-nineteenth century, the SWA Annual Open Exhibition is held in March each year at the Westminster Central Hall, Storey's Gate, London SW1, (admission free).
Aim is to exhibit the best of women artists work and features approximately 700 new works by many leading artists in a range of media, including oils, pastels, etchings, miniatures, sculptures and showcase pieces.
Membership is by election only but non-members may enter work.
To apply for submission forms write to above address. Archives are held by V&A Museum's Archive of Art and Design, Blythe House, 23 Blythe Road, London W14 0QF.
Work Stocked and Sold:
Pa. Sc.

SOCIETY OF WOOD ENGRAVERS (SWE)
North Lodge, Hamstead Marshall, Newbury, RG20 0JD.
Tel: 01635-524255. **Fax:** 01635-524255.
Personnel: *General Secretary:* Mrs Sue Brown.

The Society, founded in 1920, is dedicated to the promotion of wood engraving.
It tours an annual open selected exhibition of engravings and other relief media to about 8 venues around England. The exhibitions show the best of current work from Britain and a number of other countries.
Members and subscribers are kept in touch by an excellent bi-monthly newsletter. Any

interested person may subscribe: £15 p.a. in UK, £20 p.a. overseas.
Services and Facilities:
Art Consultancy. Commissioning Service. Friends/Society.

THE TEXTILE SOCIETY
Macclesfield Museum, Roe Street, Macclesfield, SK11 6UT. **Tel:** 01625-613210. **Fax:** 01625-617880.

UNITED SOCIETY OF ARTISTS (UA)
207 Sunny Bank Road, Potters Bar, EN6 2NJ.
Tel: 01707-851439. **Fax:** 01707-646613.

VISITING ARTS
11 Portland Place, London W1N 4EJ.
Tel: 0171-389 3019. **Fax:** 0171-389 3016.

VISUAL ARTS AND GALLERIES ASSOCIATION (VAGA)
The Old Village School, The High Street, Witcham, Ely, CB6 2LQ.
Tel: 01353-776356. **Fax:** 01353-776356.
Email *106341.327@compuserve.com*
Personnel: *Director:* Hilary Gresty. *Chair:* Stephen Poster.
The national association working for the public exhibition, presentation and development of the visual arts. The Association (membership 350 organisations and individuals) works primarily as an advocacy body on behalf of museums and galleries throughout the UK. Activities include regular briefings (eg free entry to museums and galleries; lobbying MPs etc), seminars (eg contemporary collecting policy; NESTA etc). Bi-monthly newsletter.
Services and Facilities:
Art Consultancy.

VOLUNTARY ARTS NETWORK
P.O. Box 200, Cardiff CF5 1YH. **Tel:** 01222-395395. **Fax:** 01222-397397.

WATER COLOUR SOCIETY OF WALES (CYMDEITHAS DYFRLLIW CYMRU)
4 Castle Road, Raglan, NP5 2JZ. **Tel:** 01291-690260.
Personnel: *Secretary:* Margaret Butler.

Watercolour Society of Wales
Cymdeithas Dyfrlliw Cymru

The Watercolour Society of Wales was established in 1959. A handful of artists living around Cardiff felt the need for a separate specific organisation for Watercolour artists. The Society now has a membership of fifty. It is our aim to exhibit and promote work carried out in the medium of watercolour. The artists come from all areas of Wales and their work has interesting and varied styles in technique and subject matter. Future Exhibitions: March 1998 - Museum of Modern Art, Machynlleth; June/July 1998 - Museum & Art Gallery, Brecon.

ARTS BOARDS

Arts boards, Arts councils.

ARTS COUNCILS

ARTS COUNCIL OF ENGLAND
14 Great Peter Street, London SW1P 3NQ.
Tel: *0171-333 0100.*

ARTS COUNCIL OF NORTHERN IRELAND
185 Stranmillis Road, Belfast, BT9 5DU.
Tel: *01232-381591.*
Fax: *01232 -661715.*

ARTS COUNCIL OF WALES
Museum Place, Cardiff CF1 3NX.
Tel: *01222-394711.*
Fax: *01222-221447.*
Opening times: *Mon-Fri 9-5.15*
Personnel: *Senior Visual Arts & Craft Officer, Artform Development Division:* Isabel Hitchman.
The Arts Council of Wales (ACW) is the national organisation with specific responsibility for the funding and development of the arts in Wales, including the visual arts and the crafts. It receives grants from central and local government of which the largest is from the Welsh Office. It is also the distributor of funds for the arts in Wales generated by the National Lottery. From these resources, ACW makes grants to support art activities and facilities. Some of this funding is allocated in the form of annual revenue grants to full-time arts organisations.
ACW also operates schemes which provide financial and other forms of support for individual activities and projects. ACW is a Registered Charity and is set up by Royal Charter. ACW works through the medium of both the Welsh and English languages.

THE ARTS COUNCIL/AN CHOMHAIRLE EALAION
70 Merrion Square, Dublin 2,
Tel: *00353-1-661 1840.*
Fax: *00353-1-676 1302.*
Personnel: *Visual Arts Officer:* Sarah Finlay. *Exhibition Organiser:* Helena Gorey.

SCOTTISH ARTS COUNCIL
12, Manor Place, Edinburgh EH3 7DD.
Tel: *0131-226 6051.*
Fax: *0131-225 9833.*
Personnel: *Information Officer:* Giulio Romano. Christine Galey.
The Scottish Arts Council is one of the principal channels of Government funding for the arts in Scotland. SAC exists to create a climate in which arts of quality flourish and are enjoyed by a wide range of people throughout Scotland.

REGIONAL ARTS BOARDS

EAST MIDLANDS ARTS BOARD
Mountfields House, Epinal Way, Loughborough, LE11 0QE.
Tel: *01509-218292.* **Fax:** *01509-262214.*

EASTERN ARTS BOARD
Cherry Hinton Hall, Chery Hinton Road, Cambridge, CB1 4DW.
Tel: *01223 -215355.*
Fax: *01223-248075.*
Email *info@eastern-arts.co.uk*
Opening times: *Mon-Fri 9-5.30.*
Nearest Station: *Cambridge.*
Personnel: *Visual Arts Officer:* Niki Braithwaite.

Eastern Arts Board Funded

Eastern Arts Board is the regional funding and development agency for the east of England. It is one of ten Regional Arts Boards and covers the counties of Bedfordshire, Cambridgeshire, Essex, Hertfordshire, Lincolnshire, Norfolk and Suffolk. It receives funding from the Arts Council of England, the British Film Institute, the Crafts Council and the regions Local Authorities.
The Visual and Media Arts Department supports artistic activity across contemporary visual arts, crafts, photography, multimedia, live art, cinema, television and radio.

LONDON ARTS BOARD
Elme House, 133 Long Acre, London WC2E 9AF.
Tel: *0171-240 1313.*

NORTH WEST ARTS BOARD
Manchester House, 22 Bridge Street, Manchester M3 3AB.
Tel: *0161-834 6644.*
Fax: *0161-834 6969.*

NORTHERN ARTS BOARD
9-10 Osborne Street, Newcastle-upon-Tyne NE2 1NZ
Tel: *0191-281 6334.*
Fax: *0191 281 3276.*

SOUTH EAST ARTS BOARD
10 Mount Ephraim, Tunbridge Wells, TN4 8AS
Tel: *01892-515210 ext 213.*
Fax: *01892-549383.*

SOUTH WEST ARTS
Bradninch Place, Gandy Street, Exeter, EX4 3LS.
Tel: *01392-218188.*
Fax: *01392-413554.*
Email *swarts@mail.zynet.co.uk*
Ws *http://www.swa.co.uk*
Personnel: *Chairman:* David Brierly. *Chief Executive:* Graham Long.

South West Arts is the official public body for the arts in the South West. We cover Bristol, Bath and North East Somerset, South Gloucestershire and North Somerset, Cornwall, Devon, Dorset, Gloucestershire and Somerset. We are a registered charity. Our mission is "To raise the quality of the arts in the region and make them available to the widest possible audience".
We achieve our mission through information, advice, advocacy, raising funds for and funding. South West Arts is the official adviser to the Arts Council of England on all Lottery applications from the region.

SOUTHERN ARTS BOARD
13 St. Clement Street, Winchester, SO23 9DQ.
Tel: *01962-855099.*
Fax: *01962-861186.*

WEST MIDLANDS ARTS
82 Granville Street, Birmingham B1 2LH.
Tel: *0121-631 3121, Lottery Line, 0121-693 6878.*
Fax: *0121-643 7239.*
Email *west.midarts@midnet.com*
Ws *http://www.arts.org.uk/*
Opening times: *Opening hours 9-5.*
Personnel: *Chief Executive:* Sally Luton.
The Regional Arts Board for Hereford & Worcester, Shropshire, Staffordshire, Warwickshire and the metropolitan West Midlands, offering funding, advice, information, training and planning for the arts, crafts and media.
Annual project awards are available to individual artists, crafts makers and photographers - contact Information Services for further details. Visual Arts Update is a monthly mailing of opportunities for artists and makers. Artfile, a slide index, assists artists and makers to promote their work.
Information on Arts Lottery regional venues and facilities available. Designated parking for disabled drivers, level access to building and wheelchair access to all facilities.
Services and Facilities:
Disabled Access.

YORKSHIRE & HUMBERSIDE ARTS
21 Bond Street, Dewsbury, WF13 1AX.
Tel: *01924-455555.*
Fax: *01924-466522.*
Email *yharts-info@geo2.poptel.org.uk*
Ws *http://www.arts.org.uk*
Opening times: *Mon-Thurs 9-5.30, Fri 9-5.*
Personnel: *Chief Executive:* Roger Lancaster.
Yorkshire and Humberside Arts serves the administrative area covered by the counties of West, South and North Yorkshire and the former county of Humberside, providing financial support for the arts in the region and developing public appreciation of the arts by improving access to, and the quality of, artistic activity.
Services and Facilities:
Disabled Access.

EDUCATION

Institutions by course, award/qualification, main address listing.

THE ART WORLD
DIRECTORY
1998/99 25TH EDITION

FINE ART

This section lists institutions running Fine Art courses together with the core subjects covered.

BATH SPA UNIVERSITY COLLEGE (FORMERLY BATH COLLEGE OF HIGHER EDUCATION)
Core Subjects:
Painting. Sculpture.

BRETTON HALL, COLLEGE OF THE UNIVERSITY OF LEEDS
Core Subjects:
Ceramics. Painting. Sculpture.

BYAM SHAW SCHOOL OF ART
Core Subjects:
Painting. Photography. Printmaking. Sculpture.

CAVENDISH COLLEGE
Core Subjects:
Painting. Photography. Printmaking.

CHELSEA COLLEGE OF ART AND DESIGN (LONDON INSTITUTE)
Core Subjects:
Painting. Printmaking. Sculpture.

COOMBE FARM GALLERY
Core Subjects:
Painting.

CUMBRIA COLLEGE OF ART AND DESIGN
Core Subjects:
Painting. Photography. Printmaking. Sculpture.

DARTINGTON COLLEGE OF ARTS

EDINBURGH COLLEGE OF ART
Core Subjects:
Painting. Photography. Printmaking. Sculpture.

EDINBURGH'S TELFORD COLLEGE
Core Subjects:
Photography.

GOLDSMITHS COLLEGE
Core Subjects:
Photography.

HEATHERLEY SCHOOL OF FINE ART
Core Subjects:
Painting. Printmaking. Sculpture.

THE HISTORY OF ART STUDIES
Core Subjects:
Painting. Sculpture.

HURON UNIVERSITY U.S.A. IN LONDON
Core Subjects:
Painting. Photography. Printmaking.

THE INSTITUTE
Core Subjects:
Painting. Photography. Sculpture.

KENT INSTITUTE OF ART & DESIGN AT MAIDSTONE
Core Subjects:
Painting. Photography. Printmaking. Sculpture.

KINGSTON UNIVERSITY, FACULTY OF DESIGN
Core Subjects:
Painting. Photography. Printmaking. Sculpture.

LANCASTER UNIVERSITY, SCHOOL OF CREATIVE ARTS, THE ART DEPARTMENT
Core Subjects:
Drawing. Painting. Printmaking. Sculpture.

NOTTINGHAM TRENT UNIVERSITY
Core Subjects:
Painting. Photography. Printmaking. Sculpture.

RUSKIN SCHOOL OF DRAWING AND FINE ART
Core Subjects:
Art History. Painting. Printmaking. Sculpture.

THE SLADE SCHOOL OF FINE ART
Core Subjects:
Painting. Photography. Printmaking. Sculpture.

SURREY INSTITUTE OF ART & DESIGN
Core Subjects:
Photography.

SWANSEA INSTITUTE OF HIGHER EDUCATION
Core Subjects:
Media. Painting. Photography.

THE CITY LITERARY INSTITUTE FOR ADULT STUDIES, DEPARTMENT OF VISUAL ARTS
Core Subjects:
Painting. Photography. Printmaking. Sculpture.

UNIVERSITY COLLEGE OF RIPON AND YORK ST. JOHN
Core Subjects:
Painting. Printmaking.

UNIVERSITY OF PLYMOUTH
Core Subjects:
Painting. Photography. Printmaking. Sculpture. Textiles. Time-based Media.

UNIVERSITY OF WALES, ABERYSTWYTH
Core Subjects:
Photography. Printmaking.

VISUAL ISLAMIC & TRADITIONAL ARTS DEPT.
Core Subjects:
Painting.

WARWICKSHIRE COLLEGE, SCHOOL OF ART AND DESIGN
Core Subjects:
Painting. Photography. Printmaking. Sculpture.

INDIVIDUAL COURSES

ANIMATION

CAVENDISH COLLEGE
CUMBRIA COLLEGE OF ART AND DESIGN
EDINBURGH COLLEGE OF ART
NOTTINGHAM TRENT UNIVERSITY
THE CITY LITERARY INSTITUTE FOR ADULT STUDIES, DEPARTMENT OF VISUAL ARTS
WARWICKSHIRE COLLEGE, SCHOOL OF ART AND DESIGN

ARCHITECTURE

BIRKBECK COLLEGE
CAVENDISH COLLEGE
EDINBURGH COLLEGE OF ART
THE HISTORY OF ART STUDIES
KENT INSTITUTE OF ART & DESIGN AT MAIDSTONE
NOTTINGHAM TRENT UNIVERSITY

ART HISTORY

BATH SPA UNIVERSITY COLLEGE (FORMERLY BATH COLLEGE OF HIGHER EDUCATION)
BIRKBECK COLLEGE
CHELSEA COLLEGE OF ART AND DESIGN (LONDON INSTITUTE)
CHRISTIE'S EDUCATION
CUMBRIA COLLEGE OF ART AND DESIGN
GLASGOW UNIVERSITY
THE HISTORY OF ART STUDIES
HURON UNIVERSITY U.S.A. IN LONDON
THE INSTITUTE
LANCASTER UNIVERSITY, SCHOOL OF CREATIVE ARTS, THE ART DEPARTMENT
MODERN ART STUDIES
THE NEW STUDY CENTRE
THE SLADE SCHOOL OF FINE ART
THE CITY LITERARY INSTITUTE FOR ADULT STUDIES, DEPARTMENT OF VISUAL ARTS

ART EDUCATION

University College of Ripon and
York St. John
University of Plymouth
University of Wales, Aberystwyth
Warwickshire College, School of
Art and Design

CERAMICS

Bath Spa University College
(Formerly Bath College of Higher
Education)
Cumbria College of Art and
Design
Edinburgh College of Art
Edinburgh College of Art
(Heriot-Watt University)
The Institute
Kent Institute of Art & Design at
Maidstone
Kingston University, Faculty of
Design
Nottingham Trent University
Surrey Institute of Art & Design
Swansea Institute of Higher
Education
The City Literary Institute for
Adult Studies, Department of
Visual Arts
University College of Ripon and
York St. John
University of Plymouth
Warwickshire College, School of
Art and Design

DECORATIVE ART

Nottingham Trent University

DESIGN - AUTOMOTIVE

Warwickshire College, School of
Art and Design

DESIGN - 3D

Kent Institute of Art & Design at
Maidstone
University of Plymouth

DESIGN - DISPLAY

Dundee College

DESIGN - GRAPHIC

The American College in London
Bath Spa University College
(Formerly Bath College of Higher
Education)
Cavendish College
Cumbria College of Art and
Design
Dundee College
Edinburgh College of Art

Kent Institute of Art & Design at
Maidstone
Nottingham Trent University
Swansea Institute of Higher
Education
The City Literary Institute for
Adult Studies, Department of
Visual Arts
University of Plymouth
Warwickshire College, School of
Art and Design

DESIGN - INTERIOR

Chelsea College of Art and
Design (London Institute)
Dundee College
Nottingham Trent University

DESIGN - PHOTOGRAPHY

The American College in London
Bath Spa University College
(Formerly Bath College of Higher
Education)
Birkbeck College
Bretton Hall, College of the
University of Leeds
Byam Shaw School of Art
Cavendish College
Chelsea College of Art and
Design (London Institute)
Christie's Education
Coombe Farm Gallery
Cumbria College of Art and
Design
Dartington College of Arts
Dundee College
Edinburgh College of Art
Edinburgh College of Art
(Heriot-Watt University)
Edinburgh's Telford College
Glasgow University
Goldsmiths College
Heatherley School of Fine Art
The History of Art Studies
Huron University U.S.A. in
London
The Institute
Kent Institute of Art & Design at
Maidstone
Kingston University, Faculty of
Design
Lancaster University, School of
Creative Arts, The Art
Department
Modern Art Studies
The New Study Centre
Nottingham Trent University
Ruskin School of Drawing and
Fine Art
The Slade School of Fine Art
Surrey Institute of Art & Design
Swansea Institute of Higher
Education
The City Literary Institute for
Adult Studies, Department of
Visual Arts
University College of Ripon and

York St. John
University of Plymouth
University of Wales, Aberystwyth
Visual Islamic & Traditional Arts
Dept.
Warwickshire College, School of
Art and Design

DESIGN - TYPOGRAPHIC

University of Plymouth

FURNITURE

Edinburgh College of Art
Edinburgh College of Art
(Heriot-Watt University)
The Institute
Kingston University, Faculty of
Design
Nottingham Trent University
University College of Ripon and
York St. John
University of Plymouth
Warwickshire College, School of
Art and Design

ILLUSTRATION

The American College in London
Dundee College
Edinburgh College of Art
Kent Institute of Art & Design at
Maidstone
Nottingham Trent University
Swansea Institute of Higher
Education
The City Literary Institute for
Adult Studies, Department of
Visual Arts
University of Plymouth
Warwickshire College, School of
Art and Design

JEWELLERY/SILVER

Cumbria College of Art and
Design
Edinburgh College of Art
Edinburgh College of Art
(Heriot-Watt University)
The Institute
Kent Institute of Art & Design at
Maidstone
Surrey Institute of Art & Design
The City Literary Institute for
Adult Studies, Department of
Visual Arts
University College of Ripon and
York St. John
Warwickshire College, School of
Art and Design

MEDIA

NOTTINGHAM TRENT UNIVERSITY
UNIVERSITY OF PLYMOUTH

MULTIMEDIA

SWANSEA INSTITUTE OF HIGHER
EDUCATION

PAINTING

DUNDEE COLLEGE
EDINBURGH COLLEGE OF ART
(HERIOT-WATT UNIVERSITY)

PRINTMAKING

DUNDEE COLLEGE
EDINBURGH COLLEGE OF ART
(HERIOT-WATT UNIVERSITY)

SCULPTURE

DUNDEE COLLEGE
EDINBURGH COLLEGE OF ART
(HERIOT-WATT UNIVERSITY)

STAINED GLASS

SWANSEA INSTITUTE OF HIGHER
EDUCATION

TEXTILES

BATH SPA UNIVERSITY COLLEGE
(FORMERLY BATH COLLEGE OF
HIGHER EDUCATION)
CHELSEA COLLEGE OF ART AND
DESIGN (LONDON INSTITUTE)
CUMBRIA COLLEGE OF ART AND
DESIGN
DUNDEE COLLEGE
EDINBURGH COLLEGE OF ART
GOLDSMITHS COLLEGE
KENT INSTITUTE OF ART & DESIGN AT
MAIDSTONE
NOTTINGHAM TRENT UNIVERSITY
THE CITY LITERARY INSTITUTE FOR
ADULT STUDIES, DEPARTMENT OF
VISUAL ARTS
UNIVERSITY COLLEGE OF RIPON AND
YORK ST. JOHN
WARWICKSHIRE COLLEGE, SCHOOL OF
ART AND DESIGN

AWARDS

CERT. IN PORTRAITURE

HEATHERLEY SCHOOL OF FINE ART

CERAMICS - DIPLOMA

THE CITY LITERARY INSTITUTE FOR
ADULT STUDIES, DEPARTMENT OF
VISUAL ARTS

DEGREE

THE AMERICAN COLLEGE IN LONDON
BATH SPA UNIVERSITY COLLEGE
(FORMERLY BATH COLLEGE OF
HIGHER EDUCATION)
BRETTON HALL, COLLEGE OF THE
UNIVERSITY OF LEEDS
BYAM SHAW SCHOOL OF ART
CHELSEA COLLEGE OF ART AND
DESIGN (LONDON INSTITUTE)
CHRISTIE'S EDUCATION
CUMBRIA COLLEGE OF ART AND
DESIGN
DARTINGTON COLLEGE OF ARTS
DUNDEE COLLEGE
EDINBURGH COLLEGE OF ART
GOLDSMITHS COLLEGE
HURON UNIVERSITY U.S.A. IN
LONDON
KENT INSTITUTE OF ART & DESIGN AT
MAIDSTONE
KINGSTON UNIVERSITY, FACULTY OF
DESIGN
LANCASTER UNIVERSITY, SCHOOL OF
CREATIVE ARTS, THE ART
DEPARTMENT
NOTTINGHAM TRENT UNIVERSITY
RUSKIN SCHOOL OF DRAWING AND
FINE ART
THE SLADE SCHOOL OF FINE ART
SWANSEA INSTITUTE OF HIGHER
EDUCATION
UNIVERSITY COLLEGE OF RIPON AND
YORK ST. JOHN
UNIVERSITY OF PLYMOUTH
WARWICKSHIRE COLLEGE, SCHOOL OF
ART AND DESIGN

FOUNDATION

BYAM SHAW SCHOOL OF ART
CAVENDISH COLLEGE
CHELSEA COLLEGE OF ART AND
DESIGN (LONDON INSTITUTE)
CUMBRIA COLLEGE OF ART AND
DESIGN
DUNDEE COLLEGE
HEATHERLEY SCHOOL OF FINE ART
THE HISTORY OF ART STUDIES

HURON UNIVERSITY U.S.A. IN
LONDON
KENT INSTITUTE OF ART & DESIGN AT
MAIDSTONE
SWANSEA INSTITUTE OF HIGHER
EDUCATION
THE CITY LITERARY INSTITUTE FOR
ADULT STUDIES, DEPARTMENT OF
VISUAL ARTS
WARWICKSHIRE COLLEGE, SCHOOL OF
ART AND DESIGN

PREFOUNDATION

THE INSTITUTE

POST GRADUATE

BATH SPA UNIVERSITY COLLEGE
(FORMERLY BATH COLLEGE OF HIGHER
EDUCATION)
BRETTON HALL, COLLEGE OF THE
UNIVERSITY OF LEEDS
BYAM SHAW SCHOOL OF ART
CHELSEA COLLEGE OF ART AND
DESIGN (LONDON INSTITUTE)
CHRISTIE'S EDUCATION
CUMBRIA COLLEGE OF ART AND
DESIGN
DARTINGTON COLLEGE OF ARTS
EDINBURGH COLLEGE OF ART
GLASGOW UNIVERSITY
GOLDSMITHS COLLEGE
HURON UNIVERSITY U.S.A. IN
LONDON
KENT INSTITUTE OF ART & DESIGN AT
MAIDSTONE
LANCASTER UNIVERSITY, SCHOOL OF
CREATIVE ARTS, THE ART
DEPARTMENT
THE SLADE SCHOOL OF FINE ART
SWANSEA INSTITUTE OF HIGHER
EDUCATION
UNIVERSITY COLLEGE OF RIPON AND
YORK ST. JOHN
UNIVERSITY OF PLYMOUTH
VISUAL ISLAMIC & TRADITIONAL ARTS
DEPT.
WARWICKSHIRE COLLEGE, SCHOOL OF
ART AND DESIGN

PRACTICAL COURSES

BYAM SHAW SCHOOL OF ART
HEATHERLEY SCHOOL OF FINE ART
KENT INSTITUTE OF ART & DESIGN AT
MAIDSTONE

TEACHER TRAINING

BATH SPA UNIVERSITY COLLEGE
(FORMERLY BATH COLLEGE OF HIGHER
EDUCATION)
BRETTON HALL, COLLEGE OF THE
UNIVERSITY OF LEEDS
UNIVERSITY COLLEGE OF RIPON AND
YORK ST. JOHN

ART EDUCATION

UNIVERSITY OF PLYMOUTH
WARWICKSHIRE COLLEGE, SCHOOL OF ART AND DESIGN

ADULT EDUCATION

BIRKBECK COLLEGE
CAVENDISH COLLEGE
CHRISTIE'S EDUCATION
CUMBRIA COLLEGE OF ART AND DESIGN
DUNDEE COLLEGE
HEATHERLEY SCHOOL OF FINE ART
THE HISTORY OF ART STUDIES
THE INSTITUTE
KENT INSTITUTE OF ART & DESIGN AT MAIDSTONE
THE NEW STUDY CENTRE
THE CITY LITERARY INSTITUTE FOR ADULT STUDIES, DEPARTMENT OF VISUAL ARTS
WARWICKSHIRE COLLEGE, SCHOOL OF ART AND DESIGN

MAIN ADDRESS LISTINGS

THE AMERICAN COLLEGE IN LONDON
110 Marylebone High Street, London W1M 3DB.
Tel: *0171-486 1772.*
Fax: *0171-935 8144.*
Email *admissions@acl.edu*
Nearest Underground: *Baker Street/Bond Street*
Personnel: *Director of Admissions:* Miss Karen Haygreen. *Program Chair, Visual Communication:* Mr Steve Jeppesen.

The Visual Communication Program at ACL provides outstanding educational quality in the fields of graphic design, illustration, photography and computer/multi-media design. The teaching program is well supported by an impressive range of industry standard equipment and facilities including three dedicated design studios, an Apple PowerMac computer design lab, a Multi-Media computer lab, a full-colour and black and white photographic darkroom, a photo studio and an animation

suite as well as an extensive library with Internet research resource facilities.
We have an impressive tradition of success with graduates now working across the globe in the fields of advertising, publications, graphics and multi-media design. In fact, there is a good chance you will already have seen the work of our alumni in magazines, on billboards or on television.
In 1997, a recent graduate won 5 of the British Advertising Awards including the Campaign Gold Award for Best Individual Poster; three of our students were awarded honours for their outstanding and original design work in the Royal Society for the Arts Student Design Awards and four of our graduating students were accepted on an M.A. course at one of the most selective institutions in the United Kingdom.
We believe that we can offer you a great chance to become part of this tradition of success and help you to develop the knowledge and skills needed for an exciting and fulfilling professional career.
Courses:
Design (Graphic). Illustration.
Qualifications:
Degree.

BATH SPA UNIVERSITY COLLEGE (FORMERLY BATH COLLEGE OF HIGHER EDUCATION)
Faculty of Art and Music, Sion Hill Place, Lansdown, Bath, BA1 5SF.
Tel: *01225-875725.* **Fax:** *01225-875666.*
Email *staffinitial.surname@bathspa.ac.uk*
Ws *http://www.bathspa.ac.uk/*
Nearest Station: *Bath Spa.*

The Faculty of Art and Music, which offers undergraduate and postgraduate courses, utilises both College campuses and is characterised by its wide use of practising artists, designers and musicians as part-time and associate lecturers. This policy ensures that students are in regular tutorial contact with staff who actively engage in research. Many of our staff operate internationally, resulting in a highly creative and professional environment at Bath Spa University College. Faculty courses have an excellent reputation for the quality of educational experience available to students. Work takes place in either refurbished or purpose-built specialist accommodation. The cities of Bath and Bristol, as well as ease of access to London, ensure excellent resources for creative study.
Courses:
Art History. Ceramics. Design (Graphic). Fine Art. Textiles.
Qualifications:
Degree. Post Graduate. Teacher Training.

BIRKBECK COLLEGE
Centre for Extra-Mural Studies, 26 Russell Square, London WC1B 5DQ.
Tel: *0171-631 6660.*
Fax: *0171-631 6686.*
Nearest Underground: *Russell Square.*
Personnel: *Executive Officer, Art History:* Jo Oulton.
The Centre offers about ninety part-time day/evening courses on the history of art and architecture in various centres in the Greater London area.
The courses are for adults, and all except a post-Diploma course are open to anyone, without prior qualification. The programme covers a Certificate/Diploma (equivalent to the first year of a BA); assessed courses of one or two terms; non-assessed courses; weekend study days; and a residential summer school. Classroom meetings are supplemented by gallery visits.
Emphasis is on developing ways of seeing art, thinking about it and understanding critical approaches to it.
Courses:
Architecture. Art History.
Qualifications:
Adult Education.

BRETTON HALL, COLLEGE OF THE UNIVERSITY OF LEEDS
West Bretton, Wakefield WF4 4LG.
Tel: *01924-832017.*
Fax: *01924-832016.*
Email *registry@mailhost.bretton.ac.uk*
Nearest Station: *Wakefield.*
Personnel: *Head of Fine Art:* Richard Bell.
The Fine Art Degree Programme recruits to three discrete routes, each based within a subject discipline - ceramics - painting - sculpture, offering an intensive experience in developing understanding through informed studio practice.
The diversity and range of possibilities within contemporary Fine Art practice is encouraged and nurtured by a varied range of teaching strategies. This is underpinned by a clear sense of historical and contemporary social and critical issues.
Studio accommodation is extensive and provides excellent provision across the area. The unique and highly stimulating environment of Bretton Hall and its surroundings, including the Yorkshire Sculpture Park, enhances this well established programme.
Courses:
Fine Art.
Qualifications:
Degree. Post Graduate. Teacher Training.

BYAM SHAW SCHOOL OF ART
2 Elthorne Road, Archway, London N19 4AG.
Tel: *0171-281 4111.*
Fax: *0171-281 1632.*
Email *info@byam-shaw.ac.uk*
Ws *http://www.byam-shaw.ac.uk*
Nearest Underground: *Archway.*
Personnel: *Director:* Alister Warman.
Independent Fine Art School committed to the education of intending artists. Three-year BA (Hons) in Fine Art. Foundation and

Diploma Studies. Post-graduate and Short-term studies.
Courses:
Fine Art.
Qualifications:
Degree. Foundation. Post Graduate. Practical.

CAVENDISH COLLEGE

209-212 Tottenham Court Road, London W1P 9AF. **Tel:** *0171-580 6043.* **Fax:** *0171-255 1591.* **Email** *learn@cavendish.ac.uk OR cavendis@gpo.sonnet.co.uk* **Ws** *http://www.cavendish.ac.uk* **Nearest Underground:** *Goodge Street.*

CAVENDISH COLLEGE

A Cavendish Diploma course provides each student with a solid foundation from which to enter their chosen field in art and design together with sound progression opportunities into higher education.
All courses provide an intensive and diagnostic arena of study, enabling the student to identify and maximise their creative potential across a range of interrelated disciplines.
Lectures by a large number of practising professional's give the student a clearer understanding of their chosen area of study and an insight into the routes by which they may progress towards their chosen careers. Please contact the college for further enrolment details.
Courses:
Animation. Architecture. Design (Graphic). Fine Art.
Qualifications:
Adult Education. Foundation.

CHELSEA COLLEGE OF ART AND DESIGN (LONDON INSTITUTE)
School of Art, Manresa Road, London SW3 6LS. **Tel:** *0171-514 7751.* **Fax:** *0171-514 7777.*
Nearest Underground: *South Kensington.*
Chelsea College of Art & Design is a con-

stituent college of the London Institute, the largest Art & Design education institute in Europe. The College offers a range of pace-setting courses for UK and overseas students, from Foundation through to MA and research degrees.
The College is located in central London, the centre for most art and design activity in the United Kingdom - contemporary art galleries, design practices, trade fairs, fashion houses, as well as museums, libraries and archives.
Courses:
Art History. Design (Interior). Fine Art. Textiles.
Qualifications:
Degree. Foundation. Post Graduate.

CHRISTIE'S EDUCATION
63 Old Brompton Road, London SW7 3JS. **Tel:** *0171-581 3933.* **Fax:** *0171-589 0383.* **Ws** *http://www.christies.com*
Opening times: *Mon-Fri 9-5.*
Nearest Underground: *South Kensington.*
Personnel: *Chairman:* Robert Cumming. *Administrator:* Caroline de Lane Lea.
Christie's Education runs a wide variety of challenging, specialist and general interest courses in the Fine and Decorative Arts. They cover all periods from classical antiquity to contemporary art, and range from fully validated diploma and university courses to short courses and evening classes.
Courses are run in London, Scotland, Paris, New York and Australia. All of them place great importance on training the eye and the first hand examination of works of art, with vocational as well as academic instruction. Students are of all ages, nationalities and backgrounds, and postgraduate and mature students are well catered for.
Courses:
Art History.
Qualifications:
Adult Education. Degree. Post Graduate.

COOMBE FARM GALLERY
Dittisham, Dartmouth, TQ6 0JA. **Tel:** *01803-722352.* **Fax:** *01803-722275.* **Email** *Rileyarts@AOL.com*
Opening times: *Daily 10-5. Sundays by appointment.*
Nearest Station: *Totnes.*
Personnel: *Gallery Owner:* Tina Riley. *Gallery Director:* Mark Riley. *P.R Admin.:* Gina Carter.

A contemporary art and craft gallery featuring the work of artists and makers mainly from

the West Country. The gallery shows ceramics, paintings, prints, jewellery, glass, wood and papier maché. Two or three exhibitions annually feature the work of specific artists and new young designers. Coombe Farm Studios is the educational part of the gallery where we run a variety of Fine Art and Craft courses in Devon and painting holidays abroad tutored by Paul Riley.
Courses:
Fine Art.

CUMBRIA COLLEGE OF ART AND DESIGN
Brampton Road, Carlisle, CA3 9AY. **Tel:** *01228-400300.* **Fax:** *01228-514491.* **Email** *Cum@cumbriacollart.ac.uk* **Ws** *http://www.cumbriacollart.ac.uk* **Nearest Station:** *Carlisle - 1.5 miles.* **Personnel:** *Marketing:* Allison J. Roberts. Cumbria College of Art and Design - a college in the university sector - offer a wide range of courses in the study, practice, criticism and promotion of visual, performing and media arts, crafts and design, and in heritage management. These lead to the award of BA Honours degrees and Higher National Diplomas as well as a range of BTEC National Diplomas. With the opportunity of further part time post graduate study in contemporary arts practice, cultural and heritage management, media and local history.
Courses:
Animation. Art History. Ceramics. Design (Graphic). Fine Art. Jewellery/Silversmithing. Textiles.
Qualifications:
Adult Education. Degree. Foundation. Post Graduate.

DARTINGTON COLLEGE OF ARTS
Totnes, TO9 6EJ. **Tel:** *01803-862224.* **Fax:** *01803-863569.* **Email** *registry@dartington.ac.uk* **Ws** *http://www.dartington.ac.uk* **Nearest Station:** *Totnes.* **Personnel:** *Administrator : Registry:* Margaret Eggleton.

Established in 1961 on the beautiful Dartington Hall Estate, Dartington College of Arts is well-known as a centre for innovation in the performance arts.
A 1997 Higher Education Funding Council audit commented on our "charismatic" and "innovative" teaching methods. We scored 23 out of a potential 24 points. Through partnership with the University of Plymouth, undergraduate and post-graduate awards are offered in Visual Performance (visual arts and performance), Music, Theatre, Performance Writing

and Arts Management. Students studying for BA (Hons) in any of these specialisms are encouraged to collaborate between disciplines and to experiment in emerging hybrid and multi-media art forms.
Courses:
Fine Art.
Qualifications:
Degree. Post Graduate.

DUNDEE COLLEGE
Art and Design Section, Graham Street Centre, Graham Street, Dundee DD4 9RF.
Tel: *01382-834834.*
Fax: *01382-884388.*
Personnel: *Team Leader, Graphics, Photography:* Sheila Page. *Team Leader, Fine Art, Illustration:* Anne Boyle. *Team Leader, Textiles/Interiors:* Jim Buchan.
The College offers full time courses to HND level in Design and Fine Art. Foundation courses are also offered at National Certificate level in Design areas and Fine Art. Students progress from this college to Art Colleges in Scotland, most commonly Duncan of Jordanstone College of Art, or BA courses in England. Many progress to employment directly.
Courses:
Design (Display). Design (Graphic). Design (Interior). Illustration. Painting. Printmaking. Sculpture. Textiles.
Qualifications:
Adult Education. Degree. Foundation.

EDINBURGH COLLEGE OF ART
Lauriston Place, Edinburgh EH3 9DF.
Tel: *0131-221 6000/221 6030.*
Fax: *0131-221 6089.*
Email *registration@eca.ac.uk*
Ws *http://www.eca.ac.uk*
Personnel: *Registrar:* Marian Hall.

Edinburgh
COLLEGE *of* **ART**

HERIOT-WATT UNIVERSITY

Edinburgh College of Art offers a wide range of degree courses in the fields of Art & Design and Environmental Studies.
With a student population of approximately 1700 and a reputation as a centre of excellence, the College has a lively, creative and intimate atmosphere.
Throughout the year, the College also runs a varied exhibitions programme, featuring not only work from students and staff but touring or specially curated exhibitions of local, UK or international origin.
Courses:
Animation. Architecture. Ceramics. Design (Graphic). Fine Art. Furniture. Illustration. Jewellery/Silversmithing. Textiles.
Qualifications:
Degree. Post Graduate.

EDINBURGH COLLEGE OF ART (HERIOT-WATT UNIVERSITY)
Lauriston Place, Edinburgh EH3 9DF.
Tel: *0131-221 6000.* **Fax:** *0131-221 6001.*
Email *registration@eca.ac.uk*
Ws *http://www.hw.ac.uk/eca*

Courses:
Ceramics. Furniture. Jewellery/Silversmithing. Painting. Printmaking. Sculpture.

EDINBURGH'S TELFORD COLLEGE
North Campus, Crewe Toll, Edinburgh EH4 2NZ. **Tel:** *0131-332 2491.* **Fax:** *0131-343 1218.*
Courses:
Fine Art.

GLASGOW UNIVERSITY
History of Art Department, 7 University Gardens, Glasgow G12 8QQ.
Tel: *0141-330 4097.* **Fax:** *0141-330 3513.*
Email *J.Nicholson@arthist.arts.gla.ac.uk*
Ws *http://www.arts.gla.ac.uk/ArtHist/decarts.htm*
Personnel: Gordon McFarlan.
Diploma/M. Phil in Decorative Arts. This is a one-year course run in association with Christie's which combines practical and academic approaches to the study of the decorative arts. Christie's Glasgow premises introduce students to the workings of an auction house, while current curatorial practice is studied at Glasgow's many museums.
Courses:
Art History.
Qualifications:
Post Graduate.

GOLDSMITHS COLLEGE
Lewisham Way, New Cross, London SE14 6NW.
Tel: *0171-919 7000.* **Fax:** *0171-919 7509.*
Email *admissions@gold.ac.uk*
Ws *http://www.gold.ac.uk/*
The Department of Visual Arts at Goldsmiths College is one of international distinction. In addition to teaching programmes at both undergraduate and postgraduate level, it is concerned with promoting the understanding of contemporary art through the personal endeavours of individual members of staff and through departmental initiatives.
The department is divided into two study areas - Fine Art and Textiles. The department received a 5* rating (Centre of International Excellence) in the 1996 Research Assessment Exercise, one of only two University departments to be awarded such a rating for Fine Art.
Courses:
Fine Art. Textiles.
Qualifications:
Degree. Post Graduate.

HEATHERLEY SCHOOL OF FINE ART
80 Upcerne Road, London SW10 0SH.
Tel: *0171-351 4190.* **Fax:** *0171-361 6945.*
Nearest Underground: *Fulham Broadway/Sloane Square.* BR: *Victoria*
HEATHERLEY'S TODAY - A century has passed since Thomas Heatherley retired from the school. Despite the changing pattern of art education Heatherley's has retained the atelier scheme of enrolment for its Open Studio. This allows students to join classes at any time of the academic year, on a part-time casual basis, to work from the life model. Heatherley's also offers a range of part-time

Day and Evening Courses, Easter and Summer Courses, a full time Portfolio/Foundation Course and Diploma in Portraiture Studies. Continuing Studies offers a modular programme for students who have already completed basic studies.
Courses:
Fine Art.
Qualifications:
Adult Education. Certificate in Portraiture. Foundation. Practical.

THE HISTORY OF ART STUDIES
13 South Terrace, London SW7 2TB.
Tel: *0171-584 6086.* **Fax:** *0171-584 0705.*
The History of Art Studies: Offers slide illustrated lecture courses by eminent Art Historians in the Fine Arts, (1 Year Certificate course or attending lectures only). Architecture and Decorative Arts; from the Renaissance to Modern Art. Also, Short Study Courses and Full-Time Courses commencing September. Lectures held at the Linnean Society, Burlington House, Piccadilly, London. W1. Information and brochure from Valerie Dalton.
Courses:
Architecture. Art History. Fine Art.
Qualifications:
Adult Education. Foundation.

HURON UNIVERSITY U.S.A. IN LONDON
Fine Arts Department, 58 Princes Gate, London SW7 2PS.
Tel: *0171-584 9696.* **Fax:** *0171-589 9406.*
Email *Marco-Gorin@Huron.ac.uk*
Nearest Underground: *South Kensington.*
Personnel: *Director of Admissions:* Marco Gorin.

Huron University offers a unique opportunity for students who wish to prepare for careers in Art and Design or for students who may simply wish to take a year out to study Art before entering University to undertake degree courses in other disciplines.
The campus situated on Exhibition Road Kensington has good studio, computer and photographic dark room facilities and is just two minutes walk from the Victoria and Albert, Science and Natural History museums.
The Fine Arts Department offers:- Foundation course in Art and Design, BA Major in History of Art, BA Major in Studio Arts, AA in Studio Arts, Postgraduate Diploma in Fine Art.
Courses:
Art History. Fine Art.
Qualifications:
Degree. Foundation. Post Graduate.

THE INSTITUTE

Hampstead Garden Suburb, Central Square, London NW11 7BN.
Tel: *0181-455 9951.* **Fax:** *0181-201 8063.*
Email *101320,153@compuserve.com*
Personnel: *Head of Art:* Bob Rothero.
Course Director: Barbara Jackson.

Prefoundation and Portfolio - September to March. This course in the visual arts consists of two structured terms, 27 hours per week, designed to prepare students for an art foundation course or an art degree at university. The course is suitable either for school leavers or for those mature students who wish to experience the total commitment of a full-time course in art and creative studies. Regular tutorials will be given to students as well as practical guidance and career advice. Some basic materials will be made available by the Institute but students should provide a portfolio and basic drawing equipment. A list of materials and equipment needed will be sent to successful students on acceptance to the course. Access to Art - April to June. This one term course is aimed at students interested in pursuing art to a higher level with the possibility of progressing onto the Prefoundation Course.
Courses:
Art History. Ceramics. Fine Art. Furniture. Jewellery/Silversmithing.
Qualifications:
Adult Education. Pre-foundation.

KENT INSTITUTE OF ART & DESIGN AT MAIDSTONE

Oakwood Park, Oakwood Road, Maidstone, ME16 8AG.
Tel: *01622-757286.* **Fax:** *01622-692003.*
Email *kiadmarketing@kiad.ac.uk*
Ws *http://kiad.ac.uk/kiad.htm*
Nearest Station: *Maidstone West.*
Personnel: *Exhibitions Officer:* Christine Gist. *Admissions Officer:* Gill Hall.
The Kent Institute offers a comprehensive range of courses in Art, Design and Architecture at all levels from BTEC National Diploma to Masters and Research Degrees. BA (Honours), MA Degrees and Research Degrees (M.Phil and PhD) are accredited by the University of Kent at Canterbury and Diploma and Higher National Diploma courses by BTEC.
KIAD was formed in 1987 by the merger of three well-established and thriving colleges each founded over 100 years ago in Canterbury, Maidstone and Rochester-upon-Medway. Each college runs courses dealing with specific areas of Art, Design and Architecture: Canterbury, Fine Art and Architecture; Maidstone, Visual Communication; Rochester, Three-Dimensional Design, Fashion & Clothing, Precious Metals.
Courses:
Architecture. Ceramics. Design (3-D). Design (Graphic). Fine Art. Illustration. Jewellery/Silversmithing. Textiles.
Qualifications:
Adult Education. Degree. Foundation. Post Graduate. Practical.

KINGSTON UNIVERSITY, FACULTY OF DESIGN

Knights Park, Kingston upon Thames, KT1 2QJ.
Tel: *0181-547 2000.* **Fax:** *0181-547 7011.*
Email *P.Amendt@kingston.ac.uk*
Nearest Station: *Kingston-Upon-Thames.*
Personnel: *Head of School:* Prof. Bruce Russell.
Three areas: painting, sculpture, intermedia. Emphasis on student self-management and professional practice. Printmaking, photography and computer assisted imaging inductions first year. First year structured, project led, second and third years personal research. Second year transatlantic and European exchange programme. All student contribute to public art/town and gown programme and art loan scheme. 'Aftercare' graduate students network. Inhouse gallery showing staff and student self-curated shows and new international gallery.
Courses:
Ceramics. Fine Art. Furniture.
Qualifications:
Degree.

LANCASTER UNIVERSITY, SCHOOL OF CREATIVE ARTS, THE ART DEPARTMENT

Lonsdale Hall, Bailrigg, Lancaster, LA1 4YW.
Tel: *01524-593056.* **Fax:** *01524-593056.*
Email *d.plahuta@lancaster.ac.uk OR a.heward@lancaster.ac.uk*
Ws *http://www.lancs.ac.uk/users/art/*
Personnel: *Head of Department:* Professor Nigel Whiteley.
We offer two degree schemes: Art: Practice and Theory. A fine art-based degree which integrates courses in painting, drawing, sculpture and printmaking with 20th century art history. Art: History and Culture. An art-history-based degree which focuses on the 20th century and allows you to take a limited amount of practical work. Post-graduate research degrees (M.Phil and Ph.D) also available. Lancaster is one of the leading universities in the country for the quality of teaching, research and facilities.
Courses:
Art History. Fine Art.
Qualifications:
Degree. Post Graduate.

MODERN ART STUDIES

5 Bloomsbury Place, London WC1A 2QA.
Tel: *0171-436 3630.*
Fax: *0171-436 3631.*
Email *courses@modernartstudies.demon.co.uk*
Personnel: *Principal:* Diana Weir. *Course Director:* Jean Hodgins.

M◆DERN
ART STUDIES

Christies Modern Art Studies offers full and part time courses surveying key ideas and developments from Impressionism to the present day.
The course includes slide lectures and gallery visits by distinguished art historians, critics and writers and also comprises visits to museums, galleries, auctions houses and study visits abroad.
Courses:
Art History.

THE NEW STUDY CENTRE

21 Palace Gardens Terrace, London W8 4SA.
Tel: *0171-229 3393.*
Fax: *0171-229 4220.*
Opening times: *9.30-1.*
Personnel: *Administrator:* Mrs J. Fitzgerald.
The New Study Centre, formerly known as The Study Centre for the History of the Fine and Decorative Arts, continues a tradition of more than 30 years providing opportunities for the study of art history.
The New Study Centre offers a variety of courses and lectures which cover all levels of interest and experience. 1998 courses include: The Lothbury Lectures. Monet-Velasquez-Whistler-Hockney. Four lunchtime lectures which will be given by Douglas Skeggs at The Lothbury Gallery, London EC2 on 13th January, 3rd February, 10th February and 24th February. Monarchs, Merchants and Magnates. The Fine and Decorative Arts c1660 to c1702. 6th May, 13th May, 19th May.
Three study-day visits to Greenwich, the City of London and Northamptonshire (Drayton House and Boughton House) which will provide an insight into the stimulus given to the architecture and interior furnishings of the later Stuart period by royal, mercantile and landowner patronage. History of the Decorative Arts.
The Decorative Arts Course covers the history of European furniture (mainly English and French), pottery, porcelain, silver, glass and textiles from 16th century to the present day. Two mornings each week. Optional start

dates for five, fifteen or twenty week course. The next course will begin in Autumn 1998. For details of all courses please contact The New Study Centre office.

Courses:
Art History.

Qualifications:
Adult Education.

NOTTINGHAM TRENT UNIVERSITY
Faculty of Art and Design, Dryden Street, Nottingham, NG1 4FX.
Tel: *0115-941 8418.* **Fax:** *0115-948 6403.*
Email *Eppie.Durrant@ntu.ac.uk*
Ws *http://www.ntu.ac.uk*

The Faculty of Art and Design is one of the largest and foremost in Europe, offering a wide range of courses at undergraduate and post-graduate levels.
The Faculty comprises three departments: Design, Fashion and Textiles and Visual and Performing Arts. Each department provides a related portfolio of courses offering a broad spectrum of disciplines.
All facilities are of a very high standard and most are in purpose-built accommodation.
All courses involve input from distinguished professionals, specialists and consultants who visit the Faculty on a regular basis and enhance still further the academic programmes delivered by accomplished and dedicated staff teams.

Courses:
Animation. Architecture. Ceramics. Decorative Art. Design (Graphic). Design (Interior). Fine Art. Furniture. Illustration. Media. Textiles.

Qualifications:
Degree.

RUSKIN SCHOOL OF DRAWING AND FINE ART
74 High Street, Oxford, OX1 4BG.
Tel: *01865-276940.* **Fax:** *01865-276949.*
Email *stephen.farthing@ruskin-school.ox.ac.uk*
Ws *http://www.ruskin-sch.ox.ac.uk/*
Personnel: *Ruskin Master of Drawing:* Stephen Farthing.

The Ruskin School is the Fine Art Department at Oxford University. It benefits

from a strong academic foundation, with a particular emphasis on prominent visiting lecturers, and treats the boundaries between media as permeable.
Of particular note is The Laboratory, the School's research wing, which supports the production of new work deriving from collaborations between artists and experts from the worlds of science, technology and the Humanities.
The Laboratory is administered by Paul Bonaventura and Antonia Payne and organises The Joseph Beuys Lectures and the Arts Council of England Helen Chadwick Fellowship on an annual basis.

Fine Art.
Qualifications:
Degree.

THE SLADE SCHOOL OF FINE ART
University College London Gower Street, London WC1E 6BT.
Tel: *0171-504 2313.*
Fax: *0171-380 7380.*
Email *slade.enquiries@ucl.ac.uk*
Ws *http://www.ucl.ac.uk/slade/*
Nearest Underground: *Euston, Euston Square, Warren Street.*

The Slade School of Fine Art, founded in 1871, is a department of University College London.
The Slade offers the BA in Fine Art (four years, full time) and, at graduate level, the MA and MFA (two years full time), the Graduate Diploma (one year, full time) and MPhil and PhD degrees.
Students are taught by professional artists of distinction and distinguished staff teaching art history and theoretical studies. At Undergraduate level students may specialise either in Painting, Sculpture or Fine Art Media (including film, video, printmaking, photography and electronic media). Graduate students may also specialise in theatre design.

Courses:
Art History. Fine Art.
Qualifications:
Degree. Post Graduate.

SURREY INSTITUTE OF ART & DESIGN
James Hockey Gallery, Falkner Road, Farnham, GU9 7DS.
Tel: *01252-722441.*
Fax: *01252-732241.*
Courses:
Ceramics. Fine Art. Jewellery/Silversmithing.

SWANSEA INSTITUTE OF HIGHER EDUCATION
Faculty of Art and Design, Townhill Road, Swansea SA2 0UT.
Tel: *01792-481285.* **Fax:** *01792-205305.*
Personnel: Dr. Bill Gaskins.
As a major centre of excellence for art & design higher education in Wales, the Faculty provides opportunities for students to study a wide variety of vocational and professional subjects or to undertake more academically oriented studies by choosing alternative theoretical and historical subjects.
There is also an Art and Design Foundation programme for students preparing for higher education entry, as well as future possibilities to study for a taught postgraduate degree leading to MA or the Research degrees of MPhil and PhD. Undergraduate awards include the BA (Hons) and HND and these are available on both a full-time and part-time basis.

Courses:
Ceramics. Design (Graphic). Fine Art. Illustration. Multi-Media. Architectural Stained Glass.
Qualifications:
Degree. Foundation. Post Graduate.

THE CITY LITERARY INSTITUTE FOR ADULT STUDIES, DEPARTMENT OF VISUAL ARTS
Keeley House, Keeley Street, London WC2B 4BA.
Tel: *0171-430 0547.* **Fax:** *0171-583 7500.*
Opening times: *9.30-9.*
Nearest Underground: *Holborn, Covent Garden.*
Personnel: *Head of Visual Arts:* Janet Hill. *Administrator:* Kay Hawkins.

The Department of Visual Arts offers a wide range of part-time courses for adults throughout the whole year.
Subject areas include: Art history, basketry, bookbinding, ceramics, conservation of books, documents and ceramics, design, drawing, gilding, graphic design, jewellery, life drawing, painting, picture framing, portfolio preparation, pottery, printmaking, sculpture, stained glass and textiles. The programme provides opportunities to study weekdays, in the evening and on Saturdays. Courses vary from one day schools to year long courses. Students can attend

Courses:
Animation. Art History. Ceramics. Design (Graphic). Fine Art. Illustration. Jewellery/Silversmithing. Textiles.
Qualifications:
Adult Education. Diploma in Ceramics. Foundation.

UNIVERSITY COLLEGE OF RIPON AND YORK ST. JOHN

Lord Mayor's Walk, York YO3 7EX.
Tel: *01904-656771.* **Fax:** *01904-612512.*
Email *f.coupar@ucrysj.ac.uk*
Ws *http://www.ucrysj.ac.uk*
Nearest Station: *York.*
Personnel: *Assistant Registrar (Admissions):*
Ian Waghorn. *Dean of Creative & Performing*
Arts: Finlay Coupar.

THE UNIVERSITY COLLEGE OF
RIPON & YORK
ST JOHN

The University College of Ripon & York St.
John offers degrees in art and design and technology, which are awarded by the University
of Leeds. There are also opportunities for
part-time study.
Teaching is undertaken by staff who are themselves practising artists, designers and crafts-
men/women exhibiting nationally and internationally and supported by highly qualified
and experienced technicians.
Spacious, modern studios and workshops are
resourced with state-of-the-art equipment.
All art and design programmes are studied in
the centre of York, one of Europe's premier
locations.
Courses:
Art History. Ceramics. Fine Art. Furniture.
Jewellery/Silversmithing. Textiles.
Qualifications:
Degree. Post Graduate. Teacher Training.

UNIVERSITY OF PLYMOUTH

Faculty of Arts and Education, Earl Richards
Road North, Exeter, EX2 6AS.
Tel: *01392-475022.* **Fax:** *01392-475012.*
Email *fae-admissions@plymouth.ac.uk*
Ws *http://www.fae.plym.ac.uk/*
Nearest Station: *Exeter St. Davids, Exeter*
Central.

Based in Exeter and Exmouth, the Faculty of
Arts & Education offers a wide range of programmes in Arts & Design disciplines at
undergraduate, postgraduate and research
level.
The Art & Design programme includes: Fine
Art; Design & Italian; Illustration;
Photography; Typography and 3D Design.
The Combines Arts programme includes: Art
History; Media Arts; Visual Arts, all of which
can be studied as single honours, majors or
options with another subject. Art and Design
is also a subject, specialism in the Teacher
Education programmes at upper and lower pri-
mary and secondary level.
Courses:
Art History. Ceramics. Design (3-D). Design
(Graphic). Design (Photography). Design
(Typographic). Fine Art. Furniture. Illustration.
Media.
Qualifications:
Degree. Post Graduate. Teacher Training.

UNIVERSITY OF WALES, ABERYSTWYTH

School of Art, Buarth Mawr, Aberystwyth,
SY23 1NE.
Tel: *01970-622460.* **Fax:** *01970-622461.*
Courses:
Art History. Fine Art.

VISUAL ISLAMIC & TRADITIONAL ARTS DEPT.

The Prince of Wales's Institute of Architecture,
Unit 6A, 44 Gloucester Avenue, London NW1
8JD.
Tel: *0171-916 9740.* **Fax:** *0171-916 9741.*
Email *vita@easynet.co.uk*
Opening times: *Mon-Thurs 9-8.30. Fri 9-*
5.30
Nearest Underground: *Camden/Chalk*
Farm.
Personnel: *Administrator:* R. Suzuki.
The V.I.T.A. department offers a unique
opportunity to study both the theory and the
practise of visual Islamic and traditional arts
at higher education level.
Students are encouraged to pursue their own
particular skill - whether it be painting,
wood/stone carving, jewellery, ceramics,
stained glass etc., at the same time as attend-
ing classes in geometry, calligraphy, arabesque
and others.
Courses:
Fine Art.
Qualifications:
Post Graduate.

WARWICKSHIRE COLLEGE, SCHOOL OF ART AND DESIGN

Warwick New Road, Leamington Spa, CV32
5JE.
Tel: *01926-318000.* **Fax:** *01926-318111.*
Email *enquiries@warkscol.ac.uk*
Ws *http://www.warkscol.ac.uk*
Nearest Station: *Leamington Spa/Coventry.*
Personnel: *Deputy Director:* Dean Hancox.

The School of Art & Design is a centre of
excellence. Its 600 full-time students (and
similar number attending part-time) involve
themselves in a comprehensive range of studies - from media studies to information technology and computer generated image making
as well as the traditional studies of fine art,
design, crafts and creative activities. You
would expect to find all this. But in
Leamington, you will also find an unusual
warmth and friendliness, a commitment
to high standards. You will find an outward
looking school, with close links to industry
and professional practice and an awareness of
its role in the wider community, and you may
discover an opportunity to begin a career.
The School of Art & Design encourages a
spirit of curiosity in students and staff alike.
Will you find what you're looking for? Only
you can judge. Come and see it for yourself.
Courses:
Animation. Art History. Ceramics. Design
(Automotive). Design (Graphic). Fine Art.
Furniture. Illustration.
Jewellery/Silversmithing. Textiles.
Qualifications:
Adult Education. Degree. Foundation. Post
Graduate. Teacher Training.

NOTES

ART MANAGEMENT AND PROMOTION

Art Consultants, Art Management, Digital Graphics, Electronic Services, Information Services, Marketing Services & PR, Public Art Agencies.

THE ART WORLD
DIRECTORY
1998/99 25TH EDITION

" ... well researched, highly effective and good value too" - the Design Museum

media contacts: visual arts

everything you need to know to organise successful and cost-effective publicity campaigns

Comprehensive press information service for museums, galleries, artists and curators. Databases, discs and directories listing over 1000 up-to-date visual arts correspondents in all areas of the media, from the national newspapers, to local radio programmes to internet sites; along with notes on deadlines, editorial schedules and inside advice on getting good coverage.

make sure all your exhibitions receive the best possible press coverage - subscribe to media contacts: visual arts.

Used by the National Gallery, the National Portrait Gallery, the Courtauld Institute, the Barbican Art Gallery, the Imperial War Museum, the Museum of Modern Art, Oxford, the British Museum, the Whitworth Art Gallery, the National Museums and Galleries of Scotland, Manchester City Art Gallery, White Cube and Anthony d'Offay.

Call 0171 610 9991

Subscriptions start from £95 p.a. Published by artsinform, Cooper House, 2 Michael Road, SW6 2AD
T: 0171 610 9991, F: 0171 610 9992, W: artsinform.demon.co.uk

ART MANAGEMENT & PROMOTION

ART CONSULTANTS

ALEXANDRA WETTSTEIN FINE ART C
15 Rommany Road, London SE27 9PY.
Tel: *0181-761 4580.*
Fax: *0181-473 1721.* **Email**
alexandra.wettstein@virgin.net
Ws *http://graffiti.virgin.net/alexandra.wettstein/*
Opening times: *9-6 and By appointment.*
Nearest Underground: BR:
W.Dulwich/Gypsy Hill/W. Norwood.
Personnel: *Proprietor:* Alexandra Wettstein.

Alexandra Wettstein deal primarily in the sale of recognised modern and contemporary art created from c.1880 to the present day. The business also deals in up and coming, but as yet less well known contemporary artists. Alexandra Wettstein has available unique works and limited edition works on paper as well as sculpture and ceramics.
The company will locate specific works not in stock and provides framing, restoration and valuation services irrespective of whether or not the work was originally purchased from Alexandra Wettstein Fine Art.
Services and Facilities:
Art Consultancy. Art for Offices. Commissioning Service. Parking. Valuation.
Work Stocked and Sold:
Cer. Dr. Pa. Pr. Sc.
Price range: £50 - £150,000.

ANNE BERTHOUD
4a Stanley Crescent, London W11 2NB.
Tel: *0171-229 8400.*
Fax: *0171-221 8185.*
Opening times: *By appt.*
Nearest Underground: *Notting Hill Gate.*
Personnel: *Director:* Anne Berthoud.
Contemporary British and international paintings, drawings, prints, sculpture, ceramics and photographs. Agency and organisation of exhibitions. Anne Berthoud is also personally available for consultancy services.
Services and Facilities:
Art Consultancy. Commissioning Service. Valuation.
Work Stocked and Sold:
Cer. Dr. Pa. Ph. Pr. Sc.

ART CONTACT LTD
2 Rickett Street, London SW6 1RU.
Tel: *0171-381 8655.* **Fax:** *0171-386 9015.*
Email *jt@artcontact.co.uk*
Ws *http://www.artcontact.co.uk*
Opening times: *Office hours, by appointment.*
Personnel: *Director:* Julian Thomas.

Art Contact
Art Consultants for office interiors and private clients. Rent or buy: Original works - Commissions - Prints - Sculpture - Limited Editions. Framing and Installation.
Services and Facilities:
Art Consultancy. Art for Offices. Commissioning Service. Framing. Restoration.

ART FOR OFFICES C
International Art Consultants, The Galleries, 15 Dock Street, London E1 8JL.
Tel: *0171-481 1337.* **Fax:** *0171-481 3425.*
Email *art@artservs.demon.co.uk*
Opening times: *Open Mon-Fri 9.30-6.*
Nearest Underground: *Tower Hill, Aldgate, Aldgate East.*
Personnel: *Directors:* Andrew Hutchinson, Peter Harris. Amanda Basker.
We have 20 years experience advising architects, designers and corporate clients on the planning and implementation of art programmes.
Our 10,000 square foot galleries provide a central source of art, enabling clients and specifiers to view a comprehensive range of art on a single visit to one location.
We deal directly with over 800 artists and have a large visual reference library covering art in all media which is cross referenced by style and price. This makes it possible to research works of art, or artists for commission quickly and effectively. Art can be purchased, commissioned or acquired on a flexible rental basis.
Services and Facilities:
Art Consultancy. Art for Offices. Commissioning Service. Framing. Parking.
Work Stocked and Sold:
Cer. Cra. Dr. Gla. Pa. Ph. Pr. Sc. Tx. Wd.
Price range: £100 - £50,000.

THE ART MOVEMENT
120 Beaufort Mansions, Beaufort Street, London SW3 5AE. **Tel:** *0171-351 0510, Mobile 0973-692494.* **Fax:** *0171-351 0510.*

AXLA ART CONSULTANTS C
121 Ledbury Road, London W11.
Tel: *0171-727 9724, 0171-229 7267.*

BELINDA CANOSA
38 St. Marys Grove, London W4 3LN.
Tel: *0181-747 0436.* **Fax:** *0181-995 1099.*

BRANDLER GALLERIES C
1 Coptfold Road, Brentwood, CM14 4BM.
Tel: *01277-222269.*
Fax: *01277-222786.*
Email *art.british@dial.pipex.com*
Ws *http://www.brandler-galleries.com*
Opening times: *Tues-Sat 10-5.30.*
Nearest Station: *Brentwood 400 yds, Shenfield 1 mile.*
Personnel: *Director:* John Brandler. Linda

Rodrigues.A friendly gallery just 2 miles from exit 28 on the M25 with free parking. A wide selection of prints and paintings by British old and modern masters.

Brandler Galleries

As we purchase virtually all our stock we have to choose the best examples. Without the London overheads our clients know they get a much better deal on the same artists, without having to fight to get into London with all its problems. We are happy to send photographs or E-Mail images before your trip. Clients include banks, insurance companies and collectors all wanting the best art at realistic prices.
Services and Facilities:
Art Consultancy. Art for Offices. Commissioning Service. Framing. Parking. Restoration. Valuation.
Work Stocked and Sold:
Cer. Dr. Pa. Pr. Sc.
Price range: £50 - £65,000.

BUSINESS ART GALLERIES C
New Academy Gallery, 34 Windmill Street, Fitzrovia, London W1P 1HH.
Tel: *0171-323 4700.* **Fax:** *0171-436 3059.*
Ws *http://www.screenpages.co.uk/ac/newacademy/index.html*
Opening times: *Mon-Fri 10-6 (Thurs 10-8), Sat 11-5 (closed Bank Holiday Weekends).*
Nearest Underground: *Goodge Street, Tottenham Court Road.*
Personnel: *Directors:* John Hutchings, Jill Hutchings. *Contact:* Caroline Brown.

Business Art Galleries was founded within the Royal Academy of Art in 1978 and is Britain's longest established art consultants. Now an independent company, we offer a comprehensive corporate art service including: free consultations and on-site presentation, a flexible hire scheme and special commissions.
Our two sister galleries, the New Academy Gallery and Curwen Gallery, provide us with an extensive permanent stock of work as well as a changing monthly programme of exhibitions. This includes painting, limited edition prints and sculpture from both leading and up-and-coming contemporary British artists.
Services and Facilities:
Art Consultancy. Art for Offices. Commissioning Service.
Work Stocked and Sold:
Dr. Pa. Pr. Sc.
Price range: £50 - £20,000.

COLLOMB-EAST ASSOCIATES
London **Tel:** *0171-409 1595.*

Ab *Artist's Books* **App** *Applied Art* **Cer** *Ceramics* **Cra** *Crafts* **Dec** *Decorative* **Dr** *Drawing*
Fur *Furniture* **Gla** *Glass* **Jew** *Jewellery* **Pa** *Paintings* **Ph** *Photography* **Pr** *Prints*
Sc *Sculpture* **Tx** *Textiles* **Wd** *Wood*

COODE-ADAMS MARTIN ASSOCIATES
Inworth Hall, Inworth, Colchester, CO5 9SN.
Tel: *01376-561946.* **Fax:** *01376-570318.*

DAVIES & TOOTH
5 Northfields Prospect, Putney Bridge Road, London SW18 1PE.
Tel: *0181-875 0820.* **Fax:** *0181-877 1741.*

DE PUTRON ART CONSULTANTS
27 Pattison Road, London NW2 2HL.
Tel: *0171-431 1125.* **Fax:** *0171-431 1125.*
Opening times: *By appointment only.*
Nearest Underground: *Hampstead/Golders Green.*
Personnel: *Director: Laura de Putron.*

An art consultancy that provides a professional and comprehensive service to clients in the corporate and private sectors.
It represents artists who specialise in painting, portraiture, sculpture, murals and the applied arts. These artists represent the very highest standards and are individually selected by the consultancy. They range from well-established names to the 'rising stars' who have just entered the market place.
The consultancy works directly with corporate and private clients, architects and interior designers, and offers total flexibility of service irrespective of job size and complexity.
Artwork can be purchased, rented or commissioned. Free consultation offered to all enquirers.
Services and Facilities:
Art Consultancy. Art for Offices. Commissioning Service.
Work Stocked and Sold:
App. Cer. Dr. Gla. Pa. Pr. Sc. Tx. Wd.
Price range: £100 - £50,000.

DICKSON RUSSELL ART MANAGEMENT
7 Queen Anne's Gardens, Bedford Park, London, W4 1TU.
Tel: *0181-747 3066 & 0171-733 7137.*
Fax: *0181-742 7831.*
Opening times: *By appointment.*
Nearest Underground: *Turnham Green.*
Personnel: *Directors: Rachel Dickson, Emma Russell.*
Dickson Russell provides a complete range of art management services for both corporate and private clients, to include art acquisition, exhibition curation, project management for commissioned works, and maintenance of existing collections. Art of all media and from across all periods can be sourced to suit the client's business, profile and location.
Additional services can include professional packing, shipping, restoration, framing, installation and photographing of artwork; catalogue literature, insurance updates and valuations are also undertaken. A professional fee is charged; no commission is taken on purchased artworks.
Services and Facilities:
Art Consultancy. Art for Offices. Commissioning Service. Framing. Restoration. Valuation.

EGEE ART CONSULTANCY *C*
9 Chelsea Manor Studios, Flood Street, London SW3 5SR.
Tel: *0171-351 6818.* **Fax:** *0171-376 3510.*
Email *egee.art@btinternet.com*
Ws *http://www.globebyte.co.uk/egee/egeeart.htm*
OR *http://www.egeeart.co.uk*
Opening times: *Mon-Fri 8.30-5.30, Sat by arrangement. By appointment.*
Nearest Underground: *Sloane Square or South Kensington.*
Personnel: *Director:* Dale Egee. *Sales:* Yvonne Eklund. *Art Consultant:* Kate Brown. *Administrator:* Barbara Allen.

EGEE ART CONSULTANCY

Specialists in art for the Middle East for twenty years. We have a wide range of antique and contemporary Arab and Orientalist art at our Gallery in London, our own range of editioned prints suitable for hotels and corporate interiors, and exclusive Alhambra plaques in painted resin and sterling silver.
We find art that is appropriate for the Middle East, from reproductions to fine paintings and unique commissioned works. Our clients range from private collectors to governments and corporations, and we will be pleased to discuss your artwork requirements. Please contact us for an appointment, or to request our brochures.
Services and Facilities:
Art Consultancy. Art for Offices. Commissioning Service. Framing. Restoration. Valuation.
Work Stocked and Sold:
Cra. Dr. Pa. Ph. Pr. Sc. Tx.
Price range: £50 - £35,000.

FEDERATION OF BRITISH ARTISTS
Mall Galleries, 17 Carlton House Terrace, London, SW1Y 5BD.
Tel: *0171-930 6844.* **Fax:** *0171-839 7830.*
Personnel: *Katy Letman.*
The FBA runs a Fine Art Commission and Advisory Service on behalf of nine professional art societies, including The Royal Society of Portrait Painters. In the relaxed atmosphere of the commissions room, the FBA provides the opportunity to view examples of work, including oils, pastels and watercolours by over 600 member artists.

HOWICK CONTEMPORARY ART CONSULTANTS
The Side House, 18 Parkhill Road, London NW3 2YN.
Tel: *0171-284 2614.* **Fax:** *0171-267 7861.*
Opening times: *Opening: normal office hours and visits by appointment only.*
Nearest Underground: *Belsize Park.*
Personnel: *Louisa Howick. Alistair Howick.*
A professional art consultancy providing a

comprehensive and personal service to architects, interior designers and corporate clients on a wide range of art works.

Imaginative well-researched solutions, including commissions, purchasing, and rentals within set budgets.
Services and Facilities:
Art Consultancy. Art for Offices. Commissioning Service. Framing. Parking. Restoration. Valuation.
Work Stocked and Sold:
Cer. Cra. Dec. Dr. Fur. Gla. Pa. Ph. Pr. Sc. Tx. Wd.

IMAGES, CORPORATE ART CONSULTANTS
19 Helenslea Avenue, Golders Green, London, NW11 8NE.
Tel: *0181-455 3160.*

JAMES COX CONSULTANCY
Lynton House, 48 Lynton Road, Rayners Lane, Harrow, HA2 9NN

KATHRYN BELL/FINE ART CONSULTANCY
Studio 123D, Canalot Production Studios, 222 Kensal Road, London W10 5BN.
Tel: *0181-960 0070.*
Fax: *0181-960 0209.*
Opening times: *By appt.*
Nearest Underground: *Westbourne Park.*
Personnel: *Director:* Kathryn Bell.
Our art consultancy and exhibition programme are now established in London and Tokyo.
We represent British and Japanese based artists and try to encourage a true cross cultural exchange; by bringing artists to work, exhibit and teach in the 'opposite' culture and then by including these artists in exhibitions and site specific commissions.
Our approach is independent and unique and appeals to both private and corporate collectors. The artists we have recently worked with include the sculptors Noe Aoki, Danny Lane and Vanessa Pooley, the textile artists Shelley Goldsmith and Marta Rogoyska, and the painters James Brook, Chikako Mori and Fraser Taylor.
Services and Facilities:
Art Consultancy. Art for Offices. Commissioning Service. Lectures. Valuation.
Work Stocked and Sold:
App. Dr. Gla. Pa. Ph. Pr. Sc. Tx. Wd.
Price range: £500 - £40,000.

LONDON ART CONSULTANCY *C*
29 Hollywood Road, London, SW10.
Tel: *0171-351 7711.*

Ab Artist's Books **App** Applied Art **Cer** Ceramics **Cra** Crafts
Dec Decorative **Dr** Drawing **Fur** Furniture

ART MANAGEMENT & PROMOTION

LONDON ARTFORMS *C*
*Low Ground Floor, 7-15 Rosebery Avenue,
London, EC1.* **Tel:** *0171-837 1900.*

LOUISE PICKERING FINE ART
18 Juer Street, London SW11 4RF.
Tel: *0171-228 3481.* **Fax:** *0171-585 0282.*

LYNNE STERN & LINNET FEILDING
*Art Consultancy & Management, 46 Bedford
Row, London WC1R 4LR.* **Tel:** *0171-491
8905.* **Fax:** *0171-624 7072.*
A professional art consultancy and management team with particular experience in working with corporate clients, architects and designers and in managing large and small art projects, to time schedules and budgets. Independent with wide expertise including working in the business art section at the Royal Academy; for each client project, works selected from in-depth knowledge of established and younger generation artists in a wide range of media, for purchase or commission. Management and maintenance of existing works of art and collections also provided. Awarded the Art and Work Award 1996.
Services and Facilities:
*Art Consultancy. Art for Offices. Commissioning
Service. Lectures.*

SARAH MYERSCOUGH ASSOCIATES *C*
40 South Molton Street, London W1Y 1HB.
Tel: *0171-495 0069.* **Fax:** *0171-493 2354.*
Opening times: *10-6.*
Nearest Underground: *Bond Street.*
Personnel: *Specialist Art Consultant
Contemporary Art:* Sarah Myerscough.
Enliven the office and create a stimulating work environment by collecting contemporary art. Art need not be an expensive option and if carefully selected can make a very powerful and singular statement. Contact Sarah Myerscough who gives specialist advice, on site presentations, arranges installation and aftercare to the corporate and private market.
Services and Facilities:
*Art Consultancy. Art for Offices. Commissioning
Service. Framing. Restoration. Valuation.*
Work Stocked and Sold:
App. Cra. Dr. Pa. Pr. Sc. Tx.
Price range: £100 - £100,000.

**TANJA GERTIK
FINE ART CONSULTANT**
*First Floor, 42 Welbeck Street, London W1M
7HF.* **Tel:** *0171-483 4526.* **Fax:** *0171-486
1667.*
Complete Fine Art Consultancy and comprehensive art management services for corporate and private collectors. Independent advice on the acquisition, rental and site specific commission of art. From on site presentation through project management to cataloguing and maintenance of existing art collections. Additional services include development of corporate art programmes, exhibition curating and advice on art sponsorship opportunities. Paintings, sculpture, applied arts, stained glass and textiles are sourced from artists studios, commercial galleries, auction houses and private dealers.

**UNICORN CONSULTANCY
(UNICORN PICTURES LTD)**
65 Corringway, London W5 3HB.
Tel: *0181-998 2611.* **Fax:** *0181-998 2611.*
Opening times: *Anytime, by appointment.*
Nearest Underground: *Park Royal, North
Ealing.*
Personnel: *Director:* John Simmons FRSA.
Consultant: Maurizio Castronovo. *Consultant:*
Lynne Fitzgerald.
(Established 1961). Fine art project consultants. Unicorn provides new and adventurous paintings and sculptures by award-winning British artists with rising reputations, to Parliamentary, corporate and private collections; and in-house exhibitions in corporate premises.

Ambassador for London Award 1995.
Services and Facilities:
*Art Consultancy. Art for Offices. Commissioning
Service.*
Work Stocked and Sold:
Cer. Gla. Pa. Pr. Sc. Tx.
Price range: £500 - £7,500.

WILLIAM HARDIE LTD
*Fine Art Consultants and Valuers, 15a
Blythswood Square, Glasgow G2 4BG.*
Tel: *0141-221 6780.* **Fax:** *0141-248 6237.*

WORK PLACE ART CONSULTANTS *C*
*Globe Studio, 62 Southwark Bridge, London
SE1.* **Tel:** *0171-401 9494.*

ART MANAGEMENT

ART CONNECT
P.O. Box 85, Edgeware, HA8 0UY.
Tel: *0181-906 1930.*
Personnel: Miss McNeil.

Art Connect

Art Connect are a non-profit organisation formed to help contemporary artists establish themselves within the commercial sector. Art Connect has the benefit of being managed by people experienced in commerce with valuable contacts throughout the UK and abroad, all with a common interest and love of art who understand the difficulty of an artist earning a living through their talent.
Art Connect's aim, using our commercial expertise is to help all talented artists new or established to promote and sell their work and to assist in finding new markets suited to their particular skill set.
Services and Facilities:
*Art Consultancy. Commissioning Service.
Framing. Gallery space for hire.*

ART FOR OFFICES *C*
*International Art Consultants, The Galleries, 15
Dock Street, London E1 8JL.*
Tel: *0171-481 1337.* **Fax:** *0171-481 3425.*
Email *art@artservs.demon.co.uk*
Opening times: *Open Mon-Fri 9.30-6.*
Nearest Underground: *Tower Hill,
Aldgate, Aldgate East.*
Personnel: *Directors:* Andrew Hutchinson, Peter Harris. Amanda Basker.
We have 20 years experience advising architects, designers and corporate clients on the planning and implementation of art programmes.
Our 10,000 square foot galleries provide a central source of art, enabling clients and specifiers to view a comprehensive range of art on a single visit to one location.
We deal directly with over 800 artists and have a large visual reference library covering art in all media which is cross referenced by style and price. This makes it possible to research works of art, or artists for commission quickly and effectively. Art can be purchased, commissioned or acquired on a flexible rental basis.
Services and Facilities:
*Art Consultancy. Art for Offices. Commissioning
Service. Framing. Parking.*
Work Stocked and Sold:
*Cer. Cra. Dr. Gla. Pa. Ph. Pr. Sc. Tx.
Wd.*
Price range: £100 - £50,000.

**HERITAGE LOTTERY FUND AND THE
NATIONAL HERITAGE MEMORIAL FUND**
7 Holbein Place, London SW1W 8NR.
Tel: *0171-591 6000.* **Fax:** *0171-591 6001.*

INDEPENDENT PUBLIC ARTS *C*
17 Bernard Street, Leith, Edinburgh EH6 6PW.
Tel: *0131-555 0045.* **Fax:** *0131-554 1850.*

DIGITAL GRAPHICS

RUTTERS/SCANACHROME
*16 Jacksons Lane, Great Chesterford, Saffron
Waldron, CB10 1PU.*
Tel: *01799-531049, Mobile 0973-631052.*
Fax: *01799-530651.*
Email *rutters@scanachrome.com*
Ws *www.scanachrome.com/rutters*
Personnel: Paul Rutter.
Rutters specialise in the production of one-off and short run, large format images onto a broad range of fabric and vinyl substrates where conventional printing is impractical. Applications

---

Gla Glass *Jew* Jewellery *Pa* Paintings *Ph* Photography *Pr* Prints
Sc Sculpture *Tx* Textiles *Wd* Wood

include blinds, murals, backdrops, banners, reproduction paintings and decorative hoardings for interior decor; retail, graphic and exterior use.

With a wealth of experience in all aspects of image production, Rutters can advise on a project from design through to installation.

ELECTRONIC SERVICES

THE LMR COMPUTER CONSULTANCY
19 South Walk, Wickham, BR4 9JA.
Tel: *0181-462 7740.*
Fax: *0181-462 7739.* **Email** *lmr@compuserve.com*
Personnel: Les Rodger.
For the last 15 years we have specialised in providing art clients in the UK and around the world with complete computer packages, from Single User PCs to Multi-User Networks. We design and set up stock databases, comprehensive client files, accounts systems, invoicing systems, word processing, desktop publishing, email and laptop/pc communications packages along with a complete training program in a range of today's most popular software. Telephone or fax for more information.

THESAURUS GROUP LTD
Mill Court, Furlongs, Newport, PO30 2AA.
Tel: *01983-826000.* **Fax:** *01983-826201.*
Ws *thesaurus.co.uk/*
Personnel: *Managing Director:* John Woracker.
Comprehensive pre-sale information products based on auction data from around the world giving the user access to in excess of 7,000 sales and 4 million objects each year from over 600 auction houses in the UK and North America.
Services and Facilities:
Bookshop. Valuation.

INFORMATION SERVICES

ARTISTS' GENERAL BENEVOLENT INSTITUTION
Burlington House, Piccadilly, London W1V 0DJ.
Tel: *0171-734 1193.*
Fax: *0171 734 1193.*
Personnel: *Secretary:* Miss April Connett-Dance.
A charity managed by artists to provide financial assistance for members of the profession who are in need, as result of illness, accident or old age. Widows of artists are also eligible to apply. The AGBI depends on voluntary contributions to carry out this work. There is also an Artists' Orphan Fund.

ARTSINFORM
Cooper House, 2 Michael Road, London SW6 2AD.
Tel: *0171-610 9991.* **Fax:** *0171-610 9992.*
Email *artsinform.demon.co.uk*
Opening times: *10-6.*
Nearest Underground: *Fulham Broadway.*
Personnel: *Directors:* Ms Jessica Wood, Ms Rosie Clarke.
Press information service for the visual arts. Directories, discs and databases which list over 1000 up-to-date art correspondents in the press, broadcast and electronic media; along with deadlines, editorial schedules, advance and inside information on getting press coverage for exhibitions and events. Used by hundreds of museums, galleries, artists and exhibition organisers across the UK including: the National Gallery, the British Museum, the Design Museum, the National Galleries of Scotland, the Museum of Modern Art, Oxford, Arnolfini, the Barbican Art Gallery, White Cube, Anthony d'Offay.

AXIS
Leeds Metropolitan University, Calverley Street, Leeds LS1 3HE.
Tel: *0113-283 3125.* **Fax:** *0113-283 5938.*
Email *axis@gn.apc.org*
Ws *http://www.lmu.ac.uk/ces/axis*
Opening times: *Mon-Fri 9-5.*
Personnel: *Principle Information Officer:* Cath Bentley.

For Information on Visual Artists

Axis is a visual arts service providing information about contemporary artists and craftspeople living/working in Britain. The service is free and available to all.
The information is displayed on a computer database, the Axis database. The Axis database contains each artist's CV and up to nine images of their work. Nearly 2,500 are registered.
The Axis database is available at access points around the UK. Alternatively, information can be provided over the phone and by post. Printouts of CVs and artwork images are available at nominal cost. Axis is mainly funded by the Arts Councils of England, Scotland and Wales.

THE INTERNATIONAL ARTS BUREAU
4 Baden Place, Crosby Row, London SE1 1YW.
Tel: *0171-403 6454.* **Fax:** *0171-403 2009.*
Email *lab@mcmail.com*
Opening times: *9.30-5.30.*
Nearest Underground: *London Bridge.*
Personnel: *Director:* Rod Fisher. *Manager:* Valerie Synmoie.
The International Arts Bureau is an independent agency providing information, advice, research, publications, training and consultancy on international arts issues. The Bureau offers:- a free enquiry service. Contact should be made by telephone (0171-403 7001) or by

letter or fax; free monthly one-to-one funding advice surgeries; a bi-monthly journal outlining key policy issues, prospective legislation, funding deadlines, and case studies (available on subscription); tailored training courses and information seminars on a range of international arts issues.
The Bureau is also the official UK contact point for the European Commission's cultural funding programmes - Kaleidoscope, Raphael and Ariane.
Services and Facilities:
Art Consultancy.

MARKETING SERVICES & PR

ALAN SYKES PROMOTIONS
Talkin Head Farm, Brampton, CA8 1LT.
Tel: *016977-2228.* **Fax:** *016977-2228.*
Email *alansykes@talkinhead.demon.co.uk*
Personnel: Alan Sykes.
Specialises in getting national press coverage for the arts in the regions. Has worked recently on successful publicity for Bill Viola's "The Messenger" in Durham Cathedral, Lucian Freud's exhibition at Abbot Hall, Kendal, David Mach's brick "Train" in Darlington, Andy Goldsworthy's "Sheepfolds" in Cumbria and Claes Oldenburg's "Bottle of Notes" in Middlesbrough.
Also managed publicity for campaign against closure of the Hatton Gallery at Newcastle University. "PR mastermind" - The Herald (Glasgow), September 1996, "There must be 100s of projects outside London which could use the Sykes touch," - Arts Management Weekly, November 1996, "outstanding" - The Guardian, June 1997.
Services and Facilities:
Art Consultancy. Art for Offices.

ART MARKET RESEARCH
85 Stoke Newington Church, London N16.
Tel: *0171-249 8071.*

BRIAN POTTER AND ASSOCIATES
12 Ryeworth Road, Charlton Kings, Cheltenham, GL52 6LH.
Tel: *01242-529121.* **Fax:** *01242-513495.*

JAMES KESSELL DESIGN CONSULTANTS
Meadows Edge, Gibraltar, Aylesbury, HP17 8TY. **Tel:** *01296-747446.* **Fax:** *01844-292150.*

JOHN HAYWOOD PRESS AND PUBLIC RELATIONS C
67 Gordon House, Glamis Road, London E1 9ED. **Tel:** *0171-481 3073.*

LAYZELL PUBLIC RELATIONS FOR THE ARTS
Little Orchard, Dallinghoo, Woodbridge, IP13 0LG. **Tel:** *01473-737468.* **Fax:** *01473-737750.*
Personnel: *Director:* Alistair Layzell.
Layzell Public Relations for the Arts specialise in publicity for exhibitions, events, fairs and books on the arts; the co-ordination and

organisation of festivals, openings and launches. High profile coverage has been achieved for artists, gallery owners and publishers, on national and regional television and radio and in the national and specialist art press. Marketing services.

PARKER HARRIS AND COMPANY
15 Church Street, Esher, KT10 8YZ.
Tel: 01372-462190. **Fax:** 01372-460032.
Opening times: *Open daily 9-5.*
Personnel: *Partners:* Penny Harris, Emma Parker.
Parker Harris and Company specialise in all aspects of arts administration, exhibition organising, press and public relations. As well as organising national touring events such as the Jerwood Painting Prize, The Hunting Art Prizes and the Singer Friedlander/Sunday Times Watercolour Competition, they also arrange one man shows throughout the UK and Europe, liaising between artist, gallery, buyer and press.

SUE BOND PUBLIC RELATIONS C
Boxted Hall, Boxted, Bury St. Edmunds, IP29 4JT. **Tel:** 01787-282288. **Fax:** 01787-282119.

YVONNE COURTNEY PR
5a Bramber Road, London W1A 9PA.
Tel: 0171-795 6001.

PUBLIC ART AGENCIES

CARDIFF BAY ARTS TRUST
123 Bute Street, Cardiff CF1 6AE.
Tel: 01222-488772. **Fax:** 01222 472439.
Email *Arts.Trust@ENABLIS.co.uk*
Personnel: *Director:* Sue Grayson Ford.
CBAT works as a consultant for Public Art Projects in the Cardiff Bay regeneration area. Since 1991 we have managed over 60 projects varying from environmental improvements. Workshops, artist collaborations in urban design teams to temporary and permanent artworks as part of the new and existing urban fabric.
CBAT works in collaboration with local residents, public authorities, the private sector, artists and craft workers in the initiation and implementation of commissions. Whilst concentrating its efforts in the regenerated docklands of Cardiff, CBAT is willing to consider consultancies nationwide.
Services and Facilities:
Art Consultancy. Art for Offices. Commissioning Service.

CYWAITH CYMRU - ARTWORKS WALES P
2 John Street, Cardiff CF1 5AE.
Tel: 01222-489543. **Fax:** 01222-465458.
Email *cywaith@netcomuk.co.uk*
Nearest Station: *Cardiff Central.*
Personnel: *Director:* Tamara Krikorian.
Deputy Director: Simon Fenoulhet.
Administrator: Nia Roberts.
Artworks Wales was established in 1981 as the Welsh Sculpture Trust to encourage the plac-

ing of art in the environment through commissions, exhibition and residencies.

The wide range of work covered by the organisation is supported by a strong commitment to the cultural life of Wales, seeking to bring about new work which is particular to its environment and which reflects the culture from which it comes.
Cywaith Cymru works closely with local authorities, industry, environmental groups and arts organisations. It encourages creative collaboration between artists, architects, landscape architects and developers. Registered charity No. 512006. Commissioning Service.
Services and Facilities:
Art Consultancy. Commissioning Service.
Work Stocked and Sold:
Sc.

FREE FORM ARTS TRUST
38 Dalston Lane, London E8 3AZ.
Tel: 0171-249 3394.
Fax: 0171-249 8499. **Email**
freeform@ffat1.globalnet.co.uk
Nearest Underground: *Dalston Kingsland.*
Personnel: *Associate Director:* Barbara Wheeler-Early. *Training Co-ordinator:* Patrick Burton.
Artist-led national community and public arts organisation. Regeneration of the urban landscape and social and physical environmental improvement. Partnership with clients and users at all design stages to create 'a sense of place'.
Public Art commissioning. Work based training programme for skilled artists to work with communities in public art. Examples of range of work include school and estate improvements to community festivals (Fish Quay Festival, N. Tyneside, with a million visitors a year is now part of local tradition).
Current work includes major regeneration schemes in Peckham, Bolton, Reading; project development work in Redbridge and Hove; subway decoration, Westminster.
Services and Facilities:
Art Consultancy. Commissioning Service.

PUBLIC ART COMMISSIONS AGENCY
Studio 6, Victoria Works, Vittoria Street, Jewellery Quarter, Birmingham B1 3
Tel: 0121-212 4454. **Fax:** 0121-212 4426.
Personnel: *Director:* Vivien Lovell.
London office:- *c/o 116 Commercial Street, London E1 6NF.*
The Public Art Commissions Agency is constituted as a company limited by guarantee, registered as an educational charity, and governed by a Council of Trustees.
The Agency works nationally with a wide range of public and private sector clients. Organisation objectives: the Agency's aim is to develop and carry out a programme of visual arts commissions and residencies by professional artists and craftspeople.
It ensures that work of the highest quality is produced in a context of appropriate consultation with the community for which it is intended; advocates, through collaboration with the appropriate professional and statutory bodies, that the visual arts are fully integrated into projects of architectural or environmental design. Presentations, seminars, workshops organised.
Services and Facilities:
Art Consultancy. Commissioning Service. Lectures. Workshop Facilities.

Gla *Glass* **Jew** *Jewellery* **Pa** *Paintings* **Ph** *Photography* **Pr** *Prints*
Sc *Sculpture* **Tx** *Textiles* **Wd** *Wood*

THE ARTWORLD
DIRECTORY 1998/99 **223**

NOTES

ART SERVICES

THE ART WORLD
DIRECTORY
1998/99 25TH EDITION

Additional copies of the Art World Directory.

Save more than 20%.

Use this form to buy additional copies of this edition for just £9.95 plus £2.00 p&p.

Simply complete the form below and return with your remittance to Art Review, Art World Directory, Freepost, London EC1B 1DE. *(A photocopy of the page is fine).*

Art World Directory Additional Copies Order Form.

Please send me _____ additional copy(ies) of the 1998/99 Art World Directory @ £9.95 plus £2.00 p&p each.*

I enclose my remittance for £ _____ made payable to Art Review Ltd.

Please debit my ☐ Access ☐ Visa ☐ Amex ☐ Mastercard

Card No: _____ Expiry Date _____

Signature _____ Date _____

Name _____ Address _____

_____ Postcode _____

Tel _____ (in case of queries only)

Ref: AWDF1

*The postage and packing cost relates to UK orders only, European p&p £3.00, Overseas £6.00.

CONSERVATION AND RESTORATION

THE ART WORLD
DIRECTORY
1998/99 25TH EDITION

ABBOTT & HOLDER
30 Museum Street, London WC1A 1LH.
Tel: *0171-637 3981.*
Fax: *0171-631 0575.*
Email *abbott.holder@virgin.net*
Ws *http://www.artefact.co.uk/AaH.html*
Opening times: Mon-Sat 9.30-6, Thurs
9.30-7.
Nearest Underground: *Tottenham Court Road.*
Personnel: *Partners:* Phillip Athill, John Abbott.
Over 1000 English watercolours,, drawings and prints (with some oils) 1780-1990 displayed on three gallery floors. Founded in 1936 our policy has always been to sell pictures that can be bought from income and our price range is from £50-£5,000.
We have an in-house conservator and are happy to give free advice of cleaning, restoring and framing. Every seven weeks we issue a LIST introducing 300 works to stock and announcing any particular exhibition we are featuring. Our LISTS are free and will be sent in application.
Services and Facilities:
Art Consultancy. Framing. Gallery space for hire. Restoration. Valuation.
Work Stocked and Sold:
Pr.
Price range: £50 - £5,000.

BAUMKOTTER GALLERY
63a Kensington Church Street, London, W8 4BA.
Tel: *0171-937 5171.*
Fax: *0171-938 2312.*
Opening times: Mon-Fri 9.30-6.
Nearest Underground: *High Street Kensington, Notting Hill Gate.*
Personnel: *Proprietor:* Lore Baumkotter. *Manager:* John Guy.
Nicholas Baumkotter. Picture restoration and relining of oil paintings. 14 years experience in the art trade. Restoration studio, Sutton, Surrey. Telephone: 0181-642 4404.
Services and Facilities:
Parking. Restoration.
Work Stocked and Sold:
Pa.
Price range: £500 - £60,000.

CLARE REYNOLDS
20 Gubyon Avenue, Herne Hill, London SE25.
Tel: *0171-326 0458.*

DE BEER STUDIOS
9 Old Bond Street, London W1X.
Tel: *0171-629 1470.*

DEBORAH BATES PAPER CONSERVATION & GALLERY
191 St. John's Hill, Battersea, London SW11 1TH.
Tel: *0171-223 1629.*
Fax: *0171-207 1330.*
Opening times: *Studio:* Mon-Fri 10-6. *Gallery:* Mon-Sat 10-4.
Nearest Underground: *Clapham Junction.*
Personnel: *Proprietor:* Deborah Bates.
Established in 1980 the conservation practice offers studio and on site conservation and restoration of works of art on paper: watercolours, prints, drawings and pastels for private collectors, galleries and institutions.

All staff fully qualified. Large, well equipped studio. Insurance work undertaken (flood and fire damage). Appraisal and estimates are given free. Condition and treatment reports. Framing service and advice on storage and display for preventative conservation. Delivery and collection can be arranged. Member of the Institute of Paper Conservation and listed on the register maintained by the Museum & Galleries Commission. Gallery specialising in contemporary art.
Services and Facilities:
Restoration.

G. BIGNELL PAPER ONSERVATION
45 Coronet Street, London N1. **Tel:** *0171-729 3161.*

GRAEME STOREY
The Grange, Maesbrook, Oswestry, SY10 8QP.
Tel: *0169-185260.*

HAHN & SON
47 Albemarle Street, London, W1X 8FE.
Tel: *0171-493 1630, 0171-493 9196.*

JAMES WRAY PICTURE CONSERVATION
Wood Farm, Forsyth Road, Otley Ipswich,
Tel: *01473-890286.*

LEES FINE ART RESTORERS
Unit 11, Wellington Close, Ledbury Road, London W11. **Tel:** *0171-229 3521.*

LOWE & BUTCHER
Neckinger Mills, 162-164 Abbey Street, London SE1. **Tel:** *0171-237 1113.*

PATRICIA GARNER
Arragon Conservation Studio, 55 Arragon Road, Twickenham, TW1 3NG.
Tel: *0181-892 1819, 0181-286 6153.*
Fax: *0181-891 0115.*
Opening times: *Mon-Fri 9-5.30 or by appointment.*
Nearest Station: *Twickenham.*
Personnel: *Director:* Patricia Garner.
Restoration and conservation of oil paintings from all periods to museum standard. Established 1976. Member of United Kingdom of Conservation, The International Institute of Conservation, The Association of British Picture Restorers, a listed Restorer with The Museum and Galleries Commission.
Services and Facilities:
Art for Offices. Framing. Parking. Restoration.

PAUL CONGDON-CLELFORD BA (HONS)
Bostock Close, Sparsholt, Winchester, SO21 SQH.
Tel: *01962-776495, Mobile 0441-66194.*
Fax: *01962-776495.*
Member of FATG; IPG; ABPR; GADR. This long established and specialist studio provides restoration and conservation of oil paintings on canvas and panel; including water colours, pastel and engravings and other works on paper.
Limited frame conservation is also available. Paintings in any condition including those damaged and torn can be lined and restored. Insurance claim damaged art is a speciality. Collection and delivery, together with home consultations are available throughout most of Britain. Conservator to Museums and Galleries, dealers and framers.
Services and Facilities:
Parking. Restoration.

PAUL MITCHELL LTD
99 New Bond Street, London W1Y 9LF.
Tel: *0171-493 8732 / 0860.*
Fax: *0171-409 7136.*

PLOWDEN AND SMITH
190 St. Ann's Hill, Wandsworth, London SW18 2RT.
Tel: *0181-874 4005.* **Fax:** *0181-874 7248.*

RANKINS (GLASS) COMPANY LTD.
The London Glass Centre, 24-34 Pearson Street, London E2 8JD.
Tel: *0171-729 4200.*
Fax: *0171-729 7135/9197.*
Personnel: Stephanie Graham.
Holders of the Royal Warrant for supplying low-reflective glass, Rankins are independent glass processors and glaziers situated in teh east end of London.
We specialise in fire-resistant, conservation adn low-reflective glass and carry substantial stocks of these and all stndard float glass products.
With our vast range of equipment we can ofer all teh different forms of glass processing required by the end user as well as design advice when required.
For further information please call the Rankin Sales Office.

THE STUDIO
55 Arragon Road, Twickenham, TW1 3NG.
Tel: *0181-892 1819.*
Fax: *0181-891 0115??.*

TRADE PICTURE SERVICES
Neckinger Mills, Abbey Street, London SE1.
Tel: *0171-237 4388.*

UCL PAINTING ANALYSIS
43 Gordon Square, London WC1H.
Tel: *0171-383 2090.*

WITNEY RESTORATIONS LTD.
Unit 17, Hanborough Business Park, Main Road, Long Hanborough, OX7 2LH.
Tel: *01993-883336.*
Fax: *01993-779852.*

Ab Artist's Books **App** Applied Art **Cer** Ceramics **Cra** Crafts **Dec** Decorative **Dr** Drawing **Fur** Furniture **Gla** Glass **Jew** Jewellery **Pa** Paintings **Ph** Photography **Pr** Prints **Sc** Sculpture **Tx** Textiles **Wd** Wood

FINE ART INSURANCE

Brokers, companies.

THE ART WORLD
DIRECTORY
1998/99 25TH EDITION

INSURANCE BROKERS

AON UK
Briar Cliff House, Kings Head, Farnborough, GU4 7TE. **Tel:** *01252-807321.* **Fax:** *01252-807330.*

BLACKWALL GREEN (JEWELLERY AND FINE ART)
Lambert Fenchurch House, Friary Court, Crutched Friars, London EC3N 2NP.
Tel: *0171-560 3000, Telex 8814631.*
Fax: *0171-560 3649.*

BYAS MOSLEY & CO. LTD.
International Fine Art Division, William Byas House, 14-18 St. Clare Street, London WC3N 1JX.
Tel: *0171-481 0101.* **Fax:** *0171-480 5303.*

CROWLEY COLOSSO
Friary Court, Crutched Friars, London EC3N 2NP.
Tel: *0171-560 3000.* **Fax:** *0171-560 3655.*

HISCOX PLC.
54 Leadenhall Street, London EC3 2BJ.
Tel: *0171-423 4000.* **Fax:** *0171-929 1251.*
Email *enquiry@hiscox.co.uk*
Ws *http://www.hiscox.co.uk*
Personnel: Robert Read. Annabel Fell-Clark. Emma O'Neill.
Hiscox plc is one of the leading specialist insurers in the UK, representing 30 years' experience and knowledge of providing individually tailored insurance.
By combining efficiency of service, speed and fairness of claims payment, Hiscox offers an unparalleled ranged of products to the discerning individual.

HSBC GIBBS (HCA) LTD.
Bishops Court, 27/33 Artillery Lane, London E1 7LP.
Tel: *0171-661 2360.*
Fax: *0171-377 2175.*
Opening times: *9.30-5.30 Mon-Fri.*
Nearest Underground: *Liverpool Street.*
Personnel: Bob Diggory. Tony Barratt.
Specialist insurance brokers for Art Dealers; Antique Dealers; Auction Houses; Shippers and Packers; Art Galleries and Museums; Historic Houses; Private Collections; Corporate Collections; Exhibitions; Transits; Art Trade Fairs and Jewellery. Official insurance brokers for "Art 97". A member of the HSBC Group.

JARDINE INSURANCE BROKERS INT. LTD.
Jardine House, 6 Crutched Friars, London EC3N 2HT.
Tel: *0171-528 4100, 0171-528 4444.*
Fax: *0171-528 4746.*

NEEDHAM JOBSON & CO. C
Byron House, 102 Wimbledon Hill Road, London SW19 7PB.
Tel: *0181-944 8870.*
Fax: *0181-944 8816.*

SBJ SPECIALITY LIMITED
One Hundred Whitechapel, London E1 1JG.
Tel: *0171-816 2000.* **Fax:** *0171-816 2121.*
Personnel: Christopher Bailey-West. David Lock.

Dedicated Specialist in the insurance of Fine Arts & Collectables for Private Collectors, Galleries, Museums and others connected to the art world.
For further information contact Christopher Bailey-West or David Lock.

SEDGWICK FINE ART C
Sedgwick House, The Sedgwick Centre, London E1 8DX.
Tel: *0171-377 3456.*
Fax: *0171-377 3199.*

SNEATH, KENT & STUART LTD.
Stuart House, 53/55 Scrutton Street, London EC2A 4QQ.
Tel: *0171-739 5646.* **Fax:** *0171-739 6467.*

WILLIS CORROON FINE ART
Ten Trinity Square, London EC3P 3AX.
Tel: *0171-975 2173.*
Fax: *0171-975 2447.*
Email *hallettl@wcg.co.uk*
Opening times: *Mon-Fri 9.30-5.30. 24 hours answer machine.*
Personnel: *Account Executive:* Louise Hallett.
Specialist insurance brokers working in all areas of fine art - galleries, private dealers, museums, travelling exhibitions and private collections.
We assure the best possible services at all times at the most competitive rates. We can arrange valuations and recommend storage and transport for works or art.
Services and Facilities:
Valuation.

WINDSOR I. B. LTD. (SKS)
Lyon House, 160-166 Borough High Street, London SE1 1JR.
Tel: *0171-407 7144.*
Fax: *0171-827 9312.*
Personnel: Barbara Weedon. Geoffrey Sneath. David Beck. Peter Clifford. Michael Collins.
Instant Premium Indications. Specialist Brokers to Contemporary Art Dealers, Private Collections, Antique and Fine Art Dealers, Interior Decorators. Brokers to: LAPADA; The Fine Art Trade Guild, IDDA and BAFRA. Fairs - Brokers to: World of Drawings and Watercolours, 20th Century Art Fair, Fine Art and Antiques Fair, Olympia, Chelsea Antiques Fair to name a few.

INSURANCE COMPANIES

NORDSTERN ART INSURANCE LTD.
78 Leadenhall Street, London EC3A 3DH.
Tel: *0171-626 5001.* **Fax:** *0171-626 4606.*
Personnel: Clare Pardy.

Nordstern
Art Insurance Limited

Nordstern specialises in providing insurance cover for private collectors, including contents and buildings, and for dealers, museums and exhibitions.
As part of AXA, one of he world's largest insurance groups, Nordstern offers excellent security combined with highly competitive rates, an in-depth knowledge of the art market and a fair and speedy claims settlement service.
"We believe we offer the best of both worlds" says Clare Pardy, New Business Manager, "a small well-run company which knows its own specialist market and is part of an international group with global influence".
For further information, please contact Clare Pardy or David Scully.

FINE ART PRINTERS

Fine Art Printers, Art cards.

THE ART WORLD
DIRECTORY
1998/99 25TH EDITION

FINE ART PRINTERS

ABACUS (COLOUR PRINTERS) LTD
Lowick Green, Lowick, Ulverston, LA12.8DX.
Tel: *01229-885361.* **Fax:** *01229 -885348.*
Opening times: *Mon-Sat 9-5.*
Personnel: *Directors:* John Sutcliffe, Vicki Sutcliffe.
Specialist printers to the art world - nationwide! Mail order postcards, greetings cards, posters, catalogues from your own art work. All work is in house to ensure maximum print quality and accuracy of colour to the original art work. Print members of the Fine Art Trade Guild for 10 years.
Services and Facilities:
Parking.

AMICA FINE ART PRINTING LTD.
F1 Park Hall, 40 Martell Road, London SE21 8EN.
Tel: *0181-670 6060.* **Fax:** *0181-670 0060.*

BAS PRINTERS LTD.
Over Wallop, Stockbridge, SO20 8JD.
Tel: *01264-781711.* **Fax:** *01264-781116.*

BROAD OAK COLOUR
Units A & B, 254 Broad Oak Road, Canterbury, CT2 7QH. **Tel:** *01227-767856.* **Fax:** *01227-762599.*

DAYFOLD FINE ART PRINTERS
Dayfold House, Black Moor Road, Verwood, BH31 6BE.
Tel: *01202-827141.* **Fax:** *01202-825841.*

FIDELITY COLOUR FINE ART PRINTS
8-10-12 Hornsby Square, Southfields, Lamdon, SS15 6SD. **Tel:** *01268-544066.* **Fax:** *01268-418977.*

JONES AND PALMER LTD.
95 Carver Street, Birmingham B1 3AR.
Tel: *0121-236 9007; isdn: 0121-200 8380.*
Fax: *0121-236 5513.*

NAPIER JONES
187 Gordon Road, London SE15 3RT.
Tel: *0171-277 8677.* **Fax:** *0171-639 3320.*
Email *print@napierjones.ltd.uk*
Opening times: *7-6.*
Nearest Underground: *Peckham.*
Personnel: *Managing Director:* Jennifer Jones. *Director:* Peter Clements.

NAPIER·JONES

Napier Jones has a longstanding reputation for quality printing. We are accustomed to collaborating directly with artists or galleries to produce stylish catalogues, cards or other literature for which we win awards.
Limited edition or open prints can be produced up to 28x40 inches (720x1020mm). We print using the new 'Waterless' technology which is not only more environmentally friendly but also produced improved quality. Call us for more information

NEWCASTLE FINE ART PRINTERS
9A Marquis Court, Low Prudhoe,
Tel: *01661-831086.*

NORTHUMBERLAND FINE ART PRINTERS
West Farm, Kenton Bar, Ponteland Road, Newcastle-upon-Tyne NE3 3EJ.
Tel: *0191-286 2596.*

RANELAGH COLOUR PRINTERS
Park End, South Hill Park, London NW3 2SG.
Tel: *0171-435 4400.* **Fax:** *0171-435 5635.*

ST. IVES PRINTING & PUBLISHING COMPANY
Unit 4D, Penbeagle Industrial Estate, St. Ives, TR26 2JH. **Tel:** *01736-798951.* **Fax:** *01736-795020.*

ART CARDS

THOUGHT FACTORY
Group House, 40 Waterside Road, Hamilton Industrial Park, Leicester LE5 1TL.
Tel: *0116-276 5302.* **Fax:** *0116-246 0506.*

Email *kpegroup@aol.com*
Ws *http://www.kpegroup@aol.com*
Opening times: *Mon-Thurs 8.30-5.30, Fri 8-1.30.*
Nearest Station: *Leicester London Road.*
Personnel: *Director:* Elaine King.
Open your mind to the possibilities that Thought Factory can offer. We can turn your work into print at a really competitive price. We offer Business Cards, Post Cards and Greetings Cards and you will certainly be amazed at the reproduction. Want to see more phone/fax or email us for prices, samples and promotional pack.

WEST ONE POSTCARDS
Golden House, 29 Great Pulteney Street, London W1R 3DD.
Tel: *0171-434 0235.*
Fax: *0171-434 2061.*
Personnel: Ian Brewster.
Private view and prodeuction postcards - from £110 for 1,000 full colour cards including black text on the reverse. We also supply presentation folders, envelopes, invoice pads, stationary, posters, catalogues. Design, artwork and finishing services available.

FOUNDERS

Nautilus

the fine art foundry for sculptors seeking the perfect cast

Paul Joyce
Manager

A graduate of Goldsmiths College. After ten years as a sculptor, Paul founded Nautilus with a 100lb capacity home-made furnace. Within four years he was lost wax casting up to three quarters of a ton and rapidly building a reputation as an expert in hot, cold and fume patination, constantly evolving new techniques to achieve different effects:

Charlie Dearing
Master Chaser

Charlie has no diplomas or degrees after his name. He began as a foundry labourer, straight from school. Three weeks later, he was entrusted with filing down the edges of a canopy entrance cast for the Sultan of Abu Dhabi's palace. Today, Charlie is arguably the most gifted chaser anywhere in the UK. and has a fine rapport with his sculptor clients.

Desmond Stanley
Lost Wax Caster

Desmond joined a fine art foundry straight from school, where he excelled at art. He is a leading exponent of lost wax casting, highly skilled in the delicate crafts of rubber moulding, ceramic shell investment and in the final casting process itself. His expertise goes beyond the traditional;with a wide knowledge of the latest materials and techniques.

Richard Lowther
Moulder

Rick joined Finch Seaman straight from school. His vast experience in the time-saving and cost-effective techniques of greensand moulding make him a major asset to the team; a vital link between the modern technology available in the Finch Seaman Foundry and the more traditional skills of the Nautilus team.

Ed Triplow
Welder and Chaser

After completing a Foundation course at Ravensbourne College, Ed worked as a sculptor in Wales before joining a fine art foundry, where he was apprenticed to Charlie Dearing developing a wide range of skills, including welding, brazing, patinating and chasing. He now works under Charlie in the Nautilus team.

Adrian Bennett
London Studio

After training as a sculptor for seven years at Liverpool (partly with a Fellowship) and completing a post graduate course at the RCA, Adrian was establishing himself as a sculptor when he decided to join Nautilus. He now runs their London Studio, a unique facility in many ways, and acts as the London contact.

11 Swinborne Drive, Springwood Industrial Estate, Braintree, Essex CM7 2YP

Telephone: Foundry 01 376 343222 London: 0181 692 1309 Fax: 01 376 348480

Nautilus Fine Art Foundry is a trading name of Finch Seaman Limited

AB FINE ART FOUNDRY
1 Fawe Street, London E14 6PD.
Tel: *0171-515 8052.*
Fax: *0171-987 7339.*
Personnel: Henry Abercrombie. Jerry Hughes.
A B Fine Art Foundry Ltd employs only craftspeople with a fine art background, ensuring an empathy with individual sculptors and their work.
The foundry offers a complete range of services: scaling up - armature building - mould making - lost wax and sand casting - patination - repair and restoration etc.
We have a record of reliability in meeting deadlines and maintaining high quality and good value for money.
1,700 sq ft. studio available for individual projects. If casting your work into bronze interests you and you would like to visit the workshops or discuss any projects, please phone and we will be happy to help and advise.

ALDEN ARTS
8 Reynolds Place, Crawley,
Tel: *01293-535411.*

ART BRONZE FOUNDRY (LONDON) LTD
1 Michael Road, London SW6.
Tel: *0171-736 7292.*

ART CAST
36 Southwell Road, London SE5.
Tel: *0171-733 8424.*

BRONZE AGE SCULPTURE FOUNDRY
272 Island Row, Limehouse, Docklands, London E14 7HY.
Tel: *0171-538 1388.*
Fax: *0171-538 9723.*
Email *duncanh@netcomuk.co.uk*
Ws *http://www.netcomuk.co.uk/-duncanh*
Opening times: *9-6.*
Nearest Underground: *Limehouse (Docklands Light Rail).*
Personnel: Proprietor: Mark Kennedy.

Bronze Age

Situated in London's Docklands within ten minutes of Tower Bridge, Bronze Age offers a unique personalised service to artists, using the lost wax casting technique.
Services and Facilities:
Parking.

THE BRONZE WORKS
Yaff, 111 Matilda Street, Sheffield S14 QF.
Tel: *0114-2726452.*
Fax: *0114-2761769.*

BURLEIGHFIELD ARTS LIMITED
Sculpture Casting Studio, Loudwater, High Wycombe, HP10 9RF.
Tel: *01494-521341.* **Fax:** *01494-461953.*
Email *burleighfield@compuserve.com*
Ws *http://www.polestarltd/sculpture/*
Opening times: *Weekdays 8-5.*
Personnel: Paul Dimishky.

BURLEIGHFIELD ARTS
LIMITED

Whatever your commission, large or small, our skill and experience has encouraged sculptors, established artists and students alike to entrust us with their work.
We offer a complete range of services including enlarging, casting into metal by either the sand piece or lost wax processes, finishing and erection on site anywhere in the world. For a first class, friendly and efficient service please contact us. On A40 East of roundabout at Exit 3 of M40.

CASTECK LTD
Unity Works, 42 Victoria Street, Hockley, Birmingham B1 3OE.
Tel: *0121-233 1334.* **Fax:** *0121-523 7469.*

CENTURY BRONZE
9 Camton Street, Birmingham BAT 6AR.
Tel: *0121-212 0840.*

COLIN REID GLASS
New Mills, Stod Road, Stroud, GL3 1RN.
Tel: *01453-751421.*

EAST COAST CASTING LTD
Old Iron Foundry, Norwich Road, Carbrooke, Watton, **Tel:** *01953-881741.*

FINE ART FOUNDRY
Thurning, **Tel:** *01832-293392.*

FIRTH RIXON
PO Box 6, Heath Road, Darleston, Wednesbury,
Tel: *01521-568 6222.*

HARDY NON-FERROUS METALS LTD
Vulcan Street, Middlesbrough **Tel:** *01642-247759.*

JOHN LONGBOTTOM (IRONFOUNDERS)
Broomhill Road, Bonnybridge, FK4 2AN.
Tel: *01324-812860.*

LEANDER ARCHITECTURAL
Fletcher Foundry, Hallsteads Close, Doves Holes, Buxton,
Tel: *01298-814941.* **Fax:** *01298-814970.*
Email *ted@leanderarch.demon.co.uk*
Ws *http://www.leanderarch.demon.co.uk*
Opening times: *8-5.30.*
Nearest Station: *Dove Holes.*
Personnel: *Partner:* Ted McHuay.
Leander operate a sand cast bronze and aluminium foundry specialising in plaques and bas-reliefs. The company has in-house pattern and modelling facilities and a wide range of

graphic production techniques. Leander has acquired a deserved reputation for undertaking complex and graphically precise castings in any quantity and to tight schedules. Clients include sculptors, community arts groups, English Heritage, CADW and many local authorities. Many plaques and signs are cast for export because of the foundry's experience in working with different languages and script forms.
Services and Facilities:
Disabled Access. Parking. Workshop Facilities.

LS SCULPTURE CASTING
Southfield Farm, North Lane, Weston-on-the-Green, Bicester, OX6 6RG. **Tel:** *01869-350904.* **Fax:** *01869-350904.*

LUNTS CASTINGS LTD
Middlemore Road, Birmingham B21 0BJ.
Tel: *0121-551 4301.* **Fax:** *0121-523 7954.*
Personnel: A.J. Limb.
Lunts Castings Ltd. have built on an enviable reputation for quality and service at very competitive prices, enabling the sculptor to price to sell.
We offer a collection/delivery service of both waxes and bronze. Casting is carried out for most non-ferrous and precious metals, i.e. bronze, brass, silver and gold. Many well-known sculptors are moving to the Lunts complete casting service, so put us to the test.

MERIDIAN SCULPTURE FOUNDRY LTD
Railway Arches, 842 Consort Road, London SE15 2PH.
Tel: *0171-639 2553.* **Fax:** *0171-277 9486.*
Opening times: *By appointment.*
Nearest Underground: *BR: Peckham Rye.*
Personnel: *Directors:* Megan Crofton, Jack Crofton.
Services and Facilities:
Restoration.

MIKE DAVIS FOUNDRY
St. James Street, New Bradwell, Milton Keynes, MK13 0BW.
Tel: *01908-315841.* **Fax:** *01908-511363.*
Personnel: Mike Davis.

With the backing of twenty year's experience and expertise, this friendly family based foundry offers an intimate one to one relationship with its clients and is proud to take endless pains to achieve your requirements. From small intimate, to large demanding works, we are happy to give free estimates either in foundry or at our studio. Collection and delivery can be arranged as can the on-site installation of large pieces. We employ the latest lost wax to ceramic shell process to ensure the highest possible casting quality.

MORRIS SINGER LTD

Bond Close, Kingsland, Basingstoke, RG24 0PT.
Tel: *01256-24033.* **Fax:** *01256-844565.*
Personnel: *Contact:* David J. Vallance.
Whenever you place a commission with Morris Singer Ltd., you have the confidence of knowing that it has the backing of almost 150 years of experience and many of the great artists within that time have commissioned the services of Morris Singer.

Whether your work is large or small, anywhere in the world, then we will be happy to enlarge, cast, erect on site and provide all the comprehensive services you would expect from the foremost company. We are very close to exit 6 on the M3.

NAUTILUS FINE ART FOUNDRY

Head Office and Works,
11 Swinborne Drive, Springwood Industrial Estate, Braintree, CM7 2YP.
Tel: *01376-343222 or 0181-692 1309.*
Fax: *01376-343480.*
Opening times: *7.30am-5.30pm.*
Nearest Station: *Braintree.*
Personnel: *Manager:* Paul Joyce.

Nautilus is now recognised as a leader in the art casting profession. By employing only those considered to be the best in their respective disciplines, we achieve a quality second-to-none. The facilities we can offer and the range of materials, processes and patinations available, together with our studio facilities in both Braintree and London, has resulted in us becoming one of the most comprehensive of any art foundry. To fully appreciate all that Nautilus can offer, with an opportunity to discuss your requirements with our production team, please contact Paul Joyce to arrange a visit.

PANGOLIN EDITIONS

Unit 9, Chalford Industrial Estate, Chalford, GL6 8NT.
Tel: *01453-886527.*
Fax: *01453-731499.*
Nearest Station: *Stroud.*
Personnel: *Manager:* Bob Thornycroft.
Pangolin Editions is well established as one of Britain's leading sculpture foundries casting for both national and international clients. It is one of the last foundries still practising the traditional skills of lost wax investment casting whilst CO_2 sand piece moulding is used for larger works. All bronzes are hand finished with a wide range of patinas being a foundry speciality. Our priority is craftsmanship and we aim for a strong working partnership between sculptor and foundry. We are capable-of casting on any scale and welcome enquiries by telephone, fax or in writing.

Services and Facilities:
Art Consultancy. Art for Offices. Commissioning Service. Parking. Restoration. Workshop Facilities.

ROYAL TUNBRIDGE WELLS CLASSIC CASTINGS

P.O. Box 97, Tunbridge Wells, TN2 4ZJ.
Tel: *01956-533683/01892-784379.*
Fax: *01892-784379.*

NOTES

FRAMERS

Framers, frames for hire, period frames.

THE ART WORLD
DIRECTORY
1998/99 25TH EDITION

FRAMERS

ACADEMY FRAMING
ROYAL ACADEMY OF ARTS
Burlington House, Piccadilly, London W1V 0DS.
Tel: *0171-300 5646 & 5647.* **Fax:** *0171-300 8001.*
Opening times: *Mon-Fri 10-5.*
Nearest Underground: *Green Park, Piccadilly Circus.*
Personnel: *Manager: E. Fernandes. Assistant Manager: C. Sims. Framers: T. Breen & G. Thompson. Mount Cutter: M. Taylor. Fitter: C. Medhurst.*
Academy Framing is a bespoke framers situated next to the Royal Academy Schools and serves the Royal Academy itself as well as many of the West End galleries. We are also open to members of the public offering advice on framing. We have a wide selection of mouldings, many of which are exclusive designs and can be finished in a variety of ways from staining and waxing to water gilding. All work undertaken is to the highest of conservation standards. Restoration of oils and works of paper is also available. Prices start from £5 per foot for stained and waxed finishes.
Services and Facilities:
Framing. Restoration.

ALEC DREW PICTURE FRAMES LTD
5/7 Cale Street, Chelsea Green, London SW3 3QT.
Tel: *0171-352 8716.*
Opening times: *Mon-Fri 9-5, Wed 9-6, Sat 9.30-1.*
Nearest Underground: *Sloane Square/South Kensington.*
We are well situated bespoke framers, working to a conservation standard offering a wide range of traditional and modern Factory Mouldings and Hand-Made Frames. We can also put you in touch with restorers, picture hangers, or other specialists.
Services and Facilities:
Framing. Restoration.

ARNOLD WIGGINS & SONS LTD
4 Bury Street, London SW1.
Tel: *0171-925 0195.*

ART FOR OFFICES
International Art Consultants, The Galleries, 15 Dock Street, London E1 8JL.
Tel: *0171-481 1337.* **Fax:** *0171-481 3425.*
Email *art@artservs.demon.co.uk*
Opening times: *Open Mon-Fri 9.30-6.*
Nearest Underground: *Tower Hill, Aldgate, Aldgate East.*
Personnel: *Directors: Andrew Hutchinson, Peter Harris. Amanda Basker.*
We have 20 years experience advising architects, designers and corporate clients on the planning and implementation of art programmes. Our 10,000 square foot galleries provide a central source of art, enabling clients and specifiers to view a comprehensive range of art on a single visit to one location. We deal directly with over 800 artists and have a

large visual reference library covering art in all media which is cross referenced by style and price. This makes it possible to research works of art, or artists for commission quickly and effectively. Art can be purchased, commissioned or acquired on a flexible rental basis.
Services and Facilities:
Art Consultancy. Art for Offices. Commissioning Service. Framing. Parking.
Work Stocked and Sold:
Cer. Cra. Dr. Gla. Pa. Ph. Pr. Sc. Tx. Wd.
Price range: £100 - £50,000.

ART & SOUL
G14 Belgravia Workshops, 157-163 Marlborough Road, London N19 4NF.
Tel: *0171-263 0421.* **Fax:** *0171-263 0421.*
Opening times: *Tues-Fri 9-5. Closed 1-2. Sat 10-1. (Phone to check holidays).*
Nearest Underground: *Archway, Finsbury Park.*
Personnel: *Rebecca Bramwell.*
Quality framing service. Phone for details and booklet.

ART & WOOD SUPPLIES
220 North End Road, London W14.
Tel: *0171-385 4683.*

ART WORKS
50 High Street, Walton-on-Thames, KT12 1BY.
Tel: *0800-834409.*

ARTBEAT
703 Fulham Road, London SW6.
Tel: *0171-736 0337.*

ARTBOOK LONDON
The Chambers, Chelsea Harbour, London SW10 0XF. **Tel:** *0171-349 0666.* **Fax:** *0171-349 0202.*

ARTEFACT PICTURE FRAMERS
36 Windmill Street, London W1P 1HF.
Tel: *0171-580 4878, Freephone 0500-850085.*

ARTICLES
460 Fulham Road, London SW6.
Tel: *0171-381 3204.*

ARTISTIC IMPRESSIONS
62a Queens Road, London SE15.
Tel: *0171-580 4878.*

ASHWORTH & THOMPSON
12 Baron Street, London N1.
Tel: *0171-837 6836.*

BEECHFIELD FRAMES
Arch 79, Stewarts Lane, Silverthorne Road, London SW8 3HE. **Tel:** *0171-720 9971.*

BELGRAVIA FRAMEWORKS
9 Kinnerton Street, Belgravia, London SW1X 8EA. **Tel:** *0171-245 1112.* **Fax:** *0171-245 1156.*

BISHOPSGATE FRAMING GALLERY
228 Bishopsgate, London EC2M 4QD **Tel:** *0171-247 2320.* **Fax:** *0171-247 2320.*

BLOOMSBURY FRAMING CO.
42 Theobalds Road, London WC1.
Tel: *0171-404 8140.*

BLUE JAY FRAMES
Possingworth Craft Workshops, Blackboys East, Heathfield, TN22 5HE.
Tel: *01435-866258.* **Fax:** *01435-868473.*
Opening times: *Mon-Fri 8.30-5.30.*
Nearest Station: *Uckfield.*
Personnel: *Managing Director: Simon Hayes Fisher.*
Located in the heart of Sussex, we service many museums, galleries, designers and shops, realizing that the three most important things required from a wholesale picture framer are quality, reliability and keen pricing.
We offer a full range of moulding and mount board samples at no charge to our customers and operate a free pick up and delivery service in London and the South East.
The turn around time of orders can be tailored to suit the individual customers requirements and we are confident that, having tried us once, you will find the quality and value unbeatable.
Services and Facilities:
Framing. Restoration.

C.C. GALLERIES
420 Roman Road, London E3.
Tel: *0171-980 2888.*

CHELSEA FRAME WORKS
106 Finborough Road, London SW10.
Tel: *0171-373 0180.*

CIRCA 48
17b Brecknock Road, London, N7.
Tel: *0171-485 9249.*

CONNAUGHT GALLERIES
44 Connaught Street, London W2.
Tel: *0171-723 1660.*

CORK STREET FRAMING
8 Bramber Street, London W14.
Tel: *0171-381 9211.*

COURT FRAMES MAYFAIR
8 Bourdon Street, 5-7 Sedley Place, (off Berkeley Square), London W1X 9HX.
Tel: *0171-493 3265.* **Fax:** *0171-493 8369.*

COUTTS FRAMING
75 Blythe Road, Hammersmith, London W14.
Tel: *0171-603 7475.*

DIXON BATE FRAMING
94-98 Fairfield Street, Manchester M1 2WR.
Tel: *0161-273 6974.*
Fax: *0161-274 4865.*
Opening times: *Mon-Fri 8.30-5.30, Sat 9-1.*
Personnel: *Managing Director: Jon Davies.*
One of the finest contemporary framers in the country. Bespoke hand-finished frames for the fine art market. Specialists in natural hardwoods and softwoods, stained/coloured/gilded/finished to your requirements. The largest selection of fames available in the North West, all produced with

individual attention. Full conservation framing service to the highest possible standards.

Servicing artists, dealers, galleries, private & public collections nationwide. Outstanding and beautiful framing at a sensible price.
Services and Facilities:
Framing. Parking.

DRURY LANE GALLERY
Unit 4, 30-35 Drury Lane, London WC2B 5RH.
Tel: *0171-379 7161.*
Fax: *0171-379 7161.*
Opening times: *Mon-Fri 9-6, Sat 11-5.*
Nearest Underground: *Covent Garden.*
Framing and restoration work carried out. Picture hanging and art consultancy accepted. We will source artwork - and supply framed artwork for hire.
Services and Facilities:
Art Consultancy. Art for Offices. Framing. Restoration.

FALCONER TRADE FRAMING
17 Ferdinand Street, Chalk Farm, London, NW1.
Tel: *0171-267 7777.*

FLETCHER GALLERY SERVICES
12 Kinghorn Street, London EC1A 7HT.
Tel: *0171-726 4811.*
Fax: *0171-606 1826.*

FLYING FOX FRAMING
54 Penton Street, London, N1 9QA.
Tel: *0171-833 3569.*

FRAME DESIGNS
57 Ebury Street, London SW1.
Tel: *0171-730 0533 / 0171-823 6521.*

FRAME EMPORIUM
589-591 Holloway Road, London, N19 4DJ.
Tel: *0171-263 8973.*
Fax: *0171-281 1766.*

FRAME FACTORY
1E Gleneagle Road, London SW16.
Tel: *0181-677 1882.*

FRAMERY
3 Academy Buildings, Fanshaw Street, London N1.
Tel: *0171-729 7677.*

FRAMEWORKS
9 Kinnerton Street, London SW1..
Tel: *0171-245 1112.*

FRAMING MATTERS
301 King Street, Hammersmith, London W6 9NH.
Tel: *0171-748 6631.*

FRASCO INTERNATIONAL
40 Moreton Street, London SW1V.
Tel: *0171-834 7773 / 7834.*

GALLERY 181 FRAMING AND JUST MIRRORS
141 Greyhound Road, London W6 8NJ.
Tel: *0171-385 9613.*

THE GALLERY
20 Durngate Street, Dorchester DT1 1JP.
Tel: *01305-267408.*
Fax: *01305-251429.*
Email *john.pearson1@virgin.net.uk*
Opening times: *Tues-Sat, 10-5.*
Nearest Station: *Dorchester South.*
Personnel: *Proprietor: Susie Pearson.*
A full, bespoke picture framing service is offered, to Conservation and Museum standards.
The workroom is situated on the premises enabling clients to discuss problems directly. A wide range of mouldings and mountboards are held in stock, while unusual needs can be easily obtained.
Friendly advice is available on most framing techniques. Close links are maintained with local professional oil painting and watercolour Conservationists and cleaners.
Services and Facilities:
Framing. Restoration.
Work Stocked and Sold:
Dr. Pa. Pr.
Price range: £100 - £1,000.

GLAZE & FRAME
408 Harrow Road, London W9 2HU.
Tel: *0171-266 5379.*

HADLEIGH FRAMES
11 Benwell Road, London N7.
Tel: *0171-700 1192.*

HARVARD ENTERPRISES
36-40 York Way, London N1.
Tel: *0171-278 7138.*

HOLBORN GALLERIES
70 Chancery Lane, London WC2A.
Tel: *0171-404 0678.*

INTERNATIONAL ART SUPPLIES
CP House, Otterspool Way, Watford, WD2 8HG.
Tel: *01923-210042.*
Fax: *01923-240899.*

ISLINGTON FRAMES
8 Essex Road, London N1.
Tel: *0171-359 8031.*

JOHN CAMPBELL, PICTURE FRAMERS
164 Walton Street, Kensington, London, SW3 2JL.
Tel: *0171-581 1775, 0171-584 9268.* **Fax:** *0171-581 3499.*

JOHN GILBERT
30-34 Woodfield Place, London W9.
Tel: *0171-289 3198.*

JOHN JONES ART CENTRE LTD.
Stroud Green Road, Finsbury Park, London N4 3JG.
Tel: *0171-281 5439.*
Fax: *0171-281 5956.*
Opening times: *Mon-Fri 8-6, Sat 10-5. Artshop only Sun 10-5.*
Nearest Underground: *Finsbury Park.*
Personnel: *Artshop Manager: Jason Mackie.*
John Jones Art Centre, Stroud Green Road, Finsbury Park, London N4 3JG (1 min walk from Finsbury Park station). Customer Car Parking. Tel: 0171-281 5439, Fax: 0171-281 5956.
Services and Facilities:
Bookshop. Framing. Parking. Restoration. Shop.

KEVIN D'ARTS
Unit 6, Southern Row, London W10.
Tel: *0181-964 0238.*

KINGSBRIDGE ARTS
141 Dawes Road, London SW6.
Tel: *0171-381 1133.*

LENNY VILLA
386a York Way, London N7 9LW.
Tel: *0171-700 5010.*

LITTLE VENICE FRAMES
12 Clifton Road, London W9.
Tel: *0171-286 6500.*

MAINLINE MOULDINGS
Unit 3 Hollygate Lane Industrial Park, Cotgrave, Nottingham, NG12 3JW.
Tel: *0115-989 0076.*
Fax: *0115-989 9488.*

MOSTA POSTA
86 Southwark Street, London SE1.
Tel: *0171-620 4070.*

NEW FRAMES
37 Beak Street, London W1.
Tel: *0171-437 8881.*

OLD CHURCH GALLERIES
320 Kings Road, London, SW3 5UH.
Tel: *0171-351 4649.*
Fax: *0171-351 4449.*

OXFORD EXHIBITION SERVICES
Station Road, Uffington, SN7 7QD.
Tel: *01367-820713.*
Fax: *01367-820504.*
And at Unit G6,Tavern Quay, Rope Street, Rotherhithe, London SE16 1TD. Tel: 0171-237 5646, fax: 0171-232 2254.
A comprehensive framing service specialising in frames for galleries and artists, touring exhibitions and custom designed frames.
Wide range of mouldings for modern and traditional pictures. See also: Packers and Shippers.
Services and Facilities:
Framing.

FRAMERS

Paul Mitchell Ltd
99 New Bond Street, London W1Y 9LF.
Tel: *0171-493 8732 / 0860.* **Fax:** *0171-409 7136.*

Peter Allen
27 Union Street, London SE1. **Tel:** *0171-357 8002.*

Picturesque
16 St Marys Street, Chepstow, NP6 5EW.
Tel: *01291-623000.*

Popner Picture Framing
352 Old York Road, (Formerly York Road), Wandsworth, London SW18 1SS.
Tel: *0181-871 4808.*

Portobello Framers
316 Portabello Road, London W10 5RU.

Richard Tindall
151 Tower Bridge Road, London SE1.
Tel: *0171-403 0500.*

Steve Maddox Specialist Picture Framers
Hardy House, 62 Trafalgar Road, Moseley, Birmingham B13 8BU.
Tel: *0121-449 3868.*

Timothy Newbery
39 Warple Way, London W3 0RX.
Tel: *0181-749 7002.*

Wessex Wood Mouldings
Beeston Road, Mileham,
Tel: *01328-700200, 01794-519500.*
Fax: *02438-700777, 01794-519505.*

FRAMES FOR HIRE

B2 Exhibitions
5 Peary Place, Bethnal Green, London E2 0QW.
Tel: *0181-983 1109.*

James Cox
Lynton House, 48 Lynton Road, Rayners Lane, Harrow, HA2 9NN

PERIOD FRAMES

Bourlet Fine Art Frames
32 Connaugh Street, London W2. **Tel:** *0171-724 4837.*

Brian Nicholson
Unit 1/2, St Mary's Workshop, Henderson Street, Leith, **Tel:** *0131-553 6811.*

Colin Lacey Gallery
38 Ledbury Road, London W11. **Tel:** *0171-229 9105.*

Daggett C
153 Portobello Road, London, W11 2DV.
Tel: *0171-229 2248.*

The Greenwich Gallery
9 Nevada Street, Greenwich, London, SE10 9JL.
Tel: *0181-305 1666.*
Fax: *0181-305 1666.*
Opening times: *Every day 10-5.30.*
Nearest Underground: *Docklands Light Railway. BR: Greenwich.*
Personnel: *Director: Richard F. Moy. Contact: F. Barnham.*
The Greenwich Gallery specialises in period painting, watercolours and prints from c.1750 to about 1950. Established in 1964. Have also had retrospective exhibitions of modern artists. Work in conjunction with Greenwich conservation workshops offering restoration/conservation service in all media, expert valuations and an old and modern picture framing and mounting service.
Services and Facilities:
Art for Offices. Bar. Framing. Restaurant. Restoration. Valuation.
Work Stocked and Sold:
Dr. Pa. Pr.

Howard & Stone Conservators
Unit 27 Penny Bank Chambers, 33-35 St. Johns Square, London, EC1.
Tel: *0171-490 0813.*

Jack Hopson Conservation
Holes Lane, Olney, MK46 4BX.
Tel: *01234-712306.*

John Tannous
115 Harwood Road, London, SW6.
Tel: *0171-736 7999.*
Fax: *0171-371 5237.*

Keith Elliot, Bespoke Framer
The Old Meeting Hall, Maltby Lane, Barton-Upon-Humber, DN18 5PY.
Tel: *01652-660380.*

Marguerite Marr
403 Elm Tree Court, Elm Tree Road, London, NW8.
Tel: *0171-289 0877.*

Patricia Garner
Arragon Conservation Studio, 55 Arragon Road, Twickenham, TW1 3NG.
Tel: *0181-892 1819, 0181-286 6153.*
Fax: *0181-891 0115.*
Opening times: *Mon-Fri 9-5.30 or by appointment.*
Nearest Station: *Twickenham.*
Personnel: *Director: Patricia Garner.*
Restoration and conservation of oil paintings from all periods to museum standard. Established 1976.
Member of United Kingdom of Conservation, The International Institute of Conservation, The Association of British Picture Restorers, a listed Restorer with The Museum and Galleries Commission.
Services and Facilities:
Art for Offices. Framing. Parking. Restoration.

Sebastian D'Orsai
8 Kensington Mall, London, W8.
Tel: *0171-229 3888.*

NOTES

MATERIALS & EQUIPMENT

Artists' materials, framing supplies, gallery hanging supplies.

THE ART WORLD
DIRECTORY
1998/99 25TH EDITION

ARTISTS MATERIALS

ALEC TIRANTI LTD
27 Warren Street, London W1.
Tel: *0171-636 8565.*
Fax: *0171-636 8565.* **Email**
sales@tiranti.co.uk
Ws *thttp://www.iranti.co.uk*
Opening times: *Mon-Fri 9-5.30, Sat 9.30-1.*
Personnel: *Managing Director:* J. Tiranti
Minst. Mgt.. *Directors:* Susan Tiranti Lyons
Acis, Jonathon Lyons.

Established 1895. Shop & Administration: 70
High Street, Theale, Reading, Berks. Open:
Mon-Fri 8.30-5pm, Sat 9.30-1pm.
Manufacturers and suppliers of a complete
range of sculptors' tools, materials and studio
equipment.
Publish an extensive catalogue covering tools
for stonecarving, woodcarving and modelling.
Materials for making flexible rubber moulds,
special plasters, clays, waxes, Chavant non-
drying clays, polyester resins and cold cast
resin metals, white metals and pewter, gilding
supplies, modelling and carving stands.
Services and Facilities:
Shop.

AMSTERDAM LINEN
P.O. Box 235, Hayes, UB3 1HF.
Tel: *0171-701 9500.* **Fax:** *0171-738 1488.*
Opening times: *9-5.*

✖ AMSTERDAM
✖✖ LINEN
✖

Amsterdam Linen, an international mail order
company, introduced a range of samples, ready-
to-use primed stretched linen canvases to the
UK market last year.
Reasonably priced and wonderful to work on,
these canvases have been well received by
amateur and professional artists alike. The
company has now extended its product range
to include primed and unprimed canvas on
rolls, and stretcher pieces. It will also shortly
be marketing a universal primer for oil and
acrylic surfaces. With its fine, even grain,
linen is generally considered the best support
for oils and acrylics. Additionally, it has
greater permanency than cotton, hessian and
other surfaces. But linen is usually much more
expensive and this is a deterrent for most
artists: they simply cannot afford to paint on
it! However, additional to their superb quality, another advantage of Amsterdam Linen
Canvases is that they are eminently affordable,
and there is further economy when the canvas
is bought on rolls and stretched yourself.

ATLANTIS ART MATERIALS
146 Brick Lane, London, E1 6RU.
Tel: *0171-377 8855.*

BIRD & DAVIS LTD
*45 Holmes Road, Kentish Town, London NW5
3AN.* **Tel:** *0171-485 3797.* **Fax:** *0171-284
0509.*

BURNS & HARRIS (RETAIL)
163-165 Overgate, Dundee DD1 1QS.
Tel: *01382-22591.* **Fax:** *01382-29895.*

CANONBURY ART SHOP
266 Upper Street, London N1.
Tel: *0171-226 4652.*

CONTÉ À PARIS
*Colart Fine Arts & Graphics Ltd, Whitefriars
Avenue, Harrow, HA3 5RH.*
Tel: *0181-427 4383.* **Fax:** *0181-863 7177.*

COWLING & WILCOX LTD.
26-28 Broadwick Street, London W1V 1FG.
Tel: *0171-734 9557.*
Fax: *0171-434 4513.*
Opening times: *Mon-Fri 9-6, Sat 10-5.*
Nearest Underground: *Oxford Circus,
Piccadilly Circus.*
Personnel: *Sales:* Jane Goodwin.
Widest selection of portfolios, carrying cases
and presentation books in central London. A
comprehensive range of fine, graphic and craft
materials is available, everything for students,
amateur and professional artists.
A good choice of art books kept in stock. We
offer student discount, a complete internation-
al mail order service and credit account facilities. A stock list is available on request.
Services and Facilities:
Shop.

DALER-ROWNEY
PO Box 10, Bracknell, RG12 8ST.
Tel: *01334-424621.*
Fax: *01344-486511.*

DECORATIVE ARTS CO.
5a Royal Crescent, London W11.
Tel: *0171-371 4303.*

E. PLOTON (SUNDRIES) LTD
273 Archway Road, London N6 5AA.
Tel: *0181-348 0315.*
Fax: *0181-348 3414.*
Email *ploton@ploton.co.uk*
Ws *http://www.ploton.co.uk/ploton*
Nearest Underground: *Highgate.*
Personnel: *Directors:* J. Vich, A. Vich.
This is a small family business which became a
limited company in 1948 and exports all over
the world. Our main services are the supply of
gold and silver leaf, bronze powders, metal leaf,
specialist decorative brushes and artists' materials. A mail order service is available. Please
send S.A.E. for catalogue.

ENTWISTLE THORPE
52a Earlsdon Street, Coventry CV5 6EG.
Tel: *01203-674775.*
Fax: *01203-670654.*

EUROGRAPHICS
18 St. Nicholas Street, Bristol BS1 1UB.
Tel: *01272-273467.*

FALKINER FINE PAPERS
76 Southampton Row, London WC1B.
Tel: *0171-831 1151.*

HUSSEY & KNIGHTS
*Graphics House, 60 St. Giles Street, Norwich,
NR2 1LW.* **Tel:** *01603-761030.* **Fax:** *01603-
761032.*

INTAGLIO PRINTMAKERS
62 Southwark Bridge Road, London, SE1.
Tel: *0171-928 2633.*

JAMES DINSDALE
Armley Road, Leeds LS12 2DR.
Tel: *01532-430684.*
Fax: *01532-428047.*

JOHN E. WRIGHT
15 Brick Street, Derby DE1 1DU.
Tel: *01332-44743.* **Fax:** *01332-293369.*

JOHN JONES ART CENTRE LTD.
*Stroud Green Road, Finsbury Park, London N4
3JG.*
Tel: *0171-281 5439.*
Fax: *0171-281 5956.*
Opening times: *Mon-Fri 8-6, Sat 10-5.
Artshop only Sun 10-5.*
Nearest Underground: *Finsbury Park.*
Personnel: *Artshop Manager:* Jason Mackie.
John Jones Art Centre, Stroud Green Road,
Finsbury Park, London N4 3JG (1 min walk
from Finsbury Park station). Customer Car
Parking. Tel: 0171-281 5439, Fax: 0171-281
5956.
Services and Facilities:
Bookshop. Framing. Parking. Restoration. Shop.

KEMPS
28 Buckingham Palace Road, London SW1W.
Tel: *0171-834 1610.*

L. CORNELISSEN & SON
105 Great Russell Street, London WC1B 3RY.
Tel: *0171-636 1045.*

LAMLEY ART SUPPLIES
5 Exhibition Road, London SW7 2HE.
Tel: *0171-589 1276.*

LANGFORD & HILL
*4th Floor, Hardy House, 16-18 Beak Street,
Regent Street, London W1R.*
Tel: *0171-439 0181.*

LIQUITEX UK
Ampthill Road, Bedford, MK42 9RS.

LONDON GRAPHIC CENTRE
254 Upper Richmond Road, London SW15 6TQ.
Tel: *0171-785 9797.*

PRODUCT CARAN D'ACHE/JAKAR INTERNATIONAL LTD

Hillside House, 2-6 Friern Park, London N12 9BX.
Tel: *0181-445 6376.*
Fax: *0181-445 2714.*
Personnel: *General Manager:* D.W. Finney.

Swiss Made

Exclusive distributors in the UK and Ireland of Caran D'ache (Switzerland) Artists' Materials in addition to many Art Products in the Jakar catalogue.

RUSSELL & CHAPPLE LTD.

23 Monmouth Street, Shaftsbury Avenue, London WC2H 9DE.
Tel: *0171-836 7521.*
Fax: *0171-497 0554.*
Opening times: Mon-Fri 8.30-5. Sat 10-5.
Our specialist ground floor canvas shop offers an unrivalled choice of Artists Canvases, from 8oz to 16oz per square yard, and from 36" to 162" width.
While our first floor fine art shop has a cornucopia of artists' materials, including: Artists Paper, Boards, Easels, Paints, Pastels, Brushes, Pencils and General Artists Paraphernalia, in qualities aimed at professional artists, art students and serious amateur painters. We welcome mail order customers as well as personal shoppers.
Services and Facilities:
Shop.

STAEDTLER (UK) LTD

Pontyclun, CF72 8YJ.
Tel: *01443-237421.*
Fax: *01443-237440.*
Staedtler (UK) Limited is one of the leading manufacturers of drawing and writing equipment.
A comprehensive range of art products are available, suitable for all needs, ranging from the amateur to professional artist. The range of products include high quality Mars Lumograph sketching pencils and Pigment Liners, ideal for drawing, sketching and accentuating.

STAEDTLER

Staedtler's paint Karat Liqua is a watersoluble liquid wax which can be used opaque or, by adding water, becomes a watercolour medium. Finally, the Karat Aquarell Watercolour Pencils and Crayons are extremely break resistant and unlimited palette of intermediate colours and tones can be achieved.

FRAMING SUPPLIES

PEAK ROCK

Unit 30, DRCA Business Centre, Charlotte Despard Avenue, London SW11 5HD.
Tel: *0171-498 8444, Mobile 07050-108555.*
Fax: *0171-498 8333.*
Email *peakrock@art-estore.com*
Ws *peakrock.com*
Opening times: Open 9-5.
Nearest Underground: *Battersea Park & Queenstown Road (both 2 mins walk).*
Personnel: *Sales:* Nigel Hunt, Dean Liddelow, Peter Mullen.

GALLERY HANGING SUPPLIES

FRANK B. SCRAGG & CO

68 Vittoria Street, Birmingham B1 3PB.
Tel: *0121-236 7219.*
Fax: *0121-236 3633.*
Personnel: Mr J. B. Lewis.
Frank B. Scragg & Company are a long established company dealing in a wide range of supplies for framing and hanging pictures.
For galleries, there is brass rail with hooks and chain, together with a system of sliding rods and adjustable hooks, available in various finishes. Scragg's also supply all manner of framing accessories including wire, cord, hooks and rings. A free illustrated catalogue and price list is available on request.

PEAK ROCK

Unit 30, DRCA Business Centre, Charlotte Despard Avenue, London SW11 5HD.
Tel: *0171-498 8444, Mobile 07050-108555.*
Fax: *0171-498 8333.*
Email *peakrock@art-estore.com*
Ws *http://peakrock.com*
Opening times: Open 9-5.
Nearest Underground: *Battersea Park & Queenstown Road (both 2 mins walk).*
Personnel: *Sales:* Nigel Hunt, Dean Liddelow, Peter Mullen.

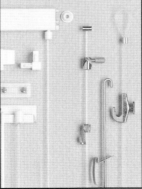

The UK's specialist in picture hanging systems, wood and metal print display browsers and sleeves, wood display easels, and portfolios, folders and sleeves.
Picture hanging systems allow optimal positioning of artwork without damage to walls. Pictures can be hung and re-hung in seconds. There is a choice of systems to match the style and practical needs of galleries, offices and homes. System components are manufactured to a high quality specification.
Print and Poster display browsers are available in black steel, natural finish oak and cherry wood and brown stained oak and cherry wood. Browser sleeves are available in various sizes, qualities and colours.

EQUIPMENT

CANUTE GALLERY SUPPLIES

Unit 4, Ashford Business Complex, Ashford, Middx.
TW15 1YQ.
Tel/Fax: *01784-251441.*
Personnel: Ms Jennifer Nugent.
IMAGE PERFECT GLASS, revolutionary 'invisible' glass gives the impression there is no glass in the finished artwork. It's invisible, you have to touch it to know its there! Eliminates the annoying effect of plain glass and the milky dullness of non-reflective glass.
No colour tinge - anti reflective benefits realised from all angles.
Recommended for all artworks, photographs and embroideries.Retains its unique properties even in triple mounting, creating a perfect image without reflection of discolouration ameliorating the craft of the framer and guaranteeing complete customer satisfaction.
Image Perfect Museum glass has all the aesthetic benefits of Image Perfect with the added advantage of 99% protection from harmful ultra violet rays.
No other glass combines this highest UV blockage with the virtually invisible viewing properties.
Manufactured by Zuel Co. 640 Hampden Avenue, St. Paul, MN 55114, USA.
Distributed in the UK through Canute Gallery Supplies, Ashford, Middlesex. Tel: 01784 251441.

CONSERVATION BY DESIGN

Timecare Works, 60 Park Road West, Bedford, Beds. MK41 7SL.
Tel: *01234-217258.*
Fax: *0234-328164.*
Email *info@conservation-by-design.co.uk*
Ws *http://www.conservation-by-design.co.uk*
Personnel: Stuart Welch, Philip Chamock, Rachel Bridger.
Conservation By Design is a company dedicated to the design and supply of high quality conservation storage and display products including acid free boxes, safe transparent polyester album pages, acid free papers and mounting board and a wide range of furniture including plan chests, picture racking, mobile shelving and museum standard glass showcases.

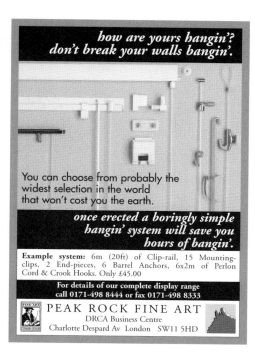

For all your Materials & Equipment needs, check out the Art Review classified

section. Published 10 times a year, it offers you the best in up-to-date

information on all aspects of art and design services. Call our subscription line

now on **0171 236 4880** or complete the subscription form on page 194.

NOTES

PACKERS & SHIPPERS

UNIT 7 BRUNEL COURT
ENTERPRISE DRIVE
OFF STATION ROAD
FOUR ASHES
WOLVERHAMPTON
WV10 7DF

- ART AND CRAFT TRANSPORT
- NATIONAL AND INTERNATIONAL
- AIR-RIDE INSULATED TRANSPORT VEHICLES
- WEEKLY TRIPS TO LONDON AND SCOTLAND
- CLIMATE CONTROLLED STORAGE
- PACKING AND SHIPPING
- CASE AND PLINTH CONSTRUCTION
- EXHIBITION HANGING
- PUBLIC SCULPTURE INSTALLATION

TEL: 01902 791797/ 790687 **FAX:** 01902 790687

PACKERS & SHIPPERS

01 Art Services
282 Richmond Road, London E8 3QS.
Tel: 0181-533 6124.
Fax: 0181-533 2718.
Opening times: Mon-Fri 9-6.
Personnel: Elizabeth Cooper.
01 Art Services Ltd is a reputable company specialising in fine art transportation and installation in London and the UK. Handling and installation of single works and exhibitions. Storage space available.

All Wheel Drive
4 Clevedale, Downend, Bristol B216 2SQ.
Tel: 0117-9836 627520/01836-627520/01272-570158. **Fax:** 01272-820505.

Anglo Pacific International Plc
Unit 1, Bush Industrial Estate, Standard Road, N. Acton, London NW10 6DF.
Tel: 0181-838 8008.
Fax: 0181-965 4954.
Email gerryward@anglopacific.co.uk
Personnel: Gerry Ward.
Specialist Packers and Shippers serving the whole world from a London head office. Offering a full range of services to meet the needs of Artists, Dealers, Collectors, Exhibitions organisers etc.
Contact Gerry, Mary or Malcolm for a free estimate or just friendly advice.

Art Handle
9 Sophia's Walk, Cathedral Road, Cardiff CF1 9LL.
Tel: 01222-233390, Mobile 0850-681004.
Fax: 01222-233390.

Art Move Ltd
Unit 3, Grant Road, London SW11 2NU.
Tel: 0700 ART MOVE .
Fax: 0171-223 0241.
Email artmove@dircon.co.uk
Opening times: Mon-Fri 9-5.30 and by appointment.
Nearest Underground: Clapham Junction.
Local, national and international transport. Climate-controlled Secure Storage approved by Museum and Galleries Commission. Worldwide Shipping. Picture Hanging and Sculpture Installation for trade, corporate and private clients. Packing and case making. Photography. Gilding and Conservation.
Services and Facilities:
Framing. Restoration.

Art Services Ltd
Unit 3, 129/131 Coldharbour Lane, London SE5 9NY.
Tel: 0171-274 5555.
Fax: 0171-737 7121.

Artlink Transport
102 Main Street, Milngavie, Glasgow.
Tel: 0141-956 5320.

C'Art
Unit 7, Brunell Court, Enterprise Drive, Off Station Road, Four Ashes, Wolverhampton WV10 7DF.
Tel: 01902-791797. **Fax:** 01902-790687.

Personnel: Angus MacDonald.
Ideally placed on the M6/M5 axis for competitive art and craft transport throughout Britain in custom built vehicles; onward transport to Europe.
Shipping and airfreight arranged worldwide. Packing and casemaking available. Hanging of single works or exhibitions; public art installation.

Cadogan Tate Fine Art Removals Ltd.
Cadogan House, Huthe Road, North Kensington, London NW10 6RS.
Tel: 0181-969 6969.
Fax: 0181-960 4567.

David Williams Specialised Transport
20 Lammas Road, Watton At Stone, SG14 3RH.
Tel: 01920-830031.
Fax: 01920-830576.
Opening times: Mon-Fri 8-8.
Specialising in all aspects of the transportation and installation of sculpture, for private and public exhibitions.
Case packing, shipping, storage, national and international transport.

Davies Turner Worldwide Movers Ltd.
Overseas House, Stewarts Road, London SW8 4UG.
Tel: 0171-622 4393.
Fax: 0171-720 3897.

Hedley's Humpers Ltd.
Units 2, 3 & 4, 97 Victoria Road, London NW10 6ND.
Tel: 0181-965 8733.
Fax: 0181-965 0249.

Lockson International Shippers, Packers & Removals of Fine Arts & Antiques
29 Broomfield Street, London EC14 6BX.
Tel: 0171-515 8600.
Fax: 0171-515 4043.

Momart Limited
(A WHOLLY OWNED SUBSIDIARY OF MOMART INTERNATIONAL PLC)
199-205 Richmond Road, London E8 3NJ.
Tel: 0181-986 3624.
Fax: 0181-533 0122.
Personnel: Managing Director: Scot Blyth.
Specialists in all aspects of Fine Art handling; experts in packing, case making, import and export services, private and exhibition installation, national and international transport (using air ride, climate control, fine art vehicles), high security storage.

Oxford Exhibition Services
Unit 7, Tavern Quay, Rope Street, London SE16 1TD.
Tel: 0171-237 5646.
Fax: 0171-232 2254.
Email enquiries@oxex.demon.co.uk
Ws www.oxex.demon.co.uk
Also at Station Road, Uffington, Oxon SN7

7QD. Tel: 01367-820713, fax: 01367-820504.

OXFORD EXHIBITION SERVICES
Oxford Exhibition Services offer a wide range of specialist fine art handling services to museums and galleries in the UK and abroad. Established in 1986 its London and Oxfordshire based staff are committed to maintaining high standards in the packing, domestic and international transport, display and storage of art works and other unique objects.

Pitt & Scott Ltd.
Eden Grove, London N7. **Tel:** 0171-607 7321/0171-607 0566.

Robinson & Foster Ltd.
75/81 Burnaby Street, London SW10 0NS.
Tel: 0171-393 3993. **Fax:** 0171-393 3906.

Shuttle Services
14 Clayton Road, Jesmond, Newcastle-upon-Tyne NE2 4RP. **Tel:** 0191-281 1397, Mobile 0831 854518. **Fax:** 0191-281 6734.

T. Rogers & Co. Ltd.
P.O. Box 8, 1a Broughton Street, London SW8 3QL. **Tel:** 0171-622 9151. **Fax:** 0171-627 3318.
Storage, packing, removal, shipping and forwarding of all works of art. Customs bonded warehousing.

Trans Euro Fine Art Division
Trans Euro Worldwide Movers, Drury Way, Brent Park, London NW10 0JN.
Tel: 0181-784 0100. **Fax:** 0181-459 3376.
Email richarde@transeuro.com
Opening times: Mon-Fri 8-6.
Personnel: Richard Edwards. Richard Bullivant.
Providing specialist packing and worldwide transportation services for the safe movement of works of art of all kinds. Secure environment controlled storage available for short and long terms. 'Climate Controlled' UK and European transport on 'Air Ride' vehicles. International exhibition transport and handling.

Transnic Ltd.
Arch 434, Gordon Grove, London SE5 9DW.
Tel: 0171-738 7555.

Transportomatic Ltd.
Ladford Covert, Ladforfields Business Park, Seighford, Stafford, ST18 9QL. **Tel:** 01785-282892. **Fax:** 01785-282802.

Vulcan International
Unit 13/14, Ascot Road, Clockhouse Lane, Feltham, TW14 8QF. **Tel:** 01784-244152.
Fax: 01784-248183.

Wingate & Johnston Ltd.
134 Queens Road, Peckham, London, SE15 2HR.
Tel: 0171-732 8123.
Fax: 0171-732 2631.

PHOTOGRAPHY

THE ART WORLD
DIRECTORY
1998/99 25TH EDITION

A. C. Cooper
10 Pollen Street, London W1R 9PH.
Tel: 0171-629 7585.

Alan Crumlish
11 Kirklee Terrace Lane, Glasgow G12 0TL.
Tel: 0141-339 5790.

Anthony Marshall
2 Riverside Cottages, New Lumford, Bakewell,
DE45 1GH. **Tel:** 01629-814787.

Antonia Reeve
11 Grosvenor Crescent, Edinburgh EH12 5EL.
Tel: 0131-337 4640.

ASP Photography
281 Sydenham Road, London SE26 5EN.
Tel: 0181-676 0836; Mobile 0956-897302.

B2 Photographic
5 Peary Place (off Roman Road), Bethnal Green,
London E2 0QW. **Tel:** 0181-983 1109.

Chris Boyle
272 Newchurch Road, Rawtenstall, BB4 7SN.
Tel: 01706-215958.

Coopers of Regent Street
207 Regent Street, London W1R 7DD.
Tel: 0171-629 6745.

Davies Colour Ltd
168 Sloper Road, Cardiff CF1 8AA.
Tel: 01222-230565.

Dawes & Billings Photographic
42 Goldstone Road, Hove, BN3 3RH.
Tel: 01273-722971.

Dennis Gilbert
11/15 Furmage Street, London SW18 4DF.
Tel: 0181-870 9051.

Frank Thurston Photography
c/o Royal College of Art, Kensington Gore,
London SW7. **Tel:** 0171-584 5020 x286.

Gabriel Weissman Applied & Fine Art
21 Cable Street Studios, 566 Cable Street,
London E1 9HB. **Tel:** 0171-780 9096.

Graham P. Matthews
Delfyd Farm, Llangennith, SA3 1JL.
Tel: 01792-386217.

Hayward Associates C
Unit 1, Shelley Farm, Ower, Romsey, SO51
6AS. **Tel:** 07000-442992.

Ian Jackson Photography
Oakgate, Southampton Road, Cadnam, SO4
2NA. **Tel:** 01703-814010.

Imagetrend
12 Chesterford Gardens, London NW3 7DE.
Tel: 0171-435 7383.

Incorporated Photographer
14 East Rise, Llanishen, Cardiff CP4 5RJ.

J.R. Photography
15 Westward Close, Uttoxeter, ST14 7BJ.
Tel: 01889-565061.

James Austin Fine Art Photography
Wysing Arts, Fox Road, Bourne, Cambridge,
CB3 7TX.
Tel: 01954-718871. **Fax:** 01954-718500.
Opening times: 9-6.
Nearest Station: Cambridge/Royston.
Personnel: James Austin.
Extensive experience of fine art photography.
Clients include National Trust, English
Heritage, Crafts Council, Christie's, Kettle's
Yard, Cambridge Colleges, Private Collections,
Artists, Craftsmen and Architects.
Subjects covered include architecture, paint-
ings, sculpture, ceramics, glass, textiles and
jewellery. Catalogue photography for
Waddington Galleries, Tate Gallery, London
and Liverpool, Henry Moore Foundation, Van
Gogh Museum, Sainsbury Centre for Visual
Arts (including catalogue of Robert and Lisa
Sainsbury collection).
Commissioned work for many books on archi-
tecture, arts and crafts. Photographic library
extensively used by History of Art departments
of universities throughout the world, and by
numerous publications on history of art and
architecture.
Services and Facilities:
Disabled Access. Parking.

John Carmichael
2 Scotts Avenue, Bromley, BR2 0LQ.
Tel: 0181-464 5869.

John Hoodless
36 Seymour Avenue, Morden, SM4 4RD.
Tel: 0181-330 3234/01323-762547;

John Penna
2 Hylands Road, Epson, KT18 7ED.
Tel: 01372-721678.

John R. Simmons C
21 Park Mansions, Prince of Wales Drive,
London SW11. **Tel:** 0171-622 0448.

Keith Meadley Photography
2 Sadberge Court, Osbaldswick, York YO1 3DR.
Tel: 01904-611109.

Kenneth Smith
6 Lussielaw Road, Edinburgh EH9 3BX.
Tel: 0131-667 6159.

Leith Photography
447 Edgeware Road, London W2.
Tel: 0171-723 5551.

Michael Hoppen Photography
Alexandra Studios, 3 Jubilee Place, London SW3
3TD.
Tel: 0171-352 3649.

Mike Smith
Durham University Oriental Museum, Elvet Hill,
Durham, DH1 3TH.
Tel: 0191-374 7911.

Norman R. Kent
Unit 5, 14 Castelnau, Barnes, London SW13
9RU.
Tel: 0181-741 9133.

P.J. Gates Photography Ltd.
94 New Bond Street, London W1Y 9LA.
Tel: 0171-629 4962.
Fax: 0171-493 4324.
Opening times: Mon-Fri 9.30-5.30.
Nearest Underground: Bond Street.
Personnel: Peter J. Gates FBIPP. Phillip
Paddock ABIPP.
The Company was formed in 1977 by P.J.
Gates and P.J. Paddock. The objective is to
provide top quality photography of works of
Art, Ancient or Modern. The company has an
international reputation, with clients through-
out the Northern Hemisphere. The clients
comprise Dealers, Collectors, and Museum
Curators.

Paul Medley
Oxford, **Tel:** 01865-72316.

Peter Waltham
Lincolnshire Archives, St. Rumbolds Street,
Lincoln, LN2 5AB.
Tel: 01522-526204.

The Photography of Art
159 Kennington Lane, London SE11 4EZ.
Tel: 0171-735 2432/0705/007 0216.
Fax: 0171-735 2627.
Email gillian@mcmail.com
Ws www.books.mcmail.com/photo.htm
Opening times: By appointment only.
Nearest Underground: Kennington.
Personnel: Director: Gillian Cargill. Co-
ordinator: Jenny Camilleri.

The Photography of Art provides artists and
galleries with a low cost professional recording
service while funding projects involving artists
and photography.
Phone for brochure on the £30 for 30 slides or
prints service.

Prudence Cuming Associates
28-29 Dover Street, London W1X 3PA.
Tel: 0171-629 6430.

Raymond Fifield
12 Lutton Bank, Lutton, Spalding, PE12 9LJ.
Tel: 01406-363951.

Rodney Todd-White
3 Clifford Street, London W1X 1RA.
Tel: 0171-734 9070/0171-287 9727.

SPACE FOR HIRE

Gallery and studio hire.

GALLERIES

ABBOTT & HOLDER
30 Museum Street, London WC1A 1LH.
Tel: *0171-637 3981.*
Fax: *0171-631 0575.*
Email *abbott.holder@virgin.net*
Ws *http://www.artefact.co.uk/AaH.html*
Opening times: Mon-Sat 9.30-6, Thurs 9.30-7.
Nearest Underground: *Tottenham Court Road.*
Personnel: *Partners:* Phillip Athill, John Abbott.
Over 1000 English watercolours,, drawings and prints (with some oils) 1780-1990 displayed on three gallery floors. Founded in 1936 our policy has always been to sell pictures that can be bought from income and our price range is from £50-£5,000.
We have an in-house conservator and are happy to give free advice of cleaning, restoring and framing. Every seven weeks we issue a LIST introducing 300 works to stock and announcing any particular exhibition we are featuring. Our LISTS are free and will be sent in application.
Services and Facilities:
Art Consultancy. Framing. Gallery space for hire. Restoration. Valuation.
Work Stocked and Sold:
Pr.
Price range: £50 - £5,000.

THE AIR GALLERY
32 Dover Street, London W1X 3RA.
Tel: *0171-409 1255 / 1516 / 1395.* **Fax:** *0171-409 1856.*

ALCHEMY GALLERY
157 Farringdon Road, London EC1R 3AD.
Tel: *0171-278 5666.*
Fax: *0171-278 9666.*

ART CONNOISSEUR GALLERY
95-97 Crawford Street, London W1H 1AN.
Tel: *0171-258 3835.*
Fax: *0171-258 3532.*

ATRIUM GALLERY, WHITELEYS
Whiteleys, Queensway, London W2 4YN.
Tel: *0171-229 8844.* **Fax:** *0171-792 8921.*

THE BARBER INSTITUTE OF FINE ARTS
The University of Birmingham, Birmingham B15 2TS. **Tel:** *0121-414 7333.*
Fax: *0121-414 3370.*
Opening times: Mon-Sat 10-5, Sun 2-5.
Nearest Station: *New Street (Main line), University (Cross City Line).*
Personnel: *Director:* Professor Richard Verdi. *Curator:* Paul Spencer-Longhurst. *Administrator:* Sophie Wilson.
One of the finest small picture galleries in the world housing an outstanding collection of old masters and modern paintings including masterpieces by Bellini, Rubens, Poussin, Murillo, Gainsborough, Rossetti, Whistler and Magritte. Among the Impressionist pictures are major works by Manet, Monet, Renoir,

Degas, Gauguin and Van Gogh. The Institute regularly holds concerts, lectures and recitals - all of which are open to the public.

It is also available for hire for seminars, receptions, concerts and private views.
Services and Facilities:
Disabled Access. Friends/Society. Gallery space for hire. Guided Tours. Lectures. Museum Shop. Parking.
Work Stocked and Sold:
Pa.

BIRD & DAVIS LTD
45 Holmes Road, Kentish Town, London NW5 3AN.
Tel: *0171-485 3797.*
Fax: *0171-284 0509.*

EBURY GALLERIES
200 Ebury Street, London, SW1.
Tel: *0171-730 8999.*

GALLERY 47
47 Great Russell Street, Bloomsbury, London WC1B 3PA.
Tel: *0171-637 4577.*

THE GALLERY IN CORK STREET
28 Cork Street, London W1X 1HB.
Tel: *0171-287 8408.*
Fax: *0171-287 2018.*
Opening times: Mon-Fri 10-6, Sat 11-4.
Nearest Underground: *Green Park/Piccadilly.*
Personnel: *Manager:* Caroline Kanter.
The Gallery in Cork Street and Gallery 27 are two stunning galleries of international reputation in "Europe's Leading Art Street".
The Gallery in Cork Street Ltd. offers our clients a unique opportunity to hold exhibitions entirely under their control in Cork Street.
The Gallery in Cork Street: 125m2 of versatile prime display area, 60 linear m of wall space, full height double window frontage. Gallery 27: 100m2 of versatile prime display area, 50 linear m of wall space, large window frontage. Excellent Presentation.
Full Management and Facility support.

Exclusive mailing list. Organisation services available by arrangement.
Services and Facilities:
Gallery space for hire.

HANOVER GALLERIES
11-13 Hanover Street, Liverpool, L1 3DN.
Tel: *0151-709 3073.*
Opening times: Tues-Sat 10.30-5.
Personnel: *Director:* E.P. Austin.
Two spacious and prestigious galleries of exceptional standard, on ground and first floors, inter-connected by a spiral staircase, wall run 85ft and 81ft respectively. Both have good natural light and 30 fully adjustable track spots per gallery. Available for rent. Details on request.
Services and Facilities:
Gallery space for hire.

HIGHGATE GALLERY
11 South Grove, Highgate, London N6 6BS.
Tel: *0181-340 3343.*
Opening times: Tues-Fri 1-5, Sat or Sun 10-4.
Nearest Underground: *Archway.*
Personnel: *Administrator:* Linden Nicoll. Hazel Solomon.
This unique C19 gallery is housed in the Highgate Literary and Scientific Institution, a busy social and cultural centre in Highgate Village.
The gallery is top-lit and spacious with 75' x 6' clear hanging space and excellent exhibition lighting.
Rates are reasonable and no commission is taken. There are nine exhibitions a year, usually of two weeks each. Slides and/or photos should be sent to the Exhibition Committee plus a CV.
Ring the Administrator on 0181-340 3343 for further details.
Services and Facilities:
Disabled Access. Gallery space for hire.

MALL GALLERIES
17 Carlton House Terrace, London SW1Y 5BD.
Tel: *0171-930 6844.*
Fax: *0171-839 7830.*
Nearest Underground: *Charing Cross/Piccadilly Circus*
The Main, East and North Galleries, totalling over 500sq. metres, are available for hire separately or in any combination. The Galleries meet British Library conditions with colour correct lighting, air conditioning and moveable screens. Please contact the above administrative address for details. See also entries under London Galleries, Art Consultants and Art Societies as 'Federation of British Artists'.
Services and Facilities:
Art Consultancy. Commissioning Service. Friends/Society. Gallery space for hire. Guided Tours. Lectures. Workshop Facilities.

OPEN SPACE GALLERY
131 Lower Marsh, London SE1 7AE.
Tel: *0171-261 1353.*

SACKVILLE GALLERY
26 Sackville Street, London W1X 1DA.
Tel: *0171-734 8104.* **Fax:** *0171-734 8104.*

SPACE FOR HIRE

SOAR GALLERY
4 Launceston Place, London W8 5RL.

YARROW GALLERY
Art Department, Oundle School, Glapthorn Road, Oundle, Peterborough, PE8 4EN.
Tel: *01832-274034.* **Fax:** *01832-274034.*
Opening times: *Mon-Fri 10.30-1 & 2.30-5, Sun 2.30-5.*
Nearest Station: *Peterborough.*
Personnel: *Director:* Roger Page.
School-sponsored exhibitions and available for hire.
Services and Facilities:
Gallery space for hire.

STUDIO SPACE FOR HIRE

ACME
44 Copperfield Road, London E3 4RR.
Tel: *0181-981 6811.*
Fax: *0181-983 0567.*

GREAT WESTERN STUDIOS
Westbourne Park, London W2.
Tel: *0171-221 0100.*

HERTFORD ROAD STUDIOS
12-14 Hertford Road, London N1.
Tel: *0171-241 0651.*

ROSEANGLE GALLERY
17 Roseangle, Dundee.
Tel: *0138-322429.*

SCULPTURE HOUSE
54-56 Mill Place, Kingston upon Thames, KT1 2LR.

SOUTH AND NORTH ARTS
133 Rye Lane, Peckham, London SE15 4ST.
Tel: *0171-635 8742.*

SPACE
8 Hoxton Street, London N1 6NG.
Tel: *0171-613 1925.*
Fax: *0171-613 1996.*
Email *spacestudios@easynet.co.uk*
Ws *http://www.ecna.org*
Personnel: *Studios Manager:* Fiona Furness.
A registered non-profit making charity established by artists in 1968. SPACE aims to provide secure well-managed studios for visual artist.
Studio buildings are situated in East and South East London. Prices per sq. ft. include rate, buildings insurance, maintenance and administration. Studios available can be short term or long term.
Sub-lets and shares are also available. Some sites are subject to waiting list. Phone for application and registration pack. Funded by the London Arts Board.

THE CABLE STREET STUDIOS
Thames House, 566 Cable Street, Limehouse, London E1 9HB.
Tel: *0171-790 1309.*
Fax: *0171-790 1309.*

NOTES

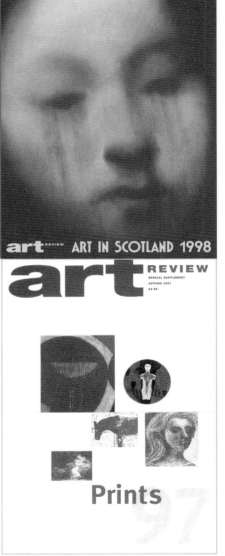

PUBLISHING

Bookshops, Book Publishers, Magazines.

THE ART WORLD
DIRECTORY
1998/99 25TH EDITION

PUTS ITS
MOUTH
WHERE
YOUR
MONEY IS

art REVIEW
THE ESSENTIAL
MONTHLY GUIDE
0171 2364880

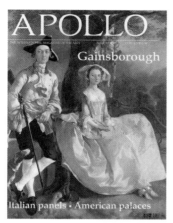

PUBLISHING

ART BOOK PUBLISHERS

ACADEMY GROUP LTD
Academy Editions, 42 Leinster Gardens, London W2 3AN. **Tel:** *0171-402 2141.*

THE APPLE PRESS
6 Blundell Street, London N7 9BH. **Tel:** *0171-700 8521.*

ART SALES INDEX LTD
1 Thames Street, Weybridge, KT13 3JG. **Tel:** *01932-856426.*

ASHGATE/SCOLAR PRESS
Gower House, Croft Road, Aldershot, GU11 3HR.
Tel: *01252-331551.* **Fax:** *01252-344405.*
Email *gower@gowerpub.demon.co.uk*
Ws *http://www.ashgate.com*
Personnel: Sarah Stilwell.
In 1998 we will publish a new, expanded and updated edition of the classic Handbook of Modern British Painting and Printmaking 1900-1990, plus new works on Glyn Philpot, Forrest Reid, C.W. Nevinson, Mary Potter, amongst others.
As part of our expanding programme of Ashgate Art History titles we will continue to publish recent research, monographs or collected essays dealing with all aspects of art and architectural history.
Please visit our website to find out about new titles and/or telephone to request a copy of our current art books catalogue.

AURUM PRESS LTD
25 Bedford Avenue, London WC1B 3AT. **Tel:** *0171-637 3225.*

BRITISH MUSEUM PRESS
46 Bloomsbury Street, London WC1B 3QQ. **Tel:** *0171-323 1234.*

BT BATSFORD
583 Fulham Road, London SW6 5BY. **Tel:** *0171-486 8484.*

CAMBRIDGE UNIVERSITY PRESS
The Edinburgh Building, Shaftesbury Road, Cambridge, CB2 2RU. **Tel:** *01223-312393.*

CASSELL PLC
Wellington House, 125 Strand, London WC2R 0BB. **Tel:** *0171-420 5582.*

COLLINS & BROWN PUBLISHERS
London House, Parkgate Road, London SW11 4NQ.
Tel: *0171-924 2575.*

CONSTABLE AND COMPANY
3 The Lanchesters, 162 Fulham Palace Road, London W6 9ER.
Tel: *0181-741 3663.*

DAVID & CHARLES
Brunel House, Forde Road, Newton Abbott, TQ1Z 4PN. **Tel:** *01626-61121.*

DORLING KINDERSLEY
9 Henrietta Street, London WC2E 8PS.
Tel: *0171-836 5411.*

FABER & FABER
3 Queen Square, London WC1N 3AU.
Tel: *0171-465 0045.*

GARNET PUBLISHING
8 Southern Court, South Street, Reading, RG1 4QF. **Tel:** *01189-597847.*

GERALD DUCKWORTH & CO LTD
48 Hoxton Square, London N1 6PB.
Tel: *0171-729 5986.*

HAMILYN OCTUPUS
Michelin House, 81 Fulham Road, London SW3 6RB. **Tel:** *0171-581 9393.*

HARRY N. ABRAMS INC
Lynton House, 7-12 Tavistock Square, London WC1H 9LB. **Tel:** *0171-391 65643.*

HODDER & STOUGHTON
Hodder Headline Book Publishing Ltd 338 Euston Road, London NW1. **Tel:** *0171-873 6000.*

J.A.B. PUBLISHING
Suite 2, Arran Place, Valnord Road, St. Peter Port, Gu1 1TL **Tel:** *01481-722460.*

LAYZELL PUBLIC RELATIONS FOR THE ARTS
Little Orchard, Dallinghoo, Woodbridge, IP13 0LG. **Tel:** *01473-737468.* **Fax:** *01473-737750.*
Personnel: *Director:* Alistair Layzell.
Layzell Public Relations for the Arts specialise in publicity for exhibitions, events, fairs and books on the arts; the co-ordination and organisation of festivals, openings and launches.
High profile coverage has been achieved for artists, gallery owners and publishers, on national and regional television and radio and in the national and specialist art press.
Marketing services.

LITTLE, BROWN & COMPANY
Brettenham House, Lancaster Place, London WC2E 7EN. **Tel:** *0171-911 8000.*

MACMILLAN PUBLISHERS LTD.
THE DICTIONARY OF ART
25 Eccleston Place, London SW1W 9NF.
Tel: *0171-881 8356.* **Fax:** *0171-881 8357.*

MANCHESTER UNIVERSITY PRESS
Oxford Road, Manchester M13 9NR.
Tel: *0161-273 5539.*
Fax: *0161-274 3346.*

METHUEN LONDON LTD
Michelin House, 81 Fulham Road, London SW3 5DT. **Tel:** *0171-581 9393.*

THE MIT PRESS LTD
Fitzroy House, 11 Chenies Street, London WC1E 7ET.
Tel: *0171-306 0603.*

OCTUPUS BOOKS LTD
Michelin House, 81 Fulham Road, London SW3 6RB. **Tel:** *0171-581 9393.*

ORION PUBLISHING
Orion House, 5 Upper St Martins Lane, London WC2H 9EA. **Tel:** *0171-240 3444.*

OXFORD UNIVERSITY PRESS
Great Clarendon Street, Oxford, OX2 6DP.
Tel: *01865-556767.*
Fax: *01865-556646.*
Ws *http://www.oup.co.uk (and specific art page), oup-usa.org/arthis/art1.html*
Oxford University Press is an international publishing house which publishes books across almost every academic subject and has become known for the highest standards of academic excellence and quality of production.
Oxford University Press publishes a wide range of art books including the new OXFORD HISTORY OF ART series, a major collection of ground-breaking, authoritative, and beautifully illustrated books by art historians at the forefront of new thinking.

PARAGON PRESS
92 Horwood Road, London SW6 4QH.
Tel: *0171-736 4024.*

PAVILION
26 Upper Ground, London SE1 9DP.
Tel: *0171-620 1666.*

PHAIDON PRESS
Regents Wharf, All Saints Street, London N1 9PA.
Tel: *0171-843 1000.*

RANDOM HOUSE
PUBLISHING
20 Vauxhall Bridge Road, London SW1V 2SA.
Tel: *0171-973 9670.*

REAKTION BOOKS
11 Rathbone Place, London W1P 1DE.
Tel: *0171-580 9928.*

ROUTLEDGE
11 New Fetter Lane, London EC4P 4EE.
Tel: *0171-583 9855.*

SCOLAR PUBLISHING
Croft Road, Aldershot, GU12 4DY.
Tel: *01252-331551.*

THAMES & HUDSON
30-34 Bloomsbury Street, London WC1B 3QB.
Tel: *0171-636 5488.*
Email *sales@thbooks.demon.co.uk*
Ws *thttp://www.hamesHudson.co.uk*

V&A PUBLICATIONS
160 Brompton Road, London SW3 1HW.
Tel: *0171-938 9663.*

YALE UNIVERSITY PRESS
23 Pond Street, London NW3 2PN.
Tel: *0171-431 4422.*

ART BOOKSHOPS

AN LANNTAIR
Town Hall, South Beach, Stornoway, HS1 2BX.
Tel: *01851-703307.* **Fax:** *01851-703307.*

ARNOLFINI GALLERY
16 Narrow Quay, Bristol BS1 4QA.
Tel: *0117-929 9191.* **Fax:** *0117-925 3876.*

ARTS BIBLIOGRAPHIC
*37 Cumberland Business Park, Cumberland
Avenue, London, NW10 7SL.*
Tel: *0181-961 4277.* **Fax:** *0181-961 8246.*
Email *sales@artsbib.com*
Ws *http://www.artsbib.com*
Arts Bibliographic is not a bookshop as such, it
is a firm of library suppliers specialising in
books and catalogues on art and design.
Their expert services are now available to the
general public as well via a website providing
mail-order facilities and information on the
latest publications: www.artsbib.com.

ASHMOLEAN MUSEUM
Beaumont Street, Oxford, OX1 2PH.
Tel: *01865-278000.*

ATRIUM BOOKSHOP
5 Cork Street, London W1.
Tel: *0171-495 0073.*

BARBICAN ART GALLERY
Level 3, Silk Street, London EC2.
Tel: *0171-382 7105.*

BEYOND WORDS
42-44 Cockburn Street, Edinburgh EH1 1PB.
Tel: *0131-226 6636.* **Fax:** *0131-226 6676.*
Opening times: Jan-Mar 1988 : Tue-Sat 10-
6, From 1 Apr 1998 : Tue-Sat 10-8, Sun-Mon
12-5.
Nearest Station: Edinburgh Waverley.
Personnel: *Proprietor:* Neil McIlwraith.
Beyond Words provides Scotland's finest selection of new photographic books. It stocks
everything for the photography enthusiast:
books on skills and techniques, cameras and
photographic technology, analysis and criticism, history of photography, photojournalism
and documentary, portraits and nudes, landscape, wildlife, travel and photographers A to
Z. Plus photographically illustrated books to
complement other interests such as social and
local history, Scotland, literature and the arts,
sport and hillwalking, gardens and travel. And
a selection of magazines, greetings and post
cards, and stationery, all complementing the
photographic theme. Beyond Words has a display space for prints, often from recently published books.
Services and Facilities:
Bookshop. Friends/Society. Gallery space for hire.

BLACKWELL'S ART & POSTER SHOP C
27 Broad Street, Oxford, OX1 2AS. **Tel:**
01865-792792. **Fax:** *01865-794143.*
Opening times: Mon-Sat 9-6, Tue 9.30-6,
Sun 11-5.

For books on every aspect of art, architecture
and design from typography to town planning.
Worldwide mail order service. Friendly,
knowledgeable staff. Orders welcomed by
phone, fax, or letter.

CRAFTS COUNCIL
*44a Pentonville Road, Islington, London N1
9BY.* **Tel:** *0171-278 7700.* **Fax:** *0171-837
6891.*

DEAN CLOUGH GALLERIES
Halifax, HX3 5AX. **Tel:** *01422-344555.*

DILLONS ARTS BOOKSHOP
8 Long Acre, London WC2. **Tel:** *0171-836
1359.*

DURHAM ART GALLERY
Aykley Heads, Durham, DH1 5TU.
Tel: *0191-384 2214.* **Fax:** *0191-386 1770.*

FOYLES BOOKSHOP
Charing Cross Road, London, WC2H 0EB.
Tel: *0171-437 5660.*

GAINSBOROUGH'S HOUSE
46 Gainsborough Street, Sudbury, CO10 6EU.
Tel: *01787-372958.* **Fax:** *01787-376991.*

THE GOLDMARK GALLERY
Orange Street, Uppingham, LE15 9SQ.
Tel: *01572-821424.*

HAYWARD GALLERY BOOKSHOP
Hayward Gallery, South Bank, London SE1.
Tel: *0171-928 3144.*

THE HENRY MOORE INSTITUTE
74 Headrow, Leeds LS1 3AA. **Tel:** *01132-
467467.* **Fax:** *01132-461481.*

**HOLBURNE MUSEUM AND CRAFTS STUDY
CENTRE**
Great Pulteney Street, Bath, BA2 4DB.
Tel: *01225-466669.*

HUNTERIAN ART GALLERY
*University of Glasgow, 82 Hillhead Street,
Glasgow G12 8QQ.*
Tel: *0141-330 5431.* **Fax:** *0141-330 3618.*

ICA BOOKSHOP
*Institute of Contemporary Arts, The Mall,
London SW1.* **Tel:** *0171-930 0493.*

INVERNESS MUSEUM & ART GALLERY
Castle Wynd, Inverness, IV2 3ED.
Tel: *01463-237114.*

LILLIE ART GALLERY
Station Road, Milngavie, Glasgow G62 8BZ.
Tel: *0141-943 3247.*

MAC (MIDLANDS ARTS CENTRE)
Cannon Hill Park, Birmingham B12 9HQ.
Tel: *0121-440 4221.* **Fax:** *0121-446 4372.*

MUSEUM OF MODERN ART
30 Pembroke Street, Oxford, OX1 1BP.
Tel: *01865-728608.* **Fax:** *01865-722733.*

NATIONAL GALLERY OF SCOTLAND
The Mound, Edinburgh EH2 2EL.
Tel: *0131-556 8921.* **Fax:** *0131-332 4939.*

NATIONAL LIBRARY OF WALES
Aberystwyth, SY23 3BW. **Tel:** *01970-632800.*

PAISLEY FINE BOOKS
17 Corsebar Crescent, Paisley, PA2 9QA.
Tel: *0141-884 2661.*

THE PHOTOGRAPHERS' GALLERY
5-8 Great Newport Street, London WC2.
Tel: *0171-831 1772.*

ROYAL ACADEMY BOOKSHOP
Royal Academy, Burlington House, London W1.
Tel: *0171-439 7438.*

ROYAL PHOTOGRAHIC SOCIETY
The Octagon, Milson Street, Bath, BA1 1DN.
Tel: *01225-462841.*

**SCOTTISH NATIONAL GALLERY OF
MODERN ART**
Belford Road, Edinburgh EH4 3DR. **Tel:** *0131-
556 8921.*

SCOTTISH NATIONAL PORTRAIT GALLERY
1 Queen Street, Edinburgh EH2 1JD.
Tel: *0131-556 8921.*

SERPENTINE GALLERY
Kensington Gardens, London W2 3XA.
Tel: *0171-402 6075.*

TATE GALLERY BOOKSHOP
Tate Gallery, Millbank, London SW1.
Tel: *0171-821 1313/834 5651.*

VICTORIA & ALBERT MUSEUM
*Cromwell Road, South Kensington, London SW7
2RL.*
Tel: *0171-938 8500/8666.* **Fax:** *0171-938
8341.*

WATERSTONE'S BOOKSHOP
193 Kensington High Street, London, W8.
Tel: *0171-937 8432.*

WHITECHAPEL BOOKSHOP
Whitechapel High Street, London E1 7QX.
Tel: *0171-522 7898 (recorded info), 0171-522
7888.*

ZWEMMERS
24 Litchfield Street, London WC2M 9NJ.
Tel: *0171-379 7886/0171-240 6995/0171-240
4158.* **Fax:** *0171-836 7049.*

FINE ART MAGAZINES

ANTIQUES BULLETIN
*2 Hampton Court Road, Harborn, Birmingham
B17 9AE.*

ANTIQUES TRADE GAZETTE
17 Whitcomb Street, London, WC2H 7PL.
Tel: *0171-930 7192.*

PUBLISHING

APOLLO
1 Castle Lane London SW1E 6DR.
Tel: *0171-233 8906.* **Fax:** *0171-233 7159.*
Personnel: *Editor:* David Ekserdjian.
Associate Publisher: Anthony Law.
Advertisement Manager: Nigel McKinley.
Assistant Editor: Polly Chiapetta. *Subscription Manager:* Kim Collins.

APOLLO
Established 1925

Completely devoted to art, antiques and works of art. Apollo is produced monthly to the highest editorial and production standards. Its articles, written by experts and lavishly illustrated cover all periods from ancient to modern.
A diary and international exhibition and book reviews appear each month, along with many colour pages of international art and antiques advertising. £7.80 per month or Annual Subscription (12 issues) £70 UK, £75 overseas, $125 USA.

ART MONTHLY
Suite 17, 126 Charing Cross Road, London WC2H 0DG.
Tel: *0171-497 0726.* **Fax:** *0171-497 0726.*

THE ART NEWSPAPER
27-29 Vauxhall Grove, London SW8 1SY.
Tel: *0171-735 3332.* **Fax:** *0171-735 3332.*

ART REVIEW
Hereford House, 24 Smithfield Street, London EC1A 9LB.
Tel: *0171-236 4880.* **Fax:** *0171-236 4881.*
Email *info@art-review.co.uk*
Ws *http://www.art-review.co.uk*
Opening times: *We never close.*
Personnel: *Editor:* David Lee. *Adverting Manager:* Alistair Rogers

Britain's leading monthly art magazine. Annual UK subscription £36; USA $69; Europe £48; Rest of World £48. Also publishers of the Art Review Art World Directory.

ARTISTS & ILLUSTRATORS
The Fitzpatrick Building, 188-194 York Way, London N7 9QR.
Tel: *0171-700 8500.* **Fax:** *0171-700 4985.*

ARTISTS NEWSLETTER
PO Box 23, Sunderland SR4 6DG.
Tel: *0191-567 3589.* **Fax:** *0191-564 1600.*

THE ARTISTS' PUBLISHING COMPANY
Caxton House, 63-65 High Street, Tenterden, TN30 6BD.
Tel: *01580-763315/3673.* **Fax:** *01580 765411.*
Personnel: *Managing Director:* I.A. Briers. Publisher of two, monthly instructional fine art magazines offering professional painting instruction in all media: Leisure Painter, for the amateur and student. Editor: Irene A.

Briers. The Artist, for the serious amateur and semi-professional. Editor: Dr Sally Bulgin.

Both magazines give up-to-date information on books, videos and art products; tuition and exhibition listings, painting courses and holidays. An invaluable marketplace for all forms of art tuition and fine arts services. Both magazines cost £2.10 per issue; subscription: £23.00.

CONTEMPORARY VISUAL ARTS
197 Knightsbridge, 8th Floor, London SW7 1RB.
Tel: *0171-823 8373.* **Fax:** *0171-823 7969.*

CRAFTS MAGAZINE
Crafts Council, 44a Pentonville Road, Islington, London N1 9BY.
Tel: *0171-278 7700.*
Fax: *0171-837 0858.*
Email *crafts@craftscouncil.org.uk*
Ws *http://www.craftscouncil.org.uk*
Nearest Underground: *Angel.*
Personnel: *Editor:* Geraldine Rudge. *Sales & Marketing Manager:* Georgina Harman.
Britain's leading Decorative and Applied Arts Magazine, featuring the best in contemporary and traditional design-led craft.
Services and Facilities:
Commissioning Service.

FRIEZE
21 Denmark Street, London WC2H 8NE.
Tel: *0171-379 1533.*
Fax: *0171-379 1521.*

MODERN PAINTERS
Universal House, 251 Tottenham Court Road, London W1P 9AD.
Tel: *0171-636 6058.*
Fax: *0171-580 5615.*

PRINT QUARTERLY PUBLICATIONS
80 Carlton Hill, London NW8 0ER.
Tel: *0171-625 6332.*
Fax: *0171-624 0960.*

RA MAGAZINE
Royal Academy of Arts, Piccadilly, London W1.
Tel: *0171-439 7438.*
Fax: *0171-287 9023.*

TATE MAGAZINE
Blueprint Media Ltd., Christ Church, Cosway Street, London NW1 5NJ.
Tel: *0171-706 4596.*

COMMERCIAL GALLERIES BY MEDIA

This section lists establishments by media speciality. Use this section to find the gallery stocking the media you require.

THE ART WORLD
DIRECTORY
1998/99 25TH EDITION

COMMERCIAL GALLERIES BY MEDIA

COMMERCIAL GALLERIES BY MEDIA

COMMERCIAL GALLERIES BY MEDIA

COMMERCIAL GALLERIES BY MEDIA

PHOTOGRAPHY

PRINTS

COMMERCIAL GALLERIES BY MEDIA

SCULPTURE

COMMERCIAL GALLERIES BY MEDIA

NOTES

ART
UNDER
£1,000

ART UNDER £1,000

Galleries selling work priced under £1,000.

THE ART WORLD
DIRECTORY
1998/99 25TH EDITION

S/T/U/V

W/X/Y/Z

NOTES

NOTES

COMMERCIAL GALLERY ARTISTS

This section lists, by gallery, a sample of the artists the gallery represents, stocks or sells.

THE ART WORLD
DIRECTORY
1998/99 25TH EDITION

198 GALLERY
(p.85)
ALIYU, Hassan
COOPER, Clement
DONKOR, Godfried
ETTIENNE, Glen
IMANI, Pablo
JONES, Sheila
KELLY, George
MANNING, Jenni
WATSON, Raymond

20TH CENTURY GALLERY
(p.60)
ANDREWS, Sybil
AUSTEN, Winifred
AUSTIN, Frederick
AUSTIN, Robert
AYRTON, Michael
BADMIN, Stanley
BLAMPIED, Edmund
BRANGWYN, Frank
BRESSLERN-ROTH, Norbertine
BROCKHURST, Gerald
BUCKLAND-WRIGHT, John
CAMERON, David Young
DODD, Francis
FARLEIGH, John
FOOKES, Ursula
GABAIN, Ethel
GILL, Eric
GRIGGS, Frorick
JANES, Norman
JOHN, Augustus
LUMSDEN, Ernest
MALET, Guy
NASH, John
NEVINSON, C.R.W.
O'CONNOR, John
RAVERAT, Gwendoline
ROYDS, Mabel
SEABY, Allen
SICKERT, Walter
THORPE, John Hall
TUNNICLIFFE, Charles Frederick
UNDERWOOD, George C. Leon
URUSHIBARA, Yoshisiro
WALES, Geoffrey
WALLOOOOOT, William
WHITE, Ethelbert
WYLLIE, William L.

ACKERMANN & JOHNSON
(p.60)
ALKEN, Henry
ANDERSON, Douglas
BOULTBEE, John
BRIGHT, Henry
BUSH, Harry
CHAMBERS, George
CONSTABLE, John
COOKE, Arthur Claude
COOKE, Edward William
COTMAN, John Sell
CROME, John
FERNELEY, John F.
GAINSBOROUGH, Thomas
GILPIN, Sawrey
GLOVER, John
GOODWIN, Albert
HAYMAN, Francis
HERRING, J.F.
HOWARD, Ken
HUGGINS, William
LADBROOKE, John Berney
LEADER, Benjamin Williams
LUNY, Thomas
MARSHALL, Ben
MCBEY, James
MORLAND, George
MUNNINGS, Sir Alfred
NASMYTH, Alexander
NASMYTH, Patrick

PRINSEP, Edward
PRITCHETT, Edward
SARTORIUS, Francis
SARTORIUS, John Nost
SCHETKY, John Christian
SMYTHE, Edward Robert
SMYTHE, Thomas
STANNARD, Joseph
STARK, James
TURNER, J.M.W.
WALTON, Henry
WARD, James
WATTS, George Frederick
WEBB, James
WOLSTENHOLME, Dean

ADAM GALLERY
(p.100)
BOND, Marj
CARTWRIGHT, Richard
DAVIE, Alan
DENARO, Melita
FOORD, Susan
FROST, Terry
GRAHAM, Brian
HARVEY, Gail
HERON, Patrick
HILTON, Roger
HOCKNEY, David
KENT, Colin
LIN, Hsiao Mei
MACMIADHACHAIN, Padraig
MCDOWELL, Leo
MOORE, Henry
NEWTON, Algernon
NICHOLSON, Ben
PHILIPSON, Robin
PIPER, John
ROBERTS, William
ROBERTSON, James
SCOTT, William
SELBY, William
SUDDABY, Rowland
WOOD, Christopher

ADVANCED GRAPHICS LONDON
(p.175)
AITCHISON, Craigie
BARTLETT, Stephen
BEATTIE, Basil
BELLANY, John
BENJAMINS, Paul
BENNETT, Mick
CAULFIELD, Patrick
FRASER, Donald Hamilton
HALTER, Ardyn
HAMMICK, Tom
HANSON, Rolf
HOYLAND, John
HUGONIN, James
IRVIN, Albert
JONES, Trevor
KEANE, John
KLEIN, Anita
MCLEAN, John
MOON, Mick
RADFORD, Matthew
RICHARDSON, Ray
SETCH, Terry
WALKER, John
WHITEFORD, Kate
WRAGG, Gary

ALAN CRISTEA GALLERY
(p.60)
AVERY, Milton
AYRES, Gillian
BASELITZ, Georg
BLAKE, Peter
BRAQUE, Georges
CAULFIELD, Patrick
CHILLIDA, Eduardo
CRAIG-MARTIN, Michael

DAVEY, Grenville
DIBBETS, Jan
DINE, Jim
DUBUFFET, Jean
FLANAGAN, Barry
FULTON, Hamish
GABO, Naum
HAMILTON, Richard
HODGKIN, Howard
HOYLAND, John
INSHAW, David
JOHNS, Jasper
JONES, Allen
JUDD, Donald
LÉGER, Fernand
LICHTENSTEIN, Roy
MANSEN, Matthias
MANSER, Antje
MATISSE, Henri
MCKEEVER, Ian
MILROY, Lisa
MIRO, Joan
MOON, Mick
MOTHERWELL, Robert
NICHOLSON, Ben
PALADINO, Mimmo
PENCK, A.R.
PICASSO, Pablo
RAINER, Arnulf
RAUSCHENBERG, Robert
ROSENQUIST, James
SALLE, David
SCULLY, Sean
SELF, Colin
STELLA, Frank
SULTAN, Donald
TAPIES, Antoni
TILSON, Joe
WALKER, John
WARHOL, Andy
WINNER, Gerd

ALBEMARLE GALLERY
(p.61)
ALARCON, Aracely
BARLOW, Jeremy
BELL, Sandra
BERBER, Mersad
BLUMENFELD, Helaine
DAVIS, James
DOMINGUEZ, Goyo
FAULKNER, Iain
FORMIN, Igor
GALLARDA, Michael
GATHERER, Stuart Luke
GOSLING, Annabel
GRAN, Elena & Michel
HOCKING, Susan-Jayne
HURTADO, Fabio
KING, Alan
KRASNOVSKY, Alexy
LANDA, Julien
LIEPKE, Malcolm
LIU, Jinchberg
MARKUS, Csaba
MCDOWELL, Leo
MCKEAN, Graham
MCKIVRAGAN, Terry
RAISSIS, Aris
REDON HUICI, Fernando
ROBINSON, Zev
ROLDEN, Alfredo
ROSSI, Carlo
SAUNDERS, Robert
SCOULLER, Glen
TELFORD, Paul
TODD WARMOUTH, Pip
WAUGH, Scott
WILLIAMS, Antony

ALEXANDRA GALLERY
(p.61)
AMOR, Steven

ASHLEY, Stuart
ATKINS, John
BLACK, Simon
CARTER, Sue
CLINTON, Joanna
COCKAYNE, Anthony
CULLEN, Patrick
DANIEL, Jane
EARLE, Nigel
GARLAND, Peter
GRANT, Cliff
HAGGARD, Henry
HUNT, Peggy
LOADER, Sue
MAY, Jane
MEI-YIM, Chris
PALAO, Edmond
POLLAK, Norma
RICHARDSON, Ilana
TCHENEGA, Mikhail
WILDMAN, P.

ALEXANDRA WETTSTEIN FINE ART
(p.219)
BAILEY, Belinda
BARKER, Dale Devereux
CAULFIELD, Patrick
CHADWICK, Lynn
COOPER, Eileen
DELANEY, Barbara
FROST, Terry
GARFIELD, Rachel
JONES, Allen
KEILLER, Anna
KITAJ, R.B.
KOWALSKY, Elaine
MATISSE, Henri
MCKELLAR, Robert
MIRO, Joan
MOORE, Henry
NEWINGTON, Charles
PAOLOZZI, Eduardo
PASMORE, Victor
PICASSO, Pablo
PIPER, Edward
PIPER, John
SUTHERLAND, Graham
SYKES, Sandy
TILSON, Joe
WAKITA, Aijiro

ALRESFORD GALLERY
(p.108)
ASHLEY, Raymond
ATKINS, David
BATES, Joan
BERRY, June
BODEN, Richard
BROWN, Bob
COATES, Tom
CUMING, Fred
DICKER, Molly
EURICH, Richard
EVANS, Ray
FAZAKERLEY, Pauline
GLANVILLE, Christopher
GOODMAN, Sheila
HANDLEY, Paul
HOLT, Rod
HUGHES, Kevin
HUNTLY, Moira
JACKSON, Mary
JOHNSEN, Arabella
KAY, Pamela
KNOWLER, Brian
LINDLEY, Brian
MCKIVERAGAN, Terry
MILLAR, Jack
PIKESLEY, Richard
TILMOUTH, Sheila
WALKER, Sandra
WHITTLESEA, Michael

COMMERCIAL GALLERY ARTISTS

ANDERSON O'DAY GRAPHICS
(p.175)
ACKROYD, Norman
COLE, Yvonne
DANIELS, Harvey
DAVEY WINTER, Jean
DELDERFIELD, Delia
FARROW, Carol
FROST, Terry
IRVIN, Albert
JONES, Ian
MCLEAN, Bruce
NEILAND, Brendan
NEVILLE, Alison
O'NEILL, Mary Rose
PIPER, John
ROWE, Carl
SHAVE, Terry
VIRGILS, Catherine
WILKINSON, Donald

ANDREW MUMMERY GALLERY
(p.61)
AKKERMAN, Philip
BACH, Michael
BLANE, Frances
BUTLER, Jeremy
CHEVSKA, Maria
EDLUND, Krista
GOTO, John
HARDING, Alexis
HEMINGTON, Tim
HOLUBITSCHKA, Hans-Jorg
HOPKINS, Louise
HUGHES, Ian
KANE, Paula
KENNEDY, Mark
MARCHAN, Javier
MORTON, Victoria
RHODES, Carol
STAFF, Craig
TODD, Graeme

ANNE FAGGIONATO
(p.61)
BACON, Francis
BALTHUS
BASELITZ, Georg
BONNARD, Pierre
DEGAS, Edgar
GAUGUIN, Paul
GIACOMETTI, Alberto
HEPWORTH, Barbara
HIRST
LICHTENSTEIN, Roy
MATISSE, Henri
MIRO, Joan
MONET, Claude
MOORE, Henry
PICASSO, Pablo
QUINN
RODIN
WARHOL, Andy
WHITEREAD, Rachel

ANNELY JUDA FINE ART
(p.61)
ACKLING, Roger
CARO, Anthony
CHILLIDA, Eduardo
CHRISTO
CLOUGH, Prunella
FULTON, Hamish
FUNAKOSHI, Katsura
GABO, Naum
GREEN, Alan
HALL, Nigel
HOCKNEY, David
KAWAMATA, Tadashi
LEAPMAN, Edwina
MALEVICH, Kasimir
MOHOLY-NAGY, Laszlo
NASH, David

POPOVA, Liubov
REYNOLDS, Alan
RODCHENKO, Alexander
VORDEMBERGE-GILDEWART,
Friedrich

**THE ANTIQUE & BOOK
COLLECTOR**
(p.111)
BELLEROCHE, Albert
BLAMPIED, Edmund
BRANGWYN, Frank
COPLEY, John
FISHWICK, Clifford
GAUDIER-BRZESKA, Henri
GILL, Eric
HILTON, Roger
JOHN, Augustus
JONES, David
KNIGHT, Laura
LE BROQUOY, Louis
LORD, Elyse
NASH, John
PISSARRO, Orovida
SPENCER, Stanley
TINDLE, David
VAUGHAN, Keith

ART ARENA GALLERY
(p.180)
KIANUSH, Katy

ART CONNOISSEUR GALLERY
(p.62)
ANTONIADIS, Joannis
AWLSON, Walter
BOLT, Ann
BOONHAM, Nigel
BURGHARDT, R.
ERSSER, Kenneth
GRAUBART, Ellen
GROSSMAN, Clare
GULIAYEV, A.C.
HECTOR, D.
JOHNSTON, Brian
KOVEN, Jacqueline
KOVEN, Leonard
KRIKHAAR, Anthony
KUELSHEIMER, Paul
LINNELL, John
LUDLOW, W.H.
MACLAGAN, Philip D.
MESSENGER, Tony
MURISON, Neil
NEEDELL, Philip G.
ONONA, Michael
OSSORY DUNLOP, Ronald
PALMER ROBINS, William
ROBB, Tom
SADEIKAITE, Ausva
SILIN, A.M.
SPENCE, Annora
TINSLEY, Francis
TOLEDANO, Edward

ART FIRST
(p.62)
BARNS-GRAHAM, Wilhelmina
COOPER, Eileen
ELWES, Luke
GARDINER, Anna
GRANT, Alistair
GUNDLE, Kimberley
HARVEY, Jake
HUNTER, Margaret
LAWRENCE, Eileen
LEVER, Gillian
LEWTY, Simon
MACALISTER, Helen
MACDONALD, Bridget
MACLEAN, Will
MAQHUBELA, Louis
MCALEER, Clement

MILROY, Jack
NEL, Karel
PIERCE, Janet
PRENTICE, David
RAE, Barbara
ROBERTSON, Iain
TOMKINS, Ridvan
TREMBATH, Su
WELSH, Ian
WHISHAW, Anthony

ART FOR OFFICES
(p.62)
BENBOW, Zoe
BLIK, Maurice
BOOTH, Martin
BROWN, John
CANNING, Neil
CARTER, Lara
CINALLI, Ricardo
DUFFY, Terry
FORD, Anita
FRESHWATER, Sally
GODWIN, Mark
HAYES, Peter
HEWITSON, Eric
HEWITT, Annabel
HOMMA, Kaori
HUMPHREYS, Ian
JACOBSON, David
JENNINGS, Helyne
JONES, Graham
KRIKHAAR, Anthony
LICHTERMAN, Heidi
LUCIEN, Simon
MARRIOT, Neale
OLINS, Rob
PALIN, Les
PLUMMER, Brian
RIBBONS, Ian
SELIGMAN, Lincoln
SIMPSON, Chris
STOK, William
VIRGILS, Katherine
WHADCOCK, Richard

THE ARTISTS STUDIO
(p.160)
PARSONS, Keith Malcolm

ARTS CENTRE
(p.140)
ANSELL, Jane
AYNSLEY, Susannah
BURNUP, Eve
DIXON, Jon
FERGUSON, Izzy
FOWNES, Sue
GATER, Claire
LAMBERT, Liz
MONCRIEFF, Alan
RICHARDSON, Joanne
RITCHEY, Jean
ROWDEN, Ken

ATHOLL GALLERY
(p.151)
ANDERSON, Anne
ARMSTRONG, Anthony
AWLSON, Walter
BARR, Shona S.M.
BIRNIE, William
BOURNE, Peter
CHEAPE, Malcolm
CLARK, Donald
GILLESPIE, Joan
GORDON, Anne
HARRIGAN, James
HARVEY, Gail
INNES, Robert
KIRKWOOD, Terry
LAW, Frances
MACFARLANE, Alice

MACMILLAN, Sheila
MITCHELL, Gordon K.
MORRICE, Ilona
PATERSON, Anda
ROSS, Iain
SPENCE, James
THOMSON, Alastair W.
TURNER, Helen
WEBSTER, Beth
WIATRER, Richard

AXIOM CENTRE FOR THE ARTS
(p.106)
BAKER, Jane E.
COOPER, Matt
CURNON, Ben
DUNLOP, Eileen
LAWSON, Helen
MARK, Michael
MORRELL, Rory
SIMPSON, Nicola
WHITE, Adam

BADA@
(p.62)
BLACKLEDGE, Robin
DUFFY, Terry

**BCA BOUKAMEL CONTEMPORARY
ART**
(p.63)
BACH, Elvira
BRAHAM, Philip
CASTELLI, Luciano
CHIA, Sandro
CLEMENTE, Francesco
CURRIE, Ken
DELPRAT, Helene
FETTING, Rainer
GAROUSTE, Gerard
GOLDIN, Nan
HÖDICKE, K.H.
LEROY, Eugene
LUPERTZ, Markus
MCINTYRE, Keith
MOURAD, Joumana
NELE, E.R.
PENCK, A.R.
PIERRE ET GILLES
SPOERRI, Daniel
TATAFIORE, Ernesto
TRAQUANDI, Gerard

BEAUX ARTS
(p.100)
ADAMS, Norman
AYRTON, Michael
BARNS-GRAHAM, Wilhelmina
BEALING, Nicola
BELLANY, John
BLACKADDER, Elizabeth
BLOW, Sandra
CHADWICK, Lynn
CINALLI, Ricardo
FEDDEN, Mary
FEILER, Paul
FRASER, Donald Hamilton
FRINK, Elisabeth
FROST, Terry
GATFIELD, Rupert
GLENDINNING, Lucy
HANSCOMB, Brian
HARTLEY, Ben
HENRY, Sean
HERMAN, Josef
HOLLAND, Harry
HOLZHANDLER, Dora
JAMMET, Lin
KANE, Martin
KLEIN, Anita
KNOX, Jack
LANTON, Andrew
MACKENZIE, Alexander

MACPHERSON, Neil
MCDONALD, James
MCLEAN, Donna
MCRAE, Jennifer
MOUNT, Paul
MUSGRAVE, Olivia
NOLAN, Sir Sydney
ORGAN, Robert
OWEN, Janet
PALTENGHI, Julian
PEARCE, Bryan
PENNY, Giles
PHILIPSON, Sir Robin
PIPER, Edward
PIPER, John
RAY, Roy
RICHARDSON, Ray
TURPIN, Louis
USTINOV, Igor

BEAUX ARTS LONDON
(p.63)
ADAMS, Norman
AITCHISON, Craigie
BELLANY, John
CHADWICK, Lynn
CINALLI, Ricardo
DILLON, Angela
FRINK, Elisabeth
HARRIS, Philip
HEPWORTH, Barbara
HERON, Patrick
HILTON, Roger
HITCHENS, Ivon
JOLLY, Nicholas
LEAMAN, Jonathon
MONKS, John
PIPER, John
RICHARDS, Ceri
RICHARDSON, Ray
SCOTT, William
SPILLER, David
SUTHERLAND, Graham
VAUGHAN, Keith

BEN URI ART SOCIETY
(p.85)
EPSTEIN, Jacob
KRAMER, Jacob
PISSARRO, Camille
PISSARRO, Lelia
PISSARRO, Lucien

BETTLES GALLERY
(p.109)
ANDREWS, Tim
ASHBY, David
BATTERHAM, Richard
BAYER, Svend
BOWEN, Clive
BURGESS, Do
CARTER, Chris
DAVIDSON, Andrew
DODD, Mike
DOHERTY, Jack
FRITH, David
GARDINER, Karen
GRAHAM, Brian
GREGORY, Ian
GRIFFITHS, Mark
HILL, Andrew
HOWARD, Ashley
JOLLY, Linda
JOYCE, Peter
KEELER, Walter
KEELEY, Laurel
KELLAM, Colin
LEACH, David
LEACH, John
MALTBY, John
MARSHALL, Anne Marie
MARSHALL, William
MASON, Andrew

MOMMENS, Ursula
MUNDY, Sue
MYERS, Emily
NOEL, Anna
NOEL, Sarah
PHILPS, Emmie
POLLEX, John
RAY, Amanda
REES, Nick
RICH, Mary
ROGERS, Phil
TREY, Marianne de
WAAL, Edmund de
WALLWORK, Alan
WARDELL, Sasha
WHITE, David

BILSTON ART GALLERY AND MUSEUM
(p.128)
COLQUITT, Jenny
GRAVESON, Sarah
MCKAY, Jain
PEEVOR, Carol
WESTWOOD, Karen

THE BLACK SHEEP GALLERY
(p.159)
ANDERSON, Ian
BAILEY, Sylvia
BOYCE, Kay
CASEY, Sandra
CHALONER, Clinton
COLLINS SHONE, Keith
COOK, David
DAVIES, Gareth
EARNSHAW, Wilfred
FOX, Judith
GADD, Gerald V.
GARDNER, Linda
GEE, Arthur
GOODWIN, Christopher
GREEN, Andrew
HALE, Vernon
HAYNES, David
HEATH, Jim
HENDERSON, Bob
HUGHES, Phil
HUGHES, Richard
KITCHIN, Mervyn
LADELL, George
LEYENS, Petra
MACMILLAN, Gregory
MCCARTHY, Linda
MCKINNON DAY, Tricia
MILLER, Michael
MOSLEY, Tony
MUNSLOW, Angela
PASKIN, John
PEAKE, Eric
PERKINS, David
PICKERING, Polly Anna
PITT, Alison
PUGH, Leuan
RUDD, Brian
SHAUGNESSY, Clare
SNOW, Philip
SYMINGTON, Rob
TAYLOR, Brian
TUFFREY, Marion
WALKER BARKER, David
WALTON, Ian
WATKINS, Meurig
WHITE, Harry
WILSON, Eric
WOODING, Tony
WOOLF, Colin

BLACKTHORN GALLERIES
(p.132)
ABBOT & ELLWOOD, Mike & Kim
BEARMAN, Paul

BEAVAN, Jenny
BECCI, Nicola
BELL, John
BIRCHWOOD, Tracy
BRISCOE, Mike
COOKSON, Delan
DARACH, Peter
DAVIES, Peter
FINLAY, Ann
FLEMING, Jim
GAURUS, Claudia
GOLDSBOROUGH, Bob
GRANT, Ken
HILLHOUSE, David
HODDER, Grant
JENNINGS, Graham
JENNINGS, Helyne
JONES, Stephen
KENNERLEY, George
LANGAN, Jane
LEWIS, Patrick
MCGILLIVRAY, Joe
MCKEILER, John
MEIKLE, Annabel
MITCHELHILL, Noon
MOORE, Jane
MURPHY, Kathie
NASH, Mandy
O'DARE, Emma
OGILVIE, Iain
PACKINSTON, Sarah
RANA, Mah
RATCLIFFE, Sally
REEVES, Stephen
RENNIE, Edward
REPTON, Joanna
ROWE, Dot
ROWE, Les
RUSHWORTH, Helen
SHILLITO, Anne Marie
WARREN, Penny
WARSHAW, Josie
WHEELDON, John
WHELAN, Jim
WILLIAMS, Wendy
WILSON O'REILLY, Christine

BLOND FINE ART
(p.107)
AYRTON, Michael
BAWDEN, Edward
BUCKLAND-WRIGHT, John
BURRA, Edward
CAULFIELD, Patrick
COOPER, Eileen
DENNY, Robyn
FEDDEN, Mary
FRINK, Elisabeth
FROST, Terry
GIBBINGS, Robert
GILL, Eric
GROSS, Anthony
HAMILTON, Richard
HAYTER, S.W.
HERMES, Gertrude
HERON, Patrick
HOCKNEY, David
HODGKIN, Howard
HOYLAND, John
HUGHES-STANTON, Blair
JONES, Allen
JONES, David
KITAJ, R.B.
KLEIN, Anita
LEIGHTON, Clare
MACKLEY, George
MOORE, Henry
NASH, John
NASH, Paul
PAOLOZZI, Eduardo
PERI, Peter Laszlo
PIPER, John
RICHARDS, Ceri

ROTHENSTEIN, Michael
SMITH, Richard
TILSON, Joe
TREVELYAN, Julian
UNDERWOOD, Leon
VAUGHAN, Keith

BOHUN GALLERY
(p.110)
BARTLETT, Charles
BOND, Marj
FEDDEN, Mary
FRASER, Donald Hamilton
FRINK, Elisabeth
HAMBLING, Maggi
HOUSTON, John
LITTLEJOHN, William
PIPER, Edward
PIPER, John
RAMSHAW, Wendy
REDFERN, June
REMFRY, David
TREVELYAN, Julian
TURPIN, Louis
VOLK, Patricia

BOUNDARY GALLERY, AGI KATZ FINE ART
(p.63)
AUERBACH, Frank
BOMBERG, David
BORNFRIEND, Jacob
BREUER-WEIL, David
BRODZKY, Horace
BROWN, Heather
CLAYDEN, Phillippa
COZENS-WALKER, Mary
CREFFIELD, Dennis
DUBSKY, Mario
EPSTEIN, Jacob
GAUDIER-BRZESKA, Henri
GOTLIB, Henryk
GREEN, Kate
HAYDEN, Henri
HERMAN, Josef
JUGASHVILI, Jacob
KESTELMAN, Morris
KOENIG, Ghisha
KOSSOFF, Leon
KRAMER, Jacob
LAWSON, Sonia
LOUDEN, Albert
MACPHERSON, Neil
MELLAND, Sylvia
MENINSKY, Bernard
PACHECO, Ana Maria
PERLMAN, Suzanne
PRENDERGAST, Peter
REDFERN, June
TRESS, David
WOLMARK, Alfred

BOURNE GALLERY
(p.114)
BALL, Gerry
BARLOW, Jeremy
BRUMMELL SMITH, Tony
CAMPBELL, Raymond
EASTON, Arthur
EASTON, Timothy
FLYNN, Dianne
GOODE, Mervyn
GRAHAM, Peter
HESELTINE, John
JARVIS, Christopher
MAKINSON, Alistair
MASCO, Pam
NAPP, David
PIERONI, Bella
PUTMAN, Salliann
SAPP, Prue
SKEA, Janet
VALENTINE-DAINES, Sherree

WALKER, Sandra
WHEATLEY, Jenny
YARDLEY, John

THE BOW HOUSE GALLERY
(p.63)
ALLBROOK, Colin
ANDREW, Nick
BAKER, Richard
BROWN, John
CARSBERG, Natasha
CLARKE, Jonathan
CLARKE, Peter
DAVEY, Caroline
DAVIES, Phyllis
ELLIS, Kate
FELTS, Shirley
FOXHALL, Peter
GALLWEY, Kate
GOLDBACHER, Fiona
GOULD, Cheryl
GRIFFITHS, Mary
HAWKEN, Anthony
HOARE, Wendy
HOLT, John
HORSFALL, Andrew
HUBBARD, Deirdre
HUGGINS, John
LIDZEY, John
LOXTON, Polly
MARSTERS, Geoff
MAYOR, Charlotte
MILBORROW, Jim
MOON, Liz
NEWMAN, Ros
NICOLL, Judith
ONIANS, Dick
PEASNALL, Claire
RICHARDS, Christine-Ann
SHUTTER, Timothy
SINCLAIR, Helen
SWEENEY, Jan
SYKES, David
SYMMONDS, Susan
TOBIAS, Alan
WESSELMAN, Frans
WESTON, David
WESTWOOD, Dennis
WYNNE, Althea
YEDIGAROFF, Marina

BRANDLER GALLERIES
(p.118)
ABRAHAMS, Ivor
BOWYER, William
BRATBY, John
BROWN, Ralph
CAMP, Jeffrey
CASSON, Sir Hugh
COCKRILL, Maurice
CONSTABLE, John
COX, Paul
CUMING, Fred
DRING, William
DUNLOP, Ronald O.
DUNSTAN, Bernard
EURICH, Richard
FEDDEN, Mary
FRINK, Elisabeth
GAINSBOROUGH, Thomas
GORE, Frederick
GOSSE, Sylvia
GREEN, Anthony
HARTILL, Brenda
HAYES, Colin
HEPPLE, Norman
HITCHENS, Ivon
HOCKNEY, David
HOWARD, Ken
JACKLIN, Bill
JOHN, Augustus
KENNY, Michael
LARUSDOTTIR, Karolina

LAWRENCE, John Frederick
LOWRY, L.S.
MILLAR, John
MOORE, Henry
PHILLIPS, Tom
PIPER, John
POTTER, Beatrix
ROONEY, Mick
RUSSELL, Calvin
SAGE, Ruth
SHEPARD, E. H.
SHEPHERD, David
SMITH, Stan
SUTHERLAND, Emma
SUTTON, Linda
SUTTON, Philip
TINDLE, David
TURNER, J.M.W.
WEIGHT, Carel

BREWHOUSE THEATRE & ARTS
CENTRE
(p.107)
BENSON, Rosemary
HIND
JONES, David
KOLLWITZ, Käthe
MOWAT, Jane
NILSSON, Jonas
OLLSSON, Eva
SHAPE
STEINBERG, Barbera
WOOLNER, John

BROUGHTON HOUSE GALLERY
(p.117)
AKED, G. D.
BALZOLA, Asun
BORLASE, Deirdre
HARTLEY, Marie
HAZELWOOD, David
HELLEWELL, Jack
KENNEDY, Richard
KRACZYNA, Swietlan
LODGE, Jean
MATTIOLI, Carlo
MCGUINNESS, Tom
MOMMENS, Norman
MUNOZ, Rie
NEWBOLT, Thomas
PIPER, John
RAVERAT, Gwen
RICHARDS, Ceri
SCHLOSS, Edith
SHREVE, Peter
VANNITHONE, Soun

THE BRUTON STREET GALLERY
(p.64)
BACKHOUSE, David
BONCOMPAIN
BOYDELL, Lucy
BROADBENT, Stephen
CROZIER, William
DE BRUYNE, Anne
ECK, Francis
FOREMAN, William
GIBBS, Leonie
GRAHAM, David
LLACER, Teresa
MACDONALD, Alan
MENDJISKY, Serge
NADAL, Carlos
QUANNE, Michael
ROYO
TWEED, Jill
VAYREDA, C.
WINTER, Faith

BUSINESS ART GALLERIES
(p.219)
ATHERTON, Barry
BEATTIE, Basil

BELSKY, Franta
BIGGER, Clare
BLACKBURN, Kenneth
BLACKMORE, Clive
BOYD HARTE, Glynn
BROKENSHIRE, John
CECIL, Roger
CLOUGH, Prunella
CORSELLIS, Jane
DINGWALL, Phoebe
DOVER, Peter
DUNSTAN, Bernard
FRASER, Donald Hamilton
FRINK, Elisabeth
GORE, Frederick
GRANT, Alistair
HARTILL, Brenda
HEPWORTH, Barbara
HERMAN, Josef
HOCKING, Susan-Jayne
HOLLIDAY, Sarah
HOYLAND, John
IRVIN, John
JAWAHIRILAL, Lallitha
JONES, Stanley
KOTZEN, Thirza
MACARA, Andrew
MACMIADHACHAIN, Padraig
MANDL, Anita
MARTIN, Ruth
MIERINS, Liamonis
MOORE, Henry
NOACH, Michele
OKI, Yuji
PIETSCH, Heinz-Dieter
PIPER, John
RICHARDS, Ceri
RICHMOND, Robin
RIZVI, Jacqueline
ROBERTS, Keith
RYAN, Paul
SCHWARZ, Hans
SHIRAISHI, Yuko
SYMONDS, Peter
VON STUMM, Johannes
WALKER, Richard
WOUDA, Marjan
WRAY, Peter

CAMBRIDGE CONTEMPORARY ART
(p.117)
APPLETON, Jeanette
BARRACLOUGH, Diana
BENDELL-BRUNELLO, Tiziana
BLUMENFELD, Helaine
BOND, Marj
BRIDGE, Eoghan
CAREY, June
CARPENTER, Pip
CARTER, David
CARTWRIGHT, Reg
CHAGALL, Marc
CHIPPERFIELD, John
CLARICE, Jonathan
CORNISH, Charlotte
DOVE, Stanley
FRASER, Donald Hamilton
FRINK, Elisabeth
GREENHALF, Rupert
GREVATTE, Jenny
GRIGSON, David
HOLLIDGE, Jane
HUDSON, Rosalind
HYSLOP, Aliisa
IRVIN, Albert
KLEIN, Anita
KONIG, Heidi
LARUSDOTTIR, Karolina
LOIZOU, Renos
MATISSE, Henri
MCINNES, Sheila
MCVEIGH, Michael
MINCHIN, Maureen

MOORE, Henry
PALSER, Alice
PENNY, Chris
PIERCE, Derek
PIPER, John
POULTON, Jane
RANDS, Rose
RICHARDSON, Ilana
RICHARDSON, Ray
RUBENS, Zoe
SPENCE, Annora
STIRLING, Dorothy
STROMRUBENS, Ursula
THOMAS, Glynn
TING, Sharon
WADE, Richard
WELCH, Robin
WHYBRON, Terry

CHANTRY HOUSE GALLERY
(p.136)
ALLEN, David
ANDERSON, Athena
BARKER, Neville
BERZINS, Valteris
BRAITHWAITE, Kevin
CROSSLEY, Donald
CUDWORTH, Jack
CURGENVEN, Michael
DURKIN, Tom
GRAY, Len
HALSEY, Mark
HASTE, J. Barrie
HOWELL, David
JONES, Mike
KEETON, Richard
LAZZERINI, Giuliana
LOGAN, Georgina
LOGAN, Lynda
LOGAN, Terry
MAYES, Emerson
NETTLESHIP, Patrick
PARKIN, John
ROXBY, Brian
RUSH, Maureen
SAVILLE, Michael
SCHOFIELD, Helen
SIBSON, John
SIMONE, Neil
VELARD, Paula
WHATMORE, Nel

THE CHILFORD HALL SCULPTURE
CENTRE
(p.192)
AUVINEN, Matti Kalevi
BENEDETTO, Michele
BLUMENFELD, Helaine
CPAJAK, Goran
CPAKAK, Giorgie
CUN-SUN, Park
GRASSI, Andrea
NEIDERMANN, Zoya
OTERO, Camilo
PENALBA, Alicia
SATO, Akiko
SCHONK, Aart
TARABELLA, Viliano

CHRIS BEETLES
(p.64)
ARCHER, Val
BADMIN, Stanley
BARTON, Rose
BATEMAN, H.M.
BEERBOHM, Max
BLAKE, Quentin
BRABAZON, Hercules Brabazon
BROOKES, Peter
DREW, Simon
DULAC, Edmund
ELGOOD, G.S.
FOREMAN, Michael

COMMERCIAL GALLERY ARTISTS

FOSTER, Birket
FOTHERBY, Lesley
GILES, Carl
GIRVAN, Geraldine
GOODWIN, Albert
GREENAWAY, Kate
HAMMOND, Roy
HILDER, Roland
HUNT, Cecil Arthur
IVORY, Lesley Anne
KNIGHT, Charles
LARRY
PEMBERTON, Muriel
PIPER, John
RACKHAM, Arthur
ROBINSON, William Heath
ROWLANDSON, Thomas
SCARFE, Gerald
SHEPARD, E. H.
SOPER, Eileen
SOPER, George
STEADMAN, Ralph
STUDDY, George "Bonzo"
TARRANT, Margaret
TYNDALE, Walter
WAIN, Louis
WYLLIE, William L.

CHRIST CHURCH PICTURE GALLERY
(p.110)
HALS, Frans
THE CARRACCI
TINTORETTO, Jacopo
VAN DYCK, Anthony
VERONESE, Paolo

THE CITY GALLERY
(p.123)
ABBOT & ELLWOOD, Mike & Kim
BELL, Cressida
BETTS, Malcolm
BOTTLE, Neil
CARNAC, Helen
COMPLIN, Jo
CORBETT, Henrietta
CURRELL, Anthony
DOWNES, Charlie
GRIFFIN, James
GRIGOR, Rachel
HAMLYN, Jane
HAMMOND, Lisa
HARDING, Angela
HARRISON, Steve
HAUKSDOTTIR, Valgerdur
HAWKINS, Amanda
HODGKISON, Trevor
HOLMES, Michelle
IMPEY, Jill
JENNINGS, Helyne
KEELER, Walter
KIRBY, Sarah
LEVI MARSHALL, Will
MCKIBBIN, Marlene
MCSWINEY, Sharon
MILLER, Linda
MURPHY, Kathie
PACKINGTON, Sarah
PARK, Rowena
RANA, Mah
RICE, Liz
RIVANS, Maria
ROBERTS, Hilary
ROSS, Vivienne
SELLARS, Julie
SMITH, Mark
STEPHENS, Ian
STODDART, Rosalind
WALTER, Josie
WILLIAMS, Penny
WILLIAMS, Sophie
WOOD, Paul
WOOD, Philip
YOUNG, A & J

COLIN JELLICOE GALLERY
(p.130)
ABBOTT, Nolan
BELL, John
BEWSHER, Steven
BOCAI, Maria Daniela
BRADY, Flo
BROWN, Sally
COUSSET, Jean-Marie
COWNIE, Allan
DAVEY, Peter Granville
DOBSON, Martin
GARDNER, Reg
GILBERT, Colin
GRANVILLE, Nicholas
HARRISON, Michael
HAWTIN, John
HENRY, Sue
HESKETH, Michael
HIGGINSON, Cliff
HILL, Debbie
HOLLAND, Christopher
JELLICOE, Colin
JESSING, Michael
JONES, Alwyn Dempster
KELLY, Francis
LAWLEY, Christine
LEACH, Krys
LEIGH, Teresa
MARTIN, Christina
MAYER, William
MITCHELL, Sue
NOBLE, Chris
PERSSON, Kariona
PICKING, John
PORTER, Robert
RITCHIE, Paul
ROLAND, Ruth
ROTHMER, Dorothy
SANDERSON, Jean
SIMIONE, Giovanni
SKOVGAARD, Kim
STANLEY, Dave
SYKES, George
TATHAM, Susan
THORNTON, Barry
VILNA, Lila
WHITTALL, Sylvia
WILLIAMS, Enid
WILLIAMS, Jackie
WILLIAMS, Peter

THE CONINGSBY GALLERY
(p.65)
ARCHER/QUINNELL
BELLINGHAM, Barbara
BURSTON, Oliver
CROWTHER, Peter
DAVIS, Paul
FRASER, Ewan
FRIEDMAN, Jim
GISSING, Nicky
HAYGARTH, Stuart
HOOGSLAG, Nanette
HUNTLEY/MUIR
JARZBOWSKA, Tamsin
KITCHING, Alan
LOCO, Gone
MANN AND MAN
MARSHAM, Sophie
MAYNARD, Peter
ZAP ART

CONNAUGHT BROWN
(p.65)
BOSHIER, Derek
CALDER, Alexander
CHAGALL, Marc
CREFFIELD, Dennis
DUBUFFET, Jean
DUFY, Raoul
HOCKNEY, David
HOLSOE, Carl
MATISSE, Henri

MIRO, Joan
MOORE, Henry
PICASSO, Pablo
PISSARRO, Lucien
RICHARDS, Paul
TSELKOV, Oleg
WARHOL, Andy
WESSELMANN, Tom

THE CONTEMPORARY PRINT SHOW & THE CONTEMPORARY PRINT FAIR
(p.)
AYRES, Gillian
BASSETT, Clare
BAXTER, Sandra
BLACKADDER, Elizabeth
BLAKE, Peter
BRETT, Simon
BUCKLAND-WRIGHT, John
BYRNE, John
CARPENTER, Pip
CRAIG-MARTIN, Michael
DESMET, Anne
FERGUSON-LEES, Dominic
FORD, Peter
FRASER, Donald Hamilton
FREUD, Lucian
FROST, Terry
FULTON, Hamish
HAMMICK, Tom
HOCKNEY, David
HODGKIN, Howard
HOUSTON, John
HOYLAND, John
HUXLEY, Jonathan
INGAMELLS, Andrew
INSHAW, David
IRVIN, Albert
JONES, Trevor
KALINOVICH, Konstantin
KIFF, Ken
KLEIN, Anita
KOENIG, Heidi
KUDRYASHOV, Oleg
LE BRUN, Christopher
LEE, Jessie
LEWANDOWSKI, Simon
MCKEEVER, Ian
MCLEAN, Bruce
MEYER, Klaus
MILROY, Lisa
MOXLEY, Susan
OULTON, Thérèse
PALADINO, Mimmo
PERRING, Susie
PETTERSON, Melvyn
RAE, Barbara
REGO, Paula
RICHARDSON, Ray
ROLLO, Sonia
SPENCE, Annora
SYKES, Sandy

COOMBE FARM GALLERY
(p.103)
AARONSON, Adam
AGAR, Nick
APPLETON, Dixie
ATTRIDGE, Claire
CASE, Lucy
CASTRO, Beatriz
CORBETT, Lydia
CRAWFORD, Phillipa
CRESSWELL, Miranda
FOX, Louise
FRYER, Jan
GILLO, Alex
HOWSE, Karen
JANCSH, Heather
JENNINGS, Helyne
LEE, Pauline
MARSTON, James
MCCRUM, Bridget

MILLER, Lynn
MUIR, Lynn
NASH, Zoe
PAMPHILLON, Elaine
POUTNEY, Beth
PROSSER, Deborah
RILEY, Paul
RILEY, Tina
ROBSON, Sue
ROWE, Judith
RUSSELL, John
SOWDEN, Claire
SPROULE, Lin
SUTTON, Jilly
THYSSEN, Keith
WHELPTON, Rob
WILSON, Douglas
WOOD, Vicky

COSKUN & CO. LTD.
(p.65)
BRAQUE, Georges
CHAGALL, Marc
DALI, Salvador
DINE, Jim
GIACOMETTI, Alberto
LÉGER, Fernand
MATISSE, Henri
MIRO, Joan
PICASSO, Pablo
WARHOL, Andy

COURCOUX & COURCOUX CONTEMPORARY ART LTD
(p.109)
ANDREW, Nick
BRODERICK, Laurence
CHRISTOPHER, Ann
CUMING, Fred
DASHWOOD, Geoffrey
DOVE, Stanley
FEDDEN, Mary
FRINK, Elisabeth
HOWARD, Ken
JANSCH, Heather
MURLEY, Lawrence
NUTTING, Iain
PRATT, Jeffrey
RUSH JANSEN, Belinda
RYDER, Sophie
TAPLIN, Guy
TAYLOR, Frank
YATES, Fred

THE CRAFT CENTRE AND DESIGN GALLERY
(p.134)
ACKROYD, Norman
AMBERY-SMITH, Vicki
BARNES, Roger
BLAKENEY, Anthony
BOTTLE, Neil
COUSENS, Cynthia
EDEN, Michael
EDEN, Victoria
FORREST, Marianne
FORRESTER, Trevor
HALE, Jennie
JACKSON-CURRIE, Lorna
KLEIN, Anita
MORTON, Grainne
PERRY, Jo
PRESTON, Paul
RICHARDS, Victoria
ROYLE, Guy
SMITH, Martin
VAN LIEFFERINGE, Katrien

CRANE KALMAN GALLERY
(p.66)
BOMBERG, David
DUBUFFET, Calder
FRANKLIN, Jenny
HAYTER, S.W.

HOFMANN, Hans
LOWNDES, Alan
LOWRY, L.S.
MOORE, Henry
NEWCOMB, Mary
NICHOLSON, Ben
NICHOLSON, Winifred
PICASSO, Pablo
RA'ANAN, Levy
ROUAULT, Georges
SMITH, Sir Mathew
SPEAR, Ruskin
STAMOS, Theodoros
SUTHERLAND, Graham
WALLIS, Alfred
WOOD, Christopher

CREFTOW GALLERY
(p.101)
BEECROFT, Jane
DUNSTAN, Sarah
FISHER, Tom
GINGELL, Lynne
MAKINEN, Seija
MULLALY, Ann
OWERS, Dione
PILCHER, Esther
SCOTT, Carol
SEARLE, Dorothy
SHELDON-FENTEN, Angela
SHERLOCK, Darrel
TAYLOR, Theo
WADSWORTH, Paul
WICKS, Jenny

CURWEN CHILFORD PRINTS
(p.117)
AARONS, Andrew
BEATTIE, Basil
BULMER, Lionel
CHEESE, Bernard
CHEESE, Chloe
CLOUGH, Prunella
COHEN, Alfred
CORSELLIS, Jane
DUNSTAN, Bernard
FRINK, Elisabeth
FROST, Anthony
HEPWORTH, Barbara
HERMAN, Josef
HERON, Patrick
HILTON, Matthew
HOGARTH, Paul
IRVIN, Albert
KEATS, Helen
KINDERSLEY, David
LIM, Kim
LYSYCIA, Tony
PAOLOZZI, Eduardo
PROCKTOR, Patrick
ROTHENSTEIN, Michael
RUSSELL, Jim
SHARP, Tony
STAYTON, Janet
SUTTON, Philip
ZUCKERMAN, Joan

CURWEN GALLERY
(p.66)
AYRES, Gillian
BEATTIE, Basil
BLACKBURN, Kenneth
BOYD HARTE, Glynn
CLOUGH, Prunella
DINGWALL, Phoebe
FRINK, Elisabeth
GIBBS, Jonathan
HEPWORTH, Barbara
HERMAN, Josef
HOYLAND, John
IRVIN, Albert
JONES, Stanley
KOTZEN, Thirza
MARTIN, Ruth

MIERINS, Laimonis
MOORE, Henry
OKI, Yuji
PIETSCH, Heinz-Dieter
PIPER, John
RICHARDS, Ceri
RICHMOND, Robin
RYAN, Paul
SCOTT, William
SHIRAISHI, Yuko
SYMONDS, Peter
VON STUMM, Johannes
WOUDA, Marjan

DANSEL GALLERY
(p.105)
BERRY, Chris
BREWER, Jane
BROMILON, Caroline
BUTLER, Nicholas
CHAPMAN, Robert
CURTIS, Hannah
DALBY, Peter
DARBY, William
DAWSON, Brian
DUGDALE, Peter
DUMOLO, Andy
DUNWORTH, Robert
GALLIMORE, Adam
GOSDEN, Colin
HALES, Dennis
HANCOCK, Brian
HENDERSON, Stephen
HENSHAW, Nicola
HIBBERT, Louise
HUNNEX, John
JACKSON, Ted
JOHNSON, Helen
JOLLIFFE, Lionel
KILVINGTON, Robert
KING, Ian
LANCASTER, Perry
LANGWORTH, Stewart
LUCRAFT, Nigel
MARKLEY, Alan
MARSH, Bert
MARSTON, James
MARTYN, Ralph
MCEWAN, Robin
MOORE, Andrew
MOTH, David
NICOLL, Judith
OXLEY, Ted
PICKARD, Simon
PIDGEN, Martin
ROY, Peter
SANDERS, Jan
SCOTT, Mike
SMITH, Robert
SOAN, Jeff
STANLEY, David
TATTERSALL, Jules
TEED, Simon
TRY, Kevin
VICKERS, Christopher
WHITE, Don

DANUSHA FINE ARTS
(p.66)
ANOBA, Valentin
ARTAMONOV, Oleksiy
ATAYAN, Gayane
HOLIMBIEUSKA, Tetyana
MAGRO, Petro
SHYSHKO, Grygoriy
VITKOUSKYI, Lev
VOLOBUEV, Eugeniy
YABLONSKA, Tetyana
YALANSKYI, Andriy
ZHUGAN, Volodymyr

DAVIS GALLERY
(p.168)
CAHILL, Patrick
CLEAR, Ciaran
CROWE, Dee
DAVIS, Gerald
HAYES, Olivia
KELLY, Joe
KLITZ, Tony
OAKLEY, George
PEARSON, Peter
TREACY, Liam
VIALE, Patrick

DE PUTRON ART CONSULTANTS
(p.220)
ADAMS, Alastair
AMIN, Sherif
APLIN, Kay
AUST, Rushton
BARRATT, Sophia
BECKER, Bernard
BENNETT, Austin
BISSET, Anna
BLACK, Simon
BORKOWSKI, Lissa
BRASON, Paul
BRYON, Beverly
CARPANINI, David
CHURCHILL, Martin
DAVID, Michele
DAVIES, Ivor
DWYER, Judy
FARQUHARSON, Mo
FIENNES, Susannah
GEAR, Nicola
HAMILTON, Susie
HARRINGTON, Heidi
HAWKENS, Anthony
JARVIS, Martin
JONES, Catrin
JONES, Graham
KILLIN, Mhairi
KINLEY, Susan
KLAPEZ, Ivan
LORD, Bernard
LOVEGROVE, Catherine
MACLEAN, Diane
MASOERO, Jeanne
MCNIVEN, Peter
MEDWAY, Sarah
MORGAN, Howard
MORLAND, Louise
MORRIS, Stuart
NICHOLAS, Peter
O'LEARY, Clare
PATSALIDES, John
PAVLENKO, Sergei
PEARSE, Deborah
PIATIGORSKY, Max
RADFORD, Diane
WHITE, Laura
WHITEHEAD, Rhonda
WILLSON, Graeme

DEVON GUILD OF CRAFTSMEN
(p.103)
ANDERSON, Blandine
ANDREWS, Tim
BOWEN, Clive
DE TREY, Marianne
EDMUNDS, Rebecca
HIGHET, Hilary
HONE, Juliet
HONNOR, Michael
KELLAM, Colin
KENDALL, Jessamine
LEACH, David
LEACH, John
MALTBY, John
MANN, Tony
PETERS, Alan
REGESTER, Dave

SEARLE, Teresa
TAJA
VINCENT, Carole
WOOD, Vicky

DEXTERITY
(p.137)
ADAM, Jane
ALDRIDGE, Lara
BERKOWITZ, Maggie
BRETT, Kate
BROCK, Hilary
BROWNE, Piers
BRUCE, Susan
BRUNSDON, John
CALVER, John
CURTIS, Eddie
DUNBAR, Emma
DUNN, John
EDEN, Mike & Vicky
FORRESTER, Trevor
GIARRUSSO, Veronique
GIBSON, Lynne
GOLDSMITH, Robert
HAMLYN, Jane
HANSON, Helen
HARTILL, Brenda
HOLDER, Guy
JOLLY, Linda
KELLAM, Colin
KERSHAW, John
KING, Mary
LANE, Peter
LANGLEY, Siddy
LAYTON, Peter
LEAR, Susie
LEECH, Kenneth
LENNOX, Grainne
MACDONELL, Alasdair Neil
MACDONELL, Sally
MALTBY, John
MOXON, Debbie
ROGERS, Paul
RUDGE, Dillon
RUDGE, Keza
RUDGE, Lawson C.
RUDGE, Lawson E.
RUSHBROOKE, Karlin
SMITH, Jane
STONES, Alan
VAN REIGERSBERG-VERSLUYS, Carlos
WALTON, Jackie
WEST, Linda
WESTGATE, Jo
WHITE, David
WHITEROD, Karen
WILLIAMS, Julian

EDITH GROVE GALLERY
(p.67)
BROWN, Paul
GILBERT, Dennis
HARE, Derek
KNIGHT, Mervyn
NAYLOR, Brenda
NIVEN, Grizel
ONIANS, Dick
PLAZZOTTA, Enzo
SHIVARG, Camilla

EGEE ART CONSULTANCY
(p.220)
AL FAKHRI, Patricia
AZZAWI, Dia
BERCHERE, N.
CARTER, Owen
CONTRERAS, Don Rafael
COOKE, Jonathan
CORRODI, Hermann
DEUTSCH, Ludwig
DIAB, Rachid
EASTHAM, Peter

COMMERCIAL GALLERY ARTISTS

GALLERY OF MODERN ART
(p.68)
ALLEN, St. Claire
BAUMAN, Lydia
BOULTING, Bridget
BROGAN, Honor
BRUGUERA, Lluis
BURKE, Peter
CARSWELL, Robbie
CLARKE, Pat
DAVIS, Derek
DAVIS, Ruth
FREEMAN, Barbara
FREUDENTHAL, Peter
GILL, Bobby
GRATZ, Thomas
HAMILTON-FINLAY, Ian
HARLEY PETERS, Jonet
HARVEY, Jake
HIRVIMAKI, Veiko
HODGSON, Carole
HOLMSEN, Brit
HOLTOM, Robin
HULLAND, Ann
HUNT, Helen
HUNT, Kate
JAQUET, Francoise
JONES, Mary Lloyd
KATZ, Tamara
MCGOWAN, Richard
MELLON, Erik
MULHOLLAND, Susan
O'BRIEN, Donagh
PARHIZGAR, Monir
ROGERS, John Boydell
ROYSTON, Gwen Joy
SHAKSPEARE, Will
SIVERTSEN, Jan
WILLIAMS, Lois
WILLIS, Simon
WILSON, Julia

GALLERY PANGOLIN
(p.105)
ABRAHAMS, Anthony
BACKHOUSE, David
BIBBY, Nick
BROWN, Ralph
BUCK, Jon
CHADWICK, Lynn
COVENTRY, Terence
DASHWOOD, Geoffrey
KINGDON, Jonathan
MANDL, Anita
MAYER, Charlotte
RYDER, Sophie

THE GALLERY
(p.105)
APPLEBY, Lynda
BARKER, Jon
BARRY, Jo
BEECROFT, Yvonne
BRAIBI, John
BROWN, Stephen
CADMAN, Michael
CLEMSON, Katie
CUTHBERT, David
CUTHBERT, Ros
DEAKIN, Liz
DESMET, Anne
ELLIS, Edwina
EMERSON, Keyna
GRADIDGE, Daphne
GRANT, Carol
GREENHAM, Peter
HAMLEY, Fiona
HICKLIN, Jason
HILL, Dennis
HUDSON, Sheila
IBBITSUN, Glen
JESTY, Ron
LIAAS, Pamela

LITTLE, Marjorie
LUNN, Jean
MARKEY, Danny
MARSHALLSAY, Fred
NASH, Paul
NEWBERRY, Angela
ORGAN, Bryan
OSBORNE, James
PICKERING, Robin
RELPH, Sue
RODDAWAY, Howard
ROSE, Alison
SALT, Jeffy
SIMPSON, Alan
STRANG, Michael
STUART, Henrietta
TOMS, Peter
UHT, John
VULLIAMY, Daphne
WALTON, Janice
WILLINGHAM, Roy

**GLASGOW PRINT STUDIO
WORKSHOP**
(p.174)
BLACKADDER, Elizabeth
BYRNE, John
CAMPBELL, Stephen
CAREY, June
COOK, Ashley
CURRIE, Ken
DAVIE, Joseph
DUFFIN, Stuart
GONZALEZ, Roberto
HOUSTON, John
HOWSON, Peter
LAMB, Elspeth
MATHIESON, Norman
MCCULLOCH, Ian
MCLEAN, Bruce
MCPHERSON, Neil
MISTRY, Dhruva
MOCK, Richard
RAE, Barbara
RICHARDSON, Ray
ROBERTSON, Murray
WISZNIEWSKI, Adrian

GOMSHALL GALLERY
(p.114)
BANNINA, Paul
COLE, Jane
LANGLEY, Siddy
MCGOWAN, Lawrence
MIDGLEY, Colin
MILLARD, Helen
MOORCROFT, Lise
NICOLL, Judith
PANNETT, Denis
PETO, Elaine
RUDGE, Lawson
VON BERTELE, Ulrich
WOOD, Michael

GOSSIPGATE GALLERY
(p.137)
ABLEWHITE, Ron
ARMSTRONG, Bob
AYRE, Ken
BROWNE, Piers
BULL, Simon
CALVER, John
CAMPBELL, John
CAMPBELL, Robert
CAWTHORNE, Gillie
CRESSWELL, Janet
CROSS, Shirley
CROSSLEY, John Cartmell
CURTIS, Eddie & Margaret
EVANS, Judy
FRY, David
GUNDREY, Walter
HUGHES, Angela

JOLLY, Tony
KING, Michael
MASSIE, Ian Scott
MCDERMOT, Andy
MORGAN-CLARKE, Paul
MOUNTAIN, Paul
PODMORE, Peter
RHODES, Kate
RIDOUT, Jim
ROGERS, Mary Ann
ROGERS, Paul
RUSSELL, Andrew
STONES, Alan
TYE, Roger
WALKER, Angela
WHITE, David

GRAHAM CLARKE
(p.112)
CLARKE, Graham

GRANT FINE ART
(p.168)
BEHAN, John
DELANEY, Eddie
DILLON, Gerard
LE BROCQUY, Louis
MCDONNELL, Hector
O'MALLEY, Tony
O'NEILL, Dan
ROWLETT, George
YEATS, Jack B.

THE GREENWICH GALLERY
(p.243)
BRATBY, John
GILRAY, James
GROSS, Anthony
SPARE, Austin Osman

**GREENWICH PRINTMAKERS
ASSOCIATION**
(p.176)
AIDA, Emiko
ALVES, Timothy
ATKINSON, Jane
BARHAM, Jean
BLACK, Maureen
BOWYER, David
CARPENTER, Pip
CARRECK, Libby
COLEBORN, Deanne
COSSEY, Mary
CROFT, Diana
CROZIER, Kathleen
DAVIES, Louise
DE MONCHAUX, Ruth
DELL, Mickey
GILBERT, Ellen
GOLDING, Gillian
GRACIA, Carmen
GRAUBART, Ellen
HAMMOND, Audrey
HANSON, Helen
HARRIS, Donald
HUXLEY, Jonathan
IRVIN, Joanna
JOHNSON, Annette
KLEIN, Anita
LYNCH, Sue
MARSHALL, Elaine
MORRIS, Elizabeth
PATEMAN, Theresa
PERRING, Susie
PRICE, Trevor
ROBSON, Sally
ROLLO, Sonia
RONAY, Jenny
SALMON, Christopher
SALTER, Anthony
SANDS, Susan
SCOVELL, Audrey
SOLLY, Phillip

STONE, Kirsten
STRACHAN, Peter
SULLOCK, Julie
WEAVER, Felicity
WRIGHT, Kevin
ZALEKI, Barbara

GRESHAM STUDIO
(p.177)
BARNS-GRAHAM, Wilhelmina
BELLANY, John
BLACKADDER, Elizabeth
BLAKE, Peter
CAULFIELD, Patrick
CLOUGH, Prunella
COE, Sue
COHEN, Alfred
FLANAGAN, Barry
FROST, Anthony
GORMLEY, Antony
GRIFFIN, Peter
HILLER, Susan
HILTON, Matthew
HOYLAND, John
JAMMET, Lin
JAQUETTE, Yvonne
KOSUTH, Joseph
LANYON, Ellen
LIM, Kim
LONG, Richard
MACH, David
MCLEAN, John
MILLER, Mellissa
NATHAN, Janet
OLDENBURG, Claes
PAOLOZZI, Eduardo
PARKER, Cornelia
PEARCE, Bryan
PENNEY, Bill
PROCKTOR, Patrick
REGO, Paula
SMITH, Kiki
TAYLOR, Jo
TURNBULL, William
WATT, Alison
WUNDERLICH, Paul

GROVE CONTEMPORARY ARTS
(p.127)
BRADBURY, Robin
ROGERS, John Boydell

HALES GALLERY
(p.69)
BICK, Andrew
CALLAN, Jonathan
CARTER, Claire
DAWSON, Ian
DE GOEDE, Leo
DEAN, Judith
HEATH, Claude
HYDE, James
LEAMAN, David
LOWE, Rachael
MCGINN, Martin
TAKAHASHI, Tomoko
WILSON, Keith
WOODS, Richard

HANOVER FINE ARTS
(p.146)
ALRED, Richard
ANDERSON, Libby
ARNSTEIN, Sylvia
ARTAMONOV, Oleksiy
BATHGATE, John
BOCHKOV, Valery
BOYLE, Lorna
BRIGGS, Maureen
BROWNING, Demetra
BRYDON, Lindsay
CAIRNCROSS, Mike
CLARK, Fay

COMMERCIAL GALLERY ARTISTS

CONBOY, Kathleen
COSMAN, Octavian
COUPER, Carolyn
CRAIG, Ronald A.H.
CRAWFORD, Anne
ERLICH, Vladimir
FERNANDES, Regina
FISH, Margo E.
HEPWORTH, Susan
JAQUES, Avril
JAQUES, Richard
JOHNSTONE, Ian S.
KUDRIAVTSEVA, Natasha
MACDONALD, Alan
MACVICAR, Marily
MAGRO, Petro
MASTIN, Ian
MCMILLAN, Margaret
MERRILEES, Roberta
NEUSTEIN, Ella
O'DONNELL, Bernie
PHILIP, Jackie
PHILLIPS, Sheena
SHARD, Elizabeth
SHYSHKO, Grygoriy
STANDEN, Peter
STEVENSON, Wendy
STRACHAN, Una
STUBBS, Rosemary
SUTHERLAND, Alan
THEYS, Freddy
VITKOVSKYI, Lev
VOLOBUEV, Eugeniy
WATLING, John
WATTS, E.B.
WILKINSON, Sarah
YALANSKYI, Andriy
ZNOBA, Valentin

HART GALLERY
(p.69)
BALDWIN, Gordon
BEVAN, Jenny
BLACKBURN, David
BOT, G.W.
BOWEN, Sian
BUTHOD-GARCON, Gisèle
CARTER, Chris
CHAMPY, Claude
DE WAAL, Edmund
DEVEREUX, Richard
DILWORTH, Steve
DOIG, Maxwell
DRAPER, Kenneth
FREEMAN, Barbara
GREAVES, Derrick
HARTMAN, John
HENDERSON, Ewen
KOCH, Gabrielle
MACALPINE, Jean
MALTBY, John
MIDDLEMISS, Jon
OWEN, Elspeth
PERRY, Richard
ROBERTS, David
ROGERS, Phil
ROSS, Duncan
SHEPPARD, Michael
STRINGER, Simon
TAYLOR, Sutton
VIROT, Camille
WALKER-BARKER, David
WEST, Jenny
WEST, Steve
WHITTAKER, Malcolm
WOOD, Tom
WRIGHT, Austin

HAYLOFT GALLERY
(p.167)
ALLEN, Barbara
VALLELY, J.B.

THE HEFFER GALLERY
(p.118)
DAY, Anthony
DENNY, Claire
FORSTER, Rosalind
GREEN, David
HARTLAND-ROWE, Marion
HOLMES, Anthea
IMMS, David
JEANS, Francis
KIRBY, Sarah
MARSTERS, Geoff
MCCALL, Charles
MICHIE, Alastair
NASON, Elaine
PERRYMAN, Margaret
POWNALL, William
REDPATH, Ophelia
SELL, Richard
SLATTERY, Nicola
STEMP, Robin
STODDART, Rosalind
STROTHER, Jane
TINGLE, Mike
WATSON, Roy
WENDLING, Caroline
WOOLLEY, Melanie

THE HENRY MOORE FOUNDATION
(p.192)
MOORE, Henry

HIGHGATE FINE ART
(p.69)
ADAMS, Norman
ATKINSON, Anthony
BAWDEN, Richard
BETOWSKI, Noel
BOYD, Jamie
BRATBY, John
BRILL, Reginald
CASCAJOSA, Enrique
CASSON, Hugh
CRONYN, Hugh
CUNDALL, Charles
DE MAYA, Nicolas
EASTON, Arthur
FEILDEN, Lucy
FLINT-SHIPMAN, Andrew
GORE, Frederick
GOWING, Laurence
GREEN, Anthony
GUAITAMACCHI, Bruno
HARRISON, Claude
HAY, Ian
HOWARD, Ken
INGAMELLS, Andrew
JAEN, Julian
LOWNDES, Rosemary
MCWHIRTER, Ishbel
PATTERSON, Doug
PEDRAZA, Jorge
QUIRKE, Michael
RIZVI, Jacqueline
ROBBINS, Richard
SOAN, Hazel
WILSON, Stuart
ZEH, Ulrich

HILDEGARD FRITZ-DENNEVILLE
FINE ARTS
(p.69)
BECKMANN, Max
CONSTABLE, John
CORINTH, Louis
EPSTEIN, Elizabeth I.
GAERTNER, Eduard
KIRCHNER, Ernst Ludwig
KLOSE, Friedrich Wilhelm
LIEBERMANN, Max
MACKE, Auguste
MEIDNER, Ludwig
MODERSOHN-BECKER, Paula

MONET, Claude
NOLDE, Emil
OLIVIER, Ferdinand
PECHSTEIN, Max
PISSARRO, Camille
RUNGE, Philipp Otto
SCHAD, Christian
TOPFFER, Wolfgang-Adam
TURNER, J.M.W.
VON DILLIS, Johann Georg
VON HOFMANN, Ludwig
VON KOBELL, Wilhelm
VON MENZEL, Adolf

HONOR OAK GALLERY
(p.69)
ACKROYD, Norman
BENSON, Rosemary
BERRY, June
BISSON, Paul
BLACKADDER, Elizabeth
CROWLEY, Graham
DAY, Gill
DEVEREUX, Jenny
FREER, Roy
HAMERSCHLAG, Margareta
Berger-
HARTRICK, A. S.
HENNELL, Thomas
HOUSTON, John
KORTOKRAKS, Rudolph
LARUSDOTTIR, Karolina
LEIGHTON, Clare
LINES, Vincent
LLOYD, Charles
MAHON, Phyllis
MARTON, George Mayer-
MCNAB, Tiffany
O'CONNOR, John
PRICE, Trevor
RAVERAT, Gwen
STAMP, Edward
TANNER, Robin
WAGNER, Erich
WINNER, Gerd
WISZNIEWSKI, Adrian

HOULDSWORTH FINE ART
(p.69)
BRAY, Richard
CHAPMAN, Jake & Dinos
COLLISHAW, Matt
CONNELLY, Robin
DAVENPORT, Ian
GALLACIO, Anya
HAPASKA, Siobhan
KIRBY, John
LOCKHEART, Gavin
MCPHAIL, Paul
MICHIE, Alastair
RADFORD, Matthew
RANDALL-PAGE, Peter
SPIVACK, Jason
STARR, Georgina
TAYLOR WOOD, Sam
WATT, Alison
WILDING, Alison
WISZNIEWSKI, Adrian
YASS, Catherine

THE HUNT GALLERY
(p.112)
HUNT, Michael John

INGLEBY GALLERY
(p.146)
AITCHENS, Ivon
AITCHISON, Craigie
BLONDES, Jeffrey
BRAY, Richard
GOLDSWORTHY, Andy
HAMILTON-FINLAY, Ian
HODGKIN, Howard

MELLIS, Margaret
NEL, Hylton
NICHOLSON, Ben
NICHOLSON, William
NICHOLSON, Winifred
SCOTT, William
SMITH, Ian McKenzie
SPIRA, Rupert
STAIR, Julian
WOOD, Christopher
YOUNG, Emily

INNOCENT FINE ART
(p.101)
BALMER, Derek
CHEESE, Chloe
COOPER, Bill
DRURY, Neil
EDWARDS, Sylvia
FROST, Anthony
FROST, Terry
GOLDEN, Lyn
GOVER, Ann
HILTON, Rose
LE GRICE, Jeremy
MCLEAN, Bruce
MURISON, Neil
NEIL, Nell
SCASE, James
SIDOLI, Dawn
SMITH, Richard
STOCKHAM, Alfred
STORK, Mary
WHITE, Caroline

JIBBY BEANE LIMITED
(p.70)
BAILEY, Beezy
BERNAOEU, Mira
BOWIE, David
CELULA, Marek
COATES, Marcus
DE ANGELIS, Davide
ENO, Brian
FARBER, Leora
KAYE, Tony
KELLY, Anthony-Noel
PAJDIC, Predrag
SMITH, Terry
WOLF, Sylvio

JILL GEORGE GALLERY
(p.70)
ADAMSON, Crawford
BENJAMINS, Paul
BREWSTER, Martyn
BULLEN, Duncan
BUTLER ADAMS, Louise
DEVEREUX BARKER, Dale
FAWCETT, Robert
FIRTH, Mark
GILLMAN, Tricia
GILMOUR, Hugh
HOLLAND, Harry
HOSIE, David
JONES, Tony
JUDKINS, Rod
LAMBERT, Alison
LEVERETT, David
MACH, David
ORR, Chris
OTA, Tsugumi
SALTER, Rebecca
STIBBON, Emma
TAYLOR, Fraser
VIRGILS, Katherine
WHITE, Peter

THE JOHN DAVIES GALLERY
(p.106)
AGGETT, Lionel
COWDY, Richard
DENTON, Kate

DUNKLEY, Keith
EVANS, Peter
PEACOCK, Brian
PRENTICE, David
SCALDWELL, Deborah
SHORT, Tanya
SORRELL, Adrian

JOHN MARTIN OF LONDON
(p.70)
ADLINGTON, Mark
COLLIS, Peter
DUHAN, Mike
DUNCAN, Ana
GIFFORD, Andrew
GORMAN, Des
GRIFFITHS, Mary
HAMEL, Francis
KELSEY, Robert
MARTIN, David
MORROCCO, Leon
WRAITH, Robert
YATES, Fred

JONATHAN COOPER
(p.70)
AUSTIN, Michael
BREAM, Antony
KIRKMAN, Jay
MATHEWS, Binny
NESSIER, Kate
NEWTON, William
OGILVY, Susan
STINTON, Gary
TOLLEY, Nicholas
WRAITH, Robert

JONATHAN POOLE
(p.106)
COWIE-SANDERS, Jill
DAVIS, Miles
HANN, Priscilla
LENNON, John
MILLS, Joan
NICHOLAS, Peter
PLISNIER, Bobby
POOLE, Jonathan
SHEPHEARD, Jean
SWEENEY, John
WESTWOOD, Denis

JONATHAN POTTER
(p.177)
BLAGU, Willem
BRAUN, Georg
CELLARIUS, Andreas
HOGENBERG, Frans
HONDIUS, Jodocus
MERCATOR, Gerard
MORDEN, Robert
ORTELIUS, Abraham
SPEED, John

JULIAN HARTNOLL
(p.71)
BLOW, Sandra
BRATBY, John
BURNE-JONES, Sir Edward
CHANNING, Stefan
COKER, Peter
CRANE, Walter
GLAVURTIC, Kristina
GREAVES, Derrick
LEIGHTON, Frederick Lord
MIDDLEDITCH, Edward
POYNTER, F.J.
SETTON, Laurence
SHAW, John Byam
SMITH, Jack
SOUZA, Francis N.
STURGESS-LIEFF, Christopher
TILSON, Joe
WATERHOUSE, John William
WATTS, George Frederick

JULIAN LAX FINE ORIGINAL PRINTS
(p.71)
AUERBACH, Frank
BLAKE, Peter
BUFFET, Bernard
CHAGALL, Marc
COLQUHOUN, Robert
FRINK, Elisabeth
HERON, Patrick
HOCKNEY, David
HODGKIN, Howard
KOSSOFF, Leon
LÉGER, Fernand
MATISSE, Henri
MIRO, Joan
MOORE, Henry
NEVINSON, C.R.W.
NICHOLSON, Ben
PASMORE, Victor
PICASSO, Pablo
PIPER, John
ROBERTS, William
ROUAULT, Georges
SCOTT, William
SUTHERLAND, Graham
VAUGHAN, Keith

KATHRYN BELL/FINE ART CONSULTANCY
(p.220)
AOKI, Noe
AUST, Rushton
BARKER, Dale Devereux
BARKER, Jo
BARKER, Patrick
BROOK, James
CONNOR, Angela
HOARE, Tessanna
JAMES, Simon
LANE, Danny
LE FEUVRE, Lucy
NORHEIM, Marit Benthe
POOLEY, Vanessa
RICHARDSON, Ray
RIDGE, Sue
ROGOYSKA, Marta
STEWART, David
TAYLOR, Fraser
TUCKER, Sian

KENTMERE HOUSE GALLERY
(p.135)
BAWDEN, Richard
BRUNSDEN, John
EVANS, Brenda
FREER, Roy
GREENWOOD, David
HELLEWELL, Jack
HUCKETT, Alfred
NEWCOMB, Tessa
PALMER, Robert
SPENCER, Liam

KERLIN GALLERY
(p.169)
CLEMENTE, Francesco
COOKE, Barrie
CROSS, Dorothy
DOHERTY, Willie
EGAN, Felim
EUN-MO, Chung
FRANCIS, Mark
GODBOLD, David
GORMAN, Richard
HAMILTON, Richard
HODGKIN, Howard
KINDNESS, John
KIPPENBERGER, Martin
MAGILL, Elizabeth
MAGUIRE, Brian
MCKENNA, Stephen
MCKEOWN, Willie

NI CHIOSAIN, Fionnuala
O'DOWD, Gwen
OEHIEN, Albert
PALADINO, Mimmo
PRENDERGAST, Kathy
SCOTT, William
SCULLY, Sean
SEAWRIGHT, Paul
SHANAHAN, Séan
SUGIMOTO, Hiroshi
TAYLOR, Marcus
UNGERS, Sibylle
WARHOL, Andy

KILVERT GALLERY
(p.161)
ARSCOTT, Peter
BISHOP, Peter
BLAKE, Carolyn
BOLTON, Helen
BRADFORD, Geoffrey
BRADFORD, Sarah
BURGOYNE, Claire
CAMPBELL, Ann
CAMPBELL, James
CARTER, Howard
CECIL, Roger
CHRISTIE, Jonathan
CUNNING, Robert
CURNEEN, Claire
FISK, Eugene
FOA, Maryclare
FOLKARD, Edward
GOSLING, Veronica
HAWKINS, Richard
HICKS-JENKINS, Clive
HOWARD, Mark
LOVEGROVE, Elizabeth
LOWERY, Dominic
MACDONALD, Robert
MARSH, Roger
MARSLAND, Kim
MATTHEWS, Sally
NICE, Derek
PARTRIDGE, Serena
PAYNE, Michael
PENNELL, Betty
PENNELL, Ronald
PEPPÉ, Jonathan
PHILLIPSON, Michael
POPHAM, Sheila
REID, Dan
RIDGWAY, Elizabeth
ROBINSON, Paddy
ROGERS, John Boydell
ROWE, Jean
SHEARER, Charles
SMITH, Thomasin
SPOWERS, Antonia
THWAITES, Sarah
TROUP, Cally
WAINWRIGHT, Elsa
WAITE, Caroline
WINDHAM, Rachel
WINDLEY, Richard
WRIGHT, Joanna

KINGFISHER GALLERY
(p.146)
ANDERSON, Anne
BAILEY, Christopher
BAILLIE, William
BALMER, Barbara
BEVAN, Anne
BLACK, Dorothy
BOAG, Francis
BOURNE, Peter
BRIDGE, Eoghan
FRASER, Donald Hamilton
KNOX, Lie
LENAGHAN, Brenda
LITTLEJOHN, William
MANBY, Simon

MELROSE, Janet
MENDELOW, Anne
MILLER, Moray
PATERSON, Anda
PATERSON, Susie
PICKARD, Baajie
PYRIE, Jenny A.
ROBERTSON, Iain
SIMMERS, Connie
SMITH, Andrew
SPENCE, James
THOMSON, Alastair
WARDMAN, Clare
WATT, Tom
WEGMULLER, Anne

LAMONT GALLERY
(p.71)
BOYDELL, Lucy
COOPER, Eileen
CRAYK, Fred
CROCKER, Andrew
CROWLEY, Graham
DUFFIN, John
GOLLON, Chris
KAVANAGH, Jim
KENNY, Michael
LAWSON, Sonia
MANNOCCI, Lino
MASON, Robin
MCLEAN, Bruce
MEDWAY, Sarah
MISTRY, Dhruva
MORETON, Nicholas
MULLINS, Nigel
MUSGRAVE, Oivia
NOBLE, Guy
O'KEEFFE, Anthony
ORR, Chris
ROONEY, Mick
SIMPSON, Abigail
SPEISER, Kira

LAURE GENILLARD GALLERY
(p.71)
ALLSOP, Douglas
CATTELAN, Maurizio
FLEURY, Sylvie
FOXCROFT, Lesley
GABELLONE, Guiseppe
HAYS, Dan
HUGHES, Dean
MASLIN, Steven
STEPANEK, Alice
TEGALA, Simon
THOMPSON, Gladstone
TIMONEY, Padraig
UMBERG, Gunter
YASS, Catherine

LENA BOYLE FINE ART
(p.72)
BROWN, Bonnie
BYARS, Hugh
CARY, Caroline
COGHILL, Sarah
COHEN, Alfred
FEDDEN, Mary
FRINK, Elisabeth
GARWOOD, Jason
GILBERT, Dennis
HALL, Clifford
HART, Simon
HERMAN, Josef
HOWSON, Peter
HUTTON, Sarah
JOHN, Augustus
MACMIADHACHAIN, Padraig
MOORE, Henry
NEWCOMB, Tessa
NICE, Derek
PASMORE, Mary
SELL, Charlotte

SUTTON, Philip
TREVELYAN, Julian
WARD, Henry
WEIGHT, Carel

LINDA BLACKSTONE GALLERY
(p.72)
BATCHELOR, Valerie
BLOCKLEY, G. John
BLOOM, Enid
BOLTON, Richard
BRENNAND, Catherine
BROWN, John
BUTLIN, Anne-Marie
CULLEN, Patrick
DAVIS, Pamela
FARRELL, Don
GYLES, Pauline
HARRISON, Stephanie
HUNTLY, Moira
KAVANAGH, Paul
KENNEDY, Matt Barber
KENT, Colin
KING, Robert
LEDGER, Janet
LIDZEY, John
MAJZLIK, Alois
MANIFOLD, Debra
MCDOWELL, Leo
MEACHER, Neil
MITCHELL, Brenda
OUTRAM, Steven
PAINE, Ken
PARSONS, Arthur
PLINCKE, J. Richard
READ, Sue
SIMMONDS, Jackie
SIMPSON, Alan
SUTTON, Charles
SYKES, David
THOMPSON, Andrew
TURNER, Jacquie
UHT, John

LINTON COURT GALLERY
(p.136)
ADAMS, Norman
BORLASE, Deirdre
BUTT, Anna
COOK, David
HOLMES, Katharine
NORTH, Kitty
ROBERTS, Tony

LION GALLERY
(p.126)
BAMFORD, Sara
BLAKE, Peter
CASSON, Ben
CHISWELL, Shelley
CRADDOCK, Martin
CROUCH, Andrew
DRAKEFORD, Bridget
DUPERNEX, Alison
EASTAUGH, Katie
EDE, Caroline
ELLIOT, George
FISHER, Sue
FURMINGER, Julie
GALL, Fiona
GILBERT, Wally
GRIFFIN, Ardyn
HICKMAN, Ken
HODGSON, Lynn
HUNT, Anita
JAGGER, Janette
JONES, David
JONES, Siobhan
KEEBLE, Victoria
KENNY, Mary
KEOGH, Rozie
KING, Deborah
KING, Marie-Therese

KIRKBY, Ruth
LE BAILLY, Virginia
LYNCH, Helen
MACKINNON, Blake
MCEVOY, Brian
MEE, Hilary
MOSSE, Michael
NOBLE, Chris
OHLSUN, Michelle
PLUMRIDGE, Caroline
PRICE, Judith
ROBERTS, Sue
ROBINSON, Yen
ROSHER, Diane
ROWLATT, Christopher
SPRIGGS, Paul
SUTCLIFFE, Malcolm
VINE, Helen
WADE, Richard
WARDLE, Richard
WINDLEY, Richard
WRIGHTSON, Ann

LOGIE STEADING ART GALLERY
(p.151)
AWLSON, Walter
BARTON, Michael
CAMERON, Elizabeth
CARTER, Pam
CHRISTIE, John
MUNRO, Arlette
MUNRO, Ian
NELSON, Harry
NICOLSON, John
ROSS, Irene
SHARPE, Chris
SMITH, Clare
SMITH, Julian

LOOK GALLERY
(p.136)
BAGLEE, Arthur
BAILEY, Caroline
BARKER, Neville
BARTHOLOMEW, James
BELL, Catherine
BIZON, Edna
BROWNE, Piers
CARRUTHERS, Rosemary
CHEALL, John
EGERTON, John
FEARN, Raymond
GILLESPIE, Bridget
GORDON, Frank
GREENWOOD, David
HEATH, Andrew
HENLEY, David
JANIN, Philippe
JONES, Derek
JONES, Mike
LAZZERINI, Giuliana
LUCKHAM, Alan
MASSIE, Ian Scott
MCCARTHY, Peter
NAYLOR, John
PARKER, Ian
PIERSON, Rosalind
PLATTS, David
RAYMOND, Oliver
RUGGERI, Anne-Marie
SKEA, Janet
SPILMAN, Neil
TAUNTON, Adrian
TILLING, Robert
TULLOH, Phoebe
TURVEY, Simon
WALTON, Jackie
WESTERGAARD, Hanne

THE LOOK
(p.104)
CASTLE, Josephine
COX, Alison

HENSHALL, Jonty
PENNY, Lisa
POUCHER, Karen
SIMS, Gentian
SMITH, Dryden
SYKES, Bill

LUMLEY CAZALET
(p.72)
BELLEROCHE, Albert
BRAQUE, Georges
CHAGALL, Marc
FRINK, Elisabeth
HELLEU, Paul
HOCKNEY, David
MATISSE, Henri
MIRO, Joan
PICASSO, Pablo
TISSOT, J.J.

LUPTON SQUARE GALLERY
(p.134)
ABRAHAMS, Rosemary
BOWMAN, Malcolm
BOYSON, Alan
BROWN, Susan
BURGESS, Jane
COURT, Stephen
CROSS, Diane
FAIRCHILD, Michael
GREENWOOD, David
HUTTON, Sarah
KIRKBY-GEDDES, Mick
MEAD, Pauline
MOUNTAIN, Keith
MUCHAN, Paul
NORTH, Suzanne
PALLISER, Neil
PASMORE, Victor
RADOS, Ivan
SPENCE, Anora
THORNTON, Barry
WALTON, Jackie

THE MAAS GALLERY
(p.72)
ALMA-TADEMA, Sir Lawrence
ANDERSON, Sophie
BRETT, John
BURNE-JONES, Sir Edward
CALDERON, Philip Hermogenes
CRANE, Walter
DADD, Richard
DE MORGAN, Evelyn
DICKSEE, Sir Frank
DOYLE, Charles Altamont
DOYLE, Richard
DRAPER, Herbert James
ETTY, William
FITZGERALD, John Anster
FRITH, William Powell
FROST, William Edward
GOODWIN, Albert
GOTCH, Thomas Cooper
GRIMSHAW, Atkinson
HUGHES, Arthur
HUGHES, E.R.
HUNT, William Holman
LANDSEER, Sir Edwin
LEIGHTON, Frederic Lord
MACLISE, Daniel
MILLAIS, Sir John
MOORE, Albert Joseph
MULREADY, William
MURRAY, Charles Fairfax
ORCHARDSON, Sir William Quiller
OSBORN, Emily Mary
PATON, Sir Joseph Noel
POYNTER, Sir Edward John
RICHMOND, George
RICHMOND, Sir William Blake
ROOKE, T.M.

ROSSETTI, Dante Gabriel
RUSKIN, John
SANDYS, Anthony Frederick Augustus
SEVERN, Arthur
SMETHAM, James
SOLOMON, Simeon
STILLMAN, Maria Spartali
STRUDWICK, John Melhuish
VON HERKOMER, Hubert
WATERHOUSE, John William
WATTS, George Frederick
WOOLMER, Alfred Joseph

MAINHILL GALLERY
(p.144)
ALEXANDER, Alan
ALEXANDER, J.S.C.
AYRTON, Michael
CARR, Tom
COEN, John
FERGUSSON, J.D.
FRINK, Elisabeth
GIBBISON, Michael
GILLIES, William
HAIG, The Earl
JOHNSTONE, William
KERR, Henry Wright
LAWRIE, Hamish
PHILIPSON, Sir Robin
SCOTT, Tom
SINCLAIR, David
THOMSON, Adam Bruce
WALKER, Andrew
WOOD, Frank
WOOD, Watson and David

MARLBOROUGH GRAPHICS
(p.73)
ARIKHA, Avigdor
AUERBACH, Frank
BACON, Francis
DAVIES, John
FREUD, Lucian
HAMBLING, Maggi
HEPWORTH, Barbara
JACKLIN, Bill
KIFF, Ken
KITAJ, R.B.
KOKOSCHKA, Oskar
LE BRUN, Christopher
MATISSE, Henri
MIRO, Joan
MOORE, Henry
NICHOLSON, Ben
OULTON, Thérèse
PASMORE, Victor
PAUL, Celia
PICASSO, Pablo
PIPER, John
REGO, Paula
SUTHERLAND, Graham
YIFEI, Chen

MARLENE ELEINI - #12,
(p.73)
BRAY, Sarah
FROST, Terry
HATHAWAY, Emma
HUBBUCH, Karl
HUGONIN, James
LAW, Bob
RICHON, Olivier
RICKETT, Sophy
ROLLINS, Tim & Kos
WALKER, John
YEHUDA, Verdi

MARTIN TINNEY GALLERY
(p.157)
CANNING, Neil
CROWTHER, Michael
ELWYN, John

GRIFFITHS, Mary
HERMAN, Josef
HOLLAND, Harry
JAMES, Shani Rhys
JOHN, Augustus
JOHN, Gwen
JONES, David
LLOYD-JONES, Mary
MACFARLANE, John
MOORE, Sally
PIPER, John
POVEY, Edward
PRENDERGAST, Peter
PRICHARD, Gwilym
RICHARDS, Ceri
SAMUEL, Mark
SINNOTT, Kevin
WILLIAMS, Claudia
WILLIAMS, Emrys
WILLIAMS, Kyffin
ZOBOLE, Ernest

MATTHIESEN FINE ART LIMITED
(p.73)
BASSANO, Jacopo
BATONI, Pompeo
BELLOTTO, Bernardo
BOUCHER, Francois
CANALETTO, Antonio
CARRACCIOLO, Giovanni
Battista
CHARDIN, Jean-Baptiste-Siméon
DELACROIX, Eugène
DI PAOLO, Giovanni
FRAGONARD, Jean-Honoré
GADDI, Agnolo
INGRES, Jean-Auguste-Dominique
LANFRANCO, Giovanni
NATTIER, Jean-Marc
PATER, Jean Baptiste
ROMANINO, Girolamo
ROSA, Salvator
VERNET, Horace
VOUET, Simon

MEDICI GALLERIES
(p.73)
CASSELDINE, Nigel
CHANDLER, Colin
CRITTENDEN, James
DEYMONAZ, Andre
HENSHAW, Nicola
HILL, Thomas
MAGILL, Anne
MARTIN, Malcolm
PENNY, Charles
RAYBOULD, Howard
RAYNES, Polly
RICH, Mary
SANDERS, Jeremy
TONKS, Godfrey
WILSON, Althea

THE MEDICI SOCIETY LIMITED
(p.177)
BRETT, Molly
BRUEGHEL, Pieter
CANALETTO, Antonio
CONSTABLE, John
DAWSON, Muriel
EDWARDS, Carlotta
ELSLEY, Arthur
HOLBEIN, Hans the Younger
LOWRY, L.S.
MILLAIS, Sir John
RAPHAEL
RENOIR, Pierre
SCOTT, Sir Peter
SHERWIN, Frank
STREVENS, John
TARRANT, Margaret
TURNER, J.M.W.
WARD, Vernon
ZINKEISEN, Doris

MERCURY GALLERY
(p.74)
ABBASSY, Samira
BLACKADDER, Elizabeth
BOULTON, Janet
CALLENDER, Robert
GENTLEMAN, David
HIRST, Barry
HOUSTON, John
KENNY, Michael
LAURIE, Simon
REMFRY, David
RIMMINGTON, Eric
ROONEY, Mick
SUTHERLAND, Carol Ann

MICHAEL WEBB FINE ART
(p.156)
ARMFIELD, Edward
ARMFIELD, George
ATKINS, Catherine J.
BERRY, Susan
BOND, W.J.J.C.
BREAKSPEAR, John
BREANSKI, Alfred Jnr
BROWNE, Barrington
CALVERT, Henry
COCKRAM, George
COX, David
DUNCAN, Edward
FIELDING, Copley
FOSTER, Birket
FOX, Henry Charles
HAGARTY, Mary S.
HARDY, Thomas Bush
HART, Thomas
HEGG, Teresa
HOLLAND, James
HOLLAND, John
HOWARD, Squire
JAMIESON, Alex
KELLY, Talbot
KEULEMANC, Johannes G.
KING, H.J. Yeand
KNELL, William Callcott
KNOWLES, Fred J.
LAIDLAY, W.J.
LINES, Henry H.
MAIDEN, Joseph
MARTIN, E.H.
MASON, Frank H.
NIGHTINGALE, Basil
PASSEY, Charles
POWELL, Alfred
RICHARDSON, Charles
RICKMAN, Philip C.
ROPE, George Thomas
SHALDERS, George
SHERRIN, Daniel
SILK, Oliver
SIMONE
SPENCELASH, Charles
VALTER, Florence
WAINWRIGHT, T.F.
WALKER, Eaton
WANE, Richard
WATSON, Robert
WATSON, William R.C. Jnr
WILLIAMS, Owen

MILMO-PENNY FINE ART LTD
(p.169)
BURKE, Augustus N.
FORBES, Stanhope
GARSTIN, Norman
GUINNESS, May
HAMILTON, Eva
HAMILTON, Letitia
HENRY, Grace
HENRY, Paul
HILL, Nathaniel
HONE, Evie
HONE, Nathaniel

JELLETT, Mainie
KAVANAGH, Joseph M.
LAVERY, John
LEECH, William J.
MOYNAN, Thomas
O BRIEN, Dermod
O'CONOR, Roderic
O'KELLY, Aloysius
O'MEARA, Frank
O'REILLY, Joseph
ORPEN, William
OSBORNE, Walter
PURSER, Sarah
RUSSELL, George
SOMERVILLE, Edith
SWANZY, Mary
THADDEUS, Henry J.
YEATS, Jack B.
YOUNG, Mabel

MONTPELLIER GALLERY
(p.106)
ADAM, Jane
ANDREWS, Martin
ANTLEY, Lynn
BALL, Peter Eugene
BALL, Sarah
BARACCO, Ugo
BARRY, Jo
BEAVAN, Jenny
BROWN, Ruta
CARTER, Chris
CHARLES, Jane
CLARKE, Terence
CLAYTON, Inge
CONRAD, Clare
DIAMANTOPOULO, Pierre
FAIRCHILD, Boy
HARTILL, Brenda
HAYES, Peter
HUBBARD, Nick
IRWIN, Bernard
JOHNSTONE, Hazel
KING-SALTER, Julian
LANCASTER, Perry
LANGLEY, Siddy
LAYTON, Peter
MACDONELL, Alasdair Neil
MACDONELL, Sally
MARSH, Bert
MOORE, Jane
PORTER, Diana
PORTWAY, Douglas
PRICE, Trevor
RICH, Mary
ROBERTS, David
RUSHBROOKE, Karlin
SCOTT, Mike
SOLVEN, Pauling
STERN, Patrick
STRICKLAND, Lesley
TAY, Eng
TOOKEY, Fleur
WARD, John
WEATHERHEAD, Ian
WRIGHT, Peter

THE MUSEUM OF MODERN ART, WALES
(p.161)
ARNOLD, Ann
ARNOLD, Graham
BALA, Iwan
BOYDELL ROGERS, John
BURGESS, Cefyn
CECIL, Roger
DAVIES, Ogwyn
ISAAC, Bert
LLOYD-JONES, Mary
PARRY, Iwan Gwyn
PRICHARD, Gwilym
WILLIAMS, Claudia

NAIRI SAHAKIAN CONTEMPORARY ART
(p.74)
ABOVIAN, Ruben
BAGDASSARIAN, Samvel
BARBER, Claire
CATTLE, Rachel
CURNEEN, Claire
DOUGLAS CAMP, Sokari
GEVORKIAN, Armen
HAMALBASHIAN, Sarkis
LEWIS, Peter
NIEDERBERGER, Christina
SAKUMA, Hana
SANSOM, Peter

NARWHAL INUIT ART GALLERY
(p.74)
ALIKASHUAK, Alex
ALIKASWA, Mark
ANGUHADLUQ, Luke
ANOWTALIK, Luke
ATCHEALAK, Davie
CURLEY, Tony
ECHALOOK, Lucassie
EMERAK, Mark
EVIK, Tommy
HOUSTON, James
IPELLIE, Family
ISHULUTAQ, Elisapee
KALVAK, Helen
KANANGINAK
KENOJUAK, Ashevak
KIGIUNA, Annie
MAMNGUQSUALUK, Victoria
MANUMIE, Tukiki
MAYOREAK, Ashoona
MEEKO, Family
MIKI, Andy
NANOGAK, Agnes
NAPATCHIE, Noah
NORTH, William
OHAITUK, Family
OONARK, Jessie
PAPIKATUK, Markoosie
PITSEOLAK, Ashoonn
POOTOOGOOK, Mosesee
PUDLO, Pudlat
QINNUAYUAK, Lucy
SAGGIATOK, John
SAGOUK, Towatuga
SALA, Family
SHAA, Qiatsuq
TAPANIE, Tommy
TIKKIVIK, Etuk
TOOKOOME, Simon
TUTSWEETOK, Lucy

THE NATIONAL TRUST FOR PLACES OF HISTORIC INTEREST OR NATURAL BEAUTY
(p.102)
BEALING, Nicola
BERESFORD-WILLIAMS, Mary
BOWEN, Clive
CHIVERS, Bruce
COLLINS, Nic
CONWAY, Diane
DAK, Richard
DYER, John
HICKS, June
HILLIARD, Victoria
HOWSE, Karen
HUGGETT, Barry
JANSCH, Heather
JENKINS, Derek & Jennifer
JOBBINS, Graham
JONES, Robert
KING, Brenda & Jeremy
LEWIN, Paul
LYONS, Philip
MALTBY, John
MATSON, Mary Lou

MCDONALD, Sue
MEAKLEBURGH, Margo
MERRY, Margaret
MICKLETHWAITE, Chrissie
NOCK, Camilla
PAGE-DAVIS, Carole
PINKETT, Neil
POLYBANK, Rebecca
PRICE, Trevor
PROSSER, Deborah
RICH, Mary
SCOTT, Rosie
SHORT, Joanne
SYMONDS, Ken
TRUMAN, Jan
TUFF, Richard
VAN DOP, Cornelis
VIGG, Bob
WADDINGTON, Andrew
WEBSTER, John
WEST, Hugh
WILD, Chris
WILLIAMS, Heather
WILLIAMS, Peter
WILLS, Barbara
WOOD, Vicki
WRIGHT, Peter

NETWORK GALLERY
(p.180)
BARKER, Nick
BOND, Jane
CUTHBERTSON, Dina
DREW, Patricia
DUFF, Norrie
DUNN, Ian
EVANS, Veronica
GILROY, Betty
GODDARD, Stephen
GOSLING, Oliver
GRAHAM, David
HOWARD, Byron
HUNT, Tom
JOHN, Augustus
KELL, Charlotte
ROLES, Suzzanne
SCHÖSSSER, Karin
STEVENS, Christopher
STREVENS, Peter
THOMAS, Phil
WINTERBURN, Thomas
WRAITH, Robbie

**NEW ACADEMY GALLERY AND
BUSINESS ART GALLERIES**
(p.74)
ATHERTON, Barry
BELSKY, Franta
BIGGER, Clare
BLACKMORE, Clive
BROKENSHIRE, John
CECIL, Roger
CORSELLIS, Jane
DOVER, Peter
DUNSTAN, Bernard
FRASER, Donald Hamilton
GORE, Frederick
GRANT, Alistair
HARTILL, Brenda
HOCKING, Susan-Jayne
HOLLIDAY, Sarah
JAWAHIRILAL, Lallitha
MACARA, Andrew
MACMIADHACHAIN, Padraig
MANDL, Anita
NOACH, Michele
PIPER, John
RIZVI, Jacqueline
ROBERTS, Keith
RUBENS, Zoe
SCHWARZ, Hans
WALKER, Richard
WRAY, Peter

**NEW ART CENTRE SCULPTURE
PARK AND GALLERY**
(p.192)
ADAMS, Robert
ARMITAGE, Kenneth
AYLIEFF, Felicity
BARRATT, Oliver
BOOTH, Chris
BURKE, Peter
BUTLER, Reg
CHADWICK, Lynn
CROWTHER, Alison
DALWOOD, Hubert
DEVEREUX, Richard
FESENMAIER, Helene
FRINK, Elisabeth
GILI, Katherine
GORMLEY, Antony
HARRISSON, Tim
HEPWORTH, Barbara
HERMES, Gertrude
HILLIARD, Karen
JOHNS, Greg
JONES, Allen
JONES, Jenifer
KENNETHSON, George
KENNY, Michael
KING, Phillip
LIM, Kim
LOWE, Jean
LYONS, Michael
MCCRUM, Bridget
MCWILLIAM, F.E.
MEADOWS, Bernard
MORRIS, Derek
MOUNT, Paul
MOWBRAY, Joanna
NEVELSON, Louise
PAOLOZZI, Eduardo
PERRY, Richard
RANCE, Victoria
RENSHAW, Richard
ROBERTS HOLMES, Paul
ROSA, Alvaro de la
SADIQ
SPENCER WATSON, Mary
SWAN, Lucy
THOMAS, Simon
TWYFORD, Kit
VINEY, Tony
WATTS, Meical
WRIGHT, Austin

NEW ASHGATE GALLERY
(p.113)
ANGUS, Nancy
BELSHER, Holly
BLOW, Sandra
BROWN, Ruta
DEAN, Graham
EASTOP, Geoffrey
FAIRCLOUGH, Michael
GRAY, Nick
GREVATTE, Jenny
HAYES, Peter
KLEIN, Anita
LAWSON, Sonia
MALENOIR, Mary
MALTBY, John
MARTINI, Babette
MILLAIS, Fiona
NEW, Keith
PARKINSON, Peter
ROBERTSON, Carol
ROSS, Vivienne
SEE-PAYNTON, Colin
SMITH, Pippa
SPACKMAN, Sarah
WHISHAW, Anthony
ZELINSKI, Pauline

NEW GRAFTON GALLERY
(p.75)
ADLINGTON, Mark
BAILEY, Julian
BOWEY, Olwyn
BOWYER, Jason
CAMPION, Oliver
CAMPION, Sue
COATES, Tom
CRAIGMYL, Anthea
CUMING, Fred
DOWLING, Jane
DUBERY, Fred
FEDDEN, Mary
GAA, Christa
GAMMON, Reg
GREENHAM, Peter
HALL, Christopher
HAYES, Colin
HERMAN, Josef
HOCKING, Susan
NASH, John
NEWLAND, Paul
PIKESLEY, Richard
ROONEY, Mick
SPENCER, Liam
SPENCER, Sarah
TODD WARMOUTH, Pip
TROTTER, Josephine
WEIGHT, Carel
WILLIAMS, Jacqueline
YEOMAN, Martin

NEWLYN ART GALLERY
(p.102)
ANNEAR, Jeremy
ARMITAGE, Catherine
ATKINS, Ray
BARNS-GRAHAM, Wilhelmina
BEALING, Nicola
BLACKMORE, Clive
BLOW, Sandra
BOURNE, Bob
BUXTON, Judy
CALONDER, Rudolf
COOK, Barrie
COOK, Richard
DOVE, Steve
DYSON, M.J.
EMANUEL, John
EVANS, Audrey
EVANS, Bernard
FINN, Michael
FREEMAN, Ralph
FROST, Antony
FROST, Terry
GILCREST, Joan
HILTON, Rose
HOGBEN, Phil
JACKSON, Kurt
JOAN, Gilcrest
JONES, Robert
LANTON, Andrew
MACKENZIE, Alexander
MAEKELBERGHE, Margo
MCCLARY, Louise
MCCLURE, Daphne
MCDOWALL, Carole
MILLER, John
MILS, June
O'CASY, Breon
PEARLE, Bryan
PILARD, Biddy
PIPER, John
PRAED, Michael
RAY, Roy
STORK, Mary
SUMRAY, Maurice
SYMMONDS, Ken
UPTON, Michael
WALKER, Roy
WATKISS, Gill
WEYERSBERG, Angela

YATES, Fred
ZIA, Parton

NORSELANDS GALLERY
(p.139)
BROWNE-WILKINSON, Fiona
CARTMEL-CROSSLEY, John
DOBSON, Bruce
DOHERTY, Joan
EVANS, Judy
GOMAR-STONE, Barbara
GOODERHAM, Paul
KELLAM, Colin
MALLINSON, Pat
MILES, Gordon
RAWLINSON, Veronica
SANDERS, Andrew
TREVENA, Shirley
WALLACE, David
WILLIAMS, Julian
WORTHY, Diana

**NORTH DOWN VISITORS AND
HERITAGE CENTRE**
(p.168)
DEVON, Gary
PRIERS, Julian

THE OCTOBER GALLERY
(p.75)
ANATSUI, El
BARTENEV, Andrey
BECKWITH, Carol
BETHE-SELASSIE, Michael
BURROUGHS, William S.
CLARKE, LeRoy
COHEN, Ira
DOUGLAS CAMP, Sokari
GLOVER, Ablade
JEGEDE, Emmanuel Taiwo
LALOUSCHEK, Elisabeth
MENDIVE, Manuel
MINIHAN, John
OLORUNTOBA, Z.O.
RUBIO, Julieta
SHAWA, Laila
WILDE, Gerald
WILLIAMS, Aubrey
ZHONG MIN, Xu

OPEN EYE GALLERY
(p.147)
BELLANY, John
BIRNIE, William
BOND, Marj
BRIDGE, Eoghan
BROWN, John
HARRIGAN, Claire
HOWSON, Peter
KNOX, Jack
LEWIS, Whyn
MANGAN, Stephen
MITCHELL, Gordon K.
MORROCCO, Alberto
MORROCCO, Leon
REDDY, Mark
RODGER, Willie
ROPER, Geoffrey
SCOFIELD, David
SCOULLER, Glen
STIRLING, Dorothy
WYLLIE, George

ORIEL PLAS GLYN-Y-WEDDW
(p.159)
AINSWORTH, George
AP TOMOS, Gwyneth
BEVAN, Vaughan
CAMPBELL, Alex
CLARK, Francis
DAVIES, Ivor
GOBLE, Tony
GROSVENOR, David

HEDLEY, John
HUWS, Elin
JONES, Anewin
JONES, Elin
MCGUTCHEON, Andrew
PELL, John
SAX-LEDGER, Maria
SEK, Karel
SELWYN, William
SUTTON, Philip
WILLIAMS, Claudia
WILLIAMS, Kyffin

OTTERTON MILL GALLERY
(p.103)
ACWORTH, Carol
CARTER, Brenda
CARTER, Kenneth
COOK, Beryl
ERLAND, Sukey
FRANCIS, Geraldine
GOLESWORTHY, Joana
HARTLEY, Ben
LANE, Martin
SMITH, Keith
STAFFORD, John
STAFFORD, Sheila

PARNHAM HOUSE
(p.105)
ATHERLEY, Karen
BARNES, Chris
BICKLEY, Geoff
BRYNE, Kate
JACKSON CURRIE, Lorna
JACKSON, Paul
JORDAN, Cecil
KEELEY, Laurel
KEMBERY, Mary
LEACH, John
MAKEPEACE, John
MARSTON, James
MCCARTHY, Sophie
MELLORS, Kate
MOTT, Keith
O'KELL, Katherine
TATTERSALL, Jules
TUTCHER, Alison
WALLACE JONES, Harriet
WILKINSON, Fiona

PATON GALLERY
(p.75)
CLARK, Jake
GUILD, Derrick
GUY, Alexander
HATTON, Nicholas
INGLIS, Judy
JAMES, Shani Rhys
LANGLEY, Jane
MABBUTT, Mary
MAJOR, Julie
OLLIVIER, Tim
PALMER, Kate
SNELL, Rosie
VARGAS, Cecilia
VENESS, Alex

PENWITH GALLERIES
(p.102)
BARNS-GRAHAM, Wilhelmina
BEDDING, John
BOURNE, Bob
CARDEW, Ara
CARDEW, Seth
CHANDLER, Jill
CONN, Roy
CORSER, Trevor
CROSS, Tom
CROSSLEY, Bob
CULWICK, Robert
DOVE, Stephen
EMANUEL, John

FEILER, Paul
FINN, Michael
FREEMAN, Ralph
FROST, Terry
HILTON, Rose
JONES, Robert
LEACH, Janet
LEGRICE, Jeremy
MAECKELBERGHE, Margo
MARSHALL, William
MCCLURE, Daphne
MCDOWALL, Carole
MCNALLY, Kathy
MILES, June
MITCHELL, Denis
MOUNT, Paul
NICHOLSON, Kate
O'CASEY, Breon
O'MALLEY, Tony
OLINER, Sheila
PEARCE, Bryan
PENDER, Jack
PRAED, Michael
RITMAN, Lieke
SEMMENS, Jennifer
STORK, Mary
SUMRAY, Maurice
SYMONDS, Ken
TRIBE, Barbara
WALKER, Rod
WALKER, Roy
WARD, Peter
WASON, Jason
WELLS, John
WILSON, Vincent

PETER POTTER GALLERY
(p.150)
ADAIR, Andrew
AMBROZEVICH, Carmen
BANKS, Claire
BOURNE, Peter
BULLICK, Vanessa
COLVIN, Elma
CONNELL, Chris
FARQUARSON, Linda
FIRTH, Jack
GRAHAM, Rosemary
HEMINGSLEY, David
HENDERSON, Ro
JASINSKY, Alfonse
KEANY, Brian
KEMP, Helen
LAW, Pat
LEE, Mandy
LENAGHAN, Brenda
LYON, Simone
MACKENZIE, Philippa
MCLEOD, Janette
MEIKLE, Annabelle
MUIR, Graham
PHILLIPS, Sheena
RHIND, Margaret
ROBINSON, Graham
RODGER, Willie
ROSS, Wendy
RUSHBROOK, Anita
SHATWELL, Valerie
STEPHEN, Sheena
STEWART, Alison
SUTTER, Archie
TURQUAND, Patti
WHITEOAKS, Sue

PETERS BARN GALLERY
(p.116)
BAILEY, Walter
BALL, Emily
DUPRÉ, Marie-Frederique
JUPP, Mo
MUNN, Annabel
PEARSON, Colin
SCOTT, Sally

STEVENSON, Liane
SULA, Artur

PICTURE HOUSE GALLERIES
(p.102)
ASPDEN, Gail
BASCOMBE, Linda
CHRISTOPHERS, Julian
COCKERALL, Rachel
COOPER, William
DAVIES, Emma
DUPLOCK, Albert
GARRITT, Daphne
GLAISTER, Fiona
HARDINGS, Sasha
HART, Simon
HOLLAND, Emma
HOSKINGS, David
KENDRICK, Jane
MICKLETHWAITE, Chrissie
RICHARDS, Mark
ROSS, Vivienne
SAVILLE, Michael
SHAKSPEARE, William
SMITH, Nicole
WARDELL, Sasha
WINDRIDGE, Eliza

PLAZZOTTA LTD
(p.76)
PLAZZOTTA, Enzo

PORTAL GALLERY
(p.76)
ALLIN, John
ANDERSON, Eddie
ARIS, Fred
BERNSTORFF, Ann
BIRKBECK, Paul
BROOMFIELD, Frances
BYRNE, John
CARTER, Bernard
CARTWRIGHT, Reg
CASTLE, Barry
CASTLE, Philip
CHEEPEN, David
CLARK, Terry
COOK, Beryl
COPAS, Ronnie
COPELAND, Mark
CORNNER, Haydn
CUDWORTH, Nick
EASBY, Steve
GRAINGER, James
HARRISON, Claude
LAWMAN, Peter
LE BAS, Philip
LEWIS, Jane
LLOYD, James
LYON, Charlotte
MCNAUGHT, James
NEVILLE, Pat
PEPPER, Reg
RICHES, Lizzie
ROONEY, Mick
ROZOT, Isabelle
TAPLIN, Guy
TURPIN, Emma
WARD, Graham
WILLIAMS, Kit

POSK GALLERY
(p.76)
BARANOWSKA, Janina
BORKOWSKI, Andrzej
DANKIEWICZ, Krystyna
DAWIDOWSKI, Andrzej
ELASZKIEWICZ, Andrzej
FALKOWSKI, Wojciech
GIERC, Danuta
HOJAK-MYSKO, Elzbieta
JACZYNSKA, Maria
JAFFE, Ilona

LOTRINGER, Ludwig
LUBOMIRSKI DE VOUX, Stefan
LURCZYNSKI, Mieczyslaw
NEKANDA-TREPKO, Halina
PIESAKOWSKA, Danuta
PYTEL, Zygmunt
SKOLIMOWSKI, Staszka
SLASKI, Peter
SMART, Alan
WERNER, Aleksander
ZOLTOWSKI, Adam
ZWOLINSKA-BRZESKI, Teresa

PRATT CONTEMPORARY ART/PRATT EDITIONS
(p.113)
ADAMS, Susan
DAVIES, Richard
EDALATPOUR, Seyed
GRATER, Julian
KENNY, Michael
KROKFORS, Kristian
NOGUEIRA FLEURY, Leonam
PACHECO, Ana Maria
RAHMANZADEH, Akram
REES ROBERTS, Marcus
ROONEY, Mick
WALKER, Denise

PRIMAVERA
(p.118)
BARKER, Patrick
BATTERHAM, Richard
BAUMAN, Lydia
BEARD, Peter
BETTS, Malcolm
BLANTHORN, Brian
BOWEN, Clive
BRENNAND WOOD, Michael
CAINES, Susan
CARTWRIGHT, Ashley
CONSTANTINIDES, Joanna
CORNWELL, Jeremy
COWEN, Gina
CREESE, Susannah
CROUCH, Andrew
DE WAAL, Edmund
FANSHAWE KATO, Jill
FORREST, Marianne
GILMOUR, Judith
HARRIS, Charmain
HENLEY, Nicola
HOUGH, Catherine
HUSSEY, Dan
KRINOS, Daphne
LAMBERT, Anna
LAYTON, Peter
LEACH, David
LONG, Maurice
MACKMAIDHACHAIN, Padraig
MALTBY, John
MANNHEIM, Catherine
MARTIN, Guy
MCDOWELL, Leo
MEDDING, Camilla
NEWCOMB, Tessa
NEWELL, Stephen
OWEN, Elspeth
PEARSON, Colin
RACE, Robert
RAMSHAW, Wendy
RAY, Jane
SCOTT, Mike
SPIRA, Rupert
TAPLIN, Guy
TOOKEY, Fleur
WATSON, Janet

PYMS GALLERY
(p.77)
CLAUSEN, George
FORBES, Stanhope
HARPIGNIES, H.J.

COMMERCIAL GALLERY ARTISTS

BAWDEN, Richard
BRUNSDON, John
BURMAN, John
CARLO, Michael
DONALDSON, Ros
DRAPER, Jill
FUCHS, Tessa
FULLER, Moss
HARKER, Janet
HASTINGS, Eveline
HENDERSON, Sue
HOUGHTON, Barrie
MORGAN, Jane
NEUSTEN, Barrie
SPAFFORD, Iola
THOMAS, Glynn
TOOKEY, John
WADE, Richard
WESTWOOD, Neil

**THE SOLOMON GALLERY
(p.169)**
BALLARD, Brian
BLACKSHAW, Basil
CHIHULY, Dale
COLLIS, Peter
COPE, Elizabeth
DUNCAN, Ana
GEOGHEGAN, Trevor
GILLESPIE, Rowan
HOGAN, Darragh
KINGSTON, Richard
LONGUEVILLE, James
LYNN, Bob
MCALLISTER, Therese
MCDONNELL, Hector
MCENTAGART, Brett
MCWILLIAM, F.E.
MOONEY, Martin
POSKITT, Frances
RICHARDSON, Victor
SPACKMAN, Sarah
STUART, Imogen
TANSEY, Francis
WARREN, Michael
WEJCHERT, Alexandra
YEATS, Jack B.

**THE SPECIAL PHOTOGRAPHER'S
COMPANY
(p.78)**
BINGHAM, Howard
BOOT, Adrian
CATANY, Toni
CLAXTON, William
CLEMENT, Etienne
CRYER, Terry
CUNNICK, Geraint
CURTIS, Edward Sheriff
DAYAN, Eddie
DOW, Beth
FONTEYNE, Karel
FRASER, Ewan
GIBSON, David H.
GILDEN, Bruce
GORMAN, Greg
GREENFIELD, Lois
GRUEN, Bob
HARRIS, Graeme
HIRSCHBERG, Tania
HOLLAND, Tracey
JAQUES, Ronny
LELE, Ouka
LEONARD, Herman
LUCAS, Cornel
MANKOWITZ, Gered
MARSDEN, Simon
MAYNE-SMITH, Sean
MCCABE, Eamonn
MCCARTNEY, Mike
MCGEE, Tony
MOLINS, Sophie
O'NEILL, Terry

PALEOLOGOU, Ettie
PARK, Clare
PARKER, Emma
REUTER, John
RIVAS, Humberto
RYAN, Barry
SAMUEL, Deborah
SUSCHITZKY, Wolfgang
TENNESON, Joyce
THORNE-THOMSEN, Ruth
TUNICK, Spencer
VARGAS, Rafael
WAITE, Charlie
WAITE, Richard
WARBURTON, Holly
WESSON, Diane
WILMER, Val
WILSON, Laura

**ST. BRANNOCK'S GALLERY
(p.121)**
BARON, Leofric
COLINSON, Roy
GLADWELL, James
GODWIN, Sheila
PARTRIDGE, Ian
POOLE, Doreen
SALMONS, John
SMITH, Michael
SPARHAM, Marie
SYMMONS, Barbara
TOWNSEND, Christine

**ST. DAVID'S HALL
(p.157)**
BEARD, Leonard
CHAPMAN, June
DARLISON, John
DEWSBURY, Gerald
EVANS, David
GILES HOBBS, Annie
HAWKINS, Des
HOWELL, Joyce
HOWELLS, Pat
HUGHES-WILLIAMS, Sylvia
HURN, Daphne
HURST, Dora
LOWRY, Arnold
LUSH, Helen
MCDONAGH, Sue
OWEN, Cyril
OWEN, Shirley Anne
TRAYNOR, Mary
WAUGH, Trevor
WHALLEY, Ann
WILLIAMS, David
WOODS, Anne

**STAR GALLERY
(p.115)**
ARMITAGE, David
BLIGHT, John
COOPER, Michael
DUBREY, Henrietta
FEDDEN, Mary
HAMMICK, Tom
LLOYD-JONES, Mary
MESSER, Peter
MOCKFORD, Harold
RIX, Ruth
ROONEY, Mick
TRAHERNE, Margaret
WILLIAMS, Charles

**STERN ART DEALERS
(p.79)**
ARMFIELD, Edward
BALE, Thomas Charles
BATES, David
CLEMENSON, Robert
COUSIN, Charles
DE BREANSKI, Alfred
DE BREANSKI, Gustave

EPSTEIN, Sir Jacob
GOODALL, Frederick
HORLOR, Joseph
KADAR, Bela
KING, H.J. Yeend
KRAMER, Jacob
MAZE, Paul
MEADOWS, William
MORRIS, Alfred
PAICE, George
PARKER, Henry H.
PASSEY, Charles
PIKE, Sidney
PISSARRO, Georges Manzana
PISSARRO, H. Claude
PISSARRO, Lelia
PISSARRO, Lucien
PISSARRO, Ludovic-Rodo
PISSARRO, Orovida
PISSARRO, Paulemile
POLLENTINE, Alfred
SCHAFER, Henri
SHERRIN, Daniel
STEELE, Edwin
VICKERS, A.H.
WALBOURN, Ernest

**STRATHEARN GALLERY AND
POTTERY
(p.151)**
AWLSON, Walter
BELL, John
BOURNE, Peter
BUSHE, Chris
CAMPBELL, Catriona
GRAY, Janice
HALSTEAD, Rebecca
HARKESS, Claire
HOLLANDS, Emma
MACLEAN, Sonas
MAGUIRE, Fiona
MAGUIRE, John
MCCARTHY, Liz
MCSTAY, Adrienne
MEIKLE, Annabel
MORRISON, John Lowrie
MUIR, Graham
PRETSELL, Philomena
ROBINSON, Neil
SCOBIE, Lara

**THE STUDIO
(p.158)**
WILSON, David
WILSON, Guy

**THE GOLDEN PLOVER STUDIO
GALLERY
(p.161)**
GIARDELLI, Arthur
GIARDELLI, Bim

**THE WILD HAWTHORN PRESS
(p.178)**
HAMILTON-FINLAY, Ian

**THROSSELLS
(p.79)**
BULBIS, Ann
DENNIS, Ann
HARRIS, Jane
KADER, Osman

**TIB LANE GALLERY
(p.131)**
BAKER, Barbara
BILLSBOROUGH, Jim
BURTON, Morag
CEBERTOWICZ, Janina
CLAYTON, Peter
CONNELL, Joan
DAVIES, John
EHRLICH, Georg

FOERSTER, Florian
FREER, Allen
FRINK, Elisabeth
GRIMSHAW, Trevor
HALLIDAY, Irene
HENDERSON, Sue
HERMAN, Josef
HOWARD, Ghislaine
KRAMER, Jacob
LACOUX, John
LLOYD, James
MCINTYRE, Donald
MCKINLAY, Don
NASH, John
OUSEY, Harry
RADFORD, Gordon
RICHARDSON, Bob
RUTHERFORD, Harry
SARKIS, Vera
SELWYN, William
SHAW, David Carson
SORRELL, Adrian
SPAFFORD, Iola
STUBBS, Rosemary
SUTHERLAND, Joan
THOMPSON, Alan
VALLETTE, Adolphe
VAUGHAN, Keith
WOOD, Michael
WOODS, Brian

**THE UNIVERSITY GALLERY
(p.139)**
CORNISH, Norman
MCGUINNESS, Tom

**UNIVERSITY OF LIMERICK - AV
GALLERY
(p.170)**
BAKER, Robert
BLODAU, Dierer
BLODAU, Peter
BYRNE, Michael
DONOVAN, Jack
HARPER, Charles
LILBURN, David
MACMAHON, Des
MURRAY, Cóilin
SHEEMY, Jim
SHINNORS, John

**VINCENT KOSMAN FINE ART
(p.148)**
ARMSTRONG, John
BELL, Vanessa
BOMBERG, David
BROWN, Hugh Boycott
CONNARD, Philip
CROSBIE, William
DUNCAN, John
DUNLOP, Ronald O.
FEDDEN, Mary
FERGUSSON, J.D.
GERTLER, Mark
GILL, Eric
GILLIES, William
GORE, Frederick
GOSSE, Sylvia
GRANT, Duncan
HALL, Clifford
HAMILTON, Maggie
HARVEY, Harold
HAYWARD, Arthur
HILTON, Roger
HOUSTON, George
KENNEDY, Cecil
LEE HANKEY, William
MAITLAND, Paul
MANSON, James B.
MAZE, Paul
MCCLURE, David
MCINTYRE, Donald
MENINSKY, Bernard

METHUEN, Lord
MORROCCO, Alberto
MOSTYN, Tom
NICHOLSON, William
PARK, James Stuart
PARK, John A.
PATERSON, James
PATERSON, Viola
PHILLIPSON, Robin
REDPATH, Anne
ROBERTSON, Eric
ROUSELL, Theodore
RUSSELL, Gyrth
SMITH, Matthew
TREVELYAN, Julian
VAUGHAN, Keith
WILLIAMS, Terrick
WOLFE, Edward
WOLMARK, Alfred
ZINKAISEN, Doris

WADDINGTON GALLERIES
(p.80)
ALBERS, Josef
ALBERS, Josef (The Estate of)
ARP, Jean
AVERY, Milton
BLAKE, Peter
CALDER, Alexander
CAULFIELD, Patrick
CHAMBERLAIN, John
CHIA, Sandro
CRAIG-MARTIN, Michael
DAVENPORT, Ian
DE KOONING, Willem
DEGAS, Edgar
DUBUFFET, Jean
ERNST, Max
FLANAGAN, Barry
FLAVIN, Dan
FRANCIS, Sam
HEPWORTH, Barbara
HERON, Patrick
HITCHENS, Ivon
HOCKNEY, David
HODGKIN, Howard
JONES, Zebedee
JUDD, Donald
KLEE, Paul
LANDY, Michael
LÉGER, Fernand
LICHTENSTEIN, Roy
LIM, Kim
LIPCHITZ, Jacques
MAGRITTE, René
MATISSE, Henri
MILROY, Lisa
MIRO, Joan
MOORE, Henry
NICHOLSON, Ben
PALADINO, Mimmo
PICABIA, Francis
PICASSO, Pablo
RAE, Fiona
RAUSCHENBERG, Robert
SAMARAS, Lucas
SCHNABEL, Julian
SPENCER, Stanley
TAPIES, Antoni
TURNBULL, William
WARHOL, Andy
WESSELMANN, Tom
WESTERMAN, H.C.
YEATS, Jack B.

THE WALK
(p.80)
BANKS, Nick
BROAD, Clive
CALEY, Vivienne
CARR, David
DAVIES, Judy
FEILDEN, Lucy
FRY, Francis

HOGAN, David
LANCASTER, Brenda
MALI
MILNE, Vincent
MORNMENT, Hannah
MORRIS, Sue
MORTIMER, Sophie
SEN, Neera
STONE, Tess
STRUTT, Susan
WALSH, Moz

WARWICK GALLERY
(p.128)
BRUNSDON, John
BURROWS, Hazel
CUMMINGS, Christine
DINGLE, Jan
DUNN, John
FAIRCHILD, Michael
FURMINGER, Julie
HUGHES, Alan
HUGHES, John
KENNEDY, Michael
MAINWARING, John
MILLINGTON, Terence
NOBLE, Chris
RICHECOEUR, Michael
ROBERTS, Ian
SCALDWELL, Deborah
SPAIN, Mark
WILSON, Richard
WOOD, Michael

THE WEST END GALLERY
(p.124)
HACKER, Sophie
HOBBS, Paul
LAMB, Jean

WEST WALES ARTS CENTRE,
(p.160)
BEARD, Leonard
CAMPBELL, James
CANNING, Neil
COKER, Peter
CRAMP, Elizabeth
CRAMP, Jonathan
CULLEN, Stephen
CURRY, Denis
HENDERSON, Ewen
JACKSON, Dilys
LOVEDAY, Ross
MACKEOWN, James
MARSH, Simon
PARTRIDGE, Josh
PAYNE, Michael
RICH, Simon
ROBERTS, Chris
ROBERTSON, Ian
THURNHAM, Chris
TRESS, David
TUDBALL, Ruthanne
VAUGHAN JONES, Martyn
VIALE, Patrick
WARD, John

WILL'S ART WAREHOUSE
(p.80)
ADAMS, Lee
AIERS, Pauleen
BASSETT, Clare
BAXTER, Sandra
BEVAN, Oliver
BOYD, Ron
COOKE, Jonathon
CROOK, Craig
DAVY, Lesley
DE KONIQSWARTER, Steven
DICKENS, Sophie
DUFFIN, John
DUFTON, John
DUMAS, Felise
EDWARDS, Nicola

ELFICK, Pennie
FAY, Helen
GILVAN, Cartwright Christopher
GRUNDY, Bronwen
HARING, Ute
HARRIS, Ian
HAXWORTH, Hetty
JAFFE, Leanne
JAMES, Simon
KENNINGTON, Sue
LANGFORD, Martin
LEASOR, Joan
LEE, Jessie
LIDDELL, Caro
LITTLE, Pauline
LODGE, Grace
MASON, Piers
MIDGLEY, Julia
MOXLEY, Susan
NOTT, Margaret
OWEN, Rachel
PINKSTER, Anna
PIPER, Ruth
PULLEN, Alison
ROBINSON, Julian
ROBINSON, Kate
RODRIGUEZ, Cristina
SMITH, Pippa
STALKER, Geoff
THOMAS, Kate
TIMMS, Melissa
TURNBALL, Chris
URQUHART, Anne
WILSON, Robert
WINTER, Tom

WISEMAN ORIGINALS
(p.81)
AITCHISON, Craigie
BRAQUE, Georges
CHAGALL, Marc
FREUD, Lucian
FRINK, Elisabeth
FROST, Terry
GIACOMETTI, Alberto
HERON, Patrick
HOCKNEY, David
HODGKIN, Howard
HOYLAND, John
MATISSE, Henri
MIRO, Joan
MOORE, Henry
PICASSO, Pablo

WOLSELEY FINE ARTS
(p.81)
ARDIZZONE, Edward
BOMBERG, David
BONNARD, Pierre
BUCKLAND-WRIGHT, John
DENIS, Maurice
DERAIN, André
DOBSON, Frank
DUNOYER DE SEGONZAC, André
GILL, Eric
GRANT, Duncan
GRETTA
HAGREEN, Philip
HOBBS, James
HOLLOWAY, Edgar
JONES, David
KLEMANN, Paul
LHOTE, André
MARQUET, Albert
NASH, Paul
PASCIN, Jules
PIPER, John
RAVERAT, Gwen
ROUSSEL, Ker Xavier
SPENCER, Stanley
THEODOSIOU, Panico
UNDERWOOD, Leon
VOLK, Patricia

VUILLARD, Edouard
YALE, Brian

WOODBINE COTTAGE GALLERY
(p.120)
BAILEY, Katy
BIBBY, Rob
BRAMBLE, Steven
COLQUITT, Peter
CURGENVEN, Michael
ENGLISH, Andy
FOSTER, Patience
GREGORY, Mac
HOLLINSHEAD, David
LAGADEC, Jean
MICALLEF, Antony
MILLIKEN, Steven
MOON, Liz
MOORE, Sarah
NEAL, Richard
PREST, Kathy
RIVETT, Simon
SIMPSON, Juliet
SLATER, Helen
WILLIAMS, Louise
YORATH, Liz
YORATH, Rowen

ZELLA GALLERY
(p.81)
ARDEN, Kitty
BAKO BITTNER, Eva
BASSETT, Clare
BROWNE, Piers
BURLEY, Maggie
CARR, Kathy
CAYMAS, Katrien
CLAYTON, Inge
CROFT, Diana
DEVEREUX BARKER, Dale
DEVEREUX, Jenny
EPPS, Melanie
FAY, Helen
FENOUGHTY, Mary
GILBERT, Ellen
GRANT, Alistair
GRAVER, Mark
GREENHALF, Robert
GRIGOR, Rachel
GROVES, Enid
HARTILL, Brenda
HASEGAWA, Shoichi
HINAEKIAN, Peggy
HUNTER, Michael
JANOWSKI, Basia
JONES, Rosamund
LIDDELL, Caro
MARCH, Carl
MARTIN, Frank
MIDGLEY, Julia
MIKHAILOVSKY, Ekaterina
NEVILLE, Alison
NOACH, Michele
PERRING, Susie
PRICE, Trevor
ROLLO, Sonia
SCUDDER, Hilary
SEARLE, Ronald
ST. CLAIR MILLER, Frances
STODDART, Rosalind
THEYS, Freddy
WHADCOCK, Richard

ZINK EDITIONS
(p.175)
ABRAHAMS, Ivor
COOPER, Eileen
COX, Alan
DE BULAT, Fiona
FROST, Terry
KANE, Michael
MCFADYEN, Jock
SINNOTT, Kevin
SMITH, Richard

ARTISTS' INDEX

This section lists, by artist, the establishments where the artist's work may be bought.

ARTISTS' INDEX

G

ARTISTS' INDEX

NOTES

GENERAL INDEX

Alphabetical index to all entries.

THE ART WORLD
DIRECTORY
1998/99 25TH EDITION

GENERAL INDEX

GENERAL INDEX

GENERAL INDEX

GENERAL INDEX

GENERAL INDEX

GENERAL INDEX

ADVERTISER'S INDEX

NOTES

NOTES

NOTES

NOTES

NOTES